Big Book of Emergency Department Psychiatry

"All clinicians in emergency departments (EDs) espouse to provide care for the whole person, yet those individuals with psychiatric and mental health conditions in EDs all too often find timely and competent care woefully lacking.

Similar to the recent trends of integrating mental health services into primary care, this book provides expertise and practical guidance for ED physicians and nurses to increase competencies for diagnosing and treating common mental health conditions.

This innovative model of care in EDs proactively and reliably addresses the majority of patients' psychiatric and mental health needs, and reserves psychiatric consultation services and transfers to psychiatric treatment facilities for those patients who cannot be adequately treated by ED clinicians."

Patricia Rutherford, RN, MS
Vice President, Institute for Healthcare Improvement (IHI)

"The authors not only have a deep understanding of emergency psychiatry but also of operational improvement. The mix makes this book a needed reference for anyone focused on a patient centered approach for this vulnerable population."

Kevin Nolan, Statistician, Improvement Advisor, and Senior Fellow
Institute for Healthcare Improvement (IHI)

"The authors have organized and written a timely and necessary book on the care of the acute psychiatric patient in the emergency department.

Over 2 million people a year seek care for behavioral healthcare problems in hospital EDs at a cost of over $4 billion.

Behavioral health patients seeking care in the emergency department have the same hopes, needs, and fears as the rest of the patients who present to our EDs for evaluation and treatment.

The ED is often an intense and stressful work environment where staff must perform rapid assessments and make swift treatment decisions.

ED staff and team members, dedicated, focused, and highly trained, too often feel overwhelmed, burdened, and at times even threatened by the need to provide care for behavioral health patients.

There is a great deal of variation in ED expertise, training, and resource allocation for emergency mental health problems, which can lead to suboptimal care and negative patient and staff experiences.

The management of acute behavioral emergencies and crisis intervention are simply and clearly described in this book. The tactics, tools, and techniques outlined here can elevate our approach to emergency department psychiatry and allow our emergency medicine colleagues to rise above our current challenges and frustrations.

Balan et al. apply approaches, lessons, and insights from both evidence-based medicine and Lean service operations to behavioral health patients, defining best practices and demonstrating the benefits and positive impact on patient care, flow, and safety.

Big Book of Emergency Department Psychiatry is a practical playbook for the challenges at hand. The authors explain simply and clearly how to get it done."

Kirk Jensen, MD, MBA, FACEP
Chief Innovation Officer, EmCare, Inc.
Chief Medical Officer, BestPractices, Inc.
Studer Faculty Member and National Speaker
Institute for Healthcare Improvement (IHI) Faculty Member

"The management of psychiatric patients seeking care in the emergency department is one of the most complex and important issues in modern emergency medicine. The patients are frequently disenfranchised and do not receive high-quality or timely medical care. As a result, these patients impose a tremendous impact on ED resources and flow.

This book provides comprehensive insights into psychiatric care in the ED and operational improvement using Lean healthcare concepts. It will help you and your leadership team create a patient-centric culture where a community of scientists continuously improve value for psychiatric patients, hospital, and society."

Jody Crane, MD, MBA
Principal, X32 Healthcare
Author of *The Definitive Guide to Emergency Department Operational*
Improvement: Employing Lean Principles with Current ED Best Practices
to Create the "No Wait" Department

"Innovative, informative, and inspiring book, with captivating stories that display the ins and outs of psychiatric emergency services. A must-read, especially the chapters on correctional emergency psychiatry and the concept of Lean in healthcare."

Mardoche Sidor, MD
Assistant Professor of Psychiatry, Columbia University
Medical Director, The Center for Alternative Sentencing and Employment Services (CASES)

"*Big Book of Emergency Department Psychiatry* is big as it should be; it is the most comprehensive text on emergency psychiatry in print. Not only does it guide one to the diagnosis and management of emergency room patients, but it also addresses operational issues in various settings. The emergency room is a team effort, and *Big Book of Emergency Department Psychiatry* includes the perspectives of its members: psychiatrist, nurse, social worker, and non-psychiatric emergency doctor. Make room for it on your bookshelf."

David W Preven, MD
Clinical Professor
Department of Psychiatry and Human Behavior
Albert Einstein College of Medicine

"Complete, accurate, and especially timely. A must-read for any emergency department leader engaged in improving care for this vulnerable population."

Seth Thomas, MD, FACEP
Director of Quality & Performance
CEP America

"*Big Book of Emergency Department Psychiatry* is empathically written and valuable to anyone that has ever experienced or cared for someone dealing with a psychiatric emergency. It has a dose of rigor, evidence, and science, it conveys the personal experience of some of our peers, and it keeps you wanting to read more. It is a tremendous compendium of the state of knowledge of the specialty and art of emergency psychiatry.

Very soon, this book will become the must-read for this specialty for trainees and experienced mental health professionals alike. I congratulate the authors on an excellent, disciplined, rigorous work that retains the human perspective while educating the reader."

Carlos Rueda MD, MBA
Chairman, Department of Psychiatry
St. Joseph's Healthcare System
Trinitas Regional Medical Center

Big Book of Emergency Department Psychiatry

Edited By
Yener Balan, MD, FAPA
Karen Murrell, MD, MBA, FACEP
Christopher Bryant Lentz, MS, MFT

CRC Press
Taylor & Francis Group
Boca Raton London New York

CRC Press is an imprint of the
Taylor & Francis Group, an **informa** business

A PRODUCTIVITY PRESS BOOK

CRC Press
Taylor & Francis Group
6000 Broken Sound Parkway NW, Suite 300
Boca Raton, FL 33487-2742

© 2018 by Taylor & Francis Group, LLC
CRC Press is an imprint of Taylor & Francis Group, an Informa business

No claim to original U.S. Government works

Printed on acid-free paper

International Standard Book Number-13: 978-1-138-19807-4 (Paperback)

International Standard Book Number-13: 978-1-138-08057-7 (Hardback)

This book contains information obtained from authentic and highly regarded sources. Reasonable efforts have been made to publish reliable data and information, but the author and publisher cannot assume responsibility for the validity of all materials or the consequences of their use. The authors and publishers have attempted to trace the copyright holders of all material reproduced in this publication and apologize to copyright holders if permission to publish in this form has not been obtained. If any copyright material has not been acknowledged, please write and let us know so we may rectify in any future reprint.

Except as permitted under U.S. Copyright Law, no part of this book may be reprinted, reproduced, transmitted, or utilized in any form by any electronic, mechanical, or other means, now known or hereafter invented, including photocopying, microfilming, and recording, or in any information storage or retrieval system, without written permission from the publishers.

For permission to photocopy or use material electronically from this work, please access www.copyright.com (http://www.copyright.com/) or contact the Copyright Clearance Center, Inc. (CCC), 222 Rosewood Drive, Danvers, MA 01923, 978-750-8400. CCC is a not-for-profit organization that provides licenses and registration for a variety of users. For organizations that have been granted a photocopy license by the CCC, a separate system of payment has been arranged.

Trademark Notice: Product or corporate names may be trademarks or registered trademarks, and are used only for identification and explanation without intent to infringe.

Library of Congress Cataloging-in-Publication Data

Names: Balan, Yener, author. | Murrell, Karen, author. |
Lentz, Christopher Bryant, author.
Title: Big book of emergency department psychiatry / Yener Balan, Karen
Murrell, Christopher Bryant Lentz.
Description: Boca Raton : Taylor & Francis, 2018. | "A CRC title, part of the
Taylor & Francis imprint, a member of the Taylor & Francis Group, the
academic division of T&F Informa plc." | Includes index.
Identifiers: LCCN 2017007189 | ISBN 9781138198074 (pbk. : alk. paper)
Subjects: LCSH: Psychiatric emergencies.
Classification: LCC RC480.6 .B35 2018 | DDC 362.2/2--dc23
LC record available at https://lccn.loc.gov/2017007189

Visit the Taylor & Francis Web site at
http://www.taylorandfrancis.com

and the CRC Press Web site at
http://www.crcpress.com

Cover design and illustration by: Nadir Balan

Contents

Preface ix
Acknowledgments xiii
Editors xv
Contributors xvii

SECTION I FRONT LINE PERSPECTIVES

1 Emergency Psychiatry: An Emergency Psychiatrist's Perspective 3
  ZORAN SVORCAN

2 Emergency Psychiatry: An Emergency Psychiatric Social Worker's Perspective 13
  ELBA FIGUEROA

3 Emergency Psychiatry: An Emergency Physician's Perspective 27
  RUWAN EKANAYAKE

4 Emergency Psychiatry: An Emergency Nurse's Perspective 39
  JENNIFER MCGRATH

SECTION II STRUCTURAL APPROACHES TO PATIENT CENTERED CARE

5 Contemporary Psychiatric Care in the Emergency Department: Care Options, Treatment Teams, and Documentation Recommendations 49
  YENER BALAN AND CHRISTOPHER LENTZ

6 Risk Assessments in the Emergency Room 91
  REBECCA FINK

7 The Myth of Medical Clearance 105
  LEV LIBET, YENER BALAN, AND SETH THOMAS

8 Discharge Planning 117
  YENER BALAN

9 Ethical Implications for the Emergency Department Psychiatrist 131
  JEFFERY KAHN

SECTION III CLINICAL CARE

10 Anxiety and Mood Disorders in an Emergency Context 147
CHRISTOPHER LENTZ

11 Psychotic Disorders in Emergency Departments 177
CHRISTOPHER LENTZ

12 The Diagnosis and Management of Substance Use Disorders in the Emergency Psychiatric Setting: A Primer 199
NOAM FAST

13 Emergency Treatment of Agitation in Delirious and Demented Patients 235
ELYSSA L. BARRON, ALEXIS BRIGGIE, AND HOWARD L. FORMAN

14 Personality Disorders: An Empathic Approach 245
YENER BALAN AND DUYGU BALAN

15 A Primer on Medical Toxicology 255
STEVEN R. OFFERMAN

SECTION IV SPECIALIZED POPULATION CARE

16 Children and Adolescents with Psychiatric Emergencies 275
GARY LELONEK

17 Correctional Emergency Psychiatry 289
NEIL LEIBOWITZ

SECTION V METHODS FOR OPERATIONAL IMPROVEMENT

18 Introduction to Emergency Psychiatry Operational Improvement 307
KAREN MURRELL

19 A Step-by-Step Guide for Improving Emergency Psychiatry 315
KAREN MURRELL AND YENER BALAN

20 Lean Flow and the Impact of the Long-Stay Patient 329
KAREN MURRELL

21 Change Management and Addressing Barriers to Improvement 339
KAREN MURRELL, YENER BALAN, AND CHRISTOPHER LENTZ

Index 345

Preface

If you are reading this, you understand the importance of the specialty of caring for patients with psychiatric needs in an emergency setting.

Our clinical experience and mounting evidence of increasing demand suggest that the need for specialized care of patients in emergency departments across the United States is critical.

We decided to write this book to delineate operational strategies, discuss treatment care modalities and methodologies, and share experiential stories of those of us caring for our fellow humans every day. In doing so, we strive to dissipate the stigma of caring for patients with emergency psychiatric needs, and to improve the overall quality of patient care.

This book was written for trainees, clinicians, hospital administrators, and, most importantly, our patients and their families and advocates. The content of the book is designed to complement other published, regimented treatment protocols, by ensuring that the human element is retained.

The field of emergency psychiatry is on the cusp of a renaissance. With legislation, such as the Mental Health Parity Act, the subsequent Addiction Equity Act, and more recently the Affordable Care Act, patients are increasingly aware of the availability of treatment options, and have deservedly demanded a fair and similar level of standard of care for their mental health needs.

Now, more than ever, we need to advocate for our patients. There is a need to create high quality, compassionate, low-cost healthcare for patients with behavioral health needs. In the uncertainty of today's political climate, mental health providers need to be prepared to provide support to the patients that they are currently caring for and initiate a safe transition to alternative mental healthcare options if needed.

Hopefully, most clinicians will be able to act within high moral and ethical boundaries and consider pro bono work for their most needy patients. The authors of this book recommend that readers reach out to their local government officials and communicate the need to ensure that our patients' mental health needs will continue to be met now and in the years to come.

With the increase in patient care demand, and the numerous opportunities for improvement in daily emergency department operations, it is imperative that a sophisticated and humane approach is adopted for the care of patients with behavioral health needs. There is no other viable choice but to go in this direction. The other option, ignoring this renaissance in the field of emergency psychiatry, would result in worsening stigmatization, marginalization, avoidance, poor patient care, patient and staff injuries, burnout, and increased costs for hospital budgets and patients.

Annually, over 2 million people seek emergency psychiatric care in U.S. hospital emergency departments, at a cost of over $4 billion. This equates to between 6% and 12% of all U.S. emergency department visits being related to psychiatric complaints. It is reflected in an average length of stay in the emergency department for patients with psychiatric needs that is double that of other patients. This in turn exacerbates emergency department overcrowding, which is a separate national issue with many repercussions.

Emergency department staff often feel burdened by patients with psychiatric needs—for no other reason than the variation in emergency department expertise and training in mental health. The anxiety of feeling underprepared as a clinician, coupled with decreased external resources for patients on disposition, can lead to inadequate care and negative patient and staff experiences.

Following this seemingly dismal patient journey often leads to inpatient hospitalization subsequent to the emergency department visit. According to Agency for Healthcare Research and Quality (n.d.) analyses, one out of every five U.S. hospitalizations involves a mental health condition, either as a primary or secondary diagnosis. An American College of Emergency Physicians (2009) survey conducted in 2008 of 328 emergency room medical directors found that 79% of survey respondents believed psychiatric patients were "boarded" in their emergency department, with a third of patients boarded for 6 hours or more. Moreover, 62% of respondents indicated that these patients received no psychiatric services while they were being boarded.

Patients are presenting to emergency departments with a plethora of psychiatric complaints and diagnoses. Over the past decade, this epidemic has led to a significant increase in patients utilizing the emergency department for quick access to treatment of psychiatric issues ranging from depression to acute psychosis. According to the Centers for Disease Control and Prevention (2009–2010), in 2009 and 2010, 24.2% of emergency department patients sought treatment for anxiety and mood disorders. In 2009 and 2010, patients sought treatment for acute psychotic episodes in U.S. emergency departments at a rate of 17.3%. Patients with substance use issues or comorbid substance use and mental disorders also add to the ever-expanding emergency department census; these patients presented to emergency departments in 2009 and 2010 at a rate of 27.7%.

Given this national increase in psychiatric complaints presenting to emergency departments, and the apparent lack of a current standardized treatment protocol in emergency psychiatric care, a solid foundation is needed for practitioners tasked with building a treatment protocol within their own emergency department. Many of the building tasks that an emergency department administrator needs to consider in the development of an effective treatment protocol include multiple factors. An effective treatment protocol may include considerations, such as patient flow and staffing models that draw from current Lean and queuing methodology and theory. Building and maintaining staff–patient rapport is especially important in working with psychiatric patients that may have extended boarding times in the emergency department. The standardization of protocols for medication management, taking into account both medical and psychiatric medications as well as proper medical clearance and methods to keep medical clearance costs down, is also important. Lastly, proper diagnostic criteria for diagnosing psychiatric disorders, ethical issues, and risk assessment are also key elements of the emergency department protocols. All these topics are discussed in this book in a patient-centric manner and with explanations of how stakeholders in the community and hospital systems benefit from this discussion.

Patient flow through an emergency department is always at the forefront of management's daily operational tasks. With the addition of a psychiatric patient population to the emergency department daily census, metrics like boarding times and average length of stay can be significantly impacted. It is here where the importance of utilizing Lean and queuing theories and methods in the ED setting becomes a key to minimizing increases in these vital metrics. Factors such as wait times in the emergency department lobby, triaging psychiatric patients, rooming them, and ultimately discharging them from the emergency department all come into play in the game of patient flow. The ultimate goal of using Lean and queuing methodologies in the ED is to reduce overall length of stay, thereby decreasing operating expenses and potentially increasing revenue.

Patient flow has a positive or negative impact on overall length of stay in the emergency department setting, but length of stay can also be affected by early and proper treatment with medications. Many of the acute psychiatric complaints that present to the emergency department can be quickly addressed by the administration of psychiatric medication, especially in cases where the patient presents with acute psychosis or agitation. Medications used to treat comorbid chronic medical conditions that the psychiatric patient presents with must also be properly reconciled and prescribed by the treating physician. The goal is to avoid possible exacerbation of the comorbid medical condition and in turn exacerbation of the psychiatric condition that the patient is presenting with.

Length of stay in the emergency department can be significantly reduced when a solid discharge plan has been developed with the help of the patient. Once the psychiatric patient is admitted to the emergency department, discharge planning must start. Discharge planning is a multifaceted endeavor that includes multiple staff and support persons directly and indirectly involved in the patient's care. Any discharge plan that is developed must be viable in order to reduce the chances that the patient ends up returning to the emergency department shortly after discharge.

Emergency department staff may find it difficult to interact and engage with some patients that present with psychiatric complaints. The importance of effective rapport-building with this population cannot be stressed enough. It is vital that any emergency department develops and implements effective patient rapport-building education and training for all staff, with an emphasis on interactions with patients presenting with psychiatric illness. A strong rapport with the patient can go a long way in terms of reducing potential job stress for the direct care staff and the frustration levels in the patient, which can lead to a reduction in potential violent episodes and hence staff injuries occurring in the emergency department setting.

What is it like, from the perspective of staff working in the emergency department setting, to interact with and treat individuals with psychiatric disorders? What do they experience on a daily basis? What do they feel and think about? What are the motivators and rewarding experiences that drive emergency department staff to work with this patient population? From the emergency department physician to the emergency department psychiatric social worker, we include chapters in this book that address the differing and similar perspectives of various emergency department staff working with psychiatric patients.

The topics discussed previously are just a taste of what the following chapters in this *Big Book of Emergency Department Psychiatry* cover. We believe that the focus on Lean processes, queuing theory, metrics, and discharge planning as well as the various emergency department staff perspectives on working with the psychiatric patient presented herein set this book apart from others in the field.

As this book is written for patients, advocates, clinicians, physicians, and hospital administrators, the tone in this varies according to the applicable audience for each chapter. The authors deliberately shift the focus of the audience to enhance a sense of empathic awareness of other audience members' experiences.

The authors of this book are here to make clear that the subspecialty of emergency psychiatric care has the same basic objectives and stages of care as the rest of medicine: establish a therapeutic relationship with the patient, treat for recovery, and ensure the maintenance of wellness.

This renaissance in the field of emergency psychiatry begins with a cultural paradigm shift. We are proud when we see the fruits of our labor and the change we bring to patients and their families, and we know that the contents of this book coupled with the cultural shift in care delivery will lead to sustainable success!

Yener Balan
Karen Murrell
Christopher Lentz

References

American College of Emergency Physicians. 2009. Psychiatric and substance abuse survey.
Centers for Disease Control and Prevention. 2009–2010. Ambulatory healthcare data. Centers for Disease Control and Prevention. http://www.cdc.gov/nchs/ahcd/web_tables.htm.
Agency for Healthcare Research and Quality. n.d. http:// www.ahrq.gov.

Resources

Brown, PC, D Hnatow, D Kuehl, 2013. Behavioral health in emergency care. In *Emergency Department Management* by Robert W. Strauss and Thom A. Mayer. New York: McGraw-Hill Education/Medical.
Centers for Medicare and Medicaid Services. n.d. The center for consumer information & insurance oversight. Centers for Medicare and Medicaid Services. http:// www.CMS.gov/cciio.
The Kennedy Forum. n.d. http://www.thekennedyforum.org.
McCourt, JD. 2011. Strategies for expediting psych admits. *Emergency Physicians Monthly*. February 14.
National Alliance on Mental Illness. n.d. http://www.nami.org.
Substance Abuse and Mental Health Services Administration. n.d. http://www.samhsa.gov.

Acknowledgments

Thank you for picking up and reading our book!

We would like to acknowledge you, the reader, for considering how things can improve for you and those you care about.

I would not be who I am today were it not for my wife, Duygu. She has expanded my heart and mind in ways I did not know were possible! Our son Evrim is my inspiration to recognize what truly matters in life—to share love and laughter.

My mother and father provided me with a compassionate foundation that allowed me to dream and confidently go out into the world. My brother and sister remind me of who I am when I dream too much, and laugh with me.

I have been fortunate to have been in the company of and learned from many phenomenal people. My pediatric surgeon, Dr. Jeanne Pamilla, changed my perception of a personally terrifying ordeal to one of hope and trust.

During medical school, Dr. Lisa Norelli opened my eyes to the level of care required by patients with behavioral health needs, it is in great part thanks to her that I chose to become a psychiatrist. During my residency, Dr. Charles Ramesar and Dr. Bernard Wyszynski had a great influence on me, and I regularly think of our conversations and try to emulate them.

My mentor, Dr. Paul Jayson, is one of the best emergency department psychiatrists in the field; Dr. Jayson taught me to be comfortable in a busy emergency department and to care for myself and my patients.

I am honored to call Dr. David Preven my friend, as he has guided me professionally and personally with compassion, wisdom, and humor for over a decade, from a time when I knew nothing, to now, when I know slightly more than nothing.

My coauthors Karen and Chris are among the nicest, smartest people I know—we have a lot of fun together doing what we do, and I am glad to be on this journey with them.

Finally, I would like to thank all of my patients, past and future, for allowing me into your lives and minds, and making me reflect on the elements required for me to be a better human.

Thank you so much.

Yener Balan

First and foremost, I want to thank my husband, Rich, and my daughters, Maggie and Emily, for their love and support throughout the years. My passion for healthcare improvement has often taken me away from home, but they have always been there cheering me on when I return. I would not be the person I am today without my very best friends John and Doug, and our amazing son Jack. Over 30 years of friendship have shaped my character and personality.

To my great friends, Chuck Noon and Jody Crane, thank you. You introduced me to the concept of lean healthcare and showed me that doing the right thing for patients can actually be easier for everyone. You continue to inspire me with your energy and enthusiasm as you change how emergency medicine is practiced around the world.

Finally, I am grateful to my coauthors, Yener Balan and Christopher Lentz, who made me look at my own biases and reminded me that emergency psychiatry is no different than any other area of medicine and that things can be better for our patients.

I have learned so much from both of you. Your dedication is truly inspiring.

Karen Murrell

I want to give, as my son would say, a "ginormous" thank you to my lovely wife, Kari, for without her strong support and enduring patience this book would not have been completed. I also want to thank my two wonderful children, Kyra and Carson, who showed great patience and understanding in tolerating the nightly *call* during the writing of this book.

Thank you to my colleague and friend, Yener Balan; it was a conversation on a plane trip from Nova Scotia that gave birth to the idea for this book.

Thank you to the contributors of this book, who took the time and energy to provide their knowledge and expertise to these pages.

Lastly, thank you to all of the patients that have helped provide me with the lived experiences and real-time education to help make this book a meaningful document.

Christopher Lentz

Editors

Yener Balan is a board-certified psychiatrist and the executive director of behavioral health for a major healthcare organization. He is a fellow of the American Psychiatric Association and has many years of experience working in high-volume community emergency departments. He is an expert in hospital operations and has given lectures and participated in workshops worldwide.

Yener was born and raised in New York City, and while he still misses the East Coast, has made a home for himself in Oakland, California, where he lives with his wife and 5-year-old son.

Karen Murrell is board certified in emergency medicine and has an MBA with a focus on operations from the physician executive MBA program at the University of Tennessee. She is the lead physician for emergency medicine of a multihospital healthcare organization and a fellow of the American College of Emergency Physicians. She is on faculty at the Institute for Healthcare Improvement and the Haslam School of Business at the University of Tennessee. Her expertise is in emergency department hospital flow and in Lean healthcare; she has lectured and published extensively on these subjects.

Karen lives in Sacramento, California, with her husband Richard, teenagers Jack, Maggie, and Emily, and their two dogs, Lucy and Larry.

Christopher Lentz is a licensed marriage and family therapist practicing in Northern California. Christopher has 20 years of experience working in the field of mental health with a range of patients, both in terms of age and ethnicity. His experience ranges from direct patient assessment and counseling in an outpatient setting to administrative leadership in an emergency department setting. Christopher has also served as a direct care mental health clinician for a publicly funded inpatient psychiatric facility, providing psychiatric assessment, diagnoses, and case management services. Christopher has acted as a frontline emergency department mental health clinician for many years, providing psychiatric assessment, diagnoses, treatment and discharge plan recommendations to emergency department care teams. He has also served as an administrator of psychiatric consultation services in one of the busiest emergency departments in Northern California, helping to transform and drive the level of psychiatric patient care to new heights.

Christopher currently has a consultative role in a major healthcare organization. He lives in Northern California with his wife and two children.

Contributors

Duygu Balan, LPCC

Elyssa L. Barron, MD

Tony Berger, MD

Alexis Briggie, PhD

Ruwan Ekanayake, MD

Noam Fast, MD

Elba Figueroa, LCSW

Rebecca Fink, MD

Howard L. Forman, MD

Jeffery Kahn, MD

Neil Leibowitz, MD, JD

Gary Lelonek, MD

Lev Libet, MD

Jennifer McGrath, RN, MS, ACNP

Teri Miller, MD

Steve R. Offerman, MD, FACMT

Zoran Svorcan, MD

Seth Thomas, MD, FACEP

Evidence-based medical practices including medication are presented in this manuscript, however the authors are not responsible for errors or any consequences from the use of this information. The authors have taken great care to ensure the accuracy of the information in this manuscript, and note that clinicians should only practice within the scope of their license and legal allowances. Any medication should be reviewed for its most current Food and Drug Administration approvals and indications, as these may change over time, and the responsibility of the use of medications and any other treatment is on the practitioner. The information in this book is not meant to replace the advice or guidance of your direct licensed care provider.

FRONT LINE PERSPECTIVES   1

Chapter 1

Emergency Psychiatry: An Emergency Psychiatrist's Perspective

Zoran Svorcan

Contents

1.1 Introduction: The Psychiatric Emergency Room 3
1.2 My Past Shaped My Practice 4
1.3 Variety of ED Settings and Staff 4
1.4 How to Keep a Positive Perspective and Have Fun at Work 5
1.5 Secondary Motivation and Malingering 6
1.6 Confusing and Mixed Incentive Structures 8
1.7 Education Systems and Their "Psychiatric Emergency" 8
1.8 Home Environment 9
1.9 Nursing Facilities 10
1.10 Substance Misuse 10
1.11 Neurodiverse Patients 11
1.12 Conclusion 12

1.1 Introduction: The Psychiatric Emergency Room

The ideas in this chapter are my own experiences and opinions on different topics within the arena of emergency psychiatry.

My first experience working in an emergency department (ED) in America was a claustrophobic one. The ED that I first worked in by New York City standards was small, and therefore by every other standard was tiny.

The psychiatric ED was simply a small room filled with nurses, psychiatry residents, medical students, psychiatric technicians, and a few attending psychiatrists. The space was so small that we only had one square yard to walk around in.

In the middle of this small room was an ominous and intimidating secretary who yelled at anyone who asked her for something. Calling her "scary" would be an understatement.

Over time, as I became used to the smallness of the psychiatric ED, psychologically it felt larger. There appeared to be more room to move around than I initially thought, and I was not afraid to respond when the phone was ringing. Ultimately, even the scary secretary became less terrifying and we became a functional team that worked well together.

Before I knew it, my first year of psychiatry residency training had come to an end.

Years passed, and toward the middle of my third year of residency, I was asked to be the chief of the psychiatric ED. At that hospital, it was called the psychiatric observation suite (POS). I accepted the offer of that position, mostly because no one had offered me any other position. I also happened to look up to the director of the ED, as he is one of the best ED psychiatrists I have ever known.

1.2 My Past Shaped My Practice

In order for you to get to know me as a person and a physician, I would like to tell you a little about my background. I am from the former Yugoslavia, now called Croatia. I graduated in Zagreb in 1995 and worked in a village near the city of Osijek. I got married and had a son. Later, I found myself torn between two sides in a four-year war. During this war, I was able to grow as a person and as a physician through my experience working as the chief of an ED at a medium-sized medical center. Given my experience working in this ED in Croatia during a time of war, I thought I had seen it all, until I moved to the United States.

As many of my fellow immigrants had done while studying for foreign medical equivalency exams, I also worked in a variety of odd jobs to support my family, while preparing for my exams.

I had the good fortune to be accepted into a psychiatry residency program at one of the best hospitals in New York City. This changed the course of my life, and was also beneficial for my family. We felt that we finally had our lives back in control, having had close to a decade stolen from us because of the war.

My prior experiences in the war led me to believe that I could handle any challenge and work in any ED in a large city. However, I then had to adjust to working in a new country, with new laws, and different societal problems for which the patients I treated came into the ED.

During this time, I was pleased to find that most of the people on the treatment team in the ED were intelligent and personable.

1.3 Variety of ED Settings and Staff

There are different types of settings in EDs for the care of behavioral health emergencies. One such type is the Comprehensive Psychiatric Emergency Program (CPEP), which is an independent unit with a short-term stay for patients. Another setting is a subsection of a general ED, where patients with psychiatric emergencies are seen by the consulting psychiatry team. The POS where I trained, and have worked for many years, is similar to the latter example.

One is required to interact with a variety of different professionals when working in an ED. These can include secretaries, nurses, technicians, security staff, medical students, residents, and other attending physicians.

Within the greater department of psychiatry, one is additionally required to interact with therapists, social workers, managers, directors, executive directors, vice chairs, and chairs.

Managing and navigating these personalities and politics can be exhausting, even before you see your first patient! I do, however, love my job, which allows me to overcome the daily political storms of the ED.

1.4 How to Keep a Positive Perspective and Have Fun at Work

One of the first steps in creating a more enjoyable working environment in an ED involves taking the time to meet and get to know the other employees with whom you will be working. It is important to focus on what their roles are, as sometimes there may be confusion as to who is responsible for what.

Try to communicate with every single person involved in the teamwork process of patient care. This results in improved relationships and patient outcomes and increased camaraderie, even for people who aren't native English speakers, like myself.

After a certain amount of time, staff will become familiar with and recognize you and your style, and you will cease being viewed as a "foreign body" in the ED. That is the point where you then become part of the ED family and the ED becomes an enjoyable and rewarding place to work.

As you become part of the ED family, your colleagues begin to trust your clinical advice, consultation recommendations, and curbside chat sessions. They entrust you as the consulting psychiatrist with their patients. Even though your new colleagues may trust your judgment in curbside conversations, it is important that you always take the time to see and assess each and every patient.

When you are working in an environment where you feel like family, and where you are accepted by everyone around you, your morale improves. When you walk into the ED at the beginning of your shift and "everyone knows your name," you feel good, and that in turn reflects on your patient care, their outcomes, and their satisfaction as well.

As you establish your political grounds and relationships in the ED, continue to spend energy on your psychiatry department colleagues as well. I have been fortunate to work with the same social worker since I was a resident. In that regard, I have not needed to establish a new relationship with a psychiatric social worker, since we have been working together for so long.

In the event that you do not know the psychiatry therapist or social worker in the ED, make the extra effort to get to know them, because they will be your closest ally and partner in the psychiatric ED.

Building these strong relationships will also foster a high level of trust between you and your direct colleagues. That is the explicit message I want to convey. Achieve positive, trust-filled relationships wherever you work. When it comes to building rapport with senior leadership, do not bother, unless you have an innate talent for it, or some desire to become an administrator.

In my opinion, administrators may say that they care about you at times, but this usually only applies when they believe that you are doing your job efficiently and are helping to contribute to their yearly bonuses. Administrators' roles can be a waste of money. The administrative dance of having an equally qualified person supervise an equally qualified person can, to the casual observer, appear to be a waste of money.

My advice is to understand these relationships and understand the senior-level politics in your hospital system. Keep up appearances that you are doing what is necessary from a hospital administrator's perspective, which almost always comes down to adherence to policies. And, by the way, good luck with that.

Just remember: "It's not personal. It's strictly business," as Michael Corleone said.

Now that you are relatively comfortable, and settled in working in the ED, a place where you spend more time than at home (excluding sleep), let us discuss the clinical work.

1.5 Secondary Motivation and Malingering

Have you ever thought of why EDs are typically more crowded in the evenings? My hospital is in the Bronx, New York, and I regularly find it interesting that few people are waiting in the ED lobby in the mornings, but in the evenings the waiting rooms are full. Typically, people work all hours of the day, and emergencies can happen any time of the day.

I hold a view that may not be popular, which is that many people use EDs as a source of primary healthcare delivery. Those who use the ED in this fashion are also underemployed or unemployed. These are my thoughts and experiences, and do not represent anyone else's. I find that people have a light lunch at 2 p.m., and then come into the ED with their "emergency." That is when the wait times increase in the lobbies and people begin to complain about the wait.

This is not only true for medical emergencies, I also see this with psychiatric emergencies. I wonder where "the voices" are earlier in the day. There is no scientific evidence indicating a preference for diurnal variation of psychosis.

How are these more prominent and problematic later in the day?

One possible cause for this could be the substance-misusing patient population. If a person uses a drug at any hour of the day that makes them hallucinate, this may explain this observation. This, however, cannot be the explanation for all patients.

The reality is that many cases that are seen and treated in the ED should not have been seen or treated in the ED. Primary care physicians' offices and psychiatry outpatient clinics are much more suitable for the majority of urgencies and self-declared emergencies that I see in EDs.

Outpatient service delivery is typically more efficient in terms of workflow and cost. Unfortunately, the reality is that a section of ED users does not have a disincentive, in terms of copayment or cost shares, to limit or influence the use of one service versus another. There is no systematic incentive or initiative to guide patients to primary care physicians or specialty care clinics, as fee-for-service models typically have a higher profit margin from their ED care delivery system.

This is not a criticism of the patient using the system itself, rather it is a criticism of the system supporting this behavior.

I have gone back and forth working in psychiatric EDs. Prior to my most recent position, I was an inpatient psychiatrist. In my 4 years working as the inpatient medical director of a small community hospital, I was responsible for staffing both the ED and the inpatient psychiatric facility.

During this time, I was able to experience working with patients both in the psychiatric ED and on the inpatient unit. Many of the patients who were admitted to these units would make false claims of hearing voices or make unsubstantiated suicidal threats or threats to harm others in order to get admitted to the hospital. Some of these patients were classified as "malingerers," which is when someone exaggerates or misrepresents an illness for secondary gain. This was an eye-opening experience for me; as a doctor in the ED, I want to and have to trust the patients' word. I am responsible for the health and wellness of my patients and have almost no other testing method for the truth other than what the patient I am interviewing tells me. Experiencing this duality of story told and exposed truth, when admitted to the unit, made me reevaluate my approach toward and appreciation of different peoples' needs.

When clinicians come across a patient whom they feel may be malingering, there are a couple of questions that may arise and decisions that will need to be made regarding what direction the clinicians will take with the patient's care.

Clinicians may ask themselves: Do I want to trust what this patient is telling me? Should I simply admit this patient to the inpatient psychiatric hospital based on their reported symptoms? Where would I be able to transfer this patient to, in order to ensure that they are getting the most appropriate level of care needed at this time?

To further explore this topic, I present the following case example:

A middle-aged male patient arrived at the ED with the chief complaint of "hearing voices telling him to kill himself and others around him." Due to the patient's psychiatric complaint, I was called in to further assess the situation. After speaking with the patient further, he also claimed that he was seeing things that were not present, and believed that there were people who wanted to harm him. During the exam, I interviewed the patient as follows:

Me: "Did those voices say anything specific?"
Patient: "They command me to kill myself by walking into traffic."
Me: "Did they tell you anything else?"
Patient: "They told me to kill everybody else. Also, I am seeing things; people want to hurt me."

Clinically, I did not think this patient would do anything to harm himself or anyone else. I was more concerned about his thought process and what I felt was a disorganization that contributed to his claims. I had the choice of sending him back out of the ED, or to admit him for further observation. To assess the patient's thought process further, and to explore his motivations, this is what I said in response:

Me: "I do not believe you, but will admit you to the inpatient unit. If you act out in any way, we will discharge you immediately."

Upon admission, the patient revealed that he was not suicidal or homicidal, and that he was homeless and knew that if he said "those things" he would be admitted.

I have unfortunately seen this many, many times, and this has been increasing in frequency due to the current economic climate. Psychiatric clinicians in the ED must balance their internal signals and experience with patients they feel will not harm themselves and instead have a secondary motivation, with those who may have the potential to do something irreversible.

When I started working solely in the ED setting, I realized that I had no leverage over a patient's inpatient disposition decisions. I am currently the physician responsible for either recommending admission or discharging home or to a hospital alternative to the ED. Given this current role, I now need to approach a malingering patient with new strategies. I am not afforded the time to continue to observe and reinterview someone when they are on an inpatient unit. The challenge is to correctly assess, diagnose, and make disposition decisions.

I have witnessed my approach to the malingering patient evolve to be even more patient centric to ensure proper clinical care. I will often ask in a way that indicates they have no choice but to leave the ED, and present them with a time line of when they will leave. As I work in an urban area that is not as safe in the middle of the night as it is during the day time, I ask if this type of patient would like to be discharged now, or if they want to wait until the morning. Patient responses range from "let me sleep on that" to "just send me out now." While I realize that an increased length of stay in an ED is undesirable, the clinical outcome and improved communication counterbalance the length of stay concern.

The ED work created a conundrum for me to solve on a daily basis. Any patient that I came across whom I believed to be malingering caused the need to determine what their motivation was for wanting to be admitted to an inpatient psychiatric unit. Depending on what I believed their ultimate motivation was for being admitted, I needed to make a decision to admit or discharge them. Inpatient psychiatric units are truly unpleasant places if one does not need to be there. It is interesting, therefore, to hear when people want to, and make up reasons to go to an inpatient psychiatric hospital.

During all the years that I have worked in the ED setting, I have felt at times that over 50% of the cases I have assessed were malingering or attempting to get admitted onto an inpatient unit for a nonclinical reason. Sometimes, I feel as if even this percentage may be underestimated, but again, this is just my opinion based on the work I have done.

1.6 Confusing and Mixed Incentive Structures

After reading this, the casual reader may be thinking that patients do not get admitted to an inpatient unit unless it is clinically necessary. You would be wrong. In my experience, this happens on a regular basis.

The current medico-legal situation is such that "safe" and "defensive" medicine is taught and reinforced. One of the main reasons why the United States has such an expensive healthcare system, excluding the cost of medications, is that we have the most expensive legal system. Why would any clinician discharge a patient who claims suicidal ideation? Same goes with homicidal ideation. Clinicians who hear someone stating they have command auditory hallucinations or paranoia are more likely to admit the patient than discharge them from the ED.

The system is tipped in favor of inpatient hospitalization. I find that it is easier to admit someone than to gather information and document in detail why someone will not be harmful to themselves or others if I discharge them.

There is a huge incentive to keep the patient in-house, to admit them. Insurance companies will pay for the admission, and patients who claim suicidal ideation are almost always admitted. The clinical documentation of the verbal interview is what distinguishes what happens or does not happen in the session.

As discussed in other sections of this book, proper discharge planning and safety planning are all time intensive and difficult, although the right thing to do. Otherwise, the care of these patients will fall to the lowest common denominator: the path of least resistance and charting laziness. Hospitals know that they will be reimbursed, and some clinicians are reluctant to either do more work or incur any liability, and therefore have a high hospitalization rate (see the "Step-by-step guide" chapter for a further exploration of these ideas).

1.7 Education Systems and Their "Psychiatric Emergency"

It now appears customary that every child who throws a temper tantrum at school gets sent to the ED for assessment by the psychiatric team. The schools claim that it is their "policy" to send these children for emergent evaluation. I refuse to believe that a 5 year old poses a danger to a teacher or staff, although that is the "chief complaint" the child is sent to the ED with, and we find ourselves in the position of being forced to conduct an entire standard clinical evaluation.

The schools often even press for inpatient psychiatric hospitalization, and will send staff members with the child and say things like "but this is the fifth time this year, doctor, that she threw her pencils down to the floor!"

How does an emergency psychiatric team respond to this? Where do we, as a society, and the field of psychology and psychiatry draw the line between misbehavior and pathology? Personally, the majority of issues that children are sent from school with fall into the misbehavior end of the spectrum. Reinforcing this type of school "policy" is concerning on many levels, and I spend my energy speaking with everyone in the school, and the child's family, to advocate for the patient, the child, and to arrange for better, more proper accommodations for the child, rather than inpatient psychiatric hospitalization.

Several generations ago, when I was elementary-school aged, no child was sent to a psychiatric hospital for similar misbehavior. Intellectually disabled children had special services at schools. They were not pushed toward hospitals. A hospital is not the place for help for these children, in my opinion. It should be provided either in the home or school environment.

1.8 Home Environment

On the other hand, the "home" these days is also a source of preventable transfers to EDs for psychiatric assessment. In the Bronx, most children coming into the ED are from foster and group homes. It took me some time to realize that "foster homes" are also business ventures where "foster parents" are paid to raise these children. The children are then raised with the absolute minimum requirements for keeping them alive, and it is no wonder that they are regular visitors to the ED. I find that these systems further reinforce psychiatric care, rather than parenting, as the primary boundary setter.

I have been told (scolded) that a "good doctor" prescribes stimulants for these children (and for their parents too) without discussion. I am dictated to prescribe these stimulants from the ED setting, for their day regimen. And then, since the ED is viewed as a one-stop convenience store for all that ails you, I am asked to prescribe something to bring the child (and the parent) down from the daytime stimulant, so they can all sleep.

Of course, I do not give in to these demands, and only prescribe medications when absolutely clinically necessary, and only those that are appropriate for the "emergency" issue with which they came in to the ED. Otherwise, and more often than not, I send these children and families back to their outpatient provider, and if they do not have one, I set them up with one, after serious doses of psycho-education and expectation setting.

I am concerned that if we do not decide to point out the financial and legal incentives and advocate for our patients, this pattern will not end. I see diagnoses of attention deficit and bipolarity being tagged onto a child's medical records with minimal thought as to how it will affect the child, and what we are doing in terms of the bigger picture. I fear we are overdiagnosing these illnesses in children to compensate for a void, and filling the gap with potentially harmful, serious medications, and traumatizing experiences such as inpatient hospitalization. We are also sitting idly as the costs for these (often unnecessary) emergency services and overprescribing patterns balloon further.

1.9 Nursing Facilities

Again, these are experiential observations, as is the intention of this chapter. There is an abundance of nursing homes in the neighborhood of my hospital. It is of no surprise that I therefore see a high number of patients sent from these nursing homes. Interestingly, mostly on Fridays. Seriously. There is little background research for why this is the case.

I do know that there is a law that nursing homes can "reserve a bed day" for up to 14 days (each state's laws on this topic likely varies, and I recommend you look into it based on the area you live in). This means that the nursing home can get reimbursed for 95% of its care expenses. This in turn means that the hospital, or ED where the patient was sent, and the nursing home are both being paid at the same time!

I can now understand that the incentive is tipped in favor of providing the nursing home staff with respite by sending the patient to the ED, and being paid for that time. The hospitals are also paid for the services they render, and utilization of federal funds, Medicaid and Medicare increases.

I encourage people to look into relationships between fee-for-service nursing homes and for-profit, inpatient psychiatric hospitals. Why would a nursing home resident end up in a psychiatric hospital? Simple. Psychiatrists are adding diagnoses such as schizophrenia, or schizoaffective disorder, or bipolar disorder to patients with dementias, which allows them to prescribe antipsychotics to these patients based on their new "diagnosis." One they never had in the previous 80 years.

The addition of black box warnings on antipsychotics for use in patients with dementias is troubling, as prescriptions have skyrocketed for these patients. And the black box warning indicates that there is an association between dementia and death with the administration of these medications.

I return here to my point of respite for nursing home workers by sending their patients to psychiatric EDs. In the inpatient settings where I have worked, I have seen upward of 50% of the patient census composed of patients with dementia, and some label of a psychotic illness, requiring "titration of medication" on a Friday.

Unless a nursing home patient has a true psychiatric condition, and is having a true, clinical emergency requiring inpatient hospitalization, I refuse to admit them. I think those physicians who do should be investigated by their boards and licensing bodies. Behavioral therapies have far fewer side effects and are more safely administered to patients with dementias. Using a low-dose antipsychotic to get your elderly patient to sleep has many more drawbacks than benefits. I strongly urge against this practice.

1.10 Substance Misuse

The next set of patients I want to discuss are those who are in the ED due to substance intoxication or withdrawal. These patients are a prime reason why, as I said earlier, you need to have good relationships with your ED colleagues.

More often than not, the ED team will consult psychiatry as soon as a patient who is high or low, drunk or hallucinating, comes into the ED. These patients can be difficult to manage due to their intoxicated state; they may be saying things that are nonsensical or they are potentially dangerous to themselves or others. They can be loud and take more time to assess and treat than a typical ED patient. These are the reasons an ED doctor will consult psychiatry.

If you are a psychiatric clinician in a new ED with new colleagues, I encourage you to do what I do. Educate your colleagues. Preemptively spend time educating, and setting treatment and medication protocols for the substance-using patient. Set expectations and service agreements between the ED and psychiatry as to when a consult should be called for these types of patients (see the chapter on care options and treatment teams for more details on service agreements).

The psychiatric diagnosis is one of exclusion, and the patient needs to be sober, or as close to sober as possible, for the psychiatric team to provide a meaningful consultation with recommendations. The reality is that achieving sobriety can also take time (up to 24 hours depending on the drug the patient took), and EDs are not set up for keeping patients that long.

True psychiatric emergencies must be taken seriously. If the patient is not known to the treatment team, and if they claim suicidality or homicidality, regardless of their intoxication state, they should be monitored in a safe environment, until sober, and continually reassessed. Psychiatric observation areas, if available in your ED, are better suited for these patients than the general ED.

Proving a patient is intoxicated can also be challenging, since I find that newer drugs are not detected in a urine toxicology screening. The dilemma is admitting the intoxicated patient, and working with them when they are sober in the inpatient unit. The policies regarding involuntary hospitalization typically require an underlying psychiatric condition, and when the patient is then sober and potentially going through withdrawal and becoming a different challenge on the inpatient unit, it is even more complicated.

The balance is between admitting and keeping the patient in the ED for observation, for the abovementioned reasons. Having discussions with ED staff and hospital protocols can be a way to solve this issue.

1.11 Neurodiverse Patients

While there is a large spectrum of illnesses that span neurodiversity, from those with lower intellectual functioning to pervasive developmental disabilities, my firm recommendation is that only patients with an acute psychiatric exacerbation of their illness should be evaluated for inpatient psychiatric hospitalization.

People can be evaluated for many different things in the ED, including receiving a consultation by the ED psychiatric team. I would rather that the discussion begins with a request for my clinical expertise, rather than the statement that I often hear: "this patient is hitting other residents and has to be hospitalized psychiatrically."

The inpatient psychiatric hospital is not an appropriate place for patients with pervasive developmental disabilities or severe intellectual disabilities, as the treating environment is not designed for neurodiverse needs. And there really is no reason for hospitals to be redesigned to meet that need. These patients need other specialized levels of care, and psychiatric nurses and technicians (techs) care for a different set of conditions.

It is unclear why I am seeing more patients with neurodiverse issues in the ED with behavioral disturbances demanding inpatient psychiatric hospitalization. I suspect that an element of caregiver burnout and the need for respite not found in other places, is one factor. It may also be the increase in incidence and aging of subsets of these populations and their caretakers. It may also be the result of direct consumer marketing and increased awareness of medications; people come in asking for sedatives and hypnotics for all conditions.

Unfortunately, by the time a patient is brought to the ED, the behavioral outbursts may indeed be direct threats of harm to themselves and others, and may require medical and other interventions. I hope that we are sensitive to the increase in these issues and look at coverage of outpatient services to prevent and reduce them, before they end up being true emergencies. And the distinction is that they may be emergencies, but not a psychiatric one requiring psychiatric hospitalization.

1.12 Conclusion

Common themes in this chapter have been enjoy what you do and be true to yourself and the reason why you are doing your work. Many external factors influence how you are able to get to where you need to go; and I find myself spending more energy, it seems, on remaining true to my profession for the benefit of my patients.

The frontline clinician must be aware of hospital metrics and economics but primarily must focus on clinical care, and do the clinically appropriate thing. I have attempted to highlight some of the current challenges I face, and those that I notice are getting more problematic, with no resolution in sight. This is why I discussed them. I hope this chapter and this book emphasize our message, that is, the need to continuously be patient centric, with all other forces peripheral to our true reason for being, which is to help our patients.

Chapter 2

Emergency Psychiatry: An Emergency Psychiatric Social Worker's Perspective

Elba Figueroa

Contents

2.1	Introduction	14
	2.1.1 Social Work as a Profession	15
2.2	Psychiatric Assessment in the Emergency Room	15
	2.2.1 Assessing for Risk of Self-Harm	16
	2.2.2 Social Media and Minors	17
	2.2.3 Assessing and Working with the Agitated Patient	17
	2.2.3.1 The ER Treatment Team and Working with the Agitated Patient	18
2.3	Working with Children and Adolescents in the Emergency Room	18
	2.3.1 Adolescent Case Review: Paranoia	19
	2.3.2 Adolescent Case Review: Suicidal Ideation	20
	2.3.3 Working with the Family of the Suicidal or Self-Injuring Child	22
2.4	The Emergency Room Psychiatric Social Worker's Role in Substance Use Assessment	22
	2.4.1 Synthetic Marijuana Crisis	23
	2.4.2 Conversing about Substance Use with Patients	23
2.5	Mental Health System Issues: The Impact on Psychiatric Social Workers and Patients	24
	2.5.1 Mental Healthcare Access Issues: The Impact on Emergency Rooms	24
2.6	Conclusion	25
Resources		26

2.1 Introduction

Working in the emergency room can be considered by some to be intimidating, but it can also be a rewarding experience, depending upon your clinical preference. In certain situations, this can be considered an intense and rapid clinical work environment, especially due to the significant systemic changes within mental health that have occurred over the past 5 years.

I am currently a psychiatric social worker at a private hospital in the Bronx. However, I have also had the opportunity to work within a city hospital known as the Health and Hospitals Corporation since 2001, immediately after September 11, 2001. I felt this was a significant time period, especially during the beginning of my social work career living in New York, and having received my master's degree. After receiving my degree, I began working at an outpatient mental health clinic in the Bronx, working with adults and geriatric patients and providing individual, group, and family psychotherapy.

Most people you speak to, who recall that dreadful day, remember it as a beautiful sunny day. On that day, I walked back home, since the police came and informed the voters at the booths to leave (primary elections were being held at the time). When I arrived home, I began watching television as the events unfolded. It felt surreal watching as each event occurred, and I couldn't help but go back and forth from the television and outside my window while everything seemed to look so normal. I just couldn't believe what I was seeing on television. I also couldn't help the agonizing feeling of helplessness, especially when only emergency workers were being allowed to go into Manhattan. This was the day of the 9/11 terrorist attacks on New York City.

As I think back, I can recall the overwhelming feeling of not being able to help in any way. I also felt moments of fear, having the harsh reality of terrorism dismantle our day-to-day lives in that one moment. I felt this was a meaningful moment to have played a part in supporting our patients, especially during such a difficult time in which I felt as if the entire nation was mourning. I remember I was interviewing at the time for social work jobs in mental health, and soon after November 2001, I was hired within the Health and Hospitals Corporation in the Bronx to work in their outpatient mental health clinic. As a requirement, social work staff were required to complete a three-month rotation within the psychiatric emergency room during the weekends.

This was a meaningful experience. Given the turmoil created by the terrorist attacks on New York, the New York State Office of Mental Health developed "Project Liberty," which began in November 2001, to provide funding to designated outside agencies and hospitals. Project Liberty's goal was to provide short-term psychotherapy and crisis intervention and counseling services throughout New York for those who lost loved ones during the attacks and for those who worked in the Twin Towers. Many of the staff, including social workers, psychiatrists, and psychologists, were designated to several sites and broken up into teams of three to provide support and counseling. I recall on several days going to different sites throughout Manhattan on the Circle Line to see the lights as families joined together to mourn those they had lost, and I recall when the Federal Bureau of Investigation conducted interviews with families during the 9/11 commission.

Over the next few months, while working in the emergency room, the outpatient clinic, and with Project Liberty, I was grateful for the experience, since it helped define me as a clinician, in helping to mold and craft my clinical framework. Multiple levels of bereavement were involved in the unambiguous loss many of the families were experiencing because they were not able to adequately bury their loved ones. It was a difficult time period, and one of the things I recall being extremely useful and beneficial, especially as a clinical social worker right out of school, was the ongoing clinical support provided to me during weekly supervision by my social work supervisor, by the psychiatric attending, at case conferences, during peer supervision, and in team meetings.

This provided me with the guidance, support, and clinical supervision I needed to help manage my caseload, not to mention what I felt when going in and listening and being present for the families, and in separating my own emotions.

2.1.1 Social Work as a Profession

Although most people consider social work as strictly providing concrete services, there is more to it than that. There is a broad spectrum within social work, and each role within this spectrum has its own job description, whether you work in a school, mental health clinic, hospital, the Administration for Children's Services, foster care, a disability department, or even state-run agencies.

Throughout my clinical practice, what always seems to stand out for me is the ongoing clinical opportunity afforded to me to discuss and present cases to a team, which initially can be nerve-racking, but, truly is a learning experience as you grow clinically in your work. There are many benefits when piecing together someone's past clinical history and helping them mend the broken parts of themselves. We must not work within a vacuum; it is our job, and I believe our obligation, to our work to continue to train and learn through conferences and training. I have found this particularly helpful having worked as a psychiatric social worker for 15 years, the last 10 years in a psychiatric emergency room. It has been especially helpful having developed my clinical skills during psychiatric assessments, especially in working with patients who present with suicidal ideations, gestures, and attempts, and psychosis, including paranoia.

I left the outpatient clinic setting and transferred to the psychiatric emergency room when I realized early on that the pressures of paperwork were decreasing the amount of time I had available within therapy sessions. I had to help expedite and streamline the workflow. At the time, I had an individual caseload, and facilitated four psychotherapy groups and one medication group.

The group experience was initially difficult since I was inexperienced; however, over time it became a rewarding experience in that I had a geriatric group, two other psychotherapy groups with a wide range of both middle-aged men and women, and a bereavement group that involved a group of 8–10 women ranging from middle aged to seniors whose children, parents, or husbands had passed away due to a medical illness or unexpected death. I recall we touched upon several different topics that pertained to the aging process, death, separation, divorce, medical illnesses, and their impact on them. We discussed and explored the obvious elephant in the room; I was the youngest person and the question was, what could I offer, being the youngest person in the room, compared to the older group members who have had numerous life experiences?

I am extremely grateful for the supervision, case presentations, and ongoing peer supervision I had on a weekly basis. I recall initially feeling inadequate, which I explored weekly during supervision. This, without a doubt, provided me with the clinical knowledge needed to work with my patients and their families.

2.2 Psychiatric Assessment in the Emergency Room

The main focus in an emergency room (ER) includes crisis intervention, suicidal risk assessment, and patient safety, and how these interplay with the work as an ER clinician. For a clinical social worker, these are essential tools, which can be utilized throughout one's practice in years to come or in whatever other clinical role is performed in the future.

Having worked in the emergency room for over 10 years has exposed me to a wide array of patients' presentations, especially at the very peak of their decompensation. As a clinician, you are exposed to working with many people of diverse religious backgrounds, races, and ethnicities whether they are children, adolescents, adults, or geriatric patients.

Patients are either brought in by their families, school, or college, or outside agencies such as foster care, the Administration for Children's Services, and outpatient clinics within the hospital and medical groups. The role of the clinical social worker, along with the interdisciplinary staff, is to determine whether the patient, once evaluated, requires an inpatient admission, or if they are safe enough to be discharged home with an outpatient appointment within 4–5 business days.

We evaluate the circumstances that brought the patient to the emergency room: If it is for psychosis, is there a history of current auditory or visual hallucinations? Are they command-type auditory hallucinations in nature, that instruct the patient to act in a certain way? Is this a new onset and how is this contributing to the patient's decompensation, which many times can occur within a psychotic episode or within a depressive episode? Please refer to the chapter on psychosis for more details on this topic.

The social worker evaluates, during the assessment and through the psychiatric interview, to determine if there were other stressors involved contributing to the symptoms. We evaluate the patient's level of functioning, sleep, and appetite. We utilize the acronym SIG-E-CAPS (sleep, loss of interest in things, guilt, energy, concentration, appetite, psychomotor retardation, or agitation and suicide) for depression or to rule out a bipolar-related episode.

The acronym WHIP LASHED (worse or "wired" when taking antidepressants, hypomania in the patient's history, irritable, psychomotor retardation or agitation, loaded family history, abrupt onset or termination of depressive bouts, seasonal or postpartum pattern, hyperphagia and hypersomnia, early age at depression onset, delusions, hallucinations or other psychotic features) is also used.

Differentiating between what is a depressive episode, as opposed to new onset or prodromal schizophrenia-related disorders is important. A helpful diagnostic tool that has proved to be useful to my practice is *Synopsis to Psychiatry* by Kaplan and Saddock.

In working with patients who have had suicidal thoughts, be they passive gestures or attempts, the most important lesson to learn is the ability to reconstruct a patient's thought process; although they might be reluctant to explore this, either due to their own guilt, the minimizing of their symptoms, or the stigma toward mental health disorders that still exists today across all cultural backgrounds.

2.2.1 Assessing for Risk of Self-Harm

A question I tend to utilize in my assessments is, "Walk me through the day you decided you were experiencing suicidal thoughts, or the day you decided you were going to kill yourself."

Some of you are saying to yourselves that that sounds either too personal or too upfront.

Keep in mind, as you are asking these important questions, that it is essential to keep track of your own "affect" and to remain calm, maintain good eye contact, and remain even toned and nonjudgmental. This may be easier said than done. I know this takes practice and working through your own countertransference in supervision, especially for most of you who may feel you are impinging upon a patient's privacy. However, once you get past this phase that prevents you from asking these questions, the patient will let their guard down and tell you their story. This is quite an important part of the role as a clinician, since we are evaluating the patient's level of safety. It is important to focus on the details, including what led them to the suicidal gesture, the frequency of their suicidal thoughts, how often they were having these thoughts, and whether it was a planned or an impulsive attempt. Did they keep this to themselves and not tell anyone, do they have a history of attempts, if so what were they, were they hospitalized due to this, was there any regret over not having succeeded in the attempt, was there a suicide note, and most importantly, is there a history of suicide attempt in their family?

2.2.2 Social Media and Minors

I cannot tell you how much social media plays a part in our work with children and adolescents who do not feel comfortable asking their family members for help, either for fear of being judged or because of their own preconceived notions of not wanting to overwhelm their parents or be a burden on them. I have evaluated cases and come across minors who are posting sexually explicit pictures of themselves, cutting themselves, bullying, or making suicidal statements either on popular social media apps or websites. It is useful to have this important conversation with the patients and their families regarding what they are posting online.

2.2.3 Assessing and Working with the Agitated Patient

Evaluating psychosis can, at times, also coincide with evaluating the safety of your patient, other patients, and staff. Over the years, having worked within a busy psychiatric emergency room in the Bronx as a clinician, I have learned that my gut reaction to situations has proved to be an essential part of my practice.

Working in a small, closed environment and paying attention to the verbal and nonverbal cues from patients has proved to be an extremely important skill. We utilize tools in the ER as a part of the training in deescalating patients in crisis; for instance, crisis prevention intervention (CPI).

By no means am I saying that physically being involved with an agitated patient, or separating the patient physically, should be an undertaking for the clinician. Most of you are already thinking, "Wait, I don't get paid to get hurt." You're absolutely correct. That said, these are lifeline tools to use while working with your team. It is important to pay attention to what or how patients arrive to your ER.

For example, was the patient brought in via emergency medical services (EMS) or police, what does the EMS report say, were they escorted by security into the ER, did they require any emergent medications? In some cases, the patient presents as internally preoccupied, distracted, or disorganized, or is hearing voices, which can be due to a possible psychosis, or the patient may be under the influence of drugs.

Be curious, ask questions, and never assume. They may have had a history of arrests or violence or exposure to the criminal justice system. The patient may have had no previous psychiatric history and is completely afraid of being locked up or being labeled as crazy given that the stigma on mental health disorders still exists.

It is also very important to obtain collateral information from family, outpatient providers, or others who are directly involved with the patient. Collateral information can also be gathered from direct care ER staff. I make it a point to speak to the nurse and ask them how the patient is behaving, before I speak to the patient.

It can help to acknowledge the patient's perspective while attempting to verbally de-escalate the situation, especially if a patient is brought into the ER and has no perceived notion of what to expect in the ER and is shocked to find out that a patient cannot leave until evaluated by the psychiatric team. The patient may consider this to be a direct violation of their rights.

As a clinician, you must be sincere and truthful with regard to acknowledging how patients feel. It can be helpful to consider the following questions as part of their initial evaluation: do they have a history of violence or noncompliance with psychiatric treatment and medication management? If so, you need to remove yourself quickly and effortlessly to inform your ER team that the patient is either psychotic, internally preoccupied, or verbally or physically agitated, and may require oral or injectable medication. A patient's prior medical history is also taken into account prior to this step.

Therefore, asking questions of either the nurse or the patient care technician is an important part of the evaluation process to determine if the patient presents with a calm or agitated demeanor, since most often they are the first ones to come in contact with the patient during the triage process.

2.2.3.1 The ER Treatment Team and Working with the Agitated Patient

This is where working within a disciplinary framework is always essential, and above all, vital in our work in an emergency room. I cannot speak for other social workers in other emergency rooms throughout the New York area, and if you ask other clinicians they may or may not have the same experiences.

I can honestly say it has been an absolute pleasure and honor to work with an essential staff over the last 10 years in the emergency room. We are staffed with two psychiatric residents who rotate every two months, medical students, psychology and social work interns, administrative assistants, four psychiatric attendings, two secretaries, nursing staff, a medical director, a chief resident, and four full-time social workers.

Over the years, I have had the pleasure of supervising a multitude of social work interns from various master's degree programs and provided them with the clinical knowledge necessary to complete suicide and safety assessments in the emergency room. This, too, has provided me with a sense of clinical fulfillment in training new graduates, as well as licensed masters of social work in the field who come to work in the emergency room. What remains constant is being able to work together as a team to keep not only the patients safe, but ourselves as well.

Everyone plays a vital role in working well together, especially during intense, stressful events when a patient becomes physically aggressive, psychotic, or is under the influence of drugs. Also essential to our staff, is having appropriately trained security personnel and fostering a positive relationship with them so they can assist the clinical staff with the de-escalation of an agitated patient. It is also important to provide security staff with information about the patient prior to their being stationed to watch a potentially aggressive or psychotic patient.

In some cases, it can be a challenge for the psychiatric team when a patient is physically located within another service, such as the medical or pediatric emergency room, and the patient is placed on a one-to-one with security. It is necessary to provide psychoeducation to fellow staff with regard to the patient's presentation and to always remain cognizant of this point is important.

2.3 Working with Children and Adolescents in the Emergency Room

Over the years, I have enjoyed working with children and adolescent psychiatric cases. I had the opportunity of providing crisis intervention services within a family dynamic framework. However, a useful part of the clinical work has been the family therapy component of the work, and how time and time again this has proved to be vital to the improvement of the patient. I have attended family therapy seminars, and I took part in a child and family therapy certificate program for a year. This has been extremely helpful in exploring the family dynamic and psychosocial stressors affecting the patients I work with.

So many children arrive to the emergency room with a multitude of family issues, such as lack of communication, bullying, lack of one or both of their parent's involvement, deaths, and history of generational trauma, abuse, and neglect. Once these familial issues are explored further, I have found it to be essential and gratifying work.

I have learned that taking one's time to explore and listen to each party is beneficial in the process of opening the lines of communication in the family, especially when trying to explore what brought them to the emergency room. Displaying empathy and bridging the issues at hand within a supportive nonjudgmental manner is extremely helpful. Participation in family sessions is also quite helpful for the patients and their families to understand the symptoms in order to help them get through the next phase of their treatment.

2.3.1 Adolescent Case Review: Paranoia

I've worked with multiple families from different ethnic backgrounds, and one case that comes to mind was a seventeen-year-old Hispanic Dominican male with no previous psychiatric history who presented with anxiety, difficulty sleeping, no previous family psychiatric history, and no history of drugs. However, he began to experience anxiety about people looking at him (he had a severe case of acne), which created a low sense of self-esteem over the last year.

He was in his high school honor's program, had no history of aggression, and was brought into the emergency room since he was pacing at night, restless, and losing concentration in class. He began to unravel and felt everyone was looking at him through the window in his room.

After a month, he was refusing to leave the house or participate in family gatherings, and he began to isolate himself. His parents reported that he began to not make sense, was talking to himself, and exhibited delusional thinking, reporting that everyone was against him and trying to hurt him and his family.

At this point, the psychiatrist and I decided he met the criteria for an inpatient psychiatric hospital admission. His parents were upset and unable to comprehend what was going on with their son. His psychosocial stressors at the time included applying for colleges, being labeled as an overachiever by his parents, and the recent death of his grandfather, to whom he felt close.

During the family meeting, his parents repeatedly stated, "Where did we go wrong?" and blamed themselves for their son's symptoms. I explored this with them further and they expressed their feelings of helplessness as they became tearful during the session in trying to understand his symptoms, his bizarre behavior, and how this impacted them as a family going forward.

I remember experiencing an overwhelming flood of emotion including sadness for them and how they felt. I recall taking a deep breath because I too felt their sense of helplessness. At one point, we were all in silence, giving them time to process as I provided education on the process of being in the hospital between the emergency room and what to expect when he was transferred to an inpatient psychiatric unit. Both parents struggled with having to leave their son in a psychiatric hospital, and what this could do or how it could impact his academic record and privacy.

I discussed with them the issues of privacy and confidentiality. I recall that it was a long process in helping to contain the parents' emotions, which often reminded me of numerous other cases when I had worked with families and helped them to process their child's presentation and inpatient psychiatric hospital admission. The parents struggled with this since this was his second ER visit; a month prior he came to the ER due to anxiety.

At that time, it was suggested by the team in the ER that he would benefit from an inpatient psychiatric admission; however, the parents felt safe taking him home at that time. I met with the parents, and although they were reluctant initially to an inpatient admission, they eventually agreed to the admission as I explored their concerns and made attempts to explain what to expect when they went to a unit. It has been a gratifying experience working with families with various psychiatric presentations including trauma, abuse, and bereavement issues.

Just being there as a support to the family and remaining silent, as difficult as this may be, allows the families to voice their concerns, especially when they feel they are relinquishing their parental rights and the hospitalization is out of their control. In addition, the families feel they are not being rushed and feel you have taken the time to listen to them, although I do realize this is not the case for every patient and family presenting to the ER.

This is an important thing to keep in mind when working with parents: keep them in the loop as to what to expect, or at least try and be as specific as possible about what to expect during their child's psychiatric evaluation. This is especially true in cases with families who are not in agreement with psychiatric medication due to their own preconceived notions about medications and mental health.

2.3.2 Adolescent Case Review: *Suicidal Ideation*

Another case that comes to mind is a 12-year-old male who presented to our ER via EMS from school for suicidal thoughts after he wrote a suicide note in a text to his paternal cousin the night before with a plan and intent to kill himself. When I went to evaluate him, I recall he presented with such a sad affect, intermittently placing his head down; however, he also appeared to be pleasant and engaged.

We discussed at length what led to the text to his cousin, since he expressed having suicidal thoughts of wanting to stab himself with a knife in his chest. He reported experiencing these thoughts for the past week almost every day for hours, although he was scared to actually do it because he did not want to cause further pain to his family or act out on the plan to kill himself.

He came from a large family with multiple siblings; his parents were divorced for 2 years, which was another stressor. He reported there was a history of depression in his family and, about a month prior, his 15-year-old cousin committed suicide by hanging herself and died subsequently due to medical complications. He stated that, after school, the day prior to the emergency room visit, he went on social media and saw the outpouring of grief her friends made on her page and he watched a video of a song his cousin's friends made in her honor.

He expressed feeling depressed, blamed himself partially for her death, wishing he could have reached out to her more. In addition, he also missed his father, was being bullied at school, and felt hopeless and helpless. We talked about the text he sent to his cousin, which we obtained from his mother who spoke with his paternal aunt and cousin. He stated he didn't want to act out on the suicide plan, he just felt like he didn't want to live any longer. He was experiencing a multitude of symptoms: not sleeping, poor appetite, grades were beginning to go down, lack of concentration, and a lack of energy.

As I probed further, I asked him about his cousin who killed herself, and we talked about how he expressed feeling regret at not having reached out sooner and wished he could have done something. He denied wanting to go with her or accompany her in death. I provided support to him and took the time to acknowledge the importance of having reached out to someone before he actually killed himself or made a gesture to do so.

We also talked about this feeling he had regarding how he should handle problems by himself. I asked him what made him think he had to solve these problems on his own, which both of his parents later corroborated. The patient expressed that it was difficult to cope after his parents divorced, and how he's had trouble communicating with his father since his father almost always wanted him to suck it up and do well, and this created the belief that he had to be strong.

The patient had to stay overnight; however, I encouraged his mother and older sister to reach out to his father to come to the hospital for a family meeting the next day. His mother and sister were open to the idea, and they wanted desperately to help the patient and expressed their fears of not wanting history to repeat itself by having the patient kill himself or keep things bottled up inside as he often did.

The next day, the patient's father came to the ER and I met with him separately; we discussed what brought his son in to the ER for an evaluation. Initially, you could tell he was trying to hold back his emotions. We discussed the family history of depression as well, and I expressed my condolences for the family's recent loss. During the family meeting, the patient's father expressed his frustration and anger toward his ex-wife; however, he also expressed wanting to be there for his son because he did not want to lose him. The patient's father agreed to an inpatient psychiatric admission.

Afterward, I met with the patient's parents together and the 23-year-old sister for a family meeting. The patient's mother expressed her frustration with her ex-husband since she's completely aware of his anger toward her with regard to what led to the divorce; however, she wanted their communication to improve for their son's sake, as he needed their support. During the session, the patient's mother expressed to his father, who was already in a new relationship for a year, that he wasn't as involved in the patient's life as he was before and that the patient considered it a loss.

The patient's father acknowledged his anger toward the mother due to his own resentment regarding the way their relationship had ended. In hearing both sides, we talked about understanding each of their perspectives while also making attempts to work as a team despite their feelings of anger and resentment toward one another. We discussed the need to help their son express himself and not try to figure things out on his own but to freely express his emotions to them.

The patient's oldest sister expressed her insight into the family's dynamics, stating that she felt as if she was in the middle or would rock the boat if she picked any sides, since many times she was the go-between for her parents during times when the father didn't want to speak to her mother. The patient's sister expressed that she didn't want her younger brother to have that same experience. After listening to her, both parents agreed that they would set aside their own unresolved emotions in order to work on the common goal to be there for their son.

Afterward, I brought the patient into the family session, and he expressed some sense of relief about opening up about his emotions since he feared what his father would say and he expressed not wanting to burden his mother. However, both parents openly expressed their support and love for the patient despite what was going on between them as adults. The patient's parents expressed to him the importance of asking for help no matter what he was experiencing and not needing to figure things out on his own. This was an emotionally taxing case, although it was gratifying, as I felt that I was able to help provide support to the whole family and, above all, provide the patient with a voice to be heard.

From many previous child and adolescent cases in which the patients expressed feeling alone, one of the best things I have learned in family therapy sessions is to help the family communicate, give a voice to their emotions, explore their perceptions, and provide support to each other.

2.3.3 Working with the Family of the Suicidal or Self-Injuring Child

When their child or adolescent requires an inpatient psychiatric hospital admission, parents often are left feeling blame, guilt, anger, and frustration, and statements such as "Where did we go wrong?" can be a common experience through this process. It's important early on to expect the unexpected and work as best as you can with the family in providing them with as much support and psychoeducation as possible.

This is not an easy task to complete at times because there may be multiple barriers involved in regard to their comprehension of their child's symptoms, coming to terms with the fact that a problem exists, their child's diagnosis, or even comprehending the mindset of their child who may have tried to kill themselves or is engaging in ongoing self-injurious behaviors that were hidden from the family.

The clinician's role is to identify and provide the support they need. I have found it beneficial to use the family systems model by Robert Schwartz since it allows the clinician to dissect the family dynamic and break it into working parts. Providing families with adequate coping strategies is especially useful in situations when the identified child or adolescent is experiencing ongoing self-injurious behavior as a way of finding relief from their mix of emotions. This can, in some cases, feel debilitating and give rise to feelings of helplessness for parents and families because it's not something they themselves may comprehend. This is where the family intervention is extremely helpful in exploring what is triggering the behavior and why.

Many times during the evaluation process we ask the patient, "What makes you cut?" Their response at times is the inability to cope with all their emotions within one given moment. We also evaluate what is their intent when they cut, what they use, how often they cut, if they hide it from family, school, or friends, how deep was the cut, and whether it was superficial or they required any suturing? Once we have explored this further, it takes away the stigma and embarrassment, which helps the patient to feel empowered to actually open up about their emotions. Parents and families often are open to these techniques, and it helps to replace feelings of helplessness with feeling empowered.

There are several techniques, such as the use of the rubber band, which focus on helping the child to cope with a desire to injure themselves. I like using some of the newer toys, such as "loom bracelets," for this purpose. Many of the kids and even the adolescents have enjoyed using these. Loom bracelets use a plastic loom that allows the child to weave colorful rubber bands into bracelets and charms. I tell the child to pick a series of colors they believe represents strength, and encourage the parents to participate in the process, which helps to elicit more support to the patient and family interaction. The use of crayons for drawing is a useful tool in evaluating children in the ER. It helps them to open up especially in cases of trauma. It is fairly economical to carry around a pack of crayons and paper if it means this technique will help your patient.

Remember with children and adolescents we must meet them where they are at if we expect them to discuss establishing any sort of adaptive change.

2.4 The Emergency Room Psychiatric Social Worker's Role in Substance Use Assessment

Substance use is always a hot topic in the ER setting. As a clinician, the assessment of substance use issues in the patient is paramount, especially when there is a previous family history of substance use. We evaluate the age of onset when they began experimenting with drug use. It is crucial in understanding the patterns of use, whether they use illicit substances to self-medicate or to avoid problems, which can lead to an addiction.

It is especially interesting to see the changes over the years with regard to drug treatment, especially with the legalization, in some states, of marijuana and the ongoing abuse of PCP, ecstasy, heroin, cocaine, opiates, benzodiazepines, and over the counter medications, and people buying prescription drugs on the streets.

Our experience in the ER via patients' reports is that they utilize certain prescription drugs to help counteract the effects of the illicit drugs they abuse. It is helpful to be aware of a drug's street name as well. You can actually obtain this information with the help of the Internet and the patients' verbal reports. This is a consistent part of our psychiatric evaluation in the ER, as it allows us to fully understand the comorbidities and the effects these drugs have on the brain, especially for those with preexisting psychiatric disorders.

2.4.1 Synthetic Marijuana Crisis

We have experienced a public health crisis over the last 2 years in New York due to the rise in use of synthetic marijuana. This has impacted both psychiatric and medical ERs, leaving our staff overwhelmed. Since the drug cannot be detected in urine toxicology screens, this leaves the staff at times puzzled as to the cause of the ER presentation.

Since April 1, 2015, articles have been circulated from the Centers for Disease Control and Prevention (CDC) to all healthcare providers asking them to be more vigilant and aware of the rise of these drugs and the potential risks of these drugs on society. K2 and Flakka, or any other synthetic marijuana, have led to a public health crisis, especially since patients have presented to the ERs agitated or psychotic, and traditional forms of injectable medications are taking longer to demonstrate, if any, physical improvements in the psychiatric ERs.

If the patient presents with multiple medical complications, one of them being cardiac issues, they have to be placed on a "one-to-one" (to be monitored by staff at all times), due to worsening physical agitation, paranoia, and delusions. We have seen the impact these drugs have on patients and their families in the ER, having witnessed up close the deterioration the abuse of these drugs can cause.

In addition, both the medical and psychiatric ERs have become, over time, detoxification units, since many of the designated detoxification units have closed down throughout the city over the last 2–3 years. People who are getting high are often not aware of the consequences and the risks involved with these drugs. Patients cite that some of the reasons they use these drugs are because they are affordable and they do not show up in a urine drug screen. However, the long-term consequences remain and their symptoms can mimic those of psychosis, aggression, and paranoia. Therefore, in conjunction with the CDC, Poison Control, social media, law enforcement, and government officials have made consistent attempts to remove access to these drugs by placing a ban on the sale of these drugs, making multiple arrests, and providing psychoeducation to people about the negative effects of these drugs.

Over the last several months, the use of multiple news outlets and signs posted in the ER triage area have been essential in providing education about the risks and hazards of these drugs to the general population.

2.4.2 Conversing about Substance Use with Patients

As healthcare providers we must continue to openly discuss these issues with the patients we treat despite our own transference issues. It is an important part of our clinical work to know what makes the patient use substances and being mindful of what their triggers are, despite their reluctance to stop.

This is also an important discussion to have with the families of the children we work with whose exposure and access to drugs over the years can at times seem similar to buying candy at their local grocery store. Some of you may or may not be open to this discussion; however, like it or not, this is an important aspect of our clinical work, especially when we are working to help the patient and their family by developing adequate coping skills and changes in their executive functioning skills to teach them adaptive techniques to cope with stress.

I am not saying you can entirely change the patient's mind; however, for some patients, it can be the pebble dropped in the pond that causes a ripple effect in their mindset over time.

2.5 Mental Health System Issues: The Impact on Psychiatric Social Workers and Patients

This takes me to the growing problem within the mental health arena resulting from systemic issues. For clinicians in the trenches, depending upon where you work, salaries overall are still less than what we deserve. Of course, this statement is based on my own personal opinion and many people out there may not agree with me on this.

You have social workers who work multiple venues including schools, foster care agencies, the Administration for Children's Services, public or privately run hospitals, medical or psychiatric settings, shelters, government agencies, intensive case management organizations, residential facilities for the disabled, nursing homes, and substance use settings.

As social work professionals, our needs are not being met in terms of salary, clinically, or otherwise. Many of you out there know what I mean when I say we get paid less to do more. Again, some of you reading this may disagree with me, but think for a moment about all of the tasks entailed within each job description that do not justify our pay grade. For many of us out there who are not being provided with enough clinical supervision, the demands and rise in caseloads have doubled, and for some tripled, over the last 5 years. Most of this can be attributed to our individual state and local government officials and changes in public policy toward cutbacks on services, not only in mental health, but also for the physically disabled, waiver services, hearing impaired, special needs population, and the list continues.

2.5.1 Mental Healthcare Access Issues: The Impact on Emergency Rooms

In my close to 10 years working in the emergency room, several psychiatric hospitals have closed, shortening, as a result, the length of stay in the hospitals. You are required to do more with less. Access to mental healthcare has been much more difficult to secure due to the closing of many outpatient mental health clinics, forcing other clinicians from other clinics to see more patients added to their caseloads. This has led to an increase in emergency room visits, which has been detrimental to our patients and their families.

I am sure I do not have to stress what a recipe for disaster this is.

There are multiple waiting lists for adults, children, and adolescents trying to obtain services, whether they are waiting for outpatient mental health, intensive case management, CSPOA applications (Children's Single Point of Access), or developmentally delayed or hearing impaired services. Making things somewhat less stressful and complicated for patients and families has become a difficult task. These are the systemic issues impacting not only our social work profession but society as a whole.

These are the harsh realities we are dealing with.

Many of you are thinking, "Well, some of these organizations have mismanaged their funds in some cases, causing a snowball effect." Another impact is the change in optimizing medical care through insurance companies that don't want to pay for services, and this resistance has caused many clinics not to accept patients whose rate of reimbursement or ability to pay for services rendered.

An example of this aired December 14, 2014, on CNN's *60 Minutes*, and it was rebroadcast on August 2, 2015 by Scott Pelley, showing insurance companies denying payment to psychiatric patients and the struggle of parents and families to access psychiatric care for their loved ones with mental illnesses.

My own personal clinical experience has shown the need to present your patient's symptoms in a way that ensures they are not denied treatment and reimbursement for treatment. The propensity toward insurance companies denying admission, places yet another barrier to access care, and likely increases the use of the ER.

Over the last couple of years, the state of New York has developed a concept of trying to provide support to families with multiple medical problems and mental health issues via "Health Homes" assistance for adults. This is a case management service via phone that is designed to help patients meet their needs and avoid unnecessary hospitalizations and decrease emergency room visits.

Over the next couple of years the modality of Health Homes will be incorporated for children and adolescents. However, this will continue to be a struggle and a barrier for some patients, since many patients may require assistance getting to appointments and navigating the mental health-care system to ensure improved compliance with outpatient care.

2.6 Conclusion

I have enjoyed this collaborative effort in writing this chapter. I do hope it offers insight into the work I do as a clinician within an ER and most importantly the work we do as mental health professionals. The one thing that remains constant is the importance of ongoing clinical supervision in any setting you are in. It has been extremely useful and essential in enhancing my clinical skills over the years.

It has afforded me the ability to be open to discussing patients and their dynamics and exploring my own transference. This has provided me with a different perspective in looking at the cases I have worked with over the years.

Remain open to working within an interdisciplinary team, which is an important component of working collaboratively with other professions. However, not everyone is exposed to these experiences in their place of employment either due to a shortage of staff or lack of supervision, or when other professions have a lack of respect for those in the field of social work.

Being aware of one's transference is a part of our work as well, and this must be explored during supervision. Especially when there are feelings of burnout or when one is feeling overwhelmed due to systemic issues or lack of staffing and supervision.

Resources

CBS News. 2015. "Denied." *60 Minutes*. August 2.
Sadock, B J, V, A Sadock, and P Ruiz. 2014. *Kaplan and Sadock's Synopsis of Psychiatry, 11th Edition*. Philadelphia, PA: Lippincott Williams and Wilkins.
Shea, S C. 1998. *Psychiatric Interviewing: The Art of Understanding: A Practical Guide for Psychiatrists, Psychologists, Counselors, Social Workers, Nurses, and Other Mental Health Professionals*. Philadelphia, PA: Saunders.
Zimmerman, M. 2013. *Interview Guide for Evaluating DSM-5 Psychiatric Disorders and the Mental Status Examination*. East Greenwich, RI: Psych Products Press.

Chapter 3

Emergency Psychiatry: An Emergency Physician's Perspective

Ruwan Ekanayake

Contents

3.1 Introduction	27
3.2 The ABCs: Airway, Breathing, and Circulation	28
3.3 Emergent Psychiatric Presentations	28
3.3.1 The Acutely Agitated Patient	28
3.3.2 The Suicidal Patient	29
3.4 After the ABCs Is the D	30
3.5 Medical Clearance	33
3.6 Substance Use	33
3.7 Poverty	34
3.8 What We Need	35
3.9 Conclusion	36
References	36
Resource	37

3.1 Introduction

Unlike other parts of this book, this chapter is going to be far less formal. There will be no discussions about randomized controlled trials or clinical policy guidelines. The goal of this chapter is to show you the thought process of an emergency medicine physician during the evaluation of a patient with psychiatric needs.

3.2 The ABCs: Airway, Breathing, and Circulation

In emergency medicine, the airway, breathing, and circulation (ABCs) come first. (Well, technically, for the last few years it has been CAB, but that doesn't sound nearly as catchy). All patient evaluations begin with the ABCs. Patients with psychiatric disease also develop medical diseases. Appendicitis, pulmonary diseases, traumatic illnesses, myocardial infarctions, and infections are just as common in patients with psychiatric disease as they are in patients without. Some illnesses may even be more prevalent. Certainly, end-stage manifestations of treatable chronic illnesses, such as stroke due to untreated hypertension or renal failure due to untreated diabetes, may be more common in patients with psychiatric disease whose thought processes prevent them from obtaining care or following treatment plans.

For better or for worse, the presentation of these critical, immediately life-threatening conditions is usually obvious. Patients with chronic obstructive pulmonary disease (COPD) exacerbation have trouble breathing, those with trauma likely have obvious injuries or clear histories.

The sad truth, however, is that there have been, and very likely will continue to be, cases where patients with acute medical conditions are improperly or less expeditiously treated due to concomitant psychiatric presentations.

This is not due to an intentional desire to treat patients with psychiatric illnesses poorly; rather, it is likely due to anchoring bias in the treating providers. Patients acting bizarrely may be assumed to be psychotic, but may actually have an altered mental status due to trauma or infection. Similarly, for patients with psychiatric disease, they may be unable to clearly convey their symptoms to treating providers, which may delay their diagnosis.

3.3 Emergent Psychiatric Presentations

There are two main types of patients with psychiatric disease who presents with significant and emergent complaints and who must be identified and treated expeditiously: the acutely agitated patient and the suicidal patient.

3.3.1 The Acutely Agitated Patient

The acutely agitated patient is one of the most challenging presentations that is encountered in the emergency department (ED). The medical staff tries to obtain information from a person who may be unable to provide any semblance of a clear history. This can range from not knowing what medications they take to something as basic as their own name. These patients can present a danger to themselves, to other patients in the emergency department, and to the emergency department staff. In those patients who present acutely agitated, with such sparsity of clinical history, it is difficult and sometimes impossible to determine if their presentation is due to an organic medical problem, substance abuse, psychiatric illness, or a combination thereof.

Often, the initial approach to these patients (after the ABCs) is the immediate medical and physical restraint of the patient (Larkin and Beautrais 2011). Physical restraints often begin with hospital security or law enforcement personnel. Frequently, emergency department staff, such as technicians, registered nurses, and or physicians may, also become involved. Unfortunately, physically restraining a person is not in the best interest of the patient or the staff. It is violent and loud and can unsurprisingly lead to further injuries to the patient. It is also common for the staff members doing the restraining to suffer injuries as well. The impact these kinds of maneuvers (such as forceful take downs) can have on other people in the ED can be profound. It may appear barbaric and cruel. Unfortunately, at times this may be necessary to provide safety for the patient and others. Physical restraints are nearly always immediately followed by medical/pharmacologic restraints. The care and safety of staff members and other personnel who are restraining a patient are also very important considerations as they are frequently caring for multiple other patients.

Pharmacologic (or chemical) restraints may take the form of antipsychotics and are administered against the patient's stated will (although the patient may not have capacity to make an appropriate decision). Administering medications against a patient's will goes against a basic tenant of healthcare and of human behavior. For physicians, it is not comfortable to order these medications. For nurses, it is not comfortable to administer these medications. Injecting another human being with a medication despite their protestations seems barbaric. Unfortunately, it is needed in order to ensure safety for the patient and the medical staff so that appropriate evaluation can begin (Petit 2005).

When an evaluation is made to use medical restraint, with the goal of reducing imminent direct danger to patient or staff, side effects to the medication administered are certainly a reality. This is taken into consideration when the emergency is that of safety versus a side effect that can be addressed once safety is established. Since medications are administered in these scenarios in emergency situations, the treating team may not even know the patient's allergies, past medical history, or previous reactions to these medications. The adverse reactions may range from mild, such as hives or prolonged sleepiness, to severe, such as anaphylaxis, cardiac abnormalities, or respiratory depression. Fortunately, for the most frequently used medications (haloperidol, droperidol, lorazepam, diphenhydramine, and olanzapine), adverse effects and true allergic reactions are exceedingly rare.

Some patient advocates and hospital accreditation organizations have stated that these types of medications are not appropriate for use and other alternatives should be considered. Some have recommended that verbal and environmental de-escalation will yield better results for the patient. This type of thinking may be correct. However, ultimately it puts the patient, medical providers, and other patients at a higher risk. Verbal and environmental de-escalation takes time and significant personnel resources, which are not available in most modern American emergency departments. Simply put: When a person presents to the emergency room angry, agitated, and violent, sometimes it feels like the ED lacks the time or resources to quiet the patient down by putting them in a quiet comforting room with soothing music for as long as it takes.

Once the patient has become more calm and cooperative (or at least not a danger to oneself or others), the medical evaluation can begin. Medical conditions, such as stroke, sepsis, encephalitis, intentional or unintentional drug injections, and substance use frequently may present with altered mental status and or agitation as their chief complaint. Thus, psychiatric illness must be considered only after these other treatable medical conditions have been ruled out. The difficulty arises when these conditions are coexisting in the same patient. For example, it is not uncommon to see a homeless patient with a history of schizophrenia, actively abusing methamphetamines, and presenting with an infection.

3.3.2 The Suicidal Patient

The suicidal patient is another patient who requires emergent evaluations. Of these patients, there are two levels of urgency when dealing with them. The first and most critically urgent presentation is a patient who has attempted suicide. The second and less critically urgent case is a patient who plans to do so but has fortunately found a way to get help prior to being able to do so.

In the United States, the main methods of successful suicide are firearms, suffocation or hanging, poisonings, and by falls. The most common method of suicide attempt is via drug overdose (Goldsmith 2002). As always, the evaluation of a person who has attempted suicide always begins with the ABCs.

Firearm and asphyxiation or hanging injuries can compromise a person's ability to maintain a patent airway, their lungs to breathe, or their heart to beat. Patients with these types of injuries are frequently critically unwell and are brought to an emergency department via ambulance. These types of injuries are typically recognized by prehospital providers and taken to appropriate trauma hospitals where an appropriate evaluation for these injuries can begin. The treatment of a patient's underlying psychiatric disease are appropriately deferred in order to stabilize any potential life-threatening injuries they may have sustained.

Unlike with firearm and hanging injuries, whether or not a person has self-poisoned with medications (or other poisons) may not be immediately obvious (please refer to Chapter 15 "A Primer on Medical Toxicology," for more information). These patients may present via ambulance or even with family and friends who simply state that "they are not acting right." In my experience, some patients may not seek medical attention at all or wait until it is too late. Much like with an agitated or violent patient, clinical history is often difficult to obtain. To put it bluntly, when people try to kill themselves, they don't always know exactly what medications they are taking or the dosages. Ingestion of more than one poison is common (e.g., acetaminophen, narcotics, and alcohol). See chapter on toxicology for more information. Furthermore, emergent interventions such as intubation may be required without having all the appropriate history. The best therapy may be delayed until more history becomes available as family and friends investigate. In such cases, a medical team has no choice but to stabilize the patient to the best of their ability, treat a presumed poison, and deal with the psychiatric illness at a later time.

Sometimes suicide attempts may not lead to severe physical trauma and a patient may have minor injuries, which can be rapidly treated. After this, a psychiatric evaluation can begin.

Another type of patient who frequently presents to emergency departments is one with suicidal ideation and fortunately without any active attempt. These patients are typically not medically unwell. They are most commonly awake, talking, and breathing on their own. Most of the time their vital signs are normal. This is reassuring because emergent medical interventions are frequently not necessary.

Despite this, it would be inappropriate to state that these patients are completely well and have no emergency conditions. It is imperative to identify those patients with suicidal ideation who are at higher risk of suicide completion. In my experience, some patients who present calm and logical may actually be at a higher risk than I had thought of committing suicide, whereas those who present in emotional extremis may be less of a risk than I had thought. There are numerous scoring systems, guidelines, and risk-stratification tools that are available to psychiatric providers to help them identify risk of suicide. This risk stratification of patients with suicidal ideation is one of the most challenging and time consuming parts of emergency psychiatric care.

3.4 After the ABCs Is the D

Trauma surgeons will tell you that the "D" in emergency medicine stands for disability. It comes after the initial ABCs in the evaluation of trauma patients. After you determine that the patient is breathing well on their own and their circulatory system is not compromised (i.e., not bleeding to death), you need to figure out where they are actually hurt. A cynical ED nurse will tell you that the "D" stands for the trade names for meperidine or hydromorphone (both of these medications' trade names start with the letter "D"), highly potent and narcotic medications that a patient with drug-seeking behaviors may request. The trauma surgeon and this cynical ED nurse are not correct. For a seasoned ED physician, the "D" stands for *disposition*. As mentioned in other parts of this book, disposition is the most important thing for the flow of patients through an ED, which allows the department the ability to see and treat more patients. This is especially important given the national psychiatric crisis and increased census of patients seeking mental health treatment in EDs.

If the ABCs are compromised, the disposition is clear. If a patient is having an issue with one of these, they are going to the operating room, the intensive care unit, or the morgue. For the rest of the patients, an experienced emergency medicine provider can often disposition patients in their minds after only a few minutes of obtaining a history. We are very good at knowing who is sick and who is not sick. We know who can safely go home and who cannot. Sometimes we will need some additional blood tests or imaging to make sure; however, we can frequently anticipate the outcome.

Psychiatric patients, however, pose an entirely different challenge. Medical diseases, such as congestive heart failure, chronic obstructive pulmonary disease, appendicitis, myocardial infarctions, and traumatic injuries are usually quite obvious based on a history and physical exam. This is not the case with psychiatric disease, and disposition may not be obvious in many psychiatric patients. To the chagrin of many emergency medicine physicians, a quick history is very rarely sufficient for psychiatric patients. In patients with a complicated psychiatric condition, an extremely thorough history is the only way to determine safe disposition. This frequently involves talking to patients at length (who may provide unreliable histories), family members, other mental health professionals, law enforcement, or other ancillary medical staff. This takes hours. Obtaining psychiatric history and corroborating information is difficult at best during weekday working hours. On Christmas Day at 2 a.m., it can be nearly impossible.

Due to the multitude of other demands on their time, emergency medicine physicians are often not able to dedicate large chunks of time to obtain all this information. As such, the majority of this work falls to ancillary psychiatric staff. They may be called therapists, psychologists, or psychiatric help professionals. These skilled individuals are the true core of the emergency psychiatric team. It is up to them to obtain a thorough and complete history for psychiatric patients. Although these professionals may not be under the same time and pressure demand that is demanded of emergency medicine physicians, their job is no less easy. Having spent some time during medical school and residency attempting to do their job I can tell you it is one of the most frustrating endeavors I have ever undertaken. The cards are stacked against these psychiatric health professionals.

Behavioral health clinicians have to deal with many hurdles in order to be able to put together a clear picture of the patient's psychiatric disease. Patients with behavioral health needs may have an altered mental status or irrational thinking impairing their ability to provide an accurate history. Personality disorders or a patient's secondary motivations (either real or due to psychiatric disease) may further complicate the picture or cause patients to lie. I have assessed patients who have changed the story they told me the next time they told their story to the behavioral health clinician. I have even heard patients change their stories as the conversation developed.

As psychiatric disease may cause inappropriate behaviors, law enforcement frequently becomes involved with psychiatric patients. Behavioral health clinicians in the emergency room must work with the legal system to obtain an appropriate history on patients and safe disposition. It is very difficult to evaluate a patient with catatonia who was brought in by law enforcement because the person was laying down on the freeway. Similarly, a patient with bipolar disorder may be in custody for performing unsafe behaviors related to drugs or alcohol. A person with acute psychosis may be behaving bizarrely in the community, which may be harmful to the patient or others.

Corroborating information may be difficult or impossible to obtain (for further information, please see the chapter on discharge planning). Patients with severe psychiatric disease may lack social support. When patients are brought to the emergency room they may not even know their own names. Even when psychiatric emergency professionals are able to contact family or friends, they may similarly be unaware of the patient's psychiatric diagnoses or treatment plans. It is common for people with psychiatric disease to live in "room and board" or "board and care" ("halfway houses") type facilities. These facilities have variable levels of supervision, and the other residents of these facilities may have no idea about their roommate's psychiatric disease. Friends and family may also be unreliable or may have secondary motivations. Even if there are friends and family involved with a patient's care, the difficulties and challenges of taking care of a person with abnormal behaviors can take a toll on them. This may cause friends or family to simply not want to help or not be able to help. It is not uncommon for a family member with psychiatric disease to be brought into an emergency department for abnormal behaviors because the family that was taking care of them has to leave town, or has a new baby, or, sadly sometimes, is having guests over.

These are some of, but certainly not all of the barriers that emergency psychiatric professionals have to deal with. Clearly obtaining an appropriate and thorough history can be a Herculean task. Despite these numerous challenges, I have found that psychiatric professionals do amazing work! They are able to contact and coordinate with psychiatrists, law enforcement, friends, and family to provide a clear history of the patient and their psychiatric disease. During my brief initial interview of a patient, I obtain one history, but when the psychiatric health professionals finds me after doing their work, I am frequently amazed at the additional information they were able to gather to help the medical team take care of the patient.

Once a full history is obtained, it is possible to really determine the disposition for these patients. If patients are determined to not be a danger to themselves or others and have appropriate outpatient follow-up care, they are discharged—much like any medical patient once their medical emergency has been stabilized. Alternatively, if it is determined that a patient is a danger to himself or others the patient clearly needs to be admitted to a psychiatric facility.

Admission to a psychiatric facility has its own set of administrative loopholes and processes that need to be followed (that discussion is beyond the scope of this chapter.) Additionally, since psychiatric care is typically not well reimbursed, there is often little motivation for psychiatric hospitals to take on new patients. Even more importantly, there are also very few psychiatric resources (hospitals and beds therein) available. This availability is critically narrowed for patients who are on government health insurance, such as Medicare or Medicaid and even worse for patients with no insurance whatsoever. Thus, for patients with psychiatric emergencies, the process of obtaining a thorough history takes many hours so they are frequently boarded in the emergency room until an appropriate disposition can be determined.

Boarding in the ED is an awful situation for the patient, the medical staff, the physicians, and for other ED patients. In hospitals I have worked in, a 24–48 hour stay in the emergency room is fairly normal for psychiatric patients. A stay of 4–5 days is not uncommon. In certain extreme cases, people are in the ED for up to 2 weeks. Most reasonable people would not feel that this is appropriate for another human being. Yet, it is what is happening in the emergency department every day across the country (Weiss et al. 2012).

Just like any other resource in the emergency department, the hiring and management of psychiatric help professions require planning, budgeting, and administrative upkeep. In emergency departments, where resources may already be stretched thin, it may be difficulty to justify hiring a psychiatric health professional when the resources may be better spent on more ventilators. All over the United States, emergency departments are decreasing in number (O'Shea 2007) and are increasing in patient volume (Skinner et al. 2014). Prioritizing the treatment and staffing required for adequate behavioral healthcare in an ED is challenging. New innovations, such as videoconferencing and telemedicine, can improve psychiatric access, especially in hospitals that are not in urban centers. However, this is also not ideal for the patient and provider and simply is a stopgap or work-around for improving care with limited resources.

3.5 Medical Clearance

In emergency medicine, medical clearance is the idea that an emergency medicine physician must rule out medical causes of altered mental status or abnormal behavior prior to a patient being psychiatrically evaluated and or hospitalized. Looking at it objectively, of course this makes sense. Putting a patient who is intoxicated or under the influence of a substance into a psychiatric hospital makes no sense. Similarly, if a patient has a head injury, a neurologic disease, an infection, or another metabolic condition that would cause abnormal behavior, psychiatric hospitalization is not the correct treatment. However, the overall process of medical clearance has become an arduous process, which does not help the patient, the providers, or the healthcare system as a whole.

Patients with known psychiatric disease who come into a medical facility and state that they are hearing voices or having psychotic thoughts or hallucinations due to medication nonadherence likely do not require a medical work up. This especially pertains to patients who are well known to the local system. Regardless, these patients must also be medically evaluated and screened in most areas of the country. These patients often do not medically require repeated medical screening each time they present.

In my local emergency department, a medical screening involves a full, complete blood panel, a chemistry panel (including liver function tests), a urine drug screen, evaluation for acetaminophen and aspirin overdoses, and sometimes a thyroid screen. In some emergency departments, a computed tomography (CT) scan of the head (regardless of traumatic physical exam findings) or a chest x-ray (to rule out asymptomatic tuberculosis) are part of the work up for medical clearance. In my experience, nearly all these tests will turn out to be negative. All this unnecessary testing has the potential to be harmful to patients, and is certainly expensive for the healthcare system (Lukens et al. 2006). Unfortunately, this testing is not left up to the discretion of the treating emergency medicine physician; rather, it is frequently determined by preexisting protocols (please see Chapter 7, "The Myth of Medical Clearance," for more information and recommendations).

3.6 Substance Use

Due to my clinical experience working with patients with comorbid substance use and psychiatric illness, I feel that stating that they may coexist may be unnecessary. Study after study has shown that patients with psychiatric disease have a higher risk of substance use, which in turn can exacerbate underlying psychiatric conditions and a person's ability to get help for them (Hartz et al. 2014). In my experience, this has also occurred over and over in the EDs that I have practiced in.

This is not to say that all people with a psychiatric disease are taking illicit substances. This is certainly not the case. Most people who have psychiatric diseases are well managed by their therapists and doctors and lead perfectly ordinary lives. Unfortunately, as an emergency room physician, this is not who I see.

Alcohol, being the most commonly used substance in the United States, can lead to medical complications such as traumatic injuries or liver disease. It can also lead to issues with law enforcement such as alcohol-related offenses. In psychiatric patients who may already be experiencing impaired judgment, it may worsen the situation.

Marijuana does not frequently play a role in emergent psychiatric pathology. However, marijuana may cause temporary abnormal behavior in patients who are not used to a psychotropic agent. In some patients, cannabis may cause a temporary acute psychosis (Barkus 2016). It may cause gastrointestinal problems, such as marijuana hyperemesis syndrome. It may be important to note that some studies suggest that use of cannabis earlier in life may be associated with schizophrenia (Gage et al. 2016), although that link is not definitive at this time. There does however seem to be a strong link between chronic cannabis use and the later development of schizophrenia (Moore et al. 2007). Marijuana's prevalence (and increasing overall acceptance) in society can lead to occasional accidental ingestions, which may cause emotional distress for patients who are not expecting it.

Cocaine mainly causes agitation and other hyperstimulated behaviors. These may exacerbate already aberrant behaviors in patients with psychiatric disease.

Heroin is a substance that is most prevalent in large urban centers. However, in the last decade, its use has spread to suburban and rural environments. In an intoxication state, heroin acts as a depressant, and can influence psychiatric clinical presentation in the ED. Heroin is one of the most addictive illicit drugs that is easily available, and its addiction leads to behaviors that may be harmful in the procurement of the drug.

Today, prescription opioids (and abuse thereof) are one of the largest public health crises that EDs and the medical community as a whole have to deal with. While clinically prescribed opioids have a legitimate medical purpose, their use frequently leads down the path of addiction and other psychiatric disease for patients. Frequently, in suburban centers, prescription opioids are among the first substances that are used by young people experimenting with illicit substances.

Methamphetamines are a significant problem for those with psychiatric disease. They are quickly becoming some of the most used drugs in certain areas of the United States (Degenhardt et al. 2010). In some areas, arrests for methamphetamine use and distribution have overtaken those for cocaine and opioids. Certain types of methamphetamines may also be as addictive as heroin. Even for patients without psychiatric disease, methamphetamine use may mimic psychiatric pathology, such as paranoia, mania, or even frank psychosis with auditory and visual hallucinations and aggressive behavior (Grant et al. 2012). As such, it becomes difficult to evaluate these patients who are taking methamphetamines to determine if they are simply under the effect of the drug, or if they actually have psychosis due to an underlying psychiatric disease. Sometimes it is both.

Other psychotropic agents and illicit substances, such as LSD, ketamine, PCP, and psychoactive mushrooms may also be used by psychiatric patients. However, acutely intoxicated patients with these drug ingestions are, on the whole, less common than the ones mentioned previously (please see the chapter on substance use for further guidance).

3.7 Poverty

Poverty is a significant socioeconomic problem, which makes the emergency department evaluation and treatment of psychiatric disease challenging. In general, patients with psychiatric disease have a more difficult time obtaining gainful employment and, subsequently, health insurance (Lehman 1995). Poverty and comorbid substance use can create financial burdens on the patient. These factors decrease their ability to pay for psychiatric help. As such, they may not have access to long-term psychiatric care. This is far from ideal. Additionally, as most of these patients are unable to pay, there is less incentive for private psychiatric hospitals to accept them as patients, as they know that their reimbursement will be minimal or none. This is the sad fact of psychiatric care within the United States, and although it is distasteful, ignoring this aspect of psychiatric illness would be foolish.

3.8 What We Need

Provision of care and availability of resources for patients with emergent and acute behavioral health needs in the United States is suboptimal. In order to create an optimal system for behavioral healthcare in the EDs, more resources and a cultural change is needed. Of course, as most people are aware, most changes can be implemented by an increase in funding.

In an ideal world, resources should be allocated to provide young people and families of children with psychiatric disease access to psychiatric care starting from a very young age. This would involve care by psychiatrists, therapists, psychotherapy, and life skills classes. This would increase the chance that a person's psychiatric illness does not end up defining their future and has more of a likelihood of becoming a manageable illness. Funding would also be provided to ensure that young people with severe psychiatric disease who are just entering the workforce are given an opportunity to be productive members of society. This would allow them to obtain gainful employment, obtain insurance for their own psychiatric care, and would perhaps decrease the frequency of substance misuse.

Psychiatrists and other psychiatric professionals should be given increased compensation (see current U.S. Parity Laws) for psychiatric care as their own well-being impacts their medical health as well. Sadly, the U.S. government's Medicare reimbursement for psychiatry is astonishingly poor, as treatments that are more invasive (such as interventional procedures and surgeries) are more highly reimbursed than therapy and or medication or medical therapy.

Increased, availability of outpatient and hospital alternative behavioral health resources would also significantly improve overall care. Enhancing existing individual and group talk therapy availabilities would be of great benefit to the community and allow for more options for disposition planning from an ED. Unfortunately, it's difficult to ascertain whether the lack of resources allocated is due to reimbursement rates, or the scarcity of availability of therapists in any given community. It may be that they are interrelated, and both exacerbate the problem.

Emergency psychiatric care would be significantly improved by the availability of dedicated psychiatric emergency departments. Those that are present are rare and are mainly at large academic urban centers. Improved emergency department physician and staff training in psychiatric care may be an appropriate first step instead of a dedicated psychiatric emergency department.

Additionally, increased psychiatrist availability in the ED specifically would be ideal. This is unfortunately a culture change, which needs to occur within medicine and psychiatry. For the most part, psychiatrists are not used to being in the ED and managing emergent psychiatric patients 24 hours a day, 7 days a week. Emergency departments are staffed by emergency medicine physicians during all hours of the day. Other specialists like surgeons understand that they may be called in at any time to perform emergency surgeries, and obstetricians understand that babies are born at any time. However, the psychiatric community in general seems to feel that emergent psychiatric care can often wait until weekday business hours. This is unacceptable. This is not to say that psychiatrists are lazy or don't want to work (nothing could be further from the truth); however, it is the ingrained expectation and culture of psychiatry as a medical specialty. While this may have been appropriate 50 years ago, it requires a rethink today. Fortunately, in some locations, this is already happening. Some post-residency fellowships in emergency psychiatry exist, but these are rare. There are hospitals where the emergency and psychiatry departments work hand in hand to ensure their patients get 24/7 care. These are fantastic improvements in the care of psychiatric disease, and the caregivers and physicians who work at these locations have my respect and commendation.

3.9 Conclusion

Psychiatric emergency medicine remains a very challenging field within emergency medicine. Fortunately, this has been recognized by governing bodies such as the American College of Emergency Physicians. Emergency psychiatric care is slowly improving nationwide. It is my hope that the readers of this book will play some role in it and become the leaders who will spearhead these changes for the patients that so deserve it.

References

Barkus, E. 2016. High-potency cannabis increases the risk of psychosis. *Evidence-Based Mental Health* 19 (2): 54.

Degenhardt, L, B Mathers, M Guarinieri, S Panda, B Phillips, S A Strathdee, M Tyndall, L Wiessing, A Wodak, and J Howard. 2010. Meth/amphetamine use and associated HIV: Implications for global policy and public health. *International Journal of Drug Policy* 21 (5): 347–358.

Gage, S H, M Hickman, and S Zammit. 2016. Association between cannabis and psychosis: Epidemiologic evidence. *Biological Psychiatry* 79 (7): 549–556.

Goldsmith, S K. 2002. *Reducing Suicide: A National Imperative.* Washington, DC: Academies Press.

Grant, K M, T D LeVan, S M Wells, M Li, S F Stoltenberg, H E Gendelman, G Carlo, and R A Bevins. 2012. Methamphetamine-associated psychosis. *Journal of Neuroimmune Pharmacology* 7 (1): 113–139.

Hartz, S M, C N Pato, H Mederios, P Cavazos-Rehg, J L Sobell, J A Knowles, L J Bierut, and M T Pato. 2014. Comorbidity of severe psychotic disorders with measures of substance use. *JAMA Psychiatry* 71 (3): 248–254.

Larkin, G L, and A L Beautrais. 2011. Behavioral disorders: Emergency assessment. In *Tintinalli's Emergency Medicine: A Comprehensive Study Guide*, by Judith Tintinalli, 1939–1946. New York: McGraw Medical.

Lehman, A F. 1995. Vocational rehabilitation in schizophrenia. *Schizophrenia Bulletin* 21 (4): 645–656.

Lukens, T W, S J Wolf, J A Edlow, S Shahabuddin, M H Allen, G W Currier, and A S Jagoda. 2006. Clinical policy: Critical issues in the diagnosis and management of the adult psychiatric patient in the emergency department. *Annals of Emergency Medicine* 79–99. doi:10.1016/j.annemergmed.2005.10.002.

Moore, T H M, S Zammit, A Lingford-Hughes, T R E Barnes, P B Jones, M Burke, and G Lewis. 2007. Cannabis use and risk of psychotic or affective mental health outcomes: A systematic review. *The Lancet* 370 (9584): 319–328. doi:10.1016/S0140-6736(07)61162-3.

Petit, J R. 2005. Management of the acutely violent patient. *Psychiatric Clinics of North America* 28 (3): 701–711.

Skinner, H, J Blanchard, and A Elixhauser. 2014. *Trends in Emergency Department Visits, 2006–2011.* H-CUP Statistical Brief #179, Rockville, MD: Agency for Healthcare Research and Quality.

Weiss, A P, G Chang, S L Rauch, J A Smallwodd, M Schechter, J Kosowsky, E Hazen et al. 2012. Patient and practice related determinants of emergency department length of stay for patients with psychiatric illness. *Annals of Emergency Medicine* 60 (2): 162–171. doi:10.1016/j.annemergmed.2012.01.037.

Resource

O'Shea, J S. 2007. *The Crisis in America's Emergency Rooms and What Can Be Done.* Executive Summary Backgrounder #2092, Washington, DC: The Heritage Foundation.

Chapter 4

Emergency Psychiatry: An Emergency Nurse's Perspective

Jennifer McGrath

Contents

4.1 Introduction..
4.2 Caring for People 39
4.3 Psychiatric Nursing Knowledge.. 40
    4.3.1 Misdiagnosis due to Medical Mimicry: A Case Study 40
        4.3.1.1 Case Study Discussion: Misdiagnosis 41
4.4 Patient and Staff Safety 41
    4.4.1 Pills and Vodka: An Unfortunate Occurrence 42
    4.4.2 Purses and Knifes: Not What the Doctor Ordered 42
4.5 Patient Coping Mechanisms.. 42
4.6 Staff Splitting.. 43
    4.6.1 You Are a Great Nurse, Unlike Your Rude Colleague: A Case Study 43
        4.6.1.1 Case Study Discussion: Staff Splitting 43
4.7 Communication with the Emergency Physician.. 44
4.8 Conclusion.. 44
        44

4.1 Introduction

I have had the privilege of being a nurse in an emergency department (ED) for 13 years—"being" a nurse, I say, versus "working" as a nurse. I consider this profession a state of being and not simply a means of paying the mortgage; money is something that can be earned from a myriad of sources. Raised in rural suburbia, I began this journey of professional "being" as a new graduate nurse who suddenly, albeit deliberately, found herself in the middle of the hornet's nest that is the glorious ED at San Francisco General Hospital. Prior to becoming a nurse, I had several years of experience as a non-licensed medical staff member working with marginalized groups in our community, including the poor, recently immigrated and undocumented, socially and academically illiterate, and people with disabilities. However, this hospital is where I was indoctrinated into an elite society of sorts.

4.2 Caring for People

The patients and my mentors in this institution both taught me early on the art of emergency nursing, more specifically, psychiatric nursing, since that is a major component of work in the ED. Thanks to several key experiences in my formative years, I learned not just how to mainline a B-52 (diphenhydramine, haloperidol 5 mg, and lorazepam 2 mg) in the acutely psychotic patient; I also learned that an otoscope cord will actually restrict cerebral blood flow when wrapped tightly around the neck of a suicidal patient. I learned the most important lesson irrespective of nursing algorithms and pharmacokinetics: these are *people* we are treating.

People.

They are *us*, and we are *them*.

While science tells us that there are genetic predispositions toward various psychiatric diagnoses, the end-of-the-day reality is that we are all potentially a step away from being on the other side of the curtain being watched by a security officer or sitter to keep us safe.

This concept of patients as people and incorporating the human aspect, even in this chaotic, sometimes nameless, faceless urban ED, led me on a path to ask these questions of myself and my colleagues, and now of you the reader:

How can we better prepare ourselves as medical care providers to never lose sight of the *people* and their journey?

How can we accomplish this without getting assaulted with a full urinal or called every awful playground name imaginable?

4.3 Psychiatric Nursing Knowledge

Before we get into the discussion of preserving the human element in the patient with psychiatric needs from a nursing perspective, it is valuable that we discuss just what "book knowledge" the ED nurse should possess in order to practice safely.

In nursing school, basic didactic teaching is provided and regurgitated by the eager nursing student. Medications are researched and medication cards are created in order to safely pass that dose of lithium during psychiatry (psych) rotation clinicals.

Many of us prayed that the patient just simply took the medication easily, without hiding the pills in their cheeks until you walked away. Some of us also prayed the patients were in the day room so we didn't actually have to dose their meds at that time, or interact with them at all for that matter.

Suddenly, one day you've graduated, and you find yourself in the middle of an urban ED where every single gurney has four leather restraints bolted to it and not many patients take their meds willingly, which is what may have landed many of them on your doorstep.

The nurse standing in this ED, and thousands just like it (big and small) across the country should be familiar with the basic defining features of commonly seen psychiatric diagnoses, their symptoms, and commonly used medications to treat them. This is paramount; you need to know what you're potentially dealing with as you march ahead. Many of our patients self-medicate with illicit drugs or misuse prescription medications. The practicing nurse should be aware of how diverse drug-induced states look and how patients present behaviorally, and how these states may mimic various medical diagnoses and their sequelae (see the chapters on substance use and toxicology for further information).

4.3.1 Misdiagnosis due to Medical Mimicry: A Case Study

Let's look at a brief case study:

The police were called to a neighborhood for the complaint of someone breaking several car windows at random. When they arrived in the neighborhood, they found a 40-year-old Caucasian male with a history of depression and post-traumatic stress disorder from severe childhood trauma. He had very rapid speech, was diaphoretic, and would not follow any commands to put down the metal pipe in his hand. He was nervously pacing and seemed to be responding to internal stimuli. He became violent when they attempted to handcuff him, so he was ultimately tased, restrained, and brought to the ED.

On arrival, he was again violent with police and staff as they attempted to take him into the department. He was given two injections of an antipsychotic and sedative and fell promptly asleep.

And sleep he did—for 3 days straight.

He barely roused, wouldn't eat, and was even occasionally incontinent of urine. Collateral information was obtained from his spouse, who told the therapist that the patient had been using cocaine and alcohol regularly for years and had most recently been on a cocaine "binge" for the last 5 days, and had slept very little.

On day three, as he awaited inpatient psychiatric placement for "grave disability," the patient could still not be awoken easily. Both the nurse and ED physician were certain the patient's behavior could be attributed to him "just sleeping it off" and no further lab or radiologic testing was ordered. Later in the day, a new nurse thoroughly examined the patient and noticed he was not moving the left side of his body. She alerted the same physician, and the patient was taken to the computed tomography (CT) scanner and was diagnosed with a large hemorrhagic stroke. After the patient was whisked to the resuscitation room for intubation, security officers (medically untrained personnel) mentioned to other staff that he had not moved that side of his body since the day before.

Since the nurse and the physician involved had taken care of many patients like this one in their careers, they knew that often patients who abuse stimulants may fall into a deep sleep once they are in the confines of the ED, as their body attempts to undo what has just been done to it. In this case, the team used the clinical symptoms and history obtained from collateral information to diagnose an intoxication and, later, a withdrawal state, and attributed their findings to an association with substance misuse. When the presentation did not continue to fit the initial diagnosis, upon reexamination, the patient was correctly diagnosed.

4.3.1.1 Case Study Discussion: Misdiagnosis

There are many good lessons in this case study. Psychiatric patients are not medically well until proven otherwise. You must perform regular physical exams on them—walking by the door and waving to them each shift does not count. You must consider a whole host of medical diagnoses to rule out initially and throughout their stay with you. Interjecting personal bias toward these at-risk patients will likely lead you down a path of doom; you will miss key elements of the patient's history, their presentation, and their diagnoses—medical and psychiatric.

By not thoroughly examining these patients you will miss such things as wounds, dysrhythmias, overdoses, endocrinologic emergencies, or even evidence of maltreatment by a caregiver or significant other. You may also overlook the evolving picture of delirium or alcohol withdrawal, both of which we know put the patient at higher risk for morbidity and mortality.

4.4 Patient and Staff Safety

Methods of staying safe as a staff member and those essential to keeping your patients safe must be incorporated at all times, starting at the beginning of their visit. Patients should have their personal belongings removed from them initially, and they should be changed into hospital attire. This removes the risk of weaponry on the unit, as well as the potential for ingestion of substances they may have brought to the hospital with them (see Chapter 5 on care options and treatment teams for further information).

4.4.1 Pills and Vodka: An Unfortunate Occurrence

I will never forget one particular experience I had while working in a busy county hospital. The other nurse I was working with in triage had checked in a patient who was accompanied by police and had come for medical clearance after a motor vehicle crash, which resulted in felony driving under the influence.

As triage nurses, we were in charge of all the front door and ambulance traffic, as well as a very long hallway where those who could not walk were camped out waiting for an available bed. My partner directed this patient and her officer to a bed halfway down the hallway to wait. They had been in our ED about 3 hours. Though the patient also told my partner she was suicidal, my partner felt the patient was being "dramatic" in an effort to avoid jail. The patient had her bag of belongings on the gurney next to her, and the officer sat across the hallway from the patient's gurney and worked on his laptop.

Suddenly, it was noted that the patient had a seizure and was found to be pulseless; she was in ventricular fibrillation (V-fib) arrest. Our staff rushed the patient to the code room, performed cardiopulmonary resuscitation (CPR), and the patient ultimately died in the ED.

Another patient down the hall told staff after the code that shortly after the patient arrived, she saw this woman drink a bottle of liquor while taking "many" pills from a bottle in her purse. An empty bottle of 90 amitriptyline and an empty pint of vodka were found in the patient's purse. This was a preventable death and, quite sadly, one I will always somehow feel partially responsible for.

4.4.2 Purses and Knifes: Not What the Doctor Ordered

Another experience happened when I worked the night shift in a different hospital. When I came back from my lunch break, I was told of a new patient I had inherited that came to the ED for feeling suicidal. The break relief nurse was easily frustrated by this patient, who was agreeable to undress and put on a patient gown, but adamantly refused to give up her purse. The nurse allowed the patient to retain her purse, turned the light off in the room, and pulled the curtain. She relayed to me how emphatic the patient was about keeping the purse with her. I immediately walked into the room and sat down on a chair next to the patient. I calmly introduced myself and asked the patient to hand her purse over with an authoritative but respectful tone. The patient, who had her head wrapped in a sheet, unveiled her face, and I could tell she had been crying for a long time. She handed me her black purse and when I looked inside of it, the only item in the bag was a knife—one of the largest I had ever seen, other than a machete.

We owe it to our patients to help keep them safe by removing these personal effects from their reach. This practice will also help keep you and your unit safe. However, often this is no easy task, and multiple staff members and security must be incorporated to accomplish the job. This is one venue where the art of psychiatric nursing in the ED has a place. Setting firm boundaries while consistently attempting to preserve the patient's dignity as a fellow human being is not only possible but essential. Psychiatric patients are a vulnerable subset of an ED population and often arrive to the hospital already feeling powerless.

It is possible to practice kindness and show empathy while sticking within those set boundaries. Many patients may not like what you and your team are asking of them, but I have found that if you explain the process in normal terms and not just psychiatric jargon, not only will they respond better to you, but they maintain some perception of power over this experience.

4.5 Patient Coping Mechanisms

Something else to keep in mind with all ED patients, but especially psychiatric patients, is that they arrive to the hospital with the same coping mechanisms they used on the outside, which is often nil. Their preexisting baggage does not go away because you asked them to put on a crisp gown and provided them with a juice box and graham crackers. Patients may react even more violently to being restrained, perhaps due to previous sexual abuse (see Chapter 14 on personality disorders for more information). You may also find that some patients actually push you to the point of physically restraining them because they have no other way to signal that they need you to take control of this situation.

4.6 Staff Splitting

As you embark on your effort of practicing empathy and kindness, be very aware of the likelihood that some of these patients will attempt to manipulate you as a means of retaining some sort of power. This may be deliberate on their part or subconscious behavior, but you, as the nurse, must be on alert. This is where the firm boundaries come in, again.

Here is another case study that depicts a frequently encountered set of behaviors you may see in some patients with behavioral health disorders.

4.6.1 You Are a Great Nurse, Unlike Your Rude Colleague: A Case Study

Lana is a 37-year-old woman brought to the ED by her mother for depressive symptoms including anhedonia, feelings of worthlessness, sadness, and tearfulness for the last 3 weeks following the recent breakup of a romantic relationship of 5 years.

She has a history of depression and two previous suicide attempts, including cutting her wrists and an attempted hanging. She has been in the ED awaiting inpatient psychiatric hospitalization for the last 48 hours when she tells her day nurse, Nicole, that she would like to complain about the night-shift nurse.

Lana tells Nicole that the night-shift nurse was very rude to her and would only give her water to drink throughout the night when she asked for juice repeatedly, for what she described as "low blood sugar." Lana reported to the nurse that she "had to drink the juice from her roommate's tray to 'stay alive.'"

Lana seemed visibly upset and began to sob when recounting the previous night's events, and the day-shift nurse became concerned. Lana thanked Nicole several times for listening and for her caring behavior. Lana even called Nicole "the best nurse I have ever had." Nicole felt very flattered and content that she had made a positive connection with Lana. Lana then asked Nicole if she could have a tray of juices and snacks with her at all times to prevent another possible occurrence of "low blood sugar." Nicole happily obliged, though this was contradictory to the department's policy of strict meal and snack times, and no other patient had received the same special treatment.

4.6.1.1 Case Study Discussion: Staff Splitting

This case study is a perfect example of the patient attempting to pit staff members against each other for personal gain. Unbeknownst to the day nurse, it is not surprising that Lana had a history of borderline personality disorder (BPD). Patients with BPD will frequently stop at nothing to manipulate staff to have their own needs met. Had Nicole been aware of what signs to watch for, including those previously mentioned, she may have been more inclined to follow the established guidelines in the ED concerning the care of patients with behavioral health needs.

Nicole may have also been better able to set firm boundaries with Lana concerning her care. Moreover, Nicole should have considered her ability, as a nurse in the ED, to provide actual medical care, including regular blood sugar checks, if she believed the patient was actually experiencing hypoglycemia versus manipulative behavior.

4.7 Communication with the Emergency Physician

In the spirit of discussing manipulative behavior, this is where we, as nurses, are transparent about the art of finessing the ED physician to get what we need to better care for our patients.

The ED nurse is the eyes and ears for the physician, as the nurse spends the most time with the patients. By presenting both subjective and objective data to the provider, the nurse is in a position to perhaps medicate the escalating patient sooner rather than later, thus preventing a meltdown leading to restraints.

In another scenario, the ED physician may hear the patient is yelling and agitated, so they opt to give the patient something like lorazepam to simply calm the patient down and keep them quiet, temporarily. The experienced ED nurse knows what the patient truly needs is medication to stop the voices of terror inside their head, and early on before they decompensate. Gone are the days of the almighty droperidol, so we must come up with better, more conscientious ways to stop the train before it smashes into the station.

4.8 Conclusion

Finally, approaching your practice in a cerebral, methodical fashion will likely pay off for all parties involved. Keep the tone of the milieu in mind and seek ways to decrease aberrant stimuli surrounding your patients.

Conversely, take note when your patients are so bored of waiting around they are apt to create mischief. You, as the nurse, have the potential to help shape your patient's experience, so use it.

Remember what an honor it is for you and the rest of your team to guide these patients, your fellow humans, to the next step on their journey toward wellness and recovery. They are with you for just a snapshot of time, and you have the ability to make a tremendous, even life-changing, impact.

STRUCTURAL APPROACHES TO PATIENT CENTERED CARE

II

Chapter 5

Contemporary Psychiatric Care in the Emergency Department: Care Options, Treatment Teams, and Documentation Recommendations

Yener Balan and Christopher Lentz

Contents

5.1 Introduction	51
5.2 Operational Processes: Benefits	51
5.2.1 Administrative Benefits	51
5.2.2 Staffing Benefits	52
5.2.3 Direct Care Staff Benefits	52
5.2.4 Patient and Advocate Benefits	52
5.2.5 Regulatory and Quality Oversight Benefits	52
5.2.6 Length of Stay Benefits	52
5.3 Appropriate Level of Care	53
5.3.1 Least Restrictive Level of Care: Is the Use of Physical and Chemical Restraints Necessary?	54
5.3.1.1 Reduction in Restraint and Seclusion Use	55
5.4 Emergency Department Workplace Safety Concerns	56
5.4.1 Improving Workplace Safety	56
5.4.1.1 Crisis Response Teams	57
5.4.1.2 Safety Committees	57

    5.4.1.3 Sign-Out Reports 58
5.5 Patient and Staff Satisfaction 58
  5.5.1 Patient Satisfaction Survey 59
  5.5.2 Patient Confidentiality 59
5.6 Measuring Success: How Do You Know If the Team Is Making a Difference? 60
5.7 Interdepartmental Memorandum of Understanding or Service Agreement 61
  5.7.1 Service Agreement: What Does This Entail? 61
5.8 Suggested Model for Staffing 62
  5.8.1 Emergency Department Physician 62
  5.8.2 Emergency Department Nurse 63
  5.8.3 Emergency Department Social Services and Discharge Planning Team 63
  5.8.4 Psychiatrist 63
  5.8.5 Mental Health Therapists 63
  5.8.6 The Security Team 63
5.9 Recommended Patient Liberties for Attire and Personal Belongings in the ED 63
5.10 Suggestions for Daily Framework 65
  5.10.1 Morning Rounds 65
  5.10.2 Template for ED Psychiatry Pre-Rounding 65
  5.10.3 Template for Treatment Update Note 66
  5.10.4 Emergency Department Nursing Rounding Note Template 68
  5.10.5 Reviewing the Patient List and Assigning Clinicians 69
5.11 Template for Initial ED Psychiatric Consultation Note 70
  5.11.1 Initial Patient Arrival Information 70
  5.11.2 History of Present Illness 71
  5.11.3 Psychiatric History 71
  5.11.4 Past Medical History 72
  5.11.5 Substance Use History 73
  5.11.6 Social History 73
    5.11.6.1 Living Situation 74
    5.11.6.2 Legal History 74
    5.11.6.3 Financial History 74
    5.11.6.4 Support System 75
  5.11.7 Mental Status Exam 75
    5.11.7.1 Appearance 75
    5.11.7.2 Behavior 75
    5.11.7.3 Demeanor/Manner 75
    5.11.7.4 Speech 76
    5.11.7.5 Mood 76
    5.11.7.6 Affect 76
    5.11.7.7 Perceptual Disturbances 76
    5.11.7.8 Thought Process 77
    5.11.7.9 Thought Content 77
    5.11.7.10 Orientation 77
    5.11.7.11 Memory 77
    5.11.7.12 Concentration 78
    5.11.7.13 Cognition 78
    5.11.7.14 Insight 78

　　　　　　5.11.7.15 Judgment 79
　　　　　　5.11.7.16 Impulse Control 79
　　　5.11.8 Risk Assessment 79
　　　　　　5.11.8.1 Assessing Suicide Risk 80
　　　　　　5.11.8.2 Assessing Homicide Risk 80
　　　　　　5.11.8.3 Assessing for Grave Disability 80
　　　　　　5.11.8.4 Risk Level Scaling 80
　　　5.11.9 Impression 81
　　　5.11.10 Diagnosis 81
　　　5.11.11 Recommendations and Plan 82
5.12 Psychiatric Reassessment 82
5.13 To Consult or Not to Consult?: Appropriate Consultations of Psychiatry in the
　　　Emergency Setting 83
5.14 Innovative Care in the Emergency Department: Dedicated Psychiatric Observation Areas....84
　　　5.14.1 Recommendations for the Dedicated Psychiatric Observation Area....... 85
5.15 Use of Handouts in the ED 86
　　　5.15.1 Welcome Letter 86
　　　5.15.2 Diagnostic-Specific Patient Education 86
　　　5.15.3 Community Resources Information 86
　　　5.15.4 Therapeutic Handouts 86
　　　5.15.5 Patient Rights and Advocacy Group Information 86
5.16 Conclusion 86
References 87
Resources 89

5.1 Introduction

The daily shift in the emergency department (ED) working on a psychiatric consultation team involves multiple facets that the treatment team, including the clinician and administration, needs to be aware of in order to ensure that the patients are receiving satisfactory care. Staff need to be properly trained for the patient's care, they need to have access to and demonstrate proficiency in appropriate documentation in the patient chart, and they need to be able to consistently communicate the treatment plan with the team. This chapter outlines recommended guidelines for the creation and implementation of treatment teams to help provide consistent and appropriate care for the patient with behavioral health needs in the ED setting. In addition to the team framework, this chapter reviews process flow and documentation standards to facilitate optimal operations.

5.2 Operational Processes: Benefits

Creating a consistent daily process that the entire treatment team can follow has numerous benefits for quality of patient care and outcomes in general. If you are an administrator reading this book, in order to create your own effective emergency department workflow dealing with the psychiatric patient population, the benefits outlined subsequently can be used to help guide you in this planning process.

5.2.1 Administrative Benefits

A consistent staffing pattern that is proven to work well provides administration the ability to address the patient flow issues that occur in an ED and hospital setting. When a clear multidisciplinary team structure is identified, budgeting and business planning can be standardized to accommodate the templated design.

5.2.2 Staffing Benefits

Having a direct manager overseeing the team that provides the psychiatric consultations and care in the ED is necessary to ensure consistent hiring practices as well as new employee training. Management oversight of the team, and the consistent procedures and processes that are followed, helps to ensure consistent positive patient outcomes and to demonstrate continued return on investment.

5.2.3 Direct Care Staff Benefits

Established clear expectations and training for direct care staff will help to ensure that patients are provided with consistent care. Use of a templated note system also ensures that consistent documentation occurs in the chart by all staff members. This ensures that federal, state, and county regulatory requirements are met.

The structured expectation of the provider also adds to a level of comfort in setting clear guidelines for staff to follow on a daily basis. While clinicians in an ED do not know what type of problems they will be tasked to solve in a given shift, having a clear structured team, established protocols, and procedures for care delivery provides a certain level of comfort to increase staff morale and decrease staff burnout.

For a multidisciplinary team, clearly delineated expectations of each member also further the sense of adding value to the team, and also add the distinction of accountability to the team and patient outcomes.

5.2.4 Patient and Advocate Benefits

Patients and their advocates can expect to see increases in consistent and empathic care within the ED setting when direct policies and daily processes are in place to help guide the treatment team. The treatment process for any given patient needs to be clearly communicated to all the parties involved in the patient's direct care. This may include the patient's advocates, family members, and the larger ED treatment team. This will create a culture of transparency that inherently expands to the patient and their advocates. The goal is also to increase the patient's understanding of what to expect during the ED visit. This allows for the advocate or patient's family to be directly involved in their care and decision-making process if needed, and to facilitate any next steps in treatment.

5.2.5 Regulatory and Quality Oversight Benefits

It is imperative that administrative staff on the ED team have a working knowledge of both state- and countywide hospital regulations specifically related to the psychiatric patient in the emergency setting. Ensuring that there are pre-established policies and procedures for medico-legal and clinical documentation hospital-wide will act as the cornerstone for support during random and routine regulatory audits.

Some of the larger regulatory issues that may arise in an emergency setting include medication procedures, such as medication over objection; use of physical and chemical restraints; involuntary psychiatric holds; risk assessment documentation; and regular clinical documentation. A standardized approach to the care of the patient in the ED that incorporates the previously mentioned regulatory requirements will allow the ED staff to work within a framework of appropriate regulatory standards.

A comprehensive system of quality oversight needs to be established and consistently maintained within the ED. This quality oversight system will include a multiple-department team, including the emergency department administration and psychiatry department administration.

Standardized quality review and improvement processes should be established that include all the departments involved. One component should be a peer-review process that addresses not only complaints, grievances, and negative outcomes, but also should include random chart audits to ensure documentation standards are being adhered to within the ED setting. Regulatory requirements including medication management, legal status, risk assessment, and use of physical or chemical restraints should be the primary focus of these documentation reviews.

To help facilitate a smooth transition between the departments and alleviate potential future conflicts hospital-wide, we recommend a memorandum of understanding or a service agreement be developed between all the involved departments. This can then be used for training staff, as well as in discussions with external partners and regulators to describe the integrated and seamless care delivery in your hospital. The use of service agreements will be discussed in further detail in a later section of this chapter.

5.2.6 Length of Stay Benefits

Long lengths of stay, also known as boarding time, for patients waiting for inpatient psychiatric hospitalization is an increasingly troubling problem nationwide (Park 2009; Zhu 2016). This is an important metric to be aware of, given that it has a potential impact on many facets of ED operations, including but not limited to quality of patient care, patient and staff satisfaction, and increased operating costs due to lengthy boarding time, as well as a potential increase in workplace safety issues and a potential for regulatory and legal violations.

It has been shown that length of stay can be decreased by organizing and using a multidisciplinary team within the ED, and establishing a system for creating safe discharge planning. When clear treatment protocols include early assessment and treatment during an ED visit, the culture is one of efficient care. As patients who can be safely sent home are identified, cared for, and discharged, the ones requiring more elaborate care in the ED and possible inpatient psychiatric hospitalization can receive the level of care they need.

The concept of using the available inpatient psychiatric hospital beds in the community wisely benefits the patients that truly need an inpatient bed. Appropriate dispositioning of patients results in improved access with the increased bed availability in the community secondary to the capacity that was created. As the cycle of patient flow continues, this naturally translates to further decreased lengths of stay in the ED.

5.3 Appropriate Level of Care

Expertise in triaging and assigning not only the level of risk of a patient, but also appropriate disposition planning, is key to ensuring that the patient is discharged to the appropriate level of care.

This applies to the time the patient spends in the ED, where the patient goes when they leave the ED, and also the frequency with which the patient has a return visit to the ED.

As discussed in the chapter on discharge planning, all factors must be taken into consideration to ensure that the treatment team is providing care that sustains beyond the immediate discharge from the ED. For example, the predictors of frequent ED use for psychiatric illness described by Chang et al. in their 2014 review article include homelessness, a cocaine-positive toxicology screen, presence of a personality disorder, Medicare insurance, and hepatobiliary disease. When the treatment team combines general predictive information with risk factors specific to the patient, which are delineated in Chapter 6 on risk assessment, the team can preemptively discuss and address these barriers and concerns with the patient, as well as plan for the appropriate level of care.

If homelessness is a driving factor for ED visits, resulting in increased inpatient psychiatric utilization, the team should focus on that, with a potential resulting factor of decreased inpatient psychiatric hospital utilization. In well-functioning hospital systems that are well connected to the community, lists of community services will be available to offer patients in need. If your hospital system has a need for a more robust system and a checklist for more resources, consider developing a taskforce to research the community resources that are available in your area. These resources may include shelter programs, food lockers, domestic violence clinics, low- to no-cost medical clinics, legal clinics, and other local not-for-profit agencies. Consumer and family advocate groups, such as the National Alliance on Mental Illness (NAMI) and other self-help groups, such as Alcoholics Anonymous (AA) or Narcotics Anonymous (NA), can also be referenced in a community resource list. Locating available community resources for a patient discharging from the ED can be a challenge, so it is beneficial to have your community resource list printed with multiple copies available for distribution. Establishing strong working relations with community agencies, such as housing authorities or shelter directors, can be of use to the ED team when a homeless patient is in need of housing upon discharge from the ED.

Treatment and care planning, when done clinically and appropriately, cater to the individual's recovery and well-being. When they are done with the added sophistication of institutional and systematic awareness, they result in even greater benefits, as described previously.

5.3.1 Least Restrictive Level of Care: Is the Use of Physical and Chemical Restraints Necessary?

It is inevitable that, at some point, the ED team will need to intervene with an agitated or violent patient to ensure that the safety of the patient and others near the patient is preserved via the use of physical restraints, seclusion, or emergent medications.

A plethora of negative effects have been identified related to the use of seclusion and restraints on patients. Strong emotional reactions, including isolation, helplessness, humiliation, shame, and a fear of future acts of restraint by staff can be a common patient experience. A resurgence of prior traumatic memories may also arise for all parties involved in the restraint (Booner et al. 2002; Fisher 1994; Larue et al. 2013). Any preexisting negative emotions that the patient was experiencing, including rejection, exclusion, and abandonment, can become intensified during the restraint episode (Holmes et al. 2004). It has also been found that the use of restraints can have a detrimental impact on the patient's chances of following through with future outpatient psychiatric care (Currier et al. 2011). In addition to the potential emotional damage that can occur, physical complications in the patient from the use of restraints, ranging from thrombosis to death, can arise (Berzlanovich et al. 2012; Busch and Shore 2000; Hem et al.

2001). Asphyxiation was found to be a common cause of death during restraint use (The Joint Commission 1998).

Given that these episodes can be physically and emotionally taxing for the patient, ED staff, and others in the vicinity of the patient, the least restrictive level of care should always be implemented prior to resorting to the use of physical or chemical restraints. One review found inconclusive evidence regarding the effectiveness and safety of using seclusion and restraints as an intervention for the agitated patient in the ED setting, recommending that these interventions are only used as a last resort (Nelstrop et al. 2006).

In the ED setting, the use of physical restraints is the most restrictive level of care possible. It is hard to imagine physically restraining a patient as being a care option, but there may be situations in which it is the only option available to ensure the safety of the patient and those around the patient. A patient who has become combative toward staff and is unable to be verbally deescalated may present a time when physical restraints are deemed necessary.

Due to the highly restrictive nature and potential negative effects of restraint use on the patient and staff, many governmental agencies have stepped in to ensure that restraint procedures in all ED or hospital settings are followed correctly. In response to a series of articles published in the *Hartford Courant* in 1998 that documented the restraint and seclusion-related deaths of 142 patients, the Healthcare Financing Administration (now called the Centers for Medicare and Medicaid [CMS]) established rights for patients and rules for the use of restraints and seclusion in any medical facility that is funded by Medicare or Medicaid (Currier and Allen 2000). The CMS restraint regulations can be found in the *Conditions of Participation* document.

The Joint Commission also created standards for the proper use of restraints and seclusion in both medical and psychiatric settings. Per CMS regulations, restraints can only be applied to ensure the immediate physical safety of the patient, staff, or others, and their use must be discontinued as soon as it is safely possible to do so. The Joint Commission standard PC.03.05.01 states "the organization uses restraint or seclusion only when it can be clinically justified or when warranted by patient behavior that threatens the physical safety of the patient, staff, or others."

If the ED team determines that the use of restraint or seclusion of the patient is necessary to preserve safety within the ED, a patient and staff debriefing session needs to occur (Richmond et al. 2012). The debriefing session is important to help the patient and staff process and reconstruct the restraint episode in a meaningful way (Larue et al. 2013), in addition to providing the patient with a needed social connection with ED staff (Holmes et al. 2004).

5.3.1.1 Reduction in Restraint and Seclusion Use

The hope of any ED administrative team is to be able to reduce the annual number of patient restraints to zero. It is imperative that ED administrators make a push for the development and implementation of a hospital-wide program that highlights behavioral modification techniques and verbal de-escalation to help prevent or limit the need for restraints (Fisher 2003; LeBel et al. 2004).

In some instances, physical restraint of a patient can be avoided by simply taking the time to actively listen to what the patient's needs are, especially if the patient is displaying any initial signs of frustration or anger (Fishkind 2002; Richmond et al. 2012; Stevenson 1991). Building rapport with the patient can also serve as an advantage, to use later on, if the patient begins to display signs of escalating agitation. If the patient also feels that rapport has been developed with the direct care staff, they will be more apt to respond to redirection and attempts at verbal de-escalation. Rapport can be quickly and easily established with a patient by doing simple things, such as introducing yourself and offering the patient a warm blanket, reading materials, or something to eat or drink.

In the ED, it is essential that the direct care staff take a few moments during the start of a new shift to speak with the patient and establish some rapport, as this may be difficult to remember to do in the chaos that can sometimes ensue in the ED.

Restraint and seclusion usage can be significantly reduced with the help of the ED or hospital administration's endorsement of the use of an alternative program, patient participation in an alternative program, culture change in the ED direct care staff, staff training on the alternative program elements, creation of metrics and analysis of the metrics, and individualized patient treatment plans (Fisher 2003; Forster et al. 1999).

The development and use of a dedicated team of ED staff who act in the role of champions for a cultural and procedural shift can, in our experience, be helpful in creating and driving the push for a reduction in the use of restraint and seclusions. This dedicated team needs to be led by the direct care staff and should be comprised of staff that display a strong passion for working with and pushing for better care of the psychiatric patient. A member of the ED administrative team should also be part of the group. The dedicated team should be given leeway by ED administration to make changes to current workflows when these changes are deemed beneficial by all parties.

5.4 Emergency Department Workplace Safety Concerns

As discussed previously, the act of restraining or secluding a patient can present the ED staff with challenges in maintaining a safe work environment. The ED can be a scary and sometimes dangerous environment to work in. Amid the normal chaos of multiple staff and gurneys constantly moving rapidly throughout the hallways and physicians buzzing in and out of various rooms, there may be screams, yelling, or threats of violence that can be heard coming from patients. It is likely that some of these patients may be experiencing a mental health crisis.

In a survey covering a 2-year span from 2009 to 2011, 54.5% of surveyed ED nurses reported experiencing some type of physical violence and verbal abuse during a typical work week. One-quarter of the nurses surveyed stated that they had experienced physical violence 20 or more times over a 3-year period (Walsh et al. 2011). One of the chapter coauthors experienced patient violence when a patient he was assessing became agitated during an assessment and kicked him in his side torso; another patient pulled out a knife and made threats to stab him when he was discussing the patient's discharge plan.

Given the potential for violence in the ED, it is important that ED staff feel safe and comfortable with the idea of coming to the workplace each and every day. Unfortunately, sometimes the stigma that is inherently attached to patients afflicted with psychiatric disorders can have a direct effect on the ED direct care staff's comfort level in caring for and treating these patients. If the ED direct care staff do not feel safe and secure in their work environment, they may have difficulty providing a quality level of care to the patient. As Maslow's hierarchy of needs shows, feeling safe and secure are basic human needs. If these basic needs are not met, the person will be unable to function at their highest potential level and ultimately both the patient and the staff member become victims to the fear that can be present while working with patients suffering from psychiatric disorders. This scenario raises a question: How can we ensure that our staff will feel safe and secure?

5.4.1 Improving Workplace Safety

Workplace safety can be improved in the emergency department psychiatric unit by utilizing a variety of approaches. The use of crisis response teams, safety committees, and open lines of communication between ED staff can help to facilitate a push in the direction of increased safety.

5.4.1.1 Crisis Response Teams

In order to address the issue of workplace safety in a psychiatric setting, many hospital systems have utilized a response team model. A behavioral health crisis response team, referred to as the behavioral emergency response team (BERT), is comprised of multidisciplinary members including a psychiatric nurse, a psychiatric technician, a psychiatrist, and a security officer who are contacted by hospital staff if an intervention is needed for an agitated or violent patient (Pestka et al. 2012).

The psychiatric nurse acts as the team lead and is the primary person responsible for assessing the needs of the situation, making recommendations for interventions to the patient's primary treatment team and developing a treatment plan for the patient. The psychiatrist is contacted if the treatment team feels that the patient may benefit from psychotropic medications, either voluntarily or emergently, or needs transfer to an inpatient psychiatric facility. The security officer acts as the primary tool for deescalating the patient and can take physical action to ensure that the safety of the patient and staff is preserved. In our experience, we have found the use of a dedicated, on-site ED psychiatric team helpful in responding to episodes of patient aggression.

The use of an overhead paged alert system can be utilized to inform all staff of a combative patient. Some healthcare facilities have utilized a color code (e.g., green) that is paged on the hospital overhead paging system for this purpose. Once the code is paged overhead, the dedicated, on-site psychiatric team, comprised of a master's- or doctoral-level mental health therapist, psychiatrist, registered nurse, emergency department technician, and security officers, meet at the location of the crisis event to determine, as a team, what level of intervention is needed to maintain a safe setting.

The on-site psychiatrist is key in being able to quickly assess and meet the patient's psychotropic medication needs. This is especially important when time is of the essence and emergent medications may need to be quickly ordered and administered to prevent a harmful situation from occurring.

The Joint Commission (2010) recommends that the use of uniformed security officers, limiting the number of visitors that patients can have, and routine screening of visitors, including wanding and bag checks, be implemented in the ED. Further recommendations from the Joint Commission for prevention of violence in the ED include adequate training and education of ED staff in the de-escalation of agitated family members of patients and education on proper incident reporting procedures to ED administration and security personnel. At times, the presence of multiple security guards (or a show of force), in and of itself, can help to prevent some acts of violence in the ED (Pestka et al. 2012). This may especially be the case with patients that present with a personality disorder, for instance, antisocial personality disorder, who are cognizant of their actions.

5.4.1.2 Safety Committees

The development and implementation of a safety committee can be an important step in making a hospital-wide cultural shift toward safety in the workplace. A safety committee should be comprised of direct care ED staff that have lived on the job experience with some of the safety issues that the ED needs to address (Severson 2011). This may include drawing upon a variety of positions within the department in order to gain a wide perspective of the current and relevant safety issues that are affecting all staff (Maurer 2013). Recruiting at least one representative from the ED nurses, ED technicians, ED physicians, security officers, ED psychiatry clinicians, ED administration, and clerical and environmental services staff can be helpful in this process.

The roles and purpose of the safety committee need to be clearly established early on during the development of the committee. The overarching role of any safety committee is the reduction and prevention of workplace injuries and illnesses (Maurer 2013). Steps to reaching this goal of improved workplace safety include open staff communication and dialogues regarding any safety concerns, especially related to staff and patient interactions. This fostering of an open communication system between the ED staff can help to create a culture shift toward improved safety.

5.4.1.3 Sign-Out Reports

Open communication, in and of itself, can easily be implemented via an ED direct-care-staff change of shift sign-out report process. Sign-out reports should occur on any ED team that has direct psychiatric patient contact, including ED nurses, ED technicians, ED psychiatry clinicians, ED physicians, and security officers. The report should be clear, concise, and provide useful information for the receiving party (Friesen et al. 2008).

In our experience, the sign-out report process was most effectively used during a warm or staff-to-staff handoff, although an established sign-out report form can also be utilized in cases where there may be breaks in the shifts of oncoming and leaving staff. For psychiatric patient sign-out purposes, the following information should be discussed or included on a sign-out report form:

- Patient's first and last name, age, and gender.
- Hospital record number.
- Brief description of the reason for the patient's ED admit.
- Current legal status of the patient. The descriptors used here may vary based on your state's psychiatric hold regulations.
- The date and time that the psychiatric hold on the patient expires.
- Pending issues including barriers to placement in a psychiatric facility or barriers to discharging the patient.
- Recent behavioral changes or concerns.

The following is an example sign-out report: John Doe is a 38-year-old male. His hospital record number is 111-3456D. He arrived to the ED via law enforcement after he was found wandering in the middle of a street naked and mumbling to himself. He is currently on an involuntary psychiatric hold that will expire on December 5th at 14:35. John is on a waiting list for a bed at the James Snider Psychiatric Treatment Center but needs a family member to bring his CPAP machine to the ED before the hospital will accept him for placement. John displayed increased agitation over the past shift and was placed in 4 point restraints after he attempted to hit his nurse.

The focus on and communication of any recent behavioral changes is key to help the new oncoming staff to be aware of any safety issues when interacting with the patient.

5.5 Patient and Staff Satisfaction

Our experience, as well as the literature (Summers 2003), suggests that with the use of clearly defined teams who are expert in direct clinical assessments of patients with behavioral health needs, patient and staff satisfaction improves.

As staff becomes more familiar with the subject matter and can engage in discussions with patients and their families, staff also feel empowered and satisfied with their own contributions to the team. This in turn reflects in the perception of the patient of feeling heard, validated, and invited to be part of the treatment planning solution.

Observable positive patient outcomes reinforce staff sense of mastery, resulting in improved staff satisfaction. This has the added benefit of a buffer against staff burnout, absenteeism, and ultimately turnover.

Another component of streamlining the operational approach to patients in the ED is by decreasing their length of stay and the use of lower acuity (as measured by Emergency Severity Index [ESI]) bed space. In other words, if there are less patients overall in an ED, the likelihood of using a hallway to care for the patient decreases, as does the potential for decreased satisfaction due to being cared for in a hallway in the ED (Stiffler 2015).

Establishing a method to capture the patient voice in a survey allows for continuous quality improvement and honest communication and introspection. A study done by Kitts et al. (2013) looked at satisfaction with psychiatry consultation services for patients and their families in a pediatric hospital. The article discusses the importance of promoting patient- and family-centered care informed by patient satisfaction levels with the services delivered, as well as the importance of having clinicians on the psychiatry team conveying their clinical impressions and recommendations to patients and their families (Kitts et al. 2013).

5.5.1 Patient Satisfaction Survey

The satisfaction survey should begin with a description of the services being provided and the purpose of the survey, such as a desire to improve quality of care based on patient care experiences and responses.

We recommend that questions in the survey start by asking if the patient was given information about the rules and policies of the environment and the care delivered. The survey should continue with questions regarding the patient's level of involvement and understanding of any medication and/or therapeutic treatment received. Key questions should be asked regarding the patient's perception of the level of involvement and satisfaction with the level of involvement received from staff on behalf of the patient and their family or advocates. Issues such as dignity, respect, and communication styles of the clinicians should be asked. Other important issues that add to a better understanding of the experience are those that pertain to perception of patient safety while in the ED, the general sense of cleanliness in the ED, and the quality of the food served, as well as feelings of comfort while being treated. We encourage surveys to also include areas for free text to answer such questions as which staff member the patient feels deserves additional recognition, as well as any other information the patient feels is important to convey to the team.

5.5.2 Patient Confidentiality

In order to help increase the patient's willingness to discuss relevant concerns and overall patient satisfaction levels over the long run, the patient must feel comfortable and at ease with the interview process in the ED setting. This comfort can be established if the patient feels that the information they are disclosing during the interview process is confidential.

Within the ED itself, it may be difficult and challenging for the psychiatric treatment team to create a private and secure area to hold the psychiatric interview in. We have experience working in busy EDs where patients are lined up in the hallways, head to foot, lying on gurneys, with little more than a curtain between them and the next patient. Several EDs we have worked in have had patients double and triple parked next to each other without any privacy screening. Due to the nature of the high volume of some of these EDs, the patients weren't even able to be divided up between those with behavioral health needs and those with other medical needs. Patients with acute psychosis, especially those experiencing paranoia, can be highly affected by this environment and may be less likely to disclose any information to the clinician.

In order to create some semblance of confidentiality within this setting, the treatment team needs to develop innovative and novel uses of ED space. In our experience, we have found that taking a patient out of the hallway and into a patient interview room, a triage room, or an unused office creates a more confidential space and allows the patient to feel more comfortable during the interview. This also has a secondary effect of increasing the rapport with the clinician, as it shows the patient that the clinician is spending extra energy to attempt to make their personal issues private.

It is important that a confidential space is created in the ED if possible in order to ensure that the hospital and the clinician are following all the established laws regarding confidentiality of patient information. There are federal, state, and county regulations around patient confidentiality that the hospital administration needs to be aware of, and the hospital must have policies in place to ensure that all ED staff are abiding by these laws.

We recommend checking in with the patient to determine their comfort level with holding the psychiatric interview within the usual ED treatment space, or give them the opportunity to hold the interview in a more private setting. If the patient opts to hold the interview in a more private area, it is important to take precautions to ensure patient and staff safety during the interview process. This will include making sure that security staff is present and a chaperone is present if the patient is the opposite gender of the interviewing clinician, or if you at all suspect any potential for accusatory interactions, regardless of the patient's gender. Again, this is simply to have a witness to protect the patient and clinician alike.

If security staff or another clinician is not available to chaperone you during the interview, it is recommended that the interview space either has a window or is easily visible to passing staff. Also, ensure that you let another treatment team member know that you will be taking the patient, to another location for an interview, regardless of how long or short a time. This serves to close the loop on transparency and open communication with staff, which is also connected with safety and privacy for the patient.

Any staff member working in the hospital, whether it be security or another staff member that you ask to chaperone during the interview process, is also bound by confidentiality laws. It can be helpful to inform the patient of this fact, and also document in the patient's chart that you had the interview with the specific staff members providing witness.

5.6 Measuring Success: How Do You Know If the Team Is Making a Difference?

Whether you have or create a psychiatric consultation service or a multidisciplinary team, it is important to have a process for quality assurance. The availability or idea of having a team makes intuitive sense, and we suggest giving thought to measuring outcomes, as discussed in Chapter 19 on metrics.

According to numerous studies, such as the review done by Sheridan et al. in 2016, as well as our experience, using a dedicated team of behavioral health clinicians significantly decreases length of stay and the need for admission to an inpatient psychiatric hospital. In the article by Sheridan et al. in 2016, titled, "The effect of a dedicated psychiatric team to pediatric emergency mental healthcare," they looked at pre- and post-intervention data, and report a 27% decrease in mean pediatric length of stay post-intervention of implementing a pediatric psychiatric team in the ED. Please refer to Chapter 19 on metrics for further details.

5.7 Interdepartmental Memorandum of Understanding or Service Agreement

Regardless of the model of healthcare delivery, the concept of integrated health and behavioral healthcare has solidified its position in the lexicon and, more importantly, in the way we think of delivering care. Due to continued concerns regarding equitable reimbursement for psychiatric services and the reality that medical–surgical hospitals and emergency departments absolutely need psychiatric services and expertise, it makes intuitive sense to collaborate.

In 2008, George Tesar wrote an article titled "Whither hospital and academic psychiatry?" that discusses recommendations for the (at the time) present and future of academic psychiatry, in which he describes the need for interdepartmental collaboration, and the need to embrace change as well as outcomes assessment. The recommendations are applicable to the field in a broader sense and continue to be very valuable.

As the reader, if you are an administrator preparing a business case and sponsoring policies to be written for your hospital, or if you are a clinical provider in a network, or if you are a patient or advocate, the common denominator in this collaborative care approach is that patients benefit significantly more in this model of care compared with when care is delivered in a siloed approach.

Data suggests that that standardized mortality ratios are twice the population average the year following an inpatient psychiatric hospitalization (Lally et al. 2015). The article, a retrospective analysis, discusses the need for further integration of medical services in psychiatric settings due to the high incidence of general hospital utilization during and after psychiatric hospitalization. The article details the breakdown of variables, including sex, diagnoses, and inpatient medical and ED utilization, as well as their lengths of stay and implications on economic costs. Lally et al. discuss the inefficient use of resources, distress on the patient, and the need to better integrate medical care provided to patients who are psychiatrically hospitalized.

5.7.1 Service Agreement: What Does This Entail?

While the focus of our book is emergency psychiatry, the concept of a service agreement, or memorandum of understanding, should extend to the medical and surgical floors as well, as patients are often initially seen in the ED and may require transfer to these floors.

The agreement should begin with which departments are involved in the care of the patient. We have worked in settings where there is one agreement that spans more than two departments, such as the internal medicine department, emergency department, and psychiatry department, and at places that prefer to have an agreement between two single departments at a time, and then cross-reference the agreements. As long as the content and communication of the agreement includes the expectations and accountabilities, the format should not matter.

A typical agreement will then describe what each clinician type does, when they do it, and what they are responsible for. Examples of clinician responsibilities may include when a shift starts and ends, what times the clinicians round on patients, to whom they report, and to whom they escalate issues.

Documentation expectations and standards, such as where the medical record notes are placed and the contents of the documentation, should also be discussed. The contents of this chapter can be used as a guide to populate the service agreement as well.

The agreement should continue with patient workflows, expectations of how the departments will interact, and their expectations of one another. Issues such as details on consultation requests, the timeline, any metrics being measured such as request of consult time to patient seen time, and seen time to documentation and disposition time should also be agreed upon and written in the service agreement.

Other pertinent topics that can be addressed and outlined in the service agreement include:

- The concept of assessment of the patient, and depending on average length of stays in the specific ED, reassessments, and what that process entails.
- Which physician writes which orders for labs and medications, who completes the legal paperwork, and who arranges for the discharge disposition.
- Whether a patient is going to be sent to an outpatient setting or an inpatient setting, the workflow should be described, as well as the accountable parties that will document the activities.
- If the patient is being transferred to an inpatient setting, the subsequent set of responsibilities, including patient belongings, who is assigned to notify the family and/or advocates about the transfer, as well as the handoff of information to the receiving facilities, should all be documented.
- If there are staffing differences based on time of day or night, those variations should also be documented, and specifically who is responsible when there are covering staff.
- Nuances such as different levels of care requirements of young children and adolescents in the ED, as well as communication guidelines for interactions with families and advocates of minors, are another issue that should not be overlooked in an agreement.
- If a patient requires medical observation status, or an inpatient medical or surgical hospitalization, the corresponding admitting departments should be part of this agreement, or a separate one, as mentioned previously. The subsequent and continued responsibilities of the psychiatric team should then be described in that portion, when a patient is on these floors.

The agreement concludes with creation and revision dates, and up-to-date signatures of the medical directors, department chiefs, and/or their designees.

5.8 Suggested Model for Staffing

5.8.1 Emergency Department Physician

This position is a cornerstone for the entire ED treatment team. They are the ultimate carriers of decision-making and responsibility for the patient's care. The emergency department physician (ED MD) is the first physician to see the patient and initiates the order for the psychiatric consultation. The ED MD acts as the main communication point for all team members regarding the patient's care. They place the final discharge orders for the patient, allowing the patient to leave the ED and return home.

5.8.2 Emergency Department Nurse

While the ED MD places the orders for the patient's care, the emergency department nurse (ED RN) acts to carry out the orders and serves as a buttress for the entire ED team. The ED RN serves as the strongest link in the ED treatment team's chain, and it is crucial that a quality RN is selected for this role.

5.8.3 Emergency Department Social Services and Discharge Planning Team

While, in our experience, we have had the ability to work with a separate ED social work team and discharge planning team, not all hospitals may have this level of staffing. The ED social work team is usually comprised of master's-level clinicians who specialize in linking patients to community resources, including areas like housing and transportation. The ED discharge planners are licensed RNs who specialize in developing a viable discharge plan for any patient in the ED. In our experience, they have been a crucial part of developing a safe discharge plan for patients suffering with neurocognitive disorders including dementia.

5.8.4 Psychiatrist

The psychiatrist is a medically trained MD who, in an ED setting, makes recommendations for psychiatric medications or can order them directly. Depending on the state where the ED is located, the psychiatrist may be able to place a patient on an involuntary psychiatric hold, compared with some states in which the ED MD is not able to place a patient on a hold.

5.8.5 Mental Health Therapists

Therapists are master's- or doctoral- (PhD or PsyD) level clinicians who specialize in providing counseling and psychotherapy to a patient suffering from psychiatric disorders. They have similar abilities as the psychiatrist to treat a patient minus the ability to write medication orders. While a therapist may seem more attractive compared with a psychiatrist to an administrator due to lower staffing costs, experience and level of comfort working in an ED setting with a psychiatric population in crisis far outweighs any cost difference between the two roles.

5.8.6 The Security Team

The security team contributes by providing 24-hour supervision of the patient and acts as the eyes and ears of the ED treatment team. The security team is able to provide information for the treatment team on the patient's daily behaviors and any visitors that have come and gone during their shift. Ongoing direct and consistent communication must take place between the security team and the rest of the ED team to ensure that all safety and patient need factors are accounted for.

5.9 Recommended Patient Liberties for Attire and Personal Belongings in the ED

Within the ED setting, the patient with behavioral health needs is sometimes categorized separately when compared with medical patients. This categorization can also flow into the liberties and attire that the patient is expected to forego per a policy that was written for the hospital. There are hospital systems that take this categorization process to the point of utilizing separate hospital gowns both in style and color for patients with behavioral health needs compared with those with other medical needs. While this practice is meant to help address patient safety issues, especially during elopement from the ED, it has a potentially unforeseen negative effect on patient morale during the ED stay.

As discussed earlier in this chapter, patient confidentiality is important to ensure, and this practice of utilizing separate gowns should be taken seriously as well, as it can create a potential breach in confidentiality if it allows the behavioral health patient to be clearly identified.

In order to avoid potential issues with violating patient confidentiality, and creating a possible rift between the psychiatric patient and medical patient populations in the ED setting, it is recommended that the psychiatric patient be provided the same liberties and access to their personal attire and belongings. While we recognize that there may be concerns with this recommendation based on patient safety issues and prejudices toward patients with behavioral health needs, all patients should be treated on equal grounds. Regardless of diagnosis or symptomatic presentation, the key factor in deciding to restrict belongings or clothing that may increase harm to patient or staff is the risk the patient poses. For example, there may be no risk difference between an older woman in the ED with a migraine who wants to look into her purse for her cell phone to call her son and an older woman in the ED with severe depression that wants to look into her purse for her cell phone to call her son. The woman with the migraine may also have the same risk level of self-harm as the patient with depression, and the clinically appropriate thing to do is to screen and appropriately assess this risk level and remove belongings accordingly.

Hospital administrators tend to create policies that are restrictive, and are often updated to be ever more restrictive, after every adverse patient outcome. While we recognize and respect the need for policies, we also want to present this thought experiment of foundational patient equality, with the sophisticated layers of removing civil liberties only when clinically indicated to reduce imminent harm.

If the hospital decides to be more lenient with their patients' liberties, we recommend clear and consistent documentation in the patient chart when liberties are either provided or restricted. For example, if the hospital policy includes removal of all belongings when in the ED, and subsequent to clinical evaluation and determination that the patient is a low risk of self-harm, the treatment team decides that the patient is allowed to have access to their personal cell phone. In this case, we recommend the physician place an actual nursing order in the chart that indicates when the order should be carried out, as well as the rationale for why the patient is able to receive the phone.

The decision to restrict or retain the patients' personal liberties should predominantly be based on observations and any symptomatic progression of the patient's current behaviors during their ED stay. For instance, if a patient arrives in a highly agitated, psychotic state, the treatment team may initially decide to restrict the patient's liberties for both patient and staff safety, and remove the patient's outerwear as well as any belongings that may be used as a device for harm. As the patient receives proper treatment and begins to show signs of improvement, the staff at this point may make a clinical judgment to allow the patient access to select belongings. The rationale behind these suggestions is to move the patient toward a path of wellness and normalcy. In the medical domain, we use the phrase "keeping vertical patients vertical" when discussing strategies to keep healthy and ambulatory patients in a state that reinforces that health and ambulation. We want to bring to the attention of the reader that placing the patient in categorized clothing and removing their belongings may inadvertently instill and reinforce the "sick role" and may discourage their advancement toward positive clinical outcomes while in the ED.

5.10 Suggestions for Daily Framework
5.10.1 Morning Rounds

Daily morning multidisciplinary team rounds are recommended. Depending on your staff, the team should include the ED MD, ED RN, ED social work team, ED discharge planning team, the behavioral health team: psychiatrists and therapists, any trainees or students, security team, nursing administration, outpatient community providers including social services, homeless outreach coordinators, a peer navigator, and intensive case managers.

While the roles of the first set of team members were expanded on earlier, the RN administration provides a bird's-eye view of the ED and can act as the conductor or air traffic controller for the ED. They are key in helping to create bed space for all patients and act as a filter for any patient-care complaints. The outpatient community providers should complement the knowledge of the ED social work and DC planning team and should ideally have the authority to help in disposition planning, as well as helping to facilitate safe transportation for the discharging patient. The peer navigator is a team member with lived mental health experience who acts as a guide for the patient in accessing outpatient mental healthcare. While navigators have an array of responsibilities, they are well versed in the availability of various treatment modalities. The navigator acts as an advocate for the patient, helping to support and empower the patient in their daily activities.

Depending on your staffing model, consider having the behavioral health clinician be responsible for pre-rounding on each patient before the morning rounds to ensure that all aspects of the patient's care is encompassed in the *treatment update* note that we recommend be generated on rounds. For example, if morning rounds begins at 8 a.m., consider having the morning clinician pre-round on all the patients at 7 a.m. to be prepared to present the information to the treatment team.

The following template is an example of the information that the morning clinician should gather prior to meeting with the rest of the treatment team in the morning rounds meeting. While this information is helpful for the treatment team in developing a daily plan for each patient, this information should not be made part of the patient's medical record. These notes are typically meant to serve as a guide for the clinician to present during rounds and not necessarily for charting purposes.

5.10.2 Template for ED Psychiatry Pre-Rounding

- Patient name, age, and gender: This is meant to alert the treatment team of any patient preferred nicknames, gender preference, or preferred pronouns.
- Legal status: This is simply the patient's current legal status within the ED. They can be classified as either voluntary, on an involuntary hold, or conserved. Most states will have a limit to the amount of time that a patient can be kept on an involuntary hold, so it is important to include the expiration date and time of the hold.
- Reason for ED admit: In addition to the patient's chief complaint, this section should also include who brought the patient to the ED and under what circumstances they were brought in.
- Placement status: This section describes what service facilities the patient has been presented to for placement from the ED. This may include inpatient psychiatric hospitals, crisis residential facilities, skilled nursing facilities, or memory care units. The patient's possible wait time for placement should also be noted.

- **Barriers to placement:** This should include every possible and real barrier to getting the patient out of the ED. This can include transportation barriers, housing issues, access to outpatient follow-up care, medical or physical barriers including need for durable medical (e.g., CPAP, a continuous positive airway pressure machine that blows air into the patient's airway to prevent the airway from collapsing) equipment, ambulatory assistance, or toileting assistance. While facilities are typically Americans with Disabilities Act (ADA) compliant, the goal is to get a patient into a facility that can accommodate the patient's needs. It is important for the treatment team to gather specific and detailed information about the patient's barriers; for example, if a patient is in a cast, the team needs to know what type of cast it is (soft vs. hard), how long the cast has been in place, and when the patient may need a follow-up exam from orthopedics.
- **Projected disposition:** This is the rounding clinician's clinical opinion on what the patient's ultimate disposition will be based on the patient's overall ED presentation and the clinician's current assessment of the patient's level of need. Options can include keeping the patient in the ED for further observation, continuing to keep the patient on an involuntary psychiatric hold for eventual transfer to an inpatient psychiatric hospital, or discharging the patient home with outpatient follow-up. The disposition decision can also be affected by factors, such as level of patient support and collateral contact information.

The pre-rounding behavioral health clinician is the primary person presenting at rounds, as the psychiatrist or designated clinician creates a *treatment update* note in the medical records.

The purpose of morning rounds is to allow all team members to discuss the needs of each patient including the patient's presenting complaint, medication management, current medication regimen, recent vital signs, dietary needs and restrictions, recent behavioral issues in the ED, patient's legal status (voluntary or involuntary psychiatric hold), placement updates regarding bed availability in the community if the patient continues to require inpatient hospitalization, any current or potential barriers to placement, any child protective services (CPS) or adult protective services (APS) or duty-to-warn reporting concerns, and who on the team will be addressing any of the issues that are brought up.

5.10.3 Template for Treatment Update Note

- **Behavioral health morning rounds:** Consider documenting that this treatment update note includes clinical reports and a medical record review, and that the patient was not directly rounded on at the time the note was created.
- **Patient name:** This simply lists the patient's first and last names to ensure that the correct patient is being documented on.
- **Patient identifying or hospital record number:** This serves as a secondary measure to ensure that the correct patient is being documented on.
- **Chief complaint:** This is a brief description of how the patient arrived at the ED, and what the reason was for their arrival. Examples of how the patient arrived are things such as by ambulance, by police, by family, or by self.
- **Patient vitals for the past 24 hours:** This is a record of the patient's vital signs taken by ED nursing staff over the past 24-hour period. This may include things such as blood pressure, heart rate, and temperature.

The purpose of this section is to either document that the patient has been stable during the ED stay, or if there are any vital sign abnormalities, that they have been identified and addressed as clinically appropriate.

- Currently prescribed medications: This section includes any medications that are standing orders while the patient is in the ED. The list should include medical as well as any psychiatric medications prescribed.

A subsection of this can include a list of medications that were prescribed on an as-needed (prn) basis, and when and for what reason they were prescribed. An example can be something like a benzodiazepine was prescribed in the evening, for a one-time dose, for symptoms of severe anxiety.

- Diet: This section should include any special dietary needs or restrictions that the patient may require during their ED stay. Typically, most ED physicians overlook the need for specific diet orders on a patient due to the usual expected quick turnaround of most of the patients that they see.

It is important that the ED physician takes the time with a patient with behavioral health needs to address their dietary needs, due to the fact that most of these patients may be boarding in the ED for extended periods of time.

- Behavioral and legal status review: This section includes any behavioral issues, changes, or concerns, and any changes in the patient's legal status that have occurred in the past 24 hours.

Documented behavioral issues in the ED should include interventions that may have required verbal de-escalation, redirection, medication administration, or physical restraints.

Comments regarding the patient's legal status should certainly include whether the patient is on an involuntary psychiatric hold or not. Another important component of a patient's legal status relates to conservatorship issues, as well as a durable power of attorney or a documented decision maker for the patient.

This section should also include any issues regarding child protective services and/or adult protective services reporting requirements or concerns. Tarasoff, also known as duty to *warn and protect*, reporting requirements vary by state, so we encourage training and education in your local state regulations. Duty-to-warn issues can be a common occurrence that an ED psychiatric team will need to handle with due diligence.

The following scenario is a clear example of when a duty to *warn and protect* obligation should be fulfilled. A middle-aged woman was brought into the ED by law enforcement after she had arrived at her local police station and showed a police officer on staff a receipt she had from a gun she had recently purchased. The officer asked the woman if she was "currently a danger to others," and she replied, "Yes, I am a danger to others." The woman reported that she had purchased the gun to use to kill a man that she recently discovered had molested her child 15 years ago. The woman disclosed that she had been drinking alcohol more frequently since the discovery of the molestation, but denied that she had a problem with alcohol. This woman was discharged home to the care of her spouse after a family meeting was held between the woman, her spouse, and the ED psychiatry team. During the meeting the woman decided that she would not pick up the gun she had purchased when it arrived at the gun shop. A duty to warn and protect the intended victim of the woman's intent to harm him was initiated by contacting local law enforcement to file a duty-to-warn report and by contacting the intended victim via phone.

- Discharge or transfer update: This section should include any current placement updates that have occurred during the past 24 hours. This may include issues such as inpatient psychiatric bed availability, any barriers to placement, skilled nursing facility placement, memory care unit placement, housing availability—halfway home, group home, specific shelters, the patient's own home, and/or family involvement.

It is important that the team notes any inpatient psychiatric hospitals that the patient was presented to and was declined a bed at, as well as the reason for refusing transfer of the patient. This information will allow the treatment team to identify potential barriers and take action to ameliorate them.

- Current medical issues: The value of this section is that it documents any "medical clearance" related barriers as well as any pending medical concerns, and who on the team is accountable for addressing the concerns and barriers. Please see Chapter 7 on medical clearance for more information regarding evidence-based guidelines.

5.10.4 Emergency Department Nursing Rounding Note Template

- Identifying information: Include any patient-identifying information, including hospital record number, name, age, and gender.
- Chief complaint: This should be similar to the chief complaint section described previously.
- Patient behaviors: This will describe the patient's directly observed behaviors by the nursing staff, including both constructive and negative behaviors. Examples may include "Patient has been calm, cooperative and polite with staff, and adherent with medications," or something like "Patient has been arguing, threatening to assault staff, and pacing by bedside."
- Medications given: This should be a listing of the medications the nurse has administered to the patient during their shift, including name, dosage, route, and frequency. Also document any noted side effects the patient may complain of, and also any patient refusals to take medication.
- Vital signs: While this is self-explanatory, the purpose in a behavioral health context is to ensure and document a period of "stability" for transfer to an inpatient psychiatric facility, if that is what is clinically indicated. This should include listing of common vital signs taken by the nurse during their shift, including temperature, blood pressure, and heart rate. If any aberrant vitals have been noted, those should be documented, with an explanation of what was done to remedy the issue.
- Substance use: Include any recent alcohol or other drugs that the patient has ingested. The importance of this is to identify any potential treatment protocols that need to be put in place in order to properly treat any potential withdrawal symptoms. This may include placing the patient on a medication regimen for alcohol or opiate withdrawal. Any information the nurse gathers should be communicated to the ED MD as well in order to ensure that the treatment team can develop an adequate care plan. The nurse will typically have more direct patient interaction compared with the ED physician, and may have developed a different level of relationship, and therefore be privier to more detailed historical background information that the ED MD should be aware of.
- Activities of daily living: This section should include a description of the patient's overall ability to carry out daily tasks such as toileting, showering, and feeding themselves. Also included will be any special care need issues such as assistance with toileting or feeding. This is important because these issues can affect these patient's ability to be transferred to a locked psychiatric inpatient hospital setting, and may steer the team in the direction of seeking out a medical-psychiatric inpatient hospital bed.

- Ambulation: This should include a brief description of the patient's ambulatory status—essentially, can they walk on their own, or do they need some type of physical or structural assistance to do so. In this section, any use of walkers, canes, wheelchairs, or prosthetic devices should be noted.
- Restraints: State any episodes of physical or chemical restraints the patient medically required during the nurse's shift. A clear rationale for the need for these restraints should also be documented in this section. Also document the name of the MD that placed the order, and the follow-up care that was implemented once the restraint was placed, and after it was discontinued.
- Legal status: This is simply a description of the patient's legal status. Examples are "voluntary" or "on a legal psychiatric hold," which will vary depending on the state where the patient receives treatment. Any changes in legal status that occur during the nurse's shift should also be noted here. For example, if the patient was taken off a psychiatric hold and was placed on voluntary status, this should be documented.
- Visitors: This section should include a list of any and all parties that have come to visit with the patient during the nurse's shift. The nurse should also include any potential problematic interactions between visitors and staff or the patient. Any restricted visitors or visitors that can be a potential support for the patient upon discharge from the ED should be noted in this section.

5.10.5 Reviewing the Patient List and Assigning Clinicians

After the morning rounds meeting has been completed, consider having the behavioral health team meet as a separate group to assign a patient caseload to each clinician on the team. A physical list of patients can be used for this purpose. Patients should be divided between the therapists and psychiatrists on the team based on current acuity and medication management needs. Ideally those patients with more acute psychiatric medication needs should be assigned to the psychiatrist and those with less urgent medication needs should be assigned to the therapist for assessment.

It is recommended that some type of system is in place where new assessments are delineated from reevaluations that are needed. Depending on the size of the team and the patient census load, consider patients that can be potentially discharged from the ED first and make the completion of their assessments or reevaluations a priority. The goal for this is to expedite their discharge from the ED, thereby allowing more capacity in the ED, and ensuring that patients are treated in the least restrictive environment and are discharged in a timely manner.

Patients that are acutely agitated and in need of medication management should also be noted to ensure that they are cared for appropriately.

Depending on the ED psychiatric daily census, the patient load can be divided in order to create maximum efficiency in the assessment process. Any highly acute cases should be divided among the psychiatrist and senior therapists or clinicians. Less acute cases can be divided among the newer, less experienced clinicians, or trainees, including interns or medical students.

It is critical that any clinician on the ED behavioral health treatment team has a clear understanding and mental picture of a comprehensive psychiatric assessment note. Clear and consistent documentation of the psychiatric assessment can be implemented by use of a template. This consistent documentation will ensure that adequate details and information that outline the clinician's thought process and observations are conveyed. The clinician should be documenting in all cases with the confidence that, if for some unforeseen reason, their note ended up in a court of law, they would feel secure with what is conveyed in the note. Another way to present the importance of clear and comprehensible chart documentation is to ask the clinician who completed the note if they would feel comfortable having the note posted on a large billboard for all bystanders to see. If they answer this question with a "no," their note should be revamped until they can answer with a "yes." The purpose of this section is to serve as a reminder that the clinician's thought and decision-making process should be clearly documented.

5.11 Template for Initial ED Psychiatric Consultation Note

The initial ED psychiatric consultation note is presented in the relevant sections that follow.

5.11.1 Initial Patient Arrival Information

- Identifying information: This includes the patient's first and last name, their age, marital status, ethnicity, and gender.
- Arrival method to the ED: This section should indicate if the patient was brought in by ambulance, was a walk in, or brought in by family or law enforcement. This will provide further information for discharge planning.

If the patient's family brought the patient in, then the family may be a good source of information.

If law enforcement brought the patient in, there may be a more acute psychiatric issue present, as well as potentially complicating legal concerns that may need to be addressed at the present visit.

If the patient was brought in by ambulance, the paperwork from EMS may provide valuable information regarding how the patient presented when they were picked up, as well as contact demographic information to further assist discharge planning.

- Legal status: This section includes information on whether the patient was brought in on a legal hold or placed on a hold by an outpatient mental health clinician.

If the patient is conserved or has a guardian, any applicable legal information can also be included in this section to ensure ongoing communication with the appropriate parties.

- Chief complaint: For this part of the note, ideally the patient's own words should be documented. The value of including this section is that it gives the ED clinician working with the patient an idea of how much insight the patient has into their own illness. This also speaks to what the patient's main concern is for coming into the ED, which will allow the treatment team to better address the main concerns of the patient, and potentially increase patient trust and rapport with the treatment team when they feel they are being heard and their needs are being met.

It is important that all clerical or nursing staff are trained in the consistent use of proper chief complaint labels as these labels ultimately act as a first guide for any ED staff treating the patient for the first time. The following examples highlight some real-life chief complaints that were used in an ED setting to describe what brought the patient in for treatment. Note that these patients were later consulted for the ED psychiatry team to assess the following:

- Suicidal, IUD removal
- Chest pain, rectal bleeding

5.11.2 History of Present Illness

This section should provide a description of what initially brought the patient into the ED, what the main concerns were, and why family or law enforcement brought the patient into the ED.

Include the most recent information on the exacerbation of their mental health symptoms that lead to this current ED visit. The time period or interval that should be addressed, typically, is the past several weeks prior to the ED arrival. Depending on the presenting complaint, this may go back to last time the patient was admitted to an inpatient psychiatric hospital. The purpose of this time frame is to paint an adequate picture upon which future clinical decisions can be built.

If the patient is currently prescribed medications, this section should include the patient's history of adherence to their regimen. If the patient is not adherent to the medication regimen, list the reasons why this has occurred, and if there are any reported side effects from the medications.

A review of the presenting symptoms should also be included in this section. The following specifiers should be documented:

- Perceived severity of the symptoms
- The self-reported duration, which can be hours, days, or weeks
- Frequency of experiencing the symptoms
- How these symptoms affect their ability to function
- Their ability to hold and maintain employment
- Their ability to form and maintain relationships with others, including family and friends

While billing and coding is certainly a valid reason to obtain as many specifiers as possible, the clinical reason to elicit this information is to allow the patient to tell their story and express how much their problems are bothering them.

5.11.3 Psychiatric History

This section should include prior outpatient therapy contacts including individual therapy, medication management, substance-use treatment, and case management services. The history of past inpatient psychiatric hospitalizations;

- Specifying the total number of hospitalizations
- When they were first hospitalized
- Their most recent hospitalization
- The reason they were hospitalized

The purpose of this is to document the patient's inpatient psychiatric hospitalization history, which can be used to help predict the patient's level of risk. This can include, but is not limited to, risks to harm self or others, risk of medication nonadherence, and risk of symptom exacerbation.

A list of the patient's prior psychiatric medications should also be obtained, including any potential issues with side effects, adherence issues, and any other known reasons for switching medications. The patient's self-reported experience of effectiveness of the medications should be taken into account in order to better address treatment planning and new medication suggestions.

This information can act as a valuable tool to the assessing psychiatrist in being able to work in collaboration with the patient to choose a viable and effective medication regime.

Prior suicide attempts, non-suicidal self-injurious behaviors, and any prior issues with aggression and violence are also pertinent to include in this section. The patient's history of suicide attempts should include the patient's first suicide attempt, their most recent suicide attempt, and their recollection of their most lethal suicide attempt to date. Any past suicide plans should also be documented in this section. Similar information should be gathered on the patient's history of violent acts toward others, toward property, and homicide attempts.

Abuse history should include prior experiences with sexual abuse, physical abuse, emotional abuse, and neglect. It is important to clarify if the patient was the perpetrator or victim in any of the disclosed abuse episodes. Especially in the elderly and disabled populations, fiduciary or financial abuse issues may be prevalent and should also be documented when appropriate.

Intimate partner violence (IPV) is often underreported in general, and the interview in the ED may help to elicit key information to further diagnose the etiology of the patient's complaints and also help connect the patient with resources. It is important that the assessing clinician is aware of the warning signs of IPV in order to properly diagnose the root of the patient's presentation.

Many patients may fabricate a bogus chief complaint in the hope of getting into a safe environment away from their abuser; the ED can act as this safe zone for some of these patients. The fabricated complaints can push the clinician's diagnostic judgment off balance, causing them to completely miss the IPV issues. A prime example of this is illustrated in the following scenario.

A woman arrived to the ED with her partner requesting to see a physician for a refill of her psychiatric medications. The ED physician consulted psychiatry staff to assess the patient due to the request for the psychiatric medications. Upon assessment by the ED psychiatry team, the patient started to become agitated and began yelling and screaming at the staff. The patient's partner was still in the treatment room with her. At this point, security officers were called to the patient's bedside and escorted the patient's partner to the lobby due to the patient's agitated state.

Once the patient's partner was escorted from the room, the patient became calm and pleasant toward the ED staff. She explained to the treating psychiatry team that she did not actually need a refill of her psychiatric medications and had only told the triage nurse this in order to get admitted into the ED in hopes of being able to be physically separated from her partner. The patient disclosed that her partner had been hitting and beating her at home, so she no longer felt safe living with her partner. At this time, social services were contacted to meet with the patient who provided her with IPV support and resources.

5.11.4 Past Medical History

Whether or not an ED clinician documents the patient's medical history in their note, it is useful to include the patient's past medical history. This section should include medical medications the patient is taking, dosages, and adherence patterns. We have experienced times where medical history or medications relating to nonpsychiatric issues become barriers to inpatient psychiatric placement, which is why we highlight the value of proper documentation of these topics.

Durable medical equipment needs, such as the use of a CPAP or other breathing machine, indwelling lines, or the need for cancer treatment or renal dialysis, should all be addressed. The schedule of treatment for things, such as dialysis as well as travel accommodations or arrangements, should also be mentioned to reduce as many barriers to a safe discharge as possible. Any past surgeries are also pertinent to document in this section.

The patient's ambulatory status should also be identified at this juncture, taking into account the possible use of canes, walkers, wheelchairs, or prosthetic devices. If the patient has any upcoming appointments or any need for medical attention, such as suture or cast removal that is scheduled, this should also be noted.

5.11.5 Substance Use History

This section should be as comprehensive as possible, as treatment options for past and current substance use will inevitably be part of the patient's treatment planning.

The following items need to be gathered from the patient interview:

- List of names of current substances used
- Method of use: For example, inhaling, ingesting, or injecting
- Age of first use
- Last reported use
- Frequency of current use: For example, daily, weekly, or monthly
- Longest period of sobriety, number of relapses, and attempts to get treatment (e.g., detoxification, rehabilitation, self-help groups such as Alcoholics and Narcotics Anonymous)
- Withdrawal effects and experiences (most importantly, alcohol withdrawal issues, such as delirium tremens and seizures)
- If they have been recently increasing (or decreasing) their current pattern and amount used

It may be of use to the ED team to note specific substance-seeking related behaviors that the patient may exhibit during their ED admit. Different states have databases that collect prescription information for controlled substances. If you are a clinician in such a state, the use of information from these databases has been linked to significant decreases in prescribed controlled substance misuse, diversion, and overdose.

Some patients will engage in behaviors to be able to access illicit substances while in the ED. In the numerous EDs we have worked in across the United States, we have witnessed examples such as patients hiding street drugs within body orifices, in the lining of their undergarments (bra lining and underwear lining, to be exact), and having family members smuggle in drugs while they visit the patient.

There may be some patients that are accustomed to being prescribed various controlled medications, such as benzodiazepines or opiates for prior treatment of preexisting conditions. These patients may have become used to receiving these medications when asking for them in a treatment or ED setting, and may continue this behavior during this ED admit. Special consideration needs to be given by the ED treatment team to these patterns of behavior, making sure that any requested medications are medically necessary.

An important reason to document this information is to assist in determining what level of care the patient needs while in the ED and what type of outpatient services the patient will benefit from being linked to upon discharge from the ED.

5.11.6 Social History

Taking note of the patient's social history can help with the discharge planning process. This information can identify potential social support that the patient may be able to rely on. Conversely, this information may also point to lapses in the patient's supports and the possible need for the ED treatment team to add additional resources to the patient discharge plan.

This section should include:

- Employment status: Specify current occupation, how long patient has been employed, any issues with recent job loss or stressors at work, and inability to find work.
- Education level: Last grade completed, if they are currently a student, any degrees obtained, and any issues or stressors at school.
- Relationship issues: Current relationship status, recent divorce, recent separation, and recent marriage or engagement.
- Family composition: Take note of the whether the patient is living in a blended family, foster family, or adopted family.

5.11.6.1 Living Situation

This section should include if the patient resides with their family, if the patient is living alone, or living with roommates.

If the patient is living in specialized care settings such as a memory care unit, a skilled nursing facility, or a group home (e.g., for the developmentally delayed) the information on these settings should be documented. Ideally, the address, owner, care provider, and contact information should be gathered as soon as possible to aid in treatment and discharge planning.

5.11.6.2 Legal History

While the individual points that we make in this section are valuable, patterns of behaviors resulting in legal ramifications are also important to note.

Consider including:

- History of arrests, dates of arrests, reason for the arrest, and if incarcerated, for how long.
- History of being placed on probation or parole.
- Prior history of being conserved, whether that includes mental health or probate conservatorship.
- Any prior history as a minor of placement in a facility, such as juvenile hall or youth authority.
- Substance use related arrests, such as driving under the influence (DUI) or possession or sale of controlled substances, should also be documented.

There are many ways the legal history adds value to the clinical assessment. A pattern of legal problems including arrests and jail or prison time may help lead to a diagnostic picture of conduct disorder or antisocial personality traits.

If the patient is connected with the legal system, collateral information may be obtained, as clinically appropriate. In most states, patient consent is required in order to contact any legal system providers that the patient is linked with. Legal providers may include parole and probation officers. A written release should be filled out by the patient in addition to documenting in the patient's chart notes that the patient gave consent to speak with the legal provider.

5.11.6.3 Financial History

The patient's current and past financial status can be affected by multiple factors. Some of these factors can include financial problems, such as debt or bankruptcy. Patients may display a history of inability to care for their finances. In these cases, it may be a benefit to the patient if a payee is assigned to manage the patient's expenses.

Include information about any sources of income, such as social security disability, government assistance, and stable employment.

5.11.6.4 Support System

This section should address any relevant collateral contacts including family members, friends, relatives, neighbors, community members, religious leaders, outpatient treatment providers, case managers, and law enforcement officials. Document if the patient gives permission to the treatment team to speak with anyone listed in their chart, what the patient asks the team to reveal or speak about, as well as that person's contact information, including a phone number.

It can be helpful, and prevent unnecessary family complaints to ED administration, if a process for alerting family or friends of the patient's plan of care is implemented. Please refer to the chapter on discharge planning for further information.

5.11.7 Mental Status Exam

If the history of present illness is viewed as a timeline of what the patient experienced up until the presentation to the ED, the mental status exam (MSE) should be viewed as a snapshot of what the patient looks like in front of you at that moment in time.

While the history of present illness theoretically shouldn't change, the MSE is the key element during reassessments of patients to determine if they are responding to treatment or not.

5.11.7.1 Appearance

This should be a brief description of the patient's outer presentation, including clothing, level of grooming and hygiene, weight, height, whether or not they appear their stated age, dentition, presence of tattoos or bodily markings, piercings, scars, evidence of past physical trauma, missing or deformation of limbs, posture, presence of accessories including prosthetics, walker, wheelchair, cane, or eye glasses.

5.11.7.2 Behavior

This should describe any observed behaviors of the patient. Descriptors can include level of calmness, whether they are cooperative with the interview, their level of engagement, including if they are withdrawn or aloof. Mention if the patient appears internally preoccupied, if they are talking to themselves, or if they are responding to internal stimuli.

Displayed episodes of aggression (verbal or physical), posturing, or tearfulness should be noted. Emotional lability, including laughing, is also an important descriptor to document. The clinician should identify whether or not these observed behaviors are appropriate for the context of the interview.

5.11.7.3 Demeanor/Manner

This section should provide a brief description of the patient's reaction to the clinician's presence and questions. Examples include being pleasant, cooperative, hostile, guarded, aloof, withdrawn, seductive or flirtatious, and defensive.

5.11.7.4 Speech

Speech can be described using the following descriptors:

- Rate, including rapid, slow, or rambling
- Quality, including monotonous, unspontaneous, or hesitant
- Quantity, including hyperverbal or mute
- Volume, including loud, soft, or whispering
- Prosody, including the rhythm or patterns of sound that the patient forms

5.11.7.5 Mood

The clinician should be aware that there can be a tendency to confuse the topics of mood and affect. We often see in documentation that clinicians incorrectly utilize these interchangeably in the mental status exam.

"Mood" is what the patient answers when you ask them, "How are you feeling?" Examples of mood are "I am fine" or "I have been depressed." This section also needs to take into consideration the patient's pattern of emotional stability over a specified time frame. This is what you document in the "history of present illness" section. What you include in the MSE section is how the patient responds to the question of how they are feeling at the time of that interview.

You can also think of this as the patient's subjective description of their current emotional state.

5.11.7.6 Affect

This is the description of the clinician's objective observation of the patient's emotional state. For example, if the patient reports feeling "depressed," and is laughing as they are answering you, the affect would be "incongruent with reported mood." These are examples of affect: euthymic, depressed, dysphoric, angry, fearful, elated, manic, labile, restricted, blunted, and flat, to name a few.

5.11.7.7 Perceptual Disturbances

This section is to include the presence or absence of auditory or visual or any other type of hallucinations or illusions. While this section can, and often is, included in the "thought content" portion of the MSE, there is value in separating this from the "thought content" section. As we often train medical students, interns and fellows, we have found that separation of this descriptor allows the trainee to be more cognizant of its importance.

Note the type and quality of the hallucination, such as command type; the nature and gender of the auditory hallucinations; and the description of the visual or other hallucinations. The value of the specific type of perceptual disturbance reported is that it can dramatically impact the clinician's differential as to the etiology of the disturbance. For example, if the patient is complaining of tactile hallucinations, "insects crawling on the body," consider possible substance use or withdrawal as a cause of the symptoms.

While there are few pathognomonic types of hallucinations that can exclusively rule out or rule in a diagnosis, the more information that is gathered will yield greater success in ultimately diagnosing and treating the patient.

5.11.7.8 Thought Process

This section should include a description of the clinician's observation of the patient's stream of thoughts and how the patient is answering questions. If a patient is asked a simple question, such as, "What did you eat for breakfast?" and they respond by saying, "Waffles," this is an example of a linear response. Conversely, if they respond by stating, "Waffles and cow, I saw a cow the other day in a field, green fields are neat," this is an example of a tangential response. As one word or thought elicits the next word or thought they continue to drift further from the main point of the question asked.

Additionally, describe the patient's level of thought organization as well as how quickly the patient develops answers and processes information during the interview. A patient may respond to a question that appears to make no logical sense; for example, if the patient is asked, "Where do you live?" and responds by saying, "Red steaks fly through the evening grounds," this is a display of thought disorganization.

5.11.7.9 Thought Content

This section is designed to capture the clinically pertinent positive and negative elements of what the patient talks about. Suicidal ideation, intent, and plan, as well as homicidal ideation, intent, and plan are included in this section. As mentioned previously, perceptual disturbances and how they affect the patient can also be included in this section.

5.11.7.10 Orientation

This section describes the patient's ability to state the following information:

- The patient's full name
- Date of birth
- Their current location (what kind of a place they are in, what the name is of the place, what floor of the hospital they are on)
- The time of day
- Current date including month and year
- Why they were brought to or came to the ED (e.g., "What brings you to the ED?")

Documentation should reflect if prompting is required, or if there are any errors in their answers, regardless of how minor.

5.11.7.11 Memory

This section should provide a brief overview of the patient's ability to answer questions regarding recent, remote and immediate recall. A test of the patient's memory is valuable in determining any cognitive deficits, including symptoms of a neurocognitive disorder. A simple test of the patient's memory can be completed by asking the patient to remember three items you ask them to remember. Typically, this is done by telling them three things (such as apple, ball, penny), and asking the patient to repeat the words. The clinician then tells the patient to remember them and that they will ask them to repeat the words in a couple of minutes. This is a good test for short-term memory recall, and when documented can be used as a "baseline" for the subsequent times the same memory test is given.

To test recent memory, we typically ask what the patient has had for breakfast that morning. The trick to this is to make sure you can corroborate the truth of the information given either from ED staff, a family member, or patient caregiver.

Remote memory can be tested by asking for personal historical information, or past experiences. This also needs to be corroborated with others that know the patient's history to ensure accuracy.

5.11.7.12 Concentration

This section includes the clinician's assessment of how the patient is able to maintain their focus. Questions to elicit intended responses include asking the patient to subtract 7 from 100 and continuing and monitoring for errors, to spell the word "WORLD" backward, and calculating the number of quarters in $2.25.

As one can imagine, the patient's education and literacy level directly impacts their ability to answer these types of questions. If that is a barrier, that should be noted and more general descriptors can be used to document the patient's ability to concentrate (e.g., poor, impaired, fair, good, or excellent).

5.11.7.13 Cognition

This section explores the patient's ability to abstract information. Examples that can be used clinically are asking the patient to interpret socially known proverbs. The typical proverb that we use is, "Those who live in glass homes should not throw stones." Our favorite proverb to teach medical students to ask the patient is, "The beard pays for the shaving."

The use of proverbs can be a double-edged sword when trying to test for the patient's cognitive ability. They, in truth, have limited use in testing the patient's true level of cognition, given their cultural specificity. We teach this to students by giving a very obscure proverb, such as the one presented previously, to paint this picture very clearly. Plus, teaching this part of the MSE is funny with that example, as we still have no idea what "The beard pays for the shaving" actually means. And to be honest, neither we nor any of our students have actually used this with a real patient. It is used for teaching and demonstration purposes only.

While functional assessment of the patient's intellectual ability (including mental retardation, borderline intellectual function, average and above average intelligence) can be useful in the outpatient realm, it has limited use within the ED setting. Obtaining background information from collateral contacts regarding the patient's intellectual ability and/or functional assessment is probably the quickest and most efficient way for the ED clinician to gather the information. This information can be useful in order to guide the treatment team in the future placement of the patient. For example, if a patient required placement from the ED into a home for individuals with developmental delays.

5.11.7.14 Insight

This is the patient's ability to provide the clinician with a description of what they feel is causing their current symptoms, in other words, their understanding of their disease process.

This may include simple statements from the patients regarding prior diagnoses they have had, and expressing the realization that the disorder they have been diagnosed with is causing their current symptom presentation.

The patient's understanding of what medications and treatment recommendations are being made is also pertinent to this section. In other words, "insight" can be conceptualized as, "Does the patient understand what is causing their current psychiatric episode?"

5.11.7.15 Judgment

This describes the patient's level of adherence to socially approved norms or behaviors. This also includes the patient's adherence to recommended treatment modalities including medications required for their illness, and their ability to make healthy choices for themselves. The hallmark of any behavioral health pathology is the direct impact it has on the person's life, and their ability to relate to others and care for themselves. This section in the MSE is the clinician's assessment of the patient's current decision-making process.

Possible questions to ask the patient to rate their level of judgment include, "If you found an addressed and stamped envelope, what would you do?" and "If you found a wallet on the street with $200 in it, what would you do?"

Depending on the patient's answer, the clinician then rates their judgment. Examples of judgment are: impaired, poor, fair, good, and excellent.

Typically, patients with a psychotic illness during an acute psychotic episode have poor insight and judgment. This can then affect the patient's decision to take prescribed medications for psychosis, resulting in continued poor insight and judgment. Substance use and acute intoxication effects can also result in poor insight and judgment. The purpose of documenting these elements in the MSE each time is to compare the current responses with responses from past exams and measure any identified improvement or decompensation.

5.11.7.16 Impulse Control

This is a brief description of the patient's current ability to maintain their composure and regulate their behavioral responses or urges during the interview. This not only includes physical dysregulation but also disruptive actions, utterances, yelling, and screaming.

It is important to note that the patient's current impulse control may be affected by any substance (illicit or prescribed) or disease process (e.g., delirium secondary to encephalitis).

Once again, the history of present illness delineates the issues that lead up to the current state, and this section is a mere snapshot of how the patient is during the interview itself. Descriptors of impulse control include, poor, marginal, fair, good, and excellent. Examples of poor impulse control include when a patient with mania begins to masturbate in the exam room in front of staff, when a patient with psychosis defecates on the floor in their room, or when a patient with personality pathology yells and threatens to call the president of the nation to complain about their services.

Now that the MSE portion has been completed, the documentation of the initial psychiatric assessment continues with the assessment of risk.

5.11.8 Risk Assessment

The risk assessment is probably one of the most important sections of the ED psychiatric assessment as many patients seen in the ED may present with suicidal or homicidal thoughts as their primary complaint.

In 2002, 7% of all psychiatric-related visits to EDs were due to suicide attempts, and suicidal ideation has been classified as being the second most common psychiatric complaint presenting to EDs (Currier and Allen 2003; Larkin et al. 2005). A comprehensive risk assessment includes documentation on any current reported suicidal thoughts, homicidal thoughts, and risk for grave disability.

This assessment area also carries legal ramifications for the patient as the assessing clinician can temporarily suspend the patient's civil liberties if they deem the patient to be at a high level of risk for harm to themselves or others, or gravely disabled.

Even though the completion of a risk assessment is paramount to the ED psychiatric evaluation, many clinicians may be reluctant to delve into the topic of suicide or homicide with their patients, but it is important that this issue is broached as many patients may not readily disclose these thoughts without prompting (Hirschfeld and Russell 1997).

5.11.8.1 Assessing Suicide Risk

An assessment for suicide risk can be started with a simple question: "Have you had any recent thoughts such as you wish you could go to sleep and never wake up or wished you were not alive?" This question can open the door to the patient's thoughts of suicide. If the patient answers "yes" to this question, the clinician will need to follow up with more in-depth questioning to elicit the patient's level of potential self-harm. Asking the patient, "Have you ever thought about ending your life or killing yourself?" can take the questioning on self-harm to the next level.

If a patient admits to having suicidal thoughts, the next step in the assessment process is asking about any plan, means to accessing the plan, and intent to carry out the plan for suicide that the patient has developed (Chang et al. 2011). Preparatory behaviors, such as writing a suicide note, making plans to give away personal possessions or property, or rehearsing the suicide plan, are important pieces of information to gather for completing the risk assessment puzzle.

5.11.8.2 Assessing Homicide Risk

A similar line of questioning can be utilized to explore homicidal thoughts.

Access to firearms or other deadly weapons needs to be addressed in cases of both suicidal and homicidal ideation. If the patient admits to having access to firearms or other weapons, your local law enforcement agency or family or friends of the patient can be contacted to help locate and remove the weapons thus decreasing the patient's ease of access to self-harm or harm to others (Barber and Miller 2014). Please see Chapter 9 on ethical issues for more information.

5.11.8.3 Assessing for Grave Disability

Grave disability, or the inability to plan for or care for one's basic needs due to a mental illness, is another area that requires a risk assessment. The basic idea is to elucidate the patient's current plan of care, essentially how do they plan to provide themselves with food, shelter, and clothing upon discharge from the ED?

Even in the legal system, a judge may make a decision to involuntarily commit a patient to a hospital for psychiatric treatment based on their perception of the patient's ability to provide for their basic needs (Holstein 1984). Simply asking the patient, "When you are discharged from the ED, how do you plan to provide yourself with food, clothing, and shelter?" is a simple way to determine the patient's self-care plan.

It is important to note that homelessness in and of itself does not constitute grave disability. Many patients may prefer to be homeless or may be in transition between housing. If a patient reports that they plan to live under the bridge overlooking the river, this can qualify as a plan for shelter.

The label "gravely disabled" can only be placed on a patient by a mental health or legal professional (e.g., judge). The patient must have a known prior or current primary psychiatric disorder, such as schizophrenia or major depression.

5.11.8.4 Risk Level Scaling

Each of the topics in the risk assessment section should be rated using a scale. We have found that the use of the labels "low, medium, and high" work well. So, a given patient can be given a risk rating of "low" for danger to self, "low" for danger to others and "high" for grave disability based on the assessing provider's clinical opinion. The label "none" should not be used as a rating in the risk assessment as it does not leave any room for clinical error in the assessment. It is important to note that any person one comes in contact with has some potential level of risk present. The scale we are talking about utilizes "low" as the base score in order to prevent the use of the label "none."

5.11.9 Impression

The impression section can be conceptualized as the clinician's initial opinion about what is causing the patient's presenting psychiatric complaint and corresponding ED admit. Another way to think about the impression is the clinician's best educated guess as to what is causing the patient's symptoms.

For example, if a patient arrives to the ED complaining of "hearing voices and paranoia," the assessing clinician's impression may be that the patient is experiencing the hallucinations and paranoid delusions due to ingestion of an illicit drug or to an underlying psychotic disorder. Once further medical testing (e.g., urine toxicology screening) has been completed, a more formal diagnostic picture can be developed.

The impression is essentially the clinician's differential diagnosis after an initial assessment of the patient has been completed.

5.11.10 Diagnosis

Historically, in prior versions of the Diagnostic and Statistical Manual of Mental Disorders (DSM), a multi-axial system for diagnosis was used. In the new version of the DSM, the American Psychiatric Association (APA) decided to move to a non-axial system of diagnosis. The point of a diagnosis is to provide a clear and comprehensive list of medical and psychiatric syndromes.

The prior multi-axial system was comprised of five axes. Axis one included the primary psychiatric or substance use disorders. Axis two included any personality or intellectual disability disorders, including syndromes such as borderline personality disorder. Axis three contained a list of any medical or neurological problems that the patient was diagnosed with. Axis four provided a list of all of the major psychosocial stressors that were affecting the patient. Lastly, Axis five was the Global Assessment of Functioning (GAF) score, which listed a rating from 0 to 100 to describe the patients overall level of daily functioning.

The current DSM uses a diagnostic system in which the patient's most prominent diagnosis is listed first followed by any secondary or less acute diagnoses. These diagnoses include medical, neurological, developmental, and intellectual disorders. Psychosocial stressors are also noted when relevant to the diagnostic picture. For example, a patient arrived at the ED with psychotic symptoms. The patient has a history of alcohol abuse, but has been sober for the past 2 years, and has prior personality issues. The patient is going through a divorce from his third wife and is at risk of being laid off from his job. The DSM-5 diagnosis for this patient could be psychotic disorder, unspecified; narcissistic personality disorder; alcohol use disorder by history; relational problems; and occupational problems.

5.11.11 Recommendations and Plan

This section of the assessment documents the clinician's treatment recommendations and overall treatment plan. Recommendations should be based on the information that has been gathered during the interview process with the patient. Topics in this section can include treatment modality; medication name, dose, and frequency; decision to admit to an inpatient psychiatric hospital or not; and recommended level of least restrictive care.

We have worked in hospitals where this section is the only section a consulting clinician will read to "get to the point" of the consult. While we strongly recommend that all clinicians read the entire note that they consulted another service on, knowing that this type of shortcut is taken, we suggest that the writer of an assessment have a strong recommendations section that references the main note.

Please be aware that while writing recommendations, scope of practice must be kept in mind. A non-MD therapist cannot make medication recommendations; they can suggest a medication consultation, or for the patient to see a psychiatrist in an outpatient appointment.

An example of discharge recommendations for a patient leaving the ED can look like this:

"It is recommended that the patient be referred to a partial hospitalization program for a minimum of 5 days in order to address their symptoms of depression. The patient will also benefit from a medication evaluation by a psychiatrist. Once the patient has completed their partial hospitalization treatment, it is recommended that they be stepped down to outpatient therapy sessions. An appointment has been made for the patient to meet with James Conner, licensed psychologist at the Sunny Gates clinic on 2/4/2016 at 5:00 p.m." We recommend that any patient, who is discharging from the ED back to the community, is scheduled an outpatient follow-up appointment whenever possible. The specific date, time, clinic name, and provider name that the patient will be meeting with should be documented.

Depending on the direction that the patient's treatment takes while in the ED, this can have a direct effect on the recommendations that are made and the ultimate plan for the patient. In instances where the patient needs to be kept in the ED setting for further treatment, the plan may involve documentation of direct accountable team members for clear action items they are responsible for completing. A chart documentation example of this follows: "The patient will be referred to medical social services for help with establishing housing or shelter. The psychiatrist will reassess the need for continued use of psychotropic medications. The discharge planning staff will call the patient's outpatient clinic for recent records. Medical social services will also be contacting the patient's mother for discharge transportation."

It is important that the assessing clinician not only document the recommendations in the chart, but that they also consult with the attending ED MD and RN and whoever they wrote down as accountable parties to verbally review the plan with.

5.12 Psychiatric Reassessment

The overall goal of treatment is to have the patient in the least restrictive environment receiving the most appropriate care. The patient should also be receiving the treatment that they need clinically.

To achieve these objectives and to update the treatment teams understanding of the patient illness process, we encourage using standardized timely reassessments of the patient's condition. As a guideline, it is recommended that a patient receive a psychiatric reassessment at a minimum of once every 8 hours to determine if they still require the current level of restrictive environment for their care.

If there are any clinical or social developments in the patient's case, these should trigger a reassessment of the patient's condition and corresponding appropriate documentation. Like the initial assessment note, the reassessment documentation should include the parties that are responsible for carrying out the plan for the patient's treatment and discharge.

The recommended minimal essential sections for a reassessment note include

- The subjective update or what the patient is reporting
- The objective update or what the clinician observes in the patient, also called the mental status exam
- A current risk assessment
- Updates to the assessment and plan of care

5.13 To Consult or Not to Consult?: Appropriate Consultations of Psychiatry in the Emergency Setting

It is the ED psychiatry consultation service's primary role to assess, make recommendations for treatment, and implement these treatment recommendations when clinically and ethically appropriate to do so. Given this role, it makes sense that an ED MD would want to place a consultation order for psychiatry on any patient they deem has a psychiatric complaint. This practice may put the ED staff's conscience at ease (Pestka et al. 2012; Suokas et al. 2015), but it can also be a costly one if the psychiatric needs of the patient could have been addressed by the primary ED treatment team.

It has been found that a consultation to the psychiatry team can add an average of another 3.5 hours to the patient's total length of stay (Langheim and Heilingenstein 2014). With the ever increasing hourly staffing costs of ED nurses, technicians, physicians, and a psychiatric consult service, any ED administrator, focused on ED operating costs, will want to strive to ensure that all psychiatric consult requests are appropriate. So, this begs these questions to be asked: When should the psychiatric consultation service be called and when should the primary ED treatment team address the patient's psychiatric need?

Prior to making any decision to consult the psychiatric team, the patient should be medically cleared by the treating ED physician and any medical causes of psychiatric symptoms should be ruled out. Also, be sure that you are consulting the correct service for the need that the patient is presenting with. For example, if your patient is primarily intoxicated and homeless, the hospital's medical social services team may be more appropriate to consult versus the psychiatric team.

Many patients presenting with neurocognitive disorders (e.g., dementia) trigger the ED treatment team to call in the psychiatric consult service for an assessment. In these cases, the hospital's discharge planning and neurology team may be more useful to consult for treatment and disposition planning purposes. The psychiatric consult service will typically be unable to arrange for a transfer of these patients to a psychiatric facility due to the fact that a neurocognitive disorder is a primary exclusionary criteria for many psychiatric hospitals.

The main question that the consulting party can ask themselves is, "Is this actually a psychiatric emergency?" If the answer to this question is a clear "yes," then consult away. If the answer is "no," this may be a patient that the primary ED treatment team can assess and create a disposition plan for. In many cases, these non-acute patients may just need a simple referral to outpatient psychiatric resources or a psychotropic medication refill, which any licensed physician is educated and trained to handle.

Substance intoxication can mimic the symptoms of various psychiatric disorders, so if the primary ED treatment team is aware that the patient is intoxicated on drugs or alcohol, they should consider holding off on consulting the ED psychiatric team until the patient is clinically sober and has been reassessed by the ED physician for any current symptoms of a psychiatric illness. Following are some common scenarios that your psychiatric consult service should and should not be called to intervene on.

Conditions that may warrant a higher threshold to consult the behavioral health team include acute psychosis, first break psychosis, suicide attempt, psychiatric medication side effects (e.g., extrapyramidal symptoms [EPS], dystonic reactions [eye rolling]), severe depression, suicidal thoughts, catatonia, mania, neurocognitive disorders with psychotic features, or other behavioral disturbances.

Conditions that may warrant a lower threshold to consult include acute substance intoxication (e.g., alcohol or methamphetamine), psychotropic medication refill requests, generalized anxiety, delirium, neurocognitive disorders without psychotic features, homelessness, transportation, or other social needs.

5.14 Innovative Care in the Emergency Department: Dedicated Psychiatric Observation Areas

Many hospital medical centers that provide emergency services to the community at large contain a locked psychiatric treatment unit that serves as an extension of the ED. For EDs that do not have these units, the halls of the ED end up taking the place of the psychiatric treatment unit.

Many of the patients admitted to these EDs sit in the hallway for days without adequate treatment of their symptoms, which is one of the impetuses for writing this book.

In order to address this issue, we recommend the following restructuring of the way the ED team thinks about space allocation for patients with behavioral health needs. A model we suggest is to organize the placement of your patient population into three categories: high acuity, moderate acuity, and low acuity. Depending on the state that you provide treatment in, use of the term "acuity" can have implications for staffing ratio requirements.

Patients that are deemed to be loud, combative, requiring higher intensity of monitoring and care should be placed in an area that has better visibility, with potential access to video monitoring, or closer to a nursing station. The way to conceptualize the process, even within the ED, is as the higher acuity patient stabilizes, and is better controlled medically and psychiatrically, they can be moved to the moderate level acuity area, and then to the lower acuity areas of the ED. Patients that are placed in the higher acuity area should be "medically cleared." The hope is that these patients have had substance intoxication or use ruled out of their diagnostic picture, but there may be occasions where this has been missed by the diagnosing ED clinician, so these patients may also end up being placed in the higher acuity psychiatric treatment area. Typical symptoms or diagnoses that may require a higher level of monitoring and care include acute psychosis, schizophrenia, schizoaffective disorders, and mania. Patients that have displayed a propensity for self-harm would also be placed in this area.

As the patient's symptoms improve while being treated in the high acuity area, the treatment team can begin to develop a transitional plan for movement to the moderate or lower acuity areas. This depends on the level of improvement that the patient displays, and the continued expected length of stay in the ED.

Many EDs have adopted an innovative approach to developing a safe and therapeutic area for their patients with psychiatric needs to be treated in. A psychiatric "guesting area" has been created as an alternative treatment milieu for the psychiatric patient population in the ED (Waunch and Conley 2011; Winokur and Senteno 2009; Winokur and Waunch 2010). Some hospital systems have used a model in which the guesting area is within the ED walls, while others have utilized a designated space outside of the ED to house patients waiting for psychiatric beds (Levin-Epstein 2015).

5.14.1 Recommendations for the Dedicated Psychiatric Observation Area

As a patient transitions from high to low acuity within the ED, the patient can be transitioned to a dedicated psychiatric observation area (DPOA). Administration may be hesitant to include a DPOA within the walls of the ED due to possible fears of an increased psychiatric census if the DPOA appears to be too welcoming for psychiatric patients within the community at large. This rhetoric should not be listened to and should be challenged as it tends to be unsubstantiated at best and anti-patient at the worst.

In order to establish a DPOA within the walls of an ED, we recommend that a designated space is identified for this purpose. The size of the DPOA will vary depending on the EDs average psychiatric patient census, patient to nurse staffing ratios and patient to security officer ratios. The DPOA should be located in a quiet area removed from the choatic environment of the ED halls; this will allow the patient a calm place to rest and recompensate toward a path of wellness.

Rather than using traditional ED gurneys within the DPOA, lounge chairs can be used, similar to a large padded reclining chair. The chairs should be large enough in size to accommodate patients of varying sizes and should be ADA compliant. The philosophy behind the use of a chair versus a traditional hospital gurney is to move the patient toward a state of normalcy and activation. Patients placed in a chair are taken out of the traditional sick role that is associated with the hospital gurney. The use of the chair allows for a change in the cultural expectations that the ED staff may hold toward the psychiatric patient, from one of a burdened person in need of care to one of a person moving toward wellness. This potential shift in staff cultural attitudes may also indirectly affect the discharge planning process for the patient as the staff encourages the patient's flight toward wellness and decreased time within the sick role. This can lead to a potential decrease in patient boarding time within the ED. The chair allows more flexibility with patient placement into the DPOA and keeps the patient sitting in an upright position. Patients should be encouraged by ED staff, including nurses and security officers, to get up out of the chair once every 30 minutes to walk around the DPOA.

A communal table can be placed in the middle of the DPOA, allowing a common area for the patients to sit at in order to engage in daily activities as a group. These activities may include eating meals, playing board or card games, or simply conversing with one another.

In order to provide a structured setting within the DPOA, a daily schedule can be developed and implemented. The schedule can include, but is not limited to, items such as wake and sleep times, meal times, hygiene times, recreational activity times, therapy times, and discharge planning sessions. It is important that staff are encouraged to keep the patients that are housed within the DPOA on a normalized daily schedule, this includes the amount of light that the patient is exposed to during a normal day. The lights within the DPOA should be kept on until the "lights out" time on the schedule has been reached.

5.15 Use of Handouts in the ED

Therapeutic handouts can be a beneficial addition to the ED psychiatric treatment teams box of treatment tools. While patients that are recompensating and are moving toward discharge may be a prime population to start using handouts with, any patient receiving treatment within the ED may also benefit from them.

5.15.1 Welcome Letter

The *welcome letter* acts as the patient's introduction to their ED treatment experience. The letter simply describes what the patient is being treated for, who will be treating them during their ED stay, and what is expected of them in order to move them toward a path of wellness and potential discharge. The letter should describe in detail any rules regarding visitation policies or patient belongings policies. It can be helpful to add staff photographs to the welcome letter so the patient can place a face with the name of their treating clinicians. Photographs of the patient's primary psychiatrist and psychiatric social worker are important as these will be the clinicians that will primarily help the patient move toward discharge.

5.15.2 Diagnostic-Specific Patient Education

The diagnostic-specific handout is meant to inform the patient about their diagnosis, the common symptoms that may be experienced with the diagnosis, and the available treatment options for remedying the symptoms. Specific handouts on diagnoses, including depression, anxiety, mood disorders, psychotic disorders, and substance use disorders, should be developed and distributed to the appropriate patients.

5.15.3 Community Resources Information

A community resources handout can be developed and distributed to any and all patients that have specific needs that they are having difficulty meeting. This handout should include contact information (addresses and phone numbers) for resources, such as housing or shelter authorities, public transportation, food lockers, low- to no-cost medical clinics, domestic violence organizations, substance abuse treatment (Alcoholic's Anonymous or Narcotic Anonymous), and the Social Security Administration.

5.15.4 Therapeutic Handouts

The therapeutic handouts should be in alignment with the information presented in the diagnostic handouts. The format can be either an individual therapeutic activity or group-based activity, which can be utilized in a DPOA within the ED. Common helpful therapeutic handout topics include mindfulness skills, cognitive-behavioral skills, and dialectical behavioral skills.

5.15.5 Patient Rights and Advocacy Group Information

These handouts should include information on county, state, and federal patient advocacy groups and a list of patient rights. It is important to note that some of the rights of the patient may be temporarily suspended if the treatment team decides that the patient needs to be placed on an involuntary psychiatric hold. The patient should be provided with a handout explaining what rights they retain while on the involuntary hold. Contact information for community advocacy groups, for example National Alliance on Mental Illness (NAMI) or Mental Health America, should also be included in this handout. The medical center or hospital system's patient complaints and grievances department contact information can also be added.

5.16 Conclusion

Congratulations on completing this lengthy, albeit informative, chapter! This chapter is meant to act as a guide for the reader through the murky waters of ED psychiatric patient care. We realize that many of the topics discussed previously may appear to have a utopian feel to them, but the hope is that you will gain a clearer picture of what is needed to help create a consistent, stable, and effective psychiatric system of care within your ED. If you are an administrator reading this chapter, you are now many steps ahead of other hospital system administrators in providing appropriate care, staffing, and cultural changes to the ED setting. If you are a patient or an advocate reading this chapter, you should now have a better understanding of what the possibilities are for raising the standards of care during an ED experience.

References

Barber, C W, and M J Miller. 2014. Reducing a suicidal person's access to lethal means of suicide: A research agenda. *American Journal of Preventative Medicine* 47 (3S2): S264–S272.

Berzlanovich, A M, J Schopfer, and W Keil. 2012. Deaths due to physical restraint. *Deutsches Arzteblatt International* 109 (3): 27–32.

Booner, G, T Lowe, D Rawcliffe, and N Wellman. 2002. Trauma for all: A pilot study of the subjective experience of physical restraint for mental health inpatients and staff in the UK. *Journal of Psychiatric and Mental Health Nursing* 9 (4): 465–473.

Busch, A B, and M F Shore. 2000. Seclusion and restraint: A review of recent literature. *Havard Review of Psychiatry* 8 (5): 261–270.

Chang, B, D Gitlin, and R Patel. 2011. The depressed patient and suicidal patient in the emergency department: Evidence based management and treatment strategies. *Emergency Medicine Practice* 13 (9): 1–23.

Currier, G W, and M H Allen. 2000. Physical and chemical restraint in the psychiatric emergency service. *Psychiatric Services* 51 (6): 717–719.

Currier, G W, and M H Allen. 2003. Organization and function of academic psychiatric emergency services. *General Hospital Psychiatry* 25 (2): 124–129.

Currier, G W, P Walsh, and D Lawrence. 2011. Physical restraints in the emergency department and attendance at subsequent outpatient psychiatric treatment. *Journal of Psychiatric Practice* 17 (6): 387–393.

Fisher, W A. 1994. Restraint and seclusion: A review of the literature. *The American Journal of Psychiatry* 151 (11): 1584–1591.

Fisher, W A. 2003. Elements of successful restraint and seclusion reduction programs and their application in a large, urban, state psychiatric hospital. *Journal of Psychiatric Practice* 9 (1): 7–15.

Fishkind, A. 2002. Calming agitation with words, not drugs: 10 commandments for safety. *Current Psychiatry*, April: 32–39. http://www.mdedge.com/currentpsychiatry/article/66121/calming-agitation-words-not-drugs-10-commandements-safety.

Forster, P, C Cavness, and M Phelps. 1999. Staff training decreases use of seclusion and restraint in an acute psychiatric hospital. *Archives of Psychiatric Nursing* 13 (5): 269–271.

Friesen, M A, S V White, and J F Byers. 2008. Handoffs: Implications for nurses. In *Patient Safety and Quality: An Evidenced Based Handbook for Nurses*, by R G Hughes, 285–314. Rockville, MD: Agency for Healthcare Reasearch and Quality.

Hem, E, O Steen, and S Opjordsmoen. 2001. Thrombosis associated with physical restraints. *Acta Psychiatrica Scandinavica* 103 (1): 73–76.

Hirschfeld, R M, and J M Russell. 1997. Assessment and treatment of suicidal patients. *The New England Journal of Medicine* 337: 910–915. doi:10.1056/NEJM199709253371307.

Holmes, D, S Kennedy, and A Perron. 2004. The mentally ill and social exclusion: A critical examination of the use of seclusion from the patient's perspective. *Issues in Mental Health Nursing* 25 (6): 559–578.

Holstein, J 1984. The placement of insanity: Assessments of grave disability and involuntary commitment decisions. *Journal of Contemporary Ethnography* 13 (1): 35–62.

Kitts, R L, K Gallagher, P Ibeziako, S Bujoreanu, G Garcia, and D R DeMaso. 2013. Parent and young adult satisfaction with psychiatry consultation services in a children's hospital. *Psychosomatics* 54 (6): 575–584.

Lally, J, Y L Wong, H Shetty, A Patel, V Srivastava, M T M Broadbent, and F Gaugran. 2015. Acute hopsital service utilization by inpatients in psychiatric hospitals. *General Hospital Psychiatry* 37 (6): 577–580.

Langheim, F J P, and E Heilingenstein. 2014. Evaluation of the timeliness of psychiatric consultations. *Journal of Clinical Medicine Research* 6 (4): 242–244.

Larkin, G L, C A Claassen, J A Emond, A J Pelletier, and C A Camargo. 2005. Trends in U.S. emergency department visits for mental health conditions, 1992 to 2001. *Psychiatric Services* 56 (6): 671–677.

Larue, C, A Dumais, R Boyer, M-H Goulet, J-P Bonin, and N Baba. 2013. The experience of seclusion and restraint in psychiatric settings: Perspectives of patients. *Issues in Mental Health Nursing* (5): 317–324. doi:10.3109/01612840.2012.753558.

LeBel, J, N Stromberg, K Duckworth, J Kerzner, R Goldstein, M Weeks, G Harper, and M Sudders. 2004. Child and adolescent inpatient restraint reduction: A state initiative to promote strength based care. *Journal of the American Academy of Child and Adolescent Psychiatry* 43 (1): 37–45.

Levin-Epstein, M. 2015. Psych units in the ED: Trend, solution, or neither? *Emergency Physicians Monthly*, November 18.

Maurer, R. 2013. Making safety committes work. *Society for Human Resource Management*. August 8. http://www.shrm.org/resourcesand tools/hr-topics/risk-management/pages/workplace-safety-committees.aspx.

Nelstrop, L, J Chandler-Oatts, W Bingley, T Bleetman, F Corr, J Cronin-Davis, F Donna-Maria, H Phil et al. 2006. A systematic review of the safety and effectiveness of restraint and seclusion as interventions for the short term management of violence in adult psychiatric inpatient settings and emergency departments. *Worldviews on Evidence Based Nursing* 3 (1): 8–18.

Park, J M, Park, L T, Siefert, C J, Abraham, M E, Fry, C R, Silvert, M S. 2009. Factors associated with extended length of stay for patients presenting to an urban psychiatric emergency service: A case control study. *Journal of Behavioral Health Services and Research* 36 (3): 300–308.

Pestka, E L, D A Hatteberg, L A Larson, A M Zwygart, D L Cox, and E E Borgen Jr. 2012. Enhancing safety in behavioral emergency situations. *Medsurg Nursing* 21 (6): 335–341.

Richmond, J S, J S Berlin, A B Holloman, G H Fishkind, S L Zeller, M P Wilson, M A Rifai, and A T Ng. 2012. Verbal de-escalation of the agitated patient: Consensus statement of the american association for emergency pschiatry project beta de-escalation workgroup. *Western Journal of Emergency Medicine* 13 (1): 17–25.

Severson, L. 2011. *Ten Steps to Enhance Healthcare Employees' Safety*. October. http://www.lockton.com/Resource_/PageResource/MKT/10%20steps%20to%20enhancing%20safety_L%20Severson_Oct%202011.pdf.

Sheridan, D C, J Sheridan, K Johnson, A Laurie, A Knapper, Fu Rongwei, S Appy, and M Hansen. 2016. The effect of a dedicated psychiaric team to pediatric emergency mental health care. *Journal of Emergency Medicine* 50 (3): e121–e128.

Stevenson, S. 1991. Heading off violence with verbal de-escalation. *Journal of Psychosocial Nursing and Mental Health Services* 29 (9): 6–9.

Stiffler, K A, and S T Wilber. 2015. Hallway patients reduce overall emergency department satisfaction. *The Journal of Emergency Medicine* 49 (2): 211–216.

Summers, M, and B Happell. 2003. Patient satisfaction with psychiatric services provided by a Melbourne tertiary hospital emergency department. *Journal of Psychiatric and Mental Health Nursing* 10 (3): 351–357.

Suokas, J, K Suominen, and J Lonnqvist. 2015. The attitudes of emergency staff toward attempted suicide patients: A comparative study before and after establishment of a psychiatric consultation service. *The Journal of Crisis Intervention and Suicide Prevention* 30: 161–165. doi:10.1027/0227-5910.30.3.161.

Tesar, G E. 2008. Whither hospital and academic psychiatry? *Psychiatric Clinics of North America* 31 (1): 27–42.

The Joint Commission. 1998. *Sentinel Event Alert: Preventing Restraint Deaths.* November 18. http://www.jointcommission.org/assets/1/18/SEA_8.pdf.

The Joint Commission. 2010. *Sentinel Event Alert: Preventing Violence in the Health Care Setting.* June 3. Oakbrook Terrace, IL: The Joint Commission.

Walsh, J, A Juarez, and L Gates. 2011. *Emergency Department Violence Surveillance Study.* Study, Des Plaines, IL: Emergency Nurses Association.

Waunch, A, and L Conley. 2011. Guesting area—an emergency department and behavioral health services colaboration. *ANCC National Magnet Conference.* Atlanta, GA: American Nurses Credentialing Center.

Wheat, S, Dschida D, and M Talen. 2016. Psychiatric emergencies. *Primary Care: Clinics in Office Practice* 43 (2): 341–354.

Winokur, B, and A Waunch. 2010. *Guesting Area: An Innovative Approach to Holding the Psychiatric ED Patient.* Des Plaines, IL: Emergency Nurses Association.

Winokur, E J, and J M Senteno. 2009. Guesting area: An alternative for boarding mental health patients seen in emergency departments. *Journal of Emergency Nursing* 35 (5): 429–433.

Zhu, J M, A Singhal, and R Y Hsia. 2016. Emergency department length of stay for psychiatric visits was significantly longer than for nonpsychiatric visits. *Health Affairs* 35 (9): 1698–1706.

Resources

Betz, M E, and E D Boudreux. 2016. Managing suicidal patients in the emergency department. *Annals of Emergency Medicine* 67 (2): 276–282.

Knox, D K, and G H Holloman. 2012. Use and avoidance of seclusion and restraint: Consensus statement of the american association for emergency psychiatry project beta seclusion and restraint workgroup. *Western Journal of Emergency Medicine* 13 (1): 35–40.

Lavakumar, M, E Gastelum, F Hussain, J Levenson, R. Wharton, P Muskin, and P Shapiro. 2013. How do you know your consult service is doing a good job? generating performance measures for c-l service effectiveness. *Psychosomatics* 54 (6): 567–574.

Smith, J L, S D Allesandro, E A Storch, B Landland-Orban, E Pracht, and J Petrila. 2016. Correlates of length of stay and boarding in florida emergency departments for patients with psychiatric diagnoses. *Psychiatric Services* 67 (11): 1169–1174.

Zun, L S. 2012. Pitfalls in the care of the psychiatric patient in the emergency department. *The Journal of Emergency Medicine* 43 (5): 829–835.

Chapter 6

Risk Assessments in the Emergency Room

Rebecca Fink

Contents

6.1 Introduction 91
6.2 Clinical Presentation: History and Physical Examination 92
6.3 Past Psychiatric History..95
6.4 Other Elements of History 97
6.5 Collateral Information 98
6.6 Synthesis of Information 100
    6.6.1 Mr. Turner: Case Example 1..100
    6.6.2 Ms. Anderson: Case Example 2 101
6.7 Risk Assessment: Key Elements 102
    6.7.1 History of Present Illness 102
    6.7.2 Psychiatric History 102
    6.7.3 Medical History 102
    6.7.4 Past Psychiatric History..102
    6.7.5 Social History...102
    6.7.6 Substance Use History..103
References 103

6.1 Introduction

You are sitting in the emergency room (ER) on call overnight, and this is your first night on call on your own. You have your large cup of coffee, plenty of snacks, and your cell phone and pager are charged and ready to go. So now you're all set for call, but there is one pressing question on your mind: What do I do if there is a patient who tells me she is suicidal? And if someone comes in and says she is homicidal, that's it—I'm running out the door, coffee in hand, and will find a nice job in the food service industry.

    Don't panic! Put that coffee cup down and take a deep breath.

In this chapter, we are going to discuss how to conduct a proper risk assessment and decide the next step in management. This way, on that night when you are the on-call resident at 3 a.m. and a patient comes in saying she is suicidal, you will have a game plan, not an escape plan.

The first question is, what is a risk assessment? What are we talking about when we say we're evaluating a patient's risk level? In psychiatry, when the term *risk assessment* is used, it is about determining the patient's potential to harm themselves and others. The risk assessment, then, involves assessing for both suicidality and homicidality. When a patient comes in to the emergency department for an evaluation, a risk assessment is a vital part of the clinician's job. The clinician needs to ascertain the potential risk for suicide, defined as the act or an instance of taking one's own life voluntarily and intentionally, or other self-injurious behavior. It is also necessary to assess for homicide, the deliberate and unlawful killing of one person by another, or other intention of harm to others. As you are reading, you may be saying, right, thanks. That seems like a huge responsibility—how do I do it? Well, it is indeed a very important job, but as long as you understand the components involved you too will be able to conduct a thorough risk assessment.

There are multiple factors that contribute to a risk assessment. As the clinician on call, you will be the detective looking for clues, and trying to get the necessary data to make your decision. Your goal will be to understand why the patient is in the ER now: What is the patient feeling, are there any current or recent stressors that may be contributing, and what is the patient's history of illness or dangerousness? Through the patient interview and the acquisition of collateral information, you will begin to get the clues you need to make your determination (Elbogen et al. 2006; Jacobs et al. 2003).

The key is to be curious: You are the detective, trying to find the pertinent information to decide whether your patient is at harm of risk to himself or others. When we are assessing risk, and looking for the clues, we are both looking for "risk factors" and also "protective factors"—aspects of a patient's life that are protective against harm. It is like you are walking through a building to investigate what has set off the smoke detector. You will want to open each door to see if something is there. If the door can be easily closed, then you close it and move on. However, if you get the sense that there may be smoke behind the door, then you'll need to investigate a bit more carefully to decide if you need to stay in that room longer to investigate further or if that door can be safely closed. When you are doing a risk assessment, you are investigating a building with several different floors. On each floor, you will need to go through the hallways and open the doors to each room on the floor.

Each section in this chapter will be a different floor. We will start by investigating the history of present illness (HPI), which covers the patient's current clinical presentation. After we've been there, we will review the elements of past psychiatric history, and then other elements of the patient's life that should be reviewed when assessing risk level. All of these aspects will be addressed as you interview the patient. The next step will be to get collateral information as necessary: It can be as helpful to get information from other people who are important in the patient's life as past treatment records. These can assist you in getting more information that you may not have received from the patient. So, without further ado, let's start our investigation.

6.2 Clinical Presentation: History and Physical Examination

Okay, so now the patient has been through triage, spoken to the nurse, and you are called to see the patient. You are going to take a deep breath and remember that you have the tools you need to interview your patient and assess for risk. You've got your investigative gear on, flashlight, and hard hat ready to (metaphorically speaking, of course). Also, keep in mind as you're going to interview the patient that he may be scared as well. Usually when patients come to the psychiatric ER, it's because they are in distress. Remember to take this into account: You will want to be respectful and straightforward with your patient. The more comfortable he is, the more he is going to be able to tell you what he's feeling. This will in turn enable you to help him in the best way possible, and make the soundest clinical decision. "Alright," you say, "I got it." Now can we talk a little more about the actual interview? Sure—let's do this!

You are now entering the first area of exploration. The first piece of data you will get is the reason that the patient was brought into the hospital. At the beginning of the interview, you will elicit the chief complaint—this is, in the patient's words, what brought her to the hospital today. Then you will want to delve into the specific symptoms that the patient has been feeling. In this chapter, we will particularly look at symptoms that will be important in determining the patient's risk level.

For example, to evaluate a patient for suicidality, you will want to ensure that you open the door to symptoms of depression. It is important to do a full depression screen, asking the patient about all the potential symptoms of depression. The depressive symptoms that are particularly significant in a risk assessment are hopelessness, helplessness, anhedonia, guilt, insomnia, and panic or anxiety. Sometimes people wonder how to evaluate for anhedonia, which is the inability to experience pleasure in normally pleasurable acts. One way to assess this is to ask the patient, "What types of things give you enjoyment or pleasure?" Patients who are experiencing anhedonia might tell you, "Nothing, Doc" or "I used to really like spending time with my grandchildren, but now I just go through the motions. I don't feel happy about it like I used to."

Another very important aspect of risk assessment is thoroughly assessing the patient for suicidality and self-injurious behavior. These questions are extremely important, whether the patient came to the hospital expressing suicidal ideation or not (Joiner 2007). You will need to assess all patients that you see in the ER for suicidality, regardless of their initial presentation. You may say to me, "Sure, that's easy to say, but when a patient is talking to me, how do I cut in and ask him if he wants to kill himself?" It seems kind of abrupt.

Ah yes, it can be tricky to figure out how to broach the topic of suicidality, particularly if the patient does not express it to you. It can be best to start off with a more general question, and then lead in to the more specific questions. Detective metaphor again: You need to first open the door and scan the room. If there is any glimpse of smoke, then you'll investigate further. Keeping that in mind, here is one approach. Start with a general question: Have you ever had thoughts of not wanting to be alive? If the patient says yes, then ask him to tell you more about that. You will want to know what those specific thoughts are, and if the patient currently has a plan to harm himself. If the patient has a plan, it is important to ask (1) what the plan is, (2) does the patient have access to the means to carry out the plan, and (3) is the patient currently thinking of carrying out the plan to harm himself (or did he attempt to do so just before coming to the hospital), what, if anything, is preventing him from attempting to harm himself?

These are all going to be very important things for you to know in order to determine the patient's level of risk. Someone who tells you, "Doc, every morning when I wake up, I am sad that I am still alive. It's been that way for years. But, I have no plan or thoughts of harming myself" is very different from, "Man, every day is getting harder and harder. For years, I have had occasional thoughts of overdosing on my pills, but these thoughts have been happening more frequently lately. A couple times I've gotten the pill bottles out and poured the pills into my hand, but then stopped myself."

Both of these patients may present to you with a chief complaint of suicidal ideation. But in the first case, the patient has chronic passive suicidal ideation: It is an ongoing symptom, has not changed in nature, and the patient has no plan or intent of harming himself. The second patient has also had chronic suicidal ideation. However, the suicidal thoughts are occurring more frequently now, and the patient has been coming close to carrying out his plan. This is why it is so important to delve into the details of the suicidality: You need to understand exactly where your patient is at.

There are a couple more important notes to keep in mind when questioning a patient about suicidality. You need a definitive answer to each of these questions before you can go on. For example, if you ask a patient if she has had thoughts of wanting to be dead and she says, "No, I have never had those thoughts" then that line of questioning can be closed. But if she says to you, "No, I haven't really had those thoughts," then you need to investigate further. I generally say, with an inquisitive tone, "Not really? What does that mean?" Don't move away from that question unless you get a definitive answer from the patient. With further questioning, she may say, "I mean, no. I have never had any suicidal ideation" or she may say, "Well, not often, but on occasion I wish I had never been born." In case 1, you could then close the door on that line of questioning. However, in case 2, you would then want to move forward with more specific questions about suicidality.

When asking about suicidality, be sure to pay close attention if the patient gives you reasons that prevent him from attempting to harm himself. As mentioned in the introduction, a good risk assessment evaluates for protective factors in addition to risk factors (Jacobs et al. 2003). Protective factors are aspects of a patient's life that are protective against harm. A patient's protective factors are extremely important in evaluating their level of risk for harm. For some people, protective factors are children or grandchildren. For others, the protective factors can be their religion, friends, or pets. If a patient tells you, "I would never try to hurt myself because I just love my dog too much," take a minute to ask about his dog. What's the dog's name, what type of dog is it, and so on. This will help you to build rapport with the patient while also getting an understanding of what is important to the patient, and potentially protective for him.

The evaluation of homicidality is also essential in a risk assessment: Does the patient have the intent to kill or harm others. As we discussed with the evaluation of suicidality, it is important to be mindful to how and when you ask questions regarding homicidality. I recommend that you do not start the interview with "Hey, any thoughts about killing anyone?" as this may have a detrimental effect on your rapport with the patient. Instead, wait until you are at an appropriate point in the interview. Following the questioning about suicidality, you can ask leading questions about homicidality. However, there may be other points in the interview where the patient's report of symptoms will lead to the questioning about homicidality.

Often, homicidal thoughts can occur concurrently with paranoid ideation, auditory hallucinations, or escalating anger and irritability. Sometimes it can be difficult to find a way to ask about paranoia. Starting with questions like "Do you ever feel like others are judging you or looking at you funny when you are on a subway or bus? Do you ever feel like anyone is out to harm you?" can be a good way to begin assessing for paranoia. If the patient answers yes to any of these, or if the patient has indicated that she feels persecuted by others or is having continual conflicts with others, ask about whether she has had any thoughts of harming them.

With auditory hallucinations, you can start with a question like "Do you ever hear voices that no one else is able to hear?" If the answer is yes, then it is important to follow up about the nature of the voices. Is there one or are there multiple voices? If auditory hallucinations are present, what do they say? Do the voices ever tell the patient to harm herself or anyone else? If the patient is having command auditory hallucinations to harm others, it will be very important to flesh these out. What exactly are the voices saying? Does the patient have intent to carry out the commands? Has the patient ever gotten close or attempted to carry out the commands to harm others? Are the command auditory hallucinations chronic and at baseline, or are they new or escalating?

The acuity of the situation will be very important in assessing risk: New and escalating symptoms will indicate a higher acuity than chronic symptoms that are at baseline. Also, if the patient is hearing derogatory voices about herself (voices that tell her she is always doing the wrong thing, she is not good enough, she should be punished), keep in mind that these may put her at higher risk of self-injurious behavior. It will be important to do a thorough suicide risk screen in that case, and to ask if those voices ever make her want to hurt herself, or if they ever tell her to harm herself.

Other symptoms to assess for in evaluating for homicidality are the patient's current level of agitation and irritability. If the patient has had escalating agitation, this can be a contributing factor to risk level. Think about how the patient was brought into the ER. If he was brought into the ER because he thought a guy on the street was looking at him funny and he started to yell at that guy and pulled out a swiss army knife, you need to have a high level of concern. If his family brings him in and says he has been thinking they are poisoning his food, and he has started to sleep with a dinner knife, you will have a higher level of concern. If he walks in of his own accord and says he has been doing alright overall, but he is volatile in the ER, raising his voice and becoming easily agitated, you will also take this into account.

Right now, the patient is in your ER, it is 3 a.m., and you are dreaming of that chocolate bar you left in the on-call room. You want to get through this interview, find out what the events were that brought this patient in now, and get that candy. But hold on, Doc! That candy isn't going anywhere, and you will get it soon. There are a few more things to keep in mind. These are questions to ask yourself: Is the patient able to cooperate in treatment? Is the patient amenable to discussing symptoms and treatment options with you during the interview, or is the patient unable to do so?

Concurrent substance use can be a significant factor in symptom exacerbation (Pulay et al. 2008). Make sure to do a thorough evaluation for alcohol and substance use, as well as a toxicology screen. Does the patient have a history of substance use? Has the substance use been ongoing, or has there been a change in the pattern of use? As we discussed previously, pay special attention when there has been a change in usage pattern. If a patient had been abstinent from substance use for a significant period of time and is now using again, or if the patient had been using from time to time but now is exhibiting an escalating pattern, this can be a contributing factor in symptom exacerbation.

Last, but certainly not least, make sure to ask if the patient currently has access to weapons or firearms. This is extremely important. If the patient does, then it will be necessary to address this while the patient is under psychiatric care, and find a way to remove the patient's access to them if necessary. If a patient has access to firearms, the patient then has a direct means to harm herself or others.

6.3 Past Psychiatric History

Think of this scenario: You have temporarily suspended your career in medicine and are now the coach of a very successful football team. The Super Bowl is coming up, and your team will be playing. You've got an excellent quarterback and you're excited about how he will perform, but you know that the Super Bowl is a high-pressure event and you're worried about how he'll do under pressure. One way to gauge how he performs under pressure is to look at his past performance in high-intensity games. Does he always perform the same as usual, or does he have a history of not playing as well in high-stakes games? If you know he had choked in a Super Bowl several years ago, you would need to find out more about what happened. What was it about that game that made him choke? Was it the intensity of the game? Was it cold or rainy that day? Was his offensive line weak? Understanding what happened to him in the past will help you to understand how he reacts in these high-stress games, which gives you clues to how he might respond in the upcoming Super Bowl. You can then anticipate that these things may happen, and how to train him accordingly.

When you are the psychiatrist in the ER, you will want to use the same tools that the NFL coach is using. In this section, we will delve into the salient aspects of a patient's psychiatric history that are important to ask when screening for risk. The patient's history can give you important clues as to the patient's current risk status. Does the patient have a history of psychiatric treatment? If so, what is the patient's diagnosis? Is there any history of a mood disorder or psychotic disorder?

Find out about past visits to the ER or inpatient hospitalizations: What was the context for each of these events? Does the patient have a history of hospitalization for suicidality or homicidality? Has the patient been compliant with treatment, or does the patient have a history of treatment noncompliance? It is important to know both whether the patient has been compliant with acute treatment (inpatient and ER) and outpatient treatment in the past. One way to find out this information is to ask the patient directly.

The following are other clues to find out: Does the patient have a history of leaving the hospital against medical advice, or a history of having to be taken to court for treatment over objection? Does the patient have a history of court-mandated outpatient treatment? In some states, such as New York, a patient can be mandated to assisted outpatient treatment (AOT) if he is "unlikely to survive safely in the community without supervision." When a patient has been mandated to AOT treatment, it is due to a clinical determination: The patient has a history of noncompliance with treatment, is unlikely to voluntarily participate in outpatient treatment, and a relapse could result in serious harm to self or others. Knowing that a patient has been court mandated to treatment is important in assessing risk: It gives you an idea of the past severity of illness and inability to comply with treatment on one's own.

If the patient has a history of suicidality or homicidality, you'll want to know the triggers or stressors that led to the event, and then what happened subsequently. Let's say your patient comes into the emergency room, and she is a 25-year-old woman expressing suicidal ideation.

After you ask questions about her current presentation, there are important questions to ask about her past (Jacobs et al. 2003). Has she been given a psychiatric diagnosis? Does she have a history of noncompliance with treatment or medications? Has she had suicidal ideation or suicide attempts in the past? Does she have a history of self-injurious behavior without intent to die (non-suicidal self-injurious behavior)? If she answers yes to any of these questions, these should be alerting you of the need to open those doors and explore these areas in detail. Firstly, what was the precise scenario? Find out the events leading up to the attempt: Did it occur due to escalating depression? Due to auditory hallucinations telling her she is worthless? Following a fight with a loved one? Following job loss? In the context of alcohol intoxication? Once you have a sense of the trigger(s) that led up to the suicide attempt, you will want to know exactly what happened. If the patient states "I took some pills" or "I cut my wrist," you will want to flesh out those statements more. If it was a pill overdose, what type of pills did she take? How many? How did she attain them? If the patient cut her wrist, what type of knife did she use, how deep was the cut, did it require medical attention?

In any of the previous scenarios, it is important to ask if the patient had intent to die when he attempted to harm himself. You will also want to go through and find out what happened following the attempt. Did the patient tell anybody? Did the patient go to the ER, or get medical or psychiatric interventions? What happened next? Also, what was the patient's response like when he realized that the attempt to harm himself was unsuccessful? Was he relieved to be alive? Was he disappointed? Was there any change in psychiatric treatment following the attempt? Is his presentation now similar to how it was then? Understanding past events in the patient's life can give you important data about the current level of dangerousness (Kessler et al. 1999).

When screening for homicidality, the same principles apply. If the patient is currently describing or exhibiting agitation, impulsivity, irritability, anger, or other symptoms that lead you to believe she may be at risk of harming others, you will want to know if she has experienced symptoms like this in the past. If she has had episodes of paranoia or auditory hallucinations in the past, what were they like? In any of the previous situations: did she have thoughts of harming others? Did she ever come close to harming anyone else, or actually harm someone? If so, it is necessary to find out specifics about that episode.

The patient may tell you, "Sure, Doc, a few years ago, right before I came into the ER, my neighbors were acting up just like they are now. They were sending poisonous gases through the air vents, and so I had my butcher knife out on the kitchen counter in case I needed to use it. Just like I had to do again today, it's out and ready for use if they attack." You may feel the sweat beginning to bead up on your forehead, wondering what to do now. What do I ask? Well, the next question is just to go in and find out more. A good next question would assess how close he was to actually attempting to harm the neighbors at that time. This patient was paranoid about his neighbors trying to harm him, which led him to feeling that he needed to be able to defend himself. He currently feels similar paranoia, so understanding what happened then may help you to determine what he might do now. Did this patient ever approach the neighbors or have any altercations with them, either verbal or physical? Did he ever approach them with the knife or have actual intent to use it? Were the police ever called? Does he have a history of harming others in any other context? Any history of arrest or incarceration? If he has not had any conflict with the neighbors, and has no history of violence, then you will certainly still want to take note of his statement, because it is significant and demonstrates symptom exacerbation. It will still be a risk factor, but less so. However, if the patient tells you that he started banging on the neighbor's door and yelling at them in the past, going after them in the hallway, or actually picking up the knife to go after them, then this is a more significant risk factor.

In addition to asking a patient about history of assaultive behavior, another potential indicator about harm to others is whether a patient has a history of other behavior that has been indicative of harm to others. People with antisocial personality traits can have an increased risk of harming others. Does this patient have a history of cruelty to animals or fire setting?

Finding out clues in a patient's psychiatric history can give you key information in making your risk assessment. With suicidality, knowing about prior suicide attempts, suicidal behavior, ideation or intent, and history of depression are key. With homicidality, history of physical or verbal altercations, assaultive behavior, homicidal ideation, intent or plan are key questions to ask (Elbogen et al. 2006).

6.4 Other Elements of History

As we discussed earlier, it is unlikely that the patient is in the ER now because she was just looking for some evening excitement and there weren't any good movies in the theaters this evening. She is having a rough time, and is likely having a symptom exacerbation. You need to be on the lookout, in addition to the psychiatric symptoms, for other things going on in her life that may be contributing to her current symptoms. Has she had recent stressors that have impacted her? As you go through the rest of the interview with your patient, use this opportunity to flesh out other elements of the patient's life that could be contributing stressors.

The social history can be very helpful in gathering information that may help you to further understand the patient's risk level, as well as the other sections of the interview (Swanson et al. 2006). You will get a chance to find out more about the patient's current stressors as you go through the social history.

In the social history, you're asking key questions to understanding the patient's life. You will be asking questions about the patient's social supports, family life, employment, and housing. Think about finding out what is important to this patient as you go through the social history. As we discussed before, it will be helpful in knowing what your patient identifies as his social supports, as these can be protective factors for him. Are there certain people, whether it be family or others that he feels particularly close to? Is religion important to him? Does he have a pet dog that he cares for?

Let's say you start by asking the patient about housing. You will want to know where she currently lives. Has there been any recent change in her living situation? Is she homeless? If so, these can be risk factors. If she has a stable, consistent source of housing, that can be a protective factor for her. Does she live with anyone else? If so, find out about who she lives with; living with someone else can be either a risk or protective factor, depending on the situation. Is there anything that feels unsafe about her housing situation? Any domestic violence or abuse?

The next important area to ask about is about the patient's family. Who is in the patient's family? What is his relationship with them like? Are they supports for him? Have there been any recent things that the patient finds protective: the birth of a child or grandchild, or a recent happy family event? Has there been anything stressful that happened recently: death, divorce, or separation? Has there been any child abuse? Are any government agencies involved, like child protective services? An unstable home environment or conflict within the family can be risk factors for symptom exacerbation. If the patient does not have family or a social support system, or if the patient is socially isolated, these are considered risk factors for symptom exacerbation.

Understanding the patient's financial situation is very important, because financial difficulties can be a significant stressor. Is the patient employed? If so, how is the patient functioning? If she has had prolonged impairment at work (or school), take note of that and find out more about it. The risk of losing her job is a risk factor in itself. Could the difficulty functioning be related to symptom exacerbation? If so, this will be important to know in understanding the current level of illness severity. If the patient is not employed, find out what her source of income is. Someone may be unemployed, but have a steady source of income from retirement benefits or social security. However, the lack of financial resources is a stressor. Other sources of income to consider are illegal activities (such as prostitution or drug dealing), which could be another risk factor.

6.5 Collateral Information

When you are interviewing the patient directly, you are getting her firsthand account of how she has been feeling, what brought her to the ER, and what her past history has been. This information is extremely valuable—you need to know how she perceives her symptoms. She is giving you a lot of diagnostic information that will be helpful in determining your next step in management. However, there are many times in which collateral information gives you extremely important information in treating the patient—information that you may not have known otherwise (Jacobs et al. 2003).

You may be wondering why that is. After all, you have just conducted a very thorough interview of the patient, and asked all the relevant questions. The patient has answered all the questions, and now you feel you're ready to sum it up, write your note, and get that patient the treatment he needs. You're feeling pretty good about your interview, and feel you are ready to make your decision about the next step in treatment. You're right—you have obtained a significant amount of data already. However, there is one more aspect to the interview process that can be extremely helpful to understanding and treating your patient. And that is collateral information.

When a patient is experiencing an acute episode of illness, it may be hard for him to give you an accurate depiction of his symptoms. If he is depressed, he may have trouble remembering all of his symptoms. He may be unable to give you a depiction of how his symptoms have changed over time. If he is manic, he may have very limited insight into the fact that he is manic right now. If he is paranoid, he may be suspicious about what you will do with the information he gives you, and he may not tell you exactly what's on his mind. These are just some examples of how the illness itself could limit the amount of information you are given. The patient also may have feelings about being in the ER, and may either minimize or enhance his depiction of the symptoms when portraying them to you. The patient may have difficulty remembering exactly what happened the last time he was hospitalized, or what medication he had been on in the past. Remember that this is likely a stressful time for the patient!

In order to get a more precise idea of both the patient's current presentation and past history, collateral information can be very helpful. Family members, friends, roommates, and anyone else who is close to the patient may be able to give you more information on how the patient has been doing in the time period leading up to the current ER visit. For example, he may have told you he has been feeling down for a while and not sleeping too well, but otherwise feeling alright. Then, when you ask his wife how she feels he has been doing, she tells you that she has to remind him to bathe and brush his teeth, he has been more irritable with their children, and he seems to be staring off into space and talking to someone who is not there at times. This would help you to understand the depth of his depression more fully, and also then to consider that the patient may be internally preoccupied. You would then want to ask the patient more questions about potential auditory hallucinations.

Family members can also be helpful in telling you if current symptoms are similar to previous episodes of symptom exacerbation. Is this the first time the patient's wife has noticed these symptoms of depression? If he has had them before, are these symptoms similar to the ones he has had in the past? Stronger? Different in any way? Along these lines, if the patient is currently undergoing outpatient mental health treatment, try to contact the patient's current providers. They can offer further information on diagnosis, any current medications, and past treatment. They can also give you an idea of how the patient has been doing in treatment, and if they have noticed any recent changes.

Another potential resource is past psychiatric records, if they are available to you. If the patient has been in mental health treatment at your hospital before (ER, inpatient, outpatient), make sure you review those records. If the patient has been in treatment elsewhere, see if you can get access to those records or speak with someone who was involved in the treatment. If the patient is currently on parole or assigned to court-mandated treatment, reach out to the parole officer or team involved in court-mandated treatment to get more information. If the patient is living in a residence or group home, contact the staff there. All of this information together will help you to get a more complete understanding of your patient. The more you can understand your patient, the better you can treat your patient. This is highly beneficial for both you and the patient, as it can ensure the best possible treatment.

Keep in mind that sometimes it is not possible to get any collateral information. An example of this might be a patient who is homeless, and was brought in by the police after getting in a verbal altercation on the street. The police have left the hospital by the time you are interviewing the patient. You try to call the police station, but the officers who brought the patient in are now off duty. When you speak to the patient, he tells you he has no family, is not in outpatient treatment, and moves around from shelter to shelter. In this case, your interview of the patient will be the sole source of diagnostic information. That's okay—this is why you conduct a thorough interview, and pay attention to both the patient's verbal interview and mental status.

Another thing to keep in mind is the patient's privacy, and use your discretion in obtaining collateral information. If family members bring the patient to the ER, it can be quite helpful to get their account of the patient's symptoms leading up to this visit. If the patient comes in without a family member but lives with others, you may want to contact them to find out more information. However, you should only contact those people that you need to speak with to get information that is relevant to your treatment of the patient. Medical and mental health providers and staff that work with the patient (like in a group home or residence) are helpful to contact as well.

6.6 Synthesis of Information

At this point, you've done a lot of investigative work to understand your patient. You have conducted a thorough interview, including assessing all relevant aspects of risk. You have then seen if you could get collateral information to flesh out your knowledge of the patient. Now you have all the tools you need to decide the patient's level of risk. This can be somewhat tricky, because there is no one algorithm to say for sure "This patient has seven risk factors, therefore, he is at _____ risk of harming himself or others." Don't stop here, shut this book in despair, and wonder why you just then read a whole chapter on risk assessment. Read on!

The reason we went over all the potential risk factors is so you can then sit down, look over the potential risk factors and protective factors that this patient has, and then decide the best level of treatment for your patient. Let's go through a couple of examples to think through how to assess risk level.

6.6.1 Mr. Turner: Case Example 1

Mr. Turner has come to the ER accompanied by his wife. He reports that he is in the hospital because, "I just haven't been feeling so well." He reports that he has been feeling down because he has been unemployed for a year, and feels like a failure that he cannot contribute financially to the family income. His wife is now the sole provider for him and their children. His wife and children are very important to him. He leaves the house to take trips to the store and spends time with friends who live nearby. He gets enjoyment out of being with his friends. He denies suicidal and homicidal ideation and auditory and visual hallucinations. He doesn't have firearms at home. He is in outpatient treatment, and is compliant with all of his outpatient appointments. When he spends time with friends, he drinks alcohol ("It used to be that I'd share one bottle of Hennessy with a few guys, but now it's one bottle for me and the rest for them to share"). He has been drinking more alcohol lately. His wife notes that she has to remind him to take a shower and brush his teeth. Although he attends outpatient treatment, he has been inconsistent with taking his medications: "I try to take them daily, Doc, but my memory isn't what it used to be. I remember to take them 2 or 3 days a week." Upon interviewing the patient, you learn that he was last hospitalized 2 years ago. At that time, he was hospitalized following a suicide attempt. He had escalating depressive symptoms and became noncompliant with medications. He was also drinking more alcohol. He became belligerent toward his wife while intoxicated, tried to hit her, then felt extremely guilty and overdosed on pills in an attempt to harm himself. His wife is concerned that his current symptoms are similar to the ones she saw 2 years ago.

Let's look at the risk and protective factors for this patient:

Protective factors: He has a healthy connection with his wife and children, he gets enjoyment out of being with friends, he denies suicidal ideation, homicidal ideation, auditory and visual hallucinations, he has no current access to firearms, and he has displayed consistent follow-up with his outpatient appointments.

Risk factors: Unemployment, guilt, increased alcohol use, decreased activities of daily living, inconsistence with medications, a past history of suicide attempt in the context of escalating depression and noncompliance with his medications.

In this case, you would have a high level of concern about the patient's risk of harm to both himself and others. He has escalating depressive symptoms, noncompliance with medications, and increased alcohol use. He has a known history of attempting harm to both himself and others in the context of these symptoms. He would be considered at a higher risk of harm.

6.6.2 Ms. Anderson: Case Example 2

Let's look at another scenario. Ms. Anderson is brought into the ER by her brother. He is exasperated, noting that she has been driving him nuts. She believes that a man named Joe comes into her house when she is not there and steals her things. She has called him multiple times a day, saying that Joe took her bathing suit, or her cigarettes, or a ring that their deceased mother had given her. These things always turn up later. She has had more concerns about Joe and has been calling her brother more frequently since their mother died a year ago. He feels she needs to go to the hospital. When you speak to Ms. Anderson, she tells you that Joe is coming into her house frequently and it's really annoying her. She calls her brother, and then feels better and goes about her daily activities. She continues to go to work daily, and has been functioning well at work. She doesn't talk about Joe when she is there. Her sleep and appetite remain intact. She is dressed nicely today, and notes that her appearance remains very important to her. She has been in ongoing outpatient treatment for 10 years, and takes risperidone 3 mg at night. She has remained consistent with that medication. She mentions that there have been times in the past where Joe comes to her house more frequently. At those times, her psychiatrist has increased her risperidone dose. Then, Joe comes around, but she doesn't feel as bothered by him. She has never been hospitalized because of Joe bothering her. She doesn't have any thoughts of hurting herself or anyone else, and denies auditory and visual hallucinations.

Now, let's look at the risk and protective factors for Ms. Anderson:

Protective factors: She has a strong connection with her brother, is taking care of her daily activities, she is functioning well at work, she is compliant with outpatient treatment and medications, and has a history of symptom improvement with increased medication dosage.

Risk factors: She has ongoing delusions, which have escalated. Her brother is concerned about her symptom exacerbation. Her mother died recently.

In synthesizing this information, it is important to take note that the patient's symptoms have not been at baseline. They have been escalating, and her brother has been concerned about them. However, she has not exhibited a deficit in functioning. She is not exhibiting harm risk to self or others. Given her past history, it is likely that an increase in risperidone dose will be sufficient to decrease her symptoms. Therefore, she is currently at low risk of harm to herself and others.

In order to make your own determination about the patient's risk level, follow a similar algorithm. Pay attention to current and past history that contributes to risk level. This will help you to determine the patient's current level of risk.

6.7 Risk Assessment: Key Elements

The following lists of risk assessment elements are meant to act as a guide for any clinician performing a psychiatric assessment in the ER setting. These elements should be kept in mind while the clinician formulates a risk assessment on any ER patient they assess. The following risk assessment elements have been adapted from information in Elbogen et al. (2006); Jacobs et al. (2003); Joiner et al. (2007); Pulay et al. (2008); and Swanson et al. (2006).

6.7.1 History of Present Illness

- Anhedonia, hopelessness, insomnia, panic attacks/anxiety
- Impulse control (poor, fair, good)
- Able to cooperate in treatment
- Suicidal behaviors, self-injurious behavior
- Suicidal ideation/intent/plan/access to means to carry out plan
- Physical threats
- Verbally abusive
- Violence: intent or plan
- Assaultive behavior
- Homicidal ideation/intent/plan/access to means to carry out plan

6.7.2 Psychiatric History

- Current/past psychiatric disorder (especially mood/psychotic)
- Multiple past psychiatric admissions
- History of discharge against medical advice
- History of noncompliance with treatment
- Court-mandated mental health treatment
- Prior suicide attempts and self-injurious behaviors (e.g., cutting or burning self)
- History of assaultive behavior
- History of cruelty to animals or fire setting

6.7.3 Medical History

- Serious medical or physical disability

6.7.4 Past Psychiatric History

- Family member with serious mental illness, suicide, and attempts

6.7.5 Social History

- Change in living situation/homelessness
- Conflict in family
- Stability of home environment
- Domestic violence
- Child protective services involvement
- Presence/absence of financial resources
- Incarceration history
- Prolonged impairment at work or school
- Social isolation, lack of family and social support system
- Access to weapons/firearms

6.7.6 Substance Use History

- Current alcohol or substance use
- History of alcohol use disorder/substance use disorder

References

Elbogen, E, R Van Dorn, J Swanson, M Swartz, and J Monahan. 2006. Treatment engagement and violence risk in mental disorders. *British Journal of Psychiatry* 189 (4): 354–360.

Jacobs, D G, R J Baldessarini, Y Conwell, J A Fawcett, L Horton, H Meltzer, C R Pfeffer, and R I Simon. 2003. *Practice Guideline for the Assessment and Treatment of Patients With Suicidal Behaviors*. Practice Guidelines, Arlington, VA: American Psychiatric Association.

Joiner, T, J Draper, H Stokes, M Knudson, A Berman, and R McKeon. 2007. Establishing standards for the assessment of suicide risk among callers to the suicide prevention hotline. *Suicide and Life Threatening Behavior* 37 (3): 353–365.

Kessler, R, G Borges, and E Walters. 1999. Prevalence of and risk factors for lifetime suicide attempts in the National Comorbidity Survey. *Archives of General Psychiatry* 56 (7): 617–626.

Pulay, A, D Dawson, D Hasin, R Goldstein, W Ruan, R Pickering, B Huang, S Chou, and B Grant. 2008. Violent behavior and DSM IV psychiatric disorders: Results from the National Epidemiologic Survey on Alcohol and Related Conditions. *Journal of Clinical Psychiatry* 69 (1): 12–22.

Swanson, J, M Swartz, R Van Dorn, E Elbogen, H Wagner, R Rosenheck, T Stroup, J McEvoy, and J Lieberman. 2006. A National Study of Violent Behavior in Persons With Schizophrenia. *Archives of General Psychiatry* 63 (5): 490–499.

Chapter 7

The Myth of Medical Clearance

Lev Libet, Yener Balan, and Seth Thomas

Contents

7.1 Introduction	105
7.2 Critical Assessment of Articles in Favor of Laboratory Screening	106
7.3 Articles in Favor of Selective Testing	107
7.4 History and Physical Examination	109
7.5 Pediatric Population	109
7.6 Unimportant Positives	110
7.7 Urine Toxicology Screen	110
7.8 Cost and Utility	111
7.9 Standardized Screening Protocols	111
7.10 Conclusion	112
7.11 Recommendations for Practice	112
References	114
Resources	116

7.1 Introduction

Behavioral emergencies constituted approximately 5.4% of all emergency department (ED) visits in 2001, which was a 40% increase over a 9-year period (Larkin et al. 2005). In 2011, there were 136 million ED visits, and by extrapolation that would mean 8,160,000 visits for behavioral emergencies in the United States in 2011 (CDC 2011). The trend of increasing ED visits for behavior health emergencies, shown more than a decade ago, has continued.

In most settings, the current practice is that the emergency physician performs a focused history and physical exam to ensure that there are no urgent medical needs. In many settings, a set of screening lab tests is required in order to "medically clear" the patient: complete blood count (CBC), Chem7, thyroid stimulating hormone (TSH), urine analysis, urine toxicology, alcohol level, acetaminophen level, beta HCG (the pregnancy hormone), and salicylate level. Further laboratory evaluation or imaging is left to the discretion of the emergency physician.

Once the patient is deemed to have no acute medical need and the presentation is thought to be purely psychiatric, care is transferred to the psychiatry service either within the hospital or to a stand-alone facility. Broderick et al. (2002) found that 35% of emergency practitioners practiced in a setting where testing was mandatory in a psychiatric medical screening exam. This was mandated by the receiving psychiatrist or receiving institution 84% of the time (Broderick et al. 2002). Some receiving institutions require a repeat alcohol level to ensure that the patient has metabolized. As the demand for the limited psychiatric beds is at an all-time high, the emergency departments cater to these demands to avoid having their patient overlooked.

The term "medical clearance" is a misnomer, as noted by previous publications (Lukens et al. 2006; Weissberg 1979; Zun 2005). It was first called into question by Weissberg in 1979, who rightfully noted that it is not only inaccurate but also potentially hazardous. The danger is in the assumption that "all" medical issues have been tended to. The American College of Emergency Physicians (ACEP) clinical policy in 2006 rewords the phrase as "focused medical assessment," which is a more accurate description. It is well known that psychiatric patients often have coexisting medical illnesses. More importantly, the behavioral emergency may be due to underlying medical pathology, medications, and substance misuse. There are numerous medical etiologies for neuropsychiatric presentations, such as electrolyte disturbances, infections, encephalopathy, thyroid dysfunction, intracranial mass, intoxication, acute withdrawal, and anti-NMDA receptor encephalitis to name a few. To make the situation more complex, the history may be limited, physical examination refused, there may be strenuous social circumstances, and a lack of social support or finances. Physicians may also subconsciously limit their interaction with this patient population due to their own biases (Zun 2012). The complexity of this population is not to be ignored. The role of the emergency physician is to perform an initial "focused medical assessment" taking into account all of the data, ensure medical stability, and decide if there are medical diagnoses that may be contributing to the psychiatric presentation.

The degree of testing required in order to perform an adequate assessment prior to transfer to a psychiatric facility has been a source of controversy since the inception of the concept. This is not the first article on the topic, and its predecessors have been comprehensive (Anfinson and Kathol 1992; Chun 2014; Gregory et al. 2004; Williams and Shepard 2000; Zun 2005).

The purpose of this chapter is to review the literature with regard to screening tests in behavioral emergencies and to highlight the growing evidence that this is an antiquated practice.

7.2 Critical Assessment of Articles in Favor of Laboratory Screening

To be sure, there are coexisting medical conditions in behavioral emergencies. The prevalence of an organic etiology for the psychiatric presentation is highly variable 0–46% (Ferguson and Dudleston 1986; Hall et al. 1981; Kolman 1984; Koranyi 1979; Reeves et al. 2010; Willett and King 1977) depending on the inclusion criteria. In these studies, the setting and referral base is highly variable and often differs from the current system.

The first two studies discussed are frequently quoted as examples of the high-rate organic etiologies of the behavioral presentation, and seem to have pushed the medical community toward aggressive screening. Koryani (1979) retrospectively reviewed his clinic patients and reported that 43% of his sample suffered "from major medical illnesses." In 51%, the physical illness aggravated the psychiatric condition, and in 18%, it was thought to be causative. Koryani wisely notes that the two specialties of psychiatry and medicine are "woven" together and neither should be assessed in a vacuum. While the study provides insight into his patient population, it cannot be extrapolated to those presenting to the emergency department, nor does it make claims about how to initially screen patients.

Hall et al. (1981) found the highest prevalence of comorbid medical problems in psychiatric patients at a rate of 80%. As a result, the authors recommended extensive testing, which included 34 panel chemistry, urine drug screen, urine analysis, CBC, electrocardiogram (ECG), and electroencephalogram (EEG). The more astounding figure is that in 46% of the patients the organic pathology was thought to be directly related to psychiatric presentation. The setting of this article differs from today's practice, however, in that it was an inpatient clinical research ward and most patients were referred from a psychiatric reception center. This article also fails to examine the clinical significance of the laboratory abnormalities or ascertain whether these abnormalities would have been predicted by history and examination alone.

Shortly thereafter, there was a barrage of publications on this topic of missed physical diagnoses potentially causing or exacerbating the behavioral presentation. Summers et al. (1981) noted that 19% of their patient population had a "medical contribution" to their psychiatric presentation. Importantly, all 19% were noted on physical examination.

In 1981, Bunce et al. published their experience on an acute medical care ward to which there was a wide range of referrals. Only 23% were capable of communication, greater than 50% had altered mental status, and 29% presented with "general weakness." It is difficult to draw conclusions about the current population referred to the psychiatric wards based on this study.

Nine years later, Riba and Hale (1990) argue that it is also important to discover the minor medical abnormalities in the screening process as this may "cue psychiatrists to the presence of biological variables." This is a vague statement, and consequently it is open to varied interpretations. The role of the emergency physician is to ensure medical stability. Biologic variables not directly related to the presentation can be further assessed by the psychiatrist or medical consultant.

A protocol was instituted at Harbor UCLA in 1994 for new-onset psychiatric presentations of adults. The protocol consisted of laboratory testing, computed tomography (CT) of head (if the symptoms were not explained), and lumbar puncture if febrile (Henneman et al. 1994). A staggering 63% were found to have an organic etiology. Of the 100 patients, however, "60 were disoriented." Altered mental status is known to be more indicative of an organic etiology rather than psychiatric. Nonetheless, it is accepted practice that new-onset behavioral emergencies require a higher level of scrutiny for organic etiologies.

Reeves et al. in 2010, retrospectively reviewed admissions to their psychiatric hospital over a 7-year period. Among admitted patients, 2.8% were found to have a medical disorder that caused or exacerbated the altered mental status. All had altered mental status on presentation, which, as previously noted, is a high-risk criteria indicating the likelihood of an underlying medical etiology. Organic etiologies at a rate of 2.8% are surprisingly low for this group.

These studies are influenced by the population selected. First, when altered mental status is part of the inclusion criteria, then organic etiologies will naturally be more prevalent. Second, a new-onset psychiatric presentation demands adequate scrutiny. Third, if you work at an inpatient research ward in 1980, receiving undifferentiated patients as your referral base, then many will have organic etiologies.

7.3 Articles in Favor of Selective Testing

While it is important to know the prevalence of organic causes of behavioral emergencies, the more relevant questions are, which patients require laboratory screening and what is the utility of the tests? The following studies assess the utility of laboratory screening directly, and a clearer answer is obtained. The more recent studies in this group also represent the current population in the emergency department setting.

In 1977, Willett and King published their experience at the Colorado psychiatric hospital at the University of Colorado Medical Center. In their introduction, they mention that facilities are instituting laboratory screening and that this is a matter of "considerable debate," foreshadowing the next nearly four decades. The laboratory values obtained were CBC, venereal disease research laboratory (VDRL), blood urea nitrogen (BUN), creatinine, glucose, cholesterol, serum glutamic-oxaloacetic transaminase (SGOT), lactate dehydrogenase (LDH), alkaline phosphatase, calcium, phosphorous, protein, bilirubin, uric acid, and urine dipstick. After discharge, the lab test results were evaluated. The data of interest is the "unexpected abnormal," which totaled 248 values. Of these values, 61% led to no action, and 21.6% were repeated and subsequently normal. Fourteen patients were found to have new diagnoses, none of which were the cause of the behavioral disturbance. There were three urinary tract infections (UTI), which were treated with antibiotics, and one dehydrated patient due to diuretics that was given hydration. There were no other urgent treatments. Four fairly minor diagnoses of 636 patients amounts to a laboratory contribution of 0.63%.

C J Thomas (1979) assessed how frequently psychiatrists used screening tests, how much information the tests provided, and whether or not it was acted upon. In addition to the tests performed in the previously mentioned study, B12, folate, erythrocyte sedimentation rate (ESR), thyroid hormones (T3 and T4), and "Routine radiology of the chest and skull were also considered" (Jacobs et al. 1997). None of the positives for syphilis were considered significant, 3 abnormal thyroid studies of 145 were treated, 8 out of 99 with abnormal B12 or folate received replacement, and 10 out of 251 skull x-rays were considered abnormal, although none were related to the psychiatric presentation. Of the laboratory tests, 8.1% were considered abnormal. Of these, more than half were not followed up on. It is not clear if they were missed or deemed insignificant by the clinician.

In 1986, Ferguson and Dudleston published the first study that attempted to identify high-risk groups to improve "the efficiency of the screening process." By this time, routine screening had "been introduced in most hospitals to assist in detection of physical illness" (Ferguson and Dudleston 1986). Of 650 patients, 22 did not receive a physical exam, which may reflect the psychiatrists' discomfort with exams. All abnormal thyroid studies were insignificant and no patient received treatment for this. Skull x-rays, still in play, were found to be of "limited value." The clinical criteria used predicted 86.4% of the laboratory abnormalities. The criteria would have missed 5 UTIs and 5 electrolyte abnormalities or only 1.5% (10 out of 650) of medical illness. High-risk groups included an age greater than 65, altered mental status, drug and alcohol abuse, and weight loss of more than 10%.

Kolman et al. (1984) specifically looked at an older age group, ages 56–94. Despite the natural tendency of the elderly to have a higher prevalence of comorbid medical illnesses, screening tests lacked utility. In their study, only 1.4% of tests led to a change in detection and treatment of an illness.

In a chart review of 785 patients, Dolan and Mushlin (1985) searched for abnormal values that yielded new clinically important information also termed "laboratory diagnoses." The rate of true positives was 1.8%, and the rate of false positives was 8 times higher. Laboratory diagnoses were made in 0.08% of the cases studied.

More than a decade later, Olshaker et al. (1997) studied 345 patients, of which 19% were found to have acute medical conditions. Of those with acute medical conditions, 94% were discovered on history alone. Of the four patients not picked up by history, one was febrile, one had anemia, and two had mild hypokalemia. Similar findings are noted in another retrospective study by Janiak and Attebettery in 2012. They found that of 148 inpatients, 1 patient had significant laboratory abnormalities. This single outlier was also febrile and tachycardic. These results differ greatly from those published by Hall et al. (1981) in the early 1980s, and speak to the difference in patient population, the objective of the study, the definition of abnormal, and the quality of the initial history and physical exam.

In a single-center prospective study in oriented patients performed by Amin and Wang (2009), there was no change in disposition based on laboratory values. Of 375 patients, only 4 patients had non-substance abuse related laboratory abnormalities that required intervention. All that were positive were found on the urine analyses.

Parmar et al. in 2012 conducted a two-center prospective study consisting of 191 patients. These patients were deemed "medically clear" and had screening labs drawn. The financial burden was also assessed at a Medicare reimbursement rate of $197 per patient. Only one patient had a change in disposition due to a positive acetaminophen level.

The logical conclusion from these studies has already been well stated by Gregory et al. (2004): "Overall, results indicate that the yield for routine laboratory investigations is fairly low." "Instead of routine laboratory screening testing in the ED, the data support more selective testing for patients at high risk of serious medical pathology." The 2006 ACEP clinical policy states: "Routine laboratory testing of all patients is of very low yield and need not be performed as part of the ED assessment."

7.4 History and Physical Examination

The medical assessment of the behavioral emergency is predicated on a good history and physical exam. Whether or not lab tests are performed, the assessment is incomplete if the basic elements are absent. Poor examination, documentation, or both of psychiatric patients have been shown on multiple occasions to the extent of a full neurologic exam being documented in only 8% of the charts (Szpakowicz and Herd 2008; Tintinalli et al. 1994).

This trend continues today, as shown by Reeves et al. (2010), an adequate medical history and an adequate physical examination were each documented 60% of the time, and an adequate assessment of cognitive function was documented only 31% of the time. There is no study stating that laboratory screening is a replacement for the physical exam. Therefore, the clinician should not feel reassured if screening tests are obtained, as it does not preclude a thorough assessment.

Screening tools have been attempted since 1977 (Jacobs et al. 1977; Shah et al. 2012; Zun and Howes 1988). The tool, akin to the mini-mental status examination, proposed by Jacobs et al. (1977), interestingly called for laboratory testing only after a certain threshold was met. Vital elements of the physical examination, as advocated by Dr. Zun, are a neurologic examination and a cognitive assessment. This should be done in the presence or absence of laboratory testing.

7.5 Pediatric Population

The rate of pediatric behavioral emergencies is 1.6–3.3% of ED visits (Mahajan et al. 2009; Sills and Bland 2002). Donofrio et al. in 2014, assessed 1082 patients who were either a danger to self, danger to others, or deemed to be gravely disabled. Of these, 80.5% had screening lab tests, with 7 having a change in disposition (0.8%); and 6 out of 7 had findings on history and physical exam. The only disposition change that was not anticipated was a positive pregnancy test, which may have been "an unnecessary admission." The authors stated that the positive pregnancy test seemed to provide a reason for refusal of admission by the receiving psychiatric facility. There was otherwise no change in management. The most common laboratory finding was a positive urine analysis at 1.8%. This is rightfully qualified in the study by the presence of asymptomatic bacteriuria in the general population at a rate of 0.9–2.0%.

Studies have also shown an increased length of stay due to laboratory screening (Fortu et al. 2009; Santillanes et al. 2014). Santillanes et al. make a case for field triage of pediatric psychiatric complaints and bypassing the ED entirely in those that meet criteria, which was 91% of their studied patients. In their cost assessment, they found that the patients occupied an emergency department bed on average for 6.8 hours, and that the average cost was $970 per patient.

7.6 Unimportant Positives

Most studies do not focus on the parameter of false positivity. Dolan and Mushlin (1985) noted a rate of eight times the number of false positives to true positives. Willett and King (1977) had nine times the rate of false positives compared with true positives. Donofrio had a TSH false positive rate of 22.9%. Several studies (Amin and Wang 2009; Donofrio et al. 2014; Ferguson and Dudleston 1986) show urine analysis to be positive for UTI, however, samples are frequently contaminated and may not be true urinary tract infections (culture is not available at the time of treatment). Sheline and Kehr (1990) found that 44.9% urine analyses were contaminated. In addition, as mentioned, those who are asymptomatic and not pregnant do not require intervention for asymptomatic bacteriuria. False positive test results are not without consequence. The prudent physician will repeat the test or ensure follow-up at greater cost and extending the length of stay.

7.7 Urine Toxicology Screen

Mental health and illicit substance use are inseparable as they are often coexisting and each influences the other. In 2007, a healthcare cost utilization project found that one in 8 emergency department visits (12 million or 12.5% of all ED visits) was for chief complaints of mental health or substance use. Of mental health and substance use visits, 11.9% were co-occurring conditions (Owens et al. 2010). The urine toxicology is felt to yield invaluable information to the psychiatrist, and is at best unhelpful for the emergency physician. In addition, the test may extend the length of stay, is costly, and may be misleading.

In general, the information regarding illicit substance use and alcohol use can be gathered during the history and physical exam. Olshaker found the self-reporting to be at 91% for illicit substances use, and 96% for alcohol use in the last 24 hours. Similar sensitivities have been found in other studies (Kroll et al. 2013; Shihabuddin et al. 2013). In the pediatric population, the self-reporting of substance abuse was lower, at 83% (Fortu et al. 2009).

More importantly, the urine toxicology does not change the disposition of a patient. Schiller et al. (2000) assessed this in a retrospective review and found no difference in disposition between those with positive urine toxicology screen ordered versus not. Shihabuddin et al. (2013) found that of 539 patients, 62 had positive urine toxicology screens with no changes in management by either emergency physicians or psychiatrists. Eisen et al. (2004) had similar results in which change in management was reviewed and none were deemed justified.

The use of a urine drug screen is of limited use in the pediatric population as well. Fortu et al. (2009) assessed 385 patients with toxicology screens performed in routine fashion in uncomplicated psychiatric complaints. Of these, 31% were positive, with none admitted for medical concerns. Again, the urine toxicology had no effect on disposition.

The results of the individual substances tested lacks nuance and requires intelligent interpretation. Multiple doses of methamphetamine, for example, can lead the urine toxicology screen to be positive for 5 to 6 days depending on the cut off used (Vandevenne et al. 2000). There are also numerous agents that provide a false positive screen such as bupropion, trazodone, ranitidine, promethazine, and chlorpromazine. Therefore, if there are no clinical features of stimulant abuse, it is difficult to attribute suicidality or psychotic features to methamphetamine. A recent study showed that methamphetamine positivity has not been shown to be associated with placing the patient on an involuntary psychiatric hold (Pomerleau et al. 2012).

Similarly, benzodiazepine positivity may be deceiving. The test detects the metabolites oxazepam and nordiazepam, but it does not distinguish between benzodiazepine types, nor does it indicate abuse. Diazepam may take up to 36 hours post-ingestion, which can lead to a potentially negative result despite intoxication. In addition, benzodiazepines with a long half-life will cause the test to be positive for up to 30 days, making the positive result irrelevant in the absence of a fitting clinical presentation (Moeller et al. 2008). It is also worth mentioning that there are illicit substances that do not appear on the toxicology screen, such as synthetic cannabinoids and synthetic cathinones.

Interpreting the drug screen is not only challenging but expensive. It is the most pricey single test ordered on the panel of tests. Reimbursement for the urine toxicology screen ranges from $133.22 (Schiller et al. 2000) to $154.00 (Fortu et al. 2009). Due to the limited and potentially misleading information provided by the urine toxicology screen, the practice of routine drug testing is not supported by the literature.

7.8 Cost and Utility

There are few attempts at examining the cost and utility of these tests. Sheline and Kehr (1990) note 20 changes in medical management. However, 9 were iron replacement and 3 were clinic referrals, leaving 8 important results with a total cost to their facility of $19,610. If this is parceled to each significant test, the cost is $2451.25 per test. Feldman and Chen (2011) evaluated inpatient child and adolescent patients. Of 142 subjects, there were 809 tests obtained, and only 4 abnormalities yielded a direct impact on care. One patient had symptoms of a UTI; a second had slight elevation in liver enzymes, which affected the choice of mood stabilizer; and a third patient was found to have new-onset diabetes. From an emergency medicine perspective, only the third patient is a clinically significant finding that would not have been found on history and examination. The total direct cost to the facility was $12,630.47. If all four tests are included as significant, it places the cost per significant results at a staggering $3,157.62 per test.

7.9 Standardized Screening Protocols

Standardized medical screening protocols for psychiatric patients have been developed and studied in the literature. Remarkably, the approach that these protocols have taken in assessing patients is similar, relying on the presence of any of the following elements to selectively drive the diagnostic evaluation (Shah et al. 2012; Zun and Downey 2007; Zun et al. 1996):

- New psychiatric conditions
- Abnormal physical examination (including focused mental status exam)
- Abnormal vital signs
- Presence of other potential acute medical problems

Zun and Downey in 2007 retrospectively assessed the application of such a protocol on their ED population, finding that although the protocol did not improve ED throughput for psychiatric patients, it did offer a significant reduction in average cost per patient with a similar rate of return to the ED for further evaluation. Shah et al. in 2012, published a retrospective analysis of 485 consecutive ED patients screened by a similar tool and subsequently transferred to a psychiatric crisis center. Their study demonstrated remarkable utility in determining which patients required further diagnostic evaluation beyond a thorough history and physical exam.

Given the evidence and potential of such protocols to reduce the cost of evaluation in an ED setting, improve quality and consistency, all while resolving conflict among emergency medicine and psychiatry colleagues, these authors are in favor of the development of these protocols. In some regions, comprehensive laboratory evaluation of psychiatric patients is an expectation placed upon local emergency departments by inpatient psychiatric facilities. The result of such an arrangement without application of contemporary evidence produces unnecessary delays, and drives up cost. The opportunity to apply sound evidence-based medicine to reduce cost while improving the quality of care is the impetus for the development of our SMART protocol (Wetzel et al. 2015). Please refer to Figure 7.1 for the SMART protocol.

Following the same tenets previously discussed, the SMART protocol will rely on the presence or absence of the following elements to guide the diagnostic evaluation:

- New psychiatric conditions
- Medical conditions that require screening
- Abnormal vital signs
- Risky presentations (age, ingestion, or mechanism of injury)
- Therapeutic drug levels that require screening

7.10 Conclusion

The mostly older studies that seem to justify the utility of routine laboratory screening in behavioral emergencies do not apply to the patient population appearing in the emergency departments today. Newer studies show that routine screening in these patients yields little information of use to the emergency physician in making medical decisions. The lab tests, particularly the urine toxicology screen, are costly and provide potentially misleading information. In the vast majority of cases, the relevant data needed to make decisions about how to medically stabilize these patients can be obtained from an adequate medical history and physical examination. A standardized screening protocol may be useful in limiting unnecessary testing.

7.11 Recommendations for Practice

- Thorough history and physical examination, including cognitive function and complete neurologic exam.
- New onset psychosis requires laboratory screening, with consideration for CT brain and lumbar puncture.

SMART Medical Clearance Form

	No*	Yes	Time Resolved
Suspect <u>New Onset</u> Psychiatric Condition? — **1**			
Medical Conditions that Require Screening? — **2**			
Diabetes (FSBS less than 60 or greater than 250)			
Possibility of pregnancy (age 12-50)			
Abnormal: — **3**			
Vital Signs?			
Temp: greater than 38.0°C (100.4°F)			
HR: less than 50 or greater than 110			
BP: less than 100 systolic or greater than 180/110 (2 consecutive readings 15 min apart)			
RR: less than 8 or greater than 22			
O_2 Sat: less than 95% on room air			
Mental Status?			
Cannot answer name, month/year and location (minimum A/O x 3)			
If clinically intoxicated, HII score 4 or more? (next page)			
Physical Exam (unclothed)?			
Risky Presentation? — **4**			
Age less than 12 or greater than 55			
Possibility of ingestion (screen all suicidal patients)			
Eating disorders			
Potential for alcohol withdrawal (daily use equal to or greater than 2 weeks)			
Ill-appearing, significant injury, prolonged struggle or "found down"			
Therapeutic Levels Needed? — **5**			
Phenytoin			
Valproic acid			
Lithium			
Digoxin			
Warfarin (INR)			

* If ALL five SMART categories are checked "NO" then the patient is considered medically cleared and no testing is indicated. If ANY category is checked "YES" then appropriate testing and/or documentation of rationale must be reflected in the medical record and time resolved must be documented above.

Date: _____ Time: _____ Completed by: _____, MD/DO

Figure 7.1 SMART medical clearance form.

- Urine pregnancy in age appropriate females.
- Four-hour acetaminophen level in patients with risk of intentional or accidental ingestion.
- Consider development of a regional standardized screening protocol.

References

Amin M, Wang J. 2009. Routine laboratory testing to evaluate for medical illness in psychiatric patients in the emergency department is largely unrevealing. *Western Journal of Emergency Medicine* 10 (2): 97–100.

Anfinson T J, Kathol R G. 1992. Screening laboratory evaluation in psychiatric patients: A review. *General Hospital Psychiatry* 14 (4): 248–257.

Broderick K B, Lerner E B, McCourt J D, Fraser E, Salerno K. 2002. Emergency physician practices and requirements regarding the medical screening examination of psychiatric patients. *Academic Emergency Medicine* 9 (1): 88–92.

Bunce D F, Jones L R, Badger L W, Jones S E. 1982. Medical illness in psychiatric patients: Barriers to diagnosis and treatment. *Southern Medical Journal* 75 (8): 941–944.

CDC (Centers for Disease Control and Prevention). 2011. National Hospital Ambulatory Medical Care Survey: 2011. Emergency Department Summary Tables. https://www.cdc.gov/nchs/data/ahcd/nhamcs_emergency/2011_ed_web_tables.pdf.

Chun T H. 2014. Medical clearance: time for this dinosaur to go extinct. *Annals of Emergency Medicine* 63 (6): 676–677. doi:10.1016/j.annemergmed.2013.11.012.

Dolan J G, Mushlin A I. 1985. Routine laboratory testing for medical disorders in psychiatric inpatients. *Archives of Internal Medicine* 145 (11): 2085–2088.

Donofrio J J, Santillanes G, McCammack B D, Lam C N, Menchine M D, Kaji A H, Claudius I A. 2014. Clinical utility of screening laboratory tests in pediatric psychiatric patients presenting to the emergency department for medical clearance. *Annals of Emergency Medicine* 63 (6): 666–675. doi:10.1016/j.annemergmed.2013.10.011.

Eisen J S, Sivilotti M L, Boyd K U, Barton D G, Fortier C J, Collier C P. 2004. Screening urine for drugs of abuse in the emergency department: Do test results affect physicians' patient care decisions? *Canadian Journal of Emergency Medicine* 6 (2): 104–111.

Feldman L, Chen Y. 2011. The utility and financial implications of obtaining routine laboratory screening upon admission for child and adolescent psychiatric inpatients. *Journal of Psychiatric Practice* 17 (5): 375–381. doi:10.1097/01.pra.0000405369.20538.84.

Ferguson B, Dudleston K. 1986. Detection of physical disorder in newly admitted psychiatric patients. *Acta Psychiatry Scandinavia* 74 (5): 485–489.

Fortu J M, Kim I K, Cooper A, Condra C, Lorenz D J, Pierce M C. 2009. Psychiatric patients in the pediatric emergency department undergoing routine urine toxicology screens for medical clearance. results and use. *Pediatric Emergency Care* 25 (6): 387–392. doi: 10.1097/PEC.0b013e3181a79305.

Gregory R J, Nihalani, N D, Rodriguez E. 2004. Medical screening in the emergency department for psychiatric admissions: A procedural analysis. *General Hospital Psychiatry* 26 (5): 405–410.

Hall R C, Beresford T P, Gardner E R, Popkin M K. 1982. The medical care of psychiatric patients. *Hospital and Community Psychiatry* 33 (1): 25–34.

Hall R C, Gardner E R, Popkin M K, Lecann A F, Stickney S K. 1981. Unrecognized physical illness prompting psychiatric admission: A prospective study. *American Journal of Psychiatry* 138 (5): 629–635.

Henneman P L, Mendoza R, Lewis R J. 1994. Prospective evaluation of emergency department medical clearance. *Annals of Emergency Medicine* 24 (4): 672–677.

Jacobs J W, Bernhard M R, Delgado A, Strain J J. 1977. Screening for organic mental syndromes in the medically Ill. *Annals of Internal Medicine* 86 (1): 40–46.

Janiak B D, Atteberry S. 2012. Medical clearance of the psychiatric patient in the emergency department. *The Journal of Emergency Medicine* 43 (5): 866–870. doi:10.1016/j.jemermed.2009.10.026.

Kolman P B. 1984. The value of laboratory investigations of elderly psychiatric patients. *Journal of Clinical Psychiatry* 45 (3): 112–116.

Koranyi E K. 1979. Morbidity and rate of undiagnosed physical illnesses in a psychiatric clinic population. *Archives of General Psychiatry* 36 (4): 414–419.

Kroll D S, Smallwood J, Chang G. 2013. Drug screens for psychiatric patients in the emergency department: Evaluation and recommendations. *Psychosomatics* 54 (1): 60–66. doi:10.1016/j.psym.2012.08.007.

Larkin G L, Claassen C A, Emond J A, Pelletier A J, Camargo C A. 2005. Trends in US emergency department visits for mental health conditions, 1992 to 2001. *Psychiatric Services* 56 (6): 671–677. doi:10.1176/appi.ps.56.6.671.

Lukens T W, Wolf S J, Edlow J A, Shahabuddin S, Allen M H, Currier G W, Jagoda A S. 2006. Clinical policy: Critical issues in the diagnosis and management of the adult psychiatric patient in the emergency department. *Annals of Emergency Medicine* 47 (1): 79–99. doi:10.1016/j.annemergmed.2005.10.002.

Mahajan P, Alpern E R, Grupp-Phelan J, Chamberlain J, Dong J, Holubkov R, Jacobs E, Stanley R, Tunik M, Sonnet M, Miller S, Foltin G L. 2009. Epidemiology of psychiatric-related visits to emergency departments in a multicenter collaborative research pediatric network. *Pediatric Emergency Care* 25 (11): 715–720. doi:10.1097/PEC.0b013e3181bec82f.

Moeller K E, Lee K C, Kissack J C. 2008. Urine drug screening: Practical guide for clinicians. *Mayo Clinic Proceedings* 83 (1): 66–76. doi:10.4065/83.1.66.

Olshaker J S, Browne B, Jerrard DA, Prendergast H, Stair T O. 1997. Medical clearance and screening of psychiatric patients in the emergency department. *Academic Emergency Medicine* 4 (2): 124–128.

Owens P L, Mutter R, Stocks C. 2010 Mental health and substance abuse-related emergency department visits among adults, 2007. *Statistical Brief #92. Healthcare Cost and Utilization Project (H-CUP). Agency for Health Care Policy and Research; 2006–2010.*

Parmar P, Goolsby C A, Udompanyanan K, Matesick L D, Burgamy K P, Mower WR.2012. Value of mandatory screening studies in emergency department patients cleared for psychiatric admission. *Western Journal of Emergency Medicine* 13 (5): 388–393. doi:10.5811/westjem.2012.1.6754.

Pomerleau A C, Sutter M E, Owen K P, Loomis E, Albertson T E, Diercks D B. 2012. Amphetamine abuse in emergency department patients undergoing psychiatric evaluation. *The Journal of Emergency Medicine* 43 (5): 798–802. doi:10.1016/j.jemermed.2012.01.040.

Reeves R R, Parker J D, Loveless P, Burke R S, Hart R H. 2010. Unrecognized physical illness prompting psychiatric admission. *Annals of Clinical Psychiatry* 22 (3): 180–185.

Riba M, Hale M. 1990. Medical clearance: Fact or fiction in the hospital emergency room. *Psychosomatics* 31 (4): 400–404. doi:10.1016/S0033-3182(90)72134-2.

Santillanes G, Donofrio J J, Lam C N, Claudius I. 2014. Is medical clearance necessary for pediatric psychiatric patients? *The Journal of Emergency Medicine* 46 (6): 800–807. doi:10.1016/j.jemermed.2013.12.003.

Schiller M J, Shumway M, Batki S L. 2000. Utility of routine drug screening in a psychiatric emergency setting. *Psychiatric Services* 51 (4): 474–478. doi:10.1176/appi.ps.51.4.474.

Shah S J, Fiorito M, McNamara. R M. 2012. A screening tool to medically clear psychiatric patients in the emergency department. *The Journal of Emergency Medicine*. 43 (5): 871–875. doi:10.1016/j.jemermed.2010.02.017.

Sheline Y, Kehr C. 1990. Cost and utility of routine admission laboratory testing for psychiatric inpatients. *General Hospital Psychiatry* 12 (5): 329–34.

Shihabuddin B S, Hack C M, Sivitz A B. 2013. Role of urine drug screening in the medical clearance of pediatric psychiatric patients. Is there one? *Pediatric Emergency Care* 29 (8): 903–906. doi:10.1097/PEC.0b013e31829e8050.

Sills M R, Bland S D. 2002. Summary statistics for pediatric psychiatric visits to US emergency departments, 1993–1999. *Pediatrics* 110 (4): e40.

Summers W K, Munoz R A, Read M R, Marsh G M. 1981. The psychiatric physical examination – part ii: Findings in 75 unselected psychiatric patients. *Journal of Clinical Psychiatry* 1981; 42 (3): 99–102.

Szpakowicz M, Herd A. 2008. "Medically cleared": How well are patients with psychiatric presentations examined by emergency physicians? *The Journal of Emergency Medicine* 35 (4):369–372. doi:10.1016/j.jemermed.2007.11.082.

Thomas C J. 1979. The use of screening investigations in psychiatry. *British Journal of Psychiatry* 135: 67–72.

Tintinalli J E, Peacock F W, Wright M A. 1994. Emergency medical evaluation of psychiatric patients. *Annals of Emergency Medicine* 23 (4): 859–862.

Vandevenne M, Vandenbussche H, Verstraete A. 2000. Detection time of drugs of abuse in urine. *Acta Clinica Belgica* 55 (6): 323–333.

Weissberg M P. 1979. Emergency room medical clearance: An educational problem. *American Journal of Psychiatry* 136 (6): 787790. doi:10.1176/ajp.136.6.787.

Wetzel A E, Thomas S, Balan Y, Hosein R, Noobakhsh A. 2015. Crisis in the emergency department: Removing barriers to timely and appropriate mental health treatment. Sierra Sacramento Valley Medical Society. Sacramento. White Paper.

Willett A B, King T. 1977. Implementation of laboratory screening procedures on a short-term psychiatry inpatient unit. *Diseases of the Nervous System* 38 (11): 867–870.

Williams E R, Shepherd S M. 2000. Medical clearance of psychiatric patients. *Emergency Medicine Clinics of North America* 18 (2): 185–198.

Zun L S. 2005. Evidence-based evaluation of psychiatric patients. *The Journal of Emergency Medicine* 28 (1): 35–9. doi:10.1016/j.jemermed.2004.10.002.

Zun L S. 2012. Pitfalls in the care of the psychiatric patient in the emergency department. *The Journal of Emergency Medicine* 43: 829–835. doi:10.1016/j.jemermed.2012.01.064.

Zun L S, Downey L. 2007. Application of a medical clearance protocol. *Primary Psychiatry* 14: 47–51.

Zun L, Howes D S. 1988. The mental status evaluation application in the emergencydepartment. *American Journal of Emergency Medicine* 6 (2): 165–172.

Zun L S, Leikin J B, Stotland N L, Blade L, Marks R C. 1996. A tool for the emergency medicine evaluation of psychiatric patients. *American Journal of Emergency Medicine* 14 (3): 329–333. doi:10.1016/S0735-6757(96)90191-6.

Resources

Drescher M J, Russell F M, Pappas M, Pepper D A. 2014. Can emergency medicine practitioners predict disposition of psychiatric patients based on a brief medical evaluation? *European Journal of Emergency Medicine* 22 (3): 188–191. doi:10.1097/MEJ.0000000000000131.

Dupouy J, Memier V, Catala H, Lavit M, Oustric S, Lapeyre-Mestre M. 2014. Does urine drug abuse screening help for managing patients? A systematic review. *Drug and Alcohol Dependence* 136: 11–20. doi:10.1016/j.drugalcdep.2013.12.009.

Hoffman R S. 1982. Diagnostic errors in the evaluation of behavioral disorders. *JAMA* 248 (8): 964–967.

Koran L M, Sox H C, Marton K I, Moltzen S, Sox C H, Kraemer H C, Imai K, Kelsey T G, Rose T G, Levin L C et al. 1989. Medical evaluation of psychiatry patients results in a state mental health system. *Archives of General Psychiatry* 46 (8): 733–740.

Smith-Kielland A, Skuterud B, Morland J. 1997. Urinary excretion of amphetamine after termination of drug abuse. *Journal of Analytical Toxicology* 21 (5): 325–329.

Wilcox C E, Bogenschutz M P, Nakazawa M, Woody G. 2013. Concordance between self-report and urine drug screen data in adolescent opioid dependent clinical trial participants. *Addictive Behavior* 38 (10): 2568–2574. doi:10.1016/j.addbeh.2013.05.015.

Chapter 8

Discharge Planning

Yener Balan

Contents

8.1 Introduction	118
8.2 The Art of Discharge Planning: Aligning Your Goals with the Patient's	118
8.2.1 Sense of Control, or Not	118
8.2.2 Perception of Loss of Control	118
8.2.2.1 Proven Techniques—That Work!	118
8.2.2.2 In the Real World	119
8.3 Your Steps to Wellness	120
8.3.1 Step 1: The Assessment	120
8.3.2 Step 2: Individualized Treatment	120
8.3.3 Step 3: Release/Transfer	121
8.4 Specific Information to Gather for the Discharge Process	121
8.5 Safety Planning	122
8.5.1 Warning Signs	122
8.5.2 Coping Strategies	123
8.5.3 Family, Social, and Professional Contacts	124
8.5.4 Keeping Me Safe	124
8.5.5 Signature Section	124
8.5.6 Children and Adolescents: Safety Planning Issues	124
8.6 Additional Barriers to Discharge Planning	125
8.6.1 Housing	125
8.6.2 Transportation	126
8.6.3 Medical Issues	126
8.7 Discussing Discharge Medications	126
8.8 Communication: What We Think We're Good At, and Can Always Improve On	126
8.9 Discharge Instructions	127
8.10 Conclusion	128
References	128
Resources	128
	129

8.1 Introduction

The main goal of any work in the emergency department (ED) is getting the patient *out* of the ED. This could either be by discharging them home, admitting them to a medical, surgical floor, or psychiatric floor (if your hospital has one), or transferring them to another hospital for whatever specialty the patient needs that your hospital does not have.

Every provider and participant in the flow of the patient's journey is in sync with the goal of getting the patient *out* of the ED. Patients are always coming into the ED, day and night—and the only way to ensure that the ED is not drowning in patients, any more than it may already seem, is to get them out. Knowingly or not, and certainly on different levels of sophistication and incentive structures, the players, from operation administrators to the patient transport technician, feel the pressure of this aligned goal.

Increased patient flow in the ED, at any one given time, increases everyone's burden and stress, potentially leading to strained patient interactions, employee interactions, and worst of all, the potential for errors. These concerns are reflected in poor doctor–nurse communication scores, patient satisfaction scores, employee satisfaction scores, and even increased patient complaints, allegations, and law suits. Long-term burdens and stressful work environments lead to provider burnout and turnover and can spiral into a feedback loop of difficulty hiring optimal candidates, feeding into the increased burden and stress for the remaining providers.

8.2 The Art of Discharge Planning: Aligning Your Goals with the Patient's

8.2.1 Sense of Control, or Not

Just like any other patient with emergency medical needs, the patient with emergency psychiatric needs will also have varying levels of understanding of what to expect from their treatment and time in the ED. The only difference is that sometimes patients with emergency psychiatric needs are kept in the ED involuntarily. Imagine compounding your psychiatric problem—anxiety, psychosis, depression, already a dreadful sense of loss of control—on top of an involuntary hold, and being told that you legally cannot leave the ED until a psychiatric inpatient bed is found for you to be transferred into!

8.2.2 Perception of Loss of Control

We have all been stuck in traffic. Imagine you are in the comfort of your own car and get frustrated at an extra couple minutes or hours of waiting longer to get to your destination. You are tired or hot or bored or have to use the restroom, although you can shift your perception and realize quickly that you have a lot more control of your environment than you initially thought you did! You can turn on the air conditioner or listen to a podcast. Worst case, you can pull over and relieve yourself at the roadside! You can even leave your car altogether and walk away.

We have all had to wait at an airport. Karen, Chris, and I were stuck in an airport going to give a workshop in Halifax, Nova Scotia on ED psychiatry and hospital operations when we were told that our connecting flight in Denver, Colorado had a computer malfunction, and that even after rebooting the computer system several times it still did not work, and we would not be able to board. The airline did nothing more to help us other than give us a business card that included the phone number to address complaints to, and wish us luck finding a connecting flight! We found one that would get us to Halifax, although it would add another 12 hours to our wait. Our emotions ranged from "super upset," to concerned we would miss the workshop, to feeling anxious about thinking that even if we made the workshop, how jet lagged we would be running into it, to being angry, to then resigning to the notion that we had nothing else to do but wait.

Although we *did* have many options—we could have gotten on a plane back home and cancelled the workshop. We could have taken a cab to a hotel and made the most of our time in Denver. We could also just stay in the airport, find a nice lounge, and eat at the all-you-can-eat cheese cubes buffet, and try to take naps until the connecting flight.

8.2.2.1 Proven Techniques—That Work!

During therapy, a powerful technique used is often having the patient learn how to shift their perception, and be able to manipulate their understanding of their situation in a healthy way to ensure recovery, maintenance, and resilience against future decompensations.

Now consider this scenario: You have a mental illness—a psychotic episode where almost by definition you do not have control over your mind, or a recent suicide attempt brought on by a sense of overwhelming loss of control, or a debilitating anxiety or panic attack that makes it feel as if you have no control and are "losing your mind."

Now think that you either go to the ED yourself because you recognize, on some level, you need help, or someone brings you to the ED because you are unable to recognize the level of help you need.

Both options can be terrifying, as EDs are busy, seemingly chaotic, very noisy, and bright places. They are suboptimal places for people without any pathology, and are even worse if you have a mind that needs healing.

If you, the patient, have had experience in the mental health system, you may know about involuntary holds and may be concerned that you may be placed on one when you go to the ED. If you do not and are told you are being placed on an involuntary hold, you also may become concerned. The common underlying theme is the loss of control, although in these instances, the loss of control, at least the loss of "freedom to leave," is very real.

Often, EDs will have security officers dressed like police officers, or actual police officers. These security personnel may or may not be armed with tasers or even guns in the ED. The purpose of security in the areas where patients with psychiatric needs are being monitored, observed, boarded is one thing, and the way they are perceived by the patient is another. Uniforms are typically darker colored, look militaristic, and the officers are commonly larger and more muscular than the average person. While this is done on purpose to ensure the safety of the patients and staff, the intended effect is one of dominance and a "show of force."

This does nothing other than further intimidate the patient in the ED, and creates a withdrawal from potential rapport building with the treatment team.

If your psychiatric issue involves anxiety, claustrophobia, paranoia, or persecutory delusions, your time in the ED is potentially made even more miserable, as you are now legally on a hold against your will, there are gigantic officers at your door restricting your ability to leave, hurt yourself, or anyone else, and you are "waiting for an inpatient psychiatric hospital bed to become available."

The ED clinicians often are at the mercy of this wait for an inpatient psychiatric bed to become available, although at the end of their shifts, the clinicians get to go home. The patient has to continue to wait, and for psychiatric bed availability, the wait may be over after a day or two waiting in the ED, or sometimes even longer.

As real time updates are difficult, or practically impossible, to give to the patient, the reality of the loss of control can set in as the patient realizes they are unable to leave; and the unknown element of exactly when a transfer is expected compounds the anxiety, adds to agitation and may lead to acting out behaviors in the ED that may have been avoided or prevented had transparency in information been available.

8.2.2.2 In the Real World

Stop signs at crosswalks in many major cities now have a countdown timer indicating when the next red or "do not cross" signal is coming. Subway and train stations have billboards that indicate in how many minutes the next subway or train will be arriving. Airport terminals have details on the status of flights, arrivals, departures, and any delays prominently displayed on numerous screens.

These interventions are all geared toward decreasing the unknown, attempting to decrease anxiety or agitation, complaints, and dissatisfaction, and to give the perception of a sense of control. With the countdown timer at the crosswalk, you can walk faster, run, or just wait until the next walk signal, based on the information given by the signal timer.

If you know how many minutes you have until your next train, or to board your next flight, you can get a cup of coffee, or use the restroom without worrying you will miss it—all adding to your sense of control.

EDs currently do not have such automated or technological mechanisms to alert one of future wait times once a disposition decision has been made. The patient is at the mercy of the clinician, who may or may not have any more information regarding the transfer time than the patient; or the clinician may not even be thinking about how this may affect the patient, and not even bring this issue up at all. This loss of control can leave the patient feeling frustrated, angry, or even depressed.

8.3 Your Steps to Wellness

In an attempt to increase a perception of control and ensure that the patient knows what all the steps are during their ED visit, we created an educational poster of what to expect during their ED visit. These posters are printed with large font and are displayed in patient care areas.

During each initial visit in the ED, as well as subsequent checkups and reassessments with the patient, we refer the patient to the poster and indicate to the patient where they are in their "steps to wellness."

This consistent information allows the clinician, including and especially the nurse, who has many more points of contact with the patient during their stay, to allow the patient the shift in perception of how much control they have over their treatment and potential discharge from the ED.

8.3.1 Step 1: The Assessment

We purposefully labeled the steps in the poster with the colors red, yellow, and green, to simulate a traffic signal. Red, indicating the first step, where we have a "full stop" in an effort to gather as much initial information as possible: We inform the patient that they will be evaluated by the medical and behavioral health teams. While we encourage reducing the number of times a patient tells their same story, we make it clear that this may be necessary, and specialists may have different ways and reasons for asking similar sounding questions.

We also inform the patient that they *may* require lab work (i.e., blood work or urine tests) to be completed or medications to be ordered and administered. This last part of the sentence was left as vague as possible, as we wanted to reduce any further potential defensiveness in the patient, but also wanted to let them know that medical lab work and medical medications are equally as important as any psychiatric medications or lab work required for psychiatric reasons.

Use of the word *may* in the second bullet point of the poster also works to alleviate any potential anxiety and stress. Not every one that is in the ED requires lab work (see the chapter on medical clearance for more information), and similarly not everyone will require medications.

Even if someone is placed on an involuntary hold, unless there is a medical or psychiatric emergency (lifesaving requirement), medications cannot be administered against the patient's will, and blood work cannot be drawn without consent. This aspect is made very clear to the patient. Direct care ED staff may also require reeducation on this point to ensure that the patient's rights are not violated.

8.3.2 Step 2: Individualized Treatment

This is the second step in the patient's steps to wellness, and the title on the poster is in the color yellow. This step is often the lengthiest part of the patient's ED stay that takes up the bulk of the clinicians' time and energy.

The first bullet point in this section of the poster is "case management," which states that we will obtain information from you, your family, friends, caregivers, and community partners, as needed to help plan for your care. One must always be cognizant of health information privacy regulations and laws, how they pertain to emergencies, and when a patient's informed consent is required to be able to reach out to the patient's collateral contacts; and the clinician must also ensure that this is explained to the patient.

We find that most often when someone is aware that our standardized protocols include obtaining collateral information to paint a broader portrait of the patient, and to optimize disposition and discharge planning, patients understand and realize they have options and choices of who the treatment team can contact to be a part of the conversation. This is empowering, and more often than not leads to an improved therapeutic alliance with the patient.

"Goal setting" in the second bullet point, states that we will work with the patient to develop individual goals for reaching and maintaining wellness. This includes every touch point with the patient during their ED stay and is documented in the medical record.

The third bullet point is "treatment," which states we will offer classes and educational support groups to help support the patient's steps toward wellness. Given that EDs are different, and community resources vary from county to county, it is imperative that the local team is aware of the services offered in their area—either through the patient's health plan, or within the community. In addition to being proper care, this indicates that the ED is one part of the journey, and we all want the patient to leave the ED with a plan, and understand that the goal is to achieve and maintain wellness.

The last point is "release planning." This poster point states that we will work with the patient, the patient's family, friends, physicians, and caregivers to establish resources and continued treatment to help maintain the patient's state of wellness.

8.3.3 Step 3: Release/Transfer

This last step of the poster is in the color green, and states that we will work with the patient to help facilitate the patient's release plans or possible transfer to a higher level of care.

Displaying the steps in this order allows patients and their families and advocates to visually see that there is a well-thought-out, standardized process. We don't assume everyone knows what we do, and we also want to ensure that all clinicians in the ED are always caring for the patients in the same manner.

Obviously, the nuances are tailored to the specific patient's medical and psychiatric needs, and lengths of stay in the ED may vary based on disposition decision; however, the sentiment and approach to every patient is similar.

8.4 Specific Information to Gather for the Discharge Process

The discharge planning process is an integral part of the patient's entire ED visit. In order to complete the discharge planning process, a clear and comprehensive discharge summary needs to be developed. While the discharge summary itself should focus on psychosocial needs, the information that needs to be gathered includes topics such as

- Where will the patient live after their discharge?
- How will the patient be returning home?
- If someone can pick up the patient, what is their contact information?
- If the patient is using public transportation, do they have the proper fare or transportation ticket?
- Is the patient living in a shelter? If so, what are the hours they can return to the shelter?
- If applicable to the presentation, where is the patient getting their food and clothing?

In addition to these seemingly basic questions, the team must also know the elements to bolster care coordination, such as

- What the plan is for outpatient follow-up, including a specific date, time, and address of the clinic for a scheduled or proposed follow-up appointments?
- If the patient has an outpatient treatment team, the contact information and consent to verify or make subsequent appointments for the patient is needed.
- If the patient is on medication, do they have the appropriate amount of medications available, and is their pharmacy accessible to them, if applicable?
- Collateral contacts (e.g., family or friends) that can be contacted to verify any information as needed, with the appropriate patient consents.

As these elements are gathered, the template of the discharge instructions and summary matures. Boonyasai et al. prepared a report in 2014 titled "Improving the Emergency Department Discharge Process: Environmental Scan Report," that we recommend reviewing, as it delineates different populations, psychiatry among them, settings, and an evaluation of the possible outcomes that arise in the ED discharge process.

8.5 Safety Planning

An increasing number of patients are seeking care in the emergency departments for suicide-related issues (Currier et al. 2015). For patients presenting with suicidal or homicidal thoughts, it may be difficult to discharge them based on the severity of the thoughts they are experiencing. Since the ED may be the only point of contact some patients have with the healthcare system regarding these serious issues, we recommend that safety planning occur during the patient's ED visit. Development of a safety plan, when clinically appropriate, with the patient's cooperation, can help alleviate some reluctance the ED clinician may feel to release the patient back into the community.

When structuring your safety plan and implementing it in the emergency department, we recommend including sections in the plan on patient warning signs, coping strategies, social and professional contacts, and specific mechanisms to maintain the patient's safety. We recommend that the safety plan template be printed out with plenty of blank space left on it so the patient can fill it out. There are multiple layers of value in having the patient fill out the form in their own handwriting.

Once the patient completes the safety plan, we recommend making a copy of it and putting a copy in their medical chart, and giving a copy to the patient to take home with them. This exercise acts to reinforce the point that this is a tool to be referred to, and dynamically updated as needed. If the patient returns to the emergency department in the future, the treating team can pull the latest safety plan up, and refer to it with the patient to determine what worked, what they were able to do, and what did not work. This allows the patient and treatment team to coordinate efforts to update the plan further for the medical chart, as well as for the patient's benefit.

8.5.1 Warning Signs

"Warning signs" is the title of the first recommended section to include in a safety plan. Questions that are most effective are those that can be easily understood, appreciated by the patient, and answered without shame, blame, or stigma. The purpose of this section is to ensure that the patient understands when their safety plan should be used.

This section should include, basically, any emotional or behavioral cues that the patient can use to indicate that they are heading toward a crisis state and may need to implement their safety plan. The overarching goal is to provide the patient with a cue in order to use their safety plan in a timely manner to keep the patient and others around them safe.

Typically, the patient is asked to think about the last time they were in a crisis situation, or in a situation that brought them into the ED, and to try to recall any thoughts, images, or emotions they were experiencing during that time. They can use this information in this first step of the safety plan.

Specifically, listing out the warning signs themselves is also important. The preprinted template can include prompts to guide the patient's responses on how to word their warning signs, such as "include thoughts, images, your thinking process, or mood or behaviors." When the language is written as if it is in the words of the patient, we have found even better adherence and appreciation of the safety planning exercise from the patient. For example, a patient that has a thought as a warning sign may write this as " … a thought I have when I feel extremely distressed is … "

Again, this section is meant to act as a guideline for the patient during a crisis, and to have pre-identified warning signs. If the safety plan is being shared, either by a minor patient and their parent or guardian, or volitionally by an adult patient, we find that self-described warning signs are even more helpful for the outside observer or patient advocate. The process of completing the safety plan, in and of itself, adds a rapport and alliance building that may not be initially anticipated.

8.5.2 Coping Strategies

In this section of the safety plan, the patient is asked what coping and self-soothing skills they use that they have found helpful during a crisis situation. It can help to prompt the patient by asking them to identify what they can do to avoid harming themselves or anyone else while in a crisis. If the patient is unable to come up with any examples that they have used, it can help to walk the patient through other coping skills that have worked for other patients in the past to see if they are willing to try those.

The discussion on coping strategies gives the patient a sense of control over their current symptoms and behaviors during a crisis. It can also give the patient hope to have this discussion and to know and learn that others have gone through similar issues, and have successfully been able to cope with what they are dealing with. As a reminder, these coping skills and strategies are written in the words of the patient, by the patient, on the page.

8.5.3 Family, Social, and Professional Contacts

For the next section of the safety plan, the patient is simply asked to provide the names and contact numbers for their main social support network, which may include family members, friends, neighbors, therapists, doctors, and clergy.

Often, patients are reluctant to add anything to this section, or say that they have no one they can call. We find that sometimes we need to provide the patient with support and reassurance to help them think of someone that may be available to help them in a time of crisis. If they truly cannot think of anyone, we have them write down the number for their outpatient provider, as well as "911" for emergency needs.

8.5.4 Keeping Me Safe

In this section, the patient is asked to think of one or two ways that they would be able to use in order to stay safe if they were in a crisis. For example, if patients are thinking of killing themselves, and had a plan to cut their wrists, they are asked to write down how they would avoid following through with that plan, and what steps they would take to keep themselves safe. Steps could include leaving the area that is upsetting them, calling "911" themselves, calling one of their support people to get them to the hospital, or calling a therapist or their primary care physician for help.

In addition to the obvious benefits to a safety plan, the *keeping me safe* section allows for this exercise to be completed in a safe environment, where the patient can start thinking about going over these scenarios, and rehearse in their mind, and with their clinician what they would do in the event of another emergency. That way the patient will have thought of it beforehand, and can either look at the written safety plan, or remember what they thought of during the development of their plan, and use the coping skills and decisions they wrote down on their plan to keep themselves safe.

8.5.5 Signature Section

We recommend having the patient sign and date the bottom of the safety plan form. It is important to note that a safety plan is not a "safety contract" and that the patient is not contracting to anything. The act of signing this completed safety plan works as a guide for the patient to use when they are in a state of crisis and acts to get them engaged and involved with their own discharge planning process.

The patient's level of participation in the development of the safety plan can also provide clues to the ED clinician, as to how likely the patient will be to follow through with the recommended treatment.

An example of using this as a guide for how willing the patient will be to participate in their outpatient treatment recommendations follows. We had a female patient that was asked to fill out the safety plan. Under the "coping skills" section, she wrote "have more kinky sex and use more drugs" as her coping mechanism. This was a clear message to us that she was not taking the exercise seriously, and we needed to approach her care from a different angle.

8.5.6 Children and Adolescents: Safety Planning Issues

The safety planning process and coordination of the plan with minors can be complicated due to the involvement of their parents or guardians. Sometimes in these cases the parents or guardians of the minor patient may be reluctant to accept the patient home, even when the treatment team is recommending that the patient be discharged home with outpatient mental health follow-up. In these cases the treatment team may need to take extra time with the parent or guardian in order to ease their fears and explain and address the concerns they have with the plan to discharge the patient home.

An example of this may occur when an adolescent is admitted to the ED due to non-suicidal self-injurious behavior (see the chapter on anxiety and mood disorders for an in-depth discussion on this topic). A common occurrence of this is when the patient makes superficial cuts to their wrist with a razor. Usually in these cases, after a full assessment and work up of the patient has been completed, the treatment team decides to discharge the patient home to their parents or guardians with outpatient follow-up in place. Sometimes due to the nature of the act of cutting themselves, the parent or guardian may feel fearful or concerned about the patient returning home. In these cases, we recommend that a safety plan is developed with the help of the parent or guardian and the patient. This will help ensure that the adult has a sense of control over the planning process, and can provide them with a guide that is in the words of the patient, or was cowritten with the patient.

We have experienced that developing safety plans together with family and or advocates can be a very rewarding experience, and quite therapeutic, in and of itself. Sometimes the discussion that takes place during this exercise happens to be the first time the parent and child has actually talked about safety planning and coping skills, and it helps both the minor patient and the adult to hear what the other is thinking, and know that it is under the clinical guidance of the treating clinician.

Sometimes after the safety plan is developed, it works to quell the concerns of the parent or guardian, and the patient can be discharged. If the parent or guardian is still reluctant to take the patient home after the safety plan is completed, it can sometimes help to hold a team meeting with the parent or guardian, the primary treating ED physician, psychiatrist, and ED mental health clinician. This meeting can provide even more education to the parent or guardian regarding the reason for the discharge decision to help reinforce those points. During the meeting, the parent or guardian can be reassured that they can always bring the patient back to the ED if their symptoms get worse, or if they have any recurrence of thoughts of wanting to hurt or kill themselves.

8.6 Additional Barriers to Discharge Planning

Barriers for inpatient psychiatric hospitalization placement are discussed in our chapter on care options and treatment teams under "barriers for placement" in the "template for ED psychiatry pre-rounding" section. The treatment team should be aware of any of the potential barriers to discharge the patient either home, to a hospital alternative program, or to a hospital setting, and be prepared to address these barriers.

8.6.1 Housing

Some of the more common barriers when trying to discharge a patient out of the ED and back into the community may include housing issues, especially if the patient is homeless, or if the patient is unable to return to the home they are in because a family member or concerned roommate is not willing to accept them back into the home. In these cases, the hospital social services team may need to get involved in order to help solidify a housing plan for the patient.

8.6.2 Transportation

Even though this is a small part of the discharge planning process, it can create a barrier and add time to the patient's ED stay. We recommend that a discussion on transportation needs and availabilities be completed as early as possible. Some hospital systems may be willing to help finance transportation resources for patients discharging from the ED, although the willingness to do this may vary.

Any way you look at the transportation issue, it is almost always less expensive to provide the cost of transportation of the patient to a safe predetermined location, out of the ED, than it is to have the patient wait in the ED for a transportation solution that may not materialize for many hours.

Regardless of which hospital one looks at, several hours in an ED is almost always more costly financially, and also increases potential liability, than the cost of a public transportation voucher, or even a taxi ride. While we don't advocate for free transportation for everyone and understand the financial barriers, we do highly recommend that hospital systems look at this issue and have a reasonable plan in place to address it. In addition to the cost angle, operationally having one less patient that does not need to be in the ED is always optimal in regard to the flow of the patients and creating capacity in the ED.

8.6.3 Medical Issues

We recommend encouraging MD-to-MD dialogue regarding any outstanding medical concerns that may be holding up the patient's transfer from the ED to the accepting facility, whether the facility is a crisis respite housing program or an inpatient psychiatric hospital.

More often than not, we see these hold ups arise around chronic medical issues that reveal lab results that are abnormal, but are the "baseline" results for the patient in question. The function of an MD-to-MD warm handoff or discussion is to reassure the accepting MD and treatment team that the abnormal lab values or findings do not represent an acute, concerning presentation.

8.7 Discussing Discharge Medications

We have experienced variation in individual clinicians' desire to, or reluctance to, start or alter an outpatient psychiatric medication regimen. We suggest that ED teams discuss an approach that is as uniform as possible to ensure patients and their advocates are aware of what they need to know about any medication changes that have occurred during the ED stay.

Reviewing any medications that were started or changed in the ED setting with the patient on discharge and documenting this medication reconciliation in the chart, as well as the informed consent established, is an important part of the discharge process. The informed consent of the medications should include education about potential side effects as well as what the patient can do if they experience them.

Within the hospital and medical network setting one practices in, the ED treatment team should establish clear policies regarding how the ED MD contacts and updates any outside providers, as well as the patient's pharmacy for medication requests.

The treatment team should have established protocols that address patient requests for medication refills. The protocol should keep in mind the time frame between the date of discharge from the ED to the patient's next outpatient appointment. This will ensure that the patient is provided with an adequate number of pills to bridge this gap in time. If it is a controlled substance that requires refill, an even more robust handoff and discharge communication should occur.

Depending on your hospital's opioid or benzodiazepine policy (see Chapter 10 on anxiety and mood disorders for more information), as well as the prescribing physician's comfort level, and the urgency of the clinical need of the patient, a controlled substance may not be prescribed upon discharge from an ED setting. In this case, proper discussion with the patient as to the reasons why the medication will not be prescribed, and offering alternatives resources, including alternate medications as well as other therapeutic options, should be offered and documented in medical chart.

8.8 Communication: What We Think We're Good At, and Can Always Improve On

The crux of successful communication during discharge planning is to always remember the key stakeholders. Communicating within silos has limited benefit, and can lead to unexpected complications including minor ones such as a duplication of efforts, and more detrimental ones such as missed treatment opportunities.

In addition to working with the patient and their families, as discussed previously, it is important to communicate with the patient's outpatient treatment team. Best case scenario, your health system has an integrated computerized medical record and notes can be electronically "routed" to other providers within the network. Worst case scenario, you have to write a note (believe it or not, some hospitals still have clinicians handwrite documents) and fax (interestingly, hospitals are among the final existing businesses that still rely on faxes) your note to the outside treatment provider.

Informing an outpatient provider of their patient's ED visit adds value on many levels. It ensures timely care, risk stratification (see the chapter on risk assessment for more information), and seamless care delivery. Depending on where you live, healthcare regulations may have specific time frames within when you must be seen post an emergency department visit.

During a patient's ED visit, if and when collateral contacts are made for further information, it is imperative that these conversations and the consent given by the patient to contact collaterals is documented in the patient chart. Especially if the collateral contact's information (e.g., friend, family, outside provider, or advocate) is beneficial to the patient's discharge plan and adds to the clinical picture, the collateral's contact information can be incorporated in any outpatient treatment planning.

Lastly, we highly recommend standardizing a procedure in which ED staff communicate with the patient's family, friends, or advocates and informs them when the patient is discharged or transferred from the ED. This must be done with the consent of the adult patient, and the purpose of the communication is to alleviate any caregiver concerns regarding where the patient went after their ED visit. If and when you obtain consent from the patient to inform an outside party of their discharge from the ED or transfer to another facility, document the consent in the patient record. This final touch of compassionate communication goes a long way to remind everyone that we are all working to ensure the health and well-being of our patients, and recognize that it takes many participating members advocating on a team to help one another.

8.9 Discharge Instructions

The final, and possibly most critical, piece of the discharge process is the patient's discharge instructions. A study looking at verbal discharge instructions found that patients are not given many chances to confirm they understand them, and that the instructions themselves are often incomplete (Vashi 2011). In 2012, Engel et al. looked at the importance of the patients' understanding of the discharge instructions, and specifically each component of the instructions and how it related to adherence and outcomes.

The instructions communicated with the patient and their family or advocates should demonstrate that there has been communication with the treatment team. We recommend that in addition to verbally going over all aspects of the discharge instructions, the patient be handed a copy of the instructions to take home with them, to refer to themselves, as well as to share with their outpatient providers.

As we are aware that some studies have found that patients tend to revisit the ED within 72 hours of their first admit at a rate of up to 18% (Han et al. 2009a), and that a deficiency in key components of discharge planning and care communication can be associated with adverse event risk (Fermazin et al. 2009), it is key for the treatment team to ensure the discharge planning is robust and not only clinically appropriate, but also realistic. For example, if transportation is an identified barrier, trying to schedule an outpatient follow-up to a clinic that is easier to access, is a simple solution and increases the likelihood of the possibility of adherence to the discharge plan.

The discharge instructions should also include a copy of the safety plan, if applicable, as well as any medication reconciliations. All communication provided to the patient should also be documented in the medical record for future reference, as needed.

8.10 Conclusion

Appropriate discharge planning and communication and documentation of the plan has numerous benefits that span from efficiencies in ED operations to improved patient care outcomes.

References

Boonyasai, R T, Ijagbemi, O M, Pham, J C, Wu, A W, Doggett, D, Fawole, O A, Bayram, J D, Levin, S, Connor, C. 2014. Improving the emergency department discharge process: Environmental scan report. *Agency for Healthcare Research and Quality*. 14 (15)-0067-EF.

Currier, G W, Brown, G K, Brenner, L A, Chesin, M, Knox, K L, Ghahramanlou-Holloway, M, Stanley, B. 2015. Rationale and study protocol for a two-part intervention: Safety planning and structured follow-up among veterans at risk for suicide and discharged from the emergency department. *Contemporary Clinical Trials.* 43: 179–184. doi:10.1016/j.cct.2015.05.003.

Engel, K G, Buckley, B A, Forth, V E, McCarthy, D M, Ellison, E P, Schmidt, M J, Adams, J G. 2012. Patient understanding of emergency department discharge instructions: Where are knowledge deficits greatest? *Academic Emergency Medicine.* 19 (9): 1035–1044. doi:10.1111/j.1553-2712.2012.01425.x.

Fermazin, M, Tahan, H, Lett, J E, McGonigal, L, Weis, M. 2009. Improving transitions of care: Emergency department to home. *National Transitions of Care Coalition.* http://www.ntocc.org/Portals/0/PDF/Resources/ImplementationPlan_EDToHome.pdf.

Han, C, Barnard A, Chapman, H. 2009a. Discharge planning in the emergency department: A comprehensive approach. *Journal of Emergency Nursing* 35 (6): 525–7. doi:10.1016/j.jen.2009.01.015.

Mariano, M T, Brooks, V, Digiacomo, M. 2006. PSYCH: A mnemonic to help psychiatric residents decrease patient handoff communications errors. *The Joint Commission Journal on Quality and Patient Safety.* 42 (7): 316–320.

Miles, J. 2009. Dear American Airlines. Boston, MA: *Mariner Books.*

Solet, D J, Norvell, J M, Rutan,t G H, Frankel, R M. 2005. Lost in translation: Challenges and opportunities in physician-to-physician communication during patient handoffs. *Academic Medicine.* 80 (12): 1094–1099.

Vashi, A, Rhodes, K. 2011. 'Sign right here and you're good to go': A content analysis of audiotaped emergency department discharge instructions. *Annals of Emergency Medicine.* 57 (4): 315–322. doi:10.1016/j.annemergmed.2010.08.024.

Resources

Betz, M E, Wintersteen, M, Boudreaux, E D, Brown, G, Capoccia, L, Currier, G, Goldstein, J, King, C, Manton, A, Stanley, B, Moutier, C, Harkavy-Friedman, J. 2016. Reducing suicide risk: Challenges and opportunities in the emergency department. *Annals of Emergency Medicine.* 68 (6): 758–765. doi:10.1016/j.annemergmed.2016.05.030.

Boudreaux, E D, Camargo, C A, Arias, S A, Sullivan, A F, Allen, M H, Goldstein, A B, Manton, A P, Espinola, J A, Miller I W. 2016. Improving suicide risk screening and detection in the emergency department. *American Journal of Preventive Medicine.* 50 (4): 445–453. doi:10.1016/j.amepre.2015.09.029.

Branch, W T., Kern, D, Haidet P, Weissmann, P, Gracey, C F, Mitchell, G, Inui, T. 2001. The patient-physician relationship. Teaching the human dimensions of care in clinical settings. *JAMA.* 286 (9): 1067–1074.

Bristow, D P, Herrick C A. 2002. Emergency department case management: The dyad team of nurse case manager and social worker improve discharge planning and patient and staff satisfaction while decreasing inappropriate admissions and costs: A literature review. *Lippincott's Case Management.* 7 (6): 243–251.

Bush, K, Gurney, D, Baxter, T, Crook, J. 2013. Safe discharge from the emergency setting. Emergency Nurses Association. https://www.ena.org/SiteCollectionDocuments/Position%20Statements/SafeDischarge.pdf.

Centers for Medicare and Medicaid Services. 2013. Revision to state operations manual (SOM), Hospital Appendix A - Interpretive Guidelines for 42 CFR 482.43, Discharge Planning. https://www.cms.gov/Medicare/Provider-Enrollment-and-Certification/SurveyCertificationGenInfo/Downloads/Survey-and-Cert-Letter-13-32.pdf.

Centers for Medicare and Medicaid Services. 2014. Discharge planning. https://www.cms.gov/Outreach-and-Education/Medicare-Learning-Network-MLN/MLNProducts/Downloads/Discharge-Planning-Booklet-ICN908184.pdf.

Chan, T C, Killeen, J P, Castillo, E, Vilke, G, Guss, D A, Feinberg, R, Friedman, L. 2009. Impact of an internet-based emergency department appointment system to access primary care at safety net community clinics. *Annals of Emergency Medicine.* 54 (2): 279–284. doi:10.1016/j.annemergmed.2008.10.030.

Han C, Barnard, A, Chapman, H. 2009b. Emergency department nurses' understanding and experiences of implementing discharge planning. *Journal of Advanced Nursing.* 65 (6): 1283–1292.

Mamon, J, Steinwachs, D M, Fahey, M, Bone, L R, Oktay, J, Klein, L. 1992. Impact of hospital discharge planning on meeting patient needs after returning home. *Health Services Research.* 27 (2): 155–175.

Moss, J E, Flower, C K, Houghton, L M, Moss, D L, Nielson, D A, Taylor, D M. 2002. A multidisciplinary care coordination team improves emergency department discharge planning practice. *Medical Journal of Australia.* 177 (8): 435–439.

Stanley, B, Brown, G. 2012. Safety planning intervention: A brief intervention to mitigate suicide risk. Special series: Working with suicidal clients: Not business as usual. *Cognitive and Behavioral Practice.* 19: 256–264.

Vaiva, G, Ducrocq, F, Meyer, P, Mathieu, D, Philippe, A, Libersa, C, Goudemand, M. 2006. Effect of telephone contact on further suicide attempts in patients discharged from an emergency department: Randomised controlled study. *BMJ.* 332 (7552): 1241–1245. doi:10.1136/bmj.332.7552.1241.

Chapter 9

Ethical Implications for the Emergency Department Psychiatrist

Jeffery Kahn

Contents

9.1 Introduction 131
    9.1.1 Ethical Choices and the Effect on the Patient 132
9.2 Ethical Case Presentations 132
    9.2.1 Case 1: The Suicidal Patient 132
        9.2.1.1 The Suicidal Patient: Ethics Case Discussion 134
    9.2.2 Case 2: The Psychotic Patient 136
        9.2.2.1 The Psychotic Patient: Ethics Case Discussion 137
    9.2.3 Case 3: The Cognitively Impaired Patient 138
        9.2.3.1 Capacity Evaluation Essentials 138
        9.2.3.2 The Cognitively Impaired Patient: Ethics Case Discussion 141
9.3 Conclusion 143
References 143
Resource 143

9.1 Introduction

In this chapter, I will be discussing some of the ethical challenges that occur while working as a psychiatrist or therapist in the emergency department (ED) of a hospital. To that end, I will be covering such topics as capacity and consent, autonomy, beneficence, non-maleficence, free will, paternalism, when to initiate a Tarasoff or refrain from initiating a Tarasoff, confidentiality, legal detainment against one's will, and physical and chemical restraints.

    The topics themselves are not that difficult to comprehend, although navigating through some of the gray areas may require a bit of self-reflection and self-examination (it's ok, it's good for you). The challenge on my part will not be to convey the content in an understandable and accurate way (that's the easy part), but to present this material in a manner that's just a little more interesting to those in the mental health arena, than say, for example, a wordy tome on the behavior of gases at low temperatures (now if that's your thing, if that's what gets you all worked up and passionate, my apologies, or rather, my sympathies). What I am trying to say, in a polite academic way, is that I will try my very best not to make this topic as boring as it can be.

All kidding aside, ethics in psychiatry is all but boring, as in many ways it represents and embodies the very heart and soul, the essence of what we strive to accomplish in the mental health field, and for many of us, it's what drew us into this field in the first place. I am speaking of our innate sense of fairness and compassion, embodied in our desire and wish to alleviate pain and suffering while treating all patients with the utmost respect, decency, and dignity that we know we all deserve. This becomes all the more important and pressing as we work with the most vulnerable and wounded among us, that is, patients in the throes of a mental health crisis.

9.1.1 Ethical Choices and the Effect on the Patient

This is tricky business, because we are often placed in the role of a paternalistic arbiter of what is right, best, or necessary for a patient's well-being, as we see it, which is often diametrically opposed to how the patients themselves may view their current situation. In fact, they may (and often do) view us as being the very agents of an authoritarian system bent on stripping them of their dignity, self-respect, and free will.

We have an awesome and profound responsibility, namely, but not limited to, acting on behalf of what is best for the patient, and not to confuse that with what is best for us (more on that later). This is all too often not as obvious and simple as it may outwardly seem. Here, thankfully, is where we may rely on well-founded ethical principles grounded in philosophy, and of course, the law, to help guide us through the morass of conflicting values, and to help us maneuver through the complexities inherent inn having to be the ones that are tasked with the responsibility of making decisions that may limit another's basic liberties: freedom of choice, freedom of movement, and freedom to care for oneself as one sees fit.

9.2 Ethical Case Presentations

To help further elucidate some of these concepts and principles, the following is a real case history, which will serve as a vehicle to weave in some of the aforementioned ethical questions and concerns. The details of course are altered only in such a way as to maintain patient confidentiality while keeping with the essence of the case. I chose to present a case that I was personally involved in so as to be able to describe the thought processes that informed my decision-making as they unfolded in the moment.

9.2.1 Case 1: The Suicidal Patient

While working as the lone psychiatrist in a very busy ED in California, I was asked to put the final *coup de grâce* in the form of upholding a 5150 psychiatric legal hold, declaring a particular young man as a danger to himself, requiring involuntary placement in a psychiatric inpatient facility. As this case was presented to me, this was expected to be a no brainer, a *fait accompli*, a slam dunk, a … well, you get the idea. The story, as gleaned from the chart, and presented to me by clinicians who had already seen him, goes something like this:

John Hardman, a 28-year-old Caucasian male, 7 years out of the military, arrived by ambulance to the ED following a serious suicide attempt by hanging; this, only 4 months on the heels of a previous suicide attempt by an overdose of medications. No matter what he said then, the combined wisdom at morning multidisciplinary team rounds was that he had enough risk factors to continue to warrant involuntary treatment at an inpatient psychiatric facility. This makes sense to me. After all, how clear does it have to be?

Well, after reviewing all the notes from his medical record, and interviewing him myself, I find that what previously seemed crystal clear, now seemed a bit clouded. Or is it just me? Am I somehow being taken in? I always err on the side of caution in these type of scenarios, so why the second thoughts? I'll tell you why: ethics (I know this may sound corny but it's true nevertheless). Let me explain by first conveying some further details of the presenting history as it unfolded to me. After which, we will use this case as a jumping off point to further define some of the concepts listed at the beginning of this chapter.

After returning home from two military tours of duty in the Middle East, Mr. Hardman struggled both emotionally and physically. Besides being shot himself, leaving him in some degree of chronic pain, he had also been diagnosed with post-traumatic stress disorder (PTSD), having been witness to and in the midst of many of the atrocities of war. He received some treatment at the Veterans Administration (VA), but never really followed up much with therapy and medications. He had been living with his girlfriend and her two children for the past several years, and was holding down a job for the past 2 years, up until 10 days prior to this admission, when he quit due to a personality clash with his immediate supervisor.

On the morning of this attempt, he stated, "I just couldn't take the pain anymore." And, with about 10 minutes of forethought, he tied a shoelace to the rafter in the garage and proceeded with his hastily drawn-out plan. He states he actually hung there for a second before the shoe lace broke, and he dropped a short distance to the floor. He then smoked a cigarette, after which he found his girlfriend, explained what happened, and asked to see a doctor. A primary care physician (PCP) examined him, found no ligature marks or other stigmata of hanging, and walked him the short distance to a waiting mental health therapist for further evaluation. He was subsequently placed on a 5150 involuntary psychiatric hold, deemed to be a danger to himself, and sent by an ambulance to the ED. The therapist's note in the chart clearly stated that after an evaluation at the ED, he recommended involuntary inpatient psychiatric hospitalization for the patient.

Upon my arrival to his room, I was met with a cordial, albeit somewhat overly formal, slender young man, neatly groomed, sitting up in his hospital bed. He was very matter of fact in relating the events that led up to his current emergency room visit. He was to the point, omitting nothing, minimizing nothing. Eye contact was sustained and seemed, at times, a bit intense. He went on to explain that he went on his own to his PCP, requesting psychiatric treatment. He said that he was just tired of maintaining the façade that he does not need help, that he is now at the point where he wants treatment, including psychotherapy and medication management, and was fully ready to engage wholeheartedly in that process.

I discussed with him the 5150 involuntary psychiatric hospitalization process, and he was adamant that he felt that it would not only be unnecessary, but it would not be therapeutic for him either. When I asked him about guarantees that he would not kill himself, he did not jump all over that with the lofty assurances I have come to expect when people are attempting to wrangle out of a legal psychiatric hold and avoid further hospitalization. Instead, he paused thoughtfully before answering, "I'm not sure anybody can really and truly make such promises, what I will say is that I never intend to attempt to take my own life again, that I finally feel truly committed to doing what is advised by professionals, and doing the work of getting better." He went on to say,

"I am not expecting it to be easy, or a magic cure, but this is where I'm at." He went on to recount his conversation with his girlfriend earlier this day, stating that she will never leave him alone, she will take him to work with her, and he will sleep on the inside of the bed, so that she would know if he gets up, "She is a very light sleeper."

I left his room without offering any assurances that he would be discharged home on that day.

Now the easiest thing for me to do, the safest and most conservative thing for me to do was to uphold his 5150 psychiatric hold and send him on his way to the next available psychiatric hospital bed. Furthermore, with all the clear documentation from several health professionals recommending the same, it would be a crazy risk to me to do so otherwise. If I were to discharge him home, and something should happen, "I'm screwed," and so my thoughts went, and went, and went. But then, this other nagging thought, deep in the background mist of my brain, began to clarify and gain momentum, and much to my initial annoyance, I asked myself, "What is in the best interest of the patient?" In other words, I was face-to-face with the very fundamental ethical concept that asks us to clearly delineate and differentiate between the patient's best interest and clinician's motives.

Paul Appelbaum (1988) described the act of hospitalizing a patient to protect oneself from potential liability as a "preventative detention." Is that what I am doing? Do I really think he is in imminent risk of leaving here and trying again? Will psychiatric hospitalization really benefit him, or am I just trying to pass the responsibility over to some other faceless psychiatrist, thereby alleviating myself of responsibility. In other words, am I just trying to cover my own ass? Damn this self-reflection business.

So here is where I sat myself down, reflected on the ethical concepts from earlier readings, and explored my own motivations and worries to see if I could cipher what would ultimately be in the best interest of the patient, and not just what would be in my own best interest. After all, he initially self-presented and reached out for help. Would it actually be counter-therapeutic to deprive him of his autonomy now? If I did so, would he ever trust mental health professionals again? Can I be thwarting an opportunity for his taking responsibility for his own mental health? Then again, he did just try to kill himself for the second time in 4 months, it would certainly be a justifiable hold, and erring on the side of caution can save lives, can save his life. Or would it? Perhaps the opposite would happen, perhaps he would lose faith in mental health treatment and would not engage in therapy that ultimately may be lifesaving for him. Is this even my problem? Don't I just need to think about what is the safest course of action right now, in this moment?

9.2.1.1 The Suicidal Patient: Ethics Case Discussion

This case example serves to highlight some of the ethical ambiguities of one of the most common decisions an ED psychiatrist faces on a daily basis; that is, to hospitalize or not to hospitalize. Furthermore, this basic and common question provides a backdrop through which to better acquaint ourselves with core ethical concepts that are not limited to this one very particular question, namely paternalism, autonomy, beneficence, non-maleficence, and confidentiality.

If I were to hospitalize this patient, I would be acting paternalistically (acting to protect the patient, whether he likes it or not). Although in our current era this concept has taken on a negative connotation, it is, in fact, often necessary to act paternalistically in order do what is right for the patient. Paternalism exists in the mental health context when we not only decide what is best for a particular patient, but when we then take action to benefit a patient, in violation of other ethical and moral codes, such as autonomy and free will.

To better understand the concept of "autonomy" in the context of medical ethics I quote author Lawrie Reznek, who in her book *The Philosophical Defense of Psychiatry*, writes, "a typically autonomous person is someone who understands the choices facing him, who is rational, who acts on the basis of desires and beliefs normally formed, and which is free from coercion... When someone is so depressed that he ceases to understand fully what he is doing and ceases to be rational, he ceases to be autonomous" (1991, 216). Whereas treating someone against their will is usually considered taking away one's autonomy, she further argues, that in cases of suicidal patients (adhering to our presumption that suicide in the context of a depressive episode is not rational), "a real respect for autonomy demands we intervene to restore it" (Reznek 1991, 216). This last statement is of utmost importance, as it not only informs our decision-making for the depressed suicidal patient, but also for those patients lacking capacity to consent to treatment based on other presentations as well, which will be discussed later in the chapter, such as the acutely psychotic patient, as well as patients with dementia, delirium, and the manic patient with or without psychosis.

For all of these scenarios, we must always ask ourselves if it is best for the patient for us to act paternalistically and take away their basic liberties and autonomy by forced detention and treatment, or would doing so create more harm (maleficence) compared with the potential benefit (beneficence). As Lawrie Reznek has implied, we must first determine if a given patient is truly autonomous when they profess to not want hospitalization, or has their mental illness already robbed them of their autonomy? As she later points out, "If a patient is not autonomous, such intervention does not diminish autonomy—it enhances it" (Reznek 1991, 218).

In the case of Mr. Hardman, is his depression such that he cannot cognitively manipulate the pros and cons of inpatient hospitalization? Is he reacting by not wanting the stigma he perceives would follow him from such treatment, and thus unable to make a rational choice in his own best interest? Or is he merely wanting to go home so he can get it right this time and use a more lethal means to end his life?

Such a fact-finding mission to determine existing autonomy is not always obvious and simple, especially in a busy ED, where the psychiatrist does not have a whole lot of time for evaluation and to obtain additional collateral information, often leading the psychiatrist to err on the side of caution by hospitalizing the patient.

9.2.1.1.1 Confidentiality and Privacy

In the case of Mr. Hardman, I was fortunate in that he readily agreed that I may talk to his girlfriend in private and before he spoke to her again. If he had not given his permission, the ethical and legal mandate of confidentiality would prevent me from making the initial contact and delivering information. Confidentiality has a long tradition, and extends to all areas of medicine. Not only would I not be able to contact her, but if she called me I would not even be able to confirm or deny his presence in the hospital (the latter in this case being a moot point, as she accompanied him to the hospital). However, without his permission, I would not be able to convey any information regarding his treatment or disposition, but the limits of confidentiality do not extend to my ability to listen to any information she should convey, provided that she be the one who contacted me.

Related to confidentiality is the issue of privacy, which poses a challenge for psychiatrists operating in a busy ED. In the case of Mr. Hardman, when I went back to interview him a second time, he was moved from a private room to a multiple occupancy room. I am required to do what is reasonable to ensure patient privacy, and in this case, the best that could be done was to pull the curtain surrounding his bed and close the door leading to the hallway, although in some situations, the latter is not advised or appropriate due to safety concerns.

9.2.1.1.2 Colleagues and Hospital Alternatives

To conclude the story of Mr. Hardman; I was fortunate in his case because not only did I get permission to speak with his girlfriend, but she was also readily available. She did confirm that they had already discussed, and he agreed to what he previously told me, that she would be with him 24 hours a day, including taking him to her work, which she assured me she was able to do, as well as the sleeping arrangements so that she could monitor his comings and goings throughout the night. This was all well and good, thought I, but was it realistic? What if he were to just bail on her while she was working, and couldn't he really just creep out of bed unnoticed if he were so inclined?

Round and round I went, and still I wasn't really comfortable enough with any of the options set out before me. So I did what all clinicians should do when faced with a situation that can't be satisfactorily resolved by continuing to obsess on the topic: I presented my dilemma to a trusted and experienced colleague, who listened thoughtfully until I finished, then said, "How about partial hospitalization?" Perfect. Why didn't I think of that? Something I didn't consider while waxing philosophic in my own private internal ruminations. (Case in point, always ask for feedback from your colleagues). Not that partial hospitalization is a panacea by any means, but it helps. Partial hospitalization, should he buy into it, provides a therapeutic milieu where group and individual therapy as well as medication management with a psychiatrist is provided 5 days a week, for approximately 5–6 hours a day. Of course, this is a voluntary program in an unlocked facility where he could still come and go as he pleased, but it does represent the next step down from the more restrictive environment of the inpatient hospital. To be frank, this was more comfortable for me because while it did provide him with more intensive treatment compared with standard outpatient care, I have to admit, (at least to myself), I also liked it because my ass felt like it just had at least a bit more coverage (not necessarily even true should there be a bad outcome, but I felt the more intensive care made a bad outcome less likely, and beyond that, a good outcome even more likely).

On my way to discuss this option with him, I wondered what I would do should he refuse. But, he did not refuse, albeit perhaps because he knew what the alternative might be. He went directly from the ED to his orientation at the partial program. Still, for the next week or so, I found myself worrying about him and wondering how he was doing, as well as frequently looking over my shoulder for that black-suited authority figure introducing himself as the attorney assigned to me by my insurance company.

The following case is a conglomeration of many cases that are commonly seen by psychiatrists in the ED. It represents for me a very different aspect of ethical considerations compared with the previous case. In the former, I was on the fence about hospitalizing a patient that I clearly thought could have legally hospitalized against his will, whereas in this next scenario, I wanted to hospitalize a patient that, legally, I could not.

9.2.2 Case 2: The Psychotic Patient

Ms. B, a 37-year-old female, presented to the emergency department after she was brought in by police after they found her wandering outside talking to herself, and not seeming to be making much sense, babbling about being in the CIA and asking us to please not interfere with her work.

During my initial interview with her, she presented with adequate grooming and hygiene, dressed appropriately for the season, initially calm without any psychomotor abnormalities, giving way to becoming more hyperkinetic as the interview progressed. She was a bit guarded at first, but generally polite and willing to engage during the interview. Her mood was a bit anxious, and her affect somewhat labile nearing toward anger while discussing specific events she was angry about, but never directed personally toward me. Her speech was of regular rate and rhythm, and a bit loud at times. Initially, her thought process was linear and goal directed, but after about 10 minutes she exhibited some tangential thoughts with occasional loosening of associations. Her thought content revealed both grandiose and persecutory delusions, ideas of reference, and auditory hallucinations (the latter not present during the interview itself). Absolutely no suicidal or homicidal thoughts. Cognitively, she was oriented to person, place, time, and situation. She was able to recall 3 out of 3 objects immediately and 2 out of 3 objects after 5 minutes. She was able to spell "world" backward, and she was able to name the last 3 presidents in succession.

Background information revealed that she had been hospitalized under similar circumstances numerous times, rarely for more than 72 hours. She had been seen by an outpatient psychiatrist numerous times, and had been prescribed several medications in the past, most recently risperidone, and prior to that, olanzapine. She stated that she had not taken her medications for about the past 2 months. She shared that the medication did help her to feel better, but was unable to elaborate as to how this was the case. She reported that she was on olanzapine when it was revealed at her appointment with her PCP that her blood sugar was high, and that her cholesterol was elevated as well. She lamented that she never had this problem before, and she was told by her PCP that it was probably due to the olanzapine. She said this made her quite angry in that she didn't believe her psychiatrist informed her of this possibility, "but I gave her a second chance and started risperidone" she said. She later read on the Internet that it could interfere with her hormones and cause her to lactate, and might prevent her from having children, "at that point I've had it, and I don't want to be on any medication again unless you can absolutely 100% guarantee that it will not have any negative effects on my body."

And on it went, and no amount of patient education would change her mind about starting medications now, the best I got is that she would be open to it in the future, should she feel like she needed it.

Although initially presenting as fairly lucid, it soon became clear that she was floridly psychotic, talking about her work with the CIA, the messages that came to her from the television, having an implant placed in her brain before she was born "so the CIA can always watch what I'm doing, please don't freak out but they're watching us right now." She went on to say that she didn't mind it, she was not afraid of them, and it just simply didn't bother her. The conversation went on in this way for the next 45 minutes.

9.2.2.1 The Psychotic Patient: Ethics Case Discussion

I felt strongly that she would benefit from a hospital stay and medications, but she wasn't having it. I wanted to hospitalize her, I felt it appropriate to briefly take away her liberty if that's what it took to get her treated and restore her to sanity (physician notes indicated that in the past she responded well to medications, which lysed her psychosis and alleviated her thought disorder).

When further evaluating her for a possible 5150 psychiatric hold and transfer to a psychiatric facility, it was revealed that she was able to articulate clearly where she lived, and how her apartment was paid for, the bus routes she would take to get there, and where she shopped for food, and how she obtained the finances to do so (she was on disability and had a payee that managed her finances). California law, as do most states' laws, has very narrow and specific criteria for being able to place someone diagnosed with a mental illness on a legal hold against their will for psychiatric evaluation, these being that the person must be deemed as an imminent danger to self or others, or grave disability, which is narrowly defined as not being able to formulate a viable plan of self-care as it applies to being able to articulate how she would go about obtaining food, clothing, and shelter. Well, she had a solid plan for obtaining food and shelter, and she appeared well-fed and clean, and in terms of clothing, she was certainly well-dressed.

It was clear that she did not meet legal criteria for involuntary hospitalization or treatment. The fact that not only did I think she should be hospitalized, but that I wished there were a way I could get her hospitalized is an example of me placing my values of what is best for her, ahead of her own values. In fact, I knew that should I ever become psychotic and refuse treatment, I would hope that I would be placed on a legal hold, sent to a psychiatric hospital, and should I refuse medication, I would hope the psychiatrist would petition the court to medicate me against my will. Reznek said it well when she wrote, "I judge it preferable to be returned to sanity again than left in a psychotic and 'free' state" (1991, 219). She goes on to elaborate that, "this implies a value judgment—that the harm of being psychotic is greater than the temporary harm of losing one's liberty. Whether a psychiatrist considers involuntary treatment justifiable will depend on his value judgments—on his weighing the values of sanity and liberty" (Reznek 1991, 219). She further argues that "If you do not want to be left in a psychotic but free state, then do not leave your patients untreated. Using this maxim, we conclude that sanity is more valuable than a temporary loss of liberty" (Reznek 1991, 219).

While I may agree with her, this still does not give us legal authority to proceed in placing the patient in question on a legal hold against her will, based on the aforementioned criteria. For me, this is an example of when my personal ethics conflict with the law.

Another common scenario the psychiatrist faces in the emergency department is to determine whether or not a patient has the capacity to consent to a medical procedure or treatment, or to leave the hospital against medical advice. Although any physician in the ED has the authority to make this determination, in the busy ED, this responsibility is often tasked to the psychiatrist. While this section will discuss some of the mechanics of how to assess capacity, the main focus will center on some of the ethical considerations that may arise from such evaluations.

9.2.3 Case 3: The Cognitively Impaired Patient

It was a Saturday, late in the afternoon, about 15 minutes before the end of my shift, when a friendly nurse found me and relayed the message that Doctor B. would really appreciate it if I would do a quick capacity evaluation on one of his patients so that the team could "move things along." She was a bit vague in presenting what she knew of the patient, saying only that it's an elderly guy with advanced dementia who either didn't want something the team thought he needed, or wanted something the team thought was inappropriate, she wasn't sure, "Hey, I'm out of here, he just asked me to find you before I left and to ask if you can please help."

Now I like Dr. B, he's a great guy, and after I'm gone there is not another psychiatrist coming in until the following day. I didn't want to leave him hanging, although I knew that the terms *quick* and *capacity evaluation* are often mutually exclusive.

9.2.3.1 Capacity Evaluation Essentials

The nuts and bolts of the formal capacity evaluation remains essentially the same as it did when Applebaum and Grisso published their article "Assessing patient's capacities to consent to treatment" in the *New England Journal of Medicine* way back in 1988. Basically, and in brief (so as to not to veer too far from the ethical issues that I know you are all dying to get into), it comes down to determining whether or not the patient has the ability to understand his current condition, which includes what the treatment is that is being proposed, why it is being recommended, as well as the potential risks and benefits of the recommended treatment, including the option of no treatment. The patient then needs to be able to manipulate the relevant information, and apply rational thought processes in coming to his decision. Rational thought process does not necessarily preclude making a decision that the evaluator may find unreasonable. The patient must then also be able to communicate his choice, and do so consistently over time.

Allen and Shuster (2002) condensed this nicely into four basic abilities, which are

1. The ability to communicate a choice
2. The ability to understand relevant information
3. The ability to appreciate the situation and its consequences
4. The ability to rationally manipulate information

With this information in mind I began reviewing the chart.

The patient is Mr. L, a 76-year-old retired PhD research biochemist who arrives back in the ED for the third time in the past year under similar circumstances. His neighbors called 911, when they found him outside acting bizarrely. He has a history of Parkinson's disease and mild cognitive impairment. He lives alone, and his only local support is his neighbor, who has been his best friend since grade school. He has a sister who lives in Oregon, but she is unable to take the patient in, as she has her own family, living with her daughter and her three young grandchildren that she is helping to raise.

A chart review and discussions with his neurologist reveal that he has not been adhering to the recommended medication regimen in the treatment of his Parkinson's disease and is now refusing some, but not all, of his medications that were ordered to be continued in the ED.

I find the patient sitting up in his chair, having just returned from the shower. He is seen in his hospital attire, fairly neatly kempt, having recently shaved, and his longish hair is brushed straight back. He smiles rather sheepishly upon approach, and immediately following introductions comments, "I'm glad you didn't come earlier, because they pretty much made me take my meds about an hour ago, and I'm not all that coherent until after I take the [carbidopa-levodopa]." His eye contact is intermittent, often reverting to a misdirected gaze off and to my right. He is cordial enough, albeit a bit suspicious, guarded, and somewhat apprehensive. He's a little fidgety, frequently readjusting his seat. A resting Parkinsonian tremor is evident in his right hand, and he tends to grip the side rail of his seat with his left hand. His mood appears more anxious and irritable than depressed, and his affect is prone toward frequent and brief seemingly nervous half smiles, which give way at times to revealing an underlying seething hostility and anger just below the surface, mostly when discussing "how my doctors think I should be taking my medications." Prosody of speech likewise occasionally reveals a touch of irritability and annoyance. Thought process is a bit tangential at times, and at other times somewhat perseverative, especially when it comes to the dominant theme of his preferred topic, which centers on him knowing more than the doctors about how and when he should be taking his medications. Mr. L states, "I was a research scientist, damn it, and know this shit better than most neurologists, and I certainly know my own body better than anyone else." He then leaned in, and whispered to me as if we were coconspirators in some sort of cabal, "They want me to take the 25/250's 4 times a day, and sometimes I will, but sometimes I take one-fourth of 1 once or twice every other day, or sometimes a whole one once a day, or I might go a few days without taking any, then take a half, and sometimes even a whole one a few times a day, it just depends how my body is feeling, I know what I am doing, believe me."

He goes on to convey that he understands that his doctors believe that "if I don't take it as prescribed, my Parkinson's symptoms might get worse, including involuntary movements, and that I may have cognitive decline. I get it. I know that is the risk, and now that I think about it, I really will try to take it more regularly, at least some of the time." When I ask why the sudden change in attitude, he states, "Well, it seems like I keep ending up here in the ER, so maybe I'm doing something wrong, I don't know."

Cognitively, he knew the month, but did not know the date or day of the week, and he was 2 years off on the year. He knew he was in the ED. He was able to recall 1 out of 3 objects after 5 minutes, and would not attempt serial sevens. He knew who the current president was, but could not name the one previous, and his guess was off by three previous presidents. He refused to participate in the Montreal Cognitive Assessment (MOCA).

I retreated into the nurses' station to confer with his attending physician, who conveyed that he was less worried about the medication piece at this point, and more concerned about the patient going back home to live alone. He was approached by the social worker who discussed alternative temporary placement options, such as going to a skilled nursing facility, a board-and-care facility, or a live-in caregiver, which the patient categorically refused. He refused not only a live-in caregiver, but he refused to have anybody ever come by to offer any type of assistance, saying only, "My friend comes by, that's all I need." I spoke with his friend who later arrived and was able to fill in some more of the details. Specifically, he said that yesterday he knew something was wrong when he noticed the patient outside of his house in his pajamas, walking aimlessly on the sidewalk, changing directions several times, and looking confused. When he came over to check on him, he noticed "a bunch of pills, lots of them, strewn all along the walkway leading to his door. When I asked him what he's doing he told me that he is just enjoying the weather."

The neighbor expressed concern because he used to be able to check in on him almost every day, but he can no longer do that as much due to his personal responsibilities that now require him to be out of town several days a week or more. "The last time I came over there after I was gone for about 5 days, the place was a mess, he was a mess, and he hardly had any food in the house. Sometimes I go and come back and he's ok, but other times, not so much."

The patient is now medically cleared, and not meeting criteria for a 5150 legal hold against his will, as his deficits are primarily cognitive rather than psychiatric, and therefore is not likely to improve from an inpatient psychiatric intervention.

He is now taking up an expensive bed in a very busy emergency department, while being medically stable and therefore no longer requiring treatment in the emergency department setting. The pressure on the staff to move him out is palpable; basically everyone would like him to be discharged as soon as possible, but he needs a safe disposition in order to be discharged from the emergency department.

As Mr. L is refusing placement or in-home care, I am asked to either give my blessing to discharge him home, which is what the patient wants, or to declare him not to have the capacity to make that decision, in which case the patient will be placed unwillingly into a care facility.

I returned to the bedside in order to explore the patient's reticence to the various options put before him, as well as to assess his capacity to make decisions regarding those options. Upon my bringing up the topic of a skilled nursing facility or a board-and-care home, he said, "Forget that. I get around just fine, and what would I do there, try to have a meaningful conversation with crazy or demented people who can't even remember to wipe their own ass? No, I don't think so." He was able to show that he understood that the staff believe he would be safer with that level of care: "They seem to think that I can't, or soon won't be able to take care of basic shit, or that I'll just wander off somewhere, get lost or put myself in danger somehow, but I'll tell you, I would rather just pack it in than dwindle away in one of those places." Regarding having help come to him, he responded, "I don't want to hang around with some stranger in my house, I'm just not comfortable with that, anyway Frank comes around and checks in on me, so if I need help, well, he's all I need."

9.2.3.2 The Cognitively Impaired Patient: Ethics Case Discussion

I head back to my office to contemplate (some may say ruminate or obsess over) this scenario, and the ethical implications involved. The main conflict from my perspective comes down to, once again, autonomy of the patient versus beneficence. If I were to continue only considering my perspective (a dangerous thing), I would feel more comfortable if he were to go to an alternative placement where he can be monitored constantly, have his medications managed appropriately, and keep him safe. It is no wonder that this would be my go-to plan of action, as my area of expertise is that of a medical doctor, so naturally I would tend toward a medical approach to this problem. Beneficence compels me to act for the good of the patient, but the good of the patient is not limited to only medical good.

In terms of minimizing harm (non-maleficence) I would do well to think more broadly, not just be limited to the potential medical harms, but also to consider the harm inflicted by relieving this patient of the autonomy to choose his own fate, which he clearly values highly. If I were to deny him being able to return home, I would not only be putting my values above his, but I would be taking action, which in my view, would benefit the patient. But to do this I will have to violate other moral and ethical codes, specifically autonomy and free will.

Just because I may find his choice unreasonable, does that mean it is the wrong choice for him? After all, did he not show that he possessed those four abilities discussed earlier in this section? Specifically, he was clearly able to communicate a choice, which is to go home, and this choice was consistent for over a period of 24 hours. He also showed that he understood the relevant information. He was able to articulate what his condition was, understood what the medical team was proposing and why, he articulated the benefit to him if he were to go to an alternative facility, the risk of going home, as well as the risk of not having home health assistance. He acknowledged that there was a risk of decompensation if he were to go home, where he lived alone. Finally, his thought process was rational, he understood the pros and cons, and essentially, he felt strongly about not wanting to go to a board-and-care home or a skilled nursing facility, and made his personal values clear, indicating that for him it would not be a life worth living. When it was suggested that this could just be temporary, he retorted, "What, suddenly I will be cured and be sharp as a tack in some doctor's estimation and they will just send me home? Somehow I don't have a lot of confidence the scenario will play out like that."

So what is my problem? Once again, the answer from an ethical standpoint seems clear based on all of the previous information. So why am I ambivalent, why am I hesitating to make this decision? Well for one, I can't seem to shake my natural bent toward paternalism, believing I have more insight into what is best for the patient than he himself has. Essentially, I am doing what Pellegrino (1994:50) described as making "the medical good of the patient the only good and subverts other goods to that good."

Additionally, I worry about a bad outcome, such as him wandering into traffic or some equally horrendous thing. And it would be my fault, or so my thinking goes. Oh, but it doesn't stop there. Just like in the discussion of the suicidal patient, there is the selfish part, the part where I have to make an effort to have my own self-interest take a back seat to the interest of the patient. It's the discomfort of me going home at the end of the day and yet again feeling that my ass is not as sufficiently covered as I would like. For me it is important to admit that to myself, so that I do not unconsciously put my own comfort level before what is best for the patient. If I'm going to do that, I at least want to be conscious of it.

Still, to quell my angst I decided to have one more go with Mr. L. This time I brought his best friend in and we met with him together. Then the magic happened—okay, maybe not magic, but it was still pretty cool. His friend carefully went over, again, that he would not be able to be there for him as often as he had been. He explained that he would be going out of town much more frequently, and just wouldn't be as available as he once was. To my surprise, the patient acted surprised, saying that he did not realize that. I'm thinking, "Is this the dementia, or did I fail to convey this in a clear and concise manner?" In looking back, I think perhaps I did gloss it over, or at least did not emphasize this point enough.

Mr. L ended up agreeing to have a home health caregiver come 4 days a week for a couple of hours, to make sure his medications were organized appropriately and that he was remembering to take them, to help keep up the house, and to make sure that there were groceries in the pantry. He asked his friend if he wouldn't mind setting that up, and the friend said he already researched it, talked to the people, and had the number handy. He was on it immediately. My first reaction was one of relief, and if truth be told, relief for myself first, feeling like I lucked out, and that my anxiety was taken care of. Oh yeah, then I'm sure I thought about how much better it will be for Mr. L to have those things taken care of. I'm sure I did, yeah, that's the ticket.

I was then reminded of the importance of not only gaining collateral information, but using those collateral sources to the fullest extent possible. I also learned the lesson of going back again and again to reinterview the patient, to make sure that all the relevant information is conveyed in a way that it really gets through, at least to the extent that it is possible given the patient's condition. I made the mistake of assuming that because I said something once or twice, that he understood it as much as he was capable of understanding all the various pieces. I think what happened was that a key piece of information (his friend being less available) was imparted early on, at a time when the patient's anxiety was at its highest, when he felt most keenly the intensity of the threat of losing his autonomy. I also believe that Mr. L having a say in how many days and for how long each day someone would come into his home, provided a modicum of empowerment for him.

A major underlying goal informing the nature of Mr. L's evaluation comes down to the question of whether or not Mr. L even had any autonomy left to lose. Honoring his decision to be discharged home does not necessarily mean preserving his autonomy to choose. As with the suicidal patient, there are times when making treatment or discharge decisions against the patient's will, is in fact intervening in order to restore autonomy. In Mr. L's case, it was a little trickier, because if he lacked the capacity to make autonomous decisions for himself, as is often the case in neurocognitive disorders, this capacity was less likely to be restored, in which case paternalism and beneficence become the guiding force by which decisions are made. Another wrinkle in this particular case is that, with him, it is conceivable that if he were at a facility where he was helped to take his medication as prescribed, it very well may improve his cognition.

There are those that argue that perhaps in recent years, in the era of patient-centered medicine, in the era where doctors and authority figures in general are less trusted than they were in the past, and patient empowerment is the overall meme of our culture, that the pendulum has swung too far toward giving autonomy so much weight, that it ultimately can lead to suboptimal care. Shuman and Barnosky (2011: 232) remind us that "Autonomy as an ethical standard is not absolute. Patients must be determined to have adequate capacity to understand and make decisions before acting on their own behalf. In other words, capacity is the standard by which conditional autonomy is expressed."

9.3 Conclusion

This chapter is by no means exhaustive. The goal here is to provide a framework where ethical principles can be called upon to help deliver the best possible care for patients that are commonly seen by psychiatrists in the emergency room setting, an environment where it can be especially challenging to deliver ethical care to difficult patients.

A grasp of the salient ethical principles discussed in this chapter is meant to provide a foundation for the consulting psychiatrist to help navigate the tensions between competing ethical principles, and to readily be aware of ethical issues as they come up. Knowing what questions to ask oneself is a key first step in understanding how one's personal values or strongly held beliefs, if not examined consciously, can impact and sometimes impede appropriate ethical clinical decisions made on behalf of patients whose values may differ from our own.

References

Allen, R S, and J L Jr. Shuster. 2002. The role of proxies in treatment decisions:evaluating functional capacity to consent to end-of-life treatments within a family context. *Behavioral Sciences and the Law* 20 (3): 235–252.

Appelbaum, P. 1988. The new preventative detention: psychiatry's problematic responsibility for the conrol of violence. *American Journal of Psychiatry* 7 (145): 799–785.

Pellegrino, E D. 1994. Patient and physician autonomy: Conflicting rights and obligations in the physician-patient relationship. *Journal of Contemporary Health Law and Policy* 10: 47–68.

Reznek, L. 1991. *The Philosophical Defense of Psychiatry*. New York: Routledge.

Shuman, A G, and A R Barnosky. 2011. Exploring the limits of autonomy. *Journal of Emergency Medicine* 40 (2): 229–232. doi:10.1016/j.jemermed.2009.02.029.

Resource

Appelbaum, P S, and T Grisso. 1988. Assessing patient's capacities to consent to treatment. *The New England Journal of Medicine* 319: 1635–1638. doi:10.1056/NEJM198812223192504.

CLINICAL CARE III

Chapter 10

Anxiety and Mood Disorders in an Emergency Context

Christopher Lentz

Contents

10.1 Introduction: Background 148
10.2 Anxiety Disorders 148
    10.2.1 Panic Disorder 149
    10.2.2 Post-Traumatic Stress Disorder 149
    10.2.3 Acute Stress Disorder 150
    10.2.4 Self-Medication of Anxiety Symptoms 150
10.3 Mood Disorders 151
    10.3.1 Depression 151
        10.3.1.1 Symptoms 152
        10.3.1.2 Assessing Depression in an Emergency Setting 153
        10.3.1.3 Suicidal Ideation and Suicide 154
        10.3.1.4 Suicidality: The Middle Ground 155
        10.3.1.5 Non-Suicidal Self-Injurious Behavior 157
        10.3.1.6 Parasuicidal Gestures 158
    10.3.2 Bipolar Disorder 158
        10.3.2.1 Mania 159
10.4 Medical Mimicry: Conditions Posing as and Associated with Anxiety or Mood Disorders 160
    10.4.1 Hypo- and Hyperthyroidism 160
10.5 Treatment Options for Anxiety and Mood Disorders 161
    10.5.1 Medications 161
        10.5.1.1 Antidepressants 161
        10.5.1.2 Anxiolytics 163
        10.5.1.3 Mood Stabilizers 165
    10.5.2 Therapy 167
        10.5.2.1 Relaxation Skills Training: Quick Interventions for the Emergency Setting 167

  10.5.2.2 Cognitive Behavioral Therapy Interventions: Changing the Patient's Frame of Mind 168
  10.5.2.3 Encouraging Patient Self-Care: The Positive Outcome on Anxiety and Mood Disorders 169
10.5 Conclusion 171
References 171

10.1 Introduction: Background

Nationally, emergency departments (EDs) are experiencing an influx of patients seeking treatment for a variety of mental health crises. Among these mental health crises, anxiety and mood disorders are common and presented in EDs at a rate of 24.2% in 2009 and 2010 (Centers for Disease Control and Prevention 2009–2010). Between 2006 and 2013, there was an overall increase of 64.5% in male patients 45–65 years old seen in EDs in the United States for depression, anxiety, or stress-related issues (Weiss et al. 2016). With the advent of federally funded national healthcare, all arenas of medical care have experienced an increase in patient census.

Disorders, with varying symptoms, ranging from panic attacks, post-traumatic stress disorder (PTSD), and generalized anxiety to major depression and mania will present in patients arriving to the ED for treatment when the symptoms they are experiencing have become acutely exacerbated and are negatively impacting the patient's ability to cope with the symptoms and participate in socially sanctioned activities of daily life. Typical anxiety disorders that we see in the ED include panic attacks, PTSD, and to a lesser degree, generalized anxiety disorder. Of the mood disorders, depression and bipolar are most often associated with self-injurious behaviors and suicidal thoughts. For example, a patient who is severely depressed may reach the point of contemplating or even making attempts to carry out suicide.

When patients present themselves for treatment, family members, friends, coworkers, or even community service agency representatives (e.g., law enforcement) may transport a patient suffering from an acute exacerbation of an anxiety or mood disturbance to the ED for help, especially when the symptoms the patient is exhibiting begin to negatively impact the people in their social network or if concern about the individual's ability to care for themselves or maintain their safety comes into question. For instance, a patient experiencing recurrent panic attacks may be unable to function at work or within their family structure.

Given the increased national presentation of anxiety and mood disorders in EDs, it is imperative that ED staff, including physicians, nurses, and psychiatric clinicians, are properly prepared to adequately treat and support patients presenting with these complaints. Anxiety and mood disorders can afflict any and all individuals. This can include your family members, friends, and even coworkers. It is important that any individual working in the ED setting understands how these disorders affect the patients that they may come across on a shift in the ED and how that patient should be treated. The treating clinician, whether it be a nurse or psychiatric social worker, needs to use insight and be aware of their own bias related to working with anxiety and mood disorders to prevent a potential damaging experience for a patient in need. For example, statements made to a patient like, "Hey, you have nothing to feel depressed about" or "Just calm yourself down, why are you allowing yourself to feel so anxious" do not help the patient feel supported and can have an iatrogenic effect.

What are the more common anxiety and mood disorders that the ED team needs to be prepared to treat? What are the common syndromes and symptoms that the ED staff should be aware of? How are these disorders treated and what methods of treatment are used in an ED setting? These are some of the pertinent questions that this chapter will answer.

10.2 Anxiety Disorders

Anxiety disorders are very prevalent in the general population with a lifetime rate of about 29% in adults (National Institute of Mental Health 2005a) and 25% in children (National Institute of Mental Health 2005b). Of all the anxiety disorders, specific phobias tend to have the highest prevalence rate (National Institute of Mental Health 2005c). In 2009 and 2010, EDs saw and treated 14.5% of all patients for anxiety-related issues out of all those treated for a primary mental disorder (Centers for Disease Control and Prevention 2009–2010).

In the ED setting, of the primary anxiety disorders, panic disorders, and exacerbations of prior acute stress symptoms are common patient presentations. Acute stress disorder may also be commonly seen in the ED, especially, if a patient has experienced any type of life-threatening trauma. Many patients that experience a primary anxiety disorder may feel debilitated during an anxiety attack and a sense of shame after the episode has ceased. It is important that ED clinicians are aware of this and act to support the patient both during and after the anxiety episode. The patient needs to be reassured that the anxiety episode is temporary and can be managed by the patient, with proper treatment, in the future. This will help to instill a sense of hope and a positive internal locus of control for the patient. Many therapeutic options exist for treating the primary anxiety disorders. Medication interventions, talk therapy, relaxation skills training, and mindfulness skills have all been used as effective treatment modalities.

10.2.1 Panic Disorder

The experience of panic disorder symptoms can create a sense of terror and a feeling of being overwhelmed for the patient coping with the illness. Many patients describe the experience of the panic attack as akin to having a heart attack or simply state that they felt like they are going to die during the episode. When the patient presents to the ED with a panic attack, there may be multiple physical complaints that are described. Racing heartbeat, shortness of breath, chest pain, dizziness, nausea, numbness in the hands or feet, and a feeling of losing control, going crazy, or dying may be experienced by the patient who has gone through a panic attack (American Psychiatric Association 2013).

In these cases, more often than not, the chief complaint tends to be a medical one due to the highly physical nature of the panic symptoms (Härter et al. 2003). Many patients with panic disorder may complain of experiencing symptoms similar to those of a heart condition (Fleet et al. 1996; Lynch and Galbraith 2003). The assigned ED physician will perform a focused medical examination and routine laboratory tests to rule out any possible medical cause for the complaint. Once the medical examination and laboratory results show normal physical functioning, the ED psychiatry team may be consulted to meet with the patient to help diagnose panic disorder. Patients that experience panic symptoms tend to frequently use ED and emergency medical services for treatment of their symptoms (Marchesi et al. 2004; Zane et al. 2003).

Typically, anxiety disorders do not require inpatient psychiatric hospitalization to treat and can be managed well on an outpatient basis (Zeller 2010). Unfortunately, a small percentage of patients that experience panic disorder may need to be psychiatrically hospitalized to help stabilize their symptoms depending on how acute the symptoms are and how severe the patient's ability to care for themselves is affected by the disorder. Suicidal thoughts may also be present in patients with anxiety disorders, especially if they reach a point in which they are unable to continue to cope with and manage their symptoms (Sareen et al. 2005; Weissman et al. 1989). These patients may also require inpatient psychiatric treatment, if they are unable to maintain their personal safety without supervision.

The *Diagnostic and Statistical Manual of Mental Disorders*, fifth edition (DSM-5) (American Psychiatric Association 2013) has provided more flexibility in the diagnostic arena for clinicians working with patients that present with panic symptoms. A panic attack can be diagnosed in a patient, provided that they meet the diagnostic criteria for the attack, with any other type of primary mental illness. For example, a patient that has been coping with major depression for many years may start to experience panic attacks. The panic attacks, in this case, can be added to the patient's diagnostic picture. This can be useful for coding and billing purposes for the treating clinician.

10.2.2 Post-Traumatic Stress Disorder

Post-traumatic stress disorder (PTSD) is, per the DSM-5, a trauma and stress-related disorder due to the main diagnostic requirement that the patient must have experienced or witnessed a stressor that they believed was life-threatening in nature. Common examples of stressors that may elicit PTSD symptoms in a patient include rape, attempted murder, surviving a natural disaster, such as an earthquake or hurricane, or war-related incidents, such as gunfire or bombings.

PTSD was initially referred to as "shell shock, bullet wind, soldier's heart or battle fatigue" when it was first identified and diagnosed in soldiers in World War I that had been through live combat experience (Jones 2010). It has become a more well-known disorder in recent decades due to soldiers experiencing war trauma in the Gulf region wars.

As stated earlier, a patient may not present to the ED requesting to be treated for PTSD in and of itself, but rather will present with a primary complaint of exacerbation of one or more of the associated symptoms of the disorder. Symptoms such as flashbacks, recurrent nightmares leading to insomnia, and consistent experiences of psychic numbing are some of the complaints the patient may request treatment for. Episodes of psychic numbing are especially important for the treating clinician to focus on as these can lead to episodes of depression and possible suicidal thoughts or eventual suicide attempts.

10.2.3 Acute Stress Disorder

Acute stress disorder is another DSM-5 trauma and stress-related disorder that any ED physician will eventually come in contact with at some point in their career due to the number of traumatic experiences that many ED patients go through that bring them to the ED for treatment. About 5% of all patients treated for a mental illness in 2009 and 2010 were treated for an acute stress reaction (Centers for Disease Control and Prevention 2009–2010).

A simple way to conceptualize the disorder is to think of it as a truncated version of PTSD. Many of the diagnostic criteria are similar between the two disorders. The main difference between the two disorders being the amount of time that the symptoms are present. In acute stress disorder, the symptoms are present for at least 3 days and can last for up to 1 month (American Psychiatric Association 2013). The most salient diagnostic criteria that still needs to be present is the actual lived experience of or witness to some type of perceived life-threatening episode.

10.2.4 Self-Medication of Anxiety Symptoms

Alcohol and drug use, such as downers, can provide quick and immediate relief for anxiety symptoms. Many of these drugs are easy to access. All a patient needs to do to help get relief for their anxiety is head to the closest convenience store and purchase a bottle of alcohol. This may be easier, quicker, and less anxiety-provoking for the patient than taking the time to call up their medical office to make an appointment to see their physician or counselor. Even though the use of alcohol and other drugs can provide the patient with quick relief from their symptoms, there are longer-term costs that the patient ends up paying. Continued use of alcohol and other drugs can lead to withdrawal symptoms, which can further increase the anxiety symptoms and create an increased physical and psychological need for the substance that acted as the quick fix for the anxiety. The act of self-medication using alcohol and drugs also increases the risk of developing depression, substance use disorders, suicidal ideation and attempts (Bolton et al. 2006; Robinson et al. 2011). These increased symptoms can ultimately lead the patient to the ED for further treatment.

The draw to utilize alcohol or other drugs can be strong for a patient due to the low cost and ease of access. This may especially be the case for patients that do not have accessibility to outpatient treatment options due to either lack of insurance coverage, funds for provider co-pays, transportation or location. Given this reality, it is important that the ED treatment team work with the patient to address any of the barriers to treatment that they may present with and encourage the use of healthy coping skills.

10.3 Mood Disorders

Major depressive disorder, dysthymia, bipolar disorder, these are some of the mental disorder diagnoses that patients presenting to an ED will seek treatment for. Each of these disorders contain symptoms that have a negative impact on the mood of the individual afflicted with the illness. The changes in the individual's mood strain the person's ability to function personally, socially, and occupationally. People coping with depression may experience an overwhelming feeling of sadness or hopelessness that prevents them from being able to function normally. Conversely, a patient that has been diagnosed with a bipolar disorder may display drastic swings in their mood, moving from high states of elation, during which they engage in reckless sometimes self-destructive behaviors, to low points of severe depression, during which they experience thoughts of killing themselves. Extreme episodes in either mood state, elation, or depression, can cause impairment in the patient's ability to function normally or keep themselves or others around them safe. These episodes can land the patient into an ED for emergent stabilization of their mood.

10.3.1 Depression

A patient is tearful and distraught while being examined by an ED physician. The patient states that she is unable to find the motivation to get out of bed every morning, let alone shower and put on her make up for the day. She reports that she has no energy, feels like she is a burden on her family and feels hopeless regarding anything in her life changing for the better. She informs the ED physician that she has been having thoughts and a desire to "fall asleep and never wake up."

This scenario has been an all too common event showing up in EDs throughout the nation. It has been found that about 10% of all patients treated for a mental illness in the ED setting were seen and treated for a depressive disorder (Centers for Disease Control and Prevention 2009–2010).

The prevalence of depression, anxiety, and stress-related disorders are even higher in some areas of the United States, reaching rates of 62% (Hakenewerth et al. 2013).

Depression can be a debilitating condition when it reaches severe levels in patients. An inability to carry out routine daily activities or the expression of suicidal thoughts may be the prompting factors that lead a patient's family to bring a patient into an ED for treatment of their depression. Many patients that reach this point may also be brought into the ED by law enforcement officers if they have been unwilling or unable to seek out treatment for their depressive symptoms on their own. Sometimes, the call to a law enforcement agency is made by concerned family members, friends, or neighbors of the patient.

10.3.1.1 Symptoms

The primary symptom that is the cornerstone of a depressive disorder diagnosis is a sad or depressed mood that the patient describes as being present for most of the day, nearly every day, for a period of 2 weeks (American Psychiatric Association 2013; National Institute of Mental Health 2016b). Patients may describe their depression using statements such as "I'm feeling blue," "I'm feeling down and out," "melancholy," or "I feel down in the dumps." Patients coping with depression may not be able to identify an external trigger for the depressed state and, many times, unfortunately, there is no socio-cultural or environmental cause for the depression. This can be a point of frustration for the patient who is left wondering why they are feeling the way they are feeling.

Brief education about the etiology of depression can help to elucidate the patient's experience and can be beneficial to a patient left in this state of bewilderment. In some patients, an external or social cause of the depression may exist and can be remedied once the external cause has been addressed. In one case, a female patient presented to the ED for treatment of a depressed mood and suicidal thoughts. She did not have a long-standing history of depression or treatment for it, but recently discovered, to her dismay, that her husband had been living a second life in another country. He had a second family with a wife and multiple children that he had created while on business trips to the country.

In addition to feeling sad or depressed, other common symptoms of depression include

- Anhedonia: This is a loss of interest or pleasure in activities or hobbies that the person once found enjoyable.
- Increased irritability or agitation: The patient may feel easily angered by the acts of others or by things they find to be frustrating.
- Restlessness: The patient feels like they are unable to sit still and may feel the need to move around.
- Psychomotor retardation: The patient's physical movements and speech may appear to be slower than normal.
- Decreased energy or feeling fatigued: The patient complains of frequently feeling tired.
- Increased or decreased appetite and corresponding weight gain or loss: The patient may display an increase in eating behavior, which can lead to weight gain or, conversely, a decrease in eating, which can lead to weight loss.
- Insomnia or hypersomnia: The patient may have difficulty falling or staying asleep at night or may display a swapping of sleep cycles in which they are unable to sleep during the night and sleep during the day.
- Decreased ability to concentrate or focus: The patient may complain of having difficulty with being able to learn or retain new information during the depressive episode.

- Feeling hopeless or worthless: Any feelings of hopelessness or worthlessness need to be addressed as these feelings can lead the patient into a cycle of depression and increase the potential for developing suicidal thoughts.
- Recurrent thoughts of death or dying: The patient may experience thoughts or images of their own death or of the topic of death in general.
- Suicidal thoughts: As stated earlier, if the patient's level of depression and feelings of hopelessness reach a high level, the patient may have thoughts of taking their own life.
- Complaints of generalized body aches or pain: It can be common for patients coping with depression to experience physical symptoms such as headaches, bodily pain, or digestive system issues. The ED physician needs to rule out any possible medical causes for these symptoms prior to pointing to depression as the culprit.

10.3.1.2 Assessing Depression in an Emergency Setting

Patients that are suffering from depression tend to have a negative view of the world around them (Beck et al. 1979). It is almost like they are wearing dark glasses that filter out any positive experiences that occur in their life. This negative view can sometimes trickle down into the patient's belief system regarding how depression can affect others around them. In essence, the patient may believe that their depression can be caught by others, similar to how another person may transmit a cold or flu to another person. It is important that the ED treatment team takes some time to properly educate the patient regarding the causes of depression, treatment options, and self-care skills. The depressed patient may also place blame on themselves for their condition. The patient needs to be assured that they are not at fault for the depression that they are experiencing.

Suicidal thoughts can and will occur in the patient population that seeks treatment in the ED setting. The topic of suicide can be a scary and intimidating subject to discuss for most people. It is important that the ED treatment team, especially the psychiatry staff, is aware of their own feelings regarding suicide. Some clinicians may be reluctant to discuss the topic due to unfounded fears that talking to the patient or asking them about suicide will cause the person to think about it more or will lead the person to act on their thoughts. The topic of suicide must be discussed in order to complete a comprehensive assessment of depression. Given that many patients that attempt suicide or successfully complete suicide had had recent contact with a healthcare professional prior to the attempt, it is important to keep in mind that the patient may not raise this topic unless they are specifically asked about it (Kemball et al. 2008).

There is some controversy regarding the consultation of psychiatry in the ED for use in assessing any patients presenting with depression as it will increase the overall length of stay for the patient. This has especially been the case with patients requiring inpatient psychiatric admission (Nicks and Manthey 2012). Regardless of the possibility of an increased length of stay, we strongly encourage that a comprehensive suicide screening takes place within the ED in order to catch and prevent any potential patient suicides. The saving of a patient's life will far outweigh, ethically, morally, and financially, any costs incurred by an increase in their ED length of stay.

Typically, we educate health plan systems to start with a brief depression assessment to open the discussion with the patient about possible suicidal thoughts. This assessment can include the use of the Patient Health Questionnaire 2 (PHQ-2) to assess for any possible depression (Kroenke et al. 2003). If the patient has any positive responses for depression found in the PHQ-2, the PHQ-9 (Kroenke and Spitzer 2002) can be administered to further assess for depression criteria and level of severity (American Psychological Association 2016). The PHQ-2 is a truncated version of the PHQ-9. The PHQ-2 contains two questions that are meant to help identify two of the main criteria for a diagnosis of depression. The answers to these two questions are rated on a four-point Likert type scale. The questions are

- Over the past 2 weeks, how often have you been bothered by any of the following problems:
  - Little interest or pleasure in doing things
  - Feeling down, depressed, or hopeless

10.3.1.3 Suicidal Ideation and Suicide

Suicidality is a complex and anxiety-provoking topic for many clinicians to think about or discuss, especially with our patients. Suicide is defined as the act of killing yourself because you do not want to continue living (Merriam-Webster 2017). Suicide is reported to be the 10th leading cause of death in the United States, with an estimated 44,000 completed suicides per year (American Foundation for Suicide Prevention n.d.). Men are more apt to attempt and successfully complete a suicide. It has been estimated that about three to four times more men, when compared with women, commit suicide (American Foundation for Suicide Prevention n.d.; Diekstra and Gulbinat 1993). Of those that complete suicide, many have had recent prior contact with a medical or mental health provider prior to the suicide (Luoma et al. 2002).

Suicidality can be conceptualized as occurring on a spectrum (Greenhill and Waslick 1997). There will be patients that come to the ED for treatment that will fall on the polar ends of this spectrum, and there will be those patients that fall somewhere in the middle ground. Patients who display passive suicidal thoughts, for example, making statements such as "some days I wish I could just go to sleep and never wake up," fall on the less acute end of the suicidality spectrum. Other patients who have been actively planning out a specific way to end their life and may have had prior suicide attempts, fall on the acute end of the suicidality spectrum.

The clinical decision process is usually straightforward with patients that fall on the polar ends of the spectrum. Those that express more passive suicidal thoughts can be discharged home from the ED with linkage to outpatient mental health services, while those that fall on the acute end of the spectrum may need to be placed on an involuntary psychiatric hold and referred for inpatient psychiatric hospitalization.

Given the wide variation that exists in suicidality, it is important that the ED treatment team adds a comprehensive suicide evaluation to their risk assessment. As stated earlier, this topic needs to be broached with the patient, as many patients may not talk about their suicidal thoughts or admit to experiencing them unless they are prompted to do so. At times, patients may come into the ED expressing vague or generalized physical complaints during the initial triage process. Later, during the ED physician's physical examination of the patient, the true nature of the patient's complaint, suicidal thoughts, may be disclosed to the ED physician or their treating nurse. Unfortunately, due to the stigma that society attaches to mental illness and suicide, many patients may be reluctant to state that this is the real reason for why they are seeking help in the ED. The patient will have fears of what will happen to them if they are honest about their thoughts of suicide. Fear of the unknown is a strong motivating factor preventing most people from taking action or attempting new things. These fears, though, can be legitimate. Patients may be afraid that if they discuss their thoughts of suicide that they will be placed in a strait jacket and shipped off to the "funny farm" or "nut house."

Patients can lose some of their civil liberties if they are deemed by the ED treatment team to be a danger to themselves and the topic of suicidality can raise these concerns in any treating clinician. It is important to remember that the suicidal thoughts in and of themselves do not create a dangerous situation for the patient.

It can help to keep in mind the statistics on how many patients do not end up killing themselves, while making a discharge decision on the patient. All in all, very few people end up killing themselves. For instance, in 2014 there were 2,626,418 recorded deaths in the United States, of these deaths 1.6% were due to suicide. Compare this to deaths caused by heart disease in the same year, which was at 23.4% of the total deaths (Kochanek et al. 2016).

Many patients experiencing suicidal thoughts, even those that have developed a plan for suicide, can be safely discharged from the ED with the development of a safety plan. The safety plan should include ways to limit a patient's access to lethal means to kill themselves. For instance, firearms are frequently cited as the most commonly used method of suicide in most completed suicides (Kochanek et al. 2016), and access to them should be asked about during the psychiaric assessment. If the patient admits to having access to firearms, steps can be taken to help ensure that this access is removed prior to discharging the patient from the ED. It is usually patients that express a strong desire to die and have lost the hope and will to live and who are contemplating suicide that need emergent intervention in the ED.

For many patients, the idea of suicide may be a way to solve an ongoing life problem that is plaguing them. With these patients, it can be helpful to use the statement "suicide is a permanent solution to a usually temporary problem." This line of thinking, that suicide is the only way to solve a problem, also points to the pessimistic frame of mind that many of these patients display while in a depressive episode. It can be difficult for these patients to conceptualize any other possible solutions for the way they are feeling.

10.3.1.4 Suicidality: The Middle Ground

Revisiting the suicidality spectrum, we stated that there are patients that will fall on the polar ends of the spectrum and those that fall in the middle ground. But, who are these middle ground patients? The ED treatment team will come in contact with patients that can be labeled chronically suicidal, those who have a secondary gain for expressing suicidal thoughts, and those who discuss wanting to die due to suffering from a chronic illness or debilitating disease. These patients can be classified as falling in the middle ground of the suicidality spectrum.

There are patients that can be classified as being chronically suicidal. These patients tend to cope with any psychosocial stressors in the world around them by shifting to a mindset of suicide. These patients may frequently come to the ED for treatment of depression and suicidal ideation anytime a new life stressor arises. They may present with the same rehearsed plan for killing themselves each time they present to the ED for treatment. Many patients with borderline personality disorder present with chronic suicidal thoughts and may be sent to an ED for treatment after a suicidal gesture (Paris 2002).

The second class of patient to fall into the middle ground of the suicidality spectrum is the patient that expresses suicidal thoughts in hopes of gaining something for themselves (Bundy et al. 2014). The gain may range from acquisition of material objects, such as a refill on a prescription of a pain killing medication, to the hope of being provided basic needs, such as placement in a shelter or housing program.

A young African American patient arrives to the ED asking to be admitted because he reports he is hearing voices telling him to kill himself by running into moving traffic in the street and that he will follow through with killing himself if he is discharged from the ED. The patient is homeless and is a frequent utilizer of ED services. The patient has been labeled a "hospital hopper" due to his frequent admits to the EDs in the area. The patient is dressed well and appears to be healthy and well nourished. The patient looks like he has shaved his face recently. Given this patient's presenting risk factors of command auditory hallucinations instructing him to kill himself and his unwillingness to commit to safety, many ED clinicians may be reluctant to discharge this patient without having access to the patient's prior medical records from other ED admits.

This case points to a relevant side note, the importance of having access to a shared electronic medical system that provides a link to medical records spanning multiple hospital systems for the treating ED clinicians. There are also simpler options of add-on treatment planning programs that will allow selected information to be shared among hospital systems. One obvious utility is behavioral health information, but the benefit to the treatment of other medical issues is also prevalent. In addition to the clinical benefits of a shared information system, these programs have demonstrated a financial benefit for the hospital systems that use them.

This patient presented a pattern of self-presenting to local EDs reporting suicidal thoughts and command hallucinations as a way to gain access to temporary shelter and a food source to provide him a safe place to metabolize his methamphetamine high. In essence, this patient's secondary gain in expressing suicidal ideation was temporary shelter, food, and providing for his basic need for safety.

There are many other common reasons for expressing suicidal ideation as a means of gaining something that the ED clinician may come in contact with. We have come across patients in the ED setting reporting that they are feeling suicidal in order to avoid a current stressor, such as a violent relationship or an upcoming court hearing. Other patients may play the suicide card in a game of manipulation in order to gain access to pain medications, for example, "If you do not refill my pain meds I will kill myself" or to get time off from work granted by the ED physician. In many of these cases, if the clinician is able to have a frank and honest conversation with the patient about what their underlying true need is and the need is able to be met, or compromised on, the report of suicidal thoughts will cease.

Any interactions with patients that present with suicidal thoughts who are frequent utilizers of the ED service must be clearly documented by the ED treatment team on each and every visit that the patient makes to the ED. A clear treatment, discharge and safety plan should be included in the documentation (Bundy et al. 2014). Even if there is an established pattern of manipulative behaviors from the patient showing that they have not attempted to kill themselves despite numerous threats to do so, these patients still can end up killing themselves accidentally. Clear, consistent, and comprehensive ED assessment notes will display that the ED treatment team provided the patient with the same consistent care that any other ED patient received. Operationally, we are recommending the use of shared medical record technology, as stated earlier, and a consistent treatment team in the ED to help enhance this process.

At times, a patient with the complex issue of death and dying will present to the ED either for ongoing treatment of a chronic debilitating medical issue or due to family or caregiver's concerns about suicidal statements that the patient has been expressing. Patients coping with chronic debilitating illnesses, such as cancer or end stage renal disease requiring dialysis, may reach a point when they begin to feel overwhelmed with their medical condition and express a desire to die or end their life in order to end their suffering. Many of these patients may not have had any prior experiences with suicidal thoughts or have never made a suicide attempt at any point in their life. In these cases, the patient's statements about wanting to die may be legitimate, as they view death as the only way to cope with the illness they are suffering from. These patient statements about death and dying may not be suicidal in nature. Many of these patients do not actually want to kill themselves, but only seek relief from their debilitating symptoms in the form of proper medication management and supportive counseling.

One of the most complex patients to assess and treat is the chronically suicidal patient. A chronically suicidal patient is a patient that expresses a desire to end their life on a daily basis. The suicidality, in a sense, becomes part of their daily mindset and can be overwhelming for both the patient's support system and providers that are attempting to treat the patient. The chronically suicidal patient can create a clinical conundrum for the ED treatment team due to the fact that the patient is expressing suicidal thoughts, but this behavior may be considered to be the patient's normal daily level of functioning. How is the treating clinician supposed to make a sound clinical judgment about the direction the patient's treatment should take? Should they psychiatrically hospitalize the patient because of the presence of suicidal thoughts or should the patient be discharged home with outpatient follow-up in place? As stated previously, there is a potential, albeit small, for patients to kill themselves, whether accidentally or intentionally, so it is imperative that the chart documentation is clear and demonstrates the thought process that the treatment team was engaged in while developing a patient's treatment plan (Litman 1989). For comprehensive information, please refer to Chapter 8 on discharge planning.

10.3.1.5 Non-Suicidal Self-Injurious Behavior

Sally, a young adult, arrived at the ED for treatment of multiple lacerations to her left wrist. She had purposely cut on her wrist with a razor blade that she had taken from a disposable razor she broke at home. Upon assessment, Sally reports that she had had an argument with her boyfriend of 3 months and he ended their relationship. Sally states that she purposely cut on her wrist with the razor in order to numb her emotional pain. This scenario is a prime example of what is termed non-suicidal self-injurious behavior (NSSIB). NSSIB is typically engaged in by a patient that has difficulty coping with emotional pain. The act of inflicting physical pain on the body is meant to dull or extinguish the flames of the emotional pain (Butler and Malone 2013; Klonsky 2007).

There are a variety of ways that patients may harm themselves using NSSIB. Cutting with razors, knives, or glass is common. In addition, patients may either burn or brand themselves with cigarettes or cigarette lighters or may simply scratch their skin, hit themselves, or bang their head on a hard surface (Butler and Malone 2013; Zetterqvist 2015). The acts of cutting and burning oneself are reported more by women, while men tend to report engaging in acts of burning or hitting themselves (Kerr et al. 2010). NSSIB is typically not engaged in for the purpose of attempting suicide, although family members or friends of the patient that engages in NSSIB may view these acts as suicide attempts, prompting them to bring the patient to an ED for a psychiatric evaluation.

Even though the intent behind NSSIB is quick relief of emotional pain, the acts to relieve the pain are, in and of themselves, acts of self-harm and can potentially lead to an accidental death. Some patients that use NSSIB on a regular basis to cope with their emotional upsets can develop a tolerance in the body to sensing pain. Many of these patients require increased amounts of pain to continue to experience the same emotional dulling response and hence can end up cutting deeper or burning themselves for longer time intervals, leading to a higher potential for accidental death. NSSIB has been found to have a higher prevalence of occurrence in the population within adolescent and young adults (Kerr et al. 2010). Adolescent girls have a higher prevalence of engaging in NSSIB compared with boys (Zetterqvist 2015). NSSIB can reach severe levels during which the patient may engage in acts that are considered self-mutilating. The patient may initially end up being admitted to the ED for medical treatment of the self-injurious act and then end up being evaluated by the psychiatric consultation service due to the treating physician's concerns about the patient's motive for the injury.

It is important that the assessing clinician note the motive behind the self-injurious behaviors. Did these patients harm themselves in order to self-soothe a perceived emotional trauma? Was the act of self-harm used to gain something that the patient wanted or needed? Did patients harm themselves in response to hearing command hallucinations or an acute delusional state? The clinician's answer to the question of motive will help determine which direction the treatment plan for the patient's ongoing psychiatric care will take.

There are cases in which a patient acts out irrationally in a psychotic episode by engaging in self-harming behavior versus doing so in order to cope with emotional pain. A patient had cut off his own ear with a knife in response to voices that he was hearing while intoxicated on methamphetamines. The patient believed that if he cut off his own ear, he would not be able to hear the voices anymore. Another patient had cut off a few of his fingers on his nondominant hand and would suck the blood from the wound because he believed ingesting his own blood in this manner made him stronger. A patient with religious-based delusions had cut off his own penis and refused to allow physicians to reattach it because he believed that God wanted him to dismember himself. A patient gouged her own eyes out with her finger nails after she heard the voice of the devil telling her to do so or others around her would die. The brief case examples presented previously would not be classified as acts of NSSIB due to the motive behind the self-injury, which in these cases was a psychotic response to hallucinations or delusional beliefs, versus the attempt to quell emotional pain.

10.3.1.6 Parasuicidal Gestures

Parasuicide is defined as "an attempted suicide in which the intent is to draw attention to a major personal problem rather than to cause death" (Collins Dictionary of Medicine 2005). Parasuicidal gestures include acts in which individuals intentionally harm themselves by making a non-lethal suicide attempt. Intentionally overdosing on a non-lethal dose of medication, cutting the wrist of the arm superficially, or attempting to hang oneself from a non-secure source, are all examples of parasuicidal gestures. Females tend to engage in parasuicidal gestures more often than their male counterparts and the act of overdosing on psychotropic medications tends to be the most common method of parasuicide (Diekstra and Gulbinat 1993; Mauri et al. 2005; Platt 1992). Just as NSSIB can lead to an accidental death if the method used is severe, so is the case with parasuicide. Parasuicidal gestures have been found to be a predicting factor in successfully completed suicides (Comtois 2002).

10.3.2 Bipolar Disorder

The experience of living with a bipolar disorder for many patients can be similar to riding the dramatic ups and downs of an emotional roller coaster. This emotional roller coaster will start by taking the patient up the steep track to the top of the hill of the elation of a manic episode and then plummet them down the steep track into the depths of a deep depression, sometimes all occurring within the same ride. Riding this emotional roller coaster of bipolar disorder can be taxing, emotionally, socially, and sometimes financially, for the patient taking this ride.

The label "bipolar" was selected to highlight the two extreme polar emotions that the patient living with this illness experiences, the high of mania and the low of severe depression. It is usually during one of these high or low episodes that the patient is brought to the ED by family or law enforcement for emergent treatment of the episode. The depressed end of the pole, if severe enough, can lead to thoughts of self-harm or suicide, while the manic end of the pole can drive patients to make poor, sometimes self-destructive, decisions that render them unable to properly care for themselves.

The incidence of bipolar episodes being treated in an ED setting is on the rise. Prevalence rates for patients treated for bipolar disorders in an ED setting have been found to range between 18% and 7% of the total number of patients treated for mental disorders (Boudreaux et al. 2006; Hakenewerth et al. 2013). The number of patients between the ages of 18 to 44 presenting to EDs in the United States for emergent treatment of bipolar disorders or psychotic disorders increased by 56.7% in females and by 61.6% in males between 2006 and 2013 (Weiss et al. 2016).

10.3.2.1 Mania

The hallmark of bipolar disorder is the manic episode, also referred to as mania. Mania can be a euphoric experience for the patient going through it. The emotional high that is felt during a manic episode can drive a patient to engage in reckless behaviors. Spending money in a frivolous manner, engaging in indiscriminate sexual encounters, and embarking on foolhardy business ventures are prime examples of these reckless behaviors (American Psychiatric Association 2013; National Institute of Mental Health 2016a).

The manic patient will exhibit an increase in activities, either goal directed or purposeless in nature, due to a feeling of being energized. This energized feeling may also keep the patient from sleeping for multiple days in a row, yet the patient may still report that they feel energized. The excess energy that the manic episode creates can also bring on an increased state of agitation, leading the patient to become angry or threatening toward others (Allen and Currier 2000). The patient's thoughts may rush through their mind as if the thoughts are racing by. These racing thoughts are usually evident while speaking with a patient in a manic episode. Their speech will be rapid and pressured and may jump rapidly from one topic to another. The patient's thoughts may be so rapid that their rate of speech is unable to keep up with the rate at which their thoughts are entering and leaving their mind.

The euphoric high that the patient can experience during a manic episode may negatively impact their level of insight (Geddes and Miklowitz 2013). Due to the euphoria that can be experienced, the manic patient may be reluctant to seek out help and may only end up receiving help at the urging of concerned family members, friends, or coworkers, or the patient may be involuntarily forced into treatment if admitted to an ED via law enforcement officers. This euphoric experience may lead patients to feel like nothing is wrong with how they are behaving or feeling. The patient may be thinking "If I am feeling wonderful, why do I need to see a psychiatrist for medication?" It has been estimated that about 10%–60%, with a median of 40%, of patients with mood disorders have issues with treatment noncompliance (Lingam and Scott 2002). Patients with bipolar disorder may, at some point, either discontinue, partially take, or overuse their prescribed psychotropic medications (Colom et al. 2005).

To qualify as a true manic episode, the change in the patient's mood and energy level needs to persist throughout most of a day and be present for at least 1 week, unless the patient requires inpatient hospitalization, then any time frame qualifies for a diagnosis of mania (American Psychiatric Association 2013). As stated earlier, the patient in a manic episode can engage in reckless, sometimes socially unacceptable behaviors. Some of these behaviors highlight the heightened sexual arousal that some patients may experience. A manic female patient admitted to the ED for emergent treatment began to masturbate while lying on the gurney in front of ED staff and her spouse. A male patient accosted a female nurse asking her to lift her top and expose her breasts and then requested that she touch his genitals.

At times, the manic episode may lead a patient to experience grandiose delusions. Another patient, during a manic state, went to a marina with paint and paint supplies he had purchased and began to paint the exterior of a sailboat that he did not own. He believed that he owned the sailboat and was an adept sailor, but in reality, he had not sailed a day in his life.

10.4 Medical Mimicry: Conditions Posing as and Associated with Anxiety or Mood Disorders

The art of conducting a proper psychiatric diagnosis can be quite a challenge in the ED setting given that the ED clinician is plagued by time constraints, large patient volumes, and limited patient medical information. The diagnostic process can be even further muddled by the presence of medical conditions that take on the appearance of or mimic the symptoms of a psychiatric disorder.

This medical mimicry can create issues with misdiagnosing an underlying medical illness as one that is psychiatric in nature or vice versa (Estroff and Gold 1984; Hentz 2008; Pies 1994). Inflammation in the body brought on by an infection can directly affect the brain and the development of depressive symptoms (Dantzer et al. 2008). Similarly, symptoms of a major depressive disorder can arise after a bout of mononucleosis (Estroff and Gold 1984). Patients coping with chronic medical illnesses can also experience mood or anxiety disorders at the same time (Simon 2001).

It has also been found that certain psychiatric illnesses are risk factors for developing medical issues or exacerbating chronic medical conditions. For instance, depression has been found to be a risk factor for the development and exacerbation of diabetes (Williams et al. 2006). An association has been found between the presence of anxiety disorders and the occurence of heart disease, high blood pressure, gastrointestinal disorders, and migraine headaches (Härter et al. 2003).

These issues highlight the importance of conducting a complete medical examination on the patient to rule out a medical cause of a psychiatric complaint that brought the patient to the ED. Although, the clinical information gleaned from a medical examination may not help to answer the "chicken or egg" question of which illness presented first. Knowing this information, the treating clinician is behooved to ask, "Am I treating a medical illness with mimicked psychiatric symptoms or a psychiatric illness that is exacerating an underlying medical illness?"

For coding and billing practices, the DSM-5 has clear explanations for how to properly code psychiatric disorders caused by medical conditions. The ED physician needs to take into account what they are treating. If the ED physician treats the symptoms of depression in a depressive disorder due to an underlying medical condition, the symptoms of depression will not resolve unless the underlying medical condition causing the depression is treated.

10.4.1 Hypo- and Hyperthyroidism

Hypothyroidism and hyperthyroidism are two endocrine system disorders that are not uncommon in patients presenting to the ED for treatment of an anxiety or mood disorder. It is important that the ED treatment team is aware that hypothyroidism and hyperthyroidism can mimic depressive symptoms (Bermudes 2002; Estroff and Gold 1984; Tallis 1993). Hyperthyroidism has also been known to mimic the symptoms seen in panic disorder, anxiety disorders, and the manic phase of bipolar disorder (Estroff and Gold 1984; Hentz 2008). Other endocrine disorders, including adrenal insufficiency, diabetes mellitus, and hyperparathyroidism, in their early stages, can mimic the symptoms seen in depression and anxiety disorders (Estroff and Gold 1984; Hutto 1999).

In order to help rule out the thyroid disorders as a potential cause of the psychiatric symptoms of patients that are presenting to the ED, the ED physician should conduct a comprehensive medical history on the patient. The patient should follow up with their primary care physician for a thyroid function test (Bermudes 2002). If the patient is placed in an inpatient psychiatric facility or discharged back home from the ED, treatment of the thyroid condition can commence.

10.5 Treatment Options for Anxiety and Mood Disorders

Once a patient, experiencing an emergency related to an anxiety or mood disorder, arrives to the ED for treatment, the ED treatment team must take steps to help stabilize the patient's symptoms. The options for treating exacerbated episodes of anxiety and mood disorders in an emergency setting are limited due to constraints on both time and space. Essentially, the ED clinician may not have the luxury of spending 45 minutes to an hour performing psychotherapy on a patient. This is something that is expected to occur in an outpatient mental health setting, and the patient needs to be provided with outpatient mental health resources prior to discharging from the ED in order to help maintain any alleviation from their symptoms that they received during their ED admit. Treatment of anxiety, depression, and bipolar disorder symptoms can occur by use of psychotherapeutic techniques, administration of psychotropic medication, or a combination of the two.

10.5.1 Medications

Psychotropic medications are an effective, efficient, and evidence-based method for treating many of the psychiatric symptoms that present to an ED setting. As stated previously, due to the time constraints and limited space in the ED, the use of traditional outpatient treatment methods, for example psychotherapy, may not be viable care options. The use of psychotropic medications can help bridge the gap in time and physical space that is inherently present in the ED setting. There are a multitude of medication options available that the ED physician or psychiatrist has at their disposal to treat either any emergent exacerbations or ongoing routine symptoms of the anxiety and mood disorders. Many of these medications are available in generic forms, which provides the prescribing physician some leeway in being able to offer effective treatment to patients with financial constraints. Subsequently, you will find a discussion on the various psychotropic medication classes and points to be mindful of when considering these as a treatment option. Please keep in mind that only clinicians licensed to prescribe medications should be making medication starting, stopping, and dosage recommendations.

While reading this section, please note that any uncited references to medication information were written in consultation with Yener Balan, MD.

10.5.1.1 Antidepressants

The antidepressant class of medications, as the name suggests, are meant to fight against the primary symptom of depression, which is a sad or depressed mood. Within this class of psychotropic medication, you will find the commonly used selective serotonin reuptake inhibitors (SSRIs) and the serotonin and norepinephrine reuptake inhibitors (SNRIs).

10.5.1.1.1 Selective Serotonin Reuptake Inhibitors

SSRIs help to relieve the depressed mood or feelings of extreme sadness in patients by preventing the neurons in the brain and other parts of the body from reuptaking the neurotransmitter serotonin from the synapse between the neurons, providing this neurotransmitter with more time to fill the synapse. Common serotonin reuptake inhibitors include sertraline, fluoxetine, citalopram, escitalopram, paroxetine, and fluvoxamine. Some of the SSRIs, for instance paroxetine, can also be used to treat symptoms of anxiety.

When considering the use of an SSRI for treating depression, the ED MD needs to take the time to elicit a comprehensive medication history from the patient. The medication history will help to rule out any potential risk for serotonin syndrome, which can be fatal to the patient if left untreated (Volpi-Abadie et al. 2013). Given the ED MD's time constraints, it may be beneficial to elicit the help of a nurse to gather the medication history from the patient.

Serotonin discontinuation syndrome, also referred to as withdrawals, can be another topic for the ED MD to be mindful of when considering adding an SSRI or SNRIs to a patient's medication regimen. This withdrawal syndrome can occur within 3 days in patients that have abruptly stopped or have been titrating down the dosage of a serotonin-based medication that was used for at least 6 weeks. Typical symptoms include dizziness, headaches, nausea, and fatigue (Haddad and Anderson 2007; Warner et al. 2006). Given the tendency for some patients to discontinue their medications, prior to prescribing a serotonin-based medicine, the ED MD needs to take this syndrome and the patient's medication adherence history into account.

10.5.1.1.2 Serotonin and Norepinephrine Reuptake Inhibitors

SNRIs are another class of antidepressant medication that are similar to the SSRIs in their use of serotonin reuptake inhibiting substances but differ in the use of substances that also prevent the reuptake of norepinephrine from the synaptic gap. The SNRIs are beneficial in treating the symptoms of both the depressive and anxiety-related disorders. Common SNRIs include desvenlafaxine, duloxetine, levomilnacipran, and venlafaxine.

As discussed previously, the prescribing physician needs to be mindful of the patient's medication history in order to limit the occurrence of a serotonin syndrome or withdrawals.

On average, newer, patented SNRIs, like any non-generic formulation of medication, are more expensive to purchase. This added cost burden may influence the patient's ability to adhere to a medication regimen that requires a brand name, costlier medication regimen.

10.5.1.1.3 Bupropion

Bupropion is an antidepressant that is used to treat both depression and addiction to nicotine. It is available as an oral medication with three available formulations: immediate release, sustained release, and extended release (Dwoskin et al. 2006). Care must be taken when prescribing bupropion in the sustained release formulation, as it can lower the seizure threshold in some patients (Sigg 1999).

10.5.1.1.4 Antidepressants Utility Within an Emergency Context

It has been questioned whether starting a patient on an antidepressant medication while in the ED has any practical utility (Lipson-Glick 2000). This questioning has stemmed from the belief that antidepressant medications can take 2–4 weeks to have a biological effect in the body. This 2–4 week time frame was based on the results from clinical trials of antidepressant medications that may not have completed multiple measurements of drug effectiveness early on during those trials (Porter and Ferrier 1999). Parker (1996) attempts to debunk the myth that antidepressant medications have a 2–4 week activation period. Parker reports one study that found a 5-day antidepressant medication activation period, in his review of the literature. Parker further shows that most of the studies he reviewed revealed that patients whose depressive symptoms resolved within 4–6 weeks showed improvement in their symptoms sometime during the first week of treatment.

Lipson-Glick (2000) discussed other historical reasons against administering a new antidepressant medication for a patient in the ED and provides the counter arguments for these reasons. She reports that these medications have no immediate effect on the patient. As stated previously, many antidepressants have been found to have a more rapid activation period than previously thought.

Clomipramine and venlafaxine, when administered in high doses early on in the treatment process, have been shown to have a rapid activation period (Porter and Ferrier 1999). In order to get medication into the patient's system sooner, it can also be a benefit to start an antidepressant medication as soon as depression is diagnosed. Patients started on an antidepressant do experience an immediate placebo response, which can provide relief from depressive symptoms (Parker 1996).

The concern that a suicidal patient may use the antidepressant medications to overdose on in a suicide attempt was also raised. The counterargument is that many of the newer antidepressant medications are medically safer. In addition, if suicidal patients were highly motivated to kill themselves, they could choose from any number of medications to overdose on.

Another argument raised against the starting of a new antidepressant is that the prescribing physician should know the patient well prior to starting a new medication. The patient's stay in the ED can be used as a safe environment in which to start them on a new medication. Many patients are experiencing longer admit times in the ED, some of these spanning multiple days, this time can be used to medically evaluate the patient for any side effects while on the new medication.

It may not be possible to reliably give an accurate diagnosis of depression in an ED setting due to the use of the single assessment. Lipson-Glick reports that studies are finding that an accurate diagnosis of depression can be formulated in an ED setting.

Communicating any changes in a patient's medication regimen to outpatient providers may be challenging to do from the ED, which may limit continuity of care. Lipson-Glick counters this by stating that if the ED providers are able to communicate any medication changes directly to the outpatient provider, then continuity of care can be established.

The decision to start or not start an antidepressant medication for a patient seeking treatment in the ED rests solely with the treating physician. Prior to making this decision, ED physicians should use the information presented earlier in this chapter to help guide their decision-making process. Consultation and advice from an experienced psychiatrist is also recommended in these cases.

10.5.1.2 Anxiolytics

Any medication that is formulated to alleviate or reduce anxiety can be categorized as an anxiolytic. The anxiolytics are primarily made up of the benzodiazepines. Some of the SSRIs, SNRIs, and tricyclic classes of medications also have anxiolytic properties and are used in the treatment of anxiety disorders.

10.5.1.2.1 Benzodiazepines

The most potent class of anxiolytics, and most prominent in the emergency setting, are the benzodiazepines. When used for anxiety-related emergencies, benzodiazepines are primarily used to treat the symptoms of a panic attack and are the most prescribed medication type for this purpose (Susman and Klee 2005). This class of medication is also commonly used to treat agitation (Rund et al. 2006) and alcohol withdrawal seizures or tremors (Sachdeva et al. 2015), two other issues commonly seen in the ED setting. Common benzodiazepines include alprazolam, clonazepam, diazepam, lorazepam, oxazepam, and chlordiazepoxide. Of these, alprazolam and clonazepam have been indicated for the treatment of panic disorder in the United States (Susman and Klee 2005).

10.5.1.2.1.1 Addictive Risks of Benzodiazepines

Benzodiazepines have a potential to create an addiction in patients that are prescribed them for treatment of anxiety-related symptoms. Shorter half-life benzodiazepines are more frequently abused by patients due to their quick anxiolytic response, albeit one that is short lived (O'Brien 2005). This includes medications such as alprazolam, midazolam, and oxazepam. It has been determined that cannabinoids, opioids, and gamma-hydroxybutyrate (GHB) have a similar addiction pathway to the benzodiazepines. These substances work to create a "high" in the brain by opening the door for high peaks in dopamine production within the dopamine-producing neurons by limiting an encumbering response in these neurons (National Institute on Drug Abuse 2012). To avoid an increased risk of addiction to the short half-life formulations, patients should be placed on a dosage taper or can be switched from a short half-life to a longer half-life formulation (Ashton 2002; O'Brien 2005; Susman and Klee 2005). Patients can also be switched to a non-benzodiazepine anxiolytic such as buspirone or hydroxyzine.

Benzodiazepines should not be prescribed for use outside of the ED setting unless it has been verified by ED staff that the patient will have close outpatient follow-up upon discharge in order to allow for close monitoring of the patient's use of the medication. Close follow-up of patient usage is important as unmonitored stoppage of benzodiazepines can lead to severe withdrawal symptoms ultimately leading to a catatonic state (Rosebush and Mazurek 1996) or patient death (Lann and Molina 2009).

Addiction to a benzodiazepine may prompt some patients to self-admit to an ED for the sole purpose of obtaining access to the medication. Patients may engage in what is considered drug-seeking behaviors to obtain a medication. Some of these behaviors include reporting the occurence of headaches, back pain, or dental pain; reporting that the pain is 10/10 or higher on a pain scale; requesting a specific medication or refill of a specific medication; or reporting that the medication was lost or stolen (Drug Enforcement Administration Diversion Control Division 1999; Grover et al. 2012).

One study found that patients that are seeking medications from an ED do so with low to moderate frequency (Grover et al. 2012). Many of these behaviors may be seen in patients seeking to obtain access specifically to opiates or other pain medications, although the reporting of uncontrolled anxiety and request for a specific anxiolytic by a patient may be seen in those with an addiction to benzodiazepines (Drug Enforcement Administration, Diversion Control Division 1999). It is important that the ED physician is aware of the common drug-seeking behaviors and make use of current drug databases, such as the Controlled Substance Utilization Review and Evaluation System (CURES) as used in California, or other nationally used prescription drug monitoring programs, in order to avoid unneccessary medication prescriptions (California Department of Justice 2013).

Hospital administrators may consider creating a benzodiazepine-prescribing policy for the ED setting that acts to limit the number of benzodiazepine prescriptions that are written for patients discharging from the ED. This type of policy may take the pressure off of the ED physician when confronted with a patient that is demanding a benzodiazepine refill and may help to decrease the number of patients using the ED to seek out their benzodiazepine refills.

10.5.1.2.2 Antidepressants with Anxiolytic Properties

Given the addictive risks associated with the benzodiazepines, the ED physician can consider the use of alternative medications to treat anxiety-related symptoms. Many of the SSRIs, SNRIs, and tricyclic antidepressants contain anxiolytic properties and are effective remedies for anxiety and panic symptoms. SSRIs that have been used to treat panic disorder include citalopram, fluvoxamine, fluoxetine, sertraline, and paroxetine (Zamorski and Albucher 2002).

Typical tricyclic medications used include imipramine and anafranil. SSRIs have higher safety and patient tolerance levels when compared with the tricyclic medications, so the SSRIs are recommended over the tricyclic medications for treating anxiety-related symptoms (Zohar and Westenberg 2000). It is recommended when using SSRIs or tricyclic medications to treat panic disorder that the patient be started on a low dose with dosage increases taking place at 7-day intervals ending with the maximum recommended dosage that the patient can tolerate (Zamorski and Albucher 2002).

Of the SNRIs, venlafaxine, desvenlafaxine, and duloxetine are used in the treatment of anxiety disorders. SNRIs are typically only used if a patient had no or a poor response to the SSRIs (Bystritsky et al. 2013). It is important to note a patient should not be prescribed SSRIs and SNRIs together as this combination can increase the chances that a serotonin syndrome will occur.

Some of these medication options can also be effective for children (Velosa and Riddle 2000). Fluoxetine has been found to be effective in the treatment of generalized anxiety disorder, separation anxiety disorder, and social phobia in children and adolescents, aged 7–17 years old (Birmaher et al. 2003). Similar findings in children were found for the SSRI fluvoxamine (Walkup et al. 2001).

Longer-term abstained resolution of anxiety is correlated with longer-term treatment, which includes talk therapy and a more consistent approach to medication. A benzodiazepine provides quick relief and leaves the body quickly. An SSRI takes longer to work in the body and requires concurrent psychotherapy to create the optimal foundation for long-term relief.

10.5.1.3 Mood Stabilizers

Mood stabilizers are the pièce de résistance in the fight against symptoms of bipolar disorder. As the name suggests, the mood stabilizers act to plateau the rising and falling of the patient's mood states. As discussed earlier, if you use the analogy of riding a rollercoaster, with its drastic peaks and falls, to describe the mood fluctuations present in bipolar disorder, the use of mood stabilizers would not stop the roller coaster ride completely, but would act to increase the length of level track in between, and decrease the size of the peaks and falls of the roller coaster track. Lithium, anticonvulsant medications, and some of the atypical antipsychotics have been used in the emergency setting to treat acute bipolar disorder symptoms (Vieta and Sanchez-Moreno 2008). The choice of pharmacological treatment will be driven by what type of bipolar symptoms the patient is currently presenting with and by their medication-response history.

10.5.1.3.1 Lithium

Lithium is a classic remedy that has been used to treat many types of disorders for more than a century. Lithium was used to treat gout in London beginning in 1840. Lithium was first used as a treatment for mania in 1871 by Dr. William Hammond, and in 1894 it was used to treat depression in Denmark. By the 1930s, physicians in Germany were using lithium to treat gall, bladder, and kidney stones, but its use in the psychiatric realm fell silent. In 1949, the Australian physician John Cade resparked the use of and interest in lithium as a treatment method for bipolar disorders (Shorter 2009).

Presently, lithium is still considered to be one of the primary treatment options for bipolar disorder. Lithium has been found to have a more effective response in the treatment of manic symptoms in patients that display an absence of depressive symptoms prior to the manic episode or, in other terms, patients that display a euphoric manic state (Swann et al. 1997; Vieta and Sanchez-Moreno 2008). It has also been shown to be a powerful medicine in the long-term maintenance of bipolar symptoms (Geddes and Miklowitz 2013).

The ED physician needs to ensure that the patient clearly understands how to manage the lithium prescription due to its potential for leading to renal failure in overdose (Haussmann et al. 2015; Timmer and Sands 1999). Lithium has one of the highest rates of ED admits due to improper use and toxicity compared with all other psychotropic medications (Hampton et al. 2014). Given this information, it is essential that the ED physician orders a laboratory test to determine the patient's current lithium blood serum level. Ordering this test will allow the ED physician to determine if the patient's lithium levels are within the medication's narrow therapeutic range. If the lithium levels are too low, there will be no therapeutic response to the medication, levels that are too high can lead to lithium toxicity and potential renal failure (Timmer and Sands 1999).

Lithium is well known for its antisuicidal effects in patients coping with bipolar disorders. There are a plethora of studies and literature reviews available that show strong evidence and support for lithium's ability to stave off suicide (Lewitzka et al. 2015). Lithium's antisuicidal effects are thought to reduce the risk of suicide by reducing the relapse of a mood disturbance and decrease aggression and impulsivity in the patient (Cipriani et al. 2013; Kovacsics et al. 2009; Tondo and Baldessarini 2011). An interesting review of the literature looked at the relationship between lithium levels found in a community's drinking water and the rates of suicide in that community. The review found that higher levels of lithium in the drinking water equated to reduced suicide rates within the surrounding population (Vita et al. 2015). See the article by Lewizka et al. (2015) for a comprehensive review of the literature on the antisuicidal properties of lithium.

10.5.1.3.2 Anticonvulsants

The anticonvulsants were originally developed for the treatment of seizures and related seizure disorders, such as epilepsy. Some of these medications were found to be beneficial in the treatment of bipolar disorder symptoms. In a review of the available literature, Vieta and Sanchez-Moreno (2008) found two anticonvulsant medications that had strong evidence for treating acute manic episodes. These medications are valproate and carbamazepine. Valproate has a quicker activation period compared with lithium and is useful in treating both acute and mixed episodes of mania. Carbamazepine has been found to be as effective as lithium in treating mania (Vieta and Sanchez-Moreno 2008).

10.5.1.3.3 Other Medication Options

Primarily used in the treatment of psychosis, antipsychotics have been found to be a better medication option for the short-term treatment of acute mania when compared with lithium and some of the anticonvulsants. Although, use of the antipsychotics for long-term treatment of bipolar disorder may not be tolerated well by some patients (Geddes and Miklowitz 2013). Olanzapine is useful in treating both acute and mixed episodes of mania and in the prevention of recurrences of mania and depression after a manic episode (Vieta and Sanchez-Moreno 2008). Risperidone, haloperidol, ziprasidone, and aripiprazole have proved efficacy in treating both acute mania and mixed manic episodes in patients with bipolar disorders (Geddes and Miklowitz 2013; Vieta and Sanchez-Moreno 2008).

10.5.2 Therapy

Medications can be a convenient and efficient way to stabilize and maintain any of the anxiety or mood disorders that may arise in the ED patient population. However, the use of psychopharmacological interventions may not be an option for the ED treatment team to rely on, especially in cases were a patient may not physically be able to tolerate medication treatment or in cases were the patient refuses this treatment option. In these cases, psychotherapeutic techniques can be used as a viable alternative. As stated earlier in this chapter, in the ED, time is of the essence so the use of time-limited interventions is recommended.

10.5.2.1 Relaxation Skills Training: Quick Interventions for the Emergency Setting

Relaxation skills training can be used to quickly alleviate acute exacerbations of anxiety or stress-related responses. Two interventions that can be easily taught to patients in the ED setting are deep breathing and progressive muscle relaxation (Corliss 2016).

I will typically start by educating the patient about the bio-psychosocial mechanisms of anxiety, focusing on the body's fight-or-flight response, and then move on to teaching them the deep-breathing skill. The patient is instructed to breathe in through the nose until they fill up their lungs, hold the air in the lungs for about a second and then slowly release all of the air out through the mouth. The patient is instructed to repeat this until they notice a change in their subjective level of distress.

The patient can rate their distress level on any type of subjective units of distress scale (Wolpe 1969). I instruct the patient to use a 10-point scale, with 0 equating to feeling completely calm and at ease and 10 equating to feeling extreme distress. So, the patient can be instructed to repeat the deep breathing until they have moved a given number of points closer to 0 on the 10-point distress scale.

The patient can combine counting along with the breathing as they are instructed to count each breathing cycle they complete. The counting acts as an alternative thought to focus on to help distract the patient from the stimulus that may have triggered their anxiety.

The patient should be encouraged to practice the deep-breathing skill while they are in a calm state of mind for about 10–20 minutes each day. The patient is informed that the daily practice is important if they want to be able to use the skill when they are feeling anxious or panicky. I let the patient know that they can practice this skill anywhere, from standing in line at the grocery store to sitting in a waiting room for a counseling appointment.

Another skill that can induce a state of relaxation in a patient and can be used in an ED setting is progressive muscle relaxation. In progressive muscle relaxation (Jacobson 1938), the patient is instructed to start at one end of their body, either the top of their head or the bottom of their feet, and tense each major muscle group for a few seconds and then relax the muscles and focus on the difference in the experience of the tense versus relaxed state. After the patient has finished tensing and relaxing each major muscle group, they are instructed to rate their level of distress on a 10-point distress scale. If the patient's rating on their distress scale remains high, they are instructed to perform another round of progressive muscle relaxation. For the creation of an even deeper state of relaxation, the deep breathing exercises can be added to the progressive muscle relaxation technique. All the patient needs to do is take a deep breath after they have completed tensing a muscle group. Similar to mastering any new skill, the patient needs to practice the progressive muscle relaxation skill on a daily basis in order to master it and achieve its full beneficial effects.

Hypnosis has also been used in EDs for treating acute anxiety and other psychiatric conditions. When used properly, hypnosis can create a deep state of relaxation in some patients (Iserson 2014; Peebles-Kleiger 2000). This deep state of relaxation can help to stabilize a patient experiencing severe anxiety. Hypnotic inductions can be performed within a few minutes to help alleviate anxiety and stress.

10.5.2.2 Cognitive Behavioral Therapy Interventions: Changing the Patient's Frame of Mind

Patients coping with symptoms of depression and anxiety can become engaged in self-statements, thoughts, or beliefs that are negative in nature and can exacerbate or increase the amount of time that the patient experiences these symptoms. Cognitive behavioral therapy (CBT) interventions target these negative thoughts and self-statements by teaching the patient how to change their frame of mind (Beck et al. 1979; Cully and Teten 2008). When a depressed, suicidal patient arrives to the ED for treatment, their patterns of negative thinking can be elicited during the psychiatric evaluation. It is important that the assessing clinician is paying attention to the patient's statements and overall beliefs about their life. This will help to identify the negative thoughts or beliefs the patient is using and will allow the clinician to develop a cognitive-based intervention to alter their thoughts.

Once the patient's negative thoughts have been identified, the ED clinician can help the patient change these thoughts by engaging in a few simple steps (Anderson 2014). Instruct the patient to

- Write realistic positive self-statements to counterpoise the negative ones.
- Identify times when positive thinking can be used in place of negative thinking.
- Begin and end each day by identifying what will be and what was positive about the day.

These steps can help the patient begin to reframe their thoughts from a negative to a positive structure.

Many depressed and anxious patients tend to lose hope about their condition and may believe that they may never feel happy or calm again in the future. One simple way to combat a patient's negativistic thinking is to instill hope within the patient (Cully and Teten 2008). This can be done simply by informing the patient that if they are motivated and want to feel better, they will eventually feel better. It may help to tell the patient that many other patients, similar to them, have been in the same situation and have received treatment and are generally feeling better about themselves and their lives. When speaking with your patients about their opportunity to feel better, be realistic and honest with them about the treatment process and the work they will be required to put into the process to feel better. If the patient is being started on a medication, the beneficial effects of the medication should be discussed in order to strengthen the patient's sense of hope, but the patient should also be educated about the limitations of the medication's effectiveness.

Even the act of engaging the patient in the development and creation of their treatment and discharge plans can help to activate the patient and move their frame of mind from one of being focused on symptoms to one of being focused on treatment and ultimately feeling better.

10.5.2.3 Encouraging Patient Self-Care: The Positive Outcome on Anxiety and Mood Disorders

Self-care can be an integral part of any patient's treatment plan. Taking care of your personal hygiene, eating healthy meals, sticking to a daily schedule, including normal sleep and wake times, and exercising can help to pull the patient away from a sick role and push them closer to a feeling of normalcy. Evidence also shows that these self-care behaviors can have a positive influence on the severity of a patient's anxiety or mood symptoms.

10.5.2.3.1 Exercise: Work Out and Feel Good

Since the beginning of the twentieth century, exercise has been shown to be an effective method for both reducing and maintaining reductions in the symptoms of depression and anxiety (Franz and Hamilton 1905). For a comprehensive review of the literature on this topic, please refer to the article by Martinsen (2008).

While in the ED, if the patient is expected to have a lengthy stay, it can be beneficial to offer the patient opportunities for physical activation. This can be accomplished by simply having a nurse or ED technician walk the patient around the halls of the ED. Allowing the patient time to stand up and stretch can also be helpful in facilitating the physical activation that the patient will need to continue once they leave the ED setting. Prior to the discharge of the patient, the ED treatment team can provide the patient with general instructions on how much exercise is recommended.

Patients with depression may have difficulty feeling motivated to perform any type of physical activity depending on the level of depression and fatigue they experience during a depressive episode. It can be helpful to acknowledge that the patient will experience days when it will take more of an effort to engage in any type of exercise. In these cases, I instruct the patient to do as much as they feel they can, even if it involves just getting outside for 5 minutes a day to walk around in the sunlight and fresh air.

10.5.2.3.2 Nutrition: What You Eat Can Affect Your Mood

It may not be a surprise to most of us, but what you eat can affect how you feel and the intensity of certain mental health symptoms. Think back to the last time you may have eaten at a fast food hamburger restaurant. How did you feel after eating your order of burger and French fries? Like most of us, it probably left you feeling like you had had a lead weight placed in your stomach and you may have felt fatigued or even drowsy. These are feelings that also can occur in depression.

In adults, consumption of a diet rich in fruit, vegetables, fish, and whole grains may lead to a reduction in depressive symptoms (Lai et al. 2014; Rao et al. 2008). A deficiency in certain fatty acids, vitamins, and minerals can have a bearing on mood states, including depression. Low levels of omega-3 fatty acids, B-complex vitamins, folate, chromium, iron, lithium, selenium, and zinc have all been found to have a connection to depression (Rao et al. 2008). Ingestion of omega-3 fatty acids, specifically docosahexaenoic acid, can help to reduce the occurence of anxiety (Jacka et al. 2013).

Children and adolescents' developing brains and ultimately their mental health are also affected by the type of food they consume. There is a direct positive relationship between a healthy diet and favorable mental states in children (O'Neil et al. 2014).

Consumption of certain substances, for instance caffeine or alcohol, may also either mimic or exacerbate anxiety or depressive symptoms. Caffeine has been known to mimic the symptoms of anxiety and simply stopping its use can alleviate the symptoms (Bruce and Lader 1989). Similarly, drinking alcoholic beverages can increase the risk for depressive symptoms (Fergusson et al. 2009). These findings highlight the importance of including nutritional counseling and a diet plan as part of the patient's comprehensive ED psychiatric treatment plan.

10.5.2.3.3 Sleep Problems? Use Sleep Hygiene

Sleep patterns are another important piece of the self-care puzzle that can have a negative or positive impact on the patient's experience with an anxiety or mood disorder. In the depressive, bipolar, and anxiety disorders, abnormal sleep patterns have been found to increase the severity of any current symptoms and can increase the chances of developing one of these disorders, especially in patients with a biological predisposition (Krystal 2006; Mellman 2006; Peterson and Benca 2006).

Sleep hygiene, defined as "the promotion of regular sleep" (Centers for Disease Control and Prevention 2014), is comprised of specific sleep-enhancing behaviors and environmental changes that can help improve the quality and duration of sleep the patient receives. It is recommended that patients who complain of sleep disturbances set up a regular and consistent sleep and wake schedule. The patient should go to sleep and wake up at the same times each day. The sleep space should be comfortable, relaxing, dark, and free from any lighted electronic devices, such as televisions, computers, or tablets. Lastly, eating large meals prior to sleep should be avoided (National Sleep Foundation 2017). Comprehensive sleep hygiene tips are available from the National Sleep Foundation and American Sleep Foundation websites.

In order to help prevent or limit exacerbations of anxiety and mood disorder symptoms, ED staff should educate and encourage the patient to utilize proper sleep hygiene techniques during their ED admit and provide written sleep hygiene guidelines upon their discharge.

10.5.2.3.4 Personal Hygiene: Stay Clean and Feel Better

The last piece of the self-care puzzle is adherence to personal hygiene. Routine personal hygiene tasks, such as bathing, brushing and flossing your teeth, and combing your hair can be one of the first things that ends up being neglected by a patient coping with depression. For some patients, the mere act of getting out of bed every day may feel like an arduous task, depending on the level of depression they experience (American Psychiatric Association 2013).

It can be beneficial for the patient experiencing depression to place themselves on a daily schedule that includes times for caring for personal hygiene needs and eating normal meals. This can begin in the ED if the ED staff encourage the patient to care for their personal hygiene. The patient should be politely offered times to bathe, brush and floss their teeth, and comb their hair as well as use or change feminine hygiene products, when needed.

Providing the patient with a personal hygiene kit can encourage the patient to think about and engage in caring for their personal hygiene. A personal hygiene kit can include toothpaste, a tooth brush, hair comb, soap, shampoo, and feminine hygiene products. It is important to note that safety considerations should be addressed prior to providing this kit to any patient who may have a propensity for harming themselves. This encouragement of the patient to care for their personal hygiene can help to move them closer to a state of normalcy and away from the sick role.

10.5 Conclusion

Anxiety, depression, and bipolar disorders can create a devastating experience for the individual living with these conditions. Major depression, PTSD, and bipolar disorder, if severe, can impair the patient's ability to function normally. At times, exacerbation of these disorders can lead a person into the ED by concerned family, friends, or neighbors. Panic attacks, suicidal thoughts, and mania can occur when these disorders reach a peak of exacerbation in the patient coping with them. The ED treatment team needs to be educated and prepared to support, adequately treat, and safely discharge patients home who present with these symptoms. The ED psychiatric services team must be able to support the ED physician in the proper assessment, diagnosis, and treatment of these disorders. The ED treatment team needs to remember to take into account co-occurring medical conditions or illnesses that may mimic the symptoms of the anxiety and mood disorders during the diagnostic process. Treatment options that are at the ED treatment team's disposal include medications, to help stabilize acute episodes of depression, anxiety, or mania, and therapeutic techniques, such as relaxation skills training and encouraging the patient to exercise, eat well, sleep properly, and bathe. The important point to remember is that these disorders can be treated and overcome if the ED staff work together in collaboration with the patient to develop a comprehensive treatment plan. Involving our patients in this process can also instill in them a sense of hope and empowerment to help them overcome the challenges that these disorders can present.

References

Allen, M H, and G W Currier. 2000. Diagnosis and treatment of mania in the psychiatric emergency service. *Psychiatric Annals* 30 (4): 258–266. doi:10.3928/0048-5713-20000401-10.

American Foundation for Suicide Prevention. n.d. Suicide statistics. *American Foundation for Suicide Prevention.* http://afsp.org/about-suicide/suicide-statistics/.

American Psychiatric Association. 2013. *Diagnostic and Statistical Manual of Mental Disorders*, fifth edition. Arlington, VA: American Psychiatric Association.

American Psychological Association. 2016. Patient health questionanaire (PHQ-9 & PHQ-2). *American Psychological Association.* http://www.apa.org/pi/about/publications/caregivers/practice settings/assessments/tools/patient-health.aspx.

Anderson, J. 2014. 5 Get-positive techniques from cognitive behavioral therapy. *Everyday Health.* June 12. http://www.everydayhealth.com/hs/major-depression-living-well/cognitive-behavioral-therapy-techniques.

Ashton, H. 2002. Benzodiazepines: How they work and how to withdraw. In *The Ashton Manual,* by Ashton Heather. Newcastle, UK: Newcastle University.

Beck, A T, A J Rush, B F Shaw, and G Emery. 1979. *Cognitive Therapy of Depression.* New York: The Guilford Press.

Bermudes, R A. 2002. Psychiatric illness or thyroid disease? Don't be misled by false lab tests. *Current Psychiatry* 1 (5): 51–61.

Birmaher, B, D A Axelson, K Monk, C Kalas, D B Clark, M Ehmann, J Bridge, J Heo, and D A Brent. 2003. Fluoxetine for the treatment of childhood anxiety disorders. *Journal of the American Academy of Child and Adolescent Psychiatry* 42 (4): 415–423.doi:10.1097/01.CHI.0000037049.04952.9F.

Bolton, J, B Cox, I Clara, and J Sareen. 2006. Use of alcohol and drugs to self medicate anxiety disorders in a nationally representative sample. *The Journal of Nervous and Mental Disease* 194 (11): 818–825.

Boudreaux, E D, C Cagande, J H Kilgannon, S Clark, and C A Jr. Camargo. 2006. Bipolar disorder screening among adult patients in an urban emergency department setting. *Primary Care Companion to the Journal of Clinical Psychiatry* 8 (6): 348–351.

Bruce, M S, and M Lader. 1989. Caffeine abstention in the management of anxiety disorders. *Psychological Medicine* 19 (1): 211–214. doi:10.1017/S003329170001117X.

Bundy, C, M Schreiber, and M Pascualy. 2014. Discharging your patients who display contingency-based suicidality: 6 steps. *Current Psychiatry* e1–e3.

Butler, A M, and K Malone. 2013. Attempted suicide v. non-suicidal self-injury: Behaviour, syndrome of diagnosis? *The British Journal of Psychiatry* 202 (5): 324–325. doi:10.1192/bjp.bp.112.113506.

Bystritsky, A, S S Khalsa, M E Cameron, and J Schiffman. 2013. Current diagnosis and treatment of anxiety disorders. *Pharmacy and Therapeutics* 38 (1): 30–38, 41–44, 57.

California Department of Justice. 2013. *CURES Prescription Drug Monitoring Program.* Sacramento, CA: California Department of Justice.

Centers for Disease Control and Prevention. 2009–2010. Ambulatory health care data. Centers for Disease Control and Prevention. http://www.cdc.gov/nchs/ahcd/web_tables.htm.

Centers for Disease Control and Prevention. 2014. Sleep Hygiene Tips. https://www.cdc.gov/sleep/about_sleep/sleep_hygiene.html.

Cipriani, A, K Hawton, S Stockton, and J R Geddes. 2013. Lithium in the prevention of suicide in mood disorders: Updated systematic review and meta-analysis. *BMJ* 346. doi:10.1136/bmj.f3646.

Collins Dictionary of Medicine 2005. Parasuicide. *Collins Dictionary of Medicine.* http://medical-dictionary.thefreedictionary.com/parasuicide.

Colom, F, E Vieta, M J Tacchi, J Sanchez-Moreno, and J Scott. 2005. Identifying and improving non-adherence in bipolar disorder. *Bipolar Disorders* 7: 24–31. doi:10.1111/j.1399-5618.2005.00248.x.

Comtois, K A. 2002. A review of interventions to reduce the prevalence of parasuicide. *Psychiatric Services* 53 (9): 1138–1144.

Corliss, J. 2016. Six relaxation techniques to reduce stress. *Harvard Health Publications.* http://www.health.harvard.edu/mind-and-mood/six-relaxation-techiques-to-reduce-stress.

Cully, J A, and A L Teten. 2008. *A Therapist's Guide to Brief Cognitive Behavioral Therapy.* Houston, TX: Department of Veterans Affairs, South Central MIRECC.

Dantzer, R, J C O'Connor, G G Freund, R W Johnson, and K W Kelley. 2008. From inflammation to sickness and depression: When the immune system subjugates the brain. *Nature Reviews Neuroscience* 9: 46–56. doi:10.1038/nrn2297.

Diekstra, R F, and W Gulbinat. 1993. The epidemiology of suicidal behaviour: A review of three continents. *World Health Statistics Quarterly. Rapport Trimestriel de Statistiques Sanitaires Mondiales* 46 (1): 52–68.

Drug Enforcement Administration, Diversion Control Division. 1999. Don't be scammed by a drug abuser. *Drug Enforcement Administration.* https://www.deadiversion.usdoj.gov/pubs/brochures/drugabuser.htm.

Dwoskin, L P, A S Rauhut, K A King-Pospisil, and M T Bardo. 2006. Review of the pharmacology and clinical profile of bupropion, an antidepressant and tobacco use cessation agent. *CNS Drug Reviews* 12 (3–4): 178–207.doi:10.1111/j.1527-3458.2006.00178.x.

Estroff, T W, and M S Gold. 1984. Psychiaric misdiagnosis. In *Advances in Psychopharmacology: Predicting and Improving Treatment Response*, by Mark S Gold, R B Lydiard and John S Carmen, 34–61. Boca Raton, FL: CRC Press.

Fergusson, D, J Boden, and J Horwood. 2009. Tests of causal links between alcohol abuse or dependence and major depression. *Archives of General Psychiatry* 66 (3): 260–266. doi:10.1001/archgenpsychiatry.2008.543.

Fleet, R P, G Dupuis, A Marchand, D Burelle, A Arsenault, and B D Beitman. 1996. Panic disorder in emergency department chest pain patients: Prevalence, comorbidity, suicidal ideation, and physician recognition. *The American Journal of Medicine* 101 (4): 371–380.

Franz, S I, and G V Hamilton. 1905. The effects of exercise upon the retardation in conditions of depression. *American Journal of Insanity* 62 (2): 239–256.

Geddes, J R, and D J Miklowitz. 2013. Treatment of bipolar disorder. *Lancet* 381 (9878). doi:10.1016/S0140-6736(13)60857-0.

Greenhill, L L, and B Waslick. 1997. Management of sucidal behavior in children and adolescents. *The Psychiatric Clinics of North America* 20 (3): 641–666.

Grover, C A, J W Elder, R J H Close, and S M Curry. 2012. How frequently are "classic" drug-seeking behaviors used by drug-seeking patients in the emergency department? *Western Journal of Emergency Medicine* 13 (5): 416–421.

Haddad, P M, and I M Anderson. 2007. Recognising and managing antidepressant discontinuation symptoms. *Advances in Psychiatric Treatment* 13 (6): 447–457. doi:10.1192/apt.bp.105.001966.

Hakenewerth, A M, J E Tintinalli, A E Waller, A Ising, and T DeSelm. 2013. *Emergency Department Visits by Patients with Mental Health Disorders—North Carolina, 2008–2010*. Morbidity and Mortality Weekly Report, Atlanta, GA: Centers frfor Disease Control and Prevention.

Hampton, L M, M Daubresse, H-Y Chang, C Alexander, and D S Budnitz. 2014. Emergency department visits by adults for psychiatric medication adverse events. *JAMA Psychiatry* 71 (9): 1006–1014. doi:10.1001/jamapsychiatry.2014.436.

Härter, M C, K P Conway, and K R Merikangas. 2003. Associations between anxiety disorders and physical illness. *European Archives of Psychiatry and Clinical Neuroscience* 253 (6): 313–320. doi:10.1007/s00406-003-0449-y.

Haussmann, R, M Bauer, S von Bonin, and P Grof. 2015. Treatment of lithium intoxication: facing the need for evidence. *International Journal of Bipolar Disorders* 3 (1): 23.

Hentz, P. 2008. Separating anxiety from physical illness. *Clinical Advisor*, March 18.

Hutto, B. 1999. The symptoms of depression in endocrine disorders. *CNS Spectrums* 4 (4): 51–61.

Iserson, K V. 2014. An hypnotic suggestion: Review of hypnosis for clinical emergency care. *The Journal of Emergency Medicine* 46 (4): 588–596.doi:10.1016/j.jemermed.2013.09.024.

Jacka, F N, J A Pasco, L J Williams, B J Meyer, R Digger, and M Berk. 2013. Dietary intake of fish and pufa, and clinical depressive and anxiety disorders in women. *British Journal of Nurition* 109: 2059–2066. doi:10.1017/S0007114512004102.

Jacobson, E. 1938. *Progressive Relaxation*. Chicago, IL: University of Chicago Press.

Jones, E. 2010. Shell shock at maghull and the maudsley: Models of psychological medicine in the UK. *Journal of the History of Medicine and Allied Sciences* 65 (3): 368–395. doi:10.1093/jhmas/jrq006.

Kemball, R S, R Gasgarth, B Johnson, and M, Houry, D Vickers. 2008. Unrecognized suicidal ideation in ED patients: Are we missing an opportunity? *The American Journal of Emergency Medicine* 26 (6): 701–705.

Kerr, P L, J J Muehlenkamp, and J M Turner. 2010. Nonsuicidal self-injury: A review of current reserach for family medicine and primary care physicians. *Journal of the American Board of Family Medicine* 23 (2): 240–259. doi:10.3122/jabfm.2010.02.090110.

Klonsky, E D. 2007. The functions of deliberate self-injury: A review of the evidence. *Clinical Psychology Review* 27 (2): 226–239. doi:10.1016/j.cpr.2006.08.002.

Kochanek, K D, S L Murphy, J Xu, and B Tejada-Vera. 2016. *Death: Final Data for 2014*. National Vital Statistics Report, Division of Vital Statistics, Atlanta, GA: Centers for Disease Control and Prevention.

Kovacsics, C E, I I Gottesman, and T D Gould. 2009. Lithium's antisuicidal efficacy: Elucidation of neurobiological targets using endophenotype strategies. *Annual Review of Pharmacology and Toxicology* 49: 175–198. doi:10.1146/annurev.pharmtox.011008.145557.

Kroenke, K, and R L Spitzer. 2002. The PHQ-9: A new depression diagnostic and severity measure. *Psychiatric Annals* 32 (9): 509–515. doi:10.3928/0048-5713-20020901-06.

Kroenke, K, R L Spitzer, and J B W Williams. 2003. The patient health questionanaire-2: Validity of a two-item depression screener. *Medical Care* 41 (11): 1284–1292.

Krystal, A D. 2006. Sleep and psychiatric disorders: future directions. *Psychiatric Clinics of North America* 29 (4): 1115–1130. doi:10.1016/j.psc.2006.09.001.

Lai, J S, S Hiles, A Bisquera, A J Hure, M McEvoy, and J Attia. 2014. A systematic review and meta-analysis of dietary patterns and depression in community-dwelling adults. *The American Journal of Clinical Nutrition* 99 (1): 181–197. doi:10.3945/ajcn.113.069880.

Lann, M A, and D K Molina. 2009. A fatal case of benzodiazepine withdrawal. *American Journal of Forensic Medicine and Pathology* 30 (2): 177–179.doi:10.1097/PAF.0b013e3181875aa0.

Lewitzka, U, E Severus, R Bauer, P Ritter, B Muller-Oerlinghausen, and M Bauer. 2015. The suicide prevention effect of lithium: More than 20 years of evidence—A narrative review". *International Journal of Bipolar Disorders* 3 (15). doi:10.1186/s40345-015-0032-2.

Lingam, R, and J Scott. 2002. Treatment non-adherence in affective disorders. *Acta Psychiatrica Scandinavica* 105 (3): 164–172. doi:10.1034/j.1600-0447.2002.1r084.x.

Lipson-Glick, R. 2000. Initiation of antidepressant medications in the emergency setting. *Psychiatric Annals* 30 (4): 251–257. doi:10.3928/0048-5713-20000401-09.

Litman, R E. 1989. Long-term treatment of chronically suicidal patients. *Bulletin of the Menniger Clinic* 53 (3): 215–28.

Luoma, J B, C E Martin, and J L Pearson. 2002. Contact with mental health and primary care providers before suicide: A review of the evidence. *The American Journal of Psychiatry* 159 (6): 909–916. doi:10.1176/appi.ajp.159.6.909.

Lynch, P, and K M Galbraith. 2003. Panic in the emergency room. *The Canadian Journal of Psychiatry* 48: 361–366.

Marchesi, C, E Brusamonti, C Borghi, A Giannini, R Di, F Minneo, C Quarantelli, and C Maggini. 2004. Anxiety and depressive disorders in an emergency department ward of a general hospital: A control study. *Energency Medicine Journal* 21 (2): 175–179.doi:10.1136/emj.2003.006957.

Martinsen, E W. 2008. Physical activity in the prevention and treatment of anxiety and depression. *Nordic Journal of Psychiatry* 62: 25–29. doi:10.1080/08039480802315640.

Mauri, M C, G Cerveri, L S Volonteri, A Fiorentini, A Colasanti, S Manfré, R Borghini, and E Pannacciulli. 2005. Parasuicide and drug self-poisoning: Analysis of the epidemiological and clinical variables of the patients admitted to the Poisoning Treatment Center (CAV), Niguarda General Hospital, Milan. *Clinical Practice and Epidemiology in Mental Health: CP & EMH* 1 (5). doi:10.1186/1745-0179-1-5.

Mellman, T. 2006. Sleep and anxiety disorders. *Psychiatric Clinics of North America* 29 (4): 1047–1058. doi:10.1016/j.psc.2006.08.005.

Merriam-Webster. 2017. Dictionary. May. http//www.merriam-webster.com.

National Institute on Drug Abuse. 2012. Well-known mechanism underlies benzodiazepines' addictive properties. *NIDA Notes*, April 19.

National Institute of Mental Health. 2005a. Any anxiety disorder among adults. National Institute of Mental Health. http://www.nimhg.gov/healtrh/statistics/prevalence/any-anxiety-disorder-among-adults.shtml.

National Instutite of Mental Health. 2005b. Any anxiety disorder among children. National Institute of Mental Health. http://www.nimh.nih.gov/health/statistics/prevalence/any-anxiety-disorder-among-children.shtml.

National Institiute of Mental Health. 2005c. Specific phobia among adults. National Institute of Mental Health. http://www.nimh.nih.gov/health/statistics/prevalence/specific-phobia-among-adults.shtml.

National Institute of Mental Health. 2016a. Bipolar disorder. National Institute of Mental Health. April. http://www.nimh.nih.gov/health/topics/bipolar-disorder/index.shtml.

National Institute of Mental Health. 2016b. Depression. National Institute of Mental Health. October. http://www.nimh.nih.gov/health/topics/depression/index.shtml#part_145397.

National Sleep Foundation. 2017. Sleep hygiene. https://sleepfoundation.org/sleep-topics/sleep-hygiene.

Nicks, B A, and D M Manthey. 2012. The impact of psychiatric patient boarding in emergency departments. *Emergency Medicine International* 1–5. doi:10.1155/2012/360308.

O'Brien, C. 2005. Benzodiazepine use, abuse, and dependence. *The Journal of Clinical Psychiatry* 66 (2): 28–33.

O'Neil, A, S E Quirk, S Housden, S L Brennan, L J Williams, J A Pasco, M Berk, and F N Jacka. 2014. Relationship between diet and mental health in children and adolescents: A systematic review. *American Journal of Public Health* 104 (10): e31–e42. doi:10.2015/AJPH.2014.302110.

Paris, J. 2002. Chronic suicidality among patients with borderline personality disorder. *Psychiatric Services* 53 (6): 738–742. doi:10.1176/appi.ps.53.6.738.

Parker, G. 1996. On lightening up: Improvement trajectories in recovery from depression. *Advances in Psychiatric Treatment* 2: 186–193.

Peebles-Kleiger, M J. 2000. The use of hypnosis in emergency medicine. *Emergency Medicine Clinics of North America* 18 (2): 327–338. doi:10.1016/S0733-8627(05)70128-0.

Peterson, M J, and R Benca. 2006. Sleep in mood disorders. *Psychiatric Clinics of North America* 29 (4): 1009–1032. doi:10.1016/j.psc.2006.09.003.

Pies, R W. 1994. Medical "mimics" of depression. *Psychiatric Annals* 24 (10): 519–520. doi:10.3928/0048-5713-19941001-08.

Platt, S. 1992. Epidemiology of suicide and parasuicide. *Journal of Psychopharmacology* 6 (2): 291–299. doi:10.1177/026988119200600202.

Porter, R, and N Ferrier. 1999. Emergency treatment of depression. *Advances in Psychiatric Treatment* 5: 3–10.

Rao, T S, M R Asha, B N Ramesh, and K S Rao. 2008. Understanding nutrition, depression and mental illness. *Indian Journal of Psychiatry* 50 (2): 77–82. doi:10.4103/0019-5545.42391.

Robinson, J, J Sareen, B J Cox, and J M Bolton. 2011. Role of self-medication in the development of comorbid anxiety and substance use disorders: A longitudinal investigation. *Archives of General Psychiatry* 68 (8): 800–807.

Rosebush, P I, and M F Mazurek. 1996. Catatonia after benzodiazepine withdrawal". *Journal of Clinical Psychopharmacology* 16 (4): 315–319.

Rund, D A, J D Ewing, K Mitzel, and N Votolato. 2006. The use of intramuscular benzodiazepines and antipsychotic agents in the treatment of acute agitation or violence in the emergency department. *Journal of Emergency Medicine* 31 (3): 317–324. doi:10/1016/jemermed.2005.09.021.

Sachdeva, A, M Choudhary, and M Chandra. 2015. Alcohol withdrawal syndrome: Benzodiazepines and beyond. *Journal of Clinical and Diagnostic Research* 9 (9): VE01–VE07.

Sareen, J, B J Cox, T O Afifi, R de Graff, G J G Asmundson, M ten Have, and M Stein. 2005. Anxiety disorders and risk for suicidal ideation and suicide attempts: A population-based longitudinal study of adults. *Archives of General Psychiatry* 62: 1249–1257.

Shorter, E. 2009. The history of lithium therapy. *Bipolar Disorders* 11 (0 2): 4–9. doi:10.1111/j.1399-5618.2009.00706.x.

Sigg, T. 1999. Recurrent seizures from sustained-release bupropion. *Journal of Toxicology* 37 (5): 634.

Simon, G E. 2001. Treating depression in patients with chronic disease. *Western Journal of Medicine; San Francisco* 175 (5): 292–293.

Susman, J, and B Klee. 2005. The role of high-potency benzodiazepines in the treatment of panic disorder. *Primary Care Companion to the Journal of Clinical Psychiatry* 7 (1): 5–11.

Swann, A C, C L Bowden, D Morris, J R Calabrese, F Petty, J G Small, S Dilsaver, and J M Davis. 1997. Depression during mania. Treatment response to lithium or divalproex. *Archives of General Psychiatry* 54 (1): 37–42.

Tallis, Frank. 1993. Primary hypothyroidism: A case for vigilance in the psychological treatment of depression. *British Journal of Clinical Psychology* 32 (3): 261–270.doi:10.1111/j.2044-8260.1993.tb01056.x.

Timmer, R T, and J M Sands. 1999. Lithium intoxication. *Journal of the American Society of Nephrology* 10 (3): 666–674.

Tondo, L, and R J Baldessarini. 2011. Can suicide be prevented? *Psychiatric Times*, February 10.

Velosa, J F, and M A Riddle. 2000. Pharmacologic treatment of anxiety disorders in children and adolescents. *Child and Adolescent Psychiatric Clinics of North America* 9 (1): 119–133.

Vieta, E, and J Sanchez-Moreno. 2008. Acute and long-term treatment of mania. *Dialogues in Clinical Neuroscience* 10 (2): 165–179.

Vita, A, L De Peri, and E Sacchetti. 2015. Lithium in drinking water and suicide prevention: A review of the evidence. *International Clinical Psychopharmacology*. 30 (1): 1–5. doi:10.1097/YIC.0000000000000048.

Volpi-Abadie, J, A M Kaye, and A D Kaye. 2013. Serotonin syndrome. *The Ochsner Journal* 13 (4): 533–540.

Walkup, J T, M J Labellarte, M A Riddle, D S Pine, L Greenhill, R Klein, M Davies et al. 2001. Fluvoxamine for the treatment of anxiety disorders in children and adolescents. *The New England Journal of Medicine* 344: 1279–1285. doi:10.1056/NEJM200104263441703.

Warner, C H, W Bobo, C Warner, S Reid, and J Rachal. 2006. Antidepressant discontinuation syndrome. *American Family Physician* 74 (3): 449–456.

Weiss, A J, M L Barrett, K Heslin, and C Stocks. 2016. *Trends in Emergency Department Visits Involving Mental and Substance Use Disorders, 2006–2013.* HCUP Statistical Brief #216, Rockville, MD: Agency for Healthcare Research and Quality. http://www.hcup-us.ahrq.gov/reports/statsbriefs/sb216-Mental-Substance-Use-Disorder-ED-Visit-Trends.pdf.

Weissman, M M, G L Klerman, J S Markowitz, and R M Ouellette. 1989. Suicidal ideation and suicide attempts in panic disorder and attacks. *The New England Journal of Medicine* 321: 1209–1214. doi:10.1056/NEJM198911023211801.

Williams, M M, R E Clouse, and P J Lustman. 2006. Treating depression to prevent diabetes and its complications: Understanding depression as a medical risk factor. *Clinical Diabetes* 24 (2): 79–86. doi:10.2337/diaclin.24.2.79.

Wolpe, J. 1969. *The Practice of Behavior Therapy.* New York: Pergamon Press.

Zamorski, M A, and R C Albucher. 2002. What to do when SSRIs fail: Eight strategies for optimizing treatment of panic disorder. *American Family Physician*, October 15: 1477–1484.

Zane, R D, A T McAfee, S Sherburne, G Billeter, and A Barsky. 2003. Panic disorder and emergency services utilization. *Academic Emergency Medicine* 10 (10): 1065–1069.

Zeller, S L. 2010. Treatment of psychiatric patients in emergency settings. *Primary Psychiatry* 17 (6): 41–47.

Zetterqvist, M. 2015. The DSM-5 diagnosis of nonsuicidal self-injury disorder: A review of the empirical literature. *Child and Adolescent Psychiatry and Mental Health* 31 (9). doi:10.1186/s13034-015-0062-7.

Zohar, J, and H G Westenberg. 2000. Anxiety disorders: A review of tricyclic antidepressants and selective serotonin reuptake inhibitors. *Acta Psychiatrica Scandinavica. Supplementum* 403: 39–49.

Chapter 11

Psychotic Disorders in Emergency Departments

Christopher Lentz

Contents

11.1	Introduction	178
11.2	Psychosis Defined	179
11.3	Auditory Hallucinations	179
11.4	Visual and Auditory Hallucinations and Illicit Substance Comorbidity	180
11.5	Tactile Hallucinations	181
11.6	Delusions	181
11.7	Thought Disorganization	183
11.8	Disorganized Behaviors	185
11.9	Catatonia	186
11.10	Diagnostic Categories of Psychotic Disorders	187
	11.10.1 Delusional Disorder	187
	11.10.2 Brief Psychotic Disorder	188
	11.10.3 Schizophreniform Disorder	188
	11.10.4 Schizophrenia	188
	11.10.5 Schizoaffective Disorder	189
	11.10.6 Depressive Disorder with Psychosis	189
	11.10.7 Bipolar Disorder with Psychosis	189
	11.10.8 Cannabis-Induced Psychosis	190
11.11	Medical Mimicry of Psychosis: A Case of Anti-N-Methyl-D-Aspartate Receptor Encephalitis	190
11.12	Paranoia as a Survival Mechanism	191
11.13	Treatment Options for Psychosis in the Emergency Department	192
	11.13.1 Antipsychotic Medications	193
	11.13.1.1 Risperidone	193
	11.13.1.2 Olanzapine	193
	11.13.1.3 Haloperidol	194

    11.13.1.4 Ziprasidone 194
    11.13.1.5 Aripiprazole 194
    11.13.1.6 Quetiapine 194
    11.13.1.7 Clozapine 194
  11.13.2 Antipsychotic Medication Side Effects 195
11.14 Conclusion 195
11.15 Key ED Survival Points for Psychosis 196
References 196
Resources 198

11.1 Introduction

"I am King Tut! I rule this world! I have many girlfriends including Taylor Swift. My girlfriends will give me money. They have lots of it! I can stay with one of them," yelled out a young African American patient who was being walked to the emergency department triage desk in handcuffs by police officers. "What is your name, sir?" asks the emergency department (ED) clerk at the desk. The patient suddenly lurches toward the clerk, writhing and struggling, pulling the chain on his handcuffs taut against his wrists, yelling, "King Tut! Call me King! King Tut! Ruler of the world and all others combined. Do you follow me? Are you with me?"

James, a young resident physician, is prepping himself to examine this new patient. James has many questions and uncertainties running through his mind as the patient is walked by his workstation and placed in room 16. "This is my first night in this ED, it is now 2 a.m., I've seen nine patients already and the attending physician wants me to talk to this guy. What the hell am I supposed to ask him?! How am I supposed to treat this guy? What medications should I recommend? I barely remember my psychiatric rotation from medical school. Damn! This is going to suck! I feel so unprepared for this. Okay, I've got to pull myself together. What was it that that psychiatrist I completed my psych rotation with in med school always reminded me of using? That's right, diphenhydramine, haloperidol, and lorazepam, the good ole B-52."

"Nurse," James yelled. "Please prepare an IM [intramuscular] dose of diphenhydramine 25 mg, haloperidol 5 mg, and lorazepam 2 mg for our new patient. Oh, yes! And contact psychiatry please. Thanks."

The previous scenario has been an increasingly common occurrence in emergency department settings over the past decade. Patients with mental illness are flocking to emergency departments with an increasing severity of psychiatric symptoms. According to the 2007 Agency for Healthcare Research and Quality, Healthcare Cost and Utilization Project, Nationwide Emergency Department Sample (Owens et al. 2010), individuals with psychotic disorders were seen in emergency departments throughout the United States at a rate of 9.9%, and per the Centers for Disease Control and Prevention (CDC)/National Center for Health Statistics National Hospital Ambulatory Medical Care Survey (Albert and McCaig 2015), 17.3% of all patients seen for treatment in EDs between 2009 and 2010 were treated for psychotic symptoms. Comparatively, there is a rate of 4.5 per 1000 individuals afflicted with nonorganic psychotic disorders in the community (Zimbroff 2003). As touched on in earlier chapters, the influx of mental health patients with psychotic symptoms into local EDs has been ignited by the decimation of outpatient resources available to these patients in many communities around the country. Access to outpatient psychiatric care for many of these patients, including medication consultations via a psychiatrist and mental health counseling or therapy via a licensed clinician, have been dwindling leaving the only option for relief of their psychiatric symptoms as a trip to the local ED. Many of the EDs are understaffed and ill-equipped to properly treat and diagnose psychotic disorders in these patients that present for help and relief of their symptoms.

It can be common for many emergency department staff to feel anxious and unprepared with being able to adequately treat psychotic disorders in the patients that present with these. Common questions that may arise when presented with a case of psychosis include: How do I properly diagnose the disorder? What treatment options are available? What symptoms do I need to be aware of? What medications will help relieve the psychotic symptoms?

11.2 Psychosis Defined

Psychosis can be defined simply as lost touch with reality. This lost touch with reality can be manifested in symptoms including delusions or false beliefs about the world, hallucinations including auditory or visual, disorganized or bizarre thoughts, and bizarre behaviors. The National Alliance on Mental Illness (NAMI) defines psychosis as "disruptions to a person's thoughts and perceptions that make it difficult for them to recognize what is real and what isn't. These disruptions are often experienced as seeing, hearing, and believing things that aren't real or having strange, persistent thoughts, behaviors, and emotions" (2016).

Experiencing psychotic symptoms can be terrifying for the patient that is attempting to cope with them and can be draining on the family, which is attempting to support the patient through this experience, as a unit. Some of the more common symptoms of psychosis that can devastate the patient's ability to focus on ordinary daily tasks include auditory hallucinations, visual hallucinations, and delusions.

Imagine yourself at work on a normal day and think back to a time when you may have experienced a stressful day on the job. It may have been difficult and emotionally taxing to work through your routine daily work stress. Now imagine this same stressful day at work with the added impediment of hearing two voices, one male and one female, constantly talking back and forth to each other about every behavior you engage in. "Look at Jack, he is typing on the computer. He is not doing a very good job with his typing. Look at him now; he is getting up to use the toilet. Now he is opening the door to the restroom. Oh, Jack is urinating in a toilet!" Another impediment may include voices that are berating you or instructing you to harm yourself or others around you. "You are a terrible person Jack. You are worthless. You are a faggot. You should just go kill yourself." These can be a common daily experience for a patient coping with a psychotic disorder.

11.3 Auditory Hallucinations

Auditory and visual hallucinations are the most commonly reported types of sensory distortions in patients with psychosis; although, tactile and olfactory hallucinations may also be present in some individuals (Barberio 2000; Mandal 2014). As stated earlier, hearing voices is the most commonly reported hallucination, followed by seeing people or animals that are not actually present. Patients presenting with psychosis will report hearing voices that talk directly to them or about them. For example, voices talking directly to the patient may ask them to perform various behaviors or may directly berate, belittle, or threaten the patient. "Jack, you need to run outside and scream." "Jack, you are in danger. We are going to kill you." Voices that talk about the patient may describe what they are doing throughout the day as if making a running commentary of the patient's daily behaviors. "Jack is now eating breakfast. He is lifting a spoon up to his face. He is chewing his cereal."

Voices can be considered to be distressing to the patient that experiences them, but sometimes, patients will report enjoying the voices they hear, especially if the voices are of a deceased loved one or a perceived guardian angel. A young African American female had presented to the emergency department with her family reporting that she was hearing and actively responding to voices. The patient reported that she enjoyed hearing the voices as the comments they made to her were comical in nature. The patient would laugh out loud and giggle in response to the voices. She also reported that one of the voices she heard was the voice of the lead singer for the rock band Nickelback, who she believed was her boyfriend.

Auditory hallucinations may also be experienced by the patient as sounds. A middle-aged Latino male arrived at the emergency department reporting that he was distressed by the experience of constantly hearing music repeating the same melody that no one else around him was able to hear.

11.4 Visual and Auditory Hallucinations and Illicit Substance Comorbidity

Voices are not the only type of hallucination that patients may present with, visual hallucinations can also be prevalent, although they are less common than auditory hallucinations. Snakes, spiders, roaches, cats, or worms, these have all been common visual hallucinations experienced by patients. The report of seeing animals or insects is a common complaint in many patients with psychosis. Patients may also report seeing people that are not present, including family members, deceased family members, or famous religious figures. "The Pope has been coming to visit me every night in my room; he is followed by a group of black cats."

Patients may also report seeing devils, demons, or even angels. These visions may sometimes be accompanied by auditory hallucinations, seeing and hearing the devil talking to the patient. Patients may commonly describe instances in which they see shadows out of the corner of their eye or in their peripheral vision, although, it is safe to be skeptical in these cases as these most likely are reports of accounts of illusions versus true hallucinations. The occurrence of hypnogogic or hypnopompic hallucinatory experiences must also be ruled out (American Psychiatric Association 2013). Hallucinatory experiences like these, which occur either when first falling asleep or upon waking up from sleep, can be a common experience for any patient.

The interplay of hallucinogenic substances must also be taken into account whenever visual or auditory hallucinations are reported. Substances such as hallucinogenic mushrooms, ecstasy, methamphetamines, or even cannabis can induce hallucinations in the average healthy person, but can compound the experience in a patient already inflicted with a psychotic disorder. Some substances, such as methamphetamines, if frequently used, can create psychotic symptoms in a patient, which may persist even after the substance has been metabolized by the body (Grant et al. 2012). Withdrawal from alcohol intoxication can also elicit auditory or visual hallucinations.

Especially in patients aged 18–30 first presenting with psychotic symptoms to the ED, the assessing clinician should include a substance-induced psychosis in their diagnostic differential (Wilkinson et al. 2014). Unfortunately, many psychiatric professionals working in EDs tend to blame psychotic symptoms on a psychotic disorder instead of a possible comorbid substance use issue (Mohr et al. 2005). In one study, it was found that one-quarter of 223 patients surveyed who presented to an ED with psychotic symptoms were later found to either have a substance-induced psychotic disorder, or no psychotic disorder at all (Mohr et al. 2005).

11.5 Tactile Hallucinations

The presence of tactile hallucinations in a patient is most often brought on by ingestion of illicit substances, for example, methamphetamine or club drugs, such as ecstasy. The presence of olfactory hallucinations may point to an underlying organic issue, such as a brain tumor, dementia process, Parkinson's disease (Chaudhury 2010), or traumatic brain injury. The most commonly reported tactile hallucinations that patients present with in an ED setting are the sensation that insects are crawling on or in the patient's skin, which is known as delusional parasitosis (Sharma and Cieraszynski 2013). These patients will present with secondary behaviors including skin picking or scratching usually engaged in to relieve the sensation of the crawling insects or in attempts to remove the delusional infestation from the skin. Many of the patients that present with skin picking behavior may also have skin lesions or open sores present on the arms or legs.

An older white male had presented to the ED with what appeared to be a severe case of tactile hallucinations coupled with delusions. This patient believed that there was an alien organism that was living inside of his body that he could feel underneath his skin. The patient believed that this organism had tendrils that had extended out and wrapped around various appendages of his body. The patient had gone as far as using a scalpel to surgically remove what he believed were alien tendrils from his arm and leg. The patient reported that he had videotaped himself removing the tendrils and had photographs of them. The patient was accompanied by a male friend who also believed that the patient's body had been invaded by an alien organism; giving a prime example of a shared psychotic disorder or "folie à deux" (the folly of two) (American Psychiatric Association 2000). In patients that present with a primary substance use disorder, the tactile hallucinations will resolve once the patient has had time to metabolize the ingested illicit substance.

Regardless of the type of hallucination the patient is experiencing, it is important to rule out other causes of the hallucinations that a patient presents with as there are many other possible etiologies of any hallucination including severe depression or mania, post-traumatic stress disorder, alcohol or other substance use, delirium tremens, sleep deprivation, a medication side effect, organic brain diseases, such as Parkinson's and dementia, eye diseases, or delirium (Barberio 2000; Chaudhury 2010).

11.6 Delusions

Patients presenting with hallucinations may also exhibit delusions, or false beliefs about the world around them, in conjunction with hallucinations, or present with delusions alone. In some of the psychotic disorders, such as schizophrenia, the patient will present with a combination of experiencing hallucinations and delusions, while in others (for instance, in delusional disorder), delusions are present in the absence of active hallucinations. A variety of delusions may arise in different patients presenting for treatment in an emergency department setting. Some common delusional types include grandiose, persecutory, jealous, somatic, and erotomanic (American Psychiatric Association 2013). Religious delusions can also be common, especially in patients presenting with a manic episode in bipolar disorder or those with schizophrenia (Brewerton 1994).

"My home is being invaded every night. They have been coming into my home and placing cameras in the rooms. They are watching me all the time." "Who has been invading your home?" "Why, the police and FBI, of course." "How have they been entering your home?" "Through the walls. They lift up the exterior wall of the house and enter my house from under the wall, then they are able to close the wall up again when they leave. They have been videotaping me with the cameras." These are the persecutory delusions of a middle-aged African American female patient that had presented to the emergency department initially with a medical complaint, but when she disclosed her delusions to the emergency department physician, psychiatry was consulted. This patient presented with a well-groomed and professionally dressed appearance and appeared normal except for the presence of her delusions.

Some delusions may appear to be plausible and believable, especially when the content of the delusions is non-bizarre in nature. A common example of this is when the patient may be accusing family members or friends of stealing money from them or items from them, when this is not actually occurring. This delusion can be commonly found in cases of major neurocognitive disorder or Alzheimer's disorder (Jeste and Finkel 2000).

Somatic complaints will frequently be reported by patients in the ED, as many patients present to the ED in hopes of having these somatic symptoms resolved. In cases where the patient presents with psychosis and bodily complaints, for instance abdominal pain or headaches, there can be a somatic delusion associated with the bodily symptom. "My stomach hurts. I have a sea urchin in my stomach that is causing the pain. Can you please remove it?" This was the complaint from a young Asian female who had actually attempted to remove what she believed was a sea urchin from her stomach by using a knife. Caution should be used in cases where the patient presents with somatic complaints. A complete medical examination should be completed to rule out any true medical cause of the somatic complaint prior to pointing to a delusion as being the cause.

A middle-aged white obese female with a history of being diagnosed with schizophrenia had presented to the ED complaining of feeling constipated. Unfortunately, the emergency department physician that was attending to the patient neglected to perform an adequate medical exam of the patient and passed off the patient's complaint of constipation as "delusions of constipation." Later, the emergency department nurse noted that the patient began to experience leakage of fecal matter from her rectum, and upon further examination by a second physician, it was found that the patient was indeed constipated. In a similar case, cited by Kraft and Babigian (1972), a woman with schizophrenia with a known history of somatic delusions presented to an ED complaining of pain from needles in her arms. Results from radiological exams showed she had needles in one of her arms from a prior self-harming event.

Somatic delusions can appear to be mundane when expressed by patients, but some grandiose delusions may contain more flair in presentation. "I work for the CIA as a special operative for President Trump. I have been working for President Trump since the age of 15. In this time, I have accumulated an amassed wealth of one billion dollars. I also worked alongside Steve Jobs and helped him develop the Apple iPad®."

The presentation of delusions themselves in a patient may not always require the need for inpatient psychiatric hospitalization as long as the delusions are not impairing the patient's ability to care for themselves and do not lead to situations in which the delusional content causes the patient to behave in a way that creates a dangerous situation for themselves or others around them. Some delusions may appear bizarre and "crazy" when described by the patient, but if the patient is able to demonstrate an ability to plan for their own self-care or has family or friends that are willing to care for them they should be discharged home.

Recall the example given earlier describing the middle-aged African American female patient who presented to the emergency department with delusions of persecution, regarding law enforcement sneaking into her home through the wall. This patient was able to be discharged home from the emergency department because, despite the delusions she presented with, she was well groomed and was able to verbalize a clear and realistic plan for caring for herself. Compare this case to the young Asian female who presented with the somatic delusion regarding having a sea urchin in her stomach. This patient had attempted to remove the urchin from her stomach with a knife and was deemed to be a danger to herself and was referred for involuntary psychiatric hospitalization to ensure her safety.

11.7 Thought Disorganization

Delusions may or may not lead to impairments in the patient's ability to care for themselves or others, but thought disorganization, for most patients, creates a barrier to self-care and the ability to plan for discharge from the emergency department. Thought disorganization can present itself in various forms ranging from loose associations, circumstantial thinking, tangential thoughts, thought blocking, thought derailing to *word salad* (American Psychiatric Association 2013; Barberio 2000). Clinician: "Where do you currently live?" Patient: "I live off of the street. My grandmother makes oatmeal. Oatmeal is lumpy. I like that new television show *60 Minutes*." This example of thought disorganization highlights the impairment that can occur in patients that present with this symptom. The majority of patients that present with this level of thought disorder will require some level of treatment intervention, this may include a level as restrictive as inpatient psychiatric hospitalization to less restrictive voluntary options, such as crisis residential placement (sending the patient to a house located in a neighborhood that runs a voluntary mental health treatment program in the house), partial hospitalization programs, or an intensive outpatient program. If the patient can identify and contact a support person, which may be a family member or friend, who is willing to help care for the patient at home, the patient can be discharged home from the emergency department. Again, the idea is to find the least restrictive plan of care for the patient that will ensure that the patient is safe and that their treatment needs are being addressed.

Word salad is one of the more impairing symptoms of thought disorder that can afflict a patient with psychosis. Word salad can present in the patient as if his thoughts were taken out of his mind, placed in a large salad bowl, and tossed around in the bowl, then removed from the bowl at random, leading to nonsensical speech and an inability to communicate one's thoughts to others (Mosby's Medical Dictionary 2009).

"Porch steps run come here. Garbage pink composition solely bags speak deodorant. Wall speaks windy hot mess."

If after reading these statements, you are thinking, "That makes no sense at all," then you can fathom how difficult it can be for the patient suffering from psychosis to be able to organize simple thoughts in his mind in order to communicate effectively with others. Although this level of thought disorganization is rare, it can and does present in patients that are admitted to the emergency department setting. A patient presenting with severe symptoms like word salad will need inpatient psychiatric hospitalization if no other social supports that are willing to care for the patient's basic needs, including family or friends, can be identified or located.

Word salad can be an impairing symptom of thought disorder, but thought disorder can also present in a patient as neologisms, clang speech, or echolalia (American Psychiatric Association 2013). When a patient is observed to be making up words, these words are called neologisms (Barberio 2000).

Neologism literally means "new word" taken from Greek *neo* = new and *logos* = word. Many new words may be created and used in society, but the neologisms created by the patient with psychosis are usually nonsensical and would not be accepted for daily use by mainstream society. "I can no longer sleep in this caculphuc."

Clang speech or associations occur when a patient uses rhyming words (Grinnell 2016a). The words that are used during the rhyme may be real words or nonsensical words. "The man walked into the green, mean, lean, clean, bean team."

Echolalia occurs when the patient repeats exactly what someone else has said (Miller-Keane Encyclopedia and Dictionary of Medicine 2003a). For example, if during the psychiatric assessment, the clinician asks, "How were you brought to the emergency department?" the patient will respond with saying, "How were you brought to the emergency department?"

Thought disorders may also be exhibited as a flight of ideas or circumstantiality. During a flight of ideas, which can occur during a manic episode in bipolar disorder or in psychotic disorders, such as schizophrenia or schizoaffective disorder, the patient will rapidly switch from one unrelated topic to another during their conversations (Grinnell 2016d).

"I ate scrambled eggs and ham for breakfast. I love watching baseball on TV. I need to go to the bank today to get money for the church donation. Do you have a restroom here?"

As you can see from the example, it may be very difficult for the patient with a flight of ideas to clearly communicate what is occurring in their mind to others. It is as if the patient's thoughts are flowing so rapidly through their mind that their mouth and tongue are unable to keep up with the flow of thoughts, hence the jumble of unrelated statements that are communicated.

Circumstantiality occurs when the patient's thought process is long-winded and convoluted in reaching its goal (Miller-Keane Encyclopedia and Dictionary of Medicine 2003b). After asking the patient that presents with circumstantial thinking a question, their response may appear to go on and on, but will eventually answer the question. Clinician: "How did you arrive to the emergency department today?" Patient: "Well, there were these two men dressed in what looked to be paramedic uniforms who pulled up to my mother's house in a large ambulance. I expected the lights on the ambulance to be flashing and the siren to be blaring, but they were not. The two men dressed liked paramedics stopped and opened the back of the ambulance and pulled out a gurney. They wheeled this gurney into the house and my mother asked me to cooperate with the men. The men asked me to get into the gurney, so I did. They strapped me down in the gurney and wheeled me into the back of the ambulance. Then the two men drove me down my mother's street to the highway. They still did not turn on the lights or the siren. We then arrived here to the emergency department."

Circumstantial thinking can be an impediment to the patient that presents with this, but it may appear to be mundane compared with the other thought disorders, such as thought insertion, broadcasting, or withdrawal (American Psychiatric Association 2013). These thought disorders, in and of themselves, will have a more bizarre presentation when observed in the patient and have a delusional quality to them.

"I keep thinking about the end of the world, the aliens keep placing these thoughts in my head, please make them stop."

Thought insertion occurs when the patient believes that someone or something other than themselves is placing distressing or disturbing thoughts into their mind (Barberio 2000; Grinnell 2016c). The accused party may be some type of religious icon, such as god or the devil, or possibly a government entity, such as the FBI or CIA.

The antithesis of thought insertion is thought withdrawal in which the patient reports that someone or something has removed or stolen thoughts from their mind (Barberio 2000). Lapses in memory or forgotten moments reported by the patient are blamed on someone removing thoughts from their mind. "I cannot remember my address because the FBI planted that memory-stealing chip in my brain."

Lastly, thought broadcasting occurs when the patient believes that others around them are able to read or know their unspoken thoughts as if they were telepathic (Barberio 2000), although there have been varied definitions on the symptom (Pawar and Spence 2003). "I don't need to tell you why I am here today. You already know. I can tell that you can hear my thoughts. Tell me what I am thinking right now."

11.8 Disorganized Behaviors

Patients presenting with disordered thoughts may be unable to care for themselves depending on the severity of the symptoms, although disorganized behaviors can be as impairing to a patient as a disorder in thoughts. Disorganized behaviors can be exhibited in the setting in simple ways, such as dressing oddly or engaging in behaviors in public that are only socially acceptable to perform in private.

Jane, a 24-year-old female, arrives to the emergency department during a hot August afternoon dressed in multiple layers of clothing including a long sleeve shirt, a hooded sweater, a formal vest, and ski jacket, wearing a single glove on one hand that she refers to as her "magic hand," and a head scarf. It is important to recognize cultural variations in what is considered to be socially appropriate dress styles.

What is considered normal in one culture may be considered bizarre or abnormal in another. Hence, making a diagnosis on a patient's appearance in and of itself should not occur. The context of where the dress style occurs should also be take into consideration. Jane's described apparel would have appeared more normal in the context of a cold wintry day versus the hot August afternoon when she arrived at the ED. Even the era of when certain dress styles or fads occur is important to consider. Take the ever-increasing popularity of body piercing and tattooing in today's mainstream culture. A few decades ago, the act of piercing one's navel, lip, or nose may have been considered odd or grotesque. Nowadays, this act is considered by many to be hip and even sexy.

Just as dress style should not be used separately to categorize a patient as being bizarre or psychotic, behaviors that are executed in public versus private settings also need to be examined from a multifactorial stance. Take, for example, the behavior of public affection, including acts of hugging and kissing. Open displays of affection in public vary depending on the culture in which you find yourself. In some cultures, any public displays of affection may be considered taboo or abnormal, while in others, it may be a normal occurrence (Public Display of Affection 2016). Even the era during which the behavior occurs will have an impact on how deviant or normal it appears to be to others in the mainstream population.

Returning to the example of public affection, if a couple were to be observed engaging in open-mouth kissing and hugging in a public area, this behavior would be considered to be more socially acceptable and normal based on today's standards compared with a few decades ago, when it would have been frowned upon. In reality, most behaviors that a patient with true psychosis may engage in would be considered bizarre and abnormal by most people during the time or era in which they occur.

Behaviors such as running or walking in the middle of a street naked while screaming out loud or masturbating in public places are clear examples of these. But even these behaviors can be explained in other ways besides psychosis. Perhaps the person running naked down the street screaming is involved in a streaking exhibition as part of a fraternity hazing event. The person masturbating in public may be engaged in an act of voyeurism versus experiencing a psychotic break or does not have the mental capacity to know the difference between socially acceptable and unacceptable behaviors, such as is the case with severely developmentally delayed persons.

Perseveration occurs when the same activity is repeated by a patient over and over (Grinnell, Perseveration 2016b; Yang et al. 2011). Julie, a young adult Asian female, is asked, "What is the current year?" "It is close to the beginning of the start of the year." When asked, "What is the current month?" "It is close to the beginning of the start of the year." When asked, "What is the current day?" "It is close to the beginning of the start of the year." The perseveration can occur in verbal expression, as shown in the previous example, or in physical movements.

Echopraxia occurs when the patient repeats exactly what someone else has done. The word is a combination of the Greek word *echo* meaning sound and *praxis* meaning action. This behavior is considered to be a normal response in young children, prior to the age of 5, in which the actions of older individuals will be repeated by the child in order to learn new, vital behaviors that may be important for normal social and physical development (Ganos et al. 2012).

In patients with schizophrenia or other psychotic disorders, the act of repeating an observed behavior has no true practical function given the context in which repeating the observed act occurs. In one case study (Hay 1955), a patient with schizophrenia was observed engaging in echopraxia in response to material they observed on television.

Patients with pervasive developmental disorders, such as autism, may also commonly exhibit echopraxia or echolalia. Sam watches the psychiatrist that is assessing him tap the tip of his nose with his finger. Sam now persistently taps the tip of his nose. Echopraxia can sometimes occur concurrently with echolalia, which is the imitation of another's speech (Marin and Gorovoy 2014).

11.9 Catatonia

Behavioral disturbances, like perseveration, which manifest in psychotic patients can be present in patients presenting with catatonia. Catatonia can be thought of as another variant of psychosis. Patients that present to the emergency department with catatonia tend to be brought in by concerned family or friends who may report that the patient has stopped speaking, moving, or eating. Typical symptoms can include mutism, posturing, stupor, refusal to eat or drink, and hypokinesis (Daniels 2009).

Psychiatric placement of the catatonic patient may be impeded by the expectations of the inpatient psychiatric hospitals that require patients to be able to ambulate, groom, and feed themselves while on the unit. Many of these patients, if they do not respond to medication treatments, end up being placed on a medical unit in the hospital from the ED for treatment of medical complications that arise from the catatonia. Examples of medical complications may include imbalances of essential minerals and vitamins brought on by the patient's negligible food intake, or dehydration from reduced or ceased fluid intake. If the patient responds well to medication treatment in the ED setting, they can recover quickly from the catatonic episode and be discharged home to the care of family.

Common medication treatment for catatonia entails the use of high-dose benzodiazepines including lorazepam (Bush et al. 1996; England et al. 2011). In some extreme cases of catatonia, where benzodiazepines have failed to resolve the condition, electroconvulsive therapy (ECT) may be used to treat the underlying symptoms, although this is usually not a readily available option in an ED (Bush et al. 1996; England et al. 2011). It is vital to the welfare of the patient that catatonia be properly diagnosed and treated in cases were the patient presents with negativism or stupor as symptoms; these may be exhibited in the patient as the cessation of food and water intake, which can eventually lead to patient demise.

Catatonia, as stated earlier, can be displayed in the patient as stupor or negativism, but the opposite behaviors may be present in some patients. Patients may be observed or described by family members to engage in very active, purposeless behaviors (Daniels 2009).

Jack, a 25-year-old male, was observed in the emergency department to be rapidly pacing around his room in a clockwise circle as he was clapping his hands together, and then he would change the direction of his pacing. Jack would not respond or stop the pacing and clapping behavior when staff would attempt to intervene to redirect his actions. This purposeless behavior, also referred to as catatonic excitement (Aronson and Thompson 1950), is another subset of possible catatonic symptoms that emergency department patients may present with. Of course, as with all diagnoses, medical and psychogenic substance-related causes need to be ruled out. Other recorded catatonic symptoms related to the psychotic disorders include posturing and waxy flexibility. Although, the most common symptom of catatonia that presented to our ED was stupor and negativism exhibited behaviorally by an extreme reduction in body movement and cessation of food and water intake.

Samantha, a 21-year-old female, was observed to be standing up with her knees locked with her arms extended straight up into the air never moving from this position. At times, Samantha would allow the nursing staff to move her arms down to her sides, but she would not move them from this position once they were placed there by the nurse. These symptoms, posturing and waxy flexibility, are less commonly seen in the ED setting. Although catatonic symptoms can co-occur with psychosis, other conditions such as underlying medical issues or affective disorders, such as major depression or bipolar disorder, can also co-occur with the syndrome (Daniels 2009; England et al. 2011).

11.10 Diagnostic Categories of Psychotic Disorders

Catatonia is just one of many key features listed in the *Diagnostic and Statistical Manual of Mental Disorders*, fifth edition (DSM-5) that help to define a psychotic disorder. The psychotic disorders, as listed in the DSM-5, fall under the section entitled "Schizophrenia and Other Psychotic Disorders," as schizophrenia is the illness that most lay people refer to when the word psychotic or crazy is mentioned.

Patients that present to an emergency department with psychotic symptoms for psychiatric help may present with a diagnostic picture that fits any of the following disorders. It is important to note, with regard to diagnosis, that not all individuals will neatly fall into any given diagnostic picture perfectly. The majority of diagnostic attempts on a person may appear to be akin to trying to fit an octagon into a circular space or sometimes even a square.

The art of diagnosis can be described as or give the feeling of pigeonholing especially when you look at the multiple diagnostic criteria that the clinician attempts to sort through and match up with the symptoms that the patient presents with. In some cases, you may be able to have five different clinicians diagnose the same patient at the same time and develop five different diagnoses based on their clinical opinions (Spurious Precision: Procedural Validity of Diagnostic Assessment in Psychotic Disorders 1995). The main point to remember is that diagnosis is not a perfect, flawless skill. When you take into account the limited time and resources that many emergency department clinicians are presented with on the job, the rates of accurate assessment and diagnosis may decline in this clinical environment.

11.10.1 Delusional Disorder

When a patient has experienced one or more delusions (false beliefs) for a period of 1 month or more, a diagnostic picture of delusional disorder can be painted (American Psychiatric

Association 2013). Delusions can present in a variety of ways and tend to be resistant to change. Sometimes this is termed as being a fixed delusion. As discussed earlier, delusions in themselves do not constitute a psychiatric emergency, but an emergency can be considered if the delusions are causing impairments in the patient's ability to keep themselves safe, others around them safe, or in caring for their basic needs including obtaining food, clothing, and shelter. If the delusions that the individual expresses are causing a strain on daily relationships with family, friends, and workplace colleagues, an outpatient treatment plan may be beneficial to consider.

11.10.2 Brief Psychotic Disorder

Jason, a 31-year-old male, presents to the emergency department with his parents who report that over the past 2 days, he has "not been himself." Jason's parents report that he has been paranoid, stating that he believes that the FBI is tracking him and has placed cameras in the house. They also report that Jason has not been sleeping over the past two nights and they have heard him holding complete conversations with himself when alone in his bedroom. They report that he has never behaved like this in the past and, as far as they know, he does not use any illicit substances. Jason's parents report that his fiancé of 2 years broke off their relationship 1 week ago. Jason's diagnostic picture can be attributed to a case of brief psychotic disorder.

In brief psychotic disorder, delusions, hallucinations, and disorganized speech or behaviors can be present. Per the DSM-5, either delusions, hallucinations, or disorganized speech must have developed suddenly (within a 2-week period) in the person and last from 1 day to less than 1 month. The person must experience an eventual remission of all symptoms at some point during the course of the episode (American Psychiatric Association 2013).

11.10.3 Schizophreniform Disorder

Many of the psychotic disorders that are listed in the DSM-5 can be viewed as differentiated between each other simply by the time intervals that the positive psychotic symptoms are present. For instance, brief psychotic disorder is diagnosed when the patient presents with delusions, hallucinations, or disorganized speech for at least 1 day or up to 1 month. In schizophreniform disorder, the same psychotic symptoms must be present for at least 1 month or up to 6 months. While in schizophrenia, the patient can exhibit positive psychotic symptoms for 1 month or longer and other symptoms, whether they are prodromal or residual, continuously for a period of at least 6 months or longer (American Psychiatric Association 2013).

11.10.4 Schizophrenia

Lisa, a 25-year-old female, is brought to the ED by her caregiver with an increase in psychotic symptoms, including paranoid delusions and auditory hallucinations. Per the caregiver's report, Lisa had stopped taking her risperidone about 1 week ago after her voices had stopped and her paranoia ceased. Lisa believed that she was cured of her psychosis and promptly stopped taking her daily dose of risperidone. This scenario is, too often, common in the ED setting. Many patients that present with a psychotic disorder display poor insight into the illness (Assessment of Insight in Psychosis 1993). This especially may be present in patients that are afflicted with predominant delusions. Some delusions may impede the patient's ability to properly manage their medications, especially if the delusional content includes paranoia regarding medications or caregiver's intentions. Some patients may believe that medications that they have been prescribed are poison or that the caregiver has done something to poison the medications. The patient, in this case, may stop taking the medications due to the paranoid delusions. Once the patient stops taking their regularly prescribed medications, their symptoms will begin to return (Subotnik et al. 2012). Depending on the severity of the symptoms, family and friends of the individual may notice the increased symptoms, become concerned, and bring their loved one to an emergency department for further evaluation and possible re-hospitalization in a psychiatric hospital. This, unfortunately, can be a revolving door for many patients.

Per the DSM-5 (American Psychiatric Association 2013), a diagnosis of schizophrenia must include at least one positive psychotic symptom, including either hallucinations, delusions, or disorganized thinking, in addition to another positive psychotic symptom or either disorganized, catatonic or negative symptoms for a period of 1 month. There also needs to be a regression in the individual's premorbid level of functioning in a major life arena such as work, relationships, or self-care. Psychotic symptoms, either positive or negative in nature, must be present for at least 6 months.

11.10.5 Schizoaffective Disorder

Schizoaffective disorder (SAD) can be characterized as the marriage of a mood disorder with a psychotic disorder. The patient can exhibit symptoms of a major depressive episode or a manic episode with positive psychotic symptoms including hallucinations, delusions or disordered thinking. Throughout the life of the illness, positive psychotic symptoms are present for a period of at least 2 weeks without the presence of a major depressive or manic episode. Symptoms from either a depressive or manic episode are evident during the lifetime of the illness (American Psychiatric Association 2013).

11.10.6 Depressive Disorder with Psychosis

Psychotic symptoms are usually equated with disorders such as schizophrenia in which the common symptoms may include hallucinations, delusions, or disorganized thinking (Dubovsky and Thomas 1992). Psychosis can be present in mood disorders, such as major depression and bipolar disorder, when the mood disorder reaches an extreme end of the mood continuum. Auditory hallucinations and delusions, which will typically present with a theme related to the mood the patient is experiencing at the time the psychosis develops, can complicate the diagnostic picture. Hallucinations may include voices that are very negative, blaming, and guilt ridden. Delusional themes can include guilt, worthlessness, or disease.

Delusions with a persecutory theme can also be common (Bowman and Raymond 1931). Jill, a 47-year-old, presents to the ED complaining of increased depressed mood over the past 3 weeks. She reports that she has not been able to get up from her bed and has been isolating herself in her room. Jill's husband reports that she has been staring off at times and looked as if she was listening to something that was not present in the room. Jill admits that at times, she has been hearing voices that tell her that she is no good as a wife and mother and that her family would be better off if she was dead. Jill believes that she may possibly die, but is unable to tell you why or how she will die.

11.10.7 Bipolar Disorder with Psychosis

Patients that may swing from the low pole of depression up to the elevated pole of mania are more likely to experience psychotic symptoms. The DSM-5 (American Psychiatric Association 2013) classifies these episodes with specifiers: *with mood-congruent psychotic features or with mood-incongruent psychotic features*. Grandiose delusions and even hallucinations may be prevalent in a patient exhibiting a full-blown manic episode. These episodes, when present, may prompt concerned loved ones to bring the patient into an emergency department for evaluation and treatment. "I am Jesus Christ! The son of God!" Or "I am the Queen of England!" are examples of false grandiose beliefs that a patient in a manic episode may present with. Paranoid thoughts may also be prevalent. The patient may believe that family members are conspiring against them. Unfortunately, if the patient begins to act on the delusional content, whether it is grandiose or paranoid in nature, they may cause harm to themselves or others around them if help is not sought out.

11.10.8 Cannabis-Induced Psychosis

Many patients that present to EDs for treatment of acute episodes of psychosis will complicate the diagnostic picture due to comorbid substance abuse issues. Cannabis is a common drug that is rapidly becoming more socially and politically acceptable. Many states in the United States have recently legalized the recreational use of cannabis and a larger number of states have legalized cannabis for treatment of certain medical conditions, for example, glaucoma.

With the increased acceptance of cannabis in social and political arenas, it has been theorized that many psychiatric patients utilize the drug as a quick way to self-medicate their psychiatric symptoms. It has been estimated that about 18.1 million people consume cannabis annually. Given this high number of cannabis users, the chances are good that ED staff will encounter a patient with cannabis use issues.

It has been found that consumption of cannabis by individuals, whether naturally or synthetically produced, and its effects can mimic schizophrenic symptoms (Radhakrishnan et al. 2014). Instances of a brief psychotic episode have also been documented in case studies in which psychotic symptoms were present in a patient for 1 month following consumption of cannabis (Wilkinson et al. 2014). The chances of developing schizophrenia later in life can be increased in patients that have a history of frequent high-dose consumption of cannabis in adolescence (Barkus 2016; Malchow et al. 2013; Radhakrishnan et al. 2014; Moore et al. 2007; Wilkinson et al. 2014).

Whenever substance use is placed as a contributing factor on the diagnostic block, a cause and effect analysis should come into play. As the old saying goes, what came first, the chicken or the egg? In these cases where a patient presents with symptoms of schizophrenia, did the cannabis use cause the schizophrenia to develop or was the schizophrenia present, or at least a biological predisposition, prior to the substance use? As stated earlier, some studies have found a relationship between cannabis use and the development of psychotic symptoms, but other studies (Malchow et al. 2013; Wilkinson et al. 2014) have theorized that the evidence to support this relationship is weak.

11.11 Medical Mimicry of Psychosis: A Case of Anti-N-Methyl-D-Aspartate Receptor Encephalitis

A 13-year-old female is admitted to the ED by her concerned mother for help after the child had exhibited drastic changes in her behavior and thought process over the past few days. The mother of the patient reports that her daughter had been behaving normally up until a few days ago when she began to complain of flu-like symptoms and then started to talk nonsensically, was laughing out loud at inappropriate times, and would make odd movements. The ED physician performed a routine medical examination of the child and was unable to diagnose any medical illness that was causing her current symptoms. A urine toxicology screening revealed that the patient was clean from any psychoactive substances that may have been causing or contributing to her symptoms. At this point, the ED physician consulted the ED psychiatric service to assess the child.

After conducting a psychiatric evaluation on the patient, the ED psychiatric services team did not feel that the patient's presentation was due to a primary psychiatric disorder due to the young age of the patient and the rapid onset of her psychotic symptoms, and recommended that the ED physician perform further medical testing to determine the cause of her psychotic symptoms. The ED physician performed a lumbar puncture and the results showed the presence of anti-N-methyl-D-aspartate (NDMA) antibodies in the child's cerebral spinal fluid. At this time, the child was transferred from the ED into a pediatric hospital. Further tests revealed that the child had developed an ovarian teratoma or tumor. The child was eventually diagnosed with a case of anti-NMDA receptor encephalitis, was treated, and recovered with a complete remission of her psychotic symptoms.

The cause of anti-NDMA receptor encephalitis has been found to be related to the presence of an ovarian teratoma, specifically a tumor containing brain or nerve tissues (Dalmau et al. 2007, 2008). It has been classified as an autoimmune disorder in which the body creates antibodies that attack the NDMA receptors in the brain, leading to inflammation of the brain tissue. During the early stages of the disorder, a patient can exhibit psychotic symptoms, similar to those of someone afflicted with schizophrenia. Common psychiatric symptoms can include delusions, hallucinations, disorganized thoughts, bizarre behaviors, mania, mood changes, and aggression (Kayser and Dalmau 2011; Kayser et al. 2013). If the disease is left untreated, the patient can enter a state of catatonia and eventually slip into a coma and die (Dalmau et al. 2008). For a detailed personal account of this unique autoimmune disease, the book *Brain on Fire—My Month of Madness*, by Susannah Cahalan (2013), is recommended.

The previous case example points to the prime goal of any medical examination, which is to identify and diagnose medical conditions that may be a cause of the patient's symptoms. This goal needs to be strived for by the ED physician whether the symptoms that the patient presents with appear to be psychiatric in nature or not. Medical and psychiatric diagnosis is an imperfect process that is subject to and affected by clinician opinion and error. If this child's symptoms had been diagnosed incorrectly as stemming from a psychiatric disorder, she would not have received the proper treatment needed to alleviate her condition. Proper medical clearance should always be strived for prior to labeling the patient's syndrome as one that is psychiatric in nature.

The issues of trust and clinical experience were key players in this case example. It is important to note that this child had been seen at a different ED the night before and was sent home by the ED treatment team. The ED psychiatry team used this information and the report from the child's mother to further add to the child's diagnostic picture. From this point, the ED psychiatric services team used their level of clinical experience with assessing psychosis and cases of new onset psychosis. The trust that was present between the ED physician and the ED psychiatric team allowed for an open dialogue between the two parties that lead to the eventual decision to perform further medical testing. This trust and experience between the treatment team members helped to ultimately save a life.

11.12 Paranoia as a Survival Mechanism

In some instances, paranoia or paranoid delusions could be conceptualized as a survival tool created by the brain. This idea was touched on early on by Silk (1921) in his discussion of delusions and hallucinations playing a role in the psychotic patient as a defense mechanism. Patients with disorders such as PTSD, who may present with the naturally occurring hypervigilance of the disorder, have learned to adapt to the environment that was observed to be a threat to the patient. So, these hypervigilant reactions, such as looking over your shoulder to see who is behind you at all times or always sitting with your back to a wall in a room, can be viewed as a way to help the person survive based on their prior exposure to a threatening stimulus.

This idea can also be applied to situations in which the paranoia that a patient exhibits is out of touch with reality, for example, patients that present with beliefs that "the Mafia" or FBI are following them and are out to harm them. The behaviors that the patient exhibits in response to the paranoid beliefs may be engaged in as a natural survival instinct. If I believe someone is out to harm or kill me, I am naturally going to want to take action to protect myself or flee from the situation, hence the innate fight-or-flight response kicks in.

Also, take the situation in which a patient may be refusing to eat certain foods from certain individuals or may be refusing medication. In many of these instances, the patient may believe that the food or medication is being poisoned and will refuse the food or medication as a way to avoid a potential life-threatening situation. This also gives the patient a certain amount of perceived control over their environment. The solution to getting these patients to eat or take their medications, especially while in the ED, may be as simple as reassuring them that they are safe and that the food or medications have not been tampered with.

Unfortunately, if the paranoia is not based in reality and is causing impairments in the person's ability to function or maintain relationships with friends or family, the person may present to an ED for evaluation.

11.13 Treatment Options for Psychosis in the Emergency Department

Patients presenting with a psychotic episode will arrive to an ED for treatment whenever the symptoms that the patient is experiencing become severe enough that family, friends, or others in the community near the patient are negatively affected by the symptoms or associated behaviors related to the symptoms.

When the task of treating a psychotic illness is presented to an ED team, the first logical question to arise is what options are available to the team for proper treatment of the symptoms. The primary and most efficient treatment for psychotic symptoms in the ED, whether caused by a primary psychiatric disorder or substance intoxication, is medication. Aripiprazole, risperidone, haloperidol, olanzapine, ziprasidone, and clozapine are some of the commonly available antipsychotic medications that an ED treatment team may have at their disposal to treat psychotic symptoms. Troubling symptoms, both for the patient and their caregivers, including paranoia, command hallucinations, thought disorganization, and agitation, can be ameliorated by rapid and properly dosed administration of the antipsychotic class of medications.

With any patient presenting to the ED for assistance, asking them if they want help and what type of help they are seeking should be the initial starting point of the interaction (Mohr et al. 2005). If medications are being sought out by the patient or a cooperative decision is made, with the patient's input, to start a medication, oral medication should be the initial treatment choice (Brown et al. 2012; Byrne 2007; Mohr et al. 2005). Intramuscular formulations of medications can be utilized to help treat an agitated and aggressive patient who is at risk of harming themselves or others and that has not responded to offers of oral medications or other calming interventions (Brown et al. 2012; Mohr et al. 2005; Zimbroff 2003).

11.13.1 Antipsychotic Medications

With any antipsychotic medication choice, the first task should be to calm the patient to the point that they are able to rationally make choices regarding their care and treatment (Brown et al. 2012). Involving the patient in the development of their treatment plan is key to building trust and rapport with the patient. Many professional associations, including the American College of Emergency Physicians (ACEP) and the American Association for Emergency Psychiatry (AAEP), recommend using a single antipsychotic medication to ameliorate agitation in psychotic patients (Brown et al. 2012; Byrne 2007). While this book is specifically geared toward evidence-based practices and approaches for patients with behavioral health emergencies, we recommend that the reader be mindful of the potential cost burden of some medication types. We direct the reader to look at the cost disparities of the IM formulations. The following antipsychotic medications should be available to most emergency department treatment teams; the listed dosages are recommended to help treat patients presenting with an exacerbation of psychotic symptoms.

While reading this section, please note that any uncited references to medication information were written in consultation with Yener Balan, MD.

11.13.1.1 Risperidone

Risperidone is listed as an atypical antipsychotic medication. Risperidone can be administered in oral or intramuscular (IM) injection form. The recommended starting minimum effective dose is 2 mg/day (Byrne 2007) in the oral form with a final target dose of 4–8 mg/day (Risperidone 2016). The maximum daily dose in oral form is 16 mg/day. The IM formulation is long-acting and is administered once every 2 weeks at 25 mg with a maximum dose of 50 mg (Risperidone 2016). Oral risperidone combined with lorazepam has been found to have similar effectiveness when compared with the use of a combination of haloperidol IM and lorazepam IM (Brown et al. 2012). Risperidone is also available in a concentrated liquid form (Zimbroff 2003) and wafers (Mohr et al. 2005), which can help to increase medication adherence with patients.

11.13.1.2 Olanzapine

Olanzapine is classified as an atypical antipsychotic medication. Olanzapine can be administered either orally or in an IM injection; 5 mg is the minimum effective daily dose of the medication in oral form (Byrne 2007). The recommended dose is 5–10 mg in IM form with a half-life of 2–15 hours (Mohr et al. 2005). The IM form should be used for 3 consecutive days or less as a maximum duration. The maximum daily dose for all forms of olanzapine is 20 mg (Mohr et al. 2005). Olanzapine can be used in place of haloperidol to treat agitation in a psychotic patient, in IM form a single dose can work within 15–45 minutes to effectively treat the problem symptoms and create a reduction in possible extrapyramidal symptoms (EPS) (Brown et al. 2012; Mohr et al. 2005; Zimbroff 2003). For patients that present with medication-compliance concerns, a rapidly dissolvable form of Olanzapine is available, which has been shown to be safe, effective, and increases rates of medication compliance (Mohr et al. 2005; Zimbroff 2003).

11.13.1.3 Haloperidol

Haloperidol is listed as a typical antipsychotic medication. Haloperidol is available in oral, IM, and IV formulations. The minimum effective daily dose is 2 mg in oral form (Byrne 2007). In IM administrations, 0.5–10 mg can be used. The half-life of the IM formulation is 10–25 hours (Mohr et al. 2005). Haloperidol is a well-researched typical antipsychotic drug known for its effective treatment of agitation in psychotic patients with the disadvantages of high rates of EPS and involuntary muscle spasms (Brown et al. 2012; Zimbroff 2003). A combination of haloperidol IM and lorazepam IM can reduce these disadvantages and still effectively treat the patient (Brown et al. 2012; Zimbroff 2003).

11.13.1.4 Ziprasidone

Ziprasidone is classified as an atypical antipsychotic. It is available in oral and IM forms. Recommended dosing for the oral form is 20 mg twice a day with a maximum dose of 100 mg twice a day. A dose of 10–20 mg/day with a maximum dose of 40 mg/day are the recommendations for the IM formulation (Mohr et al. 2005; Ziprasidone 2016). The half-life of the IM form is 4–38 hours (Mohr et al. 2005). Ziprasidone IM has the added benefits of working within 30 minutes of administration, is less sedating and has decreased occurrences of hypotension when compared with the use of haloperidol, and use of the IM form can be smoothly switched to the oral formulation (Brown et al. 2012; Mohr et al. 2005; Zimbroff 2003).

11.13.1.5 Aripiprazole

Aripiprazole is listed as an atypical antipsychotic drug. Aripiprazole is available in oral and IM extended release forms; 10–15 mg/day is the recommended initial and target dose for the oral formulation (Apripiprazole 2016; Byrne 2007). The daily maximum dose is 30 mg. The IM extended-release formulation has an initial recommended dose of 400 mg with a maintenance dose of 400 mg/month (Apripiprazole 2016).

11.13.1.6 Quetiapine

Quetiapine is listed as an atypical antipsychotic. It is available in an oral form. The recommended daily dose is 150–750 mg (Byrne 2007; Quetiapine 2016) after titrating up from an initial dose of 50 mg administered in 25 mg tablets twice a day. The maximum recommended daily dose is 750 mg.

11.13.1.7 Clozapine

Clozapine is listed as an atypical antipsychotic. Clozapine is available in oral tablets, dissolvable tablets, and in liquid oral forms. The initial recommended starting oral dose is 12.5 mg once or twice a day with a target dosage of 300–450 mg/day. The recommended maximum daily dose is 900 mg. The liquid oral formulation is available in 1 and 9 ml oral syringes (Clozapine 2016). Clozapine is well known for its calming effect on aggression, but is underutilized in the treatment of psychosis due to the health risks attached to its use, including agranulocytosis or low white blood cell counts, but it is turned to as an alternative treatment option when a patient has failed multiple trials of other antipsychotic medications (Byrne 2007; Mohr et al. 2005).

11.13.2 Antipsychotic Medication Side Effects

Whether the treating ED physician or psychiatrist chooses to medicate a psychotic patient or not may be driven by the potential side effects that a given medication can cause. Many of the side effects that can exist with the use of antipsychotic medication can range from bothersome ones such as weight gain to life-threatening ones such as neuromalignant syndrome. With choosing any medication or treatment modality, both the risks and benefits of using the medication need to be examined and shared with the patient.

Many of the antipsychotic medications that can be used to treat psychotic symptoms can cause EPS (Byrne 2007). EPS can manifest in a variety of ways in different patients depending on how the patient's individualized physiology responds to the introduction of the medication into their system. EPS can manifest in the patient as dystonia, akathisia (a feeling of restlessness and a need to move around), tremors, rigid muscles, shuffling movements while ambulating (Brown et al. 2012), and uncontrolled muscle movements, for example, the patient's eyes may involuntarily roll backward toward the head. Both typical and atypical antipsychotic medications can create EPS and raised prolactin levels in the blood leading to sexual dysfunction and milk production in the breasts (Byrne 2007).

Sedation, increased chance of seizures, weight gain, and hyperglycemia are other common antipsychotic medication side effects (Byrne 2007). More specifically, the use of intravenous haloperidol can lead to cardiac failure and potential death from a prolonged QTc interval (Brown et al. 2012). Olanzapine combined with a benzodiazepine, administered as an intramuscular injection, has caused severe low blood pressure, slow heart rate, and decreased respiration in some patients (Brown et al. 2012). Sudden death in geriatric patients has also occurred.

Benzodiazepines, such as lorazepam, which can be used alone or combined with a typical or atypical antipsychotic, can bring on unwanted side effects, such as decreased respiration, over sedation, impaired coordination, and impaired speech production (Zimbroff 2003). The selection of an appropriate, safe, and effective medication by the treating physician must take into account any and all potential life-altering side effects.

11.14 Conclusion

Psychosis, including paranoia, can be a frightening and overwhelming experience for both the patient living with the symptoms and the emergency department staff that are tasked with treating the patient's frightening symptoms. Symptoms may range from simple delusions to bizarre behaviors, such as echolalia or waxy flexibility. Many psychotic symptoms may present in patients that are acutely intoxicated on illicit substances or those in which a substance intoxication is exacerbating an underlying psychotic disorder.

The relative experience level of the ED staff, each individual clinician's comfort level in working with a patient presenting with psychotic symptoms, the overarching stigma attached to the patient presenting with psychosis, the presence of family or other support people, and the patient's ability to adjust to the stressors present in the ED environment all interact with one another to either help the patient move forward toward wellness or move backward toward illness.

ED staff need to be properly prepared to meet the needs of the psychotic patient as the chances that ED staff will encounter psychotic symptoms in patients presenting to the ED for treatment have been increasing annually with the increases in mental health complaints presenting in EDs across the country.

11.15 Key ED Survival Points for Psychosis

The following is a list of key ED survival points for psychosis:

- Substance intoxication and medical rule-outs should always be placed in the diagnostic picture.
- Safety should always be considered given the unpredictable nature of the disorder.
- Not all psychotic episodes are emergencies and require hospitalization.
- Hallucinations, delusions, and disorganized thoughts are the key symptoms.
- Other disorders may contain psychotic symptoms (e.g., bipolar disorder).

References

Albert, M, and L F McCaig. 2015. *Emergency Department Visits Related to Schizophrenia Among Adults Aged 18–64: United States, 2009–2011*. Data Brief, Hyattsville, MD: National Center for Health Statistics. http://www.cdc.gov/data/databriefs/db215.htm.

American Psychiatric Association. 2000. Schizophrenia and other psychotic disorders. In *Diagnostic and Statistical Manual of Mental Disorders*, Fourth Edition, Text Revision. Arlington, VA: American Psychiatric Press.

American Psychiatric Association. 2013. In *Diagnostic and Statistical Manual or Mental Disorders*, Fifth Edition. Arlington, VA: American Psychiatric Association.

Aronson, M J, and S V Thompson. 1950. Complications of acute catatonic excietement. *The American Journal of Psychiatry* 107 (3): 216–220. doi:10.1176/ajp.107.3.216.

Assessment of insight in psychosis. *The American Journal of Psychiatry* 150 (6): 873–879. Accessed October 27, 2016. doi:10.1176/ajp.150.6.873.

Barberio, D. 2000. Phenomenology of schizophrenia. msu.edu. August. http://msu.edu/user/barberio/schizol1.htm.

Barkus, E. 2016. High-potency cannabis increases the risk of psychosis. *Evidence-Based Mental Health* 19 (2): 54. doi:10.1136/eb-2015-102105.

Bowman, K M, and A F Raymond. 1931. A statistical study of delusions in the manic depressive psychoses. *The American Journal of Psychiatry* 88 (1): 111–121. doi:10.1176/ajp.88.1.111.

Brewerton, T D. 1994. Hyperreligiosity in psychotic disorders. *Journal of Nervous and Mental Disease* 182 (5): 302–304.

Brown, H E, J Stoklosa, and O Freudenreich. 2012. How to stabilize an acutely psychotic patient. *Current Psychiatry*, December: 10–16. http://www.mdedge/currentpsychiatry/article/64936/schizophrenia-other-psychotic-disorders/how-stabilize-acutely.

Bush, G, M Fink, G Petrides, F Dowling, and A Francis. 1996. Catatonia II treatment with lorazepam and electroconvulsive therapy. *Acta Psychiatrica Scandinavica* 93 (2): 137–143. doi:10.111/j.1600-0447.1996.tb09815.x.

Byrne, P. 2007. Managing the acute psychotic episode. *British Medical Journal* 334: 686–692. doi:10.1136/bmj.39148.668160.80.

Cahalan, S. 2013. *Brain on Fire: My Month of Madness*. New York: Simon and Schuster.

Chaudhury, S. 2010. Hallucinations: Clinical aspects and management. *Industrial Psychiatry Journal* 19 (1): 5–12. doi:10.4103/0972-6748.77625.

Dalmau, J, A J Gleichman, E G Hughes, J E Rossi, X Peng, M Lai, S K dessain, M R Rosenfeld, R Balice-Gordon, and D R Lynch. 2008. Anti-NMDA-recrpetor encephalitis: Case series and analysis of the effects of antibodies. *Lancet Neurology* 7 (12): 1091–1098. doi:10.1016/S1474-4422(08)70224-2.

Dalmau, J, E Tuzun, H Wu, J Masjuan, J E Rossi, A Voloschin, J M Baehring, H Shimazaki, R Koide, D King, W Mason, L H Sansing, M A Dichter, M R Rosenfeld, D R Lynch. 2007. Paraneoplastic anti-N-methyl-D-aspartate receptor encephalitis associated with ovarian teratoma. *Annals of Neurology* 61 (1): 25–36. doi:10.1002/ana.21050.

Daniels, J. 2009. Catatonia: Clinical aspects and neurobiological correlates. *The Journal of Neuropsychiatry and Clinical Neurosciences* 21 (4): 371–380. doi:10.1176/jnp.2009.21.4.371.

Dubovsky, S L, and M Thomas. 1992. Psychotic depression: Advances in conceptualization and treatment. *Psychiatric Services* 43 (12): 1189–1198. doi:10.1176/ps.43.12.1189.

England, M L, D Ongur, G T Konopaske, and R Karmacharya. 2011. Catatonia in psychotic patients: Clinical features and treatment response. *The Journal of Neuropsychiatry and Clinical Neurosciences* 23 (2): 223–226. doi:10.1176/jnp.23.2.jnp.223.

Ganos, C, T Ogrzal, A Schnitzler, and A Munchau. 2012. The pathophysiology of echopraxia/echolalia: Relevance to Gilles De La Tourette syndrome. *Movement Disorders* 27 (10): 1222–1229. doi:10.1002/mds.25103.

Grant, K M, T D LeVan, S M Wells, M Li, S F Stoltenberg, H E Gendelman, G Carlo, and R A Bevins. 2012. Methamphetamine-associated psychosis. *Journal of Neuroimmune Pharmacology* 7 (1): 113–139. doi:10.1007/s11481-011-9288-1.

Grinnell, R. 2016a. *Clanging*. July 17. https://psychcentral.com/encyclopedia/clanging/.

Grinnell, R. 2016b. Perseveration. *PsychCentral*. July 17. http://psychcentral.com/encyclopedia/perseveration/.

Grinnell, R. 2016c. *Thought Insertion*. July 17. http://psychcentral.com/encyclopedia/thought-insertion.

Grinnell, R. 2016d. *Thought Disorder*. July 17. http://psychcentral.com/encyclopedia/thought-disorder/.

Hay, C. 1955. Command automatism and echopraxia to television. *The American Journal of Psychiatry* 112 (1): 65–65. doi:10.1176/ajp.112.1.65.

Jeste, D V, and S I Finkel. 2000. Psychosis of Alzheimer's disease and related dementias: Diagnostic criteria for a distinct syndrome. *The American Journal of Geriatric Psychiatry* 8 (1): 29–34. doi:10.1097/00019442-200002000-00004.

Kayser, M S, and J Dalmau. 2011. Anti-NMDA receptor encephalitis in psychiatry. *Current Psychiatry Reviews* 7 (3): 189–193. doi:10.2174/157340011797183184.

Kayser, M S, M J Titulaer, N Gresa-Arribas, and J Dalmau. 2013. Frequency and characteristics of isolated psychiatric episodes in anti-NMDA receptor encephalitis. *JAMA Neurology* 70 (9): 1133–1139. doi:10.1001/jamaneurol.2013.3216.

Kraft, D P, and H M Babigian. 1972. Somatic delusion or self mutilation in a schizophrenic woman: A psychiatric emergency room case report. *The American Journal of Psychiatry* 128 (7): 893–895. doi:10.1176/ajp.128.7.893.

Malchow, B, A Hasan, P Fusar-Poli, A Schmitt, P Falkai, and T Wobrock. 2013. Cannabis abuse and brain morphology in schizophrenia: A review of the available evidence. *European Archives of Psychiatry and Clinical Neuroscience* 263 (1): 3–13. doi:10.1007/s00406-012-0346-3.

Mandal, A. 2014. Hallucination types. *News Medical* . July 24. http://www.news-medical.net/health/Hallucination-Types.aspx.

Marin, R S, and I R Gorovoy. 2014. Echothymia: Environmental dependency in the affective domain. *The Journal of Neuropsychiatry and Clinical Neurosciences* 26 (1): 92–96. doi:10.1176/appi.neuropsych.13020020.

Miller-Keane Encyclopedia and Dictionary of Medicine, Nursing, and Allied Health, Seventh Edition. 2003a. Echolalia. http://medical-dictionary.thefreedictionary.com/echolalia.

Miller-Keane Encyclopedia and Dictionary of Medicine, Nursing, and Allied Health. 2003b. Medical Dictionary, the Free Dictionary. http://medical-dictionary.thefreedictionary.com/circumstantial.

Mohr, P, J Pecenak, J Svestka, D Swingler, and T Treuer. 2005. Treatment of acute agitation in psychotic disorders. *Neuroendocrinology Letters* 26 (4): 327–335. http://www.nel.edu/26-2005_4_pdf/NEL260405R03_Mohr.pdf.

Moore, T H M, S Zammit, A Lingford-Hughes, T R E Barnes, P B Jones, M Burke, and G Lewis. 2007. Cannabis use and risk of psychotic or affective mental health outcomes: A systematic review. *The Lancet* 370 (9584): 319–328. doi:10.1016/S0140-6736(07)61162-3.

Mosby's Medical Dictionary, 8th edition. 2009. *Word Salad*. http://medical-dictionary.thefreedictionary.com/word+salad.

National Alliance on Mental Illness. 2016. Early psychosis and psychosis. nami.org. http://www.nami.org/Learn-More/Mental-Health-Conditions/Early-Psychosis-and Psychosis.

Owens, P L, R Mutter, and C Stocks. 2010. *Mental Health and Substance Abuse Related Emergency Department Visits among Adults, 2007: Statisical Brief #92*. Statistical Brief, Rockville, MD: Agency for Healthcare Research and Quality. http://www.hcup-us.ahrq.gov/reports/statbriefs/sb92.pdf.

Pawar, A V, and S A Spence. 2003. Defining thought broadcast. *The British Journal of Psychiatry* 287–291. doi:10.1192/bjp.183.4.287.

Radhakrishnan, R, S T Wilkinson, and D C D'Souza. 2014. Gone to pot: A review of the association between cannabis and psychosis. *Frontiers in Psychiatry* 5 (54). doi:10.3389/fpsyt.2014.00054.

Sharma, T R, and M C Cieraszynski. 2013. A case of delusional parasitosis in a 58 year old woman. *Primary Psychiatry*, October 30. 2016. http://primarypsychiatry.com/a-case-of-delusional-parasitosis-in-a-58-year-old-woman/.

Silk, S A. 1921. The compensatory mechanism of delusions and hallucinations. *The American Journal of Psychiatry* 77 (4): 523–542. doi:10.1176/ajp.77.4.523.

Subotnik, K L, K H Nuechterlein, J Ventura, M J Gitlin, S Marder, J Mintz, G S Hellemann, L A Thornton, and I R Singh. 2012. Risperidone nonadherence and return of positive symptoms in early course of schizophrenia. *Focus* 10 (2): 231–238. doi:10.1176/appi.focus.10.2.231.

Wilkinson, S T, R Radhakrishnan, and D C D'Sousa. 2014. Impact of cannabis use on the development of psychotic disorders. *Current Addiction Reports* 1 (2): 115–128. doi:10.1007/s40429-014-0018-7.

Yang, Y, A Raine, P Colletti, A Toga W, and K L Narr. 2011. Abnormal structural correlates of response perseveration in individuals with psychopathy. *The Journal of Neuropsychiatry and Clinical Neurosciences* 23 (1): 107–110. doi:10.1176/jnp.23.1.jnp107#.

Zimbroff, D L. 2003. Management of acute psychosis: From emergency to stabilization. *CNS Spectrums*. 8(11 Supp 12):10–5 doi:10.1017/s1092852900008130.

Resources

Drugs.com. 2016. Apripiprazole. https://www.drugs.com/dosage/apripipazole.html.
Drugs.com. 2016. Clozapine. https://www.drugs.com/dosage/clozapine.html.
Drugs.com. 2016. Quetiapine. https:www.drugs.com/dosage/quetiapine.html.
Drugs.com. 2016. Risperidone. https://www.drugs.com/dosage/risperidone.html.
Drugs.com. 2016. Ziprasidone. https://www.drugs.com/dosage/ziprasidone.html.
Gage, S H, M Hickman, and S Zammit. 2016. Association between cannabis and psychosis: Epidemiologic evidence. *Biological Psychiatry* 79 (7): 549–556. doi:10.1016/j.biopsych.2015.08.001.

McGorry P D, M C, Henry L, D J, Jackson H J, Flaum M, H S, McKenzie D, Kulkarni J, Karoly R. 1995. Spurious precision: Procedural validity of diagnostic assessment in psychotic disorders. *The American Journal of Psychiatry* 152 (2): 220–223. doi:10.1176/ajp.152.2.220.

Schanzer, B M, M B First, B Dominguez, D S Hasin, and C L M Caton. 2006. Diagnosing psychotic disorders in the emergency department in the context of substance use. *Psychiatric Services* 57 (10): 1468–1473. doi:10.1176/ps.2006.57.10.1468.

Wikipedia. 2016. Public display of affection. https://en.m.wikipedia.org/wiki/Public_display_of_affection.

Chapter 12

The Diagnosis and Management of Substance Use Disorders in the Emergency Psychiatric Setting: A Primer

Noam Fast

Contents

12.1 Introduction	201
12.2 The Substance Use Epidemic and Treatment	201
12.2.1 The Substance Use Epidemic	201
12.2.2 Substance Use: Treatment and Morbidity	201
12.3 Anatomy of Addiction: Pathways in the Brain and Major Brain Structures	202
12.3.1 Neurotransmitters of Interest in Addiction Pathways	203
12.4 Psychological Craving: Reinforcement and Conditioning	203
12.5 Research: Data Sets	203
12.6 The Motivational Matrix of Stages of Change	203
12.7 Diagnosis: Criteria and Codes	203
12.7.1 Diagnostic Criteria	204
12.8 Alcohol Disorders	205
12.8.1 Alcohol Disorder Assessment Tools	206
12.8.1.1 AUDIT C	206
12.8.1.2 AUDIT	207
12.8.2 Alcohol Effect and Metabolism	207
12.8.3 Risk and Prognostic Factors	207
12.8.4 Blood Alcohol Level Toxicity	207
12.8.5 Alcohol Withdrawal	208
12.8.5.1 Withdrawal Treatment	208
12.8.6 Comorbidity	208
	209

- 12.8.7 Medication for Alcohol Use Disorder ... 209
- 12.8.8 Wernicke Korsakoff Syndrome ... 210
  - 12.8.8.1 Wernicke Korsakoff Syndrome Treatment ... 210
- 12.9 Sedative Hypnotic and Anxiolytic-Related Disorders ... 211
  - 12.9.1 Benzodiazepines ... 211
- 12.10 Cannabis-Related Disorders ... 211
  - 12.10.1 Cannabis: Intoxication and Withdrawal ... 212
  - 12.10.2 Cannabis: Social, Legal, and Research Issues ... 212
  - 12.10.3 Synthetic Cannabis ... 212
  - 12.10.4 Cannabis and Brain Activity ... 213
  - 12.10.5 Cannabis Use Frequency Studies in Adolescents ... 213
- 12.11 Tobacco-Related Disorders ... 213
  - 12.11.1 Tobacco: Usage and Mortality Rates ... 213
  - 12.11.2 Nicotine Pharmacology ... 214
    - 12.11.2.1 Nicotine Withdrawal ... 214
  - 12.11.3 Gold Standard Treatment ... 214
  - 12.11.4 Nicotine Treatment: Preferred Options ... 215
    - 12.11.4.1 Bupropion ... 215
    - 12.11.4.2 Varenicline ... 215
    - 12.11.4.3 Second Line Nicotine Treatment Agents ... 215
    - 12.11.4.4 Nicotine Replacement Therapy ... 216
- 12.12 Opioid-Related Disorders ... 216
  - 12.12.1 Opioid Types ... 216
  - 12.12.2 Opioid Use and Emergency Department Visits ... 216
  - 12.12.3 Opioids: A Historical Time Line ... 217
    - 12.12.3.1 National Institutes of Health Consensus Panel on Opioid Addiction ... 217
  - 12.12.4 Effects of Opioid Use ... 217
    - 12.12.4.1 Withdrawal ... 217
  - 12.12.5 Opioid Overdose ... 218
    - 12.12.5.1 Opioid Overdose Facts for First Responders ... 218
  - 12.12.6 Management of Opioid Use Disorder ... 218
    - 12.12.6.1 Choices of Medication to Manage Opioid Use Disorders ... 219
    - 12.12.6.2 Methadone ... 219
    - 12.12.6.3 Naltrexone ... 219
    - 12.12.6.4 Buprenorphine ... 219
- 12.13 Stimulant-Related Disorders ... 220
  - 12.13.1 Stimulants ... 220
    - 12.13.1.1 Stimulant Intoxication and Withdrawal ... 220
  - 12.13.2 Methamphetamine: Pharmacology and Effects ... 220
    - 12.13.2.1 Methamphetamine: Addiction and Treatment ... 221
    - 12.13.2.2 Emergency Department Visits and Methamphetamine: 2007–2011 ... 221
    - 12.13.2.3 The Man Who Ate His Methamphetamine: Case Presentation ... 221
      - 12.13.2.3.1 Case Discussion ... 222
  - 12.13.3 Cocaine Use Disorder ... 223
    - 12.13.3.1 Cocaine Formulations ... 223
    - 12.13.3.2 Methylenedioxymethamphetamine ... 223

12.14 Inhalant-Related Disorders..224
    12.14.1 Inhalant Types..224
12.15 Hallucinogen-Related Disorders...224
    12.15.1 Common Hallucinogens..224
        12.15.1.1 Lysergic Acid Diethylamide..224
        12.15.1.2 Psilocybin...225
        12.15.1.3 Dimethyltryptamine..225
        12.15.1.4 Mescaline...225
        12.15.1.5 Salvia Divinorum...225
    12.15.2 Hallucinogen Neurology..225
    12.15.3 Hallucinogen Intoxication..225
        12.15.3.1 Hallucinogen-Persisting Perception Disorder....................226
12.16 Conclusion...226
References..226
Resources...231

12.1 Introduction

Patients who suffer from substance use disorders are stigmatized in the general population and even among emergency room staff and other healthcare settings (American Medical Association 2015). This chapter describes the presentation of typical patients who suffer from substance use disorders and is meant as a guide for the treatment and referral of these patients.

12.2 The Substance Use Epidemic and Treatment

12.2.1 The Substance Use Epidemic

The association of substance use disorders with significant morbidity and mortality is overwhelming: drug overdose remains the number one cause of accidental death in the United States and tobacco smoking remains the number one preventable risk factor for death (Yoon et al. 2014). Alcohol-related morbidity remains one of the top causes of U.S. healthcare spending (Hasin and Grant 2015). Increasingly, the emergency department (ED) has become the primary treatment entryway to the healthcare system for the uninsured and society at large; approximately half of all hospital inpatient admissions were referred from the ED setting (Weiss et al. 2014). There were approximately 2,460,000 ED visits that involved drug misuse or abuse in 2011 alone. In 2012, one-third of approximately 36 million young adults reported binge alcohol use in the past month with one-fifth of young adults reporting use of an illicit drug in the past month. The Treatment Episode Data Set (TEDS) reported that there were 403,756 admissions aged 18–25 to substance abuse treatment programs in 2011 (Batts et al. 2014). The number of young adults seen in an ED for the use of illicit drugs and the misuse or abuse of pharmaceuticals increased between 2005 and 2011 (Substance Abuse and Mental Health Services Administration 2014). Between 2006 and 2011, large central metropolitan areas experienced a 22% increase in the rate of ED visits over 5 years, from 31,900 to 39,000 visits per 100,000 population (Weiss et al. 2014). Between 2006 and 2011, the rate of ED visits for substance-related disorders (not including alcohol) increased 48% (Substance Abuse and Mental Health Services Administration 2013). Over the same period, ED visits for alcohol-related disorders increased 34%.

12.2.2 Substance Use: Treatment and Morbidity

The medical professionals are in a unique position to offer treatment and referral for patients with substance use disorders as they present in crises situations. Substance-using patients who miss their outpatient follow-up appointments rely on the emergency room physician, who is, at times, the first and last line of defense against chronic, debilitating medical illnesses. The implementation of systemic screening and treatment strategies has been promising, but more needs to be done to decrease emergency room utilization for substance use disorders. Nonjudgmental, patient-centered strategies are a key to the effective initiation of treatment, successful referral for substance use services, and spiritual and biological recovery. Physical exam and appropriate diagnostic studies are paramount during emergency room encounters with substance-using patients. The sequelae of substance use disorders put patients at risk for specific syndromes such as delirium tremens, gastrointestinal (GI) bleeding, psychosis, suicidality, abscesses, and sexually transmitted infections. Additionally, patients with substance use disorders tend to fail to follow up with the treatment for comorbid medical and psychiatric illness (Barthwell 1997) so that they may present in diabetic ketoacidosis for diabetes mellitus, acute chronic obstructive pulmonary disease exacerbations, as well as psychiatric decompensation. This is also why treatment and referral strategies are so important in the emergency setting: effective prevention and treatment of substance use disorders has the potential to decrease morbidity, mortality, and healthcare utilization system wide. The era when many healthcare professionals remain reluctant to engage and treat substance-using patients is hopefully coming to an end with the advent of systemic quality improvement initiatives, "meaningful use," and adherence with "core measures" (National Academies of Sciences, Engineering, and Medicine 2016). On a personal level, it is up to every healthcare professional to treat the substance-using patient with the same dignity as any other patient.

Reducing the number of premature deaths requires integrated action. This includes risk-factor reduction, screening, early intervention, and evidence-based treatments for substance use and comorbid disorders.

The social, economic, and geographic attributes of psychiatric illness and substance use disorders are constantly evolving, with new substances and behaviors appearing and growing. While the treatment for substance use disorders is effective and normalizing, only 1 of 4 users have ever received any treatment for these conditions in their lifetimes (Batts et al. 2014). Effective emergency room education, referral, and treatment strategies can improve the prognosis for patients, families, and society as a whole (Botvin 2004).

12.3 Anatomy of Addiction: Pathways in the Brain and Major Brain Structures

The overarching concept for addiction is often called a hijack of the pleasure, reward, and craving neural pathways of the brain, mainly the ventral tegmental area of the brainstem that leads to the nucleus accumbens in the cortex. That is to say, the pleasure reward system, which is normally adaptive for the organism, gets taken over by addiction and becomes maladaptive for the organism. Other areas of the brain that are involved in the addiction hijack process include the limbic system, prefrontal cortex, and basal ganglia. Additionally, patients with addiction also suffer from decreased impulse control via hypofunctioning of the prefrontal cortex. This hypofunctioning occurs in the orbitofrontal areas then moves to the cingulate area of the prefrontal cortex (Koob and Volkow 2010).

In a concept termed the *memory salience pathway*, the relief of anxiety, sadness, and pain becomes linked with the substance use experience, so that future negative emotional states trigger further cravings for the substance (Koob and Volkow 2010).

12.3.1 Neurotransmitters of Interest in Addiction Pathways

Multiple neurotransmitters, produced by the brain's nerve cells, and brain structures play an important role in the body's biological link to addiction. These neurotransmitters include dopamine in the nucleus accumbens, corticotrophin-releasing hormone in the amygdala, and glutamate in the frontal-cingulate circuit (Koob and Volkow 2010).

12.4 Psychological Craving: Reinforcement and Conditioning

Reinforcement influences rates of operant behavior, such as substance use. A substance acts as a reinforcer when self-administration increases the future likelihood of substance use. A reinforcer is any stimulus that acts to increase the future likelihood of a behavior. There are many primary reinforcers in an individual's environment that act to increase the occurrence of addictive behavior (Tiffany and Wray 2011). The common substance caffeine, found naturally occurring in many teas and coffees, is a primary reinforcer. The caffeine, when consumed, creates a pleasurable lift in energy levels and mental acuity. These pleasurable experiences act as a reinforcer and increase the likelihood of an individual consuming another cup of coffee or tea in the future.

When a reinforcer is repeatedly paired with a neutral stimulus, this stimulus can become reinforcing itself. This phenomenon is also known as Pavlovian or classical conditioning. Conditioned preference comes into play in addictions in many ways. Take, for example, the simple act of drinking your cup of morning coffee. The natural reinforcer in this case is the caffeine in the coffee. The natural lift in energy and focus that the caffeine creates in the body reinforces the person to continue to increase the consumption of coffee. Some coffee drinkers can experience a self-reported rise in energy and focus as they go through the motions of pouring the coffee into a mug and smelling its aroma, even prior to consuming the coffee. In this case, the neutral stimulus of pouring the coffee and the activation of olfactory centers in the brain from the coffee's aroma have become paired, via multiple episodes of coffee drinking, with the natural reinforcer of the caffeine in the coffee.

12.5 Research: Data Sets

Multiple data sets exist for the researcher interested in studying substance-abuse-related issues. The Drug Abuse Warning Network (DAWN) is a public health surveillance system monitoring drug-related hospital ED utilization nationwide with a focus on metropolitan areas. Other good sources of data include the 2011 and 2012 National Surveys on Drug Use and Health (NSDUHs), the 2011 Treatment Episode Data Set (TEDS+NEDS), and the 2011 Drug Abuse Warning Network (DAWN).

12.6 The Motivational Matrix of Stages of Change

The motivational matrix of stages of change is useful when conceptualizing treatment strategies for substance use and related disorders. Simply put, it is unrealistic to expect someone who is not thinking about changing to do so. Treatment must be tailored to the preparedness of the patient to change (Miller and Rose 2009). The job of the motivational interviewer includes asking open-ended and nonjudgmental questions, affirming previous positive decisions, reflecting affect, and summarizing the patient experience while eliciting "change talk." Listening, affirming, and highlighting "change talk" improves the patient's chances of effecting a lasting positive change. The matrix is based on the stages of change model developed by Prochaska and DiClemente (1983).

The change model includes five stages that an individual may move through during their therapeutic process.

The model begins with a stage called precontemplation, then progresses to contemplation, preparation, action, and maintenance. The idea is that a patient may move through each step of the change model or some may become stuck at a certain stage of change. The stages are fluid and transitional in nature. For example, a patient that is being pressured by family and friends to seek out treatment of alcohol use, but refuses to act due to being in a state of denial, could be stuck in the precontemplation stage. Other patients may progress through the stages of change in a more haphazard manner. A patient that has never received treatment for his cocaine misuse may be motivated to seek out help after discovering that an acute medical issue has developed due to his drug use. This patient may jump from a stage of precontemplation to one of preparation or even action when he schedules an appointment in the local substance abuse recovery clinic and attends his first appointment. This patient may later experience a relapse on cocaine and slip back into a state of denial causing him to refuse any further treatment. At this time, this patient would be classified in the precontemplation stage of change.

According to the model, any relapses that the patient experiences are viewed as learning experiences, which can strengthen the patient's ability to prevent future occurrences of relapse. Once the patient has moved through the action stage into the maintenance stage, they are engaging in new behaviors that create a lasting change and replace their old substance-using behavioral patterns (Prochaska and DiClemente 1983).

12.7 Diagnosis: Criteria and Codes

The Diagnostic and Statistical Manual of Mental Disorders, fifth edition (DSM-5), has attempted to standardize and clarify the substance use and related disorders (American Psychiatric Association 2013). The words abuse and dependence, themselves somewhat stigmatizing and not evidence based, have been removed from the current DSM and now the moniker *substance use disorder* is the preferred nomenclature. In addition to intoxication and withdrawal syndromes, the substance use disorders now share roughly standardized diagnostic criteria. The disorders are grouped into mild, moderate, and severe categories, based on the number of questions endorsed out of the following groupings:

- Amount/time period: The drug or activity is used more and for a longer amount of time than intended.
- Desire to cut down: Includes the inability to decrease the dosage used.
- Time spent: How much time is spent acquiring drugs or planning for drug-related activity?
- Craving: Includes both psychological and physiological cravings.
- Obligations: How many obligations are missed due to the addiction-related behaviors?
- Problems exacerbated: How many other life areas, including social, emotional, behavioral, psychological, and financial, are negatively affected by the addiction behaviors?

- Reduction in other activity: How often does the substance use take over other activities?
- Hazardous use: May include driving while intoxicated or impaired, operating heavy machinery, or child neglect/abuse.
- Continued use despite documented problems.
- Tolerance: Does the individual need increased amounts of the drug to achieve the same effect over time?
- Withdrawal: A physiological and or subjective change in neurohomeostasis.

The disorders can be amended by the amount of time the patient is in recovery:

- Early remission: 3–12 months in recovery.
- Sustained remission: 12 months or more.

12.7.1 Diagnostic Criteria

The following is a brief list of the International Statistical Classification of Diseases and Related Health Problems (ICD), tenth edition (World Health Organization 1992) diagnosis and nomenclature for substance use and related disorders including intoxication and withdrawal. The list does not include the substance-and medication-induced mental disorders, for instance, substance-induced depressive disorder or substance-induced psychotic disorder. The list includes topics of interest that may not yet be included in the DSM-5.

- Alcohol-related disorders (alcohol use disorder F10.10): Alcohol intoxication F10.129, alcohol withdrawal F10.239, alcohol-induced disorders, other alcohol-induced disorders, unspecified alcohol-related disorder F10.99.
- Caffeine-related disorders: Caffeine intoxication F15.929, caffeine withdrawal F15.93, other caffeine-induced disorders, unspecified caffeine-related disorders F15.99.
- Cannabis-related disorders: Cannabis use disorder F12.1, F12.2, cannabis intoxication F12.129, cannabis withdrawal F12.288, other Cannabis Use disorders, unspecified cannabis use disorders–F12.99.
- Hallucinogen-related disorders: Phencyclidine use disorder F16.10, other hallucinogen use disorder F16.10, phencyclidine intoxication F16.129, other hallucinogen intoxication F16.129, hallucinogen-persisting perception disorder (flashbacks F16.983), other phencyclidine-induced disorders, other hallucinogen-induced disorders, unspecified phencyclidine-related disorder F16.99, unspecified hallucinogen-related disorder F16.99.
- Inhalant-related disorders: Inhalant use disorder F18.1, F18.2, inhalant intoxication F18.129, F18.229, F18.929, other inhalant-induced disorders, unspecified inhalant-related disorders F18.99.
- Opioid-related disorders: Opioid use disorder F11.10, F11.20, opioid intoxication F11.129, F11.229, F11.929, opioid withdrawal F11.23, other opioid-induced disorders, unspecified opioid-related disorders F11.9.
- Sedative hypnotic or anxiolytic-related disorders: Sedative hypnotic or anxiolytic use disorder F13.1, F13.2, sedative hypnotic or anxiolytic intoxication F13.129, F13.229, F13.929, sedative hypnotic or anxiolytic withdrawal F13.239, F13.232, sedative hypnotic or anxiolytic-induced disorders, unspecified sedative hypnotic or anxiolytic-related disorders F13.99.

- Stimulant-related disorders: Stimulant use disorder F14, F15.10, F15.20, stimulant intoxication F15.129, F15.229. F15.929 and so on. stimulant withdrawal F14.23, F15.23, other stimulant-induced disorders, unspecified stimulant-related disorder F14.99, F15.99.
- Tobacco-related disorders: Tobacco use disorder Z72.0, F17.20, tobacco withdrawal F17.203, other tobacco-induced disorders, unspecified tobacco-related disorder F17.209.
- Other (or unknown) substance-related disorders: Other (or unknown) substance use disorder F19.1, F19.2, other (or unknown) substance intoxication F19.129, F19.229, F19.929, other (or unknown) substance withdrawal F19.239, other (or unknown) substance-induced disorders, unspecified other (or unknown) substance-related disorder F19.99.

12.8 Alcohol Disorders

The ICD 10 (World Health Organization 1992) lists many alcohol disorders that a patient may present with, including alcohol use disorder F10.10, alcohol intoxication F10.129, alcohol withdrawal F10.239, alcohol-induced disorders, other alcohol-induced disorders, and unspecified alcohol-related disorder F10.99.

Ethyl alcohol is a central nervous system depressant that is rapidly absorbed by the GI system into the bloodstream. The alcohol molecule interacts with a variety of ligands and can alter global neuronal function via modulation of both ligand and voltage gated ion channels. Neuronal communication systems involving serotonin, adenosine, dopamine, opiates, cannabinoids, and acetylcholine are altered by alcohol. Lifetime prevalence of alcoholism approaches 15% in the general population (Grant et al. 2016).

It is necessary to quantify how much a patient drinks using the following standard designation. One alcoholic drink is 0.6 ounces of pure ethanol, or roughly a 12-ounce beer or 8 ounces of malt liquor or 5 ounces of wine or 1.5 ounces of 80-proof distilled spirit. The Assessment International Guide for Monitoring Alcohol Consumption and Related Harm (World Health Organization 2000) recommends monitoring of the following:

- The frequency of alcohol use and the frequency of heavy "binge" drinking. It is essential to assess heavy quantity consumption in addition to usual frequency and quantity of consumption. The pattern corresponds to consuming five or more drinks (male) or four or more drinks (female) in about 2 hours.
- The typical number of drinks per day when alcohol is used.

12.8.1 Alcohol Disorder Assessment Tools

In order to help assess the patient presenting with possible alcohol use issues, any of a multitude of alcohol disorder assessment tools can be utilized. The CAGE, Self-administered Michigan Alcoholism Screening Test (SMAST), and Alcohol-Related Problems Survey (ARPS) are all validated screening tools. The Alcohol Use Disorders Identification Test (AUDIT) and AUDIT C are two other useful clinical tools to assess for alcohol use disorders (Fujii et al. 2016; Hagman 2016).

The AUDIT C is a brief three-item questionnaire that can help to reliably assess a patient for the presence of an alcohol use issue. The AUDIT C is a truncated version of the 10-item AUDIT questionnaire and can be used in an emergency department setting for efficient and reliable assessments of alcohol use disorders.

12.8.1.1 AUDIT C

The AUDIT C rates each survey question using a point system with a scale from 0–4 points. Each point equates to a specified time interval or number of drinks depending on the question content. The maximum score that can be reached is 12. If a patient scores 3 or more points, it is recommended that the entire AUDIT questionnaire is completed. The AUDIT C contains the following three items:

1. How often do you have a drink containing alcohol?
2. How many units of alcohol do you drink on a typical day when you are drinking?
3. How often have you had 6 or more units if female, or 8 or more if male, on a single occasion in the last year?

12.8.1.2 AUDIT

The 10-item AUDIT questionnaire is comprised of the three items contained in the AUDIT C plus 7 more items. Like the AUDIT C, the AUDIT uses a point system, ranging from 0–4 points, to rate each survey question.

There is a maximum score of 40 points for the AUDIT questionnaire. Scores of 8 or more are considered an indicator of hazardous and harmful alcohol use (Bohn et al. 1995). The remaining 7 questions in the complete AUDIT questionnaire are

4. How often during the last year have you found that you were not able to stop drinking once you had started?
5. How often during the last year have you failed to do what was normally expected from you because of drinking?
6. How often during the last year have you needed an alcoholic drink in the morning to get yourself going after a heavy drinking session?
7. How often during the last year have you had a feeling of guilt or remorse after drinking?
8. How often during the last year have you been unable to remember what happened the night before because you had been drinking?
9. Have you or someone else been injured as a result of your drinking?
10. Has a relative or friend or a doctor or another health worker been concerned about your drinking or suggested you cut down?

12.8.2 Alcohol Effect and Metabolism

Alcohol activates GABA-A receptors causing a central nervous system depressant effect. A release of opioids and dopamine also occurs. This action may interact with serotonin systems. Alcohol is metabolized by oxidation in the liver leading to acetaldehyde by alcohol dehydrogenase. Acetaldehyde leads to acetate by aldehyde dehydrogenase. Alcohol is also released unchanged by the lungs and kidney (Zakhari 2006).

12.8.3 Risk and Prognostic Factors

Alcohol use has profound negative effects on many important organ and biological systems resulting in significant increases in morbidity and mortality. Alcohol use can bring on numerous risk and prognostic factors. Neurobehavioral alterations can occur including fluctuation in mood, decreased impulse control and behavioral changes, decreased executive ability, and impaired coordination (Vonghia et al. 2008). Cardiovascular changes may include hypertension, cardiomyopathy, "beriberi," cerebrovascular accidents, and arrhythmias. Alcohol-related gastrointestinal conditions include liver inflammation, steatosis also known as "fatty liver," alcoholic hepatitis, fibrosis and cirrhosis, and pancreatitis. Alcohol use can lead to an increased risk of developing cancers, including throat, mouth, esophagus, liver, and breast (Centers for Disease Control and Prevention 2016a). Alcohol depresses immune function, which can leave an individual susceptible to increased chances of contracting pneumonia and tuberculosis. Jaundice, clubbed fingers, palmar erythema, gynecomastia, testicular atrophy, increase in aldosterone, coagulopathy, ascites, (due to hypoproteinemia, sodium, and water retention) splenomegaly, portal hypertension, varices, hematemesis, pain, and vomiting are some common signs of hepatic cirrhosis.

12.8.4 Blood Alcohol Level Toxicity

Blood alcohol level (BAL) is measured in milligrams (mg). Various physical and neurocognitive effects can occur depending on the level of alcohol consumed. The following list displays some of the common effects displayed based on the individual's BAL ranging from increased sociability to death (Zakhari 2006).

- 10–50 mg: Increase in sociable activities, reduction in anxiety impulsivity, and increased positive mood.
- 80–100 mg: Decreased ability to coordinate physical and mental functions.
- 100–200 mg: Decreased ability to coordinate gait, continued worsening mental functions including concentration.
- 200–400 mg: At this point vomiting typically occurs along with worsening of the previously mentioned symptoms leading to stupor.
- 400 mg: This BAL and above is potentially lethal for the average person.

12.8.5 Alcohol Withdrawal

Increasingly high blood alcohol levels can lead to potential serious alcohol withdrawal symptoms. Alcohol withdrawal is an issue of primary clinical concern in the emergency room setting. Alcohol withdrawal can lower the seizure threshold and severe withdrawal can progress to delirium tremens and or uncontrolled hypertension, both of which carry significant rates of mortality. The signs and symptoms associated with alcohol withdrawal include diaphoresis, tremors, elevated heart rate, blood pressure, dilated, sluggish pupils, anxiety, nausea, vomiting, chills, disorientation, hallucinations, agitation, and seizures. Delirium tremens (DTs) is another symptom of severe alcohol withdrawal associated with mental status changes, including confusion, delusions, and hallucinations. Untreated DTs frequently results in seizures and death (Kattimani and Bharadwaj 2013).

12.8.5.1 Withdrawal Treatment

Alcohol withdrawal symptoms must be treated in order to avoid further medical complications. Various benzodiazepines and anticonvulsant medications are utilized to treat withdrawal symptoms. There exists an increased risk for serious withdrawal symptoms in a patient with multiple comorbid medical problems. Elevated lab results, including MCV and AST/ALT greater than 2/1 are a red flag. A symptom-triggered approach may help to prevent overmedicating the patient. Long-acting benzodiazepines, such as chlordiazepoxide or diazepam can serve a protective role (Kattimani and Bharadwaj 2013). If patients have liver disease, lorazepam is often used because it is not metabolized by the liver. Lorazepam and diazepam also have the advantage of intravenous and intramuscular formulations.

Benzodiazepine-equivalent doses with rate of onset and half-life, including chlordiazepoxide, diazepam and lorazepam, follow:

- Chlordiazepoxide (10 mg), slow, 30–100 hours; clonazepam (0.25 mg), intermediate, 18–50 hours; diazepam (7.5 mg), rapid, 30–100 hours
- Lorazepam (1.0 mg), intermediate, 10–20 hours

Detoxification orders for the treatment of alcohol withdrawal can be adjusted to symptom severity. For moderate withdrawal symptoms or a history of withdrawal symptoms, chlordiazepoxide can be given in a 75 mg standing dose every 8 hours, and should be held off if there are any signs of sedation in the patient. Lorazepam can be administered in a 2 mg dose every 4 hours or as needed for episodes of diaphoresis or tremulousness (first dose now). Haloperidol can be used as a 2 mg dose given every 4 hours or as needed for episodes of agitation.

For severe withdrawal symptoms, monitor the patient closely. Lorazepam should be administered in a 4 mg dose intravenously upon presentation of the patient to the emergency room. The dose should be repeated in 10 minutes if the patient remains symptomatic. Lorazepam should then be provided in a 4 mg dose every hour (hold if there are any signs of sedation). Once a patient has been started on a benzodiazepine for withdrawal and no withdrawal signs emerge, the standing dose can be decreased by 25% for the next day. Always order "as needed" (PRN) medication for potential breakthrough symptoms. For patients who do not respond well to benzodiazepines, adding an anticonvulsant can be helpful. Topiramate administered in a 25–50 mg dosage twice a day or valproic acid given in a 250–1000 mg dose twice a day can be used.

Nutrition status needs to be closely monitored in patient's suffering from alcohol withdrawal. Laboratory testing including AST, ALT, magnesium (Mg) should be completed. Thiamine should be administered at a dose of 100 mg intravenous or intramuscular for 3 days due to a tendency for alcoholics to have issues with poor gastrointestinal absorption. Depleted thiamine levels can also lead to potential development of Wernicke Korsakoff syndrome.

12.8.6 Comorbidity

Many individuals who misuse alcohol also misuse other drugs, and vice versa. Psychiatric disorders often co-occur with alcohol abuse (Hasin and Grant 2015). Alcoholics were found to be two to three times more likely than nonalcoholics to also have a co-occurring anxiety disorder. Alcoholics, even former drinkers, had quadruple the risk for a major depressive episode.

12.8.7 Medication for Alcohol Use Disorder

There are currently three Food and Drug Administration (FDA)-approved medications for alcoholism (Substance Abuse and Mental Health Services Administration 2009). They include formulations of disulfiram, naltrexone, and acamprosate. There are some promising treatments for alcoholism and other addictions that are "off label" that include the antiepileptics, such as gabapentin and topiramate. Naltrexone and acamprosate work in both the recovery and relapse phase of the alcoholic illness: They decrease the cravings for alcohol and they decrease the amount of alcohol a patient drinks during relapse. Disulfiram, which inhibits acetaldehyde dehydrogenase, may cause a severe disulfiram alcohol reaction and is not the recommended first line treatment in many circumstances. Naltrexone, the opiate receptor blocker, exerts its influence by decreasing cravings for alcohol and is available in both oral and intramuscular depot formulations, though getting insurance to cover the monthly injections can be an operational challenge. Acamprosate is an effective glutamatergic compound and can be taken with opiates and does not have the side effect of potential depression. However, it must be taken three times a day and may have a time-limited diarrhea as a potential side effect (Kranzler and Gage 2008).

12.8.8 Wernicke Korsakoff Syndrome

Wernicke Korsakoff syndrome is a neurologic complication of thiamine (vitamin B1) deficiency. Two different syndromes exist according to the severity of the presenting symptoms. Wernicke encephalopathy, the first of the two syndromes, is an acute syndrome requiring emergent treatment to prevent sequelae. Korsakoff syndrome, the second of the two syndromes, is an irreversible neurologic condition. A patient afflicted with Wernicke Korsakoff syndrome may present with a triad of symptoms including encephalopathy, gait ataxia, and ocular motor dysfunction (Kattimani and Bharadwaj 2013). Encephalopathy may cause episodes of disorientation and indifference. Ocular motor dysfunction may present in a patient as nystagmus or gaze palsies. Ataxia can present as stance and gait abnormalities, due to dysfunction at the cerebellar and vestibular areas in the brain. Other symptoms may include coma, hypotension, hypothermia, and peripheral neuropathy. Some patients may develop Korsakoff psychosis during which an inability to form new memories (anterograde amnesia) occurs. Memory loss can be more severe in cases where the patient is unable to recall past information or memories (retrograde amnesia). Patients presenting with memory loss may begin making up stories (fantastic confabulation) in order to mask or fill in the missing information created by the lost memories. Visual hallucinations may also be present in Korsakoff syndrome (Kopelman et al. 2009).

12.8.8.1 Wernicke Korsakoff Syndrome Treatment

There should be a low index of suspicion used for any potential case of Korsakoff and treatment should be started immediately upon presentation of its symptoms. The patient's response to treatment can be used as a diagnostic tool to help rule out the occurrence of Korsakoff syndrome. Treatment of the syndrome will start with a complete medical evaluation. Laboratory testing including erythrocyte thiamine transketolase (ETKA), magnesium, thiamine, and albumin levels should be run. Imaging studies such as CT scan to identify enhancing low density abnormalities (periventricular and thalamic) and MRI, which provides a more sensitive imaging study, to identify increased T2 aqueduct, medial thalamus, and mammillary bodies. Thiamine, either intramuscular (IM) or intravenous (IV), is the preferred route of administration as oral thiamine can be poorly absorbed by alcoholics (Kattimani and Bharadwaj 2013; Sharp et al. 2016). Up to 500 mg 3 times a day in an inpatient setting and then oral upon discharge from an inpatient setting are recommended treatment dosages, per the Royal College of Physicians (2001). Rare side effects of thiamine treatments can include local irritation at the administration site and anaphylaxis.

12.9 Sedative Hypnotic and Anxiolytic-Related Disorders

According to the ICD 10, sedative hypnotic or anxiolytics-related disorders include the following: Sedative hypnotic or anxiolytic use disorder F13.1, F13.2, sedative hypnotic or anxiolytic intoxication F13.129, F13.229, F13.929, sedative hypnotic or anxiolytic withdrawal F13.239, F13.232, sedative hypnotic or anxiolytic-induced disorders, and unspecified sedative hypnotic or anxiolytic-related disorders F13.99.

12.9.1 Benzodiazepines

Benzodiazepines are a class of substances that have both anxiolytic and hypnotic effects. When properly used, benzodiazepines have FDA approval for panic disorders, anxiety disorders, alcohol withdrawal, epilepsy, anesthesia, and other complaints. However, there is also a "dark side" to these medications. They can be addictive and have a "street" value (particularly alprazolam due to pharmacokinetics), they can cause sedation, lethargy, a change in mental status and can be potentially fatal in overdose, especially when mixed with other sedating substances such as alcohol, opioids, and other sedative hypnotics. Moreover, the benzodiazepine withdrawal state presents with prominent agitation and irritability and can progress to seizures and death (Petursson 1994). Treatment protocols are similar to alcohol withdrawal as discussed previously.

During the 7 years from 2005–2011, almost a million (an estimated 943,032) ED visits involved benzodiazepines alone or in combination with opioid pain relievers or alcohol (Substance Abuse and Mental Health Services Administration 2014). Patients in severe benzodiazepine withdrawal should be admitted for medical detoxification, which can frequently last one week or more. Careful interview with patients can reveal the presence of a benzodiazepine use disorder and any physician prescribing these medications should document a reasonable risk versus reward rationale for their use.

New prescriptions for benzodiazepines should be avoided when possible as there are medications with fewer risks that can many times be prescribed instead of benzodiazepines (see the Chapter 10 on anxiety and mood disorders). Medications, such as the antiepileptics (topiramate 50 mg BID or gabapentin 600 TID), SSRIs (fluoxetine 20 mg daily), buspirone (15 mg TID), hydroxyzine (50 mg QID or PRN for anxiety), clonidine (0.1 mg TID or PRN for anxiety), and antipsychotics (quetiapine 50 BID or risperidone 1 mg BID) can be used in lieu of a benzodiazepine.

Benzodiazepines may carry increased risks, especially in the geriatric and substance use disordered populations. Benzodiazepines are of particular interest to the emergency room psychiatrist. Patients frequently present to emergency rooms requesting "refills" of these medications that they previously had a prescription for. Benzodiazepines are gabaergic and exert their effect on the GABA-A receptor. GABA is the main inhibitory neurotransmitter in the brain's neural network of interneurons (Harvard Health Publications 2014).

12.10 Cannabis-Related Disorders

The ICD 10 addresses cannabis use issues in the following disorders: Cannabis use disorder F12.1, F12.2, cannabis intoxication F12.129, cannabis withdrawal F12.288, other cannabis use disorders, and unspecified cannabis use disorders F12.99.

12.10.1 Cannabis: Intoxication and Withdrawal

Cannabis, also known as marijuana, is the most commonly used illegal drug in the United States. The main psychoactive (mind-altering) chemical in marijuana is delta-9-tetrahydrocannabinol, or THC. THC can cause euphoria, distorted perceptions, memory impairment, and difficulty thinking and solving problems in the user (Weinstein and Gorelick 2011; World Health Organization 1992).

A patient who has recently used marijuana may display signs of intoxication including conjunctival injection, increased appetite, dry mouth, and tachycardia, with or without perceptual changes. Withdrawal symptoms can occur after a cessation of heavy use and can develop 1 week after the last episode of using. Cannabis withdrawal symptoms can include irritability, anxiety, insomnia, weight loss, restlessness, depression, diaphoresis, chills, headaches, and abdominal pain (Weinstein and Gorelick 2011).

12.10.2 Cannabis: Social, Legal, and Research Issues

These are interesting times for cannabis. Cannabis is still a federally listed drug, but many states have decriminalized or legalized the use of cannabis for medical or recreational purposes. For example, Colorado and, more recently, California. Cannabis is available for consumption in the form of the traditional dried plant, referred to as buds, but can also come in the form of hashish, hash oil, cannabis tinctures, vaporizers, and in edible form such as candy or cookies (National Institute on Drug Abuse 2016c).

Additionally, there are many synthetic cannabinoids that are not detectable in the common toxicology screening but may cause patients to experience increased psychosis and lead to increased healthcare utilization. Certainly, cannabinoids maybe helpful for several diagnostic entities and are already available and FDA approved (such as dronabinol) in some formulations.

There are some studies lending credence that cannabis may be beneficial for patients with wasting syndromes and certain types of spasticity associated with multiple sclerosis and certain epileptic disorders (Carter and Weydt 2002; Friedman and Devinsky 2015). However, the American Academy of Addiction Psychiatry (AAAP) rejects the concept of medical marijuana as currently constituted; there are simply not enough studies about the efficacy of cannabis for many conditions. There are issues with addiction and secondary gain, and Nora Volkow, of the National Institute on Drug Abuse (NIDA), warns of certain deleterious syndromes associated with cannabis consumption, especially with developing adolescent brains (Volkow et al. 2014). The emergency psychiatrist is in a position to answer many questions from both patients and staff about cannabis. For the most part, cannabis is still seen by a majority of the medical community as an addictive and potentially dangerous substance.

12.10.3 Synthetic Cannabis

The synthetic cannabinoids are a group of cannabinoids that are synthesized and sprayed onto material and marketed as "not safe for human consumption" and sold in stores. Conventional toxicology screening does not readily identify synthetic cannabinoids, making them popular with people who are regularly tested for drugs. Synthetic cannabinoids have been implicated in several studies for having greater morbidity compared with the natural products of the hemp plant. This includes seizures, psychosis, paranoia, severe agitation and even coma and death (Auwarter et al. 2009). "Spice" and "K2" are two examples of what these synthetic cannabinoids are referred to as.

12.10.4 Cannabis and Brain Activity

Cannabinoid receptors in the brain that are G-protein coupled are activated by endocannabinoids, plant cannabinoids, and synthetic cannabinoids. Cannabis acts upon the cannabinoid G-protein coupled receptors, specifically CB1 and 2. These receptors are ordinarily activated by endocannabinoids, such as anandamide. As part of a neural communication network, the endocannabinoid system plays an important role in normal brain development and function. The highest density of cannabinoid receptors is found in parts of the brain that influence pleasure, memory, thinking, concentration, sensory and time perception, and coordinated movement. In a study completed by Vukadinovic et al. (2013), a correlation showed that cannabis-related psychosis may be linked with thalamic dysfunction due to direct effects on the calcium channels in the thalamus.

12.10.5 Cannabis Use Frequency Studies in Adolescents

In 2009, 28.5 million Americans age 12 and older had used marijuana at least once in the year prior to being surveyed. The NIDA-funded 2010 "Monitoring the Future" Study found that 13.7% of eighth graders, 27.5% of tenth graders, and 34.8% of twelfth graders had used marijuana at least once in the year prior to being surveyed. Synthetic cannabinoids were also found to be used in adolescent populations. For instance, hashish was found to be used by 10% of high school seniors surveyed with 7% of high school seniors reporting "any recent use" and 3% reporting "more frequent use" (National Institute on Drug Abuse 2016c). Research suggests that about 9% of all users become addicted and that, among those who start young, the percentage is closer to 17%. Noted negative effects of cannabis use in adolescents include psychosis, doubled rate of motor vehicle accidents, and possible thalamic effects in the brain.

Another study looked at changes in young adults' use of and opinion toward marijuana in California before and after legalization in the state. It was found that California twelfth graders as compared with their peers in other states became 25% more likely to have used marijuana in the past 30 days, 20% less likely to perceive regular marijuana use as a great health risk, 20% less likely to strongly disapprove of regular marijuana use, and 60% more likely to expect to be using marijuana 5 years in the future. A letter from Nora Volkow on the NIDA website speaks to the possible negative consequences of marijuana use in adolescence: "Regular marijuana use in adolescence is known to be part of a cluster of behaviors that can produce enduring detrimental effects and alter the trajectory of a young person's life—thwarting his or her potential. Beyond potentially lowering IQ, teen marijuana use is linked to school dropout, other drug use, mental health problems" (Volkow 2013).

12.11 Tobacco-Related Disorders

Within the ICD 10, tobacco-related disorders include: Tobacco use disorder Z72.0, F17.20, tobacco withdrawal F17.203, other tobacco-induced disorders, and unspecified tobacco-related disorder F17.209.

12.11.1 Tobacco: Usage and Mortality Rates

Tobacco is consumed by humans in a variety of ways and means, including combustion (cigarettes), heating (vaporizers), orally and nasally (betel, snuff, snus, "bandits," chewing tobacco).

Tobacco has been cultivated for thousands of years by native populations and was first exported to Europe in early 1600s. U.S. cigarette consumption has grown dramatically over the past century, but during the past decade has decreased. In 2015, 15.1% of U.S. adults, or about 36.5 million people, consumed tobacco products and this has been a decrease in usage since 2005 (20.9%) (Jamal et al. 2016). More than one-third of the world's population consumes tobacco and mortality rates are increasing worldwide.

Decades after the release of the first Surgeon General's Report in 1964, tobacco use is still the number one major modifiable risk factor for cardiovascular disease, cancer, and chronic respiratory disease, which comprise the leading causes of death in the United States (Jamal et al. 2016). Since the release of the first Surgeon General's Report, there have been 20 million premature deaths. Tobacco deaths in the United States are greater than deaths caused by AIDS, alcohol, cocaine, heroin, homicide, suicide, motor vehicle crashes, and fires combined. Rates of comorbidity are high, with substance users having elevated rates of tobacco-related disease. Some estimate that persons with psychiatric disorders comprise 40% of the population of cigarette consumers in the United States. People with mental illnesses smoke at rates that are about twice as high as the general population (Centers for Disease Control and Prevention 2016c).

12.11.2 Nicotine Pharmacology

Nicotine is a naturally occurring alkaloid and is considered one of the oldest insecticides in use. Nicotine is a stimulant that reaches the brain in around 21 seconds creating a rapid reward effect for the user. S-isomer binds to nicotinic acetylcholine receptors in the brain (Benowitz et al. 2009; Zevin et al. 1998). High concentrations of these receptors are found in the mesolimbic system and the locus coeruleus. Binding by nicotine to its receptor leads to the opening of ion channels and neuronal depolarization. Nicotine boosts release of epinephrine, norepinephrine, ACH, serotonin, GABA, glutamate, and dopamine and leads to a secondary inhibition of monoamine oxidase (MAO). Nicotine is metabolized by the liver, CYP 2A6 into cotinine, and has a half-life of 2 hours with accumulation in body tissues (Hukkanen et al. 2005). Nicotine acts to increase the metabolism of many medications and may attenuate beta-blocker, benzodiazepine, opioid, and antacid effects. There have also been procoagulant effects with prescribed estrogen medications (Zevin and Benowitz 1999). Nicotine is excreted in the urine after renal clearance.

12.11.2.1 Nicotine Withdrawal

Due to the stimulating psychobiological effects that nicotine has on the body, nicotine withdrawal symptoms, mimicking the withdrawal symptoms from stimulants, can present. Withdrawals symptoms can include irritability, depression, anxiety, restlessness, poor concentration, hyperphagia, cravings, weight gain, and delayed reaction time (Hughes and Hatsukami 1986). Withdrawal symptoms may motivate the patient to seek out treatment and help with quitting tobacco and nicotine use.

12.11.3 Gold Standard Treatment

The 2008 update to the U.S. Public Health Service (PHS) "Clinical Practice Guideline: Treating Tobacco Use and Dependence" recommends that clinicians consistently identify and document tobacco use status and treat every tobacco user seen in a healthcare setting. The PHS recommends that healthcare providers offer medication and counseling referrals such as quitlines for patients who are willing to attempt quitting, or that they offer additional treatment to help patients quit. Treatment, per PHS guidelines, should include the use of the following 5 As:

- **Ask** the patient about tobacco use.
- **Advise** tobacco users to quit.
- **Assess** the patient's willingness to attempt quitting.
- **Assist** in the quit attempt.
- **Arrange** for follow-up treatment.

12.11.4 Nicotine Treatment: Preferred Options

The treatment options that the emergency department physician or other healthcare providers have at their disposal are varied and include medications, harm reduction techniques, and nicotine replacement therapy. The physician needs to carefully weigh the benefits and consequences of each treatment option and match an option with the patient's treatment plan. Medications preferred in the treatment of tobacco use disorders are varied. Of these, bupropion and varenicline are the most widely used FDA-approved medications.

12.11.4.1 Bupropion

The recommended starting dosage is 150 mg daily for first week, prior to quit date, and then 150 mg twice a day for ongoing treatment (Henningfield et al. 2005; Roddy 2004). Use of bupropion, when compared with nicotine replacement therapy (NRT), shows no significant differences in abstinence rates (Stapleton et al. 2013). Bupropion may be contraindicated in patients with a history of seizures.

Bupropion creates dopaminergic activity in the neuronal synapses. Bupropion acts as an antagonist at the nicotinic acetylcholine receptors in the brain, thus inhibiting the action of these receptors (Roddy 2004).

12.11.4.2 Varenicline

A wide body of existing research shows that varenicline is an evidence-based treatment for nicotine use disorders. Varenicline acts as a partial nicotine agonist and antagonist that binds to nicotinic a4b2 acetylcholine receptors (Fagerstrom and Hughes 2008). Varenicline is not metabolized by the liver and is excreted in the urine. The medication can exacerbate existing psychiatric symptoms, which may make it contraindicated for those patients presenting with a comorbid psychiatric disorder.

12.11.4.3 Second Line Nicotine Treatment Agents

Even though bupropion and varenicline are widely used first line medication treatments for nicotine dependence, many patients will require a combination of treatments. Other treatments may include second line agents, such as the medications nortriptyline or clonidine. Harm-reduction methods can also be used; the principle followed here is to reduce, but not completely eliminate, the use of nicotine (Henningfield et al. 2005). Alternative treatments to the second line agents and harm reduction include deprenyl, rimnobant (Henningfield et al. 2005), methoxsalen, and naltrexone. Naltrexone may block cravings for nicotine and attenuate the reinforcing effect of the drug. The creation of a nicotine vaccine is also a hot area of research (Hartmann-Boyce et al. 2012; Henningfield et al. 2005).

12.11.4.4 Nicotine Replacement Therapy

For those patients who are more amenable to the idea of reduction in use versus abstinence, nicotine replacement therapy can be a viable and realistic treatment option. A multitude of replacement options have been found to be effective in treating the addiction. Nicotine gum can be purchased over the counter. Evidence-based treatment recommends 2 and 4 mg doses, which are available. Nicotine gum can be chewed or parked once every 2 hours. Lozenges are available in 2 and 4 mg doses and have been described by some patients as being simpler to use than the gum.

Patches are available in 7, 14, and 21 mg dosages, in addition to "double patches." Patches are applied by the patient as a single daily dose. While using the patches, the patient should maintain abstinence in the first 2 weeks of use. The patch should be rotated with each new application. Patch use has been shown to be predictive of long-term abstinence.

Nasal spray provides rapid delivery of nicotine in a .5 mg dose per spray per nostril. The spray should be administered in 1–2 doses per hour. Lastly, an inhaler in 10 mg vaporized dosages is available. The patient should use the inhaler at least 6 times per day (Henningfield et al. 2005).

12.12 Opioid-Related Disorders

The opioid-related disorders include opioid use disorder F11.10 F11.20, opioid intoxication F11.129, F11.229, F11.929, opioid withdrawal F11.23, other opioid-induced disorders, and unspecified opioid-related disorders F11.9.

12.12.1 Opioid Types

The endogenous opioid system is widespread throughout the body and has diverse functions. There are three distinct families of opioid peptides: enkephalins, endorphins, and dynorphins (Mulder et al. 1984). Opioids modulate painful stimuli as well as gastrointestinal, endocrine, and autonomic functions. Opioids also play an emotional and behavioral role evidenced by their effects on learning, craving, reward, and memory (Kosten and George 2002). The most commonly used opioids include heroin, codeine, meperidine, morphine, fentanyl, hydromorphone, methadone, opium, hydrocodone, oxycodone, acetaminophen/oxycodone, levorphanol, hydrocodone bitartrate/acetaminophen, aspirin, and oxycodone hydrochloride/aspirin (Inturrisi 2002; Trescot et al. 2008).

12.12.2 Opioid Use and Emergency Department Visits

Data from the DAWN network indicates that opioid abuse is a growing problem in the United States (Substance Abuse and Mental Health Services Administration 2013). In 2011, the overall admission rate for misuse or abuse of opioid analgesics (excluding adverse reactions) was 134.8 per 100,000, an increase of 153% compared with 2004. In the 13 states involved in the DAWN network, the top 4 opioid analgesics involved in drug-related ED visits for 2011 were various formulations of oxycodone (175,229), hydrocodone (97,183), methadone (75,693), and morphine (38,416). Between 2004 and 2011, ED admissions increased 74% for methadone, 220% for oxycodone, 96% for hydrocodone, and 144% for morphine. Heroin-related ED episodes increased from 213,118 in 2009 to 258,482 in 2011. Heroin use and its related behaviors, including lost productivity, are estimated to lead to 6 billion dollars in costs. In 2008, more than 36,000 people died from overdose, most were caused by opioid-based prescription drugs.

12.12.3 Opioids: A Historical Time Line

In the sixteenth century, the development of laudanum appeared, which was opium prepared in an alcoholic solution. In the nineteenth century, morphine was first extracted from opium in a pure form. Morphine was named after Morpheus, the Greek god of dreams. Codeine was first isolated in 1830 in France by Jean-Pierre Robiquet, to replace raw opium as medicine. In 1839, in response to China's attempt to suppress the opium traffic, the United Kingdom begins the First Opium War. During the Civil War, opioids were given to war veterans and for "woman's problems" by physicians, causing an iatrogenic addiction epidemic. Heroin was introduced in 1895 as a cough suppressant. It is estimated that 300,000 people were addicted to opiates by 1900. In 1910, the development of the hypodermic needle led to the first intravenous use of heroin. In the 1960s, the development of methadone-maintenance programs began. By 1970, publicly funded treatment programs were being developed and implemented in many areas. In 1974, the Narcotic Addict Treatment Act was passed by the U.S. Federal Government. By 1980, it is estimated that 500,000 people were addicted to opiates. In 1990, the National Institutes of Health (NIH) Consensus Panel on opioids was created (Booth 1996).

12.12.3.1 National Institutes of Health Consensus Panel on Opioid Addiction

The NIH Consensus Panel stated that opiate addiction can be effectively treated like other medical disorders. Patients should be offered medication-assisted treatment or naltrexone and efforts should be made to reduce stigma at federal and state levels. Patients in treatment live longer and have lower healthcare utilization. They also receive supportive services, psychosocial counseling, treatment of comorbid disorders, medical services, and vocational rehabilitation. Opioid addiction is treatable, not self-induced, or a failure of the patient's willpower. "The treatment is corrective, normalizing neurological processes in patients … whose function has been deranged by long-term use of powerful narcotics" (National Institute on Drug Abuse 1999).

12.12.4 Effects of Opioid Use

The misuse of opioids results in several acute and long-term effects. Signs and symptoms of acute opioid intoxication include constricted pupils, euphoria and dysphoria, slurred speech, apathy, drowsiness, loss of consciousness, coma, psychomotor agitation or retardation, decreased respiration, decreased heart rate, pulmonary edema, impaired social judgment, impaired occupational functioning, and impaired attention and memory.

12.12.4.1 Withdrawal

A withdrawal syndrome can be precipitated in humans after even a single dose of opiates has been administered. Withdrawal symptoms begin approximately 8 hours after the last dose, though the subjective effects may begin earlier. Symptoms usually peak in 2 or 3 days and then gradually taper during the next week (Schuckit 2016). Protracted withdrawal with prominent insomnia has also been reported by some patients. Opioid withdrawal occurs following discontinuation of opioids or through the administration of competitive opioid agonists or antagonists, such as buprenorphine or naloxone (Kosten and George 2002).

Signs and symptoms of opioid withdrawal include mydriasis (dilated pupils), rhinorrhea (runny nose), lacrimation (tearing), piloerection (goose bumps), nausea and vomiting, loose bowels or diarrhea, repetitive yawning, muscle spasms and pain, restlessness and anxiety, and an elevated pulse (Schuckit 2016). The Clinical Opiate Withdrawal Scale (COWS) is a common instrument used to rate a patient's severity level of opiate withdrawals (Wesson and Ling 2003). The COWS scale covers 11 common opiate-related withdrawal symptoms. Each of these symptoms is rated on a 4- to 5-point scale and a total score is calculated for all 11 symptoms. The severity ratings range from mild (score of 5–12) to severe withdrawal (score of 36 or more). For those that are interested in using the scale for clinical purposes, many versions of the scale are available on the Internet that can be copied.

12.12.5 Opioid Overdose

In 2014, there were over 47,000 overdose deaths in the United States, including over 28,000 that involved opioid analgesics. These numbers have continued to increase and reached 50,000 deaths in 2015. The opioid and heroin overdose death rates have tripled from 2000 to 2014 and the data suggests heroin overdoses will continue to rise. According to the Centers of Disease Control and Prevention, almost 50 people die every day in the United States from opioid overdose (Rudd et al. 2016). The popularity of prescription opiates remains high in the United States. With only around 5% of the world's population, the United States annually consumes more than 80% of all international opioids produced. U.S. healthcare providers write almost 300 million prescriptions annually: "That's enough for every American adult to have their own bottle of pills." Hydrocodone, morphine, oxycodone, and heroin account for a large number of overdose deaths (Centers for Disease Control and Prevention 2016b). Most methadone overdoses occur when the drug is prescribed for pain rather than for addiction treatment.

12.12.5.1 Opioid Overdose Facts for First Responders

The following information regarding opioid overdose can help guide first responders in the field. When an overdose on opioids occurs, the patient will usually present with a decrease in breathing rate, which can be fatal, especially if the person cannot be woken up. Breathing is very slow or not existent, lips or nails may seem blue, and death usually occurs 1–3 hours after overdose from intravenous opioid use, rather than suddenly. Overdose may frequently be witnessed by someone who does not recognize the danger signs or does not want to act on it. In many cases of overdose, opioids are mixed with alcohol or benzodiazepines. Naltrexone, distributed in emergency rooms and by opioid overdose responders and prescription programs, remains the treatment of choice for overdose. When appropriate, patients receiving opioid blockers should receive medication to help with the symptoms of withdrawal (Boyer 2012). Please refer to Chapter 15 on toxicology for more detailed information on this topic.

12.12.6 Management of Opioid Use Disorder

Management of opioid use disorder includes multiple facets from intervention of acute intoxication to abstinence-oriented therapy. Crisis intervention involves the reversal of the potentially lethal effects of overdose with an opioid antagonist (Boyer 2012). Harm reduction reduces morbidity and mortality associated with the use of dirty needles and overdose. In detoxification, the goal is to taper and discontinue opioid use using methadone or suboxone while providing medical screening and aftercare services. Medication-assisted replacement therapy involves using methadone in a program- or office-based treatment using suboxone. Patients may remain on agonist therapy short term, long term, or indefinitely, depending on the patient's needs. Medication-assisted replacement therapy is an evidence-based treatment model that reduces patient morbidity and mortality. Abstinence-oriented therapy is simply treatment directed at abstinence. Unfortunately, there is an increased rate of morbidity and mortality when compared with replacement therapy. However, patients may achieve a "cure" of opioid use (though many may relapse). All treatment approaches share the common goal of improving health outcomes and reducing the societal effects of opioid use. Please review the *Practice Guideline for the Treatment of Patients with Substance Use Disorders*, from the American Psychiatric Association, for an overview of treatment options (Kleber et al. 2006).

12.12.6.1 Choices of Medication to Manage Opioid Use Disorders

Management of the symptoms associated with opioid use disorders can be facilitated effectively via the use of a variety of medication options, many of which are utilized in opioid-replacement therapy programs. Methadone, naltrexone and buprenorphine are some of the more commonly used medications in opioid addiction treatment (Kosten and George 2002; Schuckit 2016; Stotts et al. 2009).

12.12.6.2 Methadone

The first demonstrated efficacy of methadone treatment for opioid dependence was published in 1965. Methadone is now the most inexpensive evidence-based treatment agent available for use in opioid-replacement therapy. Methadone treatment is usually initiated with a dose of 20–30 mg and is gradually titrated in 5–10 mg increments per day to a therapeutic dose of 60–120 mg (Kosten and George 2002). Pregnant women who are opioid dependent should be maintained on the lowest effective dose of methadone. Risk of QTc prolongation and arrhythmia led to a black box warning in 2006 (Schuckit 2016; Stotts et al. 2009).

12.12.6.3 Naltrexone

Opioid antagonists are evidence-based treatments for opioid overdose and opioid use disorder. Naltrexone has little potential for abuse because it does not produce feelings of pleasure. Naltrexone is available as a daily oral medication usually started at 50 mg or as a monthly intramuscular injection (Kosten and George 2002; Schuckit 2016; Stotts et al. 2009).

12.12.6.4 Buprenorphine

Buprenorphine is a long-acting partial opioid agonist first used in 1978 as an alternative opioid-replacement therapy. Buprenorphine binds the opioid receptor more tightly than many opioids; this can lead to an induced withdrawal if it is taken after other opioids. Conversely, if buprenorphine is used prior to other opioids, it will competitively block the effect of other opioids.

Buprenorphine offers some advantages over methadone, which include a lower risk of overdose, a longer duration of action, and availability in the office-based setting. Usually, patients start with a day 1 dose of 4 or 8 mg, which is titrated in increments of 4 mg until a therapeutic dose is reached (the maximum dose is 32 mg). Buprenorphine and methadone are the two most widely used and effective pharmacotherapies for opioid use disorder, and both have regulatory approval in the United States for this indication (Kosten and George 2002; Schuckit 2016; Stotts et al. 2009). However, physicians must register for a Drug Enforcement Administration (DEA) waiver to provide buprenorphine and have a limit on how many patients they may treat. This has been a burden for people seeking care.

12.13 Stimulant-Related Disorders

Per the ICD 10, the stimulant use disorders include stimulant use disorder F14, F15.10, and F15.20, stimulant intoxication F15.129, F15.229, F15.929, and so on, stimulant withdrawal F14.23 and F15.23, other stimulant-induced disorders, unspecified stimulant-related disorder F14.99 and 15.99, mild cocaine use disorder F14.10, moderate/severe F14.20, and amphetamine type use disorder F15.1 and F15.2.

12.13.1 Stimulants

Stimulants exert their effects via the catecholaminergic and sympathetic nervous system, for instance, norepinephrine and dopaminergic pathways. They include naturally existing alkaloids, such as those found in the coca plant and ma-huang, and synthetics compounds, such as amphetamine, lisdexamfetamine, methamphetamine, methylphenidate, and other phenethylamines (Fischman and Foltin 2016).

12.13.1.1 Stimulant Intoxication and Withdrawal

Some of the commonly abused stimulants include amphetamines, methamphetamines, and cocaine. A myriad of physiological changes can occur in a patient that is acutely intoxicated or actively withdrawing from a stimulant. According to the DSM-5, symptoms of acute intoxication can include pulse changes, mydriasis, blood pressure changes, nausea and vomiting, diaphoresis and chills, psychomotor changes, cardiovascular changes, confusion, seizures, dystonia, and coma, with or without perceptual changes (American Psychiatric Association 2013). Withdrawal symptoms can include fatigue, vivid dreams, sleep changes, increased appetite, and psychomotor changes.

12.13.2 Methamphetamine: Pharmacology and Effects

Methamphetamine is a central nervous system stimulant that is similar in structure to amphetamine. The stimulant acts to increase wakefulness, anorexia, physical activity, heart rate, blood pressure, and body temperature, and causes intense euphoria in the user. Methamphetamine increases the release of and blocks the reuptake of dopamine. Prolonged use can lead to mood fluctuations, violent thoughts and behaviors, paranoia, anxiety, prolonged insomnia, as well as severe dental problems (also known as "meth mouth"). Paranoia, visual and auditory hallucinations, and delusions can also be present (Barr et al. 2006). See the subsequent subsection titled "The Man Who Ate His Methamphetamine" for a detailed case of oral stimulant use.

12.13.2.1 Methamphetamine: Addiction and Treatment

Methamphetamine addiction is viewed as a chronic disease characterized by compulsive drug seeking with resultant neurological changes that may be irreversible. There are currently no medications approved to treat methamphetamine addiction, but a few behavioral treatment models are in use. In the *matrix model*, behavioral treatment combining behavioral therapy, family education, individual counseling, twelve-step support, drug testing, and encouragement for nondrug-related activity is used (Rawson et al. 2004). Contingency management involves providing tangible incentives for engaging in treatment and maintaining abstinence (Roll et al. 2006).

12.13.2.2 Emergency Department Visits and Methamphetamine: 2007–2011

According to the Substance Abuse and Mental Health Services Administration, Center for Behavioral Health Statistics and Quality (2014) article highlighting the DAWN Report: Emergency Department Visits Involving Methamphetamine, 2007–2011, overall, the number of methamphetamine-related (ED) visits rose from 67,954 in 2007 to 102,961 in 2011, with similar patterns seen for males and females. In 2011, a majority (62 %) of ED visits involving methamphetamine also involved other drugs; about one-quarter (29 %) of visits involved combinations with one other drug, and one-third (33%) involved combinations with two or more other drugs. In 2011, about one-fifth (22%) of methamphetamine-related visits involved combinations with marijuana, and one-sixth (16%) involved combinations with alcohol; these were the same top two drug combinations found in 2008. Of all methamphetamine-related ED visits in 2011, about 6 in 10 (64%) resulted in patients being treated and released.

12.13.2.3 The Man Who Ate His Methamphetamine: Case Presentation

Teri Miller, Yener Balan, and Tony Berger

A 44-year-old male with a history of alcohol and methamphetamine use, in remission for three years, presented to the ED stating he had been unable to sleep since using methamphetamine 3 days prior to arrival. He complained of two to three episodes of minor hemoptysis over the same period. Additional history from the family was obtained. Prior to this episode, the patient had been sober from alcohol and smoking methamphetamine for 3 years. He had no prior psychiatric history, no medical history, and was not on any current prescribed medications.

His sister reported that after the methamphetamine use 3 days prior to arrival to the ED, the patient became withdrawn but they were unsure whether this was due to depression (over his relapse) or the drug itself, and he "seemed fine."

However, "as the days went by, he became more and more erratic" culminating in the family bringing him to the ED, 3 days post-ingestion, because he believed people were trying to hurt him, throw him into jail, or kick him out.

On initial presentation, the patient was tachycardic, but all other vital signs and initial labs (complete blood count [CBC], Chem 7) were within normal limits, except for mildly elevated liver enzymes, AST and ALT (71, 77 U/L respectively). His chest X-ray was normal. His electrocardiogram (EKG). The patient was given 2 mg of lorazepam for his agitation. He was initially unable to provide urine.

Following prompt oral rehydration, his heart rate decreased to 98 BPM and his urine output returned to normal levels. At this time, the toxicology screen was found to be positive for methamphetamine. Toxicology was consulted regarding a potential caustic ingestion, but given lack of metabolic acidosis, the resolution of tachycardia with rehydration, and the lack of ongoing hemoptysis, it was thought to be unlikely that he had a significant caustic ingestion.

Four hours following presentation, the patient complained of auditory and visual hallucinations, including "flying demons." He exhibited the symptoms of acute intoxication: hyperkinetic movements, rapid speech, anxiety, and irritability. Two hours later he was reported to be "randomly jumping around on his gurney" before falling back asleep and sleeping the remainder of the night.

Approximately 24 hours following initial presentation, his confusion and anxiety had cleared and he stated he "had done something stupid" and had swallowed a "rock" of methamphetamine "about the size of an 8-ball." He reported feeling "amazed" that it took him "this long" to recover. A few hours later the patient was medically and psychiatrically cleared and discharged home with referral for outpatient follow-up for substance use treatment.

12.13.2.3.1 Case Discussion

The half-life of methamphetamine ranges from 10–20 hours depending upon history of use, dose, and urine pH and output. (Barceloux 2012; Kish 2008; Volkow et al. 2010). Metabolism is faster in acidic urine, while alkaline urine will significantly increase the half-life (Barceloux 2012).

IV administration results in the highest bioavailability, and oral intake results in the lowest bioavailability, while smoking and intranasal routes are intermediate, depending upon technique (Elsevier 2014). Peak cardiovascular and subjective effect time parallels bioavailability; effects are most rapid with IV and intranasal (15 minutes), followed by smoking (18 minutes), and finally oral ingestion (2–3 hours) (Barceloux 2012; Hart et al. 2008).

According to the available literature, the average time of presentation between oral ingestion of methamphetamine and presentation at local EDs due to symptoms correlates with the peak-effect time based upon bioavailability (3–4 hours) (Hendrickson et al. 2006; West et al. 2010).

Nevertheless, techniques used to modify or prolong the drug's effect, including wrapping the drug in plastic or paper ("parachuting") or "stuffing" drugs into vaginal or anal cavities results in altered patterns of drug uptake. In these instances, little pharmacokinetic information is available in the literature. The longest duration of symptoms after ingestion reported was 36 hours, when the plastic baggie was believed to have ruptured in a patient who forgot to leave an opening in the bag in his attempt to prolong the release of the drug for a long-distance drive (Hendrickson et al. 2006).

The average amount of methamphetamine intentionally ingested ranges widely, though the average reported is 3.5 grams (West et al. 2010), to "the size of an 8-ball." (Kiely et al. 2009) Fatalities have occurred in patients with as little as 3 grams, with comorbid cardiac conditions (Kiely et al. 2009), and in accidental ingestions of 20 grams during transportation of the drug (Takekawa et al. 2007). However, the quantity ingested is not a sensitive indicator of severity of outcome. Higher pulse rates and higher mean body temperatures, greater than 120 BPM and 38°C respectively, are associated with poor outcomes, whereas dose and presence of packaging does not appear to be related to toxicity (Matsumoto et al. 2014; West et al. 2010). It remains unclear whether it is the cumulative exposure to methamphetamine or the peak plasma concentration that correlates more to maximum increases in hyperthermia (Matsumoto et al. 2014).

Our case study represents a unique situation in which the time between oral ingestion and presentation at the ED was greater than what would be expected in the case of oral ingestion of unpackaged methamphetamine and reported cases of "parachuted" methamphetamine (over 48 hours). Some possible explanations for this delayed onset include medications that alkalize urine (such as antacids) (Elsevier 2014), variability in the quality of the methamphetamine "rock," or increased acidity of the stomach, which would delay absorption, or very clever packaging that slowed the release until it disintegrated completely resulting in a final bolus of the drug.

More importantly, this case raised several questions for future presentations of methamphetamine ingestion and the need for further research to establish best practice guidelines. These include whether imaging studies are indicated, whether the use of activated charcoal and/or polyethylene glycol is indicated, and what the important indicators for prognosis and treatment management are.

12.13.3 Cocaine Use Disorder

Cocaine use disorder is a frequent diagnosis in the psychiatric emergency room setting. Cocaine users report increased energy, alertness, sociability, euphoria, anorexia, and insomnia, and can be frequently observed with tachycardia, repetitive ticks, tremors, skin picking, diaphoresis, poor hygiene, and mydriasis.

Chronic cocaine users frequently present to the hospital with marked behavioral disturbances, including paranoia, suicidality, hallucinations, and depressive symptoms. Once stabilized, many of these patients will sleep for an extended period and then wake up and eat double portions of meals while denying any suicidality or psychosis. Stimulant withdrawal can be treated supportively, but the expressions regarding self-harm can lead to repeated inpatient hospitalizations and increased healthcare utilization (Garlow et al. 2003). Though the cocaine-induced suicidality may resolve after the patient "sleeps it off," these patients are at an elevated risk for self-harm and should not be discharged presumptively. Cocaine-associated tachycardia, abscess from intravenous use, cerebral bleeding, or uncontrolled high blood pressure can present as a medical emergency and should always be on the rule out differential during encounters with patients with cocaine addiction (Cregler and Mark 1986).

12.13.3.1 Cocaine Formulations

Some common forms of cocaine include cocaine salt and "crack" cocaine. Cocaine salt is powdered cocaine hydrochloride, which is water soluble and is used via snorting, huffing, or injection, though it can also be smoked. "Free base" or "crack" cocaine is not water soluble and is produced by heating cocaine in a basic solution; it is usually consumed by smoking and may have a higher potential for dependence and abuse (Cone 1995).

12.13.3.2 Methylenedioxymethamphetamine

Methylenedioxymethamphetamine (MDMA), also known as ecstasy or "E," is a synthetic, psychoactive drug that has similarities to both the stimulant amphetamine and the hallucinogen mescaline. MDMA was first used in the 1950s as an aid in psychotherapy. In 1985, it was classified as a schedule 1 drug. MDMA increases the activity of serotonin, dopamine, and norepinephrine within the brain. Short-term reinforcing effects include feelings of mental stimulation, emotional warmth and empathy, enhanced/altered sensory perception, and increased physical energy. Adverse health effects can include nausea, chills, sweating, teeth clenching, muscle cramping, and blurred vision. MDMA can interfere with the body's ability to regulate temperature; on rare occasions, this can be lethal. Negative after-effects include confusion, depression, sleep problems, drug craving, and anxiety (Rochester and Kirchner 1999).

12.14 Inhalant-Related Disorders

Inhalant-related Disorders, per the ICD 10, include inhalant use disorder F18.1 F18.2, inhalant intoxication F18.129 F18.229 F18.929, other inhalant-induced disorders, and unspecified inhalant-related disorders F18.99.

12.14.1 Inhalant Types

Many home and office products available for sale to the general public, such as spray paints, glue, cleaning compounds, and whipped cream makers, can contain volatile substances that have intense, but brief, psychoactive (mind-altering) properties when inhaled. These inhalants are usually abused by huffing or snorting fumes directly (or via a rag, balloon, or bag) into the mouth or nose. Most inhalants are "downers." Inhalant users report experiencing symptoms including light-headedness, vertigo, and hallucinations. Addiction to inhalants has been reported in some individuals. Chemicals found in inhalants may produce negative and potential life-threatening symptoms such as nausea or vomiting, muscle spasm, hearing loss, bone marrow damage and liver and kidney failure (National Institute on Drug Abuse 2012). Products abused as inhalants include paint thinners or removers, dry-cleaning fluids, gasoline, fabric protector spray, lighter fluid, correction fluids, felt-tip markers, electronic contact cleaners, glue, spray paints, hairspray, deodorant spray, aerosol computer cleaners, vegetable oil sprays, whipped cream aerosols or dispensers/nitrous oxide (whippets), refrigerants, chloroform, halothane, and butyl and amyl nitrites, commonly known as "poppers" (Howard et al. 2011).

12.15 Hallucinogen-Related Disorders

According to the ICD 10, hallucinogen-related disorders include phencyclidine use disorder F16.10, other hallucinogen use disorder F16.10, phencyclidine intoxication F16.129, other hallucinogen intoxication F16.129, hallucinogen-persisting perception disorder, also known as flashbacks F16.983, Other phencyclidine-induced disorders, other hallucinogen-induced disorders, unspecified phencyclidine-related disorder F16.99, and unspecified hallucinogen-related disorder F16.99.

12.15.1 Common Hallucinogens

Patients presenting to the ED with a chief complaint of hallucinations should be screened for recent and past use of any of the common hallucinogenic substances. Common hallucinogens include d-lysergic acid diethylamide (LSD), psilocybin (4-phosphoryloxy-NiN-Dimethyl tryptamine), Dimethyl tryptamine (DMT), and mescaline.

Surveys in 2015 showed that the highest rates (18.6%) of lifetime hallucinogen use occurred in individuals between the ages of 18 and 25 (National Institute on Drug Abuse 2016b). Many of the common hallucinogens have historically been used by various cultures during religious ceremonies.

12.15.1.1 Lysergic Acid Diethylamide

Lysergic Acid Diethylamide (LSD), also known as "acid," is available in many forms. It is considered to be a very potent and powerful hallucinogen altering both the user's perceptual experiences and emotional state. LSD is water soluble and is derived from lysergic acid, which is found in a rye fungus. Depending on the form that LSD is found in, it may be called by various names on the street including blotter, doses, hits, microdots, sugar cubes, trip, tabs, or window panes (National Institute on Drug Abuse 2016a).

12.15.1.2 Psilocybin

Psilocybin, also known as "magic mushrooms," "shrooms," and "boomers," produce similar effects to those of LSD. The hallucinogenic chemical is derived from mushrooms located in the tropical and subtropical climates of South America, Mexico, and the United States. It is usually ingested in a raw or dried form, mixed with food, or brewed into a tea (National Institute on Drug Abuse 2016a).

12.15.1.3 Dimethyltryptamine

Dimethyltryptamine (DMT), also known as "Dimitri," is a chemical found naturally occurring in some Amazonian plants. It is also considered a potent hallucinogen and is categorized as a schedule 1 drug. A synthetic form of the chemical can be produced in a laboratory. DMT is typically either smoked in a pipe or vaporized and inhaled by the user (National Institute on Drug Abuse 2016a).

12.15.1.4 Mescaline

Peyote (mescaline), also known as "buttons," "cactus," and "mesc," is a small spineless cactus. Concentrations of mescaline are found in buttons on the top of the cactus, which are cut out of the cactus, dried, and then chewed, or soaked or boiled in water and the liquid is consumed by the user. As with LSD and DMT, the chemical can be synthetically produced in a laboratory.

12.15.1.5 Salvia Divinorum

Salvia divinorum, also known as "diviner's sage," "magic mint," or "Sally-D," is a plant found in Mexico, and in Central and South America. It can be chewed, dried and then smoked or vaporized for inhaling (National Institute on Drug Abuse 2016a).

12.15.2 Hallucinogen Neurology

Hallucinogens work on the neural networks in the brain that utilize serotonin. The prefrontal cortex is the primary brain area affected by hallucinogen intoxication. In the brain, LSD, psilocybin, and DMT act on the 5-HT serotonin receptors (Aghajanian and Marek 1999; Glennon et al. 1984; Halberstadt and Geyer 2011; Strassman 1996).

12.15.3 Hallucinogen Intoxication

Recent use of any hallucinogen can create a plethora of perceptual and physical changes in the user. Hallucinations can occur along with altered sensory experiences, changing the user's physical manifestation of sight, audition, tactile, and olfaction. A swapping of sensory experiences called synesthesia is sometimes experienced during which the affected person will see sounds or hear colors. It can be common for the user to exhibit intense emotional states and an altered perception of the passage of time. Physical changes including increased energy, pupillary dilation, tachycardia, sweating, palpitations, blurry vision, tremors, nausea, and incoordination may occur (Bey and Patel 2007; National Institute on Drug Abuse 2016a).

12.15.3.1 Hallucinogen-Persisting Perception Disorder

Various negative consequences can present long after a hallucinogen has been used. Persistent psychosis is one long-term effect that can develop even after just one dose of a hallucinogen. Symptoms that mimic a psychotic disorder are present in persistent psychosis. Visual disturbances, thought disorganization, paranoia, and mood dysregulation are common experiences.

Hallucinogen-persisting perception disorder (HPPD) is another possible long-term effect of hallucinogen use. In HPPD, the individual can re-experience geometric hallucinations and false perceptions of movement in their peripheral vision; the individual may also experience flashes of intense color and see halos and trails from moving objects (Espiard et al. 2005). Symptoms that mimic neurological illness, such as stroke or brain tumor, can be present (Hermle et al. 2012; National Institute on Drug Abuse 2016a).

12.16 Conclusion

Hallucinogens, stimulants, alcohol, opiates, or cannabis intoxication will at some time or another present itself within your ED. With the rise of illicit substance-related ED visits, it is imperative that any ED physician and other medical staff are well educated and trained in how to screen for, diagnose, and treat substance-related disorders. Proper training and education will ensure that the treating physician has the skills and knowledge base to effectively treat the patient population presenting with primary substance use disorders, while also being able to appropriately diagnose those presenting with dual diagnosis issues, mental disorders presenting concurrently with the substance use disorders. The ED physician is the first line of treatment for many acutely intoxicated patients that present for help, whether voluntarily or involuntarily.

References

Aghajanian, G K, and G J Marek. 1999. Serotonin and hallucinogens. *Neuropsychopharmacology* 21: 16S–23S.

American Medical Association. 2015. Patients with addiction need treatment: Not stigma. *American Society of Addiction Medicine: Magazine*, December 15.

American Psychiatric Association. 2013. *Diagnostic and Statistical Manual of Mental Disorders*, fifth edition. Arlington, VA: American Psychiatric Association.

Armstrong, T D, and E J Costello. 2002. Community studies on adolescent substance use, abuse, or dependence and psychiatric comorbidity. *Journal of Consulting and Clinical Psychology* 70: 1224–1239.

Auwarter, V, S Dresen, W Weinmann, and M Muller. 2009. 'Spice' and other herbal blends: Harmless incense of cannabinoid designer drugs? *Journal of Mass Spectrometry* 44 (5): 832–837.

Barceloux, D G. 2012. *Medical Toxicology of Drug Abuse: Synthesized Chemicals and Psychoactive Plants*. Hoboken, NJ: John Wiley and Sons.

Barr, A M, W J Panenka, W G MacEwan, A E Thornton, D J Lang, W G Honer, and T Lecomte. 2006. The need for speed: An update on methamphetamine addiction. *Journal of Psychiatry and Neuroscience* 31 (5): 301–313.

Barthwell, A G. 1997. Substance use and the puzzle of adherence. *Focus* 12 (9): 1–4.

Batts, K, M Pemberton, J Bose, B Weimer, L Hendeson, M Penne, J Gfroerer, D Trunzo, and A Strashny. 2014. *Comparing and Evaluating Substance Use Treatment Utilization Estimates from the National Survey on Drug Use and Health and Othe Data Sources.* Data Review, Rockville, MD: Substance Abuse and Mental Health Services Administration.

Benowitz, N L, J Hukkanen, and P Jacob. 2009. Nicotine chemistry, metabolism, kinetics and biomarkers. *Handbook of Experimental Pharmacology* (192): 29–60.

Bey, T, and A Patel. 2007. Phencyclidine intoxication and adverse effects: A clinical and pharmacological review of an illicit drug. *The California Journal of Emergency Medicine* 8 (1): 9–14.

Bohn, M J, T F Babor, and H R Kranzler. 1995. The alcohol use disorders identification test (AUDIT): Validation of a screening instrument for use in medical settings. *Journal of Studies on Alcohol and Drugs* 56 (4): 423–432.

Booth, M. 1996. *Opium: A History.* London: Simon and Schuster.

Botvin, G J. 2004. Advancing prevention science and practice: Challenges, critical issues and future directions. *Prevention Science* 5 (1): 69–72.

Boyer, E W. 2012. Management of opioid analgesic overdose. *The New England Journal of Medicine* 367 (2): 146–155.

Carter, G T, and P Weydt. 2002. Cannabis: Old medicine with new promise for neurological disorders. *Current Opinion in Investigational Drugs* 3 (3): 437–440.

Center for Behavioral Health Statistics and Quality. 2014. The DAWN Report: Emergency department visits involving methamphetamine: 2007 to 2011. Government Statistics, Rockville, MD: Substance Abuse and Mental Health Services Administration.

Centers for Disease Control and Prevention. 2016a. Fact sheets: Alcohol use and your health. July 25. http://www.cdc.gov/alcohol/fact-sheets/alcohol-use.htm.

Centers for Disease Control and Prevention. 2016b. Injury prevention and control: Opioid overdose. December. http://www.cdc.gov/drugoverdose/data/overdose.html.

Centers for Disease Control and Prevention. 2016c. Tobacco use among adults with mental illness and substance use disorders. August 17. http://www.cdc.gov/tobacco/disparities/mental-illness-substance-use/index.htm.

Cone, E J. 1995. Pharmacokinetics and pharmacodynamics of cocaine. *Journal of Analytical Toxicology* 19 (6): 459–478.

Cregler, L L, and H Mark. 1986. Medical complications of cocaine abuse. *The New England Journal of Medicine* 315: 1495–1500.

Espiard, M-L, L Lecardeur, P Abadie, I Halbecq, and S Dollfus. 2005. Hallucinogen persisting perception disorder after psilocybin. *European Psychiatry* 20 (5): 458–460.

Fagerstrom, K, and J Hughes. 2008. Varenicline in the treatment of tobacco dependence. *Neuropsychiatric Disease and Treatment* 4 (2): 353–363.

Fischman, M W, and R W Foltin. 2016. Cocaine and the amphetamines. In *The International Handbook of Addiction Behaviour*, by Ilana B Glass. London: Routledge.

Friedman, D, and O Devinsky. 2015. Cannabinoids in the treatment of epilepsy. *The New England Journal of Medicine* 373: 1048–1058.

Fujii, H, N Nishimoto, S Yamaguchi, and K Okawa. 2016. The alcohol use disorders identification test for consumption (audit-c) is more useful than pre-existing laboratory tests for predicting hazardous drinking: A cross-sectional study. *BMC Public Health* 16 (1): 379. doi:10.1186/s12889-016-3053-6.

Garlow, S J, D Purselle, and B D'Orio. 2003. Cocaine use disorders and suicidal ideation. *Drug and Alcohol Dependence* 70 (1): 101–104.

Glennon, R A, M Titeler, and J D McKenney. 1984. Evidence for 5-HT2 involvement in the mechanism of action of hallucinogenic agents. *Life Sciences* 35 (25): 2505–2511.

Grant, B, R B Goldstein, T Saha, P S Chou, J Jung, H Zhang, R P Pickering et al. 2016. Epidemiology of DSM-5 drug use disorder: Results from the national epidemiologic survey on alcohol and related conditions: III. *Journal of the American Medical Association* 73 (1): 39–47. doi:10.1001/jamapsychiatry.2015.2132.

Hagman, B T. 2016. Performance of the AUDIT in detecting DSM-5 alcohol use disorders in college students. *Substance Use and Misuse* 51 (11): 1521–1528. doi:10.1080/10826084.2016.1188949.

Halberstadt, A L, and M A Geyer. 2011. Multiple receptors contribute to the behavioral effects of indoleamine hallucinogens. *Neuropharmacology* 61 (3): 364–381.

Hart, C L, E W Gunderson, P Audrey, M G Kirkpatrick, A Thurmond, S D Comer, and R Foltin. 2008. Acute physiological and behavioral effects of intranasal methamphetamine in humans. *Neuropsychopharmacology* 33 (8): 1847–1855. doi:10.1038/sj.npp.1301578.

Hartmann-Boyce, J, K Cahill, D Hatsukami, and J Cornuz. 2012. Nicotine vaccines for smoking cessation. *The Cochrane Database of Systematic Reviews* (8).

Harvard Health Publications. 2014. Benzodiazepines (and the alternatives). *Harvard Health Publications*. March. http://www.health.harvard.edu/newsletter_article/Benzodiazepines_and_the_alternatives.

Hasin, D S, and B F Grant. 2015. The national epidemiologic survey on alcohol and related conditions (NESARC) waves 1 an 2: Review and summary of findings. *Spcial Psychiatry Psychiatric Epidemiology* 50 (11): 1609–1640. doi:10.1007/s00127-015-1088-0.

Henningfield, J E, R V Fant, A R Buchhalter, and M L Stitzer. 2005. Pharmacotherpy for nicotine dependence. *CA: A Cancer Journal for Clinicians* 55 (5): 281–299.

Hendrickson, R G, Z Horowitz, R L Norton, and H Notenboom. 2006. "Parachuting" meth: A novel delivery method for methamphetamine and delayed-onset toxicity from "body stuffing". *Clinical Toxicology* 44 (4): 379–382. doi:10.1080/15563650600671746.

Hermle, L, M Simon, M Ruchsow, and M Geppert. 2012. Hallucinogen-persisting perception disorder. *Psychopharmacology* 2 (5): 199–205.

Howard, M O, S E Bowen, E L Garland, B E Perron, and M G Vaughn. 2011. Inhalant use and inhalant use disorders in the United States. *Addiction Science and Clinical Practice* 6 (1): 18–31.

Hughes, J R, and D Hatsukami. 1986. Signs and symptoms of tobbacco withdrawal. *Archives of General Psychiatry* 43: 289–294.

Hukkanen, J, P Jacob, and N L Benowitz. 2005. Metabolism and disposition kinectics of nicotine. *Pharmacological Reviews* 57 (1): 79–115.

Inturrisi, C E. 2002. Clinical pharmacology of opioids for pain. *Clinical Journal of Pain* 18 (4): S3–S13.

Jamal, A, B A King, L J Neff, J Whitmill, S D Babb, and C Graffunder. 2016. Current Cigarette Smoking Among Adults: United States, 2005–2015. MMWR, Altanta, GA: Centers for Disease Control and Prevention.

Kattimani, S, and B Bharadwaj. 2013. Clinical management of alcohol withdrawal: A systematic review. *Industrial Psychiatry Journal* 22 (2): 100–108.

Kiely, E, J C Lee, and L Marinetti. 2009. A fatality from an oral ingestion of methamphetamine. *Journal of Analytical Toxicology* 33 (8): 557–560. doi:10.1093/jat/33.8.557.

Kish, S J. 2008. Pharmacologic mechanisms of crystal meth. *Canadian Medical Association Journal* 178 (13): 1679–1682. doi:10.1503/cmaj.071675.

Kleber, H D, R D Weiss, R F Jr Anton, T P George, S F Greenfield, T R Kosten, C P O'Brien, B J Ransaville, E C Strain, D M Ziedonis, G Hennessy, H S Connery. 2006. *Practice Guideline for the Treatment of Patients With Substance Use Disorders*, Second edition. Arlington, VA: American Psychiatric Association.

Koob, G F, and N D Volkow. 2010. Neurocircuitry of addiction. *Neuropsychopharmacology* 35 (1): 217–238.

Kopelman, M D, A D Thomson, I Guerrini, and E J Marshall. 2009. The Korsakoff syndrome: Clinical aspects, psychology and treatment. *Alcohol and Alcoholism* 44 (2): 148–154.

Kosten, T R, and T P George. 2002. The neurobiology of opioid depedence: Implications for treatment. *Science and Practice Perspectives* 1 (1): 13–20.

Kranzler, H R, and A Gage. 2008. Acamprosate efficacy in alcohol-dependent patients: Summary of results from three pivotal trials. *The American Journal on Addictions* 17 (1): 70–76. doi:10.1080/10550490701756209.

Ling, W, D R Wesson, and D E Smith. 2005. Prescription opiate abuse. In *Substance Abuse: A Comprehensive Textbook*. 4th Edition, by Joyce H Lowinson, Pedro Ruiz, Robert B Millman and John G Langrod, 459–468. Philadelphia, PA: Lippincott Williams and Wilkins.

Matsumoto, R R, M Seminerio, R C Turner, M Robson, L Nguyen, D Miller, and J P O'Callaghan. 2014. Methamphetamine-induced toxicity: An updated review on issues related to hyperthermia. *Pharmacology* 144 (1): 28–40. doi:10.1016/j.pharmthera.2014.05.001.

Miller, W R, and G S Rose. 2009. Toward a theory of motivational interviewing. *American Psychologist* 64 (6): 527–537.

Mulder, A H, G Wardeh, F Hogenboom, and A L Frankhuyzen. 1984. K and O-Opioid receptor agonists differentially inhibit striatal dopamine and acetylcholine release. *Nature* 308: 278–280.

National Academies of Sciences, Engineering, and Medicine. 2016. *Ending Discrimination Against People with Mental and Substance Use Disorders: The Evidence for Stigma Change.* Washington, DC: The National Academies Press. doi:10.17226/23442.

National Institute on Alcohol Abuse and Alcoholism. 2007. *Helping Patients Who Drink Too Much: A Clinician's Guide: Updated 2005 Edition.* Rockville, MD: National Institute on Alcohol Abuse and Alcoholism.

National Institute on Drug Abuse. 1999. NIH consensus panel recommends expanding access to and improving methadone treatment programs for heroin addiction. *European Addiction Research* 5: 50–51.

National Institute on Drug Abuse. 2012. Inhalants. National Institute on Drug Abuse. September. http://www.drugabuse.gov/publications/drugfacts/inhalants.

National Institute on Drug Abuse. 2016a. Hallucinogens. National Institute on Drug Abuse. January. http://www.drugabuse.gov/publications/drugfacts/hallucinogens.

National Institute on Drug Abuse. 2016b. Hallucinogens: Statistics and Trends. January. http://www.drugabuse.gov/drugs-abuse/hallucinogens.

National Institute on Drug Abuse. 2016c. Marijuana. National Institute on Drug Abuse. March. http://www.drugabuse.gov/publications/drugfacts/marijuana.

Petursson, H. 1994. The benzodiazepine withdrawal syndrome. *Addiction* 89 (11): 1455–1459.

Prochaska, J, and C DiClemente. 1983. Stages and processes of self-change in smoking: Toward and integrative model of change. *Journal of Consulting and Clinical Psychology* 5: 390–395.

Rawson, R A, P Marinelli-Casey, M D Anglin, A Dickow, Y Fraizer, C Gallagher, G P Galloway et al. 2004. A multi-site comparison of psychosocial approaches for the treatment of methamphetamine depedence. *Addiction* 99 (6): 708–717.

Rochester, J A, and J T Kirchner. 1999. Ecstasy (3,4-methylenedioxymethamphetamine): History, neurochemistry, and toxicology. *Journal of the American Board of Family Medicine* 12 (2): 137–142.

Roddy, E. 2004. Bupropion and other non-nicotine pharmacotherapies. *British Medical Journal* 509: 328.

Roll, J M, N M Petry, M L Stitzer, M L Brecht, J M Peirce, M J McCann, J Blaine, M MacDonald, J DiMaria, and L L S Kellog. 2006. Contingency management for the treatment of methamphetamine use disorders. *The American Journal of Psychiatry* 163 (11): 1993–1999.

Royal College of Physicians. 2001. *Alcohol: Can the NHS Afford It?* Medical. London: Royal College of Physicians of London.

Rudd, R A, N Aleshire, J E Zibbell, and M R Gladden. 2016. Increases in Drug and Opioid Ovedose Deaths: United States, 2000–2014. MMWR, Altanta, GA: Centers for Disease Control and Prevention.

Schuckit, M A. 2016. Treatment of opioid-use disorders. Edited by Dan L Longo. *The New England Journal of Medicine* 375: 357–368.

Sharp, C S, M P Wilson, and K Nordstrom. 2016. Psychiatric emergencies for clinicians: Emergency department management of Wernicke-Korsakoff syndrome. *Journal of Emergency Medicine* 51 (4): 401–404. doi:10.1016/j.jemermed2016.05.044.

Stapleton, J, R West, P Hajek, J Wheeler, E Vangeli, Z Abdi, C O'Gara et al. 2013. Randomized trial of nicotine replacement therapy (NRT), bupropion and NRT plus bupropion for smoking cessation: Effectiveness in clinical practice. *Addiction* 108 (12): 2193–2201.

Stotts, A, C L Dodrill, and T R Kosten. 2009. Opioid dependence treatment: Options in pharmacotherapy. *Expert Opinion on Pharmacotherapy* 10 (11): 1727–1740.

Strassman, R J. 1996. Human psychopharmacology of N,N-dimethyltryptamine. *Behavioural Brain Research* 73 (1–2): 121–124.

Substance Abuse and Mental Health Services Administration. 2009. Incorporating alcohol pharmacotherapies into medical practice: A Treatment Improvement Protocol, TIP 49. Treatment Improvement Protocol, Rockville, MD: Substance Abuse and Mental Health Services Administration.

Substance Abuse and Mental Health Services Administration. 2013. The DAWN Report: Highlights of the 2011 Drug Abuse Warning Network (DAWN) Findings on Drug Related Emergency Department Visits . Government Drug Abuse Statistics, Rockville, MD: Substance Abuse and Mental Health Services Administration.

Substance Abuse and Mental Health Services Administration. 2014. Substance Abuse Treatment Before the Affordable Care Act: Trends in Social and Economic Characteristics of Facilities and Admissions, 2006 to 2011. Behavioral Health Services Information System Report, Rockville, MD: Substance Abuse and Mental Health Services Administration.

Sylvestre, D L, J M Loftis, P Hauser, S Genser, H Cesari, N Borek, T F Kresina, L B Seeff, and H Francis. 2005. Co-occurring hepatits C, substance use, and psychiatric illness: Treatment issues and developing integrated models of care. *Journal of Urban Health* 81 (4): 719–734. doi:10.1093/jurban/jth153.

Takekawa, K, T Ohmori, A Kido, and M Oya. 2007. Methamphetamine body packer: Acute poisoning death due to massive leaking of methamphetamine. *Journal of Forensic Sciences* 52 (5): 1219–1222. doi:10.1111/j.1556-4029.2007.00518.x.

Tiffany, S, and J M Wray. 2011. The clinical significance of drug craving. *Annals of the New York Academy of Sciences* 1248 (1): 1–17. doi:10.1111/j.1749-6632.2011.06298.x.

Trescot, A M, S Datta, M Lee, and H Hansen. 2008. Opioid pharmacology. *Pain Physician* 11 (2 Suppl): S133–S153.

U.S. Public Health Service. 2008. A clinical practice guideline for treating tobacco use and depedence: 2008 update. *American Journal of Preventative Medicine* 35 (2): 158–176.

Vallersnes, O M, A M Dines, D M Wood, C Yates, F Heyerdahl, K E Hovda, I Giraudon, and P I Dargan. 2016. Psychosis associated with acute recreational drug toxicity: A European case series. *BMC Psychiatry* 293 (16). doi:10.1186/s12888-016-1002-7.

Volkow, N D. 2013. Messages from the director. National Institute on Drug Abuse. March 21. http://www.drugabuse.gov/about-nida/directors-page/messages-director/2012/09/marijuanas-lasting-effects-brain.

Volkow, Nora D, Joanna S Fowler, Gene-Jack Wang, Elena Shumay, Frank Telang, Peter K Thanos, and David Alexoff. 2010. Distribution and pharmacokinetics of methamphetamine in the human body: Clinical implications. *PLOS One* 5 (12): e152569. doi:10.1371/journal.pone.0015269.

Volkow, Nora D, Ruben D Baler, Wilson M Compton, and Susan R B Weiss. 2014. Adverse health effects of marijuana use. *The New England Journal of Medicine* 370 (23): 2219–2227. doi:10.1056/NEJMra1402309.

Vonghia, L, L Leggio, A Ferrulli, M Bertini, G Gasbarrini, and G Addolorato. 2008. Acute alcohol intoxication. *European Journal of Internal Medicine* 19 (8): 561–567.

Vukadinovic, Z, M S Herman, and I Rosenzweig. 2013. Cannabis, psychosis and the thalamus: A theoretical review. *Neuroscience and Biobehavioral Reviews* 37 (4): 658–667. doi:10.1016/j.neubiorev.2013.02.013.

Warner, M, L H Chen, D M Makuc, and R N Anderson. 2011. Drug Poisoning Deaths in the United States, 1980–2008. Data Brief, Hyattsville, MD: National Center for Health Statistics.

Weinstein, A M, and D A Gorelick. 2011. Pharmacological treatment of cannabis dependence. *Current Pharmaceutical Design* 17 (14): 1351–1358.

Weiss, A J, L M Wier, C Stocks, and J Blanchard. 2014. Overview of Emergency Department Visits in the United States, 2011. HCUP Statistical Brief #174. Statistical Brief, Rockville, MD: Agency for Healthcare Research and Quality.

Wesson, D R, and W Ling. 2003. The Clinical Opiate Withdrawal Scale (COWS). *Journal of Psychoactive Drugs* 35 (2): 253–259.

West, P L, N J McKeown, and R G Hendrickson. 2010. Methamphetamine body stuffers: An observational case series. *Annals of Emergency Medicine* 55 (2): 190–197.

White, C M. 2016. Pharmacologuic, pharmacokinetic, and clinical assessment of illicitly used y-hydroxybutyrate. *The Journal of Clinical Pharmacology* 57: 33–39. doi:10.1002/jcph.767.

World Health Organization. 1992. *International Statisical Classification of Diseases and Related Health Problems 10th Revision*. Geneva, Switzerland: World Health Organization.

World Health Organization. 2000. *International Guide for Monitoring Alcohol Consumption and Related Harm*. Geneva, Switzerland: World Health Organization.

World Health Organization. 2009. *Alcohol and Injuries: Emergency Department Studies in an International Perspective.* Geneva, Switzerland: WHO Press.

Yoon, P W, B Bastian, R N Anderson, J L Collins, and H W Jaffe. 2014. Potentially Preventable Deaths from the Five Leading Causes of Death: United States, 2008–2010. Morbidity and Mortality Weekly Report, Atlanta, GA: Centers for Disease Control and Prevention, 369–374.

Zakhari, S. 2006. Overview: How is alcohol metabolized by the body? *Alcohol Research and Health* 245.

Zevin, S, and N L Benowitz. 1999. Drug interactions with tobacco smoking. An update. *Clinical Pharmacokinetics* 36 (6): 425–438.

Zevin, S, Steven G Gourlay, and Neal L Benowitz. 1998. Clinical pharmacology of nicotine. *Clinics in Dermatology* 16 (5): 557–564.

Resources

[No author listed.] 1998. Consensus panel proposes sweeping changes to improve access to methadone maintenance treatment. *American Journal of Health System Pharmacy* 55 (3): 208.

Agosti, V, E Nunes, and F Levin. 2002. Rates of psychiatric comorbidity among U.S. residents with lifetime cannabis dependence. *American Journal of Drug and Alcohol Abuse* 28: 643–652.

Albright, J A, S A Stevens, and D J Beussman. 2012. Detecting ketamine in beverage residues: Application in date rape detection. *Drug Testing and Analysis* 4 (5): 337–341. doi:10.1002/dta.335.

Armstrong, T D, and E J Costello. 2002. Community studies on adolescent substance use, abuse, or dependence and psychiatric comorbidity. *Journal of Consulting and Clinical Psychology* 70: 1224–1239.

Ascher-Svanum, H, B Zhu, D Faries, J P Lacro, and C Dolder. 2006. A prospective study of risk factors for nonadherence with antipsychotic medication in the treatment of schizophrenia. *Journal of Clinical Psychiatry* 67 (7): 1114–1123.

Ascher-Svanum, H, D E Faries, B Zhu, F R Ernst, M S Swartz, and J W Swanson. 2006. Medication adherence and long-term functional outcomes in the treatment of schizophrenia in usual care. *Journal of Clinical Psychiatry* 67 (3): 453–460.

Banys, P. 2016. Mitigation of marijuana-related legal harms to youth in California. *Journal of Psychoactive Drugs* 48 (1): 11–20. doi:10.1080/02791072.2015.1126770.

Barnett, P G, G S Zaric, and M L Brandeau. 2001. The cost-effectiveness of buprenorphine maintenance therapy for opiate addiction in the united states. *Addiction* 96 (9): 1267–1278. doi:10.1046/j.1360-0443.2001.96912676.x.

Brumback, T, N Castro, J Jacobus, and S F Tapert. 2016. Effects of marijuana use on brain structure and function: Nuroimaging findings from a neurodevelopmental perspective. *Interntional Review of Neurobiology* 129: 33–65. doi:10/1016/bs.irn.2016.06.004.

Bush, D M. 2014. *Emergency Department Visits Involving Nonmedical Use of Anti-anxiety Medication Alprazolam.* CBHSQ Report, Rockville, MD: Substance Abuse and Mental Health Services Administration.

Callon, W, M C Beach, S Saha, G Chander, I B Wilson, M B Laws, V Sharp, J Cohn, R Moore, and T P Korthuis. 2016. Assessing problematic substance use in HIV care: Which questions elicit accurate patient disclosures? *Journal of General Internal Medicine* 31 (10): 1141–1147. doi:10.1007/s11606-016-3733-z.

Campbell, C I, S Sterling, F W Chi, and A H Kline-Simon. 2016. Marijuana use and service utilization among adolescents 7 years post substance use treatment." *Drug and Alcohol Dependence* 1–7. doi:10.1016/j.drugalcdep.2016.08.012.

Center for Behavioral Health Statistics and Quality. 2013. Results from the 2012 National Survey on Drug Use and Health: Summary of National Findings. Government Statistics, Rockville, MD: Substance Abuse and Mental Health Services Administration.

Centers for Disease Control and Prevention. 2012. Community based opioid overdose prevention programs providing naloxone: United States, 2010. Morbidity and Mortality Weekly Report, Atlanta, GA: Centers for Disease Control and Prevention.

Chen, L-H, H Hedegaard, and M Warner. 2015. QuickStats: Rates of deaths from drug poisoning and drug poisoning involving opioid analgesics: United States, 1999–2013. Morbidity and Mortality Weekly Report, Atlanta, GA: Centers for Disease Control and Prevention.

Crump, C, K Sundquist, M A Winkleby, and J Sundquist. 2013. Mental disorders and risk of accidental death. *The British Journal of Psychiatry* 203 (4): 297–302. doi:10.1192/bjp.bp.112.123992.

Day, C. 2013. Benzodiazepines in Combination with Opioid Pain Relievers or Alcohol: Greater Risk or More Serious ED Visit Outcomes. CBHSQ Report, Rockville, MD: Substance Abuse and Mental Health Services Administration.

Evans, E, H Padwa, L Li, V Lin, and Y-I Hser. 2015. Heterogeneity of mental health service utilization and high mental health service use among women eight years after initiating substance use disorder treatment." *Journal of Substance Abuse Treatment* 10–19. doi:10.1016/j.sat.2015.06.021.

Grant, B F, D S Hasin, S P Chou, F S Stinson, and D A Dawson. 2004. Nicotine dependence and psychiatric disorders in the United States: Results from the national epidemiologic survey on alcohol and related conditions. *Archives of General Psychiatry* 61 (11): 1107–1115.

Hagemann, C T, A Helland, O Spigset, K A Espnes, K Ormstad, and B Schei. 2013. Ethanol and drug findings in women consulting a sexual assault center: Associations with clinical characteristics and suspicions of drug-facilitated sexual assault. *Journal of Forensic and Legal Medicine* 20 (6): 777–784. doi:10.1016/j.jflm.2013.05.005.

Hamilton, R, V Keyfes, and S S Banka. 2016. Synthetic cannabinoid abuse resulting in ST-segment elevation myocardial infarction requiring percutaneous coronary intervention. *Journal of Emergency Medicine.* doi:10.1016/j.jemermed.2016.09.023.

Hartman, R L, and M A Huestis. 2013. Cannabis effects on driving skills. *Clinical Chemistry* 59 (3): 478–492.

Henriksen, K, J B Battles, M A Keyes, and M L Grady. 2008. Advances in Patient Safety: New Directions and Alternative Approaches, Volume . Assessment. Study, Rockville, MD: Agency for Healthcare Research and Quality.

Hermann, R C, J A Chan, S E Provost, and W T Chiu. 2006. Statisical benchmarks for process measures of quality of care for mental and substance use disorders. *Psychiatric Services* 57 (10): 1461–1467.

Hudson, T J, R R Owen, C R Thrush, X Han, J M Pyne, P Thapa, and G Sullivan. 2004. A pilot study of barriers to medication adherence in schizophrenia. *Journal of Clinical Psychiatry* 65 (2): 211–216.

Huynh, C, J Tremblay, and M-J Fleury. 2016. Typologies of individuals attending an addiction rehabilitation center based on diagnosis of mental disorders. *Journal of Substance Abuse Treatment* 71: 68–78. doi:10.1016/j.sat.2016.09.007.

Johnson, N B, L D Hayes, K Brown, E C Hoo, and K A Ethier. 2014. CDC National Health Report: Leading Causes of Morbidity and Mortality and Associated Behavioral Risk and Protective Factors: United States, 2005–2013. Morbidity and Mortality Weekly Report, Atlanta, GA: Centers for Disease Control and Prevention.

Joseph, A M, M W Manseau, M Lalane, A Rajparia, and C F Lewis. 2016. Characteristics associated with synthetic cannabinoid use among patients treated in a public psychiatric emergency setting. *The American Journal of Drug and Alcohol Abuse* 1–6. doi:10.1080/00952990.2016.1240799.

Kalk, N J, A Boyd, J Strang, and E Finch. 2016. Spice and all things nasty: The challenge of synthetic cannabinoids. *BMJ* 355 (i5639). doi:10.1136/bmj.i5639.

Killaspy, H, L Marston, N Green, I Harrison, M Lean, F Holloway, T Craig, G Leavey, M Arbuthnott, L Koeser, P McCrone, R Z Omar, M King. 2016. Clinical outcomes and costs for people with complex psychosis; a naturalistic prospective cohort study of mental health rehabilitation service users in England. *BMC Psychiatry* 95 (16). doi:10.1186/s12888-016-0797-6.

Knott, A, E Dieperink, M L Willenbring, S Heit, J M Durfee, M Wingert, J R Johnson, P D Thuras, and S B Ho. 2006. Integrated psychiatric/medical care in a chronic hepatitis C clinic: Effect on antiviral treatment evaluation and outcomes. *The American Journal of Gastroenterology* 101 (10): 2254–2262. doi:10.1111/j.1572-0241.2006.00731.x.

Lee, S J, and P Levounis. 2008. Gamma hydroxybutyrate: An ethnographic study of recreational use and abuse. *Journal of Psychoactive Drugs* 40 (3): 245–253. doi:10.1080/02791072.2008.10400639.

Malfitano, A M, G Matarese, and M Bifulco. 2006. From cannabis to endocannabinoids in multiple sclerosis: A paradigm of central nervous system autoimmune diseases. *Current Drug Targets: CNS and Neurological Disorders* 4 (6): 667–675. doi:10.2174/156800705774933087.

Marcovitz, D E, K McHugh, J Volpe, V Votaw, and H S Connery. 2016. Predictors of early dropout in outpatient buprenorphine/naloxone treatment. *The American Journal on Addictions* 25 (6): 472–477. doi:10.1111/ajad.12414.

Marra, E M, M Mazer-Amirshahi, G Brooks, J van den Anker, L Pines, J M May. 2015. Benzodiazepine prescribing in older adults in U.S. ambulatory clinics and emergency departments (2001–10). *Journal of the American Geriatrics Society* 63 (10): 2074–2081.

Mitton, C R, C E Adair, G M McDougall, and G Marcoux. 2005. Continuity of care and health care costs among persons with servere mental illness. *Psychiatric Services* 56 (9): 1070–1076. doi:10.1176/appi.ps.56.9.1070.

National Institute on Alcohol Abuse and Alcoholism. 2003. *Assessing Alcohol Problems: A Guide for Clinicians and Researchers.* Rockville, MD: National Insitute on Alcohol Abuse and Alcoholism.

National Institute on Drug Abuse. 2016d. *Monitoring the Future Study: Trends in Prevlalence of Various Drugs.* Government Statistics, Rockville, MD: National Institute on Drug Abuse.

North American Quitline Consortium. 2014. North American Quitline Consortium: Promoting Evidence Bases Quitline Services Across Diverse Communities in North America. June 25. http://www.naquitline.org.

O'Malley, S. 1998. *Treatment Improvement Protocol (TIP) Series 28: Naltrexone and Alcoholism Treatment.* Rockville, MD: Substance Abuse and Mental Health Services Administration.

Palamar, J J, P Acosta, D C Ompad, and C M Cleland. 2016. Self-reported ecstasy/MDMA/"molly" use in a sample of nightclub and dance festival attendees in new york city. *Substance Use and Misuse* 52 (1): 82–91. doi:10.1080/10826084.2016.1219373.

Patrick, M E, P Wightman, R F Schoeni, and J E Schulenberg. 2012. Socioeconomic status and substance use among young adults: A comparison across constructs and drugs. *Journal of Studies on Alcohol and Drugs* 73 (5): 772–782. doi:10.15288/jsad.2012.73.772.

Puening, S E, M P Wilson, and K Nordstrom. 2017. Psychiatric emergencies for clinicians: Emergency department management of benzodiazepine withdrawal. *The Journal of Emergency Medicine* 52 (1): 66–69. doi:10.1016/j.jemermed.2016.05.035.

Puntis, S R, J Rugkasa, and T Burns. 2016. The association between continuity of care and readmission to hospital in patients with severe psychosis. *Social Psychiatry and Psychiatric Epidemiology* 51 (12): 1633–1643. doi:10.1007/s00127-016-1287-3.

Rhodes, K V, S Basseyn, R Gallop, E Noll, A Rothbard, and P Crits-Christoph. 2016. Pennsylvania's medical home initiative: Reductions in healthcare utilization and cost among Medicaid patients with medical and psychiatric comorbidities. *Journal of General Internal Medicine* 31 (11): 1373–1381. doi:10.1007/s11606-016-3734-y.

Roncero, C, N Szerman, A Teran, C Pino, J M Vazquez, E Velasco, M Garcia-Dorado, and M Casas. 2016. Professionals' perception on the management of patients with dual disorders. *Patient Preference and Adherence* 10: 1855–1868. doi:10.2147/PPA.S108678.

Smedslund, G, R C Berg, K T Hammerstrom, A Steiro, K A Leiknes, H M Dahl, and K Karlsen. 2011. *Motivational Interviewing for Substance Abuse.* Review. Oslo, Norway: The Campbell Collaboration.

Smith, Paul F. 2002. Cannabinoids in the treatment of pain and spasticity in multiple sclerosis. *Current Opinion in Investigational Drugs* 3 (6): 859–864.

Chapter 13

Emergency Treatment of Agitation in Delirious and Demented Patients

Elyssa L. Barron, Alexis Briggie, and Howard L. Forman

Contents

13.1 Introduction 235
13.2 Step 1: Don't Do Anything—Attempt Negotiation 236
13.3 Step 2: When Negotiation Has Failed—Simultaneously Assess and Act 237
    13.3.1 Non-Pharmacologic Interventions 237
    13.3.2 Pharmacologic Interventions 237
        13.3.2.1 Antipsychotics 237
        13.3.2.2 Benzodiazepines 237
        13.3.2.3 The B52 238
        13.3.2.4 Other Medication Classes 238
        13.3.2.5 Special Situations 239
13.4 Step 3: The Agitated Patient Has Been Calmed, What Now? 239
13.5 In Closing 239
References 243
    243

13.1 Introduction

Well, hello there! You may have reached for this chapter because you are on call overnight and an agitated patient has just been brought into your emergency department (ED), and you want to know how to manage it most expertly? Possibly you are just trying to educate yourself on the latest treatment of agitation in the hope that something new and more definitive has been developed since you completed your training? Regardless of your motivation for reading this chapter, allow me to lower your expectations right now. There is probably no area of psychiatry, and maybe all of medicine, where less evidence-based progress has been made than in the management of the acutely agitated patient who is demented, delirious, or both.

With that depressing start, we will now commence with sharing what is known and with making some recommendations based on the available evidence, our clinical practice at the Albert Einstein College of Medicine, and our conversations with leaders in the field of psychosomatic medicine/consultation liaison psychiatry. Following suggestions for the acute management of agitation, we will then share some clues as to what may be the underlying causes of the patient's agitation.

All discussion on medications will be done in an "off-label" fashion. There are no drugs with Food and Drug Administration (FDA) indication for acute agitation in patients with delirium or dementia. Additionally, all antipsychotics carry an explicit FDA warning of "increased death" when used to treat patients with dementia. In this chapter, we assume that, while taking this risk into account, you are also weighing the real, immediate, and substantial risk that an agitated patient poses to himself and others.

13.2 Step 1: Don't Do Anything—Attempt Negotiation

With agitation, every intervention that you attempt is fraught with risk. Therefore, the goal should be to do as little as possible while still preventing real potential harm to an agitated patient.

There are countless times that we have been asked to assess an agitated patient in the ED and are told that the patient is psychotic, delirious, demented, or intoxicated.

While all of the previously mentioned are possible reasons that a patient may be agitated, it is equally likely that the agitated patient is someone who is easily perturbed, and that there is actually no underlying pathology leading to the agitation—with the exception of poor coping mechanisms for the unpredictable, slow, and often times frightening experience of being a patient.

The patient that is agitated for reasons secondary to personality factors can often be negotiated with so that their behavior is no longer scary, dangerous, or blocking the ability for them to be cared for optimally. We suggest the following topics of inquiry:

- Is the patient in pain that is not being treated or is being under treated? There are few things that are more frustrating than coming for help and sensing that the staff is not doing anything to help you. There are real reasons for some pain not to be immediately and comprehensively treated, but there are many more times when pain is simply not being addressed while the "real problem" is being worked up by the ED physicians. While the primary concern for physicians in the ED is the overall health of the patient, most patients just want to experience relief—and can become very agitated in its absence. Treatment of pain can be the magic bullet for agitation in the emergency setting.
- Hunger causes people to do seemingly crazy things. Feeding patients may not be the chief concern of staff due to the inherently busy and serious nature of the ED, but hunger can cause real and serious side effects, including agitation. In some cases, a lack of food may even be the indirect cause of the patient's emergency visit. Although people die of starvation, the number of people dying of starvation in EDs in the United States is probably nil, while the number of patients claiming that they are "dying from hunger" approaches infinity. If there is no reason not to allow a patient to eat, ask if they are hungry and if they think they will feel better if they are given some food. The ED is not the place to fight the obesity epidemic, and the more pleasurable the food the patient consumes, the better the response you will likely have—to quote Homer Simpson, "You don't make friends with salad" (The Simpsons 1995).
- Does the patient even need to be in an ED? Estimates of avoidable ED use range as high as 56% of all visits (Weinick et al. 2003), and ED overuse is responsible for up to 38 billion

dollars of wasteful spending per year (Delaune and Everett 2008). Many times the patients who overuse these services, and those patients who are impatient, agitated, or dissatisfied with the care they are receiving, are one and the same. They may be better served by being in an environment of their choosing, such as their private doctor's office or another hospital. Many times, these patients will say something such as, "I am never coming back to this hospital; I want to leave and go to a better hospital," and very often the best response is, "We want you to go to the setting where you will feel most well-cared for."

13.3 Step 2: When Negotiation Has Failed—Simultaneously Assess and Act

If negotiation has failed and the patient remains agitated, it is unlikely that you will get a great deal of information from the patient about why they are agitated. The question, "Excuse me sir, can you please stop throwing your feces at me so that I can ask you a few questions?" is unlikely to get anyone to stop throwing feces at you.

Since the patient is likely to be in the beginning stages of the medical work up, the medical chart is unlikely to be terribly helpful in elucidating the cause of delirium. Although friends, relatives, or a physician with whom the patient has an ongoing relationship may be crucial in determining the etiology of the agitation—it is reasonable to expect that none of these people will be available in the amount of time that you will need to act.

13.3.1 Non-Pharmacologic Interventions

The first recommended action is to consider the resources available to help the patient without any pharmacologic intervention.

- Does the hospital have one-to-one observation available (sometimes called constant observation or sitters)? Can the patient remain without medication if someone is at their bedside constantly redirecting them and giving them instructions?
- Is there is an area in the ED that has less commotion or that will be less stimulating to the agitated patient?
- Can the patient be moved to an area where there is less potential for patient self-harm or harm to others? Is there a room in the ED that simply has a bed on the floor with nothing potentially dangerous suspended on the walls?

13.3.2 Pharmacologic Interventions

If non-pharmacologic interventions are ineffective, it is time to start thinking about medications to help increase safety. The vast majority of agitation cases in the ED can be managed with one agent. If one agent is ineffective, then the requirement for more than two agents is infinitesimal.

13.3.2.1 Antipsychotics

Typical and atypical antipsychotics have been shown to be effective in the management of acute agitation, regardless of whether the agitation is due to dementia or delirium. With respect to the typical antipsychotics, potency does not predict performance in the treatment of agitation (Breitbart et al. 1996; Lanctot et al. 1998). We recommend becoming familiar with one antipsychotic as your "go to" and one as your back-up agent. Using one agent on a regular basis will give you confidence in dosing and allow the staff you are working to become familiar with it, leading to fewer errors (wrong medication or wrong dose) and fewer delays (medication has to be brought from the pharmacy). Our preference is to start with haloperidol, for the following reasons:

- It is available in both oral (PO) and intramuscular (IM) formulations, with little to no dose adjustment necessary. Agitated patients may refuse medication but it is very easy to instruct the staff to "give haloperidol 5 mg PO (orally) STAT (immediately) and if PO is refused, "give haloperidol 5 mg IM STAT." This is much easier than telling the staff to "give risperidone 1 mg PO STAT, and if PO refused, give haloperidol 5 mg IM."
- There is no established maximum for haloperidol, so if it is not successful at first, you can give an additional dose soon after without fear that you will reach a ceiling above which it is no longer safe to give.
- It is widely available in most hospital systems and therefore it is likely that it will be readily available quickly. Although you may prefer using trifluoperazine for agitation, it is unlikely that you will be able to obtain it within a time frame that is of any use to your patient.

13.3.2.2 Benzodiazepines

Outside of very specific cases, there is little to no evidence supporting the treatment of agitation due to delirium or dementia with benzodiazepines (Defrancesco et al. 2015). In fact, benzodiazepines (benzos) can worsen delirium (Breitbart et al. 1996) and can actually turn nondelirious patients into delirious patients! That said, decades of clinical practice support the use of benzodiazepines in the acutely agitated patient. Allow us to use a simile. When approaching the agitated patient, think of lorazepam as a six-pack of your favorite beer. Sure, it is crisp, delicious, and will make you feel great on a hot summer day, but if you finish that six-pack in one sitting, there is going to be a price to pay. Benzos get the job done of calming the agitated patient, but the ease of use comes with the associated potential cost of worsening the patient's condition and/or making their delirium last longer. Lorazepam is our benzodiazepine of choice for several reasons. It can be given PO, IM, and intravenously (IV). It does not require the P450 system for oxidation, as it undergoes glucuronidation, so it is not contraindicated in patients with liver dysfunction. Also, it has few drug-to-drug interactions. The added benefit of using a benzodiazepine in acute agitation is that if the patient's agitation is due to alcohol or benzodiazepine withdrawal, you are treating the underlying problem in addition to the acute agitation. Benzodiazepines should be used judiciously in women who are or may be pregnant, as all of the commonly used benzodiazepines are pregnancy category D.

13.3.2.3 The B52

You may be familiar with the cocktail famously known as the "B52," made up of haloperidol 5 mg, lorazepam 2 mg, and diphenhydramine 50 mg (Urban Dictionary n.d.). In truth, we have rarely seen this mixture of medications fail to achieve its desired effect. It has been shown that haloperidol given with lorazepam has been more effective than lorazepam given alone (Bieniek et al. 1998). The problem is that you have likely now created a patient that will be so sedated as to be unable to participate in directing their care or giving the medical team important information about their history. The "B52" is well named because, just like the B52 bomber, it will get the job done but will likely cause a great deal of collateral damage.

13.3.2.4 Other Medication Classes

There is no evidence to support usage of mood stabilizers or antidepressants in the acute setting.

13.3.2.5 Special Situations

While a complete list of special cases where one should choose one agent over another, or one class over another, would be infinitely long, here are the most common situations you will face and how to proceed most safely:

- Pregnancy: Avoid benzodiazepines because of the risk of teratogenicity. Stick with an antipsychotic, like haloperidol, that has a long track record of success treating agitation and a scant record of negatively impacting the fetus (Diav-Citrin et al. 2005). Of course, if medications can be avoided in the pregnant patient, this is always preferred.
- Lewy body dementia/Parkinson's: These patients are in a hypodopaminergic state at baseline and giving them a D2 blocker (antipsychotic) will exacerbate this problem. Use benzodiazepines.
- Alcohol or benzodiazepine withdrawal: The treatment of choice in these patients is benzodiazepines and the outcome that one is trying to avoid is withdrawal seizures. Giving antipsychotics will do nothing to lower the risk of seizures and may in fact make them more likely.
- Phencyclidine (PCP) intoxication: Patients are at increased risk of rhabdomyolysis and the combination of this with antipsychotics can put the patient at cumulatively more risk of this feared outcome.
- Prolonged QTc: Studies have shown that aripiprazole has a relatively safe cardiac profile (Polcwiartek et al. 2015). It has been shown to be effective in delirium (Boettger and Breitbart 2011; Boettger et al. 2011). It is available in PO, IM, oral disintegrating tablet, and liquid form, but not all are readily available in all hospital systems. The evidence on death secondary to QTc prolongation caused by antipsychotics ranges from sparse to nonexistent. It our practice, however, when QTc is greater than 500 msec, we prefer to give benzodiazepines for agitation.

13.4 Step 3: The Agitated Patient Has Been Calmed, What Now?

It cannot be underscored enough that when the agitated patient arrives to the ED, you are unlikely to know the actual cause of agitation, especially if you are unable to verbally negotiate with the patient and they require being medicated. Once the patient has been calmed, they may not be terribly helpful in allowing you to elucidate the etiology, but you will now likely be able to review labs and speak with people who know the patient and can provide collateral information. Subsequently, we will lay out some causes of delirium and some types of dementia so that you can be helpful to the ED physicians in caring for the patient beyond the acute agitation. For delirium, as shown in Table 13.1, we are going to include some radiologic and laboratory studies that can help guide your assessment. For dementia, as shown in Table 13.2, we will list some of the defining characteristics of each type to help guide the questions you will ask. Unfortunately, with the exception of HIV dementia, the outcomes are universally dismal.

Table 13.1   Etiologies of Delirium and Suggested Workup

Etiology	Examples	Work Up
Infection	Encephalitis, meningitis, pneumonia, urinary tract infection, abscess	Vital signs, urinalysis, urine culture, chest X-ray, blood cultures, wound cultures, HIV, VDRL, lumbar puncture (if indicated), heat-CT (if indicated).
Hypoxia	Chronic hypoxia from lung disease, carbon monoxide poisoning	Pulse oximetry, ABG, chest X-ray, carbon monoxide levels
Environmental	Hypothermia, hyperthermia, sensory overload, sensory deprivation	Vital signs
Withdrawal	Benzodiazepines, alcohol, opiates	Blood alcohol level, liver function tests, urine or serum toxicology, history regarding substance abuse and prescription drugs
Acute metabolic changes	Acidosis, renal failure, hypo or hyperglycemia	Liver function tests, basic metabolic panel, calcium, blood glucose level, ABG
Endocrine abnormalities	Hypothyroidism, Hyperthyroidism	Thyroid-stimulating hormone, free T4
Vitamin deficiencies	B12 deficiency, thiamine deficiency, history of bariatric surgery, malnutrition	B12 level, trial of thiamine
Trauma	Cerebral hemorrhage, burns	Head CT (if indicated).
Pathology of the central nervous system	Subarachnoid hemorrhage, hemorrhagic or ischemic stroke, epilepsy, paraneoplastic syndrome, tumors	Head imaging, EEG, paraneoplastic markers
Toxins or drugs	Medications and polypharmacy, pesticides, alcohol, street drugs	Urine or serum toxicology, blood alcohol level, acetaminophen and salicylate levels. Some medications have been associated with delirium: anticholinergic medications, benzodiazepines, narcotics.

Table 13.2 Overview of Dementia

Etiology of Dementia	Cause	Cardinal Features
Alzheimer's	Genetic links have been found but do not account for all cases. Loss of neurons and synapses. Amyloid plaques and neurofibrillary tangles are present.	Most common type of dementia. Usually presents with gradual onset, early memory loss and a progressive course (McKhann et al. 1984).
Vascular	Ischemic or hemorrhagic infarcts affecting areas of the brain.	Less common than Alzheimer's disease, can present in several ways. The progression can be abrupt, insidious or progressive depending on the etiology (Iadecola 2013).
Lewy Body	Some genetic link but mostly sporadic collection of alpha-synuclein within neurons.	Cardinal features are fluctuating cognitive impairment, visual hallucinations and Parkinsonism (Walker et al. 2015).
Parkinson's disease	Environmental and/or genetic factors contributing to the death of dopamine producing cells in the substantia nigra. Lewy bodies can also be found.	Dementia that presents in the context of Parkinson's disease. Most patients who live 10 years after diagnosis will have dementia (Svenningsson et al. 2012).
Frontotemporal	Several genetic mutations that cause neuronal loss in the frontal and/or temporal lobes	Characterized by disinhibition, apathy, loss of empathy, compulsive behaviors, hyperorality, and dysexecutive neuropsychological profile (Rascovsky et al. 2011).
Creutzfeldt-Jakob disease (CJD)	Prion	Rapid onset of dementia often seen with myoclonus, visual, or cerebellar signs (Gambetti 2016). The most reliable diagnostic tool is brain biopsy. As this is not readily available in your neighborhood ER (or even used at all), there are two tests that can aid in the diagnosis of CJD. A CSF 14-3-3 protein analysis and an EEG. Periodic sharp wave complexes on EEG are found in two thirds of patients with CJD (Manix et al. 2015).

(Continued)

Table 13.2 (Continued)   Overview of Dementia

Etiology of Dementia	Cause	Cardinal Features
Progressive supranuclear palsy	Unknown	Uncommon. Initially presents with trouble with balance, falling, bumping into objects, and Parkinsonism (which responds poorly to levodopa). Dementia is usually seen later in the disease. Problems with eye movements (vertical gaze palsy). The key being trouble with downward gaze and upward gaze palsy can be present in normal aging (Collins et al. 1995).
Normal pressure hydrocephalus	Abnormal volume of CSF in ventricles	Look for gait disturbance and urinary incontinence to present with symptoms of dementia as the enlarged ventricles put pressure on the adjacent cortical tissue. Intracranial pressure is not usually elevated as the name suggests (Picascia et al. 2015).
Wernicke Korsakoff syndrome	Thiamine deficiency	History of alcohol abuse or malnutrition. Features of Wernicke's include ocular disturbances, gait disturbances, and mental status changes. As disease progresses (Korsakoff), the patient will present with amnesia. Aphasia, agnosia, executive function impairment, and apraxia can all be seen (Latt and Dore 2014).
Mixed	Multifactorial	Features of Alzheimer's dementia and vascular dementia (Zekry et al. 2002).
Huntington disease	Trinucleotide repeat on chromosome 4 (AD inheritance)	Most typically presents between the ages of 35 and 45. Usually presents first with choreiform movement, impairment of motor coordination, and slowing of ocular saccades (Walker 2007). Problems with memory, visuospatial abilities, and executive functioning are seen in later stages of the disease (Montoya et al. 2006).

(Continued)

Table 13.2 (Continued) Overview of Dementia

Etiology of Dementia	Cause	Cardinal Features
Wilson's disease (Hepatolenticular degeneration)	Mutations in ATP7B gene (AR inheritance) causes copper accumulation in tissue	Look for liver dysfunction. dysarthria, dystonia, tremor, Parkinsonism, choreoathetosis, and ataxia are all neurological manifestations. Can have frontal lobe dysfunction manifesting as impaired judgment and decision-making. Can have subcortical dementia, which presents as executive dysfunction, slow thinking, and memory impairment (Lorincz 2010).
Reversible causes of dementia	Hypothyroidism, neurosyphilis, B12 deficiency, Lyme disease, exposure to heavy metal	Detailed history and appropriate labs.

13.5 In Closing

When it comes to dementia and delirium leading to agitation, the first thing to consider is that these patients are fragile and the medications are fraught with risk. Whenever you can avoid pharmacologic intervention, do so! If you need to ask, try and act by ordering the minimum dose that you can reasonably expect to help. The second thing to consider is that remaining calm despite the impressive challenge of calming an agitated patient is essential to the functioning of the team you are leading.

References

Bieniek, S A, R L Ownby, A Penalver, and R A Dominguez. 1998. A double-blind study of lorazepam versus the combination of haloperidol and lorazepam in managing agitation. *Pharmacotherapy* 18 (1): 57–62.

Boettger, S, and W Breitbart. 2011. An open trial of aripiprazole for the treatment of delirium in hospitalized cancer patients. *Palliative and Supportive Care* 9 (4): 351–357.

Boettger, S, M Friedlander, W Breitbart, and S Passik. 2011. Aripiprazole and haloperidol in the treatment of delirium. *Australian and New Zealand Journal of Psychiatry* 45 (6): 477–482.

Breitbart, W, R Marotta, M M Platt, H Weisman, M Derevenco, C Grau, K Corbera, S Raymond, S Lund, and P Jacobson. 1996. A double-blind trial of haloperidol, chlorpromazine, and lorazepam in the treatment of delirium in hospitalized AIDS patients. *American Journal of Psychiatry* 153 (2): 231–237.

Collins, S J, J E Ahlskog, J E Parisi, and D M Maraganore. 1995. Progressive supranuclear palsy: Neuropathologically based diagnostic clinical criteria. *Journal of Neurology, Neurosurgery, and Psychiatry* 58 (2): 167–173.

Defrancesco, M, J Marksteiner, W W Fleischhacker, and I Blasko. 2015. Use of benzodiazepines in Alzheimer's disease: A systematic review of literature. *International Journal of Neuropsychopharmacology* 18 (10): pyv055.

Delaune, J, and W Everett. 2008. *Waste and Inefficiency in the US Health Care System: Clinical Care: A Comprehensive Analysis in Support of System-Wide Improvements.* Healthcare Study, Cambridge: New England Healthcare Institute.

Diav-Citrin, O, S Shechtman, S Ornoy, J Arnon, C Schaefer, H Garbis, M Clementi, and A Ornoy. 2005. Safety of haloperidol and penfluridol in pregnancy: A multicenter, prospective, controlled study. *Journal of Clinical Psychiatry* 66 (3): 317–322.

Gambetti, P. 2016. Creutzfeldt-Jakob Disease (CJD). Merck manual: Consumer version. http://www.merckmanuals.com/home/brain,-spinal-cord,-and-nerve-disorders/prion-diseases/creutzfeldt-jakob-disease-cjd.

Iadecola, C. 2013. The pathology of vascular dementia. *Neuron* 80 (4): 844–866.

Lanctot, K L, T S Best, N Mittmann, B A Liu, P L Oh, T R Finarson, and C A Naranjo. 1998. Efficacy and safety of neuroleptics in behavioral disorders associated with dementia. *Journal of Clinical Psychiatry* 59: 550–561.

Latt, N C, and G Dore. 2014. Thiamine in the treatment of Wernicke encephalopathy in patients with alcohol use disorders. *Internal Medicine Journal* 44 (9): 911–915.

Lorincz, M T. 2010. Neurologic Wilson's disease. *Annals of the New York Academy of Sciences* 1184: 173–187.

Manix, M, P Kalakoti, M Henry, J Thakur, R P Menger, B Guthikonda, and A Nanda. 2015. Creutzfeldt-Jakob disease: Updated diagnostic criteria, treatment algorithm, and the utility of brain biopsy. *Neurosurgical Focus* 39 (5): E2.

McKhann, G, D Drachman, M Folstein, R Katzman, D Price, and E Stadlan. 1984. Clinical diagnosis of Alzheimer's disease. *Neurology* 34 (7): 939.

Montoya, A, B H Price, M Lepage, and M Menear. 2006. Brain imaging and cognitive dysfunctions in Huntington's disease. *Journal of Psychiatry and Neuroscience* 31 (1): 21–29.

Picascia, M, R Zangaglia, S Bernini, B Minafra, E Sinforiani, and C Pacchetti. 2015. A review of cognitive impairment and differential diagnosis in idiopathic normal pressure hydrocephalus. *Functional Neurology* 30 (4): 217–228.

Polcwiartek, C, B Sneider, C Graff, D Taylor, J Meyer, J K Kanters, and Nielsen J. 2015. The cardiac safety of aripiprazole treatment in patients at high risk for torsade: A systematic review with a meta-analytic approach. *Psychopharmacology* 232 (18): 3297–3308.

Rascovsky, K, J R Hodges, D Knopman, M F Mendez, J H Kramer, J Neuhaus, J C van Swieten et al. 2011. Sensitivity of revised diagnostic criteria for the behavioral variant of frontotemporal dementia. *Brain* 134 (Pt 9): 2456–2477.

The Simpsons. 1995. Lisa the Vegetarian, Episode 5. Directed by Mark Kirkland. Written by David Cohen. Fox, October 15.

Svenningsson, P, E Westman, C Ballard, and D Aarsland. 2012. Cognitive impairment in patients with Parkinson's disease: Diagnosis, biomarkers, and treatment. *The Lancet: Neurology* 11 (8): 697–707.

Urban Dictionary. n.d. B-52. *Urban Dictionary.* http://www.urbandictionary.com/define.php?term=b-52.

Walker, F O. 2007. Huntington's disease. *The Lancet* 369 (9557): 218–228.

Walker, Z, K Possin, B F Boeve, and D Aarsland. 2015. Lewy body dementias. *The Lancet* 386 (10004): 1683–1697.

Weinick, R M, J Billings, and J M Thorpe. 2003. Ambulatory care sensitive emergency department visits: A national perspective. *Academic Emergency Medicine* 10 (5): 525.

Zekry, D, J-J Hauw, and G Gold. 2002. Mixed dementia: Epidemiology, diagnosis, and treatment. *Journal of the American Geriatrics Society* 50 (8): 1431–1438.

Chapter 14

Personality Disorders: An Empathic Approach

Yener Balan and Duygu Balan

Contents

14.1 Introduction 245
14.2 It's Not You … It's Me: Impact of Patient Care on the ED Clinician's Psyche 246
14.3 Wait … Maybe It Is You: The Patient's Expectations of Care 246
14.4 This Seems More Complicated: Patient and Clinician Social Interactions 246
14.5 When Personality Traits Become Pathological 247
14.6 You Are the Best Doctor Ever! (Spoiler Alert: You're Probably Not): The Interplay of Disordered Personality Traits with the Clinician's Personality 248
14.7 Splitting the Team 249
14.8 Maintaining Consistent Boundaries 249
14.9 Treatment Options 250
14.10 Conclusion 251
References 252
Resources 252

14.1 Introduction

The emergency department (ED) is typically the most active, energetic, and hectic area of a hospital. Those of us that work in EDs are attracted to that vibe—the energy, challenges, and rewards it can bring. Caring for people on one of the worst days of their lives, working with their loved ones, helping reduce their anxieties, and providing hope and understanding is what emergency clinicians do very well.

14.2 It's Not You ... It's Me: Impact of Patient Care on the ED Clinician's Psyche

In an ED, the clinician is on their feet and walking around for most of the 10–12 hour shift. The high-energy requirement, coupled with exposure to illness, fear, and traumas, and the occasional inability to save someone despite heroic attempts, all in the same shift, can take its toll on the clinician's body and mind.

An emergency clinician does not have a set appointment schedule, or a way to plan ahead for the types of illnesses that will be requiring care the next day. ED clinicians are prepared to care for every level of acuity of disease and human condition, literally, at all times. Since a patient with a "simple" arm laceration requiring sutures can be followed by a car accident victim requiring lifesaving interventions, clinicians become experienced in zooming in and out of the intensity of medical care, and in communicating what they are doing with the patient to their loved ones.

The mental exercise of adjusting intensities of focus throughout a shift, and walking for miles around the ED while caring for patients in different rooms, leads to fatigue, which then can lead to sleep disruptions after the shift. Studies have shown that sleep deprivation and fatigue can cause cognitive impairment, diminished processing speed, and a general dulling of responses (Williamson and Feyer 2000). While none of these are excuses for a poor attitude or poor patient care, they certainly color interactions with patients and colleagues.

Successful hospital systems and clinician groups are mindful of a work–life balance, and promote wellness to minimize and prevent the undesired sequelae of stress.

14.3 Wait ... Maybe It Is You: The Patient's Expectations of Care

A patient comes, or is brought, into the ED with certain expectations. At the heart of these expectations is the desire for expeditious attention and medical care. The expectations regarding the context of the care are those of respect and dignity. These then are tied to expectations and a desire to ultimately learn about the condition that brought them into the ED, and how to obtain follow-up care, once stabilized.

Clinicians understand these expectations—we could all ultimately become patients at a given point in our lives, and all similarly desire to obtain medical treatment when going to a medical facility. The nuances of how things are communicated, and how long or short one waits, varies depending on where in the hospital one is, and EDs are unlike any other part of the hospital.

14.4 This Seems More Complicated: Patient and Clinician Social Interactions

Any interaction we have with another person has many layers and complexities. The most immediate layer is that of the surface interaction: what one says to another, their tone of voice, facial mimics, and their body language. That is then filtered by many sublayers, including stereotypes based on past experiences, and who the person reminds you of. The greater thematic influencer is the context of the interaction itself.

Now consider the context is a hectic, noisy emergency department, with multiple coexisting potentially conflicting demands, including high quality and efficiency of patient care, expeditious treatment and discharge targets, and positive patient satisfaction scores, all the while interacting with and treating another human.

Nothing is as black or white as described previously: it isn't anyone's fault and there may not be one specific reason why an interaction goes sour. It is imperative for clinicians to appreciate this and understand that, in addition to the expectation of being treated, patients come in with their own patterns of understanding and relating to the world.

14.5 When Personality Traits Become Pathological

Just as in other diagnostic criteria for any other psychiatric illness, personality disorders are also defined by the distress and disruption in the life they cause the person with the disorder. Being angry or upset is normal; always being angry or always being upset can become problematic. Being concerned, cynical, or protective are normal reactions, and can have significant benefit to a person when appropriate. If one is always protective, or avoiding interactions that may adversely affect their relationships, this can become problematic.

The difference described is when a personality trait, the different feelings and thought patterns and reactionary styles we all have, becomes a problem.

Personality disorders are very distinct from one another. They have many different qualities and symptoms, and they all can cause significant distress and impairment in the person's social functioning. In the *Diagnostic and Statistical Manual*, fifth edition (DSM-5) (2013), personality disorders are listed in three groups based on their similarities. The groups are defined as "clusters" A, B, and C.

Cluster A personality disorders include the paranoid, schizoid, and schizotypal types. People with these disorders may be eccentric, odd, and isolative. Imagine the difference between someone who likes tabletop role-play gaming with their friends, then imagine someone who stays in their basement, playing and collecting these games, isolating and creating fantastical scenarios that they believe have a magical and real element to them. Someone can be anywhere along this spectrum, and when it interferes with their ability to form and keep relationships, to keep a job, or to function within a defined role, then it becomes "pathological."

Cluster B includes the histrionic, narcissistic, borderline, and antisocial personality disorders. Unlike people with cluster A characteristics (isolative, quiet, less dramatic), those with cluster B traits or disorders can introduce significant tension within a relationship. In an ED, patients who are more demanding, loud, or demonstrative can be lumped into a cluster B diagnosis by a frustrated clinician. This chapter is written to caution the reader that we must be significantly more sophisticated in our approach to "labeling" and to brushing someone off as having a serious, debilitating disorder, just because they are bothering you.

Cluster C includes the avoidant, dependent, and obsessive-compulsive personality disorders. These tend to be people who are fearful, or more anxious in nature.

For specific individual diagnostic criteria, please refer to the DSM-5 (2013). For a proper diagnosis of a true personality disorder, the clinician must understand the patient's long-standing pattern of relationships and behaviors. The patterns must be evident and pervasive throughout multiple domains of their lives.

A person who is theatrical and demonstrative in certain scenarios, but can present as calm and stable in other domains, may not necessarily have a personality disorder. Someone who always wants to be the center of attention, shifts emotional expressions rapidly, and is exaggerated and theatrical in numerous domains of their lives may indeed have a pathological disorder.

Now imagine someone coming into the ED who is loud, demonstrative, and demanding. The differential diagnosis for someone in this condition with these symptoms can range from a life-threatening brain injury to substance-induced euphoria to a true psychiatric manic or psychotic episode. These are examples of diagnoses that may require urgent medical intervention. Dismissing these behaviors as a "personality disorder" does the person a disservice and may have grave repercussions.

On the surface, the ED clinician understands this, and is trained to go through a diagnostic differential and ensure the ongoing safety of their patient. Consider, for a moment, a busy ED shift; the clinician has already seen 10 patients, and the police bring in another patient that presents with the traits described previously and labels them a "psych" patient.

The main purpose of writing this book is to demonstrate not only the importance of efficiencies in hospital ED operations, but also the subtleties, as described earlier, required for global treatment success.

According to a World Health Organization (WHO) personality disorders world mental health survey based on DSM-4 criteria, the prevalence of personality disorders is estimated to be around 6% for any personality disorder (Huang et al. 2009).

Even if the clinician is indeed correct, and the patient has a true diagnosis of a personality disorder, the reality is that the prevalence of medical emergencies necessitating treatment is similar to the general population. People with personality disorders, in fact, have a high comorbidity of other *psychiatric illnesses* that may also require emergent treatment.

The principles of caring for someone in the ED are the same regardless of what they come in with: diagnose, treat, and discharge. Dealing with the presenting symptoms initially is of utmost importance in the instance of a crisis. The long-term treatment of a personality disorder is typically dealt with on an outpatient basis.

14.6 You Are the Best Doctor Ever! (Spoiler Alert: You're Probably Not): The Interplay of Disordered Personality Traits with the Clinician's Personality

We teach our students regularly, and sometimes have to remind our colleagues, that whenever working with patients, we must be aware of what the motives are behind what they say to us. Why does one person say something at one time, and choose to say something different another time? This question especially applies to situations when we are given compliments or insults.

We warn students that if they feel happy and become proud when a patient tells them they are the "best doctor ever" they must also feel the same number of units of sadness and disappointment when the same patient or another says that they are the "worst doctor ever."

In an attempt to protect one's ego, we are more apt to dismiss a social interaction when someone calls us a bad name, insults us, or puts us down. We are more likely to confirm an interaction and feel validated when someone gives us praise or compares us to our colleagues favorably. Be hesitant and mindful of why you are doing that, and rather than allowing your own sense of self to be determined by a patient's comments, be aware of why the patient, or anyone for that matter, is saying what they are saying at that time.

Of course, we are not robots, and taking everything neutrally is boring, we like hearing nice things about ourselves; however, especially when working with patients with personality disorders, know that the same person that said something amazingly nice to you 5 minutes prior may have a very different set of words for you when you give them news or information they do not want to hear.

14.7 Splitting the Team

Working with a person with a personality disorder may add challenges to the treatment team dynamic that clinicians must be sensitive to. Someone with personality pathologies may manifest these as poor relational boundaries. It is important for the clinician to have consistent boundaries, as this is what the patient may be testing and pushing, consciously or subconsciously. The clinician must be open and descriptive with their role in the care of the patient, and make sure that the roles are communicated to the patient regularly.

Someone with a cluster B pathology, such as an antisocial personality disorder, may come into the ED presenting as very charming, with a grandiose sense of self, dominating, maybe even flirtatious with clinicians or other patients in the ED. Clinicians should be aware of this and should not be giving in to the patient's manipulative ways, and they should maintain clear boundaries and expectations; these should be consistent among all clinicians as well.

If not coordinated properly, the treatment may devolve into a series of crises with frequent ED visits. Demanding, attention-seeking, demonstrative personality pathology does have a correlation with a history of childhood neglect, abandonment, or physical or sexual abuse. These patients have patterns of severe emotional vulnerabilities and traumatic experiences that underlie the manifested behaviors. While approaching these patients, and any patient for that matter, it is important to remain empathic, consistent, and accepting to ensure that the focus is on message and that the same message is delivered every time.

It is not uncommon to see a scenario where one clinician provides allowances, or bends a rule, that results in disaster when another clinician takes over and tries to revert to sticking to the rules. The most common examples of these seemingly trivial deviations involve extra meal trays, visitors, and personal belongings. Hospitals and departments have specific guidelines and policies for a reason, and we encourage that you fall back on whatever policy you are thinking about deviating from or are being asked to deviate from. Doing so, adds a third "neutral" party: the "hospital." This neutral party allows you the leeway to continue to have a therapeutic relationship with your patient, while explaining the reason why you are or are not allowing something.

Similarly, it is important to take a step back if you notice that you or someone on the treatment team becomes emotional or sensitive, in an out-of-the-ordinary kind of way, when dealing with a patient. Be mindful of why and how this patient is eliciting these thoughts and emotions in you or your colleagues and point it out. Even if you aren't always psychologically minded in the way you speak, getting over this initial awkwardness and pointing it out to the team can have significant benefits for the team and the patient.

If you find yourself going an extra step for a patient, or a certain type of patient, and not others, think about why that is. Think of who they remind you of, your own reactions, and what you stand to gain from it. The elderly woman may remind you of your sweet, loving grandmother and you want to help her; the young man who is complimenting you may be someone you are sexually attracted to and you go out of your way to help. It is natural and okay to have these feelings and thoughts—it is not okay to create a harmful milieu that takes advantage of the power differential between patient and clinician.

Theoretically, all clinician–patient interactions should be more similar than they are different. Hospitals have certain principles and goals, and clinicians have codes of conduct and ethical guidelines that we adhere to. More often than not, slight variations within a single interaction do not lead to devastating consequences, although it is the slight variation that can become a larger trend if it is consistently repeated over time.

When it comes to dealing with families, case workers, or other people the patient is engaged with, it is important to assess the situation and relationship they claim to have. Obtaining collateral information and connecting with families or outside providers are key in ensuring a warm handoff and successful discharge planning. The ED clinician must make sure that the people identified are actually helpful and will add value to the clinical encounter, and that they are not feeding into the personality disorder and enabling the person's pathology.

14.8 Maintaining Consistent Boundaries

In the previous discussion of the potential for "splitting" in a treatment environment, we mentioned the need for consistency and boundaries. The variable and volatile nature of an ED can exacerbate a patient's personality pathology, which may lead to taking advantage of any variance. In order to provide an accepting and nurturing environment, the clinician must be mindful of keeping consistency within the team and themselves.

Consider this example:

Roger M. is a 46-year-old male, who came in by himself to the ED with a chief complaint of depression. He appears his stated age, is well-dressed, makes good eye contact, is articulate, answers all questions linearly, and is goal directed. He has been observed to be flirtatious with reception staff and nurses, and in discussions with the ED behavioral health therapist, he puts other patients down and boasts about himself, and at times he talks loudly and attempts to overpower the clinical interview. He denies suicidality or homicidality, denies psychotic symptoms, and says, "I really just want to get a letter of absence from work for a week."

Upon concluding the interview, the clinician states that the patient can get a letter indicating he was in the ED, but will not be getting a letter of absence for an entire week, and that he needs to follow up with his outpatient provider for ongoing treatment. The patient immediately rises from his seat, starts yelling, demanding to see his medical files, threatens to sue the hospital and the clinicians, and bangs on the door and walls, while cursing at the staff.

In an outburst, it is important to evaluate what triggered it and what happened in that moment between the clinician and the patient. Often, in that charged interaction, there is important information hidden regarding the patient's emotional state, potential for self-harm, potential for presenting as a danger to others, as well as information regarding the patient's past and history of early relationships or traumatic experiences.

It is important for the ED clinician to be mindful of their own emotional reaction to an outburst so that they can control their response and maintain their reliable, professional, empathic state. The awareness that the patient's negative attitude, in that moment, is not in fact personal will help the clinician assess the information that is presented in the form of an outburst, and really see it for what it is.

The challenge is to maintain consistency and the ability to remain in a clinical role, especially when the patient presents as overly passionate, chaotic, and demanding. It is important to remember that the clinician is a human too, a trained human, a human who is there with a decision and purpose to care for patients, a human who took on a specific role, but yet still a human, with their own emotional vulnerabilities. We encourage the ED clinician to also recognize their own personal deficits and their own feelings of anxiety or sadness or burnout, and to reach out to other colleagues, or seek their own mental health support.

14.9 Treatment Options

In addition to the behavioral interventions and strategies described previously, we encourage a cultural shift in the approach to patient care. Personality disorders require a multimodal approach to treatment, and it is imperative that the ED clinician appreciate this.

There are no Food and Drug Administration (FDA)-approved medications for personality disorders. In the outpatient world, psychiatrists work to address and alleviate other syndromes and disorders that may be comorbid, although no medication directly treats the personality, unless another true disorder is being treated, symptomatic relief, in the long term, is also better obtained through psychotherapeutic options than with medications alone.

In the ED, the requirement is to successfully diagnose, treat, and discharge safely. If symptoms of anxiety or panic are predominant, there are medications for that. Similarly, if there are acute psychotic symptoms requiring treatment, there are medications approved for psychosis. Although to ensure an accurate gathering of data, a relationship must be established with the patient.

Behavioral modification, mindfulness, and dialectical behavioral therapy are among the many approaches and psychotherapies available for use in an outpatient setting; techniques from these modalities need to be incorporated into every clinician's practice.

Patients with personality disorders, such as borderline and antisocial, may have a higher tendency for disruptive behavior in an ED, and the safety of the patient and staff is paramount. If the patient is indeed a danger to themselves or others, verbal and behavioral de-escalation techniques must be incorporated, and medications are indicated in this setting as an emergent option—in other words, to protect the life of the patient and those around the patient.

Medications should not be used as a restraint for a patient. Oral medications should be offered, when appropriate, over an injection against the patient's will. In addition to the potential legal liability of medicating someone against their will, the medications do not address the personality pathology. It is important to meet the patient's needs and demands without injuring their ego and without harming the relationship you are working to build.

For example, patients who present with narcissistic pathology, try to maintain their image of perfection and project that image onto others. Often, when these patients are faced with physical or emotional challenges, their self-image is shattered, and fragmentation occurs. This can lead to panic and feelings of loss of control, as if their world is falling apart. These patients may resort to behaviors that disrespect or disregard the ED clinician. They may challenge them, demand that the higher ranked physician treat them, or refuse treatment from an intern or resident.

We all want to be respected and acknowledged for our abilities and efforts, and no one likes it when their competence is challenged. In this moment, however, it is important to remember that the resistance stems from the patient and that it is not personal. The ED clinician must continue to maintain a competent, secure attitude and reassure the patient that the best possible treatment will be delivered.

There may also be perverse reinforcement of the acting out behaviors, and increased staff attention, commotion around the patient, and medication may be gratifying in ways that adversely affect the purpose of caring for the patient in the ED. On several occasions, we have cared for patients that have later admitted that they were sexually aroused by being medicated and sedated in the ED in response to when they created a scene and yelled and threatened to hurt themselves in front of the staff. This example is to remind the reader that self-injurious threats must be taken seriously, as patients with a history of self-mutilation and self-injury are at increased risk of suicide, and therefore medications are warranted in an emergency setting to ensure the patient's safety.

A common theme in this book is aligning goals with the patient. The care of a patient with a personality disorder is no different. When the clinician approaches a patient genuinely and sincerely to create an alliance and explore options together with the patient, the patient picks up on this, and this will help to strengthen a developing therapeutic relationship.

People with cluster B pathology, in particular, are adept at reading social cues, and are able to pick up on insincerities and discrepancies that the clinician may get away with in their interactions with other patients. As a defense mechanism, they are good at observing people and can detect motivations and subtleties. These multiple layers of thinking about yourself, your interactions, and the person in front of you, can be tiring even when that is all you are required to focus on. Add on the busy setting of an ED, and the many other things the clinician needs to pay attention to, and you can see how quickly stress levels can build. As an aside, this is typically a motivating factor for outpatient clinicians, who predominantly care for patients with personality disorders, to work in peer groups and have frequent group supervision and de-briefing sessions. Processing a case together and obtaining further treatment recommendations can add to collegiality among clinicians; they also allow for regular opportunities to build coping mechanisms and the strength required to continue caring for patients.

As the clinician stationed in an ED, if you are working on something, let the patient know. If you do not know something, or need to find out more information, let them know. Similarly, let the patient know if you will not be able to do or provide something, for whatever reason. Simply, be honest and maintain firm and consistent boundaries with your patients.

14.10 Conclusion

The approaches described previously will allow the patient and the clinician to create a therapeutic relationship, decrease risk events in the ED, and foster healthier outcomes to ensure the patient is appropriately diagnosed, treated, and safely discharged.

References

Huang, Y, Kotov, R, de Girolamo, G, Preti, A, Angermeyer, M, Benjet, C, Demyttenaere, K et al. 2009. DSM-IV personality disorders in the WHO World Mental Health surveys. *British Journal of Psychiatry* 195 (1): 46–53. doi:10.1192/bjp.bp.108.058552.

Williamson, A M, Feyer, A M. 2000. Moderate sleep deprivation produces impairments in cognition and motor performance equivalent to legally prescribed levels of alcohol intoxication. *Occupational and Environmental Medicine* 57 (10): 649–655.

Resources

American Psychiatric Association. 2013. *Diagnostic and Statistical Manual of Mental Disorders*, fifth edition. Arlington, VA: American Psychiatric Association.

Blashfield, R K, Intoccia V. 2000. Growth of the literature on the topic of personality disorders. *American Journal Psychiatry*. 157(3): 472–473. doi:10.1176/appi.ajp.157.3.472.

Boggild, A K, Heisel M H, Links, P S. 2004. Social, demographic, and clinical factors related to disruptive behaviour in hospital. *Canadian Journal Psychiatry* 49 (2): 114–118.

Gonzalez, R A, Igoumenou, A, Kallis, C, Coid, J W. 2016. Borderline personality disorder and violence in the UK population: Categorical and dimensional trait assessment. *BMC Psychiatry* 3(16):180. doi:10.1186/s12888-016-0885-7.

Hong, V. 2016. Borderline personality disorder in the emergency department: Good psychiatric management. *Harvard Review of Psychiatry* 24(5):357–366. doi:10.1097/HRP.0000000000000112.

McMain, S F, Boritz, T Z, Leybman, M J. 2015. Common strategies for cultivating a positive therapy relationship in the treatment of borderline personality disorder. *Journal of Psychotherapy Integration* 25 (1): 20–29.

Silk, K R. 2011. The process of managing medications in patients with borderline personality disorder. *Journal of Psychiatric Practice* 17(5). 311–319. doi:10.1097/01.pra.0000405361.88257.4a.

Vaillant, G E. 1992. The beginning of wisdom is never calling a patient a borderline; or, the clinical management of immature defenses in the treatment of individuals with personality disorders. *Journal of Psychotherapy Practice and Research* 1 (2): 117–134.

Wilson, M P, Pepper, D, Currier, G W, Holloman, G H, Feifel, D. 2012. The psychopharmacology of agitation: Consensus statement of the American Association for Emergency Psychiatry project BETA psychopharmocology workgroup. Western Journal of Emergency Medicine 13 (1): 26–34. doi:10.5811/westjem.2011.9.6866.

Chapter 15

A Primer on Medical Toxicology

Steven R. Offerman

Contents

15.1 Introduction 256
15.2 Risk Assessment 256
    15.2.1 Did a Potentially Toxic Ingestion Occur? 256
    15.2.2 What Phase of Poisoning Are We Seeing? 257
        15.2.2.1 Time of Ingestion 257
    15.2.3 Mixed Exposures 259
    15.2.4 Toxidromes 259
    15.2.5 What Is the Care Plan? 259
15.3 The Deadly Dozen 259
15.4 A Few Words about Urine Drugs of Abuse Screening 263
15.5 Immediate Interventions (Decontamination) 266
15.6 Treatments and Antidotes 267
    15.6.1 Supportive Care 267
    15.6.2 Naloxone 267
    15.6.3 Emergency Intralipid 268
    15.6.4 Sodium Bicarbonate 268
    15.6.5 N-acetylcysteine 269
15.7 Conclusion 270
References 270

"Sola dosis facit venenum." ("The dose makes the poison.")

Paracelsus

15.1 Introduction

Medical toxicology is a medical subspecialty focusing on the diagnosis, management, and prevention of poisoning and other adverse health effects due to medications, occupational and environmental toxins, and biological agents. It is an officially recognized medical subspecialty by the American Board of Medical Specialties (American College of Toxicology n.d.). A medical toxicologist is a physician who has completed fellowship training (usually 2 years) and provides consultation or directly manages patients affected by poisonings, overdoses, or adverse events. Because toxicology is a pathology-based specialty (as opposed to organ system-based), the subject area is necessarily broad.

In this chapter, there will only be room to scratch the surface of our field. My goal is not to convert the reader into a self-sufficient toxicologist, but provide the foundations for exceptionally strong emergency psychiatrists.

To this end, you should be able to

1. Recognize (common) potentially deadly exposures
2. Initiate important first treatments
3. Have confidence in the history, physical, and early evaluation of acute overdose patients (which is important for knowing your stuff when you call your toxicology consultant)

Surprisingly, psychiatry residents receive almost no training in medical toxicology (Ingels et al. 2003). Emergency physicians do receive toxicology training, but it is difficult to keep abreast of such a vast and ever-evolving field.

We feel very strongly that medical toxicology specialists should be easily accessible and utilized frequently. The vast majority of overdose patients are salvageable. No complicated poisoning patient should do without the benefit of physician specialist involvement. This is no different than any other ill patient in the hospital. On another note, toxicology clearance issues can be complicated and often resource-intensive. As the emergency psychiatrist, you should work closely with your toxicologist who will often save you time and can predict bad outcomes before they occur.

What would an emergency psychiatrist want to know about toxicology?

I would break down the toxicologic evaluation into three phases:

1. Risk assessment
2. Immediate interventions (decontamination/reversal)
3. Treatment/clearance

In this chapter, we will discuss how the emergency psychiatrist and toxicologist should work as a cohesive unit through these steps.

15.2 Risk Assessment

Although this discussion is necessarily over-simplified, I present this as a framework to use for basic toxicologic assessments.

15.2.1 Did a Potentially Toxic Ingestion Occur?

The first step in toxicological risk assessment is determining whether a potentially toxic ingestion occurred. This is where history becomes extremely important. Identification of the agent(s) involved can be obtained by interviewing the patient (when possible), reviewing medication lists/bottles, and discussing available xenobiotics with family members or paramedic staff. Sometimes the list of potential poisons can be narrowed using drug screens and/or serum levels (e.g., acetaminophen and salicylates). Once potential toxic exposures have been determined, they should be reviewed to determine if a risk for poisoning exists. If so, dosage determinations are then used to determine if a potentially toxic dose has been ingested. Reference tools such as Micromedex (Truven Health Analytics n.d.), can be very useful by providing information on ranges of toxicity.

Dosage estimates vary from being extremely helpful to completely useless. More often than not the importance of this historical point is dependent on the accuracy of the history, which is a subjective, bedside assessment. Unfortunately, it is impossible for a consultant to make this type of determination over the phone. Research assessments of the reliability of emergency and psychiatric patients to provide accurate histories are mixed (Kreshak et al. 2015; Monte et al. 2015; Olshaker et al. 1997).

Psychiatric patients are often able to accurately report underlying medical conditions; however, the accuracy of medication histories or toxic substance ingestion are questionable. For these reasons, meticulous histories should be collected (whenever possible) and considered, but not completely relied upon. It appears that patients who deny ingestion are more reliable than those who report overdose (Bentur et al. 2011). It is important to attempt to corroborate ingestion/overdose histories with family, friends, law enforcement, and bystanders whenever possible.

The Health Insurance Portability and Accountability Act of 1996 (HIPAA) laws regarding patient privacy must, of course, be respected as much as possible while collecting history. Histories involving "handfuls" or "bottles" of medications indicate a wide range of potential doses, though these assessments may indicate a very large numbers of pills (Choi and Choi 2015). If an accurate dosage determination can be made, resources such as Micromedex/Poisondex (Truven Health Analytics n.d.) or ToxED (Elsevier: Gold Standard n.d.) are extremely helpful in determining potential risk. Some patients may be cleared for disposition based on dosage history alone.

15.2.2 What Phase of Poisoning Are We Seeing?

Once we have determined that a potentially toxic exposure has occurred, we assess the potential phase of poisoning. Is the patient in the preclinical (absorptive), early symptomatic, quiescent, advanced clinical, or recovery phase? These phases are not entirely universal, but they apply to many common poisons. It should also be noted that the duration of these different stages is highly variable depending on the particular agent involved. Depending on the pharmacokinetics and pharmacodynamics involved, patients may progress rapidly or very slowly to the poisoning phases.

For example, sodium cyanide poisoning causes clinical poisoning within minutes, whereas acetaminophen poisoning would not manifest for many hours after ingestion. It is understood as we make this determination that some patients have not actually had a toxic exposure at all and may never enter the poisoning phases. Please refer to Table 15.1 for an explanation of these phases.

15.2.2.1 Time of Ingestion

Time of ingestion (TOI) is probably the most important historical point when assessing risk after a potentially toxic exposure. If a time of exposure can be determined, decisions regarding decontamination, immediate antidotes, observation time, and prediction of course of illness can be projected. In many ways, this is much more important than dosage estimates.

Table 15.1 Clinical Phases of Poisoning

Phase	Clinical Appearance	What Is Happening	Intervention(s)
Preclinical (absorptive)	Usually asymptomatic	GI absorption and/or metabolic conversion of the parent compound to the physiologic poison	Decontamination Observation
Early poisoning	Increasing symptoms	Increasing serum levels	Occasional decontamination Support Antidotes
Quiescent	Some poisons may have a period of relative improvement while physiologic poisoning is actually worsening	Serum levels increasing or peaking but cellular level effects are increasing	Support Specific therapies Antidotes
Late poisoning	Poisoning symptoms have peaked or are improving	Serum levels at or near peak	Support Specific therapies Antidotes
Recovery	Usually improving Possible secondary effects from earlier phases	Declining levels	Withdrawing care Address secondary injuries

The TOI can be difficult to determine for many reasons. Sometimes only a range of time is possible in which case we usually use the most conservative limit as the TOI. When taking histories regarding TOI, it may help to tie the ingestion to other historical points (e.g., "What time did you call your boyfriend?" "What was on TV?" etc.) and interview family members (e.g., "What time did he lock himself in the bathroom?"). In addition, patients often use social media near or at the time of their overdose and friends and family members may know the exact time of the overdose based on the postings. In patients presenting within 2 hours of the TOI, gastrointestinal decontamination may be a consideration. In asymptomatic patients, observation times will be based on this TOI starting point.

Patients who are in the preclinical phase of poisoning may be candidates for decontamination. They are then usually observed for progression. Patients falling into the poisoning phases (early or late) require close observation, supportive care, and specific therapies based on the toxin(s) involved. Patients who are in the recovery phase require simple supportive care, pending resolution of their symptoms and medical clearance. In some cases, secondary conditions resulting from the acute poisoning must be addressed in this phase (aspiration pneumonia, hypoxic injury, etc.).

We recommend consultation with a medical toxicologist at any phase of poisoning as we can help with potential clearance, decontamination, and/or specific treatments. Never hesitate to ask for assistance. Our internal data shows that the vast majority of clinicians appreciate toxicology consultation and feel that it adds substantially to the care of their patients (Offerman 2012).

15.2.3 Mixed Exposures

A word about mixed exposures: In my experience, mixed exposures make up approximately 25%–30% of ingestions. Not only can patients take concurrent overdoses, but there are also many combination medicines on the market. For example, acetaminophen/hydrocodone, "PM" versions of medications such as acetaminophen/diphenhydramine, and or the migraine medication that includes the combination of acetaminophen/aspirin/caffeine.

The introduction of multiple potential poisons can greatly complicate the poisoning assessment. Not only may the physician see a confusing symptom picture, but multiple ingestants often alter or effect each other's absorption and kinetics. Once again, the first step when encountering a mixed ingestion is providing good supportive care. Then a determination can be made of which (if any) poisons may be dismissed as nontoxic. The remaining agents of concern must then be assessed for need of decontamination, therapies, and period of observation. As alluded to previously, the interaction of some poisons may change the risk profiles of co-ingestants. This needs to be factored into any risk assessment.

15.2.4 Toxidromes

One important aspect of toxicologic evaluation are toxidromes. A toxidrome is defined as a group of signs and symptoms constituting the basis for a diagnosis of poisoning. Please refer to Table 15.2 for definitions of some basic toxidromes that physicians should be able to recognize. As toxicologists, we use toxidromes to assist in diagnosing which agent may be responsible for poisoning, judging the stage of poisoning, and helping to determine the severity. When consulting a toxicology specialist, you will want to describe the toxidrome you see.

Toxidrome assessment frequently does not make the poisoning diagnosis, but is a way of organizing physical signs in order to give a clue for diagnosis and possible initial treatment plan. When combined with history, toxidromes can be a powerful tool. In mixed overdose, it should be remembered that toxidromic signs may be confusing or atypical.

15.2.5 What Is the Care Plan?

Once it has been determined that a potential toxic exposure has occurred and the phase of poisoning has been determined, we can make a clinical plan. Any need for decontamination should be addressed early. Depending on the phase of poisoning, specific therapies and antidotes should be instituted. Then clearance criteria can be developed. Clearance criteria are very specific from case to case and may range from resolution of symptoms, to decreasing lab levels, to completion of hemodialysis. We recommend the development of clearance criteria early in the assessment process as this provides a therapeutic goal around which specific treatment plans may be designed. Once clearly defined clearance criteria are met, then psychiatric evaluation in preparation for safe, efficient disposition can commence. It should be noted that clearance criteria need not always be met for psychiatric evaluation to begin. In some cases, clearance is imminent and evaluations in anticipation of needed placement is completely appropriate. An example of this might be a case of early presenting acetaminophen overdose. In these cases, the chances of bad outcomes are low and the time of medical clearance is often obvious based on acetaminophen kinetics.

Table 15.2 Commonly Encountered Toxidromes

Toxidrome	Vitals	Mental Status	Pupils/Skin	Other Findings	Odor	Examples
Antimuscarinic	↑HR Nl/↑RR ↑Temp ↑BP	• Agitation (passive) • Delirium	• Mydriasis • Dry skin	• Urinary retention • Decreased bowel sounds	None	Diphenhydramine, doxylamine, numerous plant species (e.g., *Datura spp*)
Sympathomimetic	↑HR ↑RR ↑Temp ↑BP	• Agitation (likely aggressive)	• Mydriasis • Diaphoresis	• Signs of illicit drug use • Convulsions • Tremoring	None	Cocaine, methamphetamine
Cholinergic	↓/↑HR Nl/↑RR ↓Temp ↑BP	• Confused	• Miosis • Diaphoresis	• Convulsions • Bronchorrhea • Vomiting • Diarrhea • Fasciculations • Salivation • Urination	• Pesticide • Garlic	Organophosphorus pesticides
Sedative/hypnotic	Nl/↓ HR ↓RR Nl/↓ Temp ↓ BP	• Down	• Miosis to mid-range • Normal skin	• Airway instability • Hyporeflexia	None	Benzodiazepines, barbiturates
Opioid	Nl/↓ HR ↓ RR Nl/↓ Temp ↓ BP	• Down	• Miosis • Normal skin	• May see symptoms of illicit drug use • Airway instability • Hyporeflexia	None	Heroin, morphine, hydrocodone, oxycodone, clonidine

(Continued)

Table 15.2 (Continued) Commonly Encountered Toxidromes

Toxidrome	Vitals	Mental Status	Pupils/Skin	Other Findings	Odor	Examples
Serotonergic excess (AKA serotonin syndrome)	↑HR Nl RR Nl/↑ Temp ↑↓ BP	• Up • May be agitated or confused	• May have mydriasis • Normal or diaphoresis	• Recent addition or increased serotonergic agent are key, PLUS one of the following: • Spontaneous clonus • Inducible clonus with agitation or diaphoresis • Ocular clonus with agitation or diaphoresis • Tremor and hyperreflexia OR • Hypertonia, temp>100.4°F, and ocular or inducible clonus	None	SSRIs, hallucinogens, MDMA, MAOIs
"Slow and low"	↓HR Nl RR Nl Temp ↓ BP	• Normal or confused (depends primarily on BP)	• Normal pupils • Normal skin	• Hypotension with heart rate inappropriately low	None	Beta blocker, calcium channel blocker, clonidine, imadazolines, digitalis

(Continued)

Table 15.2 (Continued)   Commonly Encountered Toxidromes

Toxidrome	Vitals	Mental Status	Pupils/Skin	Other Findings	Odor	Examples
Hydrocarbon	Nl/↑HR Nl/↑RR Nl Temp Nl BP	• Confused	• Normal or mydriasis • Normal skin	• Elevated liver enzymes • Ventricular dysrhythmias • May see symptoms of "huffing" • Pneumonitis on X-ray • Increase QTc • Hypokalemia	• Chemical • Fruity	Toluene, solvents, lacquers, spray paints
Antipsychotic	Nl/↑HR Nl RR Nl Temp ↓ BP	• Sleepy to coma	• Normal or miosis • Dry, flushed skin • Salivation	• Extrapyramidal symptoms • QRS widening • Increased QTc	None	Quetiapine, risperidone, haloperidol
Ethanol	Nl/↑ HR ↓ RR Nl/↓ Temp ↑/↓ BP	• Spectrum of confused to agitated to comatose	• Normal or mydriasis • Flushed or diaphoresis	• Ataxia/incoordination • Nystagmus • Vomiting • Atrial fibrillation	• Alcohol • "Boozy"	Ethanol, Isopropanol, ethylene glycol, hand sanitizer
Withdrawal	↑HR ↑RR ↑Temp Nl/↑BP	• Normal to confused to delirium	• Normal or mydriasis • Diaphoresis	• Convulsions • Tremors • Hallucinations • Anxiety • Insomnia	None	Ethanol withdrawal, benzodiazepines withdrawal, GHB withdrawal

One of the most common questions we are asked has to do with the need for medical admission following a toxic exposure. In some cases, the need for admission is obvious based on clinical presentation (e.g., intubated patient) or the poison involved (see section on the deadly dozen). The majority of cases, however, are less clear. Often, we recommend a period of emergency department observation to determine the need for admission versus clearance for psychiatry evaluation. Examples of this might include an aspirin overdose requiring serial levels or an asymptomatic antidepressant overdose that simply needs a period of observation to determine what peak effects will occur. It is our opinion that the period of emergency department toxicologic observation should rarely exceed 6 hours. At the 6-hour mark, reassessment and disposition decisions should be made. This "rule of thumb" is designed to address emergency department flow and patient safety.

Lastly, the time of day is an important consideration for clearance. Patients meeting clearance criteria in the late-night hours should be dispositioned with caution. It should be recognized that patients leaving the hospital in the middle of the night are unlikely to be watched closely. We recommend erring on the side of extending observation until the morning if there is any question regarding medical clearance. It is for this reason that our toxicologists do not clear patients with sustained release or long-acting opioid overdose during nighttime hours.

15.3 The Deadly Dozen

Many things can kill you (see the quote by Paracelsus at the beginning of the chapter). Almost any massive ingestion could be dangerous. But, there is a short list of relatively common agents that strike real fear in the hearts of toxicologists. Table 15.3 is a list that I like to call the "deadly dozen." These agents immediately get my attention. Remember *overdose patients shouldn't die*. These are poisons that may result in serious if not fatal outcomes and should invoke maximum caution!

15.4 A Few Words About Urine Drugs of Abuse Screening

Urine drug screens are used widely as part of the psychiatric assessment. These tests are used to determine accuracy of substance use histories and as part of the clearance evaluation for psychiatric placement. Unfortunately, many of the clinicians using these tests on a daily basis have a poor understanding of their utility and potential pitfalls. Please see Chapter 7 on the myth of medical clearance for more information.

The first step in understanding urine drug screens is realizing how these tests are performed. Almost all drugs of abuse screening is performed on urine. Most common rapid drug screen testing utilizes an immunoassay technique. In brief (without going into a detailed description), the urine is exposed to a matrix containing antibodies to very specific drug molecule structures. These bind to drug molecules that may be present in the urine. Then, reagents are added to provide colorimetric indication of the presence of these molecules. The first important concept to grasp regarding drug immunoassays is that this is *not* a single test, but instead it involves multiple (often six) different tests, each with their own sensitivities and specificities. While one test may be very specific (i.e., tetrahydrocannabinol [THC] or cocaine), another may be very unreliable (e.g., amphetamine or cyclic antidepressants).

Following immunoassay assessment, positive samples may be sent for "confirmation." Confirmatory testing is usually performed using chromatography—mass spectrometry (usually LC-MS or GC-MS). In this process, the sample is propelled across a solid matrix, which separates

Table 15.3 The "Deadly Dozen" Poisons That Should Get Your Immediate Attention

Toxin	Deadliness	Setting	Antidote(s)	Comments
Calcium channel blockers	★★★★★	Antihypertensive medications	Emergency intralipid Calcium Glucagon High dose insulin therapy Pressors	Common and very deadly. Hypotension is the precursor of doom. Early decontamination may be lifesaving.
Aspirin/salicylates	★★★	OTC analgesic	Sodium bicarbonate Hemodialysis	A sneaky poison that is very common but occasionally kills. Hyperthermia or AMS are poor prognostic indicators.
Acetaminophen	★★	OTC analgesic	N-acetylcysteine	Treatable but so common that it kills patients every year.
Long-acting opioids	★★★★	Rx analgesics	Naloxone Naloxone infusion	Simple supportive care saves these patients. Overly aggressive clearance or neglect kills patients every year.
Bupropion	★★	Atypical antidepressant	Emergency intralipid Benzodiazepines Sodium bicarbonate	Usually benign. Causes seizures. Large overdoses can be deadly and hard to manage.
Venlafaxine	★★★	Atypical antidepressant	Emergency intralipid Benzodiazepines Sodium bicarbonate	Also often benign but rarely causes death in large overdoses. Repeated seizures are a poor prognostic sign.
Carbon monoxide	★★★★	Toxic gas	High-flow oxygen Hyperbaric oxygen (HBO)	The use of HBO is heavily debated. We are believers. Long-term outcomes can be devastating. We prefer to give patients every chance to recover.

(Continued)

Table 15.3 (Continued) The "Deadly Dozen" Poisons That Should Get Your Immediate Attention

Toxin	Deadliness	Setting	Antidote(s)	Comments
Organophosphorus pesticides	★★★★	Insecticide	AW support, Atropine, Pralidoxime, Diazepam	Unusual but very deadly. Aggressive antidotal therapy may be life-saving.
Cyanide	★★★★★	Poison gas, artificial nail remover	Hydroxocobalamin, Sodium thiosulfate	Extremely unusual poisoning, however may occur in the setting of smoke inhalation. Meticulous supportive care and antidotal therapy are keys.
VW class III antidysrhythmics	★★★	Cardiac medications	Emergency intralipid, Sodium bicarbonate, Lidocaine	Uncommon antidysrhythmic medications. Aggressive bicarbonate for ECG changes may be lifesaving.
Toxic alcohols (methanol, ethylene glycol, diethylene glycol)	★★★	Antifreeze, windshield wiper fluid	Fomepizole, Leukovorin, Pyridoxine, Hemodialysis	Relatively common but deadly. Aggressive treatment saves lives. Clearance can be complicated in patients who report ingestion but appear well.
Tricyclic antidepressants	★★★	Antidepressant medications	Emergency intralipid, Sodium bicarbonate, Benzodiazepines	Used to be the most common cause of overdose deaths. Now less common.

A Primer on Medical Toxicology ■ 265

constituent molecules based on their individual characteristics (e.g., drag coefficients). As the molecules exit chromatography, a spectrometer determines their molecular mass. This testing is extremely sensitive and specific. Most importantly, it essentially confirms, when positive, the presence of substances in the urine.

The other particularly important concept to understand regarding drug screening is that while screens may suggest exposure, they do not provide any information regarding TOI, intoxication, or level of impairment. Because drug screens may remain positive for long periods after exposure, a positive qualitative drug screen cannot diagnose acute intoxication. For example, THC is highly lipid soluble and may be retained in the body for weeks after exposure in heavy marijuana users. Therefore, a positive THC screen may purely be indicative of exposure days or weeks before the current presentation. While the combination of drugs screening and clinical examination may be helpful, over-reliance on drug screen results is a pitfall.

Lastly, the emergency psychiatrist should remember that urine drugs screens look for only a handful of potential intoxicants—these are only a short list of relatively common drugs of abuse. Because there are thousands (maybe millions) of possible intoxicating substances and drug use patterns are constantly changing, many potential agents are not identified by standard drug screening. Overall, the diagnosis of drug intoxication is a historical and clinical diagnosis. The drug screen is typically a limited tool to help provide exposure information and rarely changes early management.

15.5 Immediate Interventions (Decontamination)

Gastrointestinal (GI) decontamination describes attempts to prevent or decrease absorption of swallowed poisons from the stomach or intestines. This is a highly controversial topic in toxicology. While it seems logical that removal of poisons from the GI tract would improve outcomes in poisoned patients, in practice, this is not straightforward. Induced emesis (ipecac), gastric lavage (stomach pumping), activated charcoal, cathartics, and bowel irrigation are a few of the current and historical methods that have been used for decontamination. Induced emesis and gastric lavage are rarely, if ever, indicated. These techniques have not been shown to alter clinical outcomes, carry inherent risks, and are very timing sensitive, thus making them unlikely to confer any benefit.

Activated charcoal is the most commonly utilized form of GI decontamination used in the setting of overdose. Activated charcoal refers to a process of superheating charcoal in order to increase its adsorptive power. The superheating process vastly increases the surface area of the charcoal matrix, thereby binding poison molecules allowing them to be safely eliminated out of the body. The challenge is administering the activated charcoal when the poison is still early in the GI tract and before it is absorbed into the body. Research has shown little benefit to administering activated charcoal after 1 hour from TOI. For this reason, we rarely recommend charcoal outside of the first 1–2 hours from the time of ingestion. Exclusive of timing, there are three other reasons not to give activated charcoal (contraindications): The toxin ingested isn't adsorbed by charcoal, there is a risk of caustic injury with vomiting, and there is a risk of aspiration.

In the universe of poisons there are numerous agents that are not well adsorbed. I use the mnemonic "LIE," which stands for lithium, iron (and other metals), and ethanol (and ethylene glycol, methanol). These agents are not well absorbed by activated charcoal. Ingestion of caustic agents, such as acids or lye, is also a contraindication for charcoal because of the risk of esophageal burns by inducing emesis with doses of oral charcoal in addition to poor endoscopy findings with activated charcoal. Lastly, anytime charcoal is considered in the setting of a sedative hypnotic overdose we must assess the risks of aspiration versus possible benefits. In most cases of simple sedative overdose, patients will do well with supportive care. Risking aspiration may overshadow any foreseen benefit. However, if a patient ingested a sedative hypnotic agent in combination with something more deadly (such as a calcium channel blocker), charcoal would be clearly indicated. It should be noted that use of charcoal in the setting of a "protected" airway is also not without risk. In clinical and bronchoscopy studies, it has been shown that even intubated patients can have charcoal beyond the endotracheal tube cuff and in the lower airways (Moll et al. 1999).

Multiple-dose activated charcoal and whole-bowel irrigation are advanced GI decontamination techniques that are sometimes employed. These are used in very specific circumstances and are beyond the scope of this chapter. Similarly, hemodialysis is employed in certain situations to increase clearance of toxins from the blood. Discussion of the scenarios where dialysis may be indicated is also outside the scope of this chapter and only should be considered in consultation with a medical toxicologist.

15.6 Treatments and Antidotes

A prolonged discussion regarding interventions for toxic/poisoned patients is beyond the scope of this chapter. Instead we will focus on five immediate interventions that may save a life. The emergency psychiatrist should be well versed in these maneuvers as they could make a critical difference.

15.6.1 Supportive Care

We often say that toxicologists are simply experts in good supportive care. This is because the majority of our patients will survive with supportive measures alone. Perhaps the most striking example of this is our history with sedative hypnotic overdoses (barbiturates, benzodiazepines, etc.). In years past, many (analeptic) agents were used in attempts to stimulate or "wake up" patients after these overdoses. In the 1940s, there were studies that simply showed that airway support and ventilation (if needed) were all that these patients needed (Clemmesen and Nilsson 1961; Wax 1997). All emergency psychiatrists need to pay close attention to the ABCs and general supportive care. This includes the interventions outlined in your advanced cardiac life support (ACLS) training. Being an expert in good supportive care will buy you time and, in many instances, be all that your patient needs for a good outcome.

15.6.2 Naloxone

The number of overdose deaths is increasing in recent years. In fact, deaths related to overdose now exceed motor vehicle accident deaths, with the primary driver being opioid overdoses (Centers for Disease Control and Prevention 2016). Naloxone is a competitive antagonist at the mu opioid receptor. It has few adverse effects and almost no side effects, with the primary unwanted effect being the potential for precipitation of withdrawal in opioid-addicted individuals. While there are multiple past reports of clinical response with non-opioid overdoses (clonidine, imidazolines, ethanol, valproate, and benzodiazepines), these responses are inconsistent when studied. We expect little to no effect from naloxone when given in the absence of opioid agents.

In the setting of acute overdose, the primary reason to give naloxone is the reversal of respiratory depression and airway instability. In the setting of isolated opioid overdose, naloxone is extremely effective. The initial dose is 0.2–2 mg intravenously (0.01 mg/kg in children). This dose may be repeated every 2–3 minutes until reversal is achieved (max 10 mg). In order to avoid precipitation of withdrawal, one should consider lower doses in patients suspected to be opioid dependent. It should be noted that high doses might be required in large overdoses or with long-acting opioids. While the intravenous route is preferred, naloxone is effective when given subcutaneously (0.4–2 mg dose), intramuscularly (0.4–2 mg dose), or intranasally (4 mg dose). Although intravenous naloxone has the most rapid onset of action (1–2 minutes), in prehospital studies looking at naloxone for reversal of opioid overdose, administration of subcutaneous naloxone (2–4 minute onset) resulted in equivalent time to reversal compared with starting an IV, then administering naloxone intravenously (Wanger et al. 1998). Intranasal naloxone may also be used in prehospital and emergency department settings. This route has a similar safety profile and time to reversal when compared with parenteral routes (Kerr et al. 2009; Dowling et al. 2008).

The expected duration of effect for naloxone is 1–2 hours (elimination half-life of 60–90 minutes). Therefore, re-dosing may be necessary as the duration of many opioids exceeds this time window. In cases where repeat dosing has been needed more than once (and the patient is not intubated), we usually recommend starting a naloxone infusion. Naloxone infusion dosing is the "effective dose"/hour or 0.4–1 mg/hour. The infusion is then titrated to the desired effect (based on mental status and respiratory status).

Because of the recent epidemic of opioid addiction and increases in opioid overdoses, interest in home prescriptions of naloxone has also increased. The idea here is that family members can immediately treat certain high-risk patients upon signs of overdose. These, for example, are patients with high-dose opioid prescriptions, those taking multiple psychotropic medications, with high-risk comorbid conditions, and/or known heroin users. There are now injection and intranasal products available for prescribing. In patients taking opioids who are considered high-risk, physicians should consider concurrently prescribing home naloxone. Please refer to Chapter 12 on substance use for more information.

15.6.3 Emergency Intralipid

Use of a 2% intralipid solution for treatment of lipid-soluble medications is a relatively new therapy. Emergency or "rescue" intralipid therapy has its beginnings in the anesthesia literature where it was found to be helpful for treatment of inadvertent intravascular administration of local anesthetics. It is primarily used in the setting of cardiovascular collapse, recurrent seizures, and other life-threatening events. The indications have been expanded and there are numerous reports of intralipid therapy used successfully for different lipid-soluble medications. Intralipid therapy has been used for local anesthetics, calcium channel blockers, selected antidepressants, and propranolol poisoning. There are few adverse effects reported associated with intralipid administration. Emergency intralipid dosing is as follows: 1.5 mL mL/kg of the 20% intralipid solution bolus, followed by 0.25 mL/kg/min over 30–60 minutes. We recommend that intralipid therapy usually be given in conjunction with a medical toxicology consultation.

15.6.4 Sodium Bicarbonate

Sodium bicarbonate is an important antidote in medical toxicology and may be lifesaving in cases of cardiovascular poisoning. There are many poisons that have the ability to block cardiac sodium channels resulting in QRS widening (QRS > 100–200 ms) on the surface electrocardiogram and the potential for cardiac dysrhythmias. Some common xenobiotics causing sodium channel blockade are tricyclic antidepressants, diphenhydramine, cocaine, and Von Williams class I antidysrhythmics. The finding of QRS widening in a poisoned patient should prompt serious consideration of sodium bicarbonate, especially in the setting of cardiovascular instability and/or ventricular dysrhythmia. Incidentally, sodium bicarbonate also may be lifesaving in cases of severe hyperkalemia, which is another common cause of QRS widening in unstable/poisoned patients. We recommend boluses of sodium bicarbonate (1–2 mEq/kg IV push) that can be repeated until QRS narrowing occurs. Sodium bicarbonate is also beneficial in altering the urine pH to enhance the elimination of the xenobiotic. This is most commonly performed with acute or chronic salicylate poisonings.

15.6.5 N-acetylcysteine

N-acetylcysteine (NAC) is an important sulfhydryl donor that is used as the primary treatment of acetaminophen (APAP) poisoning. While NAC may not always be considered time emergent or provide rapid reversal of poisoning, it is nonetheless one of the most important antidotes we use in toxicology. Acetaminophen poisoning is extremely common and continues to result in significant morbidity and mortality. Although the principles of NAC use are simple, questions about its use in clinical situations are frequent. When given early in the course of acetaminophen overdose, NAC is almost universally (100%) effective. Its safety profile is very good.

Patient's presenting after APAP overdose must be risk-stratified to determine the need for NAC therapy. In order to risk-stratify these patients, we divide them into two categories: Those that may be placed on the Rumack-Matthews nomogram (RMN) and those that cannot. The RMN can be used in cases of acute APAP overdose that present within 24 hours of the ingestion. "Acute" overdose is generally defined in studies as occurring within a 4-hour window. When using the RMN, a serum APAP level must be measured between 4 and 24 hours. The level is then compared against the nomogram line (reproductions of the nomogram and/or calculators are easy to find on the Internet). Patients with levels above the line require NAC treatment, and those below the line need no treatment and can be cleared. It should be noted that two nomogram lines exist: the "200 mg/L" (upper) line and the slightly more conservative "150 mg/L" (lower) line (so named based on the 4-hour toxic threshold level). We use the "200 mg/L" line for risk-stratification. I use the "150 mg/L" line only when historical uncertainty exists to provide more therapeutic cushion. The RMN is an extremely effective tool when applied correctly and has been used by medical toxicologists for over 30 years.

Patients with chronic overdose, repeated exposures, unknown TOI, or presenting late cannot be risk-stratified with the RMN. In these cases we measure a serum acetaminophen level and liver enzymes (AST, ALT). If the APAP level is <10 mcg/mL and there is normal AST/ALT (<59 IU/L), the patient does not require therapy and can be cleared. If the APAP level is above 10 mg/dL or liver enzymes are abnormal, NAC therapy should be started.

Two NAC preparations are available: oral and intravenous (acetylcysteine). These are essentially identical formulations (20% NAC solution) with the latter being approved for intravenous use. Patients starting NAC early (within 8–10 hours of ingestion) are expected to recover. Therefore, in early presenting patients, NAC can be withheld until initial lab results are obtained. Late presenting patients should receive the NAC loading dose while awaiting lab results. Oral dosing consists of a 140 mg/kg load, followed by 70 mg/kg every 4 hours. Serving oral NAC in a covered cup, mixing with juice (or diet soda), and a concomitant anti-emetic may help to improve palatability.

If vomiting occurs within 1 hour of loading dose, it is repeated or the patient can be converted to IV dosing. Oral NAC has been used for years successfully and may even be preferential to IV dosing as the antidote is absorbed directly into the portal circulation. Oral NAC allergy is essentially unheard of.

Intravenous dosing consists of a 150 mg/kg load given over 1 hour followed by two infusion doses. The first infusion being 50 mg/kg given over 4 hours followed by a second infusion of 100 mg/kg given over 16 hours. The primary downside of intravenous NAC is the potential for associated hypersensitivity reactions (anaphylaxis/anaphylactic). Use of a 1-hour loading protocol has dramatically reduced the numbers of hypersensitivity reactions. If a mild reaction occurs, often the dose can be restarted at a slower rate following antihistamine and steroid treatment. For more severe reactions, the patient should be converted to oral NAC dosing.

Clearance from NAC antidote therapy is a slightly more complicated discussion. We recommend the use of a toxicology specialist to assist in decision-making regarding when to stop therapy. In the past, 72-hour NAC regimens were recommended. Today, decisions regarding NAC clearance are entirely labs-driven. In short, we are looking for a serum acetaminophen level of <10–20 mg/L and normal (or normalizing) liver enzymes to stop NAC therapy.

Lastly, those patients that present early, following an acute overdose of APAP, often have short hospital stays. We recommend psychiatric consultation as early as possible since there is no anticipated altered mentation and the length of hospital stay is likely to be less than 24 hours.

15.7 Conclusion

Medically toxicology is a broad, non-organ-system-based specialty. While the numbers of potential poisons and clinical scenarios are vast, the fundamental principles of toxicological assessment, stages of poisoning, and initial care can be mastered. Watch out for the "deadly dozen," consider decontamination early, and become a master of strong supportive care. The immediate use of certain antidotes may be lifesaving; however, many should be administered in collaboration with a medical toxicologist. We highly recommend utilization of a toxicology specialist to aid in the safest and most efficient treatment of your emergency psychiatric patients.

References

American College of Toxicology. n.d. Introduction to medical toxicology. *American College of Medical Toxicology.* http://www.acmt.net/overview.html.

Bentur, Y, Y Lurie, A Tamir, D C Keyes, and F Basis. 2011. Reliability of history of acetaminophen ingestion in intentional drug overdose patients. *Human and Experimental Toxicology* 30 (1): 44–50.

Centers for Disease Control and Prevention. 2016. Injury prevention and control: Opioid overdose. December. http://www.cdc.gov/drugoverdose/data/overdose.html.

Choi, H S, and Y H Choi. 2015. Accuracy of tablet counts estimated by members of the public and healthcare professionals. *Clinical and Experimental Emergency Medicine* 2 (3): 168–173.

Clemmesen, C, and E Nilsson. 1961. Therapeutic trends in the treatment of barbiturate poisoning the Scandinavian method. *Clinical Pharmacology* 2 (2): 220–229.

Dowling, J, G K Isbister, C M Kirkpatrick, D Naidoo, and A Graudins. 2008. Population pharmacokinetics of intravenous, intramuscular, and intranasal naloxone in human volunteers. *Therapeutic Drug Monitoring* 30 (4): 490–496.

Elsevier: Gold Standard. n.d. Tox ED: The clinician's toxicology resource. Elsevier: Clinical Decision Support. http://www.toxed-ip.com/ToxEdSolutions.aspx?epm=2_1.

Ingels, M, D F Marks, and R Clark. 2003. A survey of medical toxicology training in psychiatry residency programs. *Academic Psychiatry* 27 (1): 50–53.

Kerr, D, A Kelly, P Dietze, D Jolley, and B Barger. 2009. Radomized controlled trial comparing the effectiveness and safety of intranasal and intramuscular naloxone for the treatment of suspected heroin overdose. *Addiction* 104: 2067–2074.

Kreshak, A A, G Wardi, and C A Tomaszewski. 2015. The accuracy of emergency department medication history as determined by mass spectrometry analysis of urine: A pilot study. *Journal of Emergency Medicine* 48 (3): 382–386.

Moll, J, W Kerns, C Tomaszewski, and R Rutherfoord. 1999. Incidence of aspiration pneumonia in intubated patients receiving activated charcoal. *Journal of Emergency Medicine* 17 (2): 279–283.

Monte, A A, K J Heard, Hoppe J A, V Vasiliou, and F J Gonzalez. 2015. The accuracy of self-reported drug ingestion histories in emergency department patients. *Journal of Clinical Pharmacology* 55 (1): 33–38.

Offerman, S R. 2012. Informal survey of Kaiser Permanente emergency physicians regarding the use of the regional toxicology service. Unpublished data.

Olshaker, J S, B Browne, D A Jerrard, H Prendergast, and T Stair. 1997. Medical clearance and screening of psychiatric patients in the emergency department. *Academic Emergency Medicine* 4: 124–128.

Truven Health Analytics. n.d. Micromedex toxicology management. *Microdex Solutions.* http://micromedex.com/toxicology-management.

Wanger, K, L Brough, I Macmillan, J Goulding, L MacPhail, and J M Christenson. 1998. Intravenous vs subcutaneous naloxone for out-of-hospital management of presumed opioid overdose. *Academic Emergency Medicine* 5 (4): 293–299.

Wax, P M. 1997. Analeptic use in clinical toxicology: A historical appraisal. *Journal of Toxicology. Clinical Toxicology* 35 (2): 203–209.

SPECIALIZED POPULATION CARE IV

Chapter 16

Children and Adolescents with Psychiatric Emergencies

Gary Lelonek

Contents

16.1 Introduction 276
16.2 The Rise of Child and Adolescent Psychiatric Emergency Visits 276
16.3 The Emergency Department Assessment 277
    16.3.1 Interview Considerations 278
    16.3.2 The Evaluation 278
16.4 Interventions 278
16.5 Legal Issues 279
    16.5.1 Child Abuse 280
16.6 Emergency Department Presentations 280
    16.6.1 Agitation in the Emergency Department 280
    16.6.2 Externalizing Behavioral Disorders 281
    16.6.3 High-Risk Behaviors 282
    16.6.4 Autism 283
    16.6.5 School Refusal 283
    16.6.6 Non-Suicidal Self-Injurious Behavior 283
    16.6.7 Suicidal Ideation and Behaviors 284
    16.6.8 Depression 285
    16.6.9 Anxiety 286
    16.6.10 Psychosis 286
    16.6.11 Hyperactivity 286
    16.6.12 Eating Disorders 287
16.7 Conclusion 287
References 287
Resource 288

16.1 Introduction

The emergency department (ED) is often the destination for a child in crisis. The crisis is triggered by a change in a child or their environment. The changing developmental needs of children and adolescents stresses the child and their environment. From infancy to adulthood, children's lives progress through tremendous changes. Development includes physical, psychosocial, identity, cognitive, psychosexual, and moral areas of life. Concomitantly, children must meet the demands of their environment; family, peers, and school. Freud, Erikson, Piaget, and Kohlberg have studied and sequenced development. Erickson's first 5 stages of development span the first 18 years of life, and afterward he designates 3 more stages of development covering the next 60 years.

Adult life is relatively stable compared with the first 18 years of life. Yet, parents are equally changing to adapt to the needs of each of their children's development, while attending to their own developmental and life demands. The environment for the child must be dynamic and fluid. The child, in their family system, is constantly balancing the drive toward differentiation with the need to be integrated into their family and social group.

Parents have to foster an environment for the development of the child from an egocentric dependent infant to an independent empathic person. The parents must model living a life with rules and limits, striving for self-improvement for their children to value the limits, rules and moral goals that parents set in place. Children need their home environments to be safe, consistent, and without hypocrisy. In any household, development takes on a multigenerational perspective as different generations living together are navigating their personal developmental needs while adapting to the changing needs of the family around them. Every child presents to the department as a member of a unit whose needs are not being met.

The maturing child constantly challenges authority for autonomy while the supporting adult sets limits. The limit setting accounts for the child's age, maturity level, and previously demonstrated "good" judgment. The road to adulthood is littered with challenges and obstacles. In addition to the stress of the changes naturally experienced through development, a child's well-being is dependent on the family, school, and community in which they live. Any change that stresses these systems has the potential to precipitate a crisis. The goal of the department assessment is to determine whether outpatient resources are available to restore equilibrium to the system.

16.2 The Rise of Child and Adolescent Psychiatric Emergency Visits

Mental health problems and self-harm are leading causes of morbidity and mortality of children. The Centers for Disease Control and Prevention (CDC) lists the leading causes of death in 10–14-year-olds as accidents, accounting for 30% of total deaths, malignant neoplasms at 16.2%, intentional self-harm at 9.1%, followed by assault at 5.1%. For adolescents ages 15–19 years old, accidents are the leading cause of death at 41.7%, followed by assault at 16.8%, and intentional self-harm at 15.2% (Heron 2013). One-fourth of youth experiences a mental disorder during the past year and about one-third across their lifetimes (Merikangas et al. 2009).

Child psychiatric department visits have been on the rise. From 1993 to 1999 ED pediatric mental health visits accounted for 1.6% of all ED visits (Sills and Bland 2002). During that time, the visits for suicidal attempts, self-injury, and psychosis was stable, suggesting that the overall rise in ED pediatric mental health visits may have been attributable to nonurgent complaints more appropriately managed by a primary mental health provider. The pediatric ED at Yale University noted an increase of 59% in psychiatric illness-related visits between 1995 and 1999 (Santucci et al. 2000). National percentages of total visits, visit counts, and population rates were calculated, overall and by race, age, and sex. ED visits for mental health issues increased from 4.4% of all visits in 2001 to 7.2% in 2011 (Simon and Schoendorf 2014).

The rise of ED visits is connected to the decrease of inpatient hospital beds, without a concomitant increase in outpatient services, and a zero-tolerance policy for agitation or threat of violence by school systems. In the 2011–2012 school year, there were 3435 calls to the emergency medical services (EMS) by New York City schools, costing at least 4.4 million dollars (Brill 2013). Of these, 947 calls were to handle disruptive or dangerous kids, costing 1.2 million dollars (Rosen 2013). These referrals have gained the name "psychiatric suspensions" with schools illegally mandating a psychiatric assessment before returning to the classroom. According to a study, only 3% of the kids brought to an emergency department from school were admitted to the hospital (Rosen 2013). Many of these referrals stem from zero tolerance and the citywide standards on discipline and intervention of the board of education. The practice of removing misbehaving students by EMS is traumatic to the students, and a costly waste of EMS and hospital resources.

The national youth risk behavior survey (YRBS) monitors health-risk behaviors that contribute to the leading causes of death, disability, and social problems among youth and adults in the United States. The national YRBS is conducted every 2 years during the spring semester and provides data representative of ninth- through twelfth-grade students in public and private schools throughout the United States. In 2013, 39.1% of women and 20.8% of males reported feeling sad 2 weeks in a row, reducing some usual activities. Overall, 17% seriously considered attempting suicide, 13.6% made a plan, 8% attempted suicide, and 2.7% received medical treatment for their attempt (Centers for Disease Control and Prevention 2016b). Rotheram-Borus (2000) reported that fewer than 50% of adolescents seen for suicidal behavior in the ED were ever referred for treatment, and, even when they were referred, compliance with treatment was low. Another study revealed that only one-fifth of these children receive necessary treatment.

16.3 The Emergency Department Assessment

Since the presentation of a child to the department represents an imbalance between the child and the environment, the assessment addresses the reasons for the imbalance. In addition to addressing the safety of the child, the ED visit should act as an intervention that acts as a vehicle of change to the child's situation. From 2003 to 2005, the rate of repeat visits was 24.4%. Among patients with repeat visits, the average number of psychiatric-related return visits was two. More than 2 psychiatric-related ED visits occurred in 18.3% (Mahajan et al. 2009) of cases.

Grandparents are increasingly the caregivers for their grandchildren. Since 1970, the number of grandparents serving as primary caregivers for their grandchildren has steadily increased. Nationally, about 3% of all households contain both grandparents and grandchildren, with more than 60% of these households maintained by a grandparent. About 2.7 million grandparents were "grandparent caregivers" (those who had primary responsibility for grandchildren under 18 years living with them) (Ellis and Simmons 2014). About one in three grandparent-maintained households had no parent present—17% of these households had two grandparents present and 15% of households had just a grandmother present. These grandparents are often dealing with their own continued development and often-deteriorating health and in Erikson's models may be continuing earlier stages of development or in the throes of "integrity versus despair."

16.3.1 Interview Considerations

The first step of the assessment is to establish the safety of the child in the ED. Attention is focused on signs requiring immediate intervention, such as psychomotor agitation, aggressiveness, alterations in the level of consciousness, and suicidal behavior. Preferably, the child psychiatry section of the ED should decrease stimulation and decrease access to potentially dangerous materials. Changing the child into a hospital gown both removes weapons or drugs that might be used to hurt themselves or others and decreases the risk of elopement. The presence of hospital security helps to create an environment of limit setting and safety for the child and hospital staff. When a child presents with agitation, their behavior should be addressed in the least restrictive manner while maintaining the safety of the child, other patients, and staff. After placing the child in a secure environment has failed to ease their agitation, chemical and physical restraints are used as necessary and appropriate.

16.3.2 The Evaluation

The first step of the evaluation is to speak with the parents and child explaining the structure of the evaluation, discuss confidentiality, including the child's right to confidentiality, and to set the expectations of the department visit. The child and parent are given the opportunity to speak with the mental health professional individually. In addition to confidentiality and building rapport with both parties, the privacy ensures that information is shared freely; children and parents can share whatever information they feel is pertinent without concern for disappointing, blaming, or implicating each other. The person who referred the patient provides collateral information about the events that precipitated the referral. Common referral sources are the parents, school, residence, foster care agencies, or outpatient providers. A medical exam may be needed to address any injuries and potential etiologies for the decompensation. Observing the interaction and behavior of the child and their guardian can inform the evaluating clinician about their relationship.

16.4 Interventions

The disposition, after the department evaluation, takes into consideration the immediate risk the child presents to themselves or others. The risk assessment includes weighing the child's risk and protective factors as an outpatient participant against the risks and benefits of hospitalization. The criterion for involuntary hospitalization for children, as it is with adults, is that the child poses an imminent risk to themselves or others or is unable to care for themselves. Most children are admitted on a voluntary status since their parents are legally responsible for making decisions for them. If the parents refuse hospitalization, and the physician assesses that the patient is an imminent threat to self or others, the patient can be admitted on an involuntary status. If the behavior is unlikely to be modified by hospitalization, then hospitalization presents a greater risk. Risk of hospitalization includes removal from family and school. This demonstrates to the child that they are not able to deal with their distress, reinforcing the concept that they cannot be responsible for their safety. The child is stripped of their civil liberty when placed on a locked unit and placed in an environment with children who are potentially dangerous or engaging in maladaptive coping strategies. When hospitalization is not indicated, then the disposition focuses on modifying risk factors for the child; including increased parental observation, decreased access to means of hurting themselves, and increased access to mental health professionals. The interventions form the "safety plan" and include having the child develop a safety plan to seek help when they need it including informing parents or calling 911 when they are unable to keep themselves safe, for instance, when experiencing suicidal or homicidal ideation.

16.5 Legal Issues

The following is based on the New York legal code. Please consult with your local state laws.

Parents have the right to make informed decisions about the healthcare for their minor child including the administration of psychiatric drugs. This requires an adequate explanation of the proposed procedure or treatment that presents a risk to the patient's health. Informed consent is not required for routine care, such as diagnostic blood tests and a physical exam. Normally, a patient has the right to refuse treatment, even if it means the patient may die. Parents must act in the child's best interest. They cannot refuse life-sustaining treatment unless the prognosis for the child is poor. For minors (under 18) either parent can consent *in loco parentis*.

Minors can consent if emancipated, for contraception, for treatment of sexually transmitted infections, abortion, obstetrical care or child delivery, HIV testing, donating blood, and mental health treatment in some settings. A minor is considered emancipated if he/she has ever been married, he/she is the parent (mother or father) of a child, and is financially self-supporting and living away from the parental home. Consent should be obtained from the emancipated minor for their treatment or treatment of the minor's child(ren). A doctor does not need proof to rely on the information provided by the minor. "Anyone who acts in good faith, based on the representation by a person that he is eligible to consent … shall be deemed to have received effective consent" (New York Public Health Law 2504. Enabling Certain Persons to Consent for Certain Medical, Dental, Health and Hospital Services n.d.).

If a minor can consent, then the minor is financially responsible for any medical treatment provided. If parents cover the insurance, they may receive an explanation of benefits (EOB) and the minor should be warned. If a minor is mentally ill or developmentally disabled, a guardian's consent must be obtained prior to treatment. Minors are entitled to confidentiality with the exception of those who are dangerousness to self or others. A minor older than 12 may be notified of any request by a qualified person to review the minor's medical information. If the minor objects, the doctor may deny the request. A doctor may also deny access to the child's medical records to a guardian if release could reasonably be expected to cause substantial and identifiable harm to the physician–patient relationship. The Health Insurance Portability and Accountability Act (HIPAA) also includes exceptions for denying access to a guardian when violence or abuse is a factor.

A doctor is not obligated to recognize the person as the patient's legal representative if they reasonably believe

- The patient has been or may be subjected to domestic violence, abuse, or neglect by the person.
- Treating the person as the legal representative could endanger the patient and, in the covered entity's professional judgment, it is not in the best interests of the patient to treat the person as the patient's legal representative.

If the doctor receives an authorization signed by a parent or guardian and is uncertain about the individual's relationship to the patient, the doctor should request verification. If a minor's parents have separated and a legal determination of custody is pending, either parent may give consent for treatment.

Both parents have equal rights. If there is a question about custody and which parent can consent, we should ask for the court order or separation agreement (legal affairs can review this). If there is a disagreement between the parents about necessary treatment, we need to consider court intervention. A minor, over the age of 16 and under 18, may apply for admission to a mental hygiene facility and, in the director's discretion, be admitted either as a voluntary patient upon his or her own application or upon the application of the minor's parent, legal guardian, or next of kin. A patient under 16 may be received only as a voluntary patient upon the application of a parent, legal guardian, or next of kin.

16.5.1 Child Abuse

Mental health professionals are mandated reporters of suspected child abuse. When a child or their parent, guardian, custodian, or legally responsible person comes before the doctor in his/her professional capacity and states personal knowledge of facts that, taken as true, would constitute child abuse or maltreatment, the doctor is legally required to report the alleged abuse. If the doctor reasonably believes that a child presenting for treatment has been or is being neglected or abused by his or her parents or by a person legally responsible for the child's care, the doctor must report the alleged abuse. The most important aspect of the evaluation of potential maltreat is assuring the physical and emotional safety of the child. Many children present to the ED after a referral from their school and child protective services. Other referrals are generated after the child has presented for treatment of an injury in the community.

The role of the mental health emergency provider is to assess the child's risk for danger to self or others. Doctors and mental health providers are mandated to report to authorities any suspected abuse to the offices of child protective services. A report is filed with the office of child protective services. If it is believed that the child is in imminent danger, the child may be kept in the hospital until child protective services can find safe placement for the child.

16.6 Emergency Department Presentations

Behavioral issues, attention deficit hyperactivity disorder (ADHD), depression, and neurotic disorders are common problems. Different age groups can manifest different presentations. The following points list some of the more common disorders and the ages in which they typically surface:

- Under 5 years old: Behavioral issue, night terrors, ADHD, concussion, convulsions
- 5–9 years old: Behavioral issue, ADHD, neurotic disorder, affective, psychosis
- 10–14 years old: Behavioral issue, depression, neurotic disorder, ADHD, affective
- 15 years and older: Depression, neurotic disorder, alcohol (EtOH), behavioral issue, major depressive disorder (MDD) (Mahajan et al. 2009).

16.6.1 Agitation in the Emergency Department

Agitation is a common cause for referral to the department. The goal is to use the least restrictive intervention to address the agitation. If the child can be verbally redirected, it is helpful to ask them what helps to calm them down. If it is possible and safe, they should be given the opportunity to use music, drawing, or writing to calm down. Children are sensitive to exhaustion, hunger, and changes in their environment. Offering them something to eat or drink is an easy intervention that has great potential benefit with low risk of harm.

If the child is unable to de-escalate by modifying their environment or using coping skills, medication can be administered. Administering a dose of the patient's regular medication is preferable to introducing a new medication to their system. If the child is acutely agitated and dangerous, then the use of intramuscular medication is warranted to maintain the safety of the child and those around them. Injectable medication including antipsychotics, benzodiazepines, and anticholinergics are commonly used for agitation. Children are generally more medication naïve, physiologically smaller than adults, and metabolize medication differently. A good rule is to administer lower starting doses of these medications.

Physical restraints can be used when other less restrictive interventions fail to address the dangerousness of the situation. Either a doctor or a nurse initiates restraints. Check with your local state laws regarding length of the restraint order based on age. Restraints should be released when the patient is no longer an imminent threat to self or others.

16.6.2 Externalizing Behavioral Disorders

Children who externalize aggressive or oppositional behaviors are often at risk for developing conduct disorder (CD) and oppositional defiant disorder (ODD). CD is characterized by four types of behaviors: aggressive behavior, destructiveness, deceitfulness, and violation of rules. The aggressive aspect involves threatening or causing physical harm. It may include fighting, bullying, being cruel to others or animals, using weapons, and forcing another into sexual activity. The destructive behavior involves intentional destruction of property, such as arson (deliberate fire setting) and vandalism (harming another person's property). Deceitful behavior includes repeated lying, shoplifting, or breaking into homes or cars in order to steal. Violation of rules involves going against accepted rules of society or engaging in behavior that is not appropriate for the person's age. These behaviors may include running away, skipping school, playing pranks, or being sexually active at a very young age.

The *Diagnostic and Statistical Manual of Mental Disorders*, fifth edition (DSM-5) criteria for the diagnosis of ODD show a pattern of behavior that includes at least four symptoms from any of these categories—angry and irritable mood; argumentative and defiant behavior; or vindictiveness. The behavior causes significant problems at work, school, or home and occurs on its own, rather than as part of the course of another mental health problem, such as a substance use disorder, depression, or bipolar disorder (American Psychiatric Association 2013).

Kids with oppositional behavior are referred to the department for becoming defiant toward their parents, school staff, or for argumentative behaviors resulting in aggression toward others or property. The children can either present as oppositional or calm and cooperative in the ED. In the absence of an imminent threat to self or others that hospitalization could treat, there is no benefit to an acute short hospitalization for a child with ODD or CD. The child could benefit from changes in their environment, including consideration of maintaining stronger limits, persons in need of supervision (PINS) petition, use of law enforcement, or residential placement.

PINS is a term used to describe a child, under the age of 18, who has committed a status offense, for example, running away, using marijuana or skipping school. PINS petition is a written request asking the family court to get involved when other efforts to control a child have failed. These behaviors benefit from treatments that focus on a multisystemic therapy (MST). MST focuses on improving family functioning because it is theorized that improvements in family functioning mediate improvements in peer relationships, school functioning, and participation in the community (Henggeler 2011).

16.6.3 High-Risk Behaviors

During adolescence, kids test boundaries, trying to manage autonomy while parents are simultaneously adjusting to their needs and setting limits as dictated by their demonstration of good judgment. Biologically, risk taking is managed by the frontal lobe of the brain, which continues to develop until reaching full maturity at about 26 years old. Until that point, people are more likely to engage in higher-risk activity that they would tolerate when the frontal lobe reaches maturity.

Risky and potentially dangerous behaviors can be a sign of possible social or family problems, poor supervision, or more serious mental illness. School truancy, running away, experimentation with drugs, gang involvement, and risky sexual behaviors can derail and even threaten the life of an adolescent who does not yet have the ability to fully cope with these adult issues and decisions and does not yet understand the long-term consequences of their behavior. It is imperative that the warning signs of risky behaviors are recognized.

Risky behavior is evaluated by determining the impact these behaviors have on the child's normal level of functioning, how the behavior compares with normal adolescent behavior, or changes in the individual's behavior or level of functioning. Any behavior that adversely affects the adolescent's ability to function academically, socially, or with their family is cause for concern. These behaviors could be due to an underlying mood disorder, psychotic disorder, experimentation with drugs, trauma, post-traumatic stress disorder, a behavioral disorder like ADHD, or disruptive behaviors, like ODD or CD. High-risk behaviors are best addressed early on to decrease the long-term morbidity of these behaviors while also increasing the likelihood of modifying the child's decision-making process and establishing a positive pattern of behavior.

In the ED, children present after they have engaged in a high-risk behavior that is beyond what the parents will tolerate. The evaluation focuses on assessing for the dangerousness of the behaviors and whether the behavior is rooted in a mood or psychotic disorder that could be modified with a hospitalization or is the result of the adolescent's poor judgment. If the child's presentation does not warrant acute inpatient hospitalization, the next step is using the department presentation as an opportunity to offer an intervention that can address the balance of autonomy and limit setting. This means assessing whether the high-risk behavior is best modified by engaging the child or their environment.

Individual therapy can address the risky behavior of most children. Family therapy can be helpful in strengthening the family's structure and ability to set limits. Medication management referrals are indicated when there is a mood, psychotic, or impulsive etiology to the child's behaviors. When available, in-home crisis intervention can bring the intervention to the main battle ground of the home. When there is inadequate supervision, child protective services should be involved for possible neglect. A child with proper adult supervision is at much lower risk than a child on the street alone or unsupervised with friends.

Additionally, the department presentation can be used as an opportunity to help the adolescent and their parents engage in open conversation about difficult topics like sex, drugs, or poor academic performance. While these are not topics that the adolescent or parent typically feel comfortable discussing with each other, having a mental health professional to discuss these topics with can help them address any confused or conflicted thoughts they may have about these issues. The mental health provider can help provide a nonjudgmental environment for the adolescent to disclose and explore these difficult topics. Having the opportunity to view these topics from both the parent's and adolescent's perspective can help both the parents and the child better appreciate the behaviors and their risks and sets the ground work for further exploration after leaving the ED.

16.6.4 Autism

The rate of autism spectrum disorder (ASD) is on the rise nationally, with 1 in 68 children afflicted with this disorder. As such, there has been a corresponding increase in ED visits. Common presentations include; multiple medical problems, especially seizures, disorders with behavioral activation, engaging in self-stimulatory repetitive behaviors, which can be aggressive toward self or others and includes head banging and biting. Caretakers are challenged by the child's aggressive behavior. Children with autism who present to the ED often have sleep-related issues. Children with autism manifest with sensitivity to stimulation of any of the senses: vision, hearing, touch, taste, and smell.

Like all other presentations, during the evaluation, it is important to determine whether the patient is presenting due to a change in the patient or in their environment. All children are sensitive to change in their routine. Due to their limitations in communicating their needs and their sensory sensitivities, children with autism are more susceptible to decompensating when there is a change in their routine.

The ED environment is over stimulating to neurotypical children and even more so to children with ASD. Patients with ASD and other developmental delays should be triaged with higher acuity due to their increased sensitivity to stimulation and change in routine. Addressing the environmental stimulation at home and in the ED can decrease the agitation of the child and potentially affect the disposition. Interventions that decrease stimulus activation include lowering lighting; decreasing alarms, phone, and TV volume, taking the child's tactile sensitivities into account; understanding that they need certain food or certain food preparations; and addressing any unpleasant smells. Activities in the department that contain different textures, colors, smells, and sounds can be beneficial. To help decrease stimulation on a child with ASD, noise-canceling headphones are helpful.

16.6.5 School Refusal

School refusal can be daunting because the child often will absolutely not go to school or will have severe tantrums when brought to school, without any clear-cut reason. While school refusal is not an acute emergency situation, it is a common reason for department referral. School refusal can be related to anxiety, ADHD, ODD, bullying, depression, and CD. A therapist working intensively with the school and the family can gradually get the child to come back to school. These children should not be referred for homeschooling, because this reinforces their worry about school, and the longer a child is out of school, the harder it is to get him or her to return to school (Hella and Bernstein 2012).

16.6.6 Non-Suicidal Self-Injurious Behavior

Non-Suicidal Self-Injurious Behavior (NSSIB) "involves intentionally injuring oneself in a manner that often results in damage to body tissue but without any conscience suicide intent" (Miller et al. 2007). The prevalence of NSSIB has been increasing with reports of 16%–18% of adolescents in community studies and between 12% and 35% in college populations.

Adolescents engage in NSSIB for various reasons. NSSIB functions as a form of avoidance and escape from unwanted emotions (Gratz et al. 2013). The act of NSSIB helps the individual to regulate emotional distress. NSSIB is a risk factor for suicidal behaviors. As the ED is a potential anxiety-provoking environment, and presumably the patient has been brought to the ED under circumstances that someone feels that they are a potential danger to themselves, it is important to ensure that the patient won't engage in NSSIB while in the ED. They should be changed into a gown, with supervision as per your institution's guidelines, asked if they have anything with them to cut themselves, and their belongings should be searched or locked away during the evaluation.

Evaluation of the child with NSSIB includes inquiring about the frequency, intensity, places on the body where they cut, what objects are used for cutting, triggers, exploring their intention when engaging in NSSIB, and its function. NSSIB is a sign of another underlying mood or personality pathology. It is important to understand the function of the behavior so that the referral can be targeted at addressing alternative coping strategies. Diagnoses associated with NSSIB include depression, anxiety, PTSD, and borderline personality disorder. In the ED, parents should be involved in having a discussion with the patient regarding the NSSIB to assist them in understanding its dangerousness.

Medically, the patient's immunizations should be reviewed to learn whether a tetanus immunization is warranted. This is especially important if the child has used any metal objects to cut themselves. Medical evaluation should include a full-body exam for cutting, as patients often cut in covered areas of the body. The medical evaluation should address whether stitches are needed or other medical care is required for the cuts.

In the absence of an immediate danger to self or others, patients who engage in NSSIB do not warrant admission to the restrictive setting on the inpatient unit. Discussion with the patient regarding the sterility of the objects that they use is important to decrease the potential morbidity of their behaviors. Parents are advised to lock away all potential sharp items commonly found in the home, including razors, knives, and scissors. Patients should disclose the location of or give their parents the utensil they are using to cut themselves. Referrals to therapists who work with NSSIB or who have been trained in dialectical behavioral therapy (DBT) have been demonstrated to help address the underlying triggers of the self-harming behaviors. A referral to a child psychiatrist for a medication evaluation may also be warranted to address the severity of an underlying mood disorder.

16.6.7 Suicidal Ideation and Behaviors

Adolescent suicide is a major health problem in the United States and worldwide. Researchers have found that between 31% and 50% of suicide attempters have previously attempted, with a quarter reattempting within the 3 months of their initial attempt (Lewinsohn et al. 1996). Miller and Taylor (2005) studied the YRBS data and determined that the more problematic behaviors that the adolescent engages in, the higher their risk is of engaging in suicidal behaviors. Suicidal behaviors include completed suicide, attempts, and ideation. As previously mentioned, in 2013, 39.1% of women and 20.8% of men reported feeling sad 2 weeks in a row, with a reported reduction in some usual activities. Overall, 17% seriously considered attempting suicide, 13.6% made a plan, 8% attempted and 2.7% received medical treatment for their attempt (Centers for Disease Control and Prevention 2016). Rotheram-Borus (2000) reported that fewer than 50% of adolescents seen for suicidal behavior in the ED were ever referred for treatment, and, even when they were referred, compliance with treatment was low. Another study revealed that only one-fifth of these children receive necessary treatment. In the ED, suicide attempts warrant inpatient psychiatric hospitalization as the patient is an imminent threat of harm to self and has demonstrated that they are not safe in their current environment.

Suicidal ideation (SI) is a common reason for referral to the ED. The evaluation of children with suicidal ideation is similar to evaluating an adult with SI. The evaluation seeks to define the nature of the ideation from passive, for example, wishing they would not wake up or they would not be alive; to intermittent SI; to a more persistent SI in the absence of a plan or intent; to SI with a plan but without intent; and finally SI with plan and intent. The increasing severity of the SI increases the potential imminent threat of the patient to themselves, thereby reaching the level needed to tip the risk to benefit scale in favor of the benefit of hospitalization over the potential risk of discharging the patient to their current level of care.

When parents are against hospitalization, the evaluation focuses on whether the patient continues to be an imminent danger to self and would need an involuntary hospitalization, and whether the guardian addresses the safety concerns of the home environment. If a parent increases the safety of the home environment with increased observation, and an appointment is scheduled with the outpatient mental health provider within 24 h, the child can be sent home. The child must demonstrate that they no longer endorse a plan or intend to engage in suicidal behavior, and the parents must demonstrate an understanding of the responsibility of caring for a child who has suicidal thoughts. If these conditions are present, then an involuntary hospitalization may not be warranted. The patient and parents should be offered hospitalization as a clear recommendation. When documenting the patient encounter, a clear recommendation for hospitalization should be noted with the parents' reasons for refusal of the hospitalization and how the parents and patient address the safety concerns in the home environment. Safety planning includes locking away all potentially lethal objects in the home including all weapons, sharps, poisons, and pills.

16.6.8 Depression

Depression in adolescents can present differently than it does in adults. Adolescents can present with irritability or increased isolation as their primary complaint in the ED. The evaluation in the ED focuses on the extent that the depression is impacting the patient's functioning in their environment and their ability to care for themselves. Exploration of suicidal ideation includes current plan, intent, history of suicide attempts, while weighing the protective factors of their support system, engagement in safety planning, and accessibility to professional mental healthcare. Disclosure of suicidal ideation warrants breaching the confidentiality of the child and bringing the support system into an open conversation with the child. When the child is not an imminent danger to self, the ability to tolerate the risks of discharging a child with suicidal ideation pivot on the ability of the child to disclose their ideation to their guardian. It is important to counsel the child that a guardian feels safer when the child is open with their suicidal feelings rather than when a child attempts to protect their guardians from their sad feelings.

Children who are not caring for themselves with decreased eating or limited self-care, reach the threshold of being unable to care for themselves and meet criteria for inpatient hospitalization. Even in the absence of suicidal ideation, an involuntary hospitalization is warranted when the parents have a history of neglect of the patient or the patient's non-suicidal symptoms of depression are on the precipice of being an imminent threat to their life.

16.6.9 Anxiety

Fear and worry are normal emotional experiences common in most children. When the fear impacts the child's functioning, parents should discuss with their pediatrician the cause of the excessive anxiety and appropriate treatment options. Anxiety often manifests with somatic complaints, including unexplained stomach problems and headaches. Moodiness with irritability, tearfulness, and angry outbursts are symptoms of anxiety, which help the child avoid the anxiety-provoking stimulus. Common presentations of anxiety in the child department include school anxiety, separation anxiety, obsessive-compulsive disorder, and panic disorder. Panic disorder with agoraphobia can interfere with the child's ability to attend school, and leave the home. Uncontrolled panic attacks are grounds to consider voluntary psychiatric hospitalization and initiation of medication management. School anxiety and separation anxiety disorder require behavioral interventions and parental training with a therapist to address the underlying cause of the anxiety and the reinforcement of the behavior that interferes with the ability to extinguish the behavior.

16.6.10 Psychosis

Most children who report visual or auditory hallucinations do not have a psychotic illness. Developmentally children transition from a realm of fantasy to reality. Young children fluidly live between the fantasy world and reality and have difficulty distinguishing between them. Young children love to tell stories. As the mind develops, reality testing matures. An imaginary friend is on the spectrum of normal development. The function of the imaginary friend should be investigated. While an imaginary friend could be part of normal development, they could develop in the setting of environmental stressors, abuse, and disorders including depression or anxiety.

Childhood-onset psychosis before age 13 is very rare. Early-onset schizophrenia (EOS) usually occurs before age 18. The diagnosis uses the same criteria as adults, which are outlined in the DSM-5 (American Psychiatric Association 2013). In addition to the presence of two of the following: hallucinations, disorganized speech, disorganized behavior, and negative symptoms for 6 months, there should be a significant decline in social or occupational functioning. The social and academic declines should predate the other symptoms. When a child presents to the ED all other potential etiologies of hallucinations should be ruled out before considering schizophrenia.

Many of the symptoms seen in people with schizophrenia are also found in people with depression, bipolar disorder, or other illnesses. As a result, studies have found that misdiagnosis is common. Developmental disorders that impair speech and language function can be misdiagnosed as psychosis. Many children with a mood disorder report auditory hallucinations when stressed. Children with depression report negative thoughts that are disturbing and have trouble describing the phenomena other than as a voice. The hallucinations of schizophrenia are more likely to be unconnected with the child's mood or a specific time of day.

In the ED, it is important to work up the patient for potential causes of psychosis that would need medical treatment. Routine labs typically access baseline blood counts, renal, thyroid, and liver function, and electrolyte levels, which are important for monitoring any side effects of medications. If there is an acute onset of the symptoms, a toxicology screen can help clarify whether the patient has been exposed to illicit drugs. In the presence of a history of seizure symptoms or neurologic symptoms, neuroimaging and completion of an electroencephalogram are indicated. Children with EOS are at increased risk for suicide and should be thoroughly screened. The family should be informed that there is no evidence that psychological or social factors cause schizophrenia (McClellan et al. 2013).

16.6.11 Hyperactivity

The CDC reports that "approximately 11% of children 4–17 years of age (6.4 million) have been diagnosed with ADHD as of 2011. The percentage of children with an ADHD diagnosis continues to increase, from 7.8% in 2003 to 9.5% in 2007, and to 11.0% in 2011" (Centers for Disease Control and Prevention 2016a). Children with ADHD typically present when the child starts childcare or school. The increased structural demands stress the ability of the young child to effectively cope and thrive in those environments. In the classroom, the child's hyperactivity and aggressive behaviors are magnified and disruptive to the child's ability to work in the classroom and form relationships with peers. The episodes of hyperactivity are difficult to contain and when the behaviors escalate to agitation and aggression the child presents to the emergency room. Children with ADHD are better able to inhibit their hyperactive and inattentive tendencies in the morning. As the day progresses their brains are less effective at inhibiting their ADHD behaviors. During the psychiatric evaluation, which is often conducted in the afternoon when children with ADHD are less inhibited, the hyperactive behavior can be observed, as well as the parent–child interaction. The patient should manifest their behaviors in at least two settings, and have six or more of the inattentive or hyperactive/impulsive behaviors. Patients can be referred for behavioral therapy or/and medication management in an outpatient setting.

16.6.12 Eating Disorders

Children with eating disorders who present to the ED need to be medically cleared before admission to a psychiatric unit is considered. A medically unstable patient should be admitted to the medical unit and followed by psychosomatic psychiatry. If medically cleared and the patient is expressing suicidal ideation (SI), homicidal ideation (HI), or inability to care for themselves, psychiatry should be consulted to evaluate whether the patient presentation represents an imminent danger to themselves, warranting inpatient psychiatric hospitalization. American Academy of Child Adolescent Psychiatry (AACAP) practice parameters report that "there is no evidence that psychiatric hospitalization for eating disorders is more effective than outpatient treatment" (Lock et al. 2015). Patients with eating disorders need specialized outpatient care. Residential and day treatment programs may be useful. In the community, the patient should be treated by a multidisciplinary team including a pediatrician, psychotherapist, and dietician. A child psychiatrist can be consulted for psychotropic medication management. Family-based treatment "is effective and superior in comparison to individual treatment."

16.7 Conclusion

The increase in child and adolescent psychiatric admits to EDs nationwide is a concerning societal issue that needs to be addressed. The psychiatric assessment and treatment of minors can be a challenging endeavor for any ED psychiatric team to undertake. Overall, in the outpatient arena, there is a lack of child psychiatrists to meet the expanding population of children who need their care. Due to this shortage in community providers, the ED psychiatric services team ends up bridging this gap in outpatient services. Children with acute mental health needs are being treated in the ED setting for many issues that an outpatient provider can address. The ED treatment team needs to be prepared to assess, support, treat, and disposition any children presenting with mental disturbances.

References

American Psychiatric Association. 2013. *Diagnostic and Statistical Manual of Mental Disorders*, fifth edition. Arlington, VA: American Psychiatric Association.

Brill, S. 2013. Bitter pill: Why medical bills are killing us. *Time*, April 4.

Centers for Disease Control and Prevention. 2016a. Attention-Deficit/Hyperactivity Disorder (ADHD). Centers for Disease Control and Prevention. October 5. http://www.cdc.gov/ncbddd/adhd/data.html.

Centers for Disease Control and Prevention. 2016b. Youth Risk Behavior Surveillance System (YRBSS). Centers for Disease Control and Prevention. August 11. http://cdc.gov/healthyyouth/data/yrbs/index.htm.

Ellis, R R, and Tavia S. 2014. *Coresident Grandparents and Their Grandchildren: 2012.* Census Study, Washington DC: United States Census Bureau.

Gratz, K L, M T Tull, and R Levy. 2013. Randomized controlled trial and uncontrolled 9-month follow-up of an adjunctive emotion regulation group therapy for deliberate self-harm among women with borderline personality disorder. *Psychological Medicine* 44 (10): 2099–2112.

Hella, B and G A Bernstein. 2012. Panic disorder and school refusal. *Child and Adolescent Psychiatric Clinics of North America* 21 (3): 593–606.

Henggeler, S W. 2011. Efficacy studies to large-scale transport: The development and validation of multisystemic therapy programs. *Annual Review of Clinical Psychology* 7: 351–381. doi:10.1146/annurev-clinpsy-032210-104615.

Heron, M. 2013. Deaths: Leading Causes for 2010. National Vital Statistics Report, Atlanta, GA: Centers for Disease Control and Prevention.

Lewinsohn, P M, Paul R, and John R S. 1996. Adolescent suicidal ideation and attempts: Prevalence, risk factors, and clinical implications. *Clinical Psychology: Science and Practice* 3 (1): 25–46.

Lock, J, M C La Via, and CQI AACAP. 2015. Practice parameter for the assessment and treatment of children and adolescents with eating disorders. *Journal of the American Academy of Child and Adolescent Psychiatry* 54 (5): 412–425.

Mahajan, P, E R Alpern, Jackie G-P, James C, Lydia D, Richard H, Elizabeth J et al. 2009. Epidemology of psychiatric-related visits to emergency departments in a multicenter collaborative research pediatric network. Perdiatric Emergency Care 25 (11): 715–720.

McClellan, J, Saundra S, and AACAP. 2013. Practice parameter for the assessment and treatment of children and adolescents with schizophrenia. *Journal of the American Academy of Child and Adolescent Psychiatry* 52 (9): 976–990.

Merikangas, K R, E F Nakamura, and R C Kessler. 2009. Epidemiology of mental disorders in children and adolescents. *Dialogues in Clinical Neuroscience* 11 (1): 7–20.

Miller, A L, J H Rathus, and Marsha L. 2007. *Dialectical Behavior Therapy With Suicidal Adolescents.* New York: Guliford Press.

Miller, T R, and D M Taylor. 2005. Adolescent suicidality: Who will ideate, who will act? *Suicide and Life Threatening Behavior* 35 (4): 425–435.

Rosen, D. 2013. Arresting a teen girl for dozing off in class? Why normal kid behavior is treated as a crime or psychiatric disorder: What happened to kids being kids? *Alternet.* May 16. http://alternet.org/civil-liberties/arresting-teen-gril-dozing-class-why-normal-kid-behavior-treated-crime-or.

Rotheram-Borus, M J, J Piacentini, C Cantwell, T R Belin, and J Song. 2000. The 18-month impact of an emergency room intervention for adolescent female suicide attempters. *Journal of Consulting and Clinical Psychology* 68 (6): 1081–1093.

Santucci, K, J Sather, and M Douglas. 2000. Psychiatry-related visits to the pediatric emergency department: A growing epidemic? *Pediatric Research* 47 (4 suppl 2): 117A.

Sills, M R, and S D Bland. 2002. Summary statistics for pediatric psychiatric vsits to us emergency departments, 1993–1999. *Pediatrics* 110 (4): e40.

Simon, A E, and K C Schoendorf. 2014. Emergency department visits for mental health conditions among US Children, 2001–2011. *Clinical Pediatrics* 53 (14): 1359–1366. doi:10.1177/000992814541806.

Resource

Find Law. n.d. New York Public Health Law 2504. Enabling certain persons to consent for certain medical, dental, health and hospital services. Find Law. http://codes.findlaw.com/ny/public-health-law/pbh-sect-2504.html.

Chapter 17

Correctional Emergency Psychiatry

Neil Leibowitz

Contents

17.1	Overview	290
17.2	Types of Correctional Facilities	290
17.3	Cost Implications	290
17.4	Legal Overview	291
17.5	Capacity	292
17.6	Intake and the New Admissions Process	292
17.7	Encounters Confidentiality and Safety	294
	17.7.1 Confidentiality Exceptions	294
17.8	Drug Use	295
17.9	Suicide Risk in Corrections	295
	17.9.1 Non-Suicidal Self-Injury	296
17.10	Injuries	297
17.11	Medication Issues	297
17.12	Agitation as a Result of Confinement	297
17.13	Cell Extractions and Use of Force	298
17.14	De-Escalation	298
17.15	Psychiatrist's Role in the Disciplinary Proceeding	298
17.16	Hunger Strikes	299
17.17	Court-Ordered Evaluations	299
17.18	Treatment of Corrections Officers	300
17.19	Tele-Health	300
17.20	Summary	300
References		300
Resources		302

17.1 Overview

Over 2 million Americans are currently incarcerated. The United States represents 5% of the world's population but houses nearly 25% of the world's incarcerated (Collier 2014). The number of inmates with significant mental illness has skyrocketed over the last 50 years. There are many theories for this. In part, this has been the result of deinstitutionalization, which began in the 1950s. A second important cause has been the War on Drugs. As more mentally ill patients left long-term hospitals, and outpatient needs for housing and treatment have not kept pace with demand, jails and prisons have become de facto psychiatric hospitals. Persons with mental illness are 64% more likely to be arrested than those without mental health problems (Theinhaus and Piasecki 2007). It is only in the last few years that this has been recognized as a public health crisis. Currently, many municipalities are making efforts to increase diversion and alternatives to incarceration; however, it is unclear whether the proper resources are in place to make this strategy successful.

Regardless of the reasons, providing emergent psychiatric care and crisis management is an imperative skill for those practicing behind bars. Providing these types of interventions is more complex in correctional settings than typical emergency rooms. Among the many issues that will discussed are physical plant design issues, difficulty providing proper supervision, and issues with the custodial nature in corrections. A major take-home point is that the correctional facility was not conceived as a place to provide mental healthcare to the significantly mentally ill population.

17.2 Types of Correctional Facilities

Correctional facilities can be categorized several ways in the United States, but the main grouping is prisons and jails. Jails are where pretrial detainees are held. A pretrial detainee is someone who has been arrested, charged, and then either not given bail or cannot afford bail. They remain in this status until their case is adjudicated. After a person is convicted, and if they are sentenced to more than one year, they are transferred to prison. Those that are sentenced to under a year generally serve the sentence in jail. There are other types of facilities, such as juvenile detention centers for minors and detention centers (e.g., Guantanamo Bay). In terms of size, there is a great deal of variability. There are small county jails, which may have an average daily population of 100 or less and large jails or prisons where 2500 inmates may be housed in a single structure (Minton 2011).

Jails tend to be more volatile as the length of stay is often brief and the inmates generally are coming from the community (or street). The population turns over up to 25 times a year in jails (Weedon 2003). Many of the clinical scenarios mirror those seen in an emergency room. Prison tends to be a more stable population as the inmates can be there for years (or life) and are often transferred after spending time in jail where they have already been stabilized. As such, it is easier to deliver psychiatric services in prison where there are fewer acute clinical situations. With this in mind, the focus of this chapter will be primarily on the jail system.

17.3 Cost Implications

When patients require inpatient levels of care or interventions that cannot be done at the correctional facility, the correctional system generally sends patients out to local emergency rooms or hospitals. There are a limited number of correctional facilities that have onsite inpatient psychiatric care or hospitals, these facilities are the exception rather than the rule. When a patient needs to go out to an emergency room, the impact on cost is substantial. In addition to the cost associated with the emergency room visit, each inmate must have custodial supervision. Often, the officers that accompany the inmate remain with him/her, this can often mean overtime pay for them. Typical emergency department visits can take 12–20 hours from the time the inmate is sent (including transportation). The average cost of an emergency department visit in the correctional system above and beyond the typical cost associated with standard emergent care is often several thousand dollars more than a typical emergency room visit (Schaenman et al. 2013).

Emergency rooms around the country, with few exceptions are, ill-equipped to handle detainees. Hospitals have legitimate safety concerns with comingling detainees with community patients. Corrections has concerns regarding the ability to be in a secure space where the inmate cannot obtain contraband. From a business perspective, hospitals do not want their community patients to have to comingle with detainees, out of concern that patients will be averse to seeking emergency care in a hospital that puts them in proximity to prisoners.

Many emergency rooms have a relatively small footprint. Inmates tend to require more space due to the desire on both corrections and hospital administrators and staff not to comingle the civilian and inmate population. This can create backup in the emergency room and affect their workflow.

17.4 Legal Overview

To understand healthcare in corrections it is important to provide a brief legal overview (note that this is only a cursory summary and there is significant case law related to this topic). Care in correctional facilities is unique in that inmates are afforded a constitutional right to healthcare.

Upon entry into the correctional system, the governing body (county, state, federal) is required to provide for all necessities for life that incarcerated persons are unable to obtain on their own. This is interpreted as food, clothing, shelter, and medical care. The Supreme Court has recognized that under the 8th Amendment barring cruel and unusual punishment (for prisoners) and the 14th amendment due process clause (for jails/pretrial detainees), inmates have the right to healthcare (Cohen 1988). In 1976, in Estelle v. Gamble (429 U.S. 97, 1976) the Supreme Court held that it is unconstitutional for prison officials to be "deliberately indifferent" to the serious medical needs of prisoners in their custody. In 1977, in Bowring v. Mills (551 F.2d 44, 4th Cir. 1977) the federal courts extended this ruling to psychiatric care equating it with medical treatment.

Standards of care in correctional facilities tend to vary state by state. Unlike hospitals, there is no federal regulating body such as the Joint Commission (JACHO) for the healthcare provided in jails. However, the American Correctional Association (ACA) has published standards for correctional institutions, and the National Commission on Correctional Healthcare (NCCHC) has published healthcare standards for correctional facilities (American Correctional Association 2010; National Commission on Correctional Healthcare 2014a; National Commission on Correctional Healthcare 2014b). These standards are not mandated, although many facilities are accredited by the NCCHC and voluntarily agree to comply with the standards. It is important to be aware that even complying with these standards does not guarantee 24-hours-a-day mental healthcare. In small facilities, the presence of a psychiatrist may be limited to just a few hours a week.

17.5 Capacity

Decision-making capacity represents an important acute assessment for psychiatrists in correctional settings. It is also an area of correctional healthcare where neither the hospital setting nor the outpatient setting properly mirrors the clinical scenarios that the emergency psychiatrist faces.

As in the hospital, any physician may make capacity determinations. Psychiatrists are the specialists in complex capacity scenarios. A large percentage of capacity cases relate to refusal of healthcare at intake. As mentioned earlier, since many inmates are arrested off the street, it is important that they be properly evaluated at intake for acute medical problems including withdrawal. Clinical reasons for refusal may be due to acute mental illness, intoxication, acute withdrawal, or even delirium. An important reason for refusal is that inmates are often upset and volatile at the time of arrest and need some adjustment to the system. It is important to use therapeutic skills to engage the patient in a capacity evaluation, which may lead to compliance. The process from arrest to triage by a medical professional can take up to 48 hours. During that time, many inmates have not had any medication (diabetes, blood pressure, etc.) or treatment. There are systems that have a pre-arraignment screening where the goal is to avoid preventable medical morbidity and mortality due to delay of treatment (Cloud 2015; Fishman 2016). The psychiatrist should pay close attention to missed medical conditions and withdrawal symptoms and be prepared to send the patient to the hospital or re-refer them to the internist for clinical management.

During the course of an incarceration, capacity evaluations may be requested due to refusals of treatment. Common referrals are due to refusals of treatment for long-term illnesses, such as diabetes treatment (finger sticks or insulin) or life-threatening illnesses such as cancer treatment. It is important for the psychiatrist to discuss the case with the medical team requesting the consult due to the unique nature of the correctional setting. As it is not a hospital, opportunities for medication over objection may not be available. For example, a patient with a hypertensive urgency may lack capacity to refuse his blood pressure medications. However, in a case like this, correctional care is akin to an outpatient clinic. If the patient refuses, the only intervention would be to send the inmate to the emergency room. While sad, the same paradigm would apply to a patient with cancer refusing treatment. In the majority of cases, the only intervention would be to hospitalize the inmate when he/she refuses if medically necessary.

A controversial area in correctional emergency care is capacity assessments due to refusal of emergency care or a refusal of transfer to a higher level of care. Corrections facilities transport patients offsite for a plethora of healthcare related reasons. Low-risk transfers are usually done by officers in corrections vehicles. High-risk situations (such as an acute myocardial infarction) are transferred via ambulance. While the percentage is low, a surprising number of patients refuse ambulance transfer. It is unclear whether a capacity evaluation is required given that the physician, by activating emergency medical services (EMS), may imply that a medical emergency and capacity would not be required. However, due to limitations in subacute care or situations where the degree of the emergency is not as clear, a capacity evaluation may be required in order to transfer the inmate over their objection. Key reasons for refusal of transfer that would warrant a determination of lack of capacity relate to a passive suicide attempt or psychosis (such as delusions relating to the transfer).

17.6 Intake and the New Admissions Process

The first point of contact an inmate makes with a healthcare provider is during intake. Intake is the admission process into a correctional facility. It involves activities by corrections officers, such as a search of the inmate and an orientation where the inmate receives the rules of the facility. Traditionally, after that portion of the intake is done there is a triage process, which may be conducted, usually by a nurse or a physician.

Intake is a particularly precarious time in jails. Many inmates are coming directly from the streets and it is difficult to establish a working diagnosis and hence ascertain what treatments are needed.

The general standard is that new inmates have a health screen within 4 hours (National Commission on Correctional Healthcare 2014a; National Commission on Correctional Healthcare 2014b). This includes a mental health and substance abuse screen. In small facilities, this information may be gathered by a corrections officer who has received supplemental health training. In larger facilities, this is often done by nurses (although other health professionals may be used). Inmates with abnormal behaviors or acute findings may be referred to psychiatry urgently. Major risks at this time relate to suicidality, acute psychosis and intoxication, or withdrawal. It is worth reiterating that in the majority of facilities, there is no 24-hour psychiatric coverage and emergencies may need to be handled by nurses overnight with phone guidance by the psychiatric provider.

The three key areas of screening on intake are for substance intoxication and withdrawal, suicidality, and psychosis. Many facilities use a checklist for suicidality. A proper screening should include a detailed substance abuse history focusing on acute intoxication and withdrawal in order to identify those inmates that may require a detox protocol or enhanced monitoring. Inmates may hide a history of substance use for fear that it will negatively impact their case. Generally, correctional facilities have standardized withdrawal protocols that include tools to evaluate symptoms (such as the clinical institute withdrawal assessment of alcohol scale [CIWA], or clinical opiate withdrawal scale [COWS], etc.). Based on the results, benzodiazepine tapers for alcohol and benzodiazepines use can be used. A limited number of facilities use methadone or buprenorphine and naloxone tapers for opiate use, and the majority provide supportive symptom management with mediations such as clonidine.

Symptom-triggered therapy may be used for inmates at low risk of acute withdrawal. Although it requires more medication, due to the challenges of monitoring. Unless the inmate is in a setting with a high degree of monitoring such as an infirmary, for those at high risk of withdrawal, use of a taper is a safer alternative. Complicated withdrawal (i.e., liver cirrhosis) should be managed at either an infirmary or hospital setting.

There have been many deaths related to overdose or acute withdrawal. In addition to the difficulty in getting an adequate substance use history, this can be due to a delay in presenting the patient to a physician due to a lengthy arrangement period, contraband (drugs) smuggled in by the inmate or peers, or a healthcare provider missing the signs and symptoms of withdrawal or overdose. Due to the risk of overdose, Rikers has given both the medical and custodial staff inhaled naloxone to use in the event of an unconscious patient. Efforts like these can decrease mortality rates.

The other reason for a complete substance use assessment is that jail suicide is closely linked with substance use. Half of completed suicides in lockup occur in inmates with a history of substance abuse (Hayes 2005). Many of these may be due to intoxication or withdrawal.

Many immediate psychiatric evaluations that occur upon intake are due to altered mental status. Psychiatrists must rule out acute intoxication, substance-induced psychosis, or withdrawal in these scenarios. In addition to withdrawal, stimulant intoxication, including primarily from amphetamines and cocaine, can present as psychosis. More recently, synthetic marijuana (such as Spice or K2) has become a drug of abuse in correctional settings (Schoenly 2015). This is in part because it does not show up in urine drug screens. Generally, this type of intoxication would need to be managed in a medical setting.

The paradigm that alcohol and benzodiazepine withdrawal can be life-threatening and opiate withdrawal is merely uncomfortable does not apply in correctional facilities. Once an inmate is housed, they may not have the level of access to medical care that civilians have. Additionally, in the housing area, the corrections officers are the eyes and ears and may not recognize signs and symptoms of decompensation due to withdrawal. While not common, death due to dehydration secondary to heroin or other opioid withdrawal is a significant risk and should not be taken lightly. Psychiatrists should ensure that symptom management and appropriate follow-up occur.

17.7 Encounters Confidentiality and Safety

The balance between privacy and security is a particularly challenging one in correctional settings. Often, facilities are older structures and were not designed with patient confidentiality in mind. Depending on the setting, patients may be seen in cubicles or an office within eyesight of an officer. In more acute instances, the visit can take place in their housing area (cell side) or in other places in the facility (such as in the yard or on a corrections bus).

Whenever possible, encounters should be conducted in private settings. Providers in correctional settings may choose to have inmates with a history of aggression toward staff or corrections officers be cuffed, in other facilities this may be mandated. Due to safety concerns, careful attention is placed on the location of correctional officers. Correctional officers should be at a distance where possible to ensure safety of staff, but they should be beyond earshot of the encounter if possible. In settings where there are additional safety concerns, the corrections officer may be present in the room or cubicle. For these visits, the officer becomes part of the treatment team and is bound by confidentiality. It is important to explain to the officer and the inmate that the officer is bound by confidentiality rules as a member of the treatment team. Otherwise, the evaluation may be inaccurate due to inmate concerns that the officer will share the inmate's health information with other officers or inmates. Unfortunately, at times, inmate information is shared with other inmates. This is particularly problematic when an inmate has a pedophilia charge. There is a hierarchy among inmates and those with certain charges are at an enormous safety risk.

One other important consideration is charge history. It is important from a clinical standpoint to know what an inmate is charged or convicted of. Knowing whether it is his first incarceration or whether he is facing serious charges can help guide the evaluation. These are risk factors in assessing suicidality. Also, knowing that a patient was arrested for multiple assaults or for assaulting a healthcare worker may influence decisions, such as whether to have a patient cuffed or have a security chaperone in the room during that visit.

17.7.1 Confidentiality Exceptions

Confidentiality of information obtained during treatment is generally protected in treatment of detainees. However, along with standard community exceptions, such as acute risk of suicidal or of homicidal behaviors, other additional limitations may be warranted. Other exceptions include information regarding an escape, dangerous contraband (such as weapons), and information requiring coordination of care with corrections (such as communicating the need to have a patient transported to an oncologist, which would essentially require the disclosure that the inmate is suffering from cancer). As mentioned previously, certain exceptions to confidentiality during the visit due to provider safety are also permitted.

Prisoners represent a protected class. As such, detainees do not have the ability to consent to sex. The Prison Rape Elimination Act (PREA) overrides confidentiality, and any instance of reported sexual assault must be reported in accordance with the facilities protocol. This extends to acts reported while incarcerated relating to any sexual assault occurring in a custodial setting.

Private space in the standard doctor–patient interaction is very important. In correctional settings it is paramount, as inmates with mental illness represent a vulnerable population that may be targeted. If privacy cannot be achieved, it may lead to patients not seeking treatment or not fully disclosing critical information. A refusal to leave the cell and come to the clinic should not be seen as a refusal until discussed with the inmate. They may fear seeking help due to risk of harm from another inmate or officer retaliation. Clearly, in acute situations such as concern of a patient decompensating, a patient may be seen in a less than ideal location such as their cell.

17.8 Drug Use

More than 50% of inmates have a substance use disorder at the time of their entry into the criminal justice system (Rich et al. 2011). This has significant treatment implications as mentioned in the previous discussion about intake. The emergency psychiatrist should never discount acute intoxication just because the inmate has been in the facility for a long period of time.

As mentioned previously, there is significant access to contraband in correctional facilities. It cannot be assumed that inmates are drug free. One real life example is an inmate in isolation that was found to have a cell phone, marijuana, cocaine, and a razor in his cell. Drugs may get smuggled to inmates via officers, civilian staff, visitors, newly arrested inmates, or even through cleverer ways, such as melting buprenorphine and putting it on the back of postage stamps. Overdoses occur in correctional facilities relatively often. These occur with inmates both new to the system and with a relatively long-length of stay (Salinger 2015; St John 2016).

Given that addiction rates among the incarcerated are very high, inmates may abuse whatever drugs they can obtain. Drugs may be laced or be impure. Epidemics that have affected the community have spread to jails and prisons with tainted drugs, most recently with tainted marijuana (Bassett 2015). Finally, medications that are often used to treat mental illness, such as quetiapine or bupropion can be crushed and inhaled. The emergency psychiatrist should always keep intoxication in the differential diagnosis. It is recommended that officers and health staff carry naloxone in the event of an unconscious inmate.

17.9 Suicide Risk in Corrections

One of the most common emergency referrals in correctional facilities is for suicidality. This can be either due to a self-harm event, an inmate claiming to have suicidal thoughts, a family member or friend informing the facility staff that the inmate is at high risk of suicide, or a referral from an officer or inmate in the inmate's housing area. Suicide risk in correctional facilities is higher than that of the general population. It is the leading cause of death in jails and the fifth leading cause in prisons (Noonan 2012). Depending on methodology and type of facility, the suicide rate may be several times higher than that of the community (National Institute of Corrections 2010). Incarceration, in and of itself, is a risk factor for suicide. Heightened times of risk occur during admission, times of new or additional legal charges, setbacks in an inmate's case, receipt of long sentences or unexpected outcomes, receipt of bad news or a bad phone call, in times after a trauma (assault), times of increased isolation or segregation, or due to an increased acuity of mental illness. Suicide risk rating assessments designed for correctional institutions may be used in concert with clinical judgment to properly evaluate the inmate's risk level for suicide.

It is important to not just dismiss self-harm as a manipulative gesture, and the psychiatrist must take these events seriously. As in all suicide assessments, addressing the underlying issue is important in management. However, in the short term, the inmate may require enhanced supervision. Correctional facilities all have protocols for when an inmate is identified as an acute risk of attempting suicide. This entails active monitoring, either in person or via video. Where active staff monitoring cannot safely be done in the correctional facility, the patient should be transferred to the hospital.

17.9.1 Non-Suicidal Self-Injury

Acts designed to cause self-harm but not death represent a significant cause of emergency referrals in a correctional setting. These include ingesting, banging, cutting, and burning. The methods of non-suicidal self-injury (NSSI) can be shocking. Certain inmates swallow items that they can get a hold of. We treated an inmate who over the course of his incarceration (approximately 2 years) swallowed over 100 items including plastic forks, spoons, and batteries. He had more than 30 endoscopic procedures to retrieve items he swallowed that presented a risk of perforation. Another major management issue is inmates who open wounds creating significant infection risk. There are many cases where NSSI went awry and resulted in a completed suicide.

These events can occur in conjunction with or in the absence of underlying psychiatric disorders. Although they are more common in inmates with personality disorders (cluster B and mixed), they can also present in psychotic disorders, mood disorders, and in inmates with developmental delay (American Psychiatric Association 2015). Whether in conjunction with a psychiatric disorder or not, environmental or interpersonal factors may be the trigger.

While typical community diagnoses and behaviors, such as borderline behavior may be the cause of NSSI, other causes are related to safety or location. An inmate may feel unsafe in his housing area secondary to a conflict with another inmate, custodial staff, or due to gang affiliations. The act is an attempt to be moved to a safer location. Self-harm may also be a way for an inmate to assert control and autonomy in an environment where they have limited control. It can also be a method to retaliate against staff.

Recent studies have shown that, independent of underlying diagnoses, rates of NSSI for inmates in segregation are higher than those of inmates in other types of housing areas (Kaba et al. 2014). It is important that the treating provider attempt to find the precipitant for the behavior, and if security related, discuss this with corrections staff to determine the appropriate course of action.

At times, inmates may self-harm for secondary gain. Reasons include desire to be placed in a setting such as a hospital, which may have easier visitation, be safer, or have better food, or to be transferred to a different housing unit. It is important for the psychiatrist to conduct a full assessment and create a plan that minimizes the risk of occurrence, rather than focusing on whether the self-harm was in fact a suicide attempt or not. This includes partnering with the medical and custodial team, as these patients are often high utilizers of healthcare and are highly disruptive. At times these inmates require a suicide watch or enhanced observation due to the increased risk of self-harm, even though they do not actually want to kill themselves.

Additionally, suicidal ideation represents a large number of emergency referrals. As in the NSSI, it is critical to find the underlying reason for the ideation and to develop an appropriate treatment to help mitigate the risk of a suicide.

17.10 Injuries

When evaluating an inmate due to an acute referral, the psychiatrist should also be wary of inmates that present with multiple medical injuries that do not seem consistent; for example, a 25-year-old inmate with 4 slip and falls in a 2-month period. This can indicate trauma of either a physical or sexual nature and presents an opportunity for the psychiatrist to try to elicit the true nature of these injuries. While in many cases the inmate will not volunteer information, asking about it may improve the therapeutic alliance and allow the treating psychiatrist to elicit important information.

17.11 Medication Issues

In correctional facilities, there is the ability to give immediate (STAT) medications for patients in acute need; for example, when the inmate has psychotic aggression. However, the environment is one where it may be challenging to properly supervise the patient after administration of the medication. While oral STAT doses of psychotropic medications are common, STAT injections are much less frequent in correctional institutions. It is often difficult to administer STAT medications in the correctional facility housing area and the patient must be brought to the clinic. The risk of harm to both the inmate and the staff during the administration of these medications is great. Additionally, most of the nursing and correctional staff are not trained to safely administer STAT injections in a crisis situation.

Often, patients are referred for potential overdoses of prescription medication. Psychiatrists in correctional settings should be aware that it is possible that inmates are concealing their medications (via "cheeking") and either hoarding them to commit suicide or selling them to other inmates. These allegations should be investigated and the inmates should receive appropriate medical attention where needed.

17.12 Agitation as a Result of Confinement

Agitation is a cause of psychiatric emergencies. Agitation sometimes occurs as a result of psychiatric decompensation. However, it can also be the result of confinement or a combination of the two problems. Inmates with mental illness often struggle with confinement, especially in a segregation or isolation setting. This can lead to psychosis including paranoia and hallucinations as well as aggression and suicidality (Scharff Smith 2006). Other acting out behaviors can be seen in extreme cases, such as ingestion of dangerous objects (forks, spoons, batteries, etc.) or feces smearing. In cases where the agitation is a result of confinement, part of the treatment may be a medical order to temporarily remove the inmate from the setting they are in to a safer setting for that individual.

17.13 Cell Extractions and Use of Force

There are numerous reasons for an inmate to refuse to leave their cell. Examples include not wanting to go to court, not wanting the cell to be searched, or acute psychiatric decompensation. Generally, when an inmate needs to be extracted from a cell, these events are governed by correctional policies and procedures even if dealing with mentally ill inmates. It is common for these procedures to call for mental health intervention prior to the use of force or extraction of a mentally ill patient. This involves the treatment provider going to the patient and attempting to convince them to voluntarily comply with the correctional officer's request. This is a setting where the psychiatrist can use their de-escalation skills to get the inmate to comply. In many situations, the inmate wants to make their needs known or needs to feel they have some control of the situation, and with some coaxing, risk of harm to the inmate and corrections staff can be avoided. Part of the evaluation is to determine if the inmate is refusing to leave due to psychiatric decompensation. If that is determined to be the case, then the psychiatrist will then advise corrections on the best way to treat the inmate. If the cause is not due to mental illness and attempts to get the inmate to comply fail, then rather than authorize the use of force to extract the inmate, the psychiatrist will let the corrections officer know mental illness is not the cause of the inmate's refusal to leave the cell.

17.14 De-Escalation

Another emergent role for correctional providers is that of de-escalation. Inmates may require interventions to avert dangerous situations. Implementation of crisis intervention teams made up of corrections officers and treatment providers may be deployed to manage acute situations and avoid uses of force. Crisis intervention has been increasingly used by police forces around the country to de-escalate situations (Compton et al. 2008). It is just being introduced in correctional settings as jurisdictions come to the realization that using force to de-escalate conflicts is not effective.

17.15 Psychiatrist's Role in the Disciplinary Proceeding

In routine correctional care, psychiatrists may be asked to evaluate an inmate to determine if it is appropriate to place the inmate in a disciplinary or solitary setting. Inmate are placed in solitary confinement due to breaking jail or prison's rules, the reasons can range from having contraband to assaulting an officer. This evaluation looks only at the inmate's psychiatric stability to be in isolation for long periods of time. While most of the time these evaluations occur in the course of routine interactions, for certain high-level offenses such as an assault on staff, these may be emergency referrals. These interactions invoke difficult ethical issues such as dual loyalty. However, the psychiatrist should limit his involvement to determining if there is a psychiatric condition and the extent that the condition caused the behavior that led to the infraction. While preferably, the person conducting the evaluation should not be the inmate's treating clinician, in a STAT setting, this may not be feasible. Informed consent should be obtained and any limitation on confidentiality should be explained. While nuanced, the psychiatrist should not be a decision maker in the disciplinary process due to ethical concerns.

In a clear-cut example, an inmate was produced for a STAT evaluation to be cleared for isolation after an assault on staff. After the evaluation, the psychiatrist determined that the inmate was acutely psychotic and it was unsafe to place him in solitary confinement. The inmate was then sent to the local hospital for admission to the inpatient forensic unit.

The American Psychiatric Association (2000) determined that no inmate should be placed in segregation (23-hour isolation with limited stimulation and social interactions) solely due to symptoms of mental illness, unless there is immediate danger for which there is no other reasonable temporary alternative. If an inmate is placed in seclusion due to mental illness, it should be for a short duration, with appropriate monitoring and treatment, and only until he is able to be transferred to an adequate clinical setting. Whether psychiatrists should be involved in the evaluation for clearance or not is currently being debated, and the clinician's role in this evaluation may change significantly in the next decade (National Commission on Correctional Healthcare 2014a; World Medical Association 2007).

Segregation is differentiated from seclusion for mental health and clinical reasons and from medical isolation due to a risk of communicable diseases. Seclusion and restraint in the community tends to be governed by regulations established by the Centers for Medicare and Medicaid Services. Most correctional facilities do not participate in Medicare or Medicaid systems, hence in the majority of facilities, those rules have not been adopted. In facilities that have the capacity to order seclusion and restraint, it should be done in the same manner as in community settings and in appropriate settings (Metzner et al. 2007).

17.16 Hunger Strikes

Hunger strikes are considered an expression of free speech. Hunger strikes may be considered a medical emergency and the psychiatrist may be called upon to issue a determination of capacity to make an informed decision regarding continuing the hunger strike. While these are more prevalent in detention facilities housing political prisoners or persons at risk of deportation, they also occur in other types of correctional facilities. However, data on hunger strikes in jails and prisons are rare. The role of the psychiatrist is to evaluate the reasons for the hunger strike, the medical stability, and the inmate's capacity, which includes psychiatric conditions as well as their understanding of the consequences of their actions (Crosby et al. 2007).

In the emergent setting, the role of the psychiatrist is to determine if mental illness is a cause for the hunger strike. Mental health causes for a hunger strike may be related to psychosis or delusions that surround the food, such as the belief that corrections officers are poisoning the food. Other causes may be related to depression and a desire to commit suicide, an eating disorder or self-care. In these cases, if the inmate is found to have an acute mental illness that is causing the hunger strike (and thus lacks capacity), then treatment should be started including intravenous fluids and nasogastric feedings.

17.17 Court-Ordered Evaluations

It is common for an inmate to act out in court. A judge may order an evaluation or place an inmate on a suicide watch. These acts are not binding and are treated as STAT requests for evaluation. The treating psychiatrist should act on the basis of his risk assessment and evaluation while looking at the reasoning of the referring person (judge, attorney, etc.) as a source of collateral information. At times the inmate has issues warranting treatment. However, other times the inmate may be upset over the court proceeding or act out for reasons that don't warrant a change in his treatment plan.

17.18 Treatment of Corrections Officers

During the course of care in a correctional facility, staff may be called on to treat correction officers or other civilians. The cause of this may be due to a referral from medicine, such as anxiety or alternatively may be secondary to trauma. One instance is after an inmate suicide. In addition to checking in with inmates in the housing area and assessing them for trauma, there may be staff who are also traumatized by the event. Particularly at risk, are the officers that found the inmate and the first responders. However, any officer who had contact with that inmate, such as those assigned to his housing area may require care. Treatment of non-inmates tends to be only on an acute, single visit basis. Follow-up care, if necessary, is then done by community providers.

17.19 Tele-Health

As mentioned previously, most facilities do not have 24-hour psychiatry coverage. Larger systems of care, such as New York City, have 24-hour psychiatry, but even that is limited and often involves coverage by one psychiatrist for several facilities that are available for consult. In many cases, smaller facilities, such as county correctional facilities may not even have psychiatrist phone coverage on the overnight shift (National Commission on Correctional Healthcare 2014a; National Commission on Correctional Healthcare 2014b).

In cases where patient emergencies arise, the nurse may be able to call an on-call psychiatrist to guide him through the situation. This often leads to limited interventions or overtreatment in increased emergency room runs. Tele-psychiatry offers an important emerging way to provide improved care in these clinical situations. In addition to clinical visits, tele-psychiatry can also be used in an adjunctive manner as a way to properly observe an inmate after a crisis or for side effects or responses to STAT medication.

17.20 Summary

Correctional emergency psychiatry incorporates many of the facets of emergency room psychiatry. The increase in both the number and severity of mental illness in incarcerated populations has made the need for emergency psychiatry important. On an acute basis, treatment of suicidality, psychosis and drug intoxication and withdrawal make up a large share of the cases treated; as illustrated, there are unique scenarios faced in corrections that require specialized training to handle.

The custodial relationship and security issues create complex situations and treatment paradigms. For the correctional emergency psychiatrist, it is important to be attuned to the unique ethical issues that arise in providing this care and the additional patient risks associated with patients requiring acute care in the correctional setting.

References

American Correctional Association. 2010. *Core Jail Standards*. Alexandria, VA: American Correctional Association.

American Psychiatric Association. 2000. *Psychiatric Services in Jails and Prisons*, second edition. Washington DC: American Psychiatric Association.

American Psychiatric Association. 2013. *Diagnostic and Statistical Manual of Mental Disorders*, fifth edition. Arlington, VA: American Psychiatric Association.

American Psychiatric Association. 2015. *Psychiatric Services in Correctional Facilities*, third edition. Washington DC: American Psychiatric Association.

Bassett, M T. 2015. *2015 Advisory #6: Increase in Synthetic Cannabinoid (Marijuana): Related Adverse Events and Emergency Department Visits.* New York, April 17.

Cloud, D. 2015. Improving the health of arrestees: The pre-arraignment screening initiative. *Vera Institute of Justice.*. http://archive.vera.org/project/improving-health-arrestees-pre-arraignment-screening-initiative.

Cohen, F. 1988. *The Mentally Disordered Inmate and the Law.* Kingston, NJ: Civic Research Institute.

Collier, L. 2014. Incarceration Nation. *Monitor on Psychology*, October: 56.

Compton, M T, Masuma B, A C Watson, and J R Oliva. 2008. A comprehensive review of extant reserach on crisis intervention team (cit) program. *Journal of the American Academy of Psychiatry and the Law Online* 36 (1): 47–55.

Crosby, S S, C M Apovian, and Michael G. 2007. Hunger strikes, force-feeding, and physician's responsibilities. *The Journal of the American Medical Association* 298 (5): 563–566. doi:10.1001/jama.298.5.563.

Fishman, L. 2016. NYC health + hospitals expands pre-arraignment health screening at manhattan detention center. *NYC Health + Hospitals.* November 4. http://www.nychealthandhospitals.org/hhc/html/news/press-release-20161104-NYC-Health-Hospitals-expands-pre-arraignment-health-screening-at-manhattan-detention-center.shtml.

Hayes, L M. 2005. Suicide prevention in correctional facilities. In *Handbook of Correctional Mental Health*, by Charles L Scott and Joan B Gerbasi, 69–88. Washington DC: American Psychiatric Publishing.

Kaba, F, Andrea L, Sarah G-K, James H, David L, Howard A, Daniel S et al. 2014. Solitary confinement and risk of self harm among jail inmates. *American Journal of Public Health* 104 (3): 442–447. doi:10.2105/AJPH.2013.301742.

Metzner, J L, Kenneth T, John L, William R, P R Recupero, and Diane S. 2007. The use of restaint and seclusion in correctional mental health care. *Journal of the American Academy of Psychiatry and the Law* 35 (4): 417–425.

Minton, T D. 2011. *Jail Inmates at Midyear 2010: Statistical Tables.* Statistical Tables, Washington DC: Bureau of Justice Statistics.

National Commission on Correctional Healthcare. 2014a. *Jail Health Standards.* Chicago, IL: National Commission on Correctional Healthcare.

National Commission on Correctional Healthcare. 2014b. *Prison Health Standards.* Chicago, IL: National Commission on Correctional Healthcare.

National Institute of Corrections. 2010. *National Study of Jail Suicide: 20 Years Later.* National Study, Washington DC: National Institute of Corrections.

Noonan, M E. 2012. *Mortality in Local Jails and State Prisons, 2000–2010: Statistical Tables.* Statistical Tables, Washington DC: Bureau of Justice Statistics.

Rich, J D, S E Wakeman, and S L Dickman. 2011. Medicine and the epidemic of incarceration in the united states. *New England Journal of Medicine* 364 (22): 2081–2083.

Salinger, T. 2015. Six westchester county inmates suffer apparent drug overdoses: Police. *New York Daily News*, July 20.

Schaenman, P, Elizabeth D, Reed J, and Reena C. 2013. *Opportunities for Cost Savings in Corrections Without Sacrificing Service Quality: Inmate Health Care.* Washington DC: Urban Institute.

Scharff S, Peter. 2006. The effects of solitary confinement on prison inmates: A brief history and review of the literature. *Crime and Justice* 34 (1): 441–528. doi:10.1086/500626.

Schoenly, L. 2015. Synthetic marijuana: A very real contraband hazard. Correctionsone.com. August 25. http://www.correctionsone.com/lorry-schoenly/articles/8720953-Synthetic-marijuana-A-very-real-contraband-hazard/.

St J, Paige. 2016. Illegal drugs are flowing into california's most guarded prisons and killing death row inmates. *Los Angeles Times*, August 24.
Weedon, J R. 2003. The role of jail is growing in the community. *Corrections Today*, April 1.
World Medical Association. 2007. WMA declaration of hamburg concerning support for medical doctors refusing to participate in, or condone, the use of torture or other forms of cruel, inhuman or degrading treatment. WMA.Net. May. http://www.wma.net/en/30publications/10policies/c19/.

Resources

Appelbaum, K L, J M Hickey, and Ira P. 2001. The role of correctional officers in multidisciplinary mental health care in prisons. *Psychiatric Services* 52 (10): 1343–1347. doi:10.1176/appi.ps.52.10.1343.
Appelbaum, K L, J A Savageau, R L Trestman, J L Metzner, and Jacques B. 2011. A national survey of self-injurious behavior in american prisons. *Psychiatric Services* 62 (3): 285–290. doi:10.1176/appi.ps.62.3.285.
Beck, A J, and T A Hughes. 2005. *Prison Rape Elimination Act of 2003: Sexual Violence Reported by Correctional Authorities 2004.* Bureau of Justice Statistics Special Report, Washington DC: U.S. Department of Justice.
Beck, A J, Marcus B, Rachel C, and Christopher K. 2013. *Sexual Victimization in Prisons and Jails Reported by Inmates.* National Survey, Washington DC: Bureau of Justice Statistics.
Centers for Medicare and Medicaid Services. 2016. Chapter 2: The Certification Process. In *State Operations Manual*, by Centers for Medicare and Medicaid Services, 2018–2020. Baltimore, MD: Centers for Medicare and Medicaid Services.
Fiscella, K, Naomi P, Sean M, and Paul F. 2004. Alcohol and opiate withdrawal in US jails. *American Journal of Public Health* 94 (9): 1522–1524.
Human Rights Watch. 2003. *Ill Equipped: U.S. Prisons and Offenders with Mental Illness.* New York: Human Rights Watch.
Karberg, J C, and D J James. 2002. *Substance Dependence, Abuse, and Treatment of Jail Inmates.* Special Report, Washington DC: Burea of Justice Statistics.
Knoll, J L. 2010. Suicide in correctional settings: Assessment, prevention, and professional liability. *Journal of Correctional Health Care* 16 (3): 188–204. doi:10.1177/1078345810366457.
Matlin, D. 2005. *Prisons: Inside the New America: From Vernooykill Creek to Abu Ghraib.* Berkley, CA: North Atlantic Books.
Metzner, J L, Fred C, L S Grossman, and R M Wettstein. 2000. Treatment in jails and prisons. In *Treatment of Offenders with Mental Disorders*, by Robert M Wettstein, 211–263. New York: Guilford Press.
Mumola, C J. 2005. *Suicide and Homicide in State Prisons and Local Jails.* Bureau of Justice Statistics Special Report, Washington DC: U.S. Department of Justice.
National Center on Institutions and Alternatives. 1995. *Prison Suicide: An Overview and Guide to Prevention.* Mansfield, MA: National Institute of Corrections.
National Commission on Correctional Healthcare. 2004. *Standards for Opioid Treatment in Correctional Facilities.* Chicago, IL: National Commission on Correctional Healthcare.
National Commission on Correctional Healthcare. 2008. *Standards for Mental Health Services in Correctional Facilities.* Chicago, IL: National Commission on Correctional Healthcare.
Peters, R H. 1992. Referral and screening for substance abuse treatment in jails. *The Journal of Mental Health Administration* 19 (1): 53–75. doi:10.1007/BF02521308.
Pierre, J M, Igor S, D A Wirshing, and W C Wirshing. 2004. Letter to the editor: Intranasal quetiapine abuse. *The American Journal of Psychiatry* 161 (9): 1718–1718. doi:10.1176/appi.ajp.161.9.1718.
Theinhaus, O J, and Melissa P. 2007. *Correctional Psychiatry: Practice Guidelines and Strategies.* Kigston, New Jersey: Civics Research Incorporated.
Thienhaus, O J, and Melissa P. 1997. Assessment of suicide risk. *Psychiatric Services* 48 (3): 293–294. doi:10.1176/ps.48.3.293.

Tonry, M. 2004. *Thinking About Crime: Sense and Sensibility in American Penal Culture.* New York: Oxford University Press.

U.S. Department of Justice. 2012. 28 CFR part 155: National standards to prevent, detect, and respond to prison rape; final rule. *Federal Register*, June 20: 37105-37232.

V

METHODS FOR OPERATIONAL IMPROVEMENT

Chapter 18

Introduction to Emergency Psychiatry Operational Improvement

Karen Murrell

Contents

18.1 Introduction 307
18.2 Background 308
18.3 Lean Defined 308
18.4 Case Study 309
18.5 Conclusion 312
References 313
Resources 313

18.1 Introduction

The purpose of the chapters in this section is to give the reader practical knowledge to improve emergency department psychiatric operations. It is very easy to obtain the knowledge of what needs to be done, but it is very different to transform this knowledge into real operational improvement. These chapters will provide a template for improvement and recommend resources if more in-depth research is required. Particularly in an area with as much cultural bias as emergency psychiatry, having a disciplined methodology for process improvement is key.

The basis of our improvement efforts will be designed around the Lean production system developed by the Japanese car company, Toyota. This system translates well into medical improvement. The core of the Lean production system is continuous improvement, promotion of "flow" through a system, disciplined methodologies for improvement, elimination of waste, and leadership development. Before designing a new system, we need to understand the current state of the system; in most cases, care is disjointed and chaotic.

18.2 Background

Sirens blaring, continuous beeping, chaos, and congestion. This is the emergency department (ED) in a nutshell. The ED is the doorway to the hospital serving people at some of the toughest times of their lives. The ED is open to all, 24/7, and there is no safety valve when capacity is reached. It is hard to imagine a worse place for restful healing. Now imagine if you were hearing voices that you could not control, felt out of touch with reality, and were having trouble controlling your actions. You come to the ED for help and instead of being placed in an area of quiet and calm, you are plopped right into the middle of this turbulent environment. You are seen by a doctor who robotically asks you if you have any medical concerns and does not ask you about your mental health. You are poked for blood, asked to urinate, all of your belongings are taken away, and you are put in a gurney in a hallway. A security guard stands by your side watching you continuously, bright lights are on at all times, and people are walking by you day and night without making any eye contact. Finally, a member of the psychiatric team comes to talk to you, but it is with a clipboard in the middle of the hall. They briefly ask you what is wrong and then leave again. You try to maintain control, but finally the stimulus is too much and you begin to yell for help and ask to leave. Instead of being asked about your concerns, you are injected with needles. Your arms and legs are tied until finally you fall asleep. This tragic situation occurs in EDs across the country every day, but it can be improved.

Mental illness is recognized as a growing problem throughout the world. An estimated one in four people have a diagnosable mental illness or substance use disorder at any given time (National Institute of Mental Health 2017). As community services are cut and budgets dwindle, the ED becomes the point of access to care for many patients. Many EDs across the country have found that Lean process improvement methodologies have helped them eliminate waits and provide improved care to patients. These same principles can be applied to the care of patients with psychiatric emergencies.

18.3 Lean Defined

Lean is an operations management approach to eliminating waste in a system. It was first described after a study of the success of the Toyota manufacturing system. Toyota surprised the car manufacturing world when they developed their "just in time" method of production. While other car companies had extensive inventory of parts built up in their warehouses, Toyota developed a "just in time" inventory system where the product flowed through the system with minimal waste—a "pull" system from the customer. This system meant that if there was a defective part identified, the worker immediately stopped the line and problems were fixed in real time.

Contrast this with other companies with piles of inventory where a problem would be identified months after production. This created a culture where everyone strived for continuous improvement.

Ohno (Liker 2004) developed the concept of "seven wastes" that are key in development of a Lean system:

- Overproduction (manufacturing an item before it is required)
- Waiting (idle time)
- Transporting
- Inappropriate processing

- Unnecessary inventory
- Excess motion
- Defects

In their book, *Lean Thinking*, James Womack and Daniel Jones (1996) describe the five-step process necessary for Lean manufacturing: defining customer value, defining the value stream, making the process "flow," "pulling" from the customer, and striving for excellence.

How does this apply the healthcare? These same applications can be used to transform healthcare operations, although it is a very complex service operation.

The key principles in Lean healthcare are (Crane and Noon 2011)

- Focusing on patient value
- Eliminating waste
- Promoting flow through the system
- Creating a culture of continuous improvement

Consider these principles in relation to ED psychiatry. Imagine if you were a patient coming into the ED, what would be of value to you?

Value in healthcare is the things that bring the patient closer to wellness: assessment by a clinician, medications if indicated, and a safe discharge or admission plan that is developed without delay.

Consider in relation to the seven wastes described previously:

- Overproduction: Unnecessary lab tests being ordered.
- Waiting (idle time): Waiting for hours or days for an inpatient psychiatric bed to become available.
- Transporting: Transport to an inpatient facility when active treatment in the ED could have allowed for discharge.
- Inappropriate processing: Being seen by a therapist when medication adjustments are indicated.
- Unnecessary inventory: Unnecessary supplies and equipment.
- Excess motion: Movement from place to place in order to find equipment, fax forms, multiple phone calls for placement.
- Defects: Any activity not done right the first time is waste. Ordering the wrong medication, calling repeatedly for patient placement, redraws of labs.

For all of us who work in emergency psychiatry, it is clear that there is much waste in the system. Emergency psychiatry in its current state would be an antonym to smooth flow. In the next sections, we will look at a case study where Lean principles improved an ED, then look at Lean tools that can be learned and applied quickly. Finally, a roadmap for improvement will be provided for the reader.

18.4 Case Study

This case study illustrates a systematic improvement effort in an emergency department. There are a number of tools that can be employed during a Lean transformation. This case study will illustrate how Lean can be used to transform an ED with an introduction to each step. The tools will then be discussed in greater detail in the next chapter with recommendations for ED psychiatry.

This story takes place at a West Coast hospital in the United States, a community hospital located in a city of 480,000 with a surrounding population approaching 2 million people. The ED has patient volumes of 120,000 visits per year with 41 licensed ED beds. The process improvement journey began in 2007 when new ED management with Lean training formed an ED team consisting of physicians, nursing, and ancillary staff members. The committee was committed to improve flow through the ED.

In late 2006, the ED was in crisis. ED volumes had increased from just over 60,000 in 2005 to 75,000 in 2009. There was little incentive to put patients in rooms, multiple rooms were being held for anticipated ambulances, there were inpatient holds, and patient and employee satisfaction was low. There were multiple hours of ambulance diversion. It was clear that the ED needed change.

By setting a vision and using Lean methodology, the department was able to make sustained improvements that catapulted them to becoming leaders in emergency medicine flow nationally. By teaching and reinforcing Lean methodology to frontline staff, the ED created a "community of scientists" that look at change and process improvement as part of their daily work routine. Helpful changes included development of patient "streams" that created high acuity beds for patients, and the creation of teams in the ED for improved communication and patient care. Even more important was the cultural transformation in the department that created ownership of each patient. This idea of improving both process and culture is key when making any change.

When the committee first met, they decided on a long-term *vision* for where they wanted the emergency department to go. This vision is key in any Lean transformation and helps to guide the team when deciding what projects to focus on. The committee decided their goal was "to be the best emergency department in America." They created a banner and posted it in the department, and the goal was communicated multiple times to all staff. This may sound unattainable, but having this vision helped guide the team as they moved forward.

As an aside, having a *multidisciplinary team* working on flow was invaluable. A key component of Lean is ideas from frontline staff—"going to the gemba" as it is called (Liker 2004). This means going to where the work is done to learn about problems and solutions and not just sitting in a conference room.

Lean is not a top-down approach. The fundamental idea of creating processes that are better for patients but easier for the staff is key. In this ED, the team consisted of about 15 people from all disciplines within the ED as well as ED leadership. While the team included only 15 people, the team continuously emphasized process improvement and Lean methodology to all staff. This consisted of frequent discussions at change of shift and even "bathroom Lean," where short bursts of Lean information was posted. All staff knew they could provide input and could request to join the committee at any time.

Before starting on any projects, the team identified *key metrics* so they would know that their work was improving patient care. In this project, key metrics were identified as follows:

- Patient arrivals by hour of the day by acuity level (see Figure 18.1)
- Admission and discharge percentages
- Door to doctor
- Doctor to disposition
- Disposition to departure
- Total length of stay, both overall and by patient acuity level

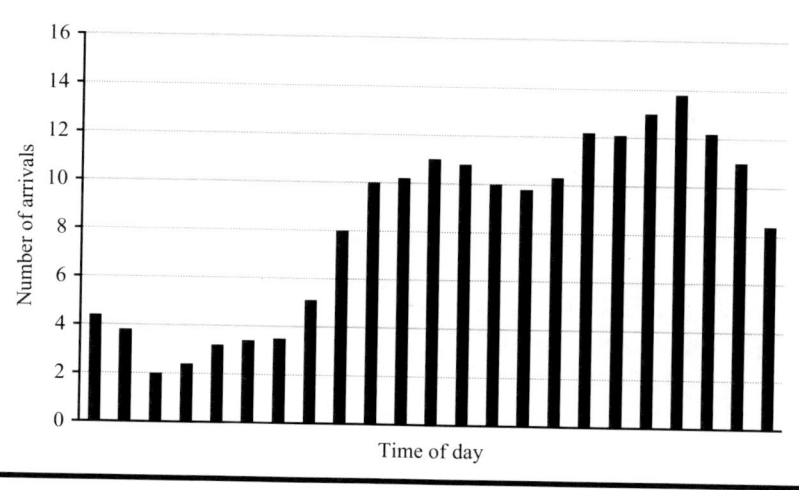

Figure 18.1 ED arrivals by hour of day.

- Left-without-being-seen percentage (this is when a patient arrives for treatment and decides to leave usually because of wait times)
- Ambulance diversion hours (again, when the ED is too busy and closes its door to ambulances requiring a trip to an ED, i.e., farther away)

As an aside, when improving ED psychiatry work, the priorities will change. In an ED, the disposition to departure metric is usually measured in minutes, while for psychiatric patients this can be hours or days. This requires different projects, but the processes are the same. Figure 18.1 illustrates ED arrivals by hour of day for a single ED, but interestingly enough the arrival patterns look the same for most EDs in the country, with the arrival line shifting up or down depending on volume.

In a national study of U.S. ED visits for psychiatric complaints by time of presentation, the graph also looked similar (Doshi et al. 2005). The challenge with these patients is the long length of stay and lack of resources that makes it difficult to staff by arrival pattern.

Now that the team had identified metrics, they considered where to start their improvement journey. They decided to start with something completely under control of the ED as a first step.

In 2007, the first project the team implemented was a "rapid care" process for low acuity patients. The throughput committee identified multiple barriers that were in place that prevented a patient from seeing a provider.

Prior to the rapid care process, the patient flow was similar to many other EDs. On arrival, patients were met by a clerk/greeter who determined if there was a need for immediate rooming into the patient care area. There were multiple delays for noncritical patients prior to evaluation by a physician.

The team decided to hold a *Kaizen event* to make these improvements. A Kaizen event is usually a 3–5 day event with the objective of changing a process for the better within the time frame. There is a clear framework, and the goal is a disruptive innovation where a process is looked in a very systematic way.

One of the first steps in a Kaizen event is doing a *value stream map* of the process. This map identifies activities that are of value to the patient versus those non-value-added activities that can be eliminated.

In this case, the triage and admitting processes were streamlined to remove waste. A rapid care physician was placed in an area immediately adjacent to the triage area, which decreased unnecessary movement and allowed the physician to immediately address triage questions, thus decreasing mis-triages. The rapid care physician was closely partnered with one nurse to increase efficiency through improved communication and teamwork.

This process was initiated as a trial in February 2007, although it looked very different than it does today. In the spirit of Lean, there were multiple trials and continuous improvement until the final process was identified.

Following the initiation of this system, the flow process was much improved for patients presenting to the ED with a low acuity complaint. Metrics showed dramatic improvement immediately, with a length of stay that dropped in half for these patients. The left-without-being-seen metric dropped from 4.5% on average to under 1% where it has remained since. Interestingly, creating this system for low acuity patients (about 25% of total volume) also created capacity in the main ED for the high acuity patients.

The total length of stay for all patients dropped from 4.23 hours to just over 3 hours. Patient and staff satisfaction were much improved as well.

Basic *queuing theory* states that the only way to increase capacity is to decrease arrivals and/or to decrease length of stay. This project did both things for the main ED: it decreased arrivals to the main ED beds as these patients were "triaged to home," and decreased length of stay by allowing main ED staff to focus on the sicker patients.

After this project, hospital administration began to take notice of the positive changes in the ED. They visited and talked with staff involved in the project and had them present to the hospital. This project and the tangible recognition by leadership led to the cultural change in the department. While the rapid care system was designed to improve care for low acuity patients, the staff began to take ownership for all patients. Rooms were no longer held for possible ambulance arrivals and patients were roomed more quickly.

The throughput group then identified another area for potential improvement. The ED had 41 beds that were geographically spread far apart. Physicians complained about caring for patients at opposite ends of the department, and nurses complained about the lack of communication.

The team again developed a value stream map as well as a *spaghetti diagram* that showed how much walking each team member was doing. A spaghetti diagram uses a continuous flow line and traces the path of a person or activity through a process. It is eye-opening to identify redundancies and excess movement in a process.

The throughput group decided to do a trial with a team assignment system. Each team consisted of one physician and two or three nurses working together. Each team got eight beds in close proximity. Patients were assigned in the waiting room to a team. All staff knew the goal of decreasing length of stay to increase capacity, and data was collected on arrival to provider and total length of stay. Best practices were shared with staff.

After implementation, physicians and nursing staff reported improved job satisfaction and better patient care because of the team approach. The physicians reported a sense of ownership for patients in the waiting room.

18.5 Conclusion

A key principle of Lean is continuous improvement. The team has changed over the years, but many more projects have been done in the ED. This systematic way of improving processes has enabled the ED to overcome challenges with a volume increasing from 67,000 in 2007 to over 120,000 in 2016.

It also means that in times of crisis, all of the ED staff has a clear vision of the goal, and processes do not fall apart. The use of Lean methodology has been pivotal in creating this sustained operational change. Engaging the frontline staff and utilizing a bottom-up approach has provided sustained results. In the next chapters, each of these Lean processes will be described in more detail with an operational guide to improving ED psychiatry.

References

Crane, J, and Chuck N. 2011. *The Definitive Guide to Emergency Department Operational Improvement.* New York: CRC Press.

Doshi, A, Boudreaux E D., Nan W, Pelletier A J., and Camargo C A. 2005. National Study of US Emergency Department visits for attempted suicide and self-inflicted injury, 1997–2001. *Annals of Emergency Medicine* 46(4): 369–375. doi:10.1016/j.annemergmed.2005.04.018.

Liker, J K. 2004. *The Toyota Way: 14 Management Principles from the World's Greatest Manufacturer.* New York: McGraw-Hill.

National Institute of Mental Health. 2017. n.d. Statistics. https://www.nimh.nih.gov/health/statistics/index.shtml.

Womack, J P., and Jones D T. 1996. *Lean Thinking: Banish Waste and Create Wealth in Your Corporation.* New York: Simon & Schuster.

Resources

Goldratt, E M., and Jeff C. 2004. *The Goal: A Process of Ongoing Improvement.* Great Barrington, MA: North River Press.

Jensen, K. 2007. *Leadership for Smooth Patient Flow: Improved Outcomes, Improved Service, Improved Bottom Line.* Chicago, IL: Health Administration Press.

Song, H, Tucker A L., and Murrell K L. 2015. The diseconomies of queue pooling: An empirical investigation of emergency department length of stay. *Management Science.* 61(12):3032–3053. doi:10.1287/mnsc.2014.2118.

Chapter 19

A Step-by-Step Guide for Improving Emergency Psychiatry

Karen Murrell and Yener Balan

Contents

19.1 Starting Your Lean Journey in Emergency Psychiatry Improvement 315
19.2 Vision, Leadership, and Creation of a Process Improvement Team 316
19.3 Metrics 317
    19.3.1 Operational Metrics 318
    19.3.2 Quality Metrics 319
    19.3.3 Diagnosis Specific Metrics 319
    19.3.4 Demographic Metrics 320
    19.3.5 Cost Metrics 320
19.4 Value Stream Mapping and the Kaizen Event 320
    19.4.1 Definitions 323
    19.4.2 Kaizen Event Schedule 323
19.5 Conclusion 326
References 326
Resources 327

19.1 Starting Your Lean Journey in Emergency Psychiatry Improvement

Every great journey starts at the beginning. Everyone would like a "quick fix" to this complex problem, but unfortunately that does not exist. This will be a war won in small steps, one after the other. The goal will be to create systems that are much better for patients, easier for the staff, and provide organizational value.

    This chapter will provide you with a series of tools to assist in guiding operational improvements. The solutions suggested here require a completely different mindset than the traditional model. It requires commitment to excellent patient care, focus on Lean healthcare methodology, and creation of a "community of scientists" focused on continuous improvement. This disciplined approach to improvement yields lasting results.

Change requires two key elements: process and culture. Process entails looking critically at every operation and the creation of care paths that standardize patient care and make it easy for staff to do the right thing. Patients with a psychiatric condition should be treated no differently than a patient with chest pain. Care plans should be individualized with medications and treatments tailored to the individual patient.

Culture—especially in this patient population—means we look at all traditional stereotypes, blow them up, toss them out, and then seek the same excellent patient care we give to our medical patients. The goal is to look at the patients as a whole and consider how changes affect each area of the care continuum: outpatient, the emergency department (ED), and inpatient.

By moving out of our silos we bring about change. We make more beds available to the community by treating patients in the ED and discharging them home when clinically appropriate. Patients who are treated with medication in the ED are better by the time they are hospitalized and have a shorter length of stay. Establishing linkages with the outpatient system means that more patients can be discharged home where they do better. Staff are happier and safer when patients are treated appropriately. Most importantly, psychiatric patients will receive the same excellent customized care we provide our medical patients.

Of all areas in emergency medicine, cultural biases are most evident in the care of psychiatric patients. As change is implemented, addressing these biases openly will be a crucial first step.

Change requires two key elements: creating a patient-centered culture and well-defined processes that are transparent to all staff. Examining every operation with the input of the frontline staff is critical for process improvement.

19.2 Vision, Leadership, and Creation of a Process Improvement Team

The first step in starting a project is having a core leadership team. These can be formal leaders within a department or someone who is designated, but three things are key: a true interest in solving the problem creatively, the ability to motivate and inspire coworkers, and the authority to drive change.

Change in this sphere is mandatory, but people naturally do not like change, and it will be up to the leaders to hold the course when there is pressure from all sides.

We believe the keys to successful leadership are as follows:

- Being a servant leader. This means valuing the opinions of others, cultivating trust among the team, developing new leaders, and encouraging the team. A servant leader acts with humility.
- Helping the team to set a vision.
- Critical and out-of-the-box thinking. This is especially important in this field, where it will be critical to cross traditional boundaries. For instance, the ED team may need to reach out to law enforcement or community partners.
- Embrace change and be a cheerleader for new processes. The leader will need to support the team as changes are operationalized.

- Integrity at all times.
- Lastly, we encourage having fun as you "fight the good fight."

Once leaders are identified, it is time to create the "ED psychiatry flow team." Before the team is recruited, there should be a meeting with hospital and ED administrators, and an agreement should be made that the team will have time to do this important work. Especially at the start, there will need to be at least weekly meetings and time for improvement events. The return on this investment will be found in decreased length of stay for patients, decreased quality issues, improved patient and staff satisfaction, and fewer workplace injuries.

The ED psychiatry flow team should be multidisciplinary, with physicians (ideally an ED MD and a psychiatrist), nurses, ED technicians, and therapists. This can be individualized depending on the resources in your ED. An ideal size is 7–10 main team members with an ad hoc contingency. It is key that everyone in this group is committed to moving the initiative forward and has a passion for ED psychiatric operational improvement.

Okay, so now we are on *day one*, what to do with this monumental task?

The first essential step is identifying the long-term vision of care for patients. This vision should not be small. It should be a stretch goal for what the group would design if they were in an ideal world with unlimited resources and were creating something from scratch. This vision is what every process improvement project along the way will be working toward; it will start to change the culture in the ED.

An example for this would be, "Our goal is to provide caring, compassionate, world-class care without delay to every patient with psychiatric needs in our ED. We want to set the standard for emergency psychiatry."

This is just an example, but the goal should be lofty enough that it inspires everyone involved. Once a vision statement is developed, it should be shared with all staff and be posted prominently. Sharing the "why" with the staff with a patient story can also help with cultural change.

19.3 Metrics

Before starting any improvement journey, it is important to know how you will measure improvement and what initial goal the team is shooting for. Metrics are important, but they need to be considered very carefully.

One metric in isolation can derail an entire system if people are working toward a metric and not toward the vision. Whenever metrics are reviewed, they should be shared in context with the overarching goal the team has established. Make sure that the improvements benefit the system as a whole. This helps to break down these silos, so common in healthcare, and helps areas converge.

When possible, there should be a single data set for all areas of operations. Having this robust discussion is beneficial to the organization as a whole. Here we specifically focus on ED psychiatry metrics, but the system-level approach avoids unwanted secondary effects.

An example would be the 4-hour rule for emergency medicine in England (Mason et al. 2012). This target states that at least 98% of patients must be seen, treated, and admitted or discharged in under 4 hours. There were monetary consequences for not reaching the goal. While there were positive effects, the unwanted consequence was that patients who could have been treated for a few more hours and discharged home were admitted to the hospital—moving the problem downstream.

Table 19.1 Example of High-Level Continuum of Psychiatry Goals

One Data Set		
Operations/Finance		
Inpatient	*Emergency*	*Outpatient*
• Streamline access to inpatient beds • Improve communication with ED pre-hospitalization and outpatient post discharge • Transparent bed availability • Staffing for demand	• Active treatment • ED psychiatric observation area • Standardized charting • Improve communication with inpatient and outpatient for best care • Staffing for demand	• Streamlined treatment modalities by diagnosis • Specialty clinics • Improve primary care psychiatry pathways • Improve communication with inpatient and ED for best care • Staffing for demand
Continuum of Care		

In ED psychiatry, setting a metric of arrival to discharge based on a certain time would yield a similar result. It is always better to keep the higher goal of excellent patient care with benefit to the system and to keep the patient a bit longer if an admission can be avoided. See Table 19.1 for an example of a continuum data set for psychiatry.

Metrics in emergency psychiatry can be divided into several categories: operational, quality, diagnosis specific, and demographic and cost metrics. Metrics allow tackling the problem one small step at a time with continuous improvement.

For example, rather than looking at total boarding time in general, work to streamline small areas. This will be a war won in minutes, not in hours. While it may not be immediately possible to achieve all these recommended metrics, getting basic operational metrics right (even if manually pulled from the records) will drive performance and start cultural change.

19.3.1 Operational Metrics

The operational metrics that you choose to drive performance and cultural change in your department will vary based on the goals of your department and program. The following are key examples of metrics that can help drive change in any program:

- Arrivals by hour of day, day of week, and month of the year. Yearly trends are also helpful.
- Disposition percentages: percentage admitted, discharged to home, or discharged to alternative care facilities. Our experience is that active treatment in the ED decreases the need for inpatient psychiatric admission. Creating this community capacity benefits the system as a whole.
- Length of stay by disposition type. Having this by hour of day and day of the week can be helpful. The aim in a perfect system is an even length of stay across the 24 hours. This is difficult in emergency psychiatry because of community resources, but it is telling when length of stay increases with arrivals after business hours. One caveat, especially for emergency psychiatric data, involves the presence of wide variations and outliers. Using the median or *winsorizing* the data (defined as limiting extreme values in the statistical data to reduce the effect of outliers) may be advisable to ensure the team is focused on the correct metric.

- Time from arrival to initial ED MD evaluation.
- Time from arrival to initial evaluation by the psychiatry team.
- Time from arrival to initial medication administration. Unless there is a psychiatrist immediately available, the ED physician should write for the initial medications. In our experience, the majority of ED psychiatric patients can benefit from medication to alleviate their symptoms. Too often, patients are boarded for hours or days with no treatment given. Having standardized protocols for medication developed in partnership between the ED and psychiatry departments will make this easier to do.
- Medical and psychiatric reevaluations of the patient by lengths of stay. Many patients are determined to need psychiatric hospitalization on initial arrival, but with medication, treatment, and time, a large percentage can be safely discharged home upon reevaluation. At a minimum, each patient should be reevaluated medically and psychiatrically every 8 hours. This is a standard of care that ensures high quality and that patients are discharged to the appropriate level.
- Patient arrival sources: self-presentation, police, ambulance, or transfer from clinic, assisted living, or inpatient facilities.
- Rate of recidivism, as defined by return to the ED. We recommend looking at 2-day, 7-day, and 30-day return rates. These cutoffs are valuable in identifying issues relating to discharge from the ED, care delivered at the inpatient unit, and inadequacies of outpatient and community resources, respectively. These metrics are then to be shared in the appropriate venue in the context of the overarching vision. This in turn emphasizes open communication and ultimately accountability.

19.3.2 Quality Metrics

- Rates of medical and system errors including mortality rates.
- Rates of self-injurious behavior in the ED.
- Elopement rates. This can also include "left without treatment" rates and "left against medical advice" rates.
- Rates of assault in the ED, delineated by victim, staff, or patient. This certainly can be linked with cost metrics, in that medical malpractice suits as well as worker compensation claims affect the system adversely as well. Our experience is that active and tailored treatment in the ED decreases the occurrences of these issues.
- Rates of restraint use. While physical restraints are easiest to identify, we encourage administrators to evaluate the practice of administering medications against the will of the patient, and how it classifies as "chemical" restraint within the system.
- Patient and staff satisfaction. This is a population that has been neglected when looking at patient satisfaction. Advocating for including these patients in the current satisfaction surveys, or the creation of a new survey may be required.
- Prescriptions written. The purpose of this metric is to establish trends and goals such as decreasing unnecessary controlled substance prescriptions (e.g., opioid and benzodiazepines) from the ED.

19.3.3 Diagnosis Specific Metrics

- Primary psychiatric disorders and disposition by diagnosis.
- Substance use disorders and disposition by diagnosis. Knowing what substances of use are prevalent in the area can help with community advocacy for programs.

- Comorbid medical conditions.
- Secondary medical diagnoses in patients with psychiatric disorders. This can include chief complaint diagnoses, such as (self-inflicted) laceration, or overdose.

19.3.4 Demographic Metrics

- Adult versus minor. This should include age distribution (pediatric, adolescent, adult, geriatric).
- Gender. This can provide specific needs that may not have been initially considered.
- Ethnicity. This can be used to identify cultural barriers to treatment, and there may be community resources specific to the population.
- Geographic information. Again, this can be used to target community areas where more resources may be needed.

19.3.5 Cost Metrics

- Staffing costs. This should include hourly rates for the MD, the nurse, the technician, and security costs. In addition to base salary, include benefits, time off from work related to staff injury, and required temporary staffing.
- Cost per case. This emphasizes how psychiatry is not different than any other field of medicine. In addition to staffing costs, this metric includes cost of real estate and general operating expenses. We are familiar with cost-per-case in the operation room, and suggest similar use for psychiatry. This helps when discussing needed resources with administration and further strengthens ties between departments.
- Medication use. Some medications cost upward of $1000 per dose versus other medications that cost significantly less with the same efficacy. In addition to cost consciousness, this also impacts the decision on discharge medications, and in turn the likelihood of adherence to a medication as an outpatient (i.e., if the medication is more expensive, the patient is less likely to fill it).

These metrics are not meant to be all-encompassing, but should be used to generate conversations around what is possible.

19.4 Value Stream Mapping and the Kaizen Event

So, at this point, the team has been assembled, the vision for the program has been determined, there have been introductory meetings between the ED and the psychiatry teams, and doable metrics have been considered and obtained.

It is now time for the first project.

Before discussing the Kaizen event, there is one more recommendation for the team. Spend 4–8 hours following a patient through the system. This is eye-opening and really illustrates the waste in the system. Patients will be very kind when told about the work going on to improve processes and that "they are helping science." Obviously, in psychiatry, patient confidentiality is key, and picking the right patient is important. Even just being a "fly on the wall" and watching patients flow through the system is helpful before starting a process improvement event.

Value stream mapping is the next important knowledge skill critical for the team. Value stream mapping looks at a process from beginning to end but is simple and easy to understand. It provides a clear language for everyone on the team and shines a light on "value added" versus "non-value added" activities.

A value-added activity in medicine is anything that brings the patient closer to wellness, is done right the first time, and provides services the patient would pay for.

Non-value-added activities are everything else.

The only exception is "business required" activities, which may be necessary for the organization, but not necessarily value added for the patient. A value stream is defined as all the actions from beginning to end required to treat a patient.

For a Kaizen event, the defined value stream starts from the initial event in the charter to the completion of the process. Simple materials are used to create a model of the value stream during a Kaizen event, with sticky notes of different colors used to describe the initial process, a second color for value-added activities, and a third color for non-value-added activities.

As the map is constructed, the team "goes to the gemba," which means going to where the work is done. If a team constructs the map without really looking at the process, many times there will be wide variation in what is described.

The first step in the process is gathering the team and introducing them to value stream mapping. The team then goes to the clinical area and does a brief walkthrough of the entire process. Then the team goes back to the staging area and creates a preliminary map of the process. See Figure 19.1 for an example of a written value stream map.

After the initial value stream is created, a second more detailed walkthrough is done. Team members are asked to time specific workflows, and activities are timed for several cycles looking at maximum and minimum times for activities. The team carefully considers time, areas where waits occur, movement of the patient and the staff, and sources of variation. Following this, the group

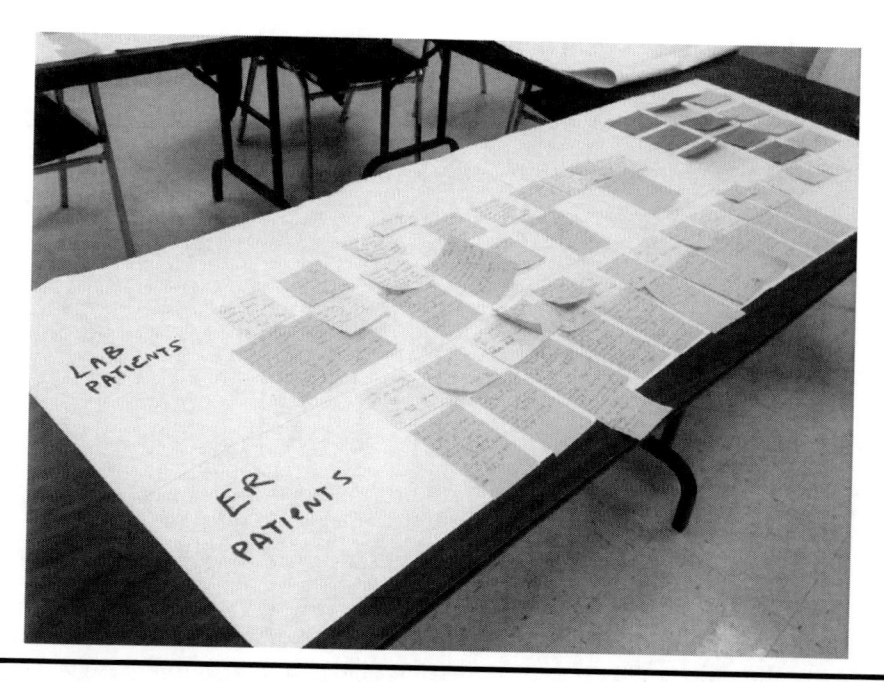

Figure 19.1 Example of a written value stream map.

322 ■ *Big Book of Emergency Department Psychiatry*

returns and thinks carefully about value-added versus non-value-added activities in the process and where there are areas of waste that could be eliminated.

It is interesting to also determine a "value added ratio." This divides the time for value-added activities versus time for non-value-added activities. Often in healthcare, this ratio can be in the single digits. The goal for process improvement is to drive this ratio up. Examples of value stream maps and the ratio for an ED project can be found in Figures 19.1 and 19.2.

One of the best ways to use the knowledge obtained in a value stream map is with a Kaizen event. As discussed, Kaizen events are improvement events that span 3–5 days with specific targets for improvement. The Kaizen team is composed of members from each area of the patient care team and must be strongly supported by senior leadership.

Figure 19.2 Example of a calculated odds ratio in an ED flow project. *Note:* In this case, the team calculated the ratio based on steps rather than time. Only 7 out of 41 steps in the operations were considered value added for the patient (17%).

When targeting the first project, picking something that would be considered a "low-hanging fruit," with a high probability of accomplishment, assures future success. This event should be carefully planned and the assistance of a process improvement expert is helpful.

Kaizen is a Japanese word that means improvement, and in business it refers to activities that continuously improve all functions and involve everyone, from the CEO to frontline workers. A Kaizen event takes a process, looks at it in-depth, and by the end of the week, the entire process is disrupted and the new process is ready to be implemented (although several iterations of small tests of change may be needed) (Graban and Swartz 2012). This event emphasizes creativity over capital. Members of the group should be identified for their "can do" attitude and "out-of-the-box" thinking. A Kaizen event can be excellent for team building and can unify everyone around the common vision.

Careful planning is needed for the event. The sponsoring lead, the ED psychiatry lead for the Kaizen event, and the process improvement expert (if available) should meet and discuss both the scope and the logistics for the event. Especially in ED psychiatry, it is easy to find multiple areas that need to be improved and have an unclear direction, leading to an ineffective and costly event.

Things that work well for a Kaizen event are patient flow (for instance "ED rounding," patient placement workflows), standard work ("a scheduled day for boarded psychiatric patients"), and environmental changes. Before the event, it is also helpful for the sponsors to outline a charter for the group. This will be a rough draft to guide the Kaizen group as they move toward a goal. An example charter is shown in Table 19.2. It is also important to communicate to as many departmental staff as possible that this event will be occurring and what to expect. This should be a very positive communication, and staff not involved should be told about opportunities for future Kaizen events. Staff should be informed that their input is important especially before final implementation of the process.

19.4.1 Definitions

- *Title and case for action*: This is the reason the Kaizen event is taking place. Both problem statement and benefits should be described.
- *Sponsor*: The administrative leader, local team leader, and facilitator should be listed. The administrator should have the authority to remove barriers and authorize changes.
- *Project description and scope*: This is a description of the project, and sets limits for what the work will entail. It should be clear and concise.
- *Brief description of the process*: A brief description of the current state.
- *Expected outcomes*: This describes the metrics that will be monitored with current states and goals for improvement. The team can change this during the Kaizen event.
- *Team members*: A list of all team members. Adjust this on the first day if there are additional members.

19.4.2 Kaizen Event Schedule

The Kaizen event traditionally lasts 5 days, although 3 days is possible. The schedule is well-defined and guides the team to develop nontraditional solutions.

Day 1: The first day of a Kaizen event starts with a leadership message. The sponsoring leader congratulates the team, empowers them to do the work, and talks about the end results and their importance.

Table 19.2 Sample Charter for an ED Psychiatry Project

Title	Scheduled Day for Emergency Psychiatry Patients
Case for action	Scheduling the day will reduce missed medications, prevent ordering errors, improve therapeutic milieu, and improve patient and staff satisfaction.
Sponsors	Dr. John Smith, Kate Jones
Project description and scope	The event will address all ED psychiatric patients who need observation for more than 8 hours in the ED. The process begins after the ED physician determines immediate discharge is not possible and observation is required, and ends when they leave the ED.
Brief description of the process	The ED physician sees the patient. Initial labs and medications are ordered. The patient is undressed and their belongings are collected and the patient is placed in a room. The patient is seen by a psychiatric social worker for evaluation. The patient is placed in a psychiatry appropriate room and monitored. The patient is reassessed in the morning, seen by a psychiatrist for nuanced medication recommendation and discharged or monitored until an inpatient bed is available.
Expected outcomes and benefit	Currently only 60% of psychiatric patients have medications prescribed by the ED physician (target is 90%). 90% of patients held overnight have diets ordered (target is 100%). 80% of patients have reassessments before 10 a.m. (goal is 90%).
Team members	Jacob Smith, Bonnie Jones, Sam Long, Eleanor McGuire, Maggie Del Duca, Emily Wells, Daniel Adams, Jonathan Corbin, Frank Holden, Larry Pham

Leadership encourages the team to reach out for help if obstacles are encountered along the way. Team introductions are made and the leader reviews the expectations for the event.

It is important to have baseline knowledge, so there is usually a review of Lean healthcare principles and the methodology. Value stream mapping, value-added versus non-value-added activities, waste in healthcare, and value-added ratios are defined.

The team is encouraged to listen to all ideas, to avoid saying "no," and to keep an open mind. Thinking out-of-the-box is encouraged, like an architect designing a building from the ground up.

Following this, the charter is reviewed. Modifications can be made to the problem statement. There should then be a discussion of outcomes including metrics for the Kaizen event.

Once the charter is completed, the value stream activity occurs. Everyone will believe they know the process, but it is very important for the entire team to look at the activity together.

By the end of this first day, the initial map should be in place and the team can begin to define value-added versus non-value-added activities.

The day closes with the leader encouraging the team to think about what they have observed throughout the day, and leader reviews the process map.

Day 2: The second day is pivotal.

The day begins with a review of the current map. Areas of disagreement are resolved by returning to where care is given (back to the ED). Each point of the map is considered carefully, and the team decides whether it is value added or non-value added from a *patient* perspective.

The team considers the value added ratios and begins to look for pain points where queuing is occurring. After this, the team brainstorming session occurs. It is important that the facilitators let the group know that during this period of time, all ideas are welcome and thinking out-of-the-box is encouraged. This type of thinking is known as divergent. The more ideas generated the better. Each idea is written on an individual sticky note. After this, the team takes a break, and the leaders and facilitators begin to collate the ideas into themes.

Ideas that fit the Kaizen event are kept, others that may be helpful later are placed in a "parking lot" for future consideration. Now that the ideas are collated, convergent thinking comes into play. The team considers which ideas to implement during the Kaizen event while creating a future state map. The future state map is constructed with an operational mindset for implementation the next day.

Day 2 ends with a report to administration. At this time, the team reviews all they have accomplished, from value stream mapping to brainstorming to future state mapping. The value added ratio should be shared as well. This is usually eye-opening, as it is revealed how much time is spent on activities that do not help the patient or the organization.

Day 3: After a productive second day, the team returns with the goal of implementing the future state.

The team is divided into work groups with a focus on layout, standard work, and visual systems and tools. Teams are encouraged to update each other frequently and have open communication. This is the time where facility experts who have been placed on alert by administration may be called on to help with things like information technology or movement of equipment.

In the afternoon, all team members converge and decide on the final process to trial, what metrics will be measured (likely manually), and the roles of each of the team members. Someone is assigned to create a patient satisfaction survey to use during the trial. Administrative leadership returns to give their final approval for the process, the trial, and any resources needed. A communication is put out to the department that a new trial will be occurring the next day.

Day 4: The fourth day is all about implementation.

First thing in the morning, the new process is reviewed and roles are assigned to each team member. The conference room becomes a "war room" for discussion of changes needed in real time as the process trial commences.

The team moves to the emergency department and gives an in-depth briefing to staff working that day. One effective method for buy-in is to have the Kaizen team members take on the roles in the new process and have department staff act as observers and timers with clipboards and stopwatches.

It is unusual to come up with a perfect process the first time, so these observations are critical. Someone should also be assigned to administer patient surveys as they exit. This trial runs for 4–8 hours.

If the idea is clearly an improvement and is easy to implement, then the Kaizen event results in a permanent change from that day forward. More often, there are logistical and communication plans that need to be developed with further trials and implementation needed. Day 4 ends with a wrap-up and discussion about the trial.

Day 5: On this final day, the team prepares a formal presentation to share with leadership.

The team works together to describe the Kaizen journey and collates the data collected to demonstrate the success of the project. Pictures from the week are added to the presentation. The summary report should include work from each day, the brainstorming that occurred, metrics that were collected, and the value added ratios in the before and after process.

Following this, and most importantly, the team needs to develop a future action plan. This part of the process is critical, and it is where many teams fail. There must be a clear time line for future trials and final implementation. Each person should be given an assignment and meeting times should be determined. Whenever possible, a formal project manager should be assigned to hold the team accountable. If that is not possible, the team leader takes on this role and responsibility to ensure the work of the week is not lost. Day 5 ends with members of the Kaizen event giving a formal presentation to leadership and a celebration of the week's work.

19.5 Conclusion

Kaizen events are very effective for creative change management, but the final points of close follow through and team member accountability are crucial. There is a spectrum of human behaviors in every organization; resistance should be expected and even embraced.

Some people will be champions of the new idea and help in any way they can. This is a small percentage of people. Helpers are loyal followers but do not aggressively push the new process.

A larger contingency will be composed of placid bystanders who will not resist your plans and will do what they are told, but will not engage in the process.

Then there will be resistors and skeptics who will push back at every step of the way. They will expect the process to fail, and will actively try to derail activities. These people should be engaged and made to feel that their voices are heard. They should also be educated on the fact that a return to the status quo is not possible.

It is human nature to resist change. Expecting this and working through it keeps team morale high. Expect 90 days of pain with any new process and continue to push forward until the new process becomes part of departmental culture.

This cycle of change continues to be repeated. Of note, many process improvement items do not require this full-scale event to implement. For smaller, clearly beneficial projects, the team can work together and create the system and simply implement it.

One example in ED psychiatry is morning rounds where the ED and psychiatry team come together and review all patients (see Chapter 5 on care options and treatment teams). This would not require a full Kaizen event, but would require administrative oversight and buy-in.

Now the reader is aware of process improvement principles, metrics required, and expected cultural barriers. Begin your process improvement journey and have fun!

References

Graban, M and Swartz. J E. 2012. *Healthcare Kaizen: Engaging Front-Line Staff in Sustainable Continuous Improvements*. New York: CRC Press.

Mason, S, Weber E J., Joanne C, Jennifer F, and Thomas L. 2012. Time patients spend in the emergency department: England's 4-hour rule—A case of hitting the target but missing the point? *Annals of Emergency Medicine*. 59 (5): 341–349. doi:10.1016/j.annemergmed.2011.08.017.

Resources

Cachon, G, and Christian T. 2013. *Matching Supply with Demand: An Introduction to Operations Management*. New York: McGraw-Hill.

Crane, J, and Chuck N. 2011. *The Definitive Guide to Emergency Department Operational Improvement*. New York: CRC Press.

Jones, P, and Karen S. 2010. The four hour target to reduce emergency department "waiting time": A systematic review of clinical outcomes. *Emergency Medicine Australasia* 22(5): 391–398. doi:10.1111/j.1742-6723.2010.01330.x.

Liker, J K. 2004. *The Toyota Way: 14 Management Principles from the World's Greatest Manufacturer*. New York: McGraw-Hill.

Liker, J K., and Convis G L. 2011. *The Toyota Way to Lean Leadership: Achieving and Sustaining Excellence through Leadership Development*. New York: McGraw-Hill.

Liker, J K., and George T. 2014. *Developing Lean Leaders at All Levels: A Practical Guide*. Winnipeg, Canada: Lean Leadership Institute Publishing.

Noon, C. 2011. Queue Calculator. X32 Healthcare. http://www.x32healthcare.com/Documents/2011_QueueCalc.xls.

Womack, J P., and Jones D T. 1996. *Lean Thinking: Banish Waste and Create Wealth in Your Corporation*. New York: Simon & Schuster.

Chapter 20

Lean Flow and the Impact of the Long-Stay Patient

Karen Murrell

Contents

20.1 Introduction 329
20.2 Background 330
20.3 Queues in ED Psychiatry 330
20.4 Utilization 331
20.5 Improving Queue Performance 334
    20.5.1 Reduce the Rate of Arrivals 334
    20.5.2 Increase the Rate of Service 335
    20.5.3 Reduce Variation in Service 335
    20.5.4 Reduce Variation in Arrivals 336
20.6 Effect of the Long-Stay Psychiatric Patient on ED Operations 336
20.7 Conclusion 337
References 337
Resources 337

20.1 Introduction

Imagine your 16-year-old daughter breaks up with her boyfriend and is despondent. She grabs a handful of ibuprofen and swallows them. You rush her to the emergency department (ED). A caring and compassionate nurse greets her and takes her to a room. The ED doctor sees her immediately, and labs and medication for abdominal discomfort are ordered. While waiting for the labs, she is seen by a therapist who comforts her and develops a safety plan in collaboration with you. Your daughter is discharged home several hours later feeling much better with a plan for close follow-up with the therapist the next day.

    This experience is very unlikely to occur in medicine today. It does illustrate the concept of lean flow in ED psychiatry. From the moment your daughter arrived to when she was discharged, she was engaged in value-added activities bringing her closer to wellness. The activities also occurred in parallel instead of serially, making use of every valuable minute. In this chapter, lean flow in relation to ED psychiatry will be discussed. This is almost an oxymoron in most of American medicine today! The impact of the "long-stay" patient on ED operations will also be considered with strategies to improve operations.

20.2 Background

Lean flow was originally used to describe movement of parts in the Toyota Production Company (Liker and Convis 2011). As discussed in Chapter 18, Toyota was different than other car companies. Other companies produced huge inventories of materials that sat in warehouses and were pulled upon when ready. Toyota had a "just in time" mentality, where cars were built as they were ordered. The car "flowed" through production from beginning to end with no delays or piles of inventory between. This was obviously less expensive, but an even more important side effect was that errors were identified and fixed immediately. With a fender that had been made months ago and stored in a warehouse, it was almost impossible to trace what had happened. Toyota developed a process where the entire line would stop when a defect was identified, and the problem could be solved in real time.

Obviously, this has huge ramifications for healthcare, where defects can have tremendous consequences for patient care. Healthcare is a bit different than a factory because, for the most part, value is not found in a tangible product. The delivery of care is given at the same time that it is consumed. So, the concept of lean healthcare is moving a patient from one value-added activity to another with minimal wait unless the patient needs therapeutic time for healing.

What causes time delays in healthcare? Non-value-added activities or waiting are the only two causes. An example of a non-value-added activity for our patient would be redrawing labs because the first set was hemolyzed and could not be analyzed by the lab. Waiting would be if the patient was not seen by psychiatry until all the labs were back and the patient was deemed "medically clear," even though she was awake, alert, and ready to get treatment by a therapist.

In this analysis, a basic knowledge of queuing theory is very helpful. Queuing theory is the mathematical study of waiting lines (or queues). It is a branch of operations research and was first described in 1909 by an engineer, Agner Erlang, who worked for the Copenhagen Telephone Exchange (Queuing Theory History n.d.). While this is a mathematical specialty, some basic knowledge will help direct where process improvement efforts should be focused while at the same time decreasing patient wait time in the ED.

20.3 Queues in ED Psychiatry

When you look at the queues for a psychiatric patient presenting for treatment in the ED, they are virtually everywhere! The patient waits for triage, waits for a bed, waits for evaluation by an ED nurse, and then the ED physician, until the patient finally gets to talk to someone from psychiatry. Often this is many hours to days! Then consider the queues for the acute patients after evaluation: waiting for medication, waiting for placement in an inpatient unit, waiting for the ambulance transfer. For the patient involved in this tortuous process, the value-added activities are few and far between.

Let's start to consider basic operations in psychiatry to illustrate this theory. In the clinic, we have a therapist who has four patients scheduled an hour for return visits. The value of four is called the *arrival rate* and is expressed in terms of units/period of time. Suppose it takes her 20 minutes to see each patient. This can be converted into a *service rate* of 20/60 or 3 patients per hour. Will there be any waiting? Of course! There are four patients arriving and she can only see three. She will fall behind by one patient per hour.

What if we decreased patients to three arrivals per hour. Will there be waiting? She has the capacity to take care of three patients. The answer is *it depends*. If patients arrive and leave *exactly* every 20 minutes, there will be no waiting. The problem is that this is totally unrealistic in the real world. Every patient is different, with different treatment needs and concerns. That is why developing a system where the service rate is less than the arrival rate is crucial for all service operations. Another interesting aspect of queuing theory is when the utilization of a server goes over 80%, any additional work will cause wait times to go up exponentially. Remember this as we continue our discussion.

Now consider emergency psychiatry where arrivals are much more unpredictable than a clinic setting and length of stay is much longer. Rather than arriving every 20 minutes, patients arrive every 3 hours on average, but the standard deviation is huge and the time required for care is much longer. So, the *arrival rate* is lower, but the time for service is much longer (e.g., *lower service rate of one patient per hour*). This arrival pattern is called a *Poisson arrival process* (developed by a French mathematician Simeon Poisson) (Statistics: The Poisson Distribution 2007). Poisson arrivals do not occur in a nice regular pattern. Instead, each component is independent of the other and arrivals occur close together or very widely spaced apart. As an example, in one ED they have an average of 10 arrivals a day. One day in September, 3 patients arrive in a 20 minute period starting at 7 a.m. The other seven patients are scattered throughout the day. The next day from 7 to 10 a.m. there are no psychiatric patients at all. The nature of a Poisson process is how random it appears. This gives a much more realistic view for ED psychiatry than the clinic view. The variation along with wide standard deviation in time needed for treatment and the multiple queues for each ED psychiatric patients make it particularly challenging.

20.4 Utilization

Let's go back to our clinic example. Now we have a therapist that sees two return appointments an hour, with the capacity to see three. We can estimate her utilization as follows: on average, she has 2 patients arriving each hour and each patient needs 20 minutes of service time. So, each hour, on average, she has 40 minutes of therapy work arriving to a server (the therapist) with 60 minutes available each hour. Dividing 40/60 gives us an estimated utilization of 66%. So, on average, the therapist will be busy 66% and idle 34% of the time. So, if the clinic manager walks by he will see the therapist idle 34% of the time, but will still be getting complaints about people waiting to see her. Why? The answer lies in *variation*.

There is a free program called Queue Calc (Noon 2011) that helps to understand these principles. Using this program, you can enter in the number of servers (the number of staff doing the same work), the arrival rate (e.g., two per hour), and the service rate (again in terms of capacity per time unit or three an hour). You then add something called the coefficient of variation. The coefficient of variation is a marker for the variation in a process. The number is between 0 and 1. Those processes with a coefficient of variation of 0 (very rare in healthcare) have no variation, while those with a coefficient of 1 have maximal variation. For instance, clinic arrivals for the most part are less random so the coefficient of variation would be low, while ED arrivals are more random and the coefficient of variation would be closer to 1. There are mathematical models for determining exactly what this number is, but just understanding this basic principle and trying different examples with it using the model is helpful. When you alter the coefficient of variation for service time, it can often show that standardizing a process even if it takes a bit longer can decrease waiting times. Thinking about all aspects of care carefully with an eye to decrease waiting times is key. Consider Table 20.1, which illustrates a clinic example with data taken from the Queue Calc program.

Here are some of the variables defined for understanding:

- Number of servers = number of therapists we are evaluating (one in this case).
- Arrival rate = number of patients arriving per hour.
- Service rate = number of patients the therapist can see an hour.
- Coefficient of variation for inter-arrival time. In this example, the number is 0.25 (remember it can be between 0 and 1). This indicates that for the most part, the arrivals are regular, but some patients still come early or late for the appointment.
- Coefficient of variation of service time. For this example, the coefficient of variation was 0.5, a bit higher than the inter-arrival time. This reflects the work done. Most patients can be seen in a certain time frame, but some patients will take less time and others much more.

After we put in these variables the program tells us how many patients will be waiting and for how long. In this example, there is plenty of capacity and the number waiting in line (or in the queue) is less than one. The average waiting time is listed as 0.104. This is 0.104 of an hour, or 6 minutes waiting time. The system is well aligned now to avoid waiting, but the server (therapist) is only 66% utilized (so will be idle 34% of the time).

Now imagine the manager sees that the therapist is sitting idle for a good portion of her time and decides to add one *new* appointment (with wider variation in treatment times and needs)

Table 20.1 Queuing Example for a Clinic Schedule

Basic Inputs	
Number of servers	1
Arrival rate	2
Service rate capacity of each server	3
Coefficient of variation of inter-arrival time	0.25
Coefficient of variation of service time	0.5
Basic Outputs	
The waiting line: Average number waiting in queue	0.208
Average waiting time	0.104
Average utilization of servers	66.67%

Table 20.2 What Happens When Additional Workload and Variation Are Added to a Server (This Case, a Therapist in the Clinic)

Basic Inputs	
Number of servers	1
Arrival rate	2.5
Service rate capacity of each server	3
Coefficient of variation of inter-arrival time	0.25
Coefficient of variation of service time	0.75
Basic Outputs	
The waiting line: Average number waiting in queue	1.302
Average waiting time	0.521
Average utilization of servers	83.33%

every 2 hours. Table 20.2 illustrates what happens when variation (new appointments have more variation than return appointments) and utilization is increased. Look at the output section of the table. Now the number of people waiting to be seen has increased to 1.3 and the average time to see the therapist has increased to 0.521 of an hour or 31 minutes.

Now let's introduce even more variation into the problem. Consider an emergency department instead of a clinic. Emergency arrivals are much less predictable than the clinic (in fact a random arrival process for the most part) and times to triage also vary considerably because of patient demographics, clothing, and so on. We have a triage nurse who can triage a patient in 12 minutes on average (so she can triage 5 patients per hour) and we have 4.6 arrivals an hour. So, the triage nurse is busy for 55.2 minutes out of 60 minutes (12 minutes × 4.6 arrivals an hour) for a utilization rate of 92%. For 8% of the time, she is idle. Please refer to Table 20.3. In queuing theory, when utilization goes over 80%, waiting times grow *exponentially*. Just adding variation to the process (random ED arrivals with variation in time to triage) and with arrivals that bring utilization to over 90%, the average number of patients waiting to be triaged is over 10 and the time waiting for triage is 2.3 hours! This is an obviously unacceptable system, but how does one improve it?

There are only a few ways:

- Add additional servers (another nurse to the process, which will obviously be costly).
- Decrease the arrival rate (look at schedules, try to get more patients seen elsewhere).
- Increase the service rate. Look at every step in a process and consider if it is necessary. Take some steps off a heavily used server and shift to someone who is less utilized. (For instance, if the therapist is making follow-up appointments, shift to a less busy secretary).
- Decrease the coefficient of variation. Standardize procedures as much as possible.

Table 20.3 What Happens in an Environment Where Variation Is Much Higher in Arrivals and Service Rate and a Server Is Highly Utilized: When a Server Is Over 80% Utilized, Waiting Time Goes up Exponentially

Basic Inputs	
Number of servers =	1
Arrival rate =	4.6
Service rate capacity of each server =	5
Coefficient of variation of inter-arrival time =	1
Coefficient of variation of service time =	1
Basic Outputs	
The waiting line: Average number waiting in queue =	10.58
Average waiting time =	2.3
Average utilization of servers =	92.0%

Further strategies for improvement will be discussed in the next section.

20.5 Improving Queue Performance

How can we improve poorly functioning queues within emergency psychiatry? There are a few basic principles for every improvement:

Reduce server utilization:

- Reduce the rate of arrivals
- Increase the rate of service

Reduce variation:

- Reduce the variation in arrivals
- Reduce the variation in service

How can we do this within the constraints of emergency psychiatry? Here are several thoughts to help generate ideas.

20.5.1 Reduce the Rate of Arrivals

Strategies for reducing the rate of arrivals

- On a high level, starting with partnerships with clinics and community resources to increase access and decrease arrivals to the ED.
- Active treatment in the ED with increased discharge rate to create inpatient community capacity.
- Looking closely at readmissions with a focus on decreasing ED arrivals (look at inpatient quality, community resources, outpatient access).
- Partnerships with local law enforcement to ensure a round robin distribution of patients in the community.
- Avoiding unnecessary lab testing to decrease utilization of the nurse or lab tech.
- Simple patients can be seen by the emergency physician and discharged by protocol to avoid burdening the psychiatric team.

20.5.2 Increase the Rate of Service

The basic principle here is standardized workflows to decrease non-value added time by workers: always consider practices that are better for the patient but easier for the people doing the work. Avoid overproduction of patients (e.g., unnecessary testing).

Strategies for increasing the rate of service:

- Cohort patients in one location to avoid movement. Assign staff to this area who have a passion for psychiatry.
- Avoid unnecessary lab testing.
- Have all supplies needed to care for patients and an area for belongings close by.
- Move a medication dispensing station to the area for medication administration.
- If call centers are used, have them present the patient to multiple locations simultaneously.
- Create a standardized charting template so staff can spend more quality time with patients and be more productive.

20.5.3 Reduce Variation in Service

It is impossible to remove all variation since there is such diagnostic diversity in this patient population. That said, there are ways to minimize variation:

- Agreements between psychiatry and ED physicians for initial medication by diagnosis
- Standardized arrival processes for patients
- Templates for charting
- Agreements with local inpatient psychiatric hospitals on streamlined admission processes
- Agreements between ED, therapist, and psychiatrist on who performs each aspect of care
- Morning rounds with a checklist to ensure all patients get excellent care and no medical or psychiatric concerns are missed

See Chapter 5 on care options and treatment teams for a detailed discussion of how this will work in an ED psychiatry program.

20.5.4 Reduce Variation in Arrivals

This will require some creativity in emergency psychiatry arrivals. As we discussed before, arrivals occur in a Poisson process so not much can be done for ED arrivals except partnerships with law enforcement and local agencies to provide access. There can, however, be decreased arrivals to other queues that the patient goes through. An excellent example is unnecessary lab testing. If we avoid this, it creates a more standardized process with less variation in blood draws to this server.

20.6 Effect of the Long-Stay Psychiatric Patient on ED Operations

As noted throughout the book, the number of emergency psychiatric patients is increasing nationally with dwindling outpatient and inpatient services. This results in further pressure on ED capacity. These patients have a disproportionate impact on the ED because of the much longer length of stay than medical patients. A way to think of it is that most EDs have a length of stay of about 3 hours for medical patients. A psychiatric patient may stay over 24 hours. The bed is a server in this case and the service rate has just gone from approximately eight patients a day to one! A small cohort of patients with this outlier length of stay can increase average length of stay in an ED markedly. Dr. Bichescu and Dr. Noon from the University of Tennessee created a model to show the effect of length of stay on ED bed capacity (Noon et al. n.d.). They ran a simulation model for one hospital system where the average daily arrivals of psychiatric patients were approximately 10 patients a day in a Poisson distribution. Patients averaged 8 hours in the ED, with a minimum of 2 hours and a maximum of 24 hours. The beds occupied varied from 0 at one point to a maximum of 10 beds occupied, and the average was 7. This is what happened in many EDs before the crisis in inpatient bed capacity worsened. The system was not ideal, but it was tolerable for ED operations.

Now consider what is happening around the country in many EDs with diminished inpatient and community resources. There are no inpatient beds available, so average lengths of stay increase. For this example, we chose 12 hours for average length of stay. Now there are more long-stay patients who need inpatient hospitalization, but there is no place for them to go, and now the longest length of stay goes up to 3 days. While there are only 10 arrivals a day, there is decreased outflow from the system and longer lengths of stay. When this model was used, it showed up to 24 ED beds would be occupied with psychiatric patients! Just adding 4 hours to length of stay and a few outlier patients meant that, instead of 7 beds being occupied, now up to 24 beds were being occupied. Seventeen beds have not become available for patients with medical emergencies in the ED. A considerable problem around the country is that these boarded patients are often not getting any treatment either. So the ED is full, the waiting room is full, and poor quality care is being delivered. There is a better way.

These queuing models dramatically illustrate the need for a new model of care. The classic ED care model provided medical stabilization, a psychiatry consult to decide disposition, and then set a goal to place patients and get them out of the department as soon as possible. With our current constraints nationally on inpatient beds, it is even more critical that we have a new model where we begin tailored psychiatric treatment as soon as possible and try to prevent admissions (when clinically appropriate) to the inpatient psychiatric hospital to create capacity.

This will require an entirely different mindset for both emergency medicine and psychiatry. Treatment should start with the ED team on arrival; staffing for psychiatry should be critically assessed with consideration for a dedicated treatment team when volume thresholds are reached. This can be in person or via tele-psychiatry. The ED psychiatric team must change their strategy.

In the past, initial assessment has been the goal, but now patients must be assessed, a treatment plan must be developed, and then reassessment must occur. Patients and families need to be actively involved when clinically possible. They should be told on arrival that treatment is starting immediately, and if they can be discharged home safely from the ED, that will be the goal. This new model will reduce the need for inpatient psychiatric beds, but the effect will be felt most if EDs in the community are following this protocol. Active treatment should have the effect of decreasing length of stay for patients in the ED.

20.7 Conclusion

The concepts presented in this chapter are a start to help improve flow for emergency psychiatry patients. Unfortunately, unless more capacity is created in the community, there will always be waiting. If and when these concepts are used, and a system is created where patients are actively treated and community resources are optimized, the situation will improve.

References

Liker, J K., and Convis G L. 2011. *The Toyota Way to Lean Leadership: Achieving and Sustaining Excellence through Leadership Development*. New York: McGraw-Hill.

Noon, C. 2011. Queue Calculator. X32 Healthcare. http://www.x32healthcare.com/Documents/2011_QueueCalc.xls.

Noon, C, Yener B, Karen M, and Bogdan B. n.d. A simulation model for analyzing a dedicated psychiatric care unit within an emergency department. Emeetingsonline. https://informs.emeetingsonline.com/emeetings/informs/265/paper/86538.pdf.

Resources

Cachon, G, and Christian T. 2013. *Matching Supply with Demand: An Introduction to Operations Management*. New York: McGraw-Hill.

Crane, J, and Chuck Noon. 2011. *The Definitive Guide to Emergency Department Operational Improvement*. New York: CRC Press.

Jensen, K. 2007. *Leadership for Smooth Patient Flow: Improved Outcomes, Improved Service, Improved Bottom Line*. Chicago, IL: Health Administration Press.

Song, H, Tucker A L., and Murrell K L.. 2015. The diseconomies of queue pooling: An empirical investigation of emergency department length of stay. *Management Science*. 61 (12): 3032–3053. doi:10.1287/mnsc.2014.2118.

UMassAmherst. 2007. "Statistics: The Poisson distribution." UMass Amherst. https://www.umass.edu/wsp/resources/poisson/.

University of Windsor. Queueing theory history. https://web2.uwindsor.ca/math/hlynka/qhist.html.

Chapter 21

Change Management and Addressing Barriers to Improvement

Karen Murrell, Yener Balan, and Christopher Lentz

Contents

21.1 Introduction 339
21.2 Barriers 339
    21.2.1 Historical Barriers 340
    21.2.2 Cultural Barriers 340
21.3 Breaking Down Cultural Barriers 340
21.4 Change Management Principles 341
21.5 Conclusion 343
References 343
Resources 344

21.1 Introduction

This book is designed for everyone, from hospital administrators to patients. It contains information and perspectives relevant to readers who are industry professionals' and to those looking to gain insights into improving care and operational standards of practice. After years of "fighting the good fight," we have learned that addressing the need for change management and barriers to improvement must be done with finesse to ensure the longevity of these changes.

21.2 Barriers

While the list of barriers may appear daunting, the cultural and historical barriers that impact you and your team need to be researched, clearly understood, and overcome in order to make real change.

21.2.1 Historical Barriers

Historically, inpatient psychiatric hospitalization was the standard, and often the only treatment option for patients requiring moderate to severe psychiatric care. The deinstitutionalization and reduced funding for inpatient psychiatric facilities that began in the 1960s in the United States had an impact on how providers were reimbursed and how the field of psychiatry evolved. Even in the last two decades, the number of inpatient psychiatric hospitals, number of inpatient psychiatric beds, and general hospitals with psychiatric care units has continued to drop (Halmer et al. 2015).

Fast-forward to today, and we see that most psychiatrists and therapists practice outpatient treatment rather than inpatient or emergency psychiatry. Due to this shifting trend, there are less trained psychiatrists and therapists interested in filling these much-needed positions. This creates a large pool of unmet needs for patients with behavioral health crises that are using the emergency departments (EDs) at increasing rates.

There has been direct cost-shifting from the inpatient psychiatric units to EDs. While there are some fee-for-service areas with plenty of beds, the incentive to admit, and long lengths of stay for patients, the majority of the country does not have this luxury. It is the "luck of the draw" for the patient—based on geography—that determines what kind of inpatient care is available.

The treatment of minors and adolescents should be an area of separate focus when expertise required is addressed, as should any measurement mechanism, as most minors seen in EDs for behavioral health crises are cared for by clinicians that do not have specialized child psychiatric training (Chun et al. 2015). We are also aware that the length of stay in EDs for minors requiring psychiatric care is longer than for minors with other medical issues, resulting in higher rates of inpatient admission (Case et al. 2011).

We have discussed metrics extensively in this book, but these metrics, thresholds, and benchmarks must also be based on community constraints. The ED psychiatric team must act as an outspoken advocate for their patients, and must move out of their comfort zone and push for increased resources for these vulnerable patients.

21.2.2 Cultural Barriers

There are a number of cultural barriers surrounding emergency psychiatry. There is a paucity of education in both medical and nursing schools about care for the patient with psychiatric needs. Combined with this, are the myths and misconceptions that exist, such as "psychiatric patients are unpredictable and violent," they are uneducated, or most of them are poor or homeless.

There is also an assumption of causality, people ask themselves why patients cannot "snap out of" their depression. No medically trained person would consider asking this question for a condition like diabetes, but it is rampant in psychiatry.

In the community, there is also stigma and shame that contributes to a reluctance to discuss psychiatric disorders. These are both familial and cultural barriers. There is also a lack of understanding by both staff and providers that psychiatric illnesses can remit and resolve. The challenge of overcoming these barriers can make changes in emergency psychiatry even more difficult. This means that being consistent and following a well-thought-out change management strategy is even more important.

21.3 Breaking Down Cultural Barriers

The stigma attached to working with patients with emergency psychiatric needs must be carefully examined by hospital administration. It is important that all staff working with this patient population learn to treat them equally and with the same dignity and respect that they would any other ED patient. There are many ways a hospital administrator can create a cultural shift within the hospital system. One possible solution is to create a team of champions comprised of direct care staff, administration, and a patient advocate. This team can work together to create new avenues of process improvement within the ED psychiatric care program. Ideally, passionate and motivated staff should lead this team of champions. This initial burst of energy is required to disseminate new ideas and process changes throughout the hospital system. The difference in approaching current staff and newly hired staff has its own set of differing challenges.

Another foundation that this team of champions can build on is found at the very beginning, when a new employee is onboarded. A carefully thought-out new employee orientation that provides specific cultural examples that fit in with the vision of the organization has proved very successful in our experience. We refer the reader to Chapter 5 on care options, treatment teams, and operational improvement for further details. Consider using elements from these chapters for your new employee orientation, as well as ongoing cultural-change workshops.

We have experience creating a team of champions. We were pleasantly surprised to find many people asking to join the team. The patient-centric changes we implemented resonated with the staff. We found that nurses and even ED MDs with minimal to no interest in specifically working with psychiatric patients changed their minds and became the newest advocates for culturally appropriate care. When the "why" of the vision was discussed and was "metabolized," we saw many barriers overcome.

21.4 Change Management Principles

John Kotter, the illustrious author, has created one elegant model for change management that fits well within the context of psychiatry (Kotter 1996). He created a defined eight-step process that fits well into our model for change. The subsequent italicized words are from his model; they are followed by our thoughts on adapting the model to emergency psychiatry.

1. *Establish a sense of urgency.* Looking at local data and that from community resources is essential. Go out of your comfort zone and go to state, county, or city meetings where emergency psychiatry is being discussed. Be vocal and learn about the problem and find out who your advocates are in the community. Create the catalyst for change—even one person can do this.

    Nationally, a sense of urgency already exists within ED psychiatric programs due to the high influx of patients seeking psychiatric care in emergency settings. The hospital administrator can use this increase in psychiatric care needs, created by a lack of community resources, as the impetus for change. The use of metrics, as described in Chapter 19 in the guide to improve emergency psychiatry, is a valuable method for the administrator to communicate this need for change.

2. *Form a powerful coalition.* Create your improvement group with a multidisciplinary team willing to "fight the good fight" for improved patient care. Work together to develop a vision and create a short- and long-term plan to reach the goal. As touched on earlier in the "breaking down cultural barriers" section, creating a team of champions has great utility in developing and sustaining new avenues for a strong cultural shift.

3. *Create a vision.* Nothing is more important than a clear concise vision for your team, and when possible, for your community. Be a constant voice for quality improvement and

change, and remember this is a war won one step at a time. This should be a high-reaching vision that strives for the care everyone would want for themselves and their loved ones.
4. *Communicating the vision*. Use every channel and vehicle of communication possible. Post the vision everywhere, talk about it positively as much as possible, and recruit new members to your coalition. This guiding vision will start to change the culture of your entire organization. In our experience, we have found it useful to using posters that describe strategic steps to realize the vision, as they are typically read by staff as well as patients. We described such an example in Chapter 5 on care options and treatment teams. Team meetings can also be used to communicate the vision of change to the entire audience, and they allow for discussion and the opportunity to answer questions. These question-and-answer sessions can help to reinforce the message of the vision.
5. *Empower others to act on the vision*. If you are in a leadership position, make it clear that the vision is a priority for the organization. If you are not in a leadership position, meet with leaders and share the vision; strategies to achieve it, including metrics; and your hope that the organization will embrace the vision. More often than not, leadership will be receptive to visions that aim to improve the quality of operations. It is surprising how often high-quality patient care makes fiscal sense as well. Hospital administrators should strive to make positive changes within their systems of care. This is especially pertinent in emergency psychiatry care settings where systems are not as optimized as elsewhere. In order to facilitate change within this care setting, the administration may need to employ ideas and actions that are considered nontraditional. As described in Chapter 19 in the step-by-step guide for improving emergency psychiatry, the administrator should empower the frontline staff to make real changes.
6. *Plan for and create short-term wins*. Striving for short-term wins that beget longer-term results is one of the main reasons why we have emphasized process improvement methodology. Systematically improving one system at a time will eventually turn your vision into a reality.

    Recognition and reward systems work, and we recommend you develop a method to implement regular recognition of team members. We are all inclined to repeat what has been reinforced with public recognition, especially when it is accompanied by a reward.

    These methods have an impact on morale and bolster loyalty to the process, team, and organization. One of the larger wins the organization strives for is a cultural shift, which will be evinced in the changes in staff perceptions of patient care.
7. *Consolidate improvements and produce more change*. Just one quick win gives the team credibility and removes barriers to the next project. In order to help consolidate improvements, it is useful to present your work at many different forums, including local and national conferences.

    As you are becoming more familiar with your organization's barriers and need to reach out further into the community, we suggest seeking connections that span organizations at various levels. Policy and procedures within the organization are one thing, influencing policy and even legislation is another. Be a continuous force for change.

    Remember Sisyphus and how he was condemned to an eternity of rolling a boulder uphill and watching it roll back down again (Camus 1965)? At times, we have found ourselves empathizing with the experience of Sisyphus. Change management is an arduous task, as many forces will push the boulder backward. We recommend persistent dedication to the task of achieving change and improvements. As it relates to change management, our experience is

that if you have not asked something at least 30 times, you have not started. Overcoming organizational inertia is achieved through a mindset of continuous improvement.
8. *Institutionalize new approaches*. Once you have a successful process, share this within your organization and community. If you are in a position to do so, promote forward-thinking leaders who share your vision. The writing of this book represents a way to share successful ideas with a broad range of potential change-management champions.

21.5 Conclusion

The premise behind any process in managing change involves breaking down the larger goal to reach your vision into smaller workable projects. Remember, once more, that this is a war won with multiple small steps.

The creation of a cultural shift that espouses a patient-centered approach with caring and compassionate providers will take time and fortitude. We have discussed the perspectives of the direct care staff and their experiences in working with patients in behavioral health crises. We then covered direct ways to structure and manage patient care for an emergency psychiatry program. Direct clinical issues, including assessment and diagnosis of primary psychiatric issues, were discussed, and then we specified methods of care for treating specialized populations, including minors and those incarcerated. Lastly, we concluded with specific principles for improving operations.

As you create a culture that demands excellence and embraces change, expect a high level of resistance, but look for the smaller percentage of those that are passionate and motivated to move toward a positive cultural change.

For hospital clinicians and administrators, we look forward to hearing about both your successes and the barriers you have encountered implementing what you have learned. For patients and advocates, we look forward to hearing about what you learned in the process of becoming an armchair lean consultant and welcome your thoughts on how these systems can be improved.

Since you have gotten to this point in the book, you are likely passionate about these issues. We encourage our readers to continue to "fight the good fight" and focus on the reality that patient-centered care and the system-improvement strategies we have recommended improves the entire system for both patients and people caring for them. As you move forward and share these ideas, others will be attracted to your passion and energy. These ideas will gain momentum and change the field of emergency psychiatry.

References

Case, S D, Case, B G, Olfson, M, Linakis, J G, Laska, E M. 2011. Length of stay of pediatric mental health emergency department visits in the United States. *Journal of the American Academy of Child and Adolescent Psychiatry*. 50 (11): 1110–1119.

Camus, A. 1965. *The Myth of Sisyphus, and Other Essays*. London: H. Hamilton.

Chun, T H, Katz, E R, Duffy, S J, Gerson, R S. 2015. Challenges of managing pediatric mental health crises in the emergency department. *Child and Adolescent Psychiatric Clinics of North America*. 24 (1): 21–40.

Halmer, T C, Beall, R C, Shah, A A, Dark, C. 2015. Health policy considerations in treating mental and behavioral health emergencies in the United States. *Emergency Medicine Clinics of North America*. 33 (4): 875–891.

Kotter, J P. 1996. *Leading Change*. Boston, MA: Harvard Business School Press.

Resources

Liker, J K, and Convis, G L. 2011. *The Toyota Way to Lean Leadership: Achieving and Sustaining Excellence Through Leadership Development.* New York: McGraw-Hill.

Liker, J K, and George T. 2014. *Developing Lean Leaders at All Levels: A Practical Guide.* Winnipeg, Canada: Lean Leadership Institute Publishing.

Song, H, Tucker, A L, Murrell K L, and Vinson D R. n.d. Public relative performance feedback in complex service systems: Improving productivity through the adoption of best practices. *SSRN Electronic Journal.* doi:10.2139/ssrn.2673829.

Index

AACAP. *see* American Academy of Child Adolescent Psychiatry (AACAP)
ABCs. *see* airway, breathing, and circulation (ABCs)
ACEP. *see* American College of Emergency Physicians (ACEP)
acutely agitated patient, 28–29
acute stress disorder, 150
ADHD. *see* attention deficit hyperactivity disorder (ADHD)
administrative benefits, 52
agitated patient, social worker with, 17–18
agitation
    child and adolescent psychiatric emergency, 280–281
    and correctional emergency psychiatry, 297
    emergency treatment
        antipsychotics, 237–238
        B52, 238–239
        benzodiazepines, 238
        and delirium, 240
        and dementia, 241–243
        negotiation, 236–237
        non-pharmacologic interventions, 237
        overview, 235–236
        pharmacologic interventions, 237–239
        special situations, 239
airway, breathing, and circulation (ABCs), 28
alcohol disorders
    assessment tools, 206–207
    blood alcohol level (BAL), 208
    comorbidity, 209
    effect and metabolism, 207
    medication for, 209–210
    risk and prognostic factors, 207–208
    Wernicke Korsakoff syndrome, 210
    withdrawal treatment, 208–209
American Academy of Child Adolescent Psychiatry (AACAP), 287
American College of Emergency Physicians (ACEP), 106
anticonvulsants, 166
antidepressants, 161–163
    bupropion, 162
    within emergency context, 162–163
    selective serotonin reuptake inhibitors (SSRIs), 162
    serotonin and norepinephrine reuptake inhibitors (SNRIs), 162
anti-N-methyl-D-aspartate receptor encephalitis, 190–191
antipsychotics, 237–238
anxiety
    child and adolescent psychiatric emergency, 285–286
anxiety disorders
    acute stress disorder, 150
    antidepressants, 161–163
        bupropion, 162
        within emergency context, 162–163
        selective serotonin reuptake inhibitors (SSRIs), 162
        serotonin and norepinephrine reuptake inhibitors (SNRIs), 162
    anxiolytics
        benzodiazepines, 164–165
    hypo- and hyperthyroidism, 160–161
    mood stabilizers
        anticonvulsants, 166
        lithium, 166
    overview, 148–149
    panic disorder, 149–150
    post-traumatic stress disorder (PTSD), 150
    self-medication, 151
    therapy
        cognitive behavioral therapy interventions, 168–169
        exercise, 169
        nutrition, 169–170
        personal hygiene, 170–171
        relaxation skills training, 167–168
        sleep hygiene, 170
Appelbaum, Paul, 134
aripiprazole, 194
arrival rate, 331
ASD. *see* autism spectrum disorder (ASD)
attention deficit hyperactivity disorder (ADHD), 280
auditory hallucinations, 179–180
    and visual, 180
autism spectrum disorder (ASD), 283

B52, and agitation, 238–239
BAL. *see* blood alcohol level (BAL)

behavioral disorders
  child and adolescent psychiatric emergency, 281–282
behavioral emergency response team (BERT), 57
benzodiazepines, 164–165, 238
BERT. *see* behavioral emergency response team (BERT)
bipolar disorder, 40, 189–190
  mania, 159–160
blood alcohol level (BAL), 208
brief psychotic disorder, 188
buprenorphine, 219–220
bupropion, 162, 215

cannabis-induced psychotic disorder, 190
cannabis-related disorders
  and brain activity, 213
  intoxication and withdrawal, 212
  social, legal, and research issues, 212
  studies in adolescents, 213
  synthetic cannabis, 212
catatonia, 186–187
CD. *see* conduct disorder (CD)
CDC. *see* Centers for Disease Control and Prevention (CDC)
cell extractions, and correctional emergency psychiatry, 298
Centers for Disease Control and Prevention (CDC), 276
change management
  barriers
    breaking, 340–341
    cultural, 340
    historical, 340
  overview, 339
  principles, 341–343
child abuse, 280
child and adolescent psychiatric emergency
  and agitation, 280–281
  and anxiety, 285–286
  autism, 283
  and child abuse, 280
  depression, 285
  description, 276–277
  and eating disorders, 287
  evaluation, 278
  externalizing behavioral disorders, 281–282
  high-risk behaviors, 282–283
  and hyperactivity, 286–287
  interventions, 278–279
  interview considerations, 278
  legal issues, 279–280
  non-suicidal self-injurious behavior (NSSIB), 283–284
  overview, 276
  and psychosis, 286
  school refusal, 283
  suicidal ideation and behaviors, 284–285
children and adolescents
  social work/social worker with, 18–21

clozapine, 194
cocaine use disorder, 223
community resources information, 86
comorbidity, 209
  illicit substance, 180
Comprehensive Psychiatric Emergency Program (CPEP), 4
conduct disorder (CD), 281
correctional emergency psychiatry
  admissions process, 292–294
  and agitation, 297
  and cell extractions, 298
  confidentiality and safety, 294–295
  cost implications, 290–291
  court-ordered evaluations, 299
  decision-making capacity, 292
  and de-escalation, 298
  drug use, 295
  hunger strikes, 299
  injuries, 297
  legal overview, 291
  medication issues, 297
  non-suicidal self-injury (NSSI), 296–297
  overview, 290
  psychiatrist's role in, 298–299
  suicide risk in, 295–297
  tele-health, 300
  treatment of officers, 300
  types of, 290
cost implications, and correctional emergency psychiatry, 290–291
cost metrics, 320
CPEP. *see* Comprehensive Psychiatric Emergency Program (CPEP)
crisis response teams, 57

DBT. *see* dialectical behavioral therapy (DBT)
decision-making, and correctional emergency psychiatry, 292
dedicated psychiatric observation areas (DPOA), 84–86
de-escalation, and correctional emergency psychiatry, 298
delirium, and emergency treatment, 240
delusional disorder, 187–188
delusions, 181–183
  paranoia/paranoid, 191–192
dementia, and emergency treatment, 241–243
demographic metrics, 320
depression, 151–158, 285
  in emergency setting, 153–154
  non-suicidal self-injurious behavior (NSSIB), 157–158
  parasuicidal gestures, 158
  suicidal ideation and suicide, 154–157
  symptoms, 152–153
depressive disorder, 189
diagnosis specific metrics, 319–320

Diagnostic and Statistical Manual of Mental Disorders
　　fifth edition (DSM-5), 281
diagnostic-specific patient education, 86
dialectical behavioral therapy (DBT), 284
dimethyltryptamine (DMT), 225
direct care staff benefits, 52
disability evaluation, in ED, 30–33
discharge planning
　　barriers to
　　　　housing issues, 126
　　　　medical issues, 126
　　　　transportation, 126
　　communication, 127–128
　　goals of, 118–120
　　instructions, 128
　　medications, 126–127
　　overview, 118
　　process, 122
　　safety planning
　　　　children and adolescents, 125
　　　　coping strategies, 124
　　　　family, social, and professional contacts, 124
　　　　keeping me safe section, 124
　　　　signature section, 124–125
　　　　warning signs, 123
　　wellness steps
　　　　assessment, 120–121
　　　　individualized treatment, 121
　　　　release/transfer, 121–122
disorganized psychotic behaviors, 185–186
DMT. *see* dimethyltryptamine (DMT)
DPOA. *see* dedicated psychiatric observation areas (DPOA)
drug use, and correctional emergency psychiatry, 295
DSM-5. *see Diagnostic and Statistical Manual of Mental Disorders* fifth edition (DSM-5)

early onset schizophrenia (EOS), 286
eating disorders
　　child and adolescent psychiatric emergency, 287
emergency department (ED) psychiatry
　　correctional
　　　　admissions process, 292–294
　　　　and agitation, 297
　　　　and cell extractions, 298
　　　　confidentiality and safety, 294–295
　　　　cost implications, 290–291
　　　　court-ordered evaluations, 299
　　　　decision-making capacity, 292
　　　　and de-escalation, 298
　　　　drug use, 295
　　　　hunger strikes, 299
　　　　injuries, 297
　　　　legal overview, 291
　　　　medication issues, 297
　　　　non-suicidal self-injury (NSSI), 296–297
　　　　overview, 290

　　　　psychiatrist's role in, 298–299
　　　　suicide risk in, 295–297
　　　　tele-health, 300
　　　　treatment of officers, 300
　　　　types of, 290
　　and education systems, 8–9
　　ethical challenges
　　　　cognitively impaired patient case, 138–143
　　　　effect on patient, 132
　　　　overview, 131–132
　　　　psychotic patient case, 136–138
　　　　suicidal patient case, 132–136
　　home environment, 9
　　and incentive structures, 8
　　motivation and malingering, 6–8
　　and neurodiverse patients, 11–12
　　and nursing facilities, 10
　　and nursing knowledge
　　　　caring for people, 40
　　　　communication with emergency physician, 44
　　　　description, 40–42
　　　　overview, 39–40
　　　　patient and staff safety, 42–43
　　　　patient coping mechanisms, 43
　　　　staff splitting, 43–44
　　operational improvement
　　　　background, 308
　　　　case study, 309–312
　　　　lean system, 308–309
　　　　overview, 307
　　physician's role
　　　　acutely agitated patient, 28–29
　　　　airway, breathing, and circulation (ABCs), 28
　　　　disability evaluation, 30–33
　　　　medical clearance, 30–33
　　　　overview, 27
　　　　poverty, 34–35
　　　　requirements, 35–36
　　　　substance use, 33–34
　　　　suicidal patient, 29–30
　　practicing, 4
　　process improvement
　　　　cost metrics, 320
　　　　demographic metrics, 320
　　　　diagnosis specific metrics, 319–320
　　　　and Kaizen events, 320–326
　　　　operational metrics, 318–319
　　　　overview, 315–316
　　　　quality metrics, 319
　　　　team creation, 316–317
　　　　value stream mapping, 320–326
　　psychiatric emergency room, 3–4
　　queues in, 330–331
　　settings and staff, 4–5
　　and social work
　　　　with agitated patient, 17–18
　　　　with children and adolescents, 18–21

emergency room (ER), 15–16
    with family of suicidal or self-injuring child, 22
    mental health system issues, 24–25
    overview, 14–15
    as profession, 15
    role in substance use assessment, 22–24
    self-harm risk assessment, 16–17
    social media and minors, 17
    synthetic marijuana crisis, 23
  and substance misuse, 10–11
  and working environment, 5–6
emergency intralipid, 268
emergency medical services (EMS), 277
emergency room (ER), 15–16
emergency treatment, of agitation
    antipsychotics, 237–238
    B52, 238–239
    benzodiazepines, 238
    and delirium, 240
    and dementia, 241–243
    negotiation, 236–237
    non-pharmacologic interventions, 237
    overview, 235–236
    pharmacologic interventions, 237–239
    special situations, 239
EMS. *see* emergency medical services (EMS)
EOS. *see* early onset schizophrenia (EOS)
ER. *see* emergency room (ER)
ethical challenges
    cognitively impaired patient case, 138–143
    effect on patient, 132
    overview, 131–132
    psychotic patient case, 136–138
    suicidal patient case, 132–136
        colleagues and hospital alternatives, 136
        confidentiality and privacy, 135–136
        ethics case discussion, 134–135

gastrointestinal (GI) decontamination, 266–267
GI. *see* gastrointestinal (GI) decontamination
gold standard treatment, 214–215

hallucinogen-persisting perception disorder (HPPD), 226
hallucinogen-related disorders
    dimethyltryptamine (DMT), 225
    hallucinogen-persisting perception disorder (HPPD), 226
    intoxication, 225–226
    lysergic acid diethylamide (LSD), 224–225
    mescaline, 225
    neurology, 225
    psilocybin, 225
    salvia divinorum, 225
haloperidol, 194
Health Insurance Portability and Accountability Act (HIPAA), 279

HI. *see* homicidal ideation (HI)
high-risk behaviors, 282–283
HIPAA. *see* Health Insurance Portability and Accountability Act (HIPAA)
history of present illness (HPI), 92
homicidal ideation (HI), 287
HPI. *see* history of present illness (HPI)
HPPD. *see* hallucinogen-persisting perception disorder (HPPD)
hunger strikes, 299
hyperactivity, 286–287
hypo- and hyperthyroidism, 160–161

illicit substance comorbidity, 180
inhalant-related disorders, 224
injuries, and correctional emergency psychiatry, 297

Joint Commission, 57

Kaizen events, 320–326
Kotter, John, 341

Lean flow
    background, 330
    effect of long-stay psychiatric patient, 336
    improving queue performance
        increasing rate of service, 335
        reducing rate of arrivals, 334–335
        reducing variation in arrivals, 335
    overview, 329–330
    queues in ED psychiatry, 330–331
    utilization, 331–334
lean system, 308–309
length of stay benefits, 53
lithium mood stabilizers, 166
LSD. *see* lysergic acid diethylamide (LSD)
lysergic acid diethylamide (LSD), 224–225

medical clearance
    cost and utility, 111
    critical assessment, 106–107
    history and physical examination, 109
    overview, 105–106
    pediatric population, 109–110
    physician's role, in ED, 30–33
    selective testing, 107–109
    standardized screening protocols, 111–112
    unimportant positives, 110
    urine toxicology screen, 110–111
Medical toxicology
    deadly dozen, 263
    gastrointestinal (GI) decontamination, 266–267
    overview, 256
    risk assessment
        care plan, 259–263
        mixed exposures, 259

time of ingestion (TOI), 257–259
toxic ingestion, 256–257
toxidromes, 259
treatments and antidotes
emergency intralipid, 268
N-acetylcysteine (NAC), 269–270
naloxone, 267–268
sodium bicarbonate, 268–269
supportive care, 267
urine drugs of abuse screening, 263–266
medication issues, and correctional emergency psychiatry, 297
mental health system issues, 24–25
mental status exam (MSE)
affect, 76
appearance, 75
behavior, 75
cognition, 78
concentration, 78
impulse control, 79
insight, 78–79
judgment, 79
memory, 77–78
mood, 76
orientation, 77
perceptual disturbances, 76
speech, 76
thought content, 77
thought process, 77
mescaline, 225
methadone, 219
methamphetamine, 220–222
metrics, for ED
cost, 320
demographic, 320
diagnosis specific, 319–320
operational, 318–319
quality, 319
mood disorders
antidepressants, 161–163
bupropion, 162
within emergency context, 162–163
selective serotonin reuptake inhibitors (SSRIs), 162
serotonin and norepinephrine reuptake inhibitors (SNRIs), 162
anxiolytics
benzodiazepines, 164–165
bipolar disorder
mania, 159–160
depression, 151–158
in emergency setting, 153–154
non-suicidal self-injurious behavior (NSSIB), 157–158
parasuicidal gestures, 158
suicidal ideation and suicide, 154–157
symptoms, 152–153

hypo- and hyperthyroidism, 160–161
mood stabilizers
anticonvulsants, 166
lithium, 166
overview, 148–149
therapy
cognitive behavioral therapy interventions, 168–169
exercise, 169
nutrition, 169–170
personal hygiene, 170–171
relaxation skills training, 167–168
sleep hygiene, 170
mood stabilizers
anticonvulsants, 166
lithium, 166
MSE. *see* mental status exam (MSE)

NAC. *see* N-acetylcysteine (NAC)
N-acetylcysteine (NAC), 269–270
naloxone, 267–268
naltrexone, 219
NAMI. *see* National Alliance on Mental Illness (NAMI)
National Alliance on Mental Illness (NAMI), 179
neurodiverse patients, 11–12
nicotine pharmacology, 214
nicotine replacement therapy, 216
NIH Consensus Panel, 217
non-pharmacologic interventions, 237
non-suicidal self-injurious behavior (NSSIB), 283–284
depression, 157–158
non-suicidal self-injury (NSSI), 296–297
NSSI. *see* non-suicidal self-injury (NSSI)
NSSIB. *see* non-suicidal self-injurious behavior (NSSIB)
nursing knowledge
caring for people, 40
communication with emergency physician, 44
description, 40–42
overview, 39–40
patient and staff safety, 42–43
patient coping mechanisms, 43
staff splitting, 43–44

ODD. *see* oppositional defiant disorder (ODD)
olanzapine, 193
operational improvement
background, 308
case study, 309–312
lean system, 308–309
overview, 307
operational metrics, 318–319
operational processes
administrative benefits, 52
direct care staff benefits, 52
length of stay benefits, 53
patient and advocate benefits, 52
regulatory and quality oversight benefits, 52–53
staffing benefits, 52

opioid-related disorders
    buprenorphine, 219–220
    effects of, 217–218
    historical time line, 217
    management of, 218–220
    methadone, 219
    naltrexone, 219
    NIH Consensus Panel, 217
    overdose facts, 218
    types, 216
    use and emergency department visits, 216–217
oppositional defiant disorder (ODD), 281

panic disorder, 149–150
paranoia/paranoid delusions, 191–192
parasuicidal gestures, 158
patient and advocate benefits, 52
patient rights and advocacy group information, 86–87
patient social history, 73–75
    financial history, 74–75
    legal history, 74
    living situation, 74
    support system, 74–75
personality disorders
    clinician's personality, 248
    diagnostic criteria, 247–248
    overview, 245
    patient and clinician social interactions, 246–247
    patient care impact, 246
    patient's expectations of care, 246
    treatment
        consistency and boundaries, 250
        options, 251–252
        team splitting, 249–250
persons in need of supervision (PINS), 281
pharmacologic interventions, and agitation, 237–239
The Philosophical Defense of Psychiatry (Reznek), 135
physician's role, in ED
    acutely agitated patient, 28–29
    airway, breathing, and circulation (ABCs), 28
    disability evaluation, 30–33
    medical clearance, 30–33
    overview, 27
    poverty, 34–35
    requirements, 35–36
    substance use, 33–34
    suicidal patient, 29–30
PINS. *see* persons in need of supervision (PINS)
Poisson arrival process, 331
post-traumatic stress disorder (PTSD), 150
PREA. *see* Prison Rape Elimination Act (PREA)
Prison Rape Elimination Act (PREA), 295
process improvement, of ED psychiatry
    cost metrics, 320
    demographic metrics, 320
    diagnosis specific metrics, 319–320
    and Kaizen events, 320–326

operational metrics, 318–319
overview, 315–316
quality metrics, 319
team creation, 316–317
value stream mapping, 320–326
psilocybin, 225
psychiatric emergency room, 3–4
psychosis, 286
psychotic disorders
    anti-N-methyl-D-aspartate receptor encephalitis, 190–191
    auditory hallucinations, 179–180
        and visual, 180
    catatonia, 186–187
    definition, 179
    delusions, 181–183
    diagnostic categories of
        bipolar disorder, 189–190
        brief psychotic disorder, 188
        cannabis-induced, 190
        delusional disorder, 187–188
        depressive disorder, 189
        schizoaffective disorder (SAD), 189
        schizophrenia, 188–189
        schizophreniform disorder, 188
    disorganized behaviors, 185–186
    illicit substance comorbidity, 180
    overview, 178–179
    paranoia/paranoid delusions, 191–192
    tactile hallucinations, 181
    thought disorganization, 183–185
    treatment options for
        antipsychotic medications, 193–194
        aripiprazole, 194
        clozapine, 194
        haloperidol, 194
        medication side effects, 195
        olanzapine, 193
        quetiapine, 194
        risperidone, 193
        ziprasidone, 194
PTSD. *see* post-traumatic stress disorder (PTSD)

quality metrics, 319
quetiapine, 194
queuing theory, 330

regulatory and quality oversight benefits, 52–53
Reznek, Lawrie, 135
risk assessment
    and treatment teams, 79–81
Risk assessment
    collateral information, 98–100
    elements of history, 97–98
    history and physical examination, 92–95
    key elements, 102–103
    overview, 91–92

past psychiatric history, 95–97
synthesis of information, 100–102
and toxicology
  care plan, 259–263
  mixed exposures, 259
  time of ingestion (TOI), 257–259
  toxic ingestion, 256–257
  toxidromes, 259
risperidone, 193

SAD. *see* schizoaffective disorder (SAD)
safety committees, 57–58
safety planning, and discharge
  children and adolescents, 125
  coping strategies, 124
  family, social, and professional contacts, 124
  keeping me safe section, 124
  signature section, 124–125
  warning signs, 123
salvia divinorum, 225
schizoaffective disorder (SAD), 189
schizophrenia, 188–189
schizophreniform disorder, 188
school refusal
  child and adolescent psychiatric emergency, 283
second line nicotine treatment agents, 215–216
sedative hypnotic and anxiolytic-related disorders, 211
selective serotonin reuptake inhibitors (SSRIs), 162
self-harm risk assessment, 16–17
serotonin and norepinephrine reuptake inhibitors (SNRIs), 162
service agreement, 61–62
service rate, 331
SI. *see* suicidal ideation (SI)
sign-out reports, 58
SNRIs. *see* serotonin and norepinephrine reuptake inhibitors (SNRIs)
social work/social worker
  with agitated patient, 17–18
  with children and adolescents, 18–21
  emergency room (ER), 15–16
  with family of suicidal or self-injuring child, 22
  mental health system issues, 24–25
  overview, 14–15
  as profession, 15
  role in substance use assessment, 22–24
  self-harm risk assessment, 16–17
  social media and minors, 17
  synthetic marijuana crisis, 23
sodium bicarbonate, 268–269
SSRIs. *see* selective serotonin reuptake inhibitors (SSRIs)
staffing benefits, 52
stimulant-related disorders
  case discussion, 222–223
  cocaine use disorder, 223
  methamphetamine, 220–222
  stimulants, 220

substance use
  and physician's role, 33–34
  social worker role in assessment, 22–24
substance use disorders
  alcohol disorders
    assessment tools, 206–207
    blood alcohol level (BAL), 208
    comorbidity, 209
    effect and metabolism, 207
    medication for, 209–210
    risk and prognostic factors, 207–208
    Wernicke Korsakoff syndrome, 210
    withdrawal treatment, 208–209
  anatomy of addiction, 202–203
  cannabis-related disorders
    and brain activity, 213
    intoxication and withdrawal, 212
    social, legal, and research issues, 212
    studies in adolescents, 213
    synthetic cannabis, 212
  criteria and codes, 204–206
  data sets, 203
  hallucinogen-related disorders
    dimethyltryptamine (DMT), 225
    hallucinogen-persisting perception disorder (HPPD), 226
    intoxication, 225–226
    lysergic acid diethylamide (LSD), 224–225
    mescaline, 225
    neurology, 225
    psilocybin, 225
    salvia divinorum, 225
  inhalant-related disorders, 224
  motivational matrix of change stages, 203–204
  opioid-related disorders
    buprenorphine, 219–220
    effects of, 217–218
    historical time line, 217
    management of, 218–220
    methadone, 219
    naltrexone, 219
    NIH Consensus Panel, 217
    overdose facts, 218
    types, 216
    use and emergency department visits, 216–217
  overview, 201
  reinforcement and conditioning, 203
  sedative hypnotic and anxiolytic-related disorders, 211
  stimulant-related disorders
    case discussion, 222–223
    cocaine use disorder, 223
    methamphetamine, 220–222
    stimulants, 220
  tobacco-related disorders
    bupropion, 215
    gold standard treatment, 214–215

nicotine pharmacology, 214
nicotine replacement therapy, 216
second line nicotine treatment agents, 215–216
usage and mortality rates, 213–214
varenicline, 215
treatment and morbidity, 202
substance use history, 73
suicidal ideation and suicide
depression, 154–157
suicidal ideation (SI), 287
and behaviors, 284–285
suicidal patient, 29–30
suicide risk, in correctional emergency psychiatry, 295–297
synthetic marijuana crisis, 23

tactile hallucinations, 181
tele-health, 300
therapeutic handouts
community resources information, 86
diagnostic-specific patient education, 86
patient rights and advocacy group information, 86–87
welcome letter, 86
therapy, for anxiety and mood disorders
cognitive behavioral therapy interventions, 168–169
exercise, 169
nutrition, 169–170
personal hygiene, 170–171
relaxation skills training, 167–168
sleep hygiene, 170
thought disorganization, 183–185
time of ingestion (TOI), 257–259
tobacco-related disorders
bupropion, 215
gold standard treatment, 214–215
nicotine pharmacology, 214
nicotine replacement therapy, 216
second line nicotine treatment agents, 215–216
usage and mortality rates, 213–214
varenicline, 215
TOI. *see* time of ingestion (TOI)
toxic ingestion, 256–257
toxicological risk assessment
care plan, 259–263
mixed exposures, 259
time of ingestion (TOI), 257–259
toxic ingestion, 256–257
toxidromes, 259
toxidromes, 259
treatment teams
appropriate level of care, 53–56
consultation service, 83–84
dedicated psychiatric observation areas (DPOA), 84–86
diagnosis, 81–82
discharge planning team, 63

ED psychiatry pre-rounding, 65–66
and emergency department
nurse, 63
nursing rounding note template, 68–69
physician, 62
social services, 63
history of present illness, 71
impression, 81
initial patient arrival information, 70–71
mental health therapists, 63
mental status exam (MSE)
affect, 76
appearance, 75
behavior, 75
cognition, 78
concentration, 78
impulse control, 79
insight, 78–79
judgment, 79
memory, 77–78
mood, 76
orientation, 77
perceptual disturbances, 76
speech, 76
thought content, 77
thought process, 77
morning rounds, 65
operational processes
administrative benefits, 52
direct care staff benefits, 52
length of stay benefits, 53
patient and advocate benefits, 52
regulatory and quality oversight benefits, 52–53
staffing benefits, 52
overview, 51
past medical history, 72–73
patient liberties, 63–64
patient satisfaction survey, 59
performance measurement, 60–61
psychiatric history, 71–72
psychiatric reassessment, 82–83
psychiatrist, 63
recommendations and plan, 82
reviewing patient list, 69–70
and risk assessment, 79–81
security team, 63
service agreement, 61–62
social history, 73–75
financial history, 74–75
legal history, 74
living situation, 74
support system, 74–75
substance use history, 73
therapeutic handouts
community resources information, 86
diagnostic-specific patient education, 86

patient rights and advocacy group information, 86–87
welcome letter, 86
treatment update note, 66–68
workplace safety concerns
crisis response teams, 57
safety committees, 57–58
sign-out reports, 58
treatment update note, 66–68

Urine drug screens, 263–266

value stream mapping, 320–326
varenicline, 215

visual hallucinations, 180

welcome letter handouts, 86
Wernicke Korsakoff syndrome, 210
workplace safety concerns
crisis response teams, 57
safety committees, 57–58
sign-out reports, 58

youth risk behavior survey (YRBS), 277
YRBS. *see* youth risk behavior survey (YRBS)

ziprasidone, 194